D0098340

DAILY JOY

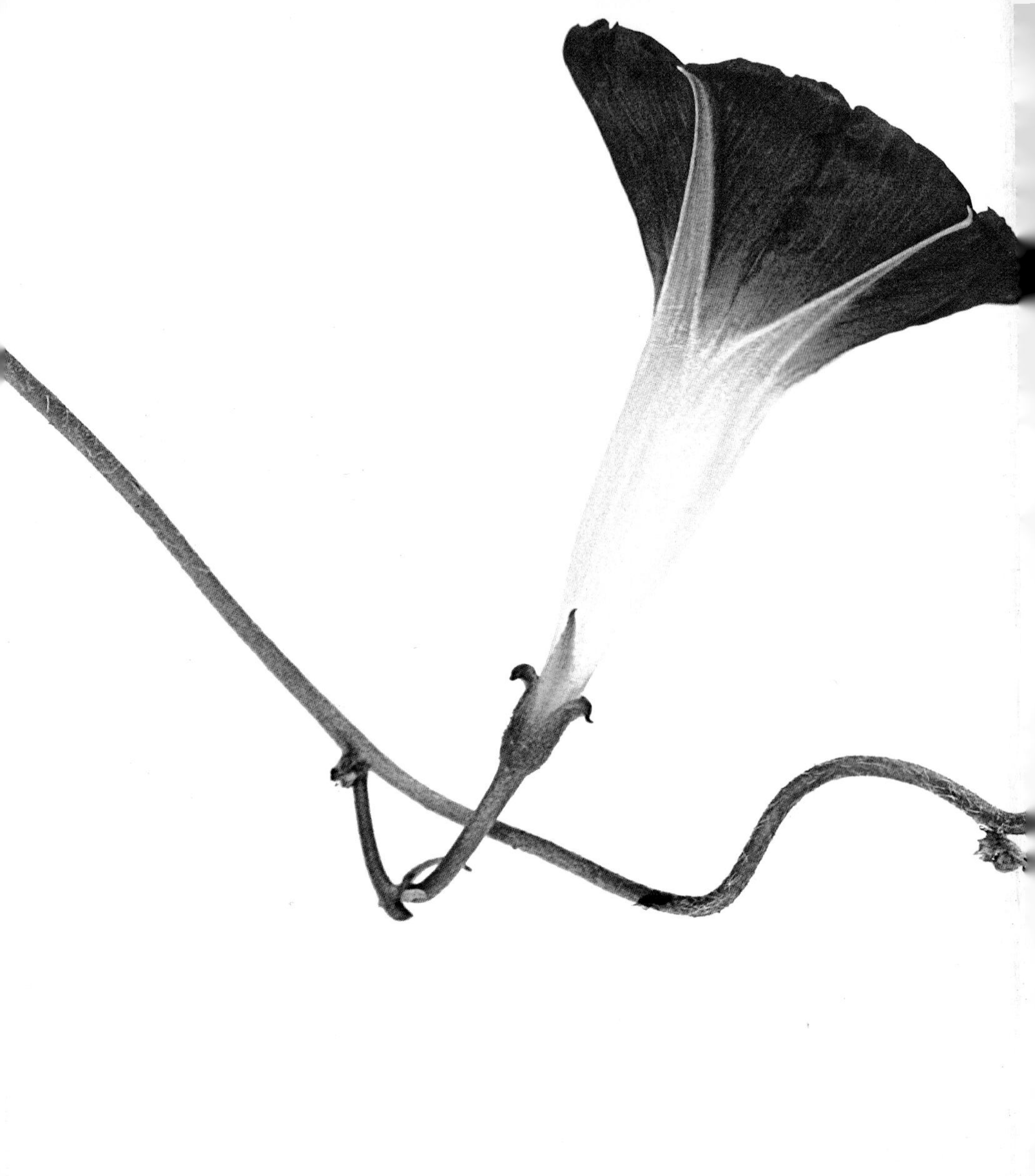

DAILY JOY

365 DAYS OF INSPIRATION

Photos and Wisdom to Lift Your Spirit

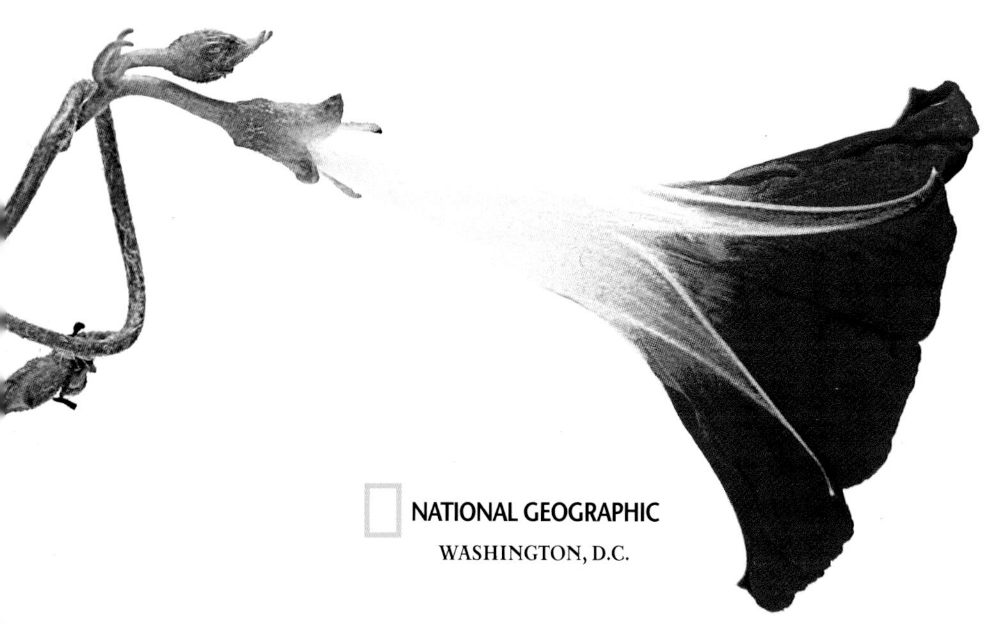

NATIONAL GEOGRAPHIC
WASHINGTON, D.C.

Published by the National Geographic Society

ISBN: 978-1-4262-0967-3

The National Geographic Society is one of the world's largest nonprofit scientific and educational organizations. Founded in 1888 to "increase and diffuse geographic knowledge," the Society's mission is to inspire people to care about the planet. It reaches more than 400 million people worldwide each month through its official journal, *National Geographic,* and other magazines; National Geographic Channel; television documentaries; music; radio; films; books; DVDs; maps; exhibitions; live events; school publishing programs; interactive media; and merchandise. National Geographic has funded more than 10,000 scientific research, conservation, and exploration projects and supports an education program promoting geographic literacy.

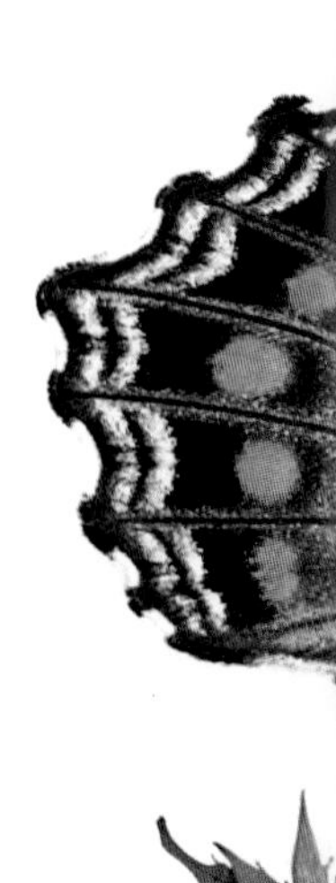

For more information, visit **www.nationalgeographic.com.**

National Geographic Society
1145 17th Street N.W.
Washington, D.C. 20036-4688 U.S.A.

For information about special discounts for bulk purchases, please contact National Geographic Books Special Sales: **ngspecsales@ngs.org**

For rights or permissions inquiries, please contact National Geographic Books Subsidiary Rights: **ngbookrights@ngs.org**

Interior design by Cinda Rose

Printed in China
15/CCOS/3

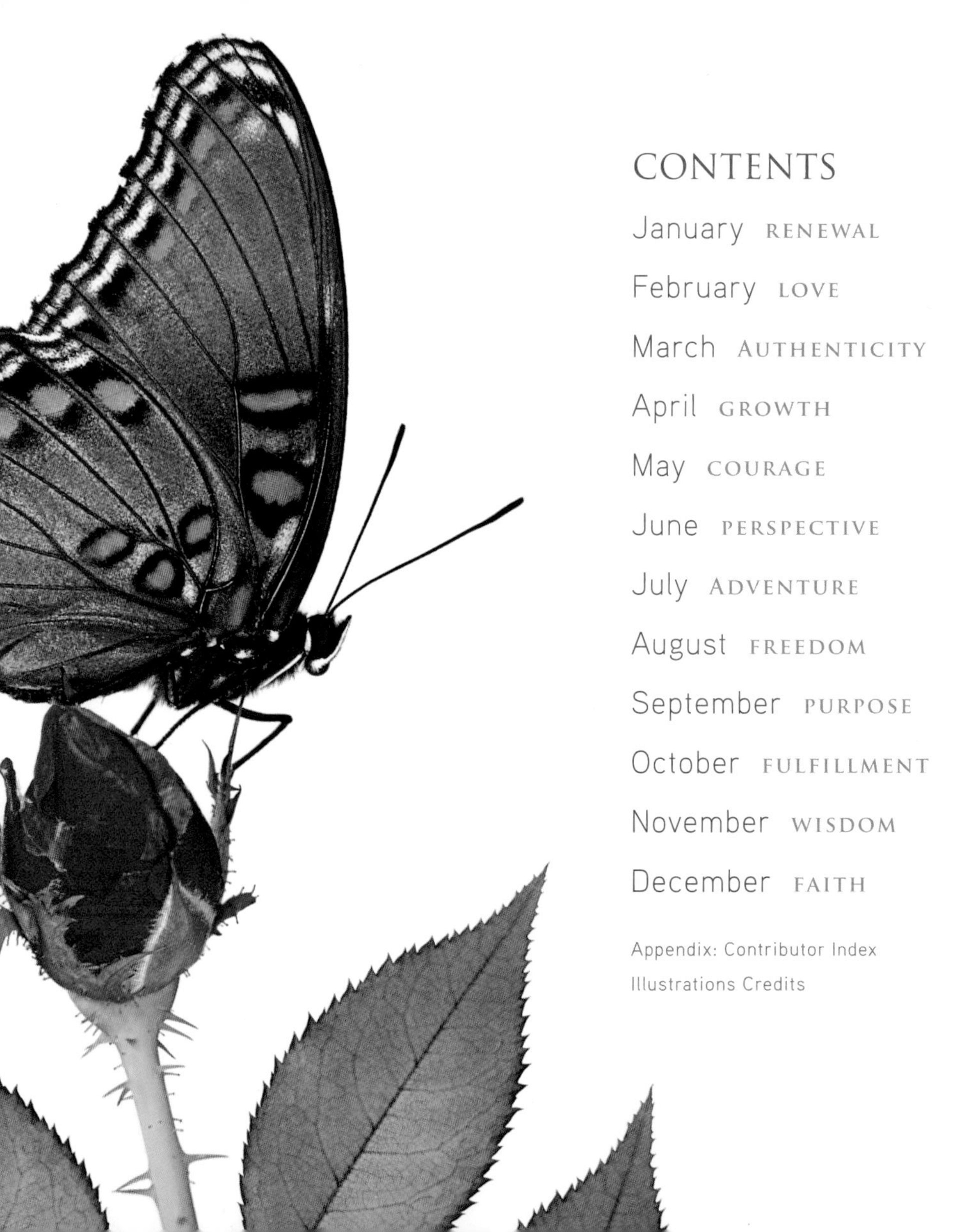

CONTENTS

RENEWAL

January

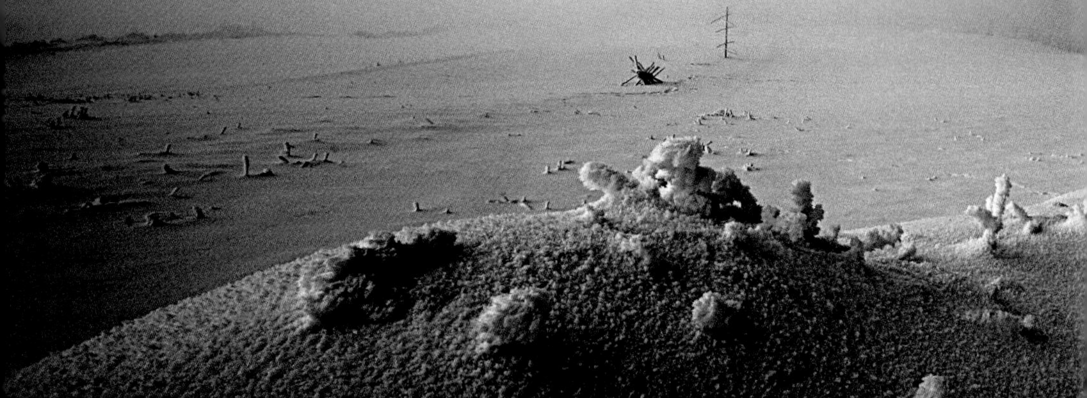

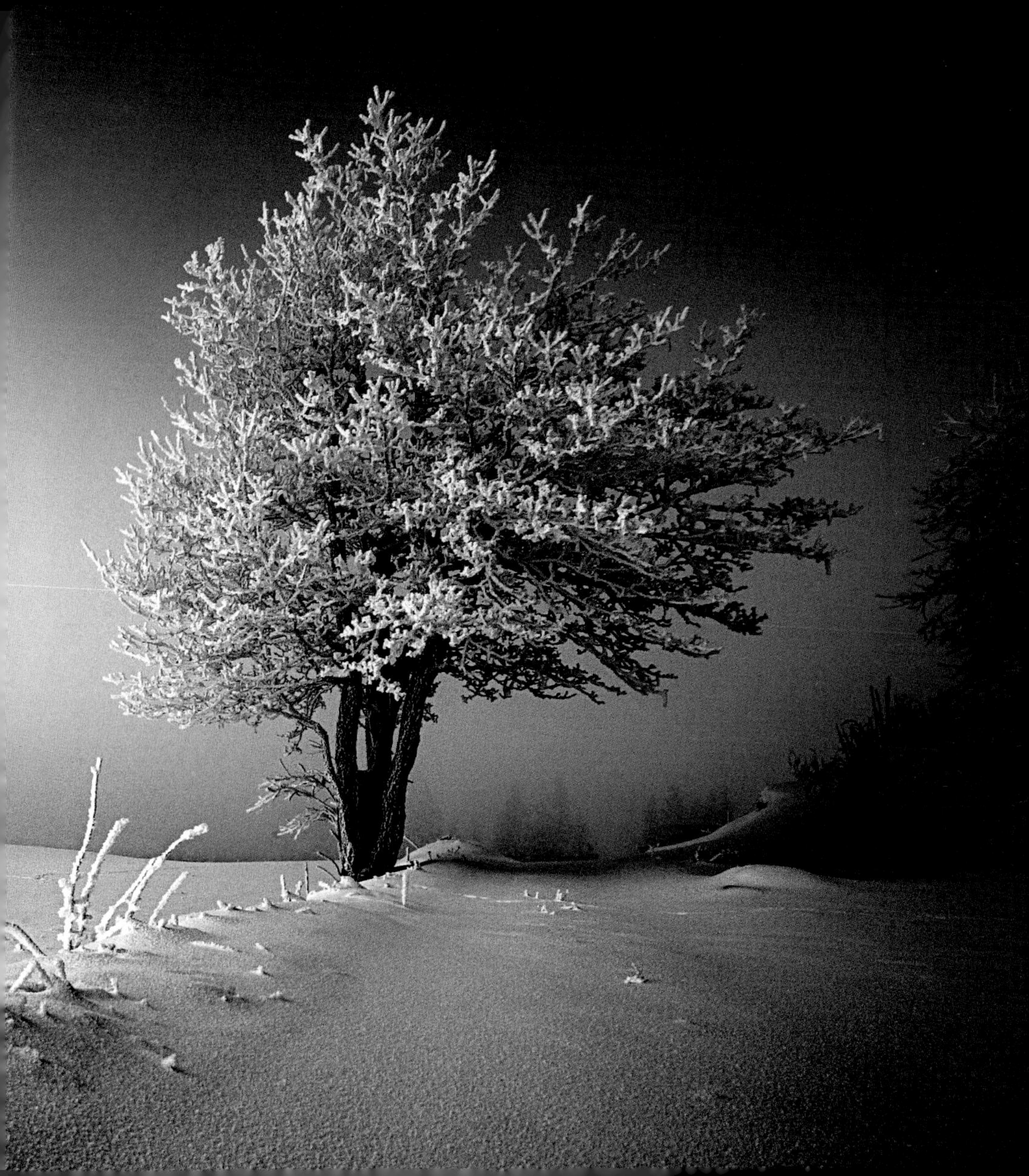

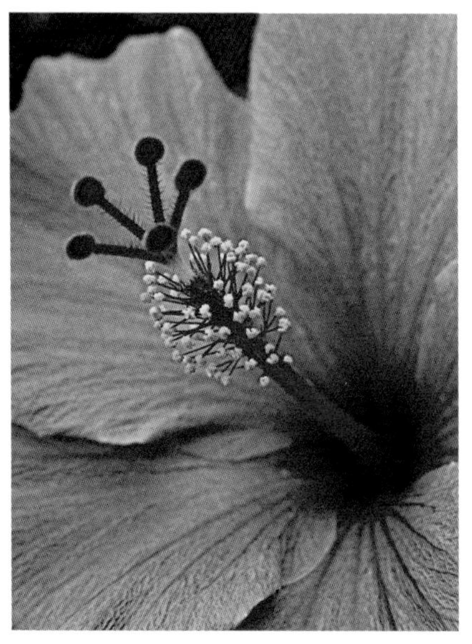

JANUARY *1*

And now let us welcome the new year—full of things that have never been.

~ Rainer Maria Rilke

January 2

Just where you are—
that's the place to start.

~ Pema Chödrön

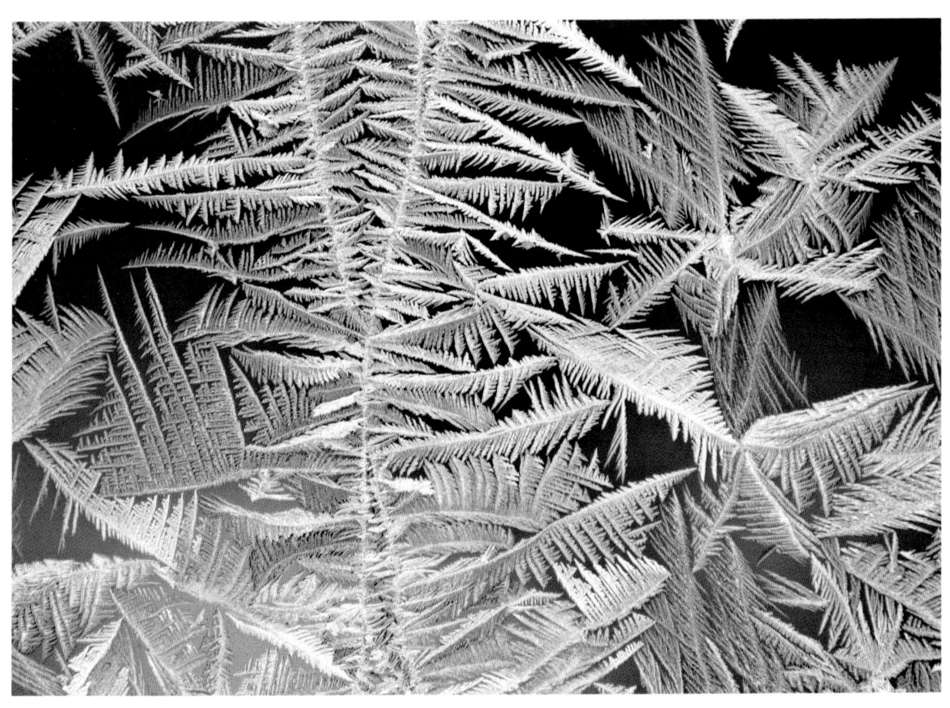

January 3

A pessimist
sees the difficulty
in every opportunity;
an optimist
sees the opportunity
in every difficulty.

~ Sir Winston Churchill

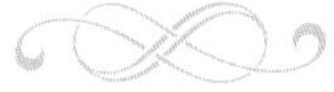

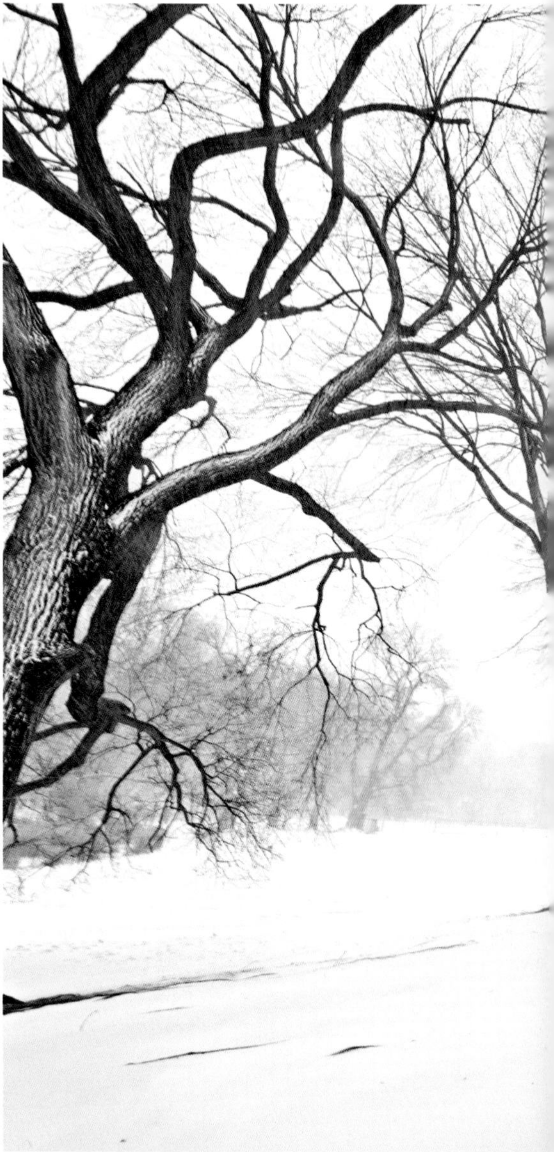

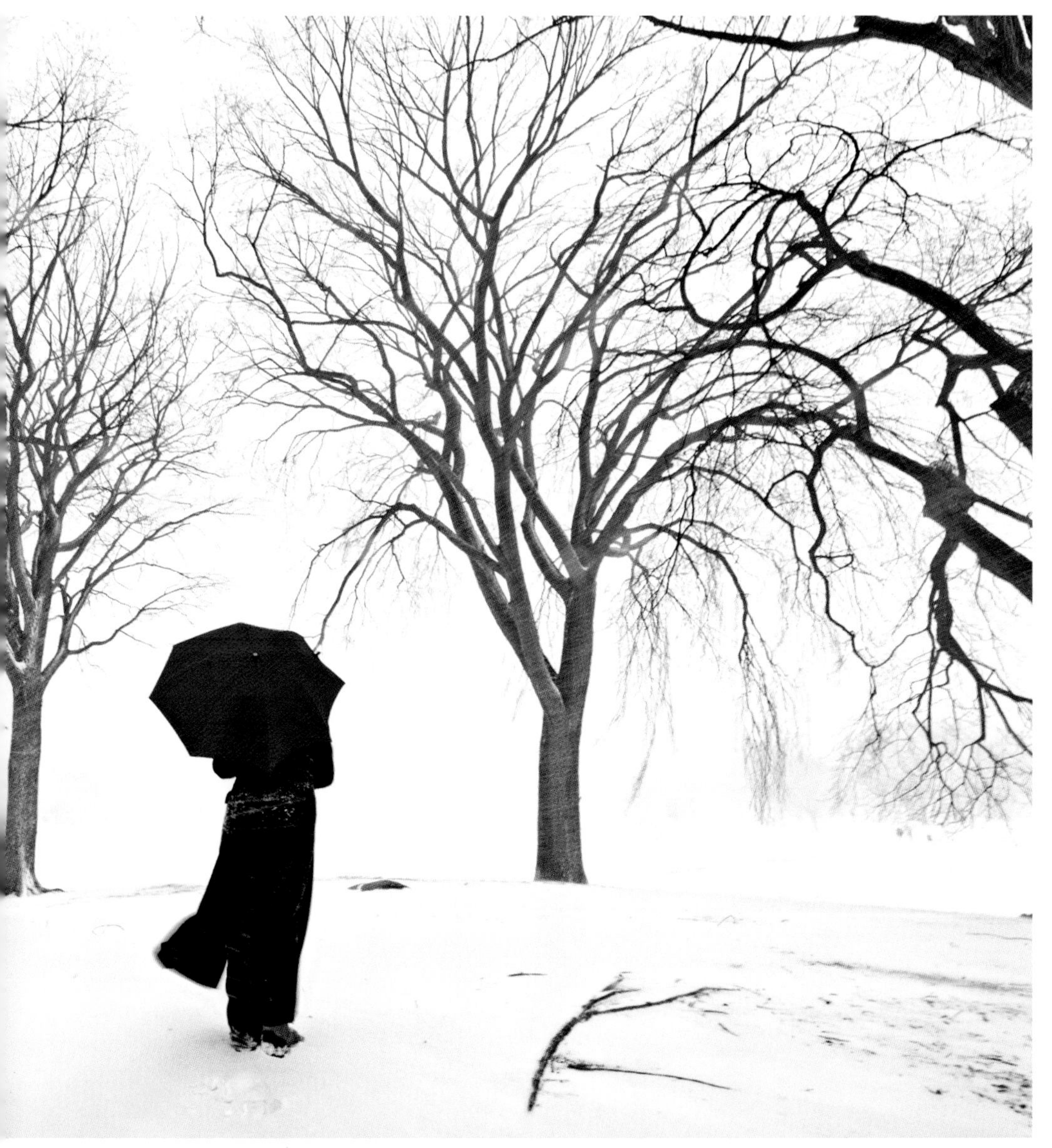

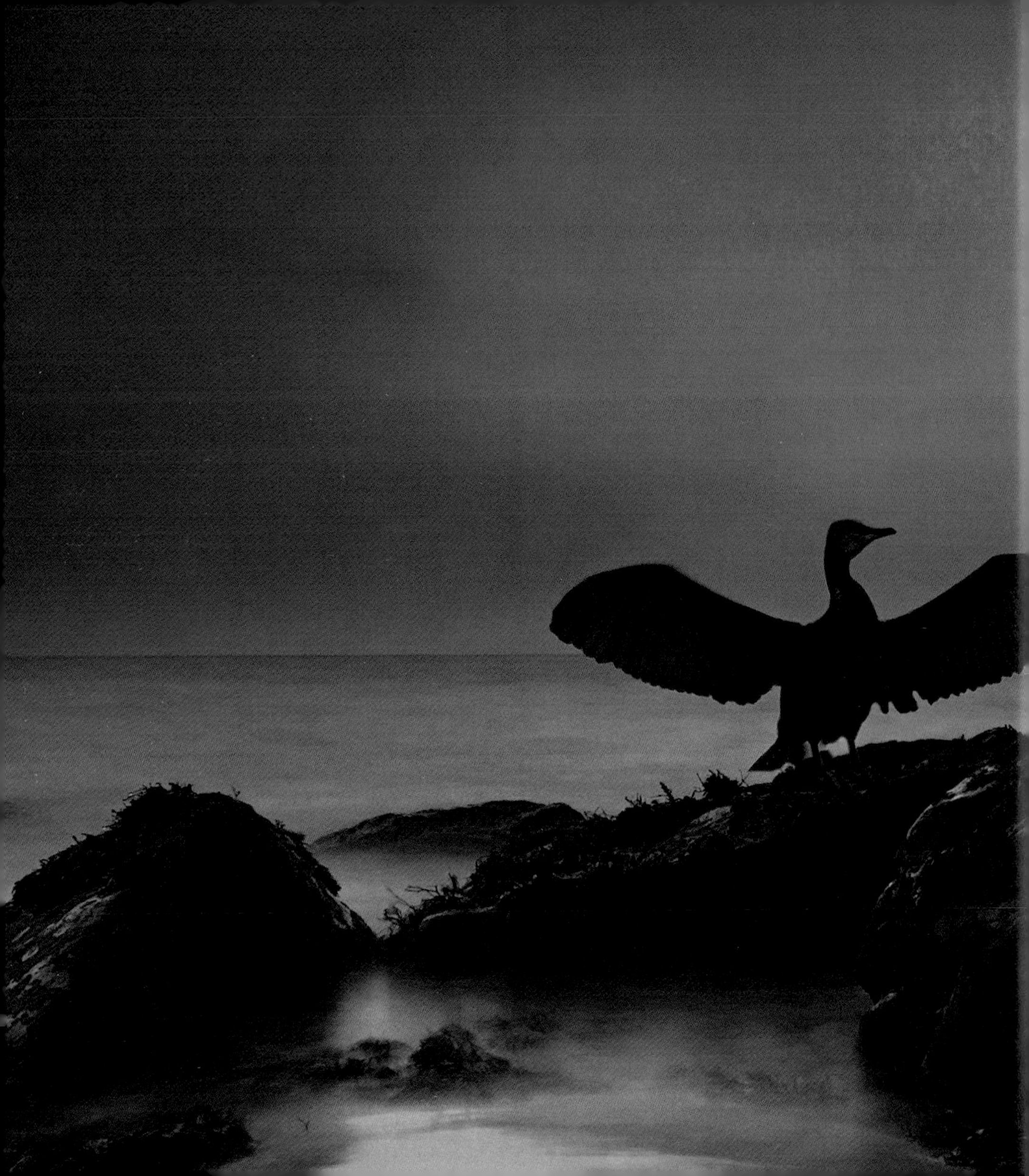

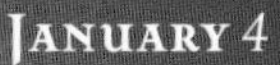

Dance, when you're broken open.
Dance, if you've torn the bandage off.
Dance in the middle of the fighting.
Dance in your blood.
Dance when you're perfectly free.

~ Rumi

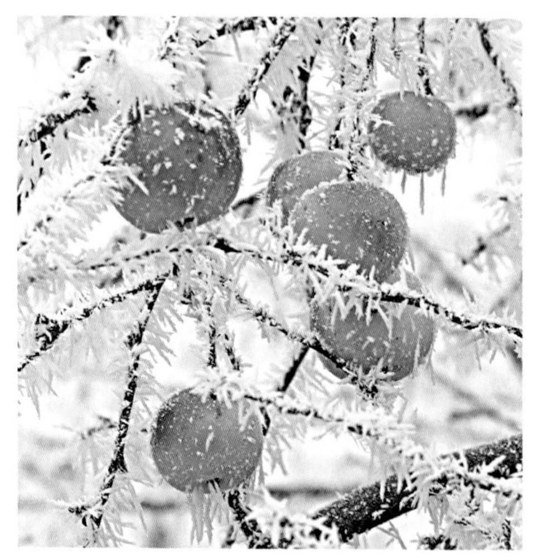

JANUARY 5

Sometimes our fate resembles
a fruit tree in winter.
Who would think
that those branches
would turn green again
and blossom?
But we hope it; we know it.

~ Johann Wolfgang von Goethe

JANUARY 6

Hope smiles on the threshold
of the year to come,
whispering that it will be happier.

~ Alfred, Lord Tennyson

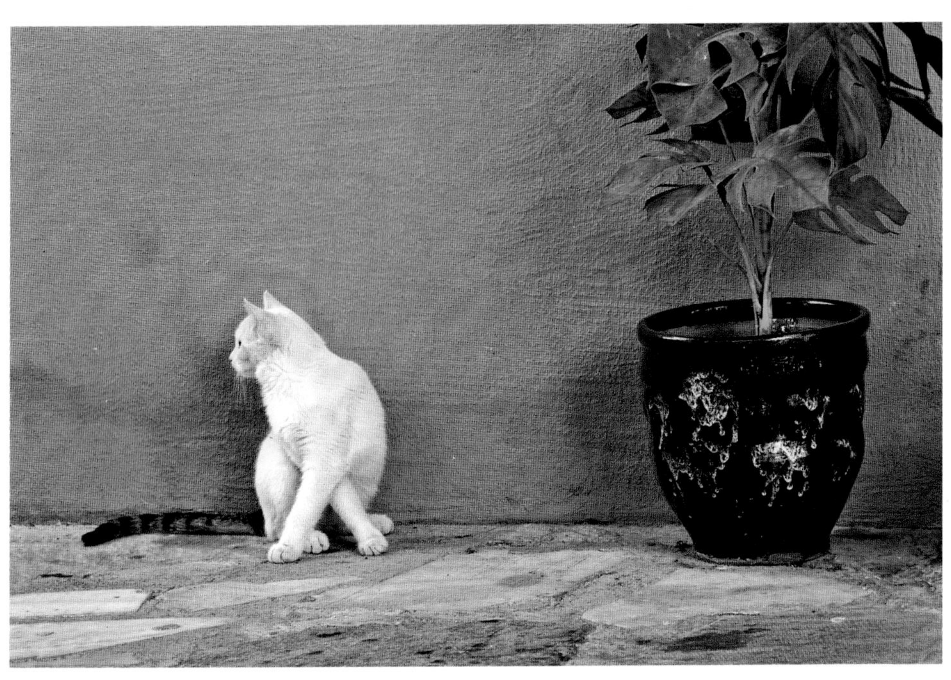

JANUARY 7

We must be willing
to get rid of the life
we've planned,
so as to have the life
that is waiting for us.

~ Joseph Campbell

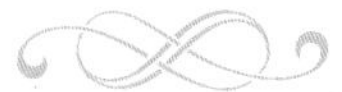

JANUARY 8

Action and reaction, ebb and flow, trial and error, change—this is the rhythm of living. Out of our over-confidence, fear; out of our fear, clearer vision, fresh hope. And out of hope, progress.

~ Bruce Barton

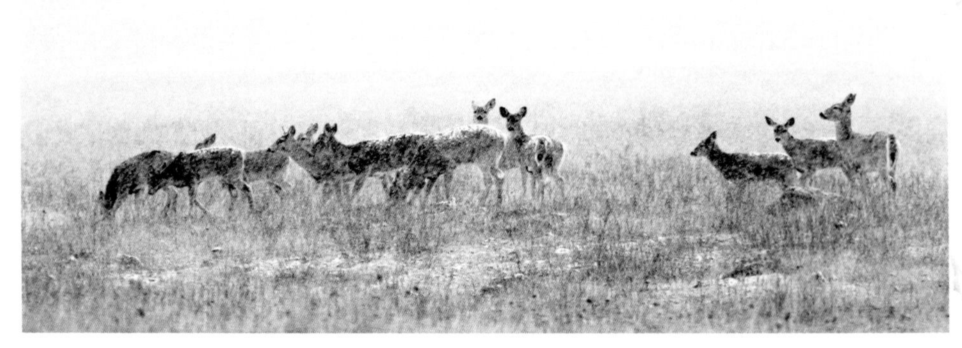

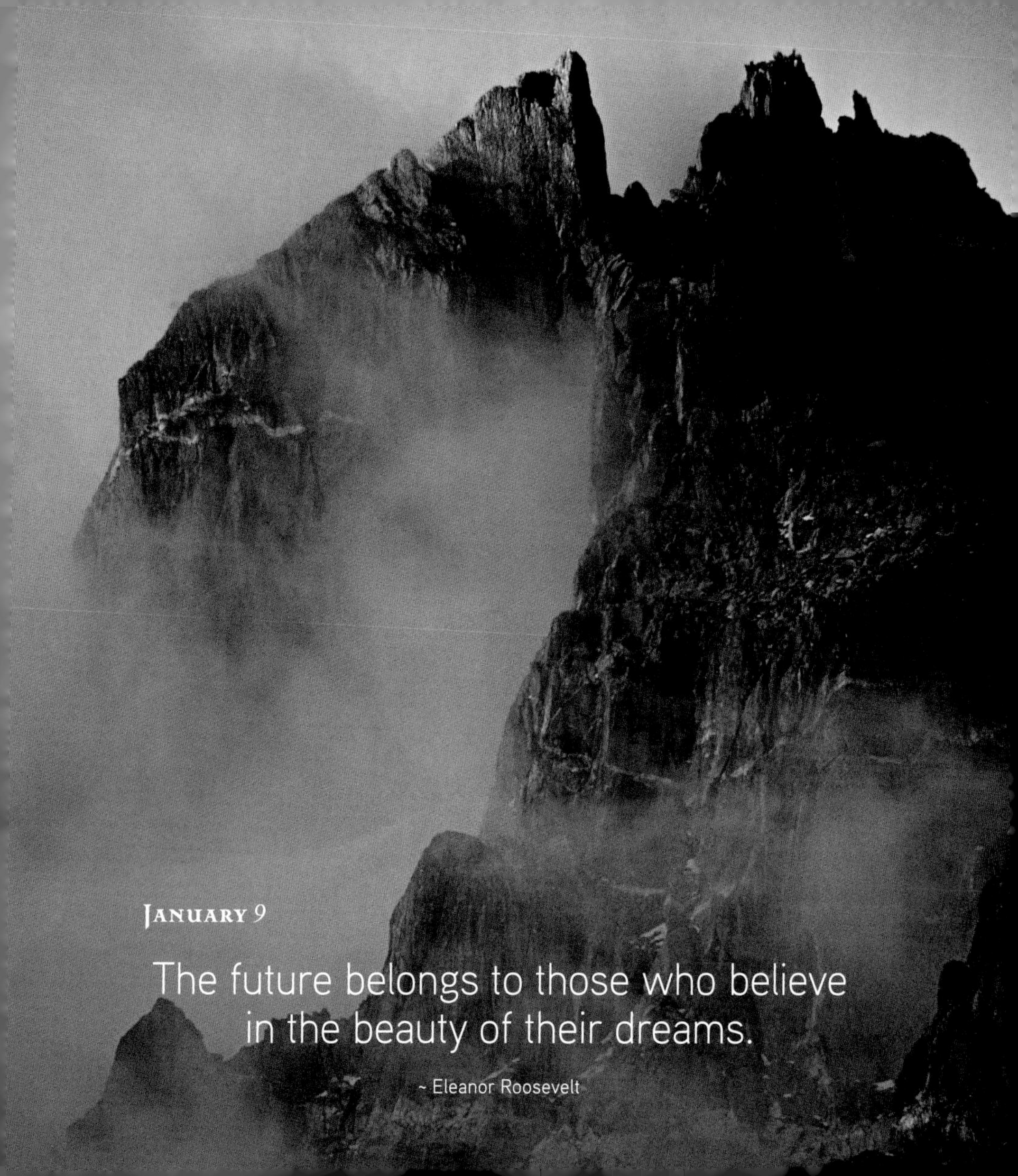

JANUARY 9

The future belongs to those who believe in the beauty of their dreams.

~ Eleanor Roosevelt

January 10

What lies behind us
and what lies before us
are small matters
compared to what lies
within us.

~ Ralph Waldo Emerson

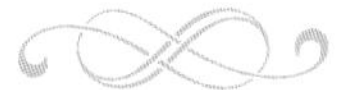

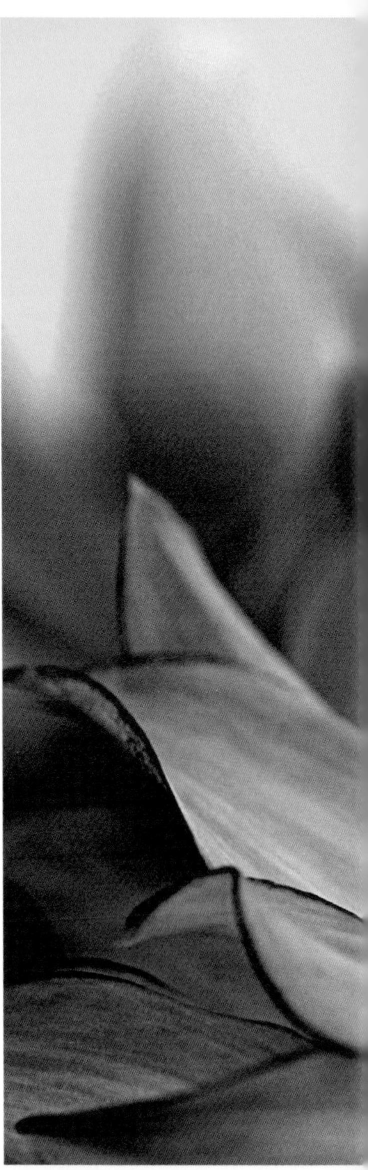

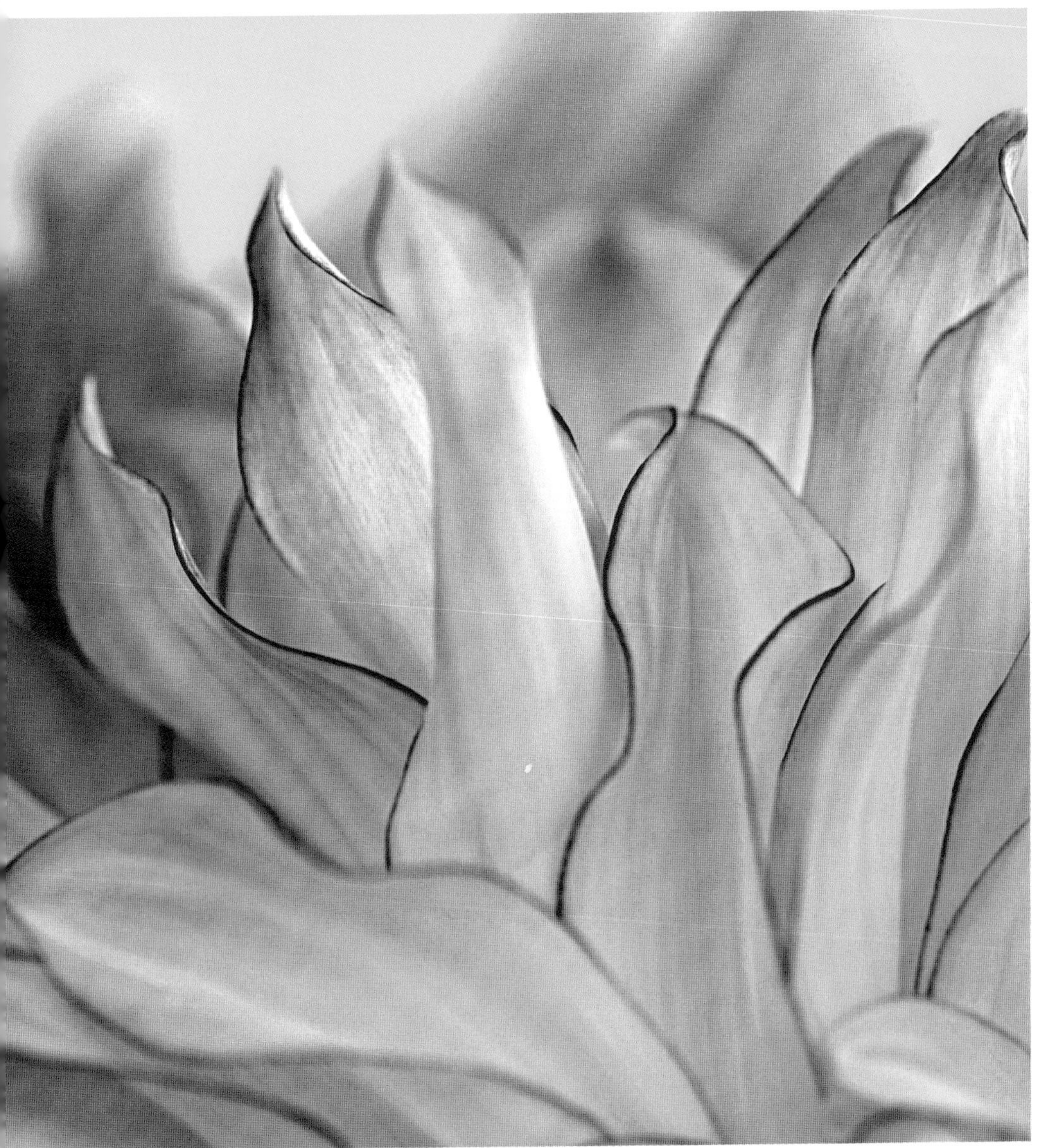

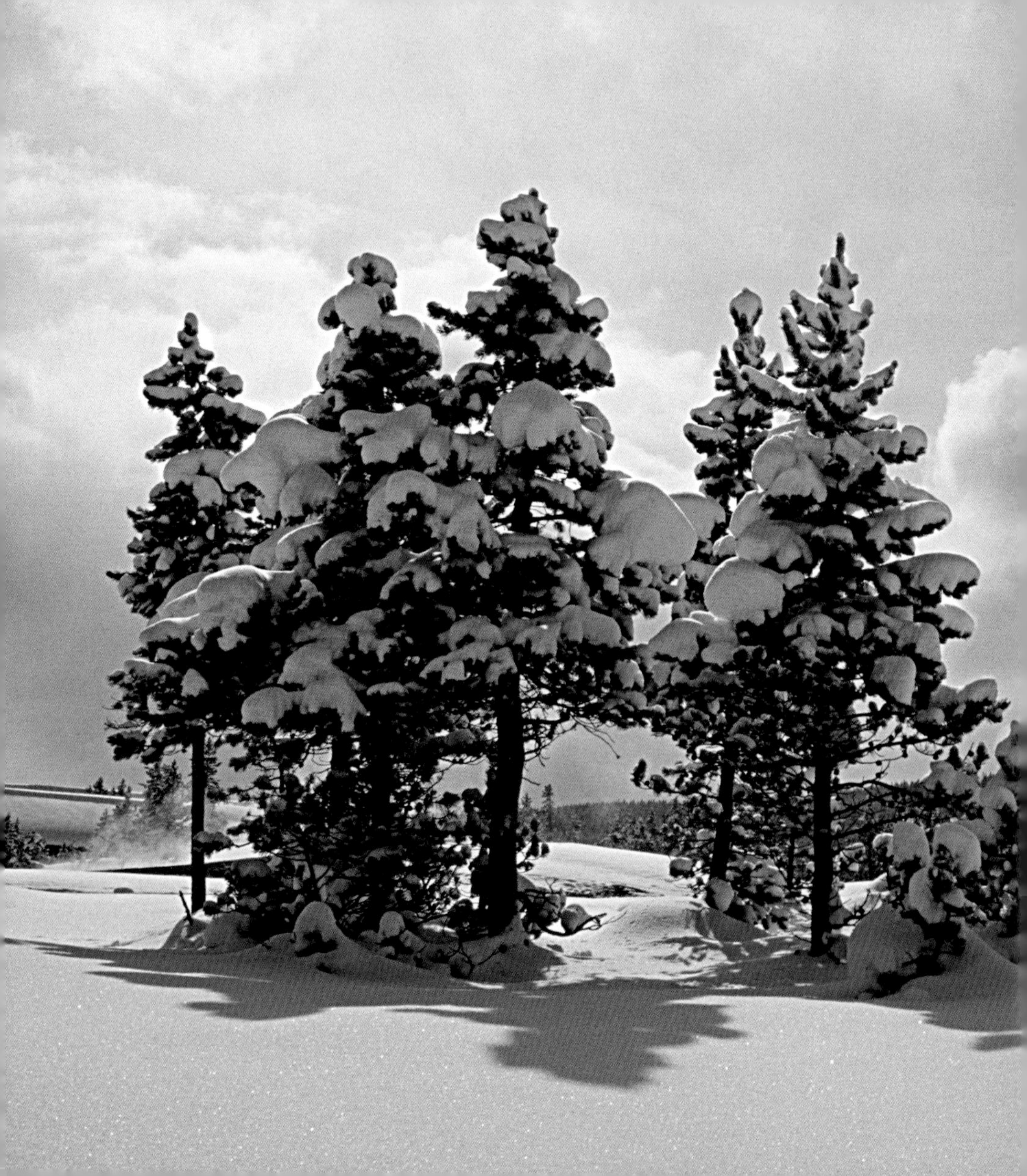

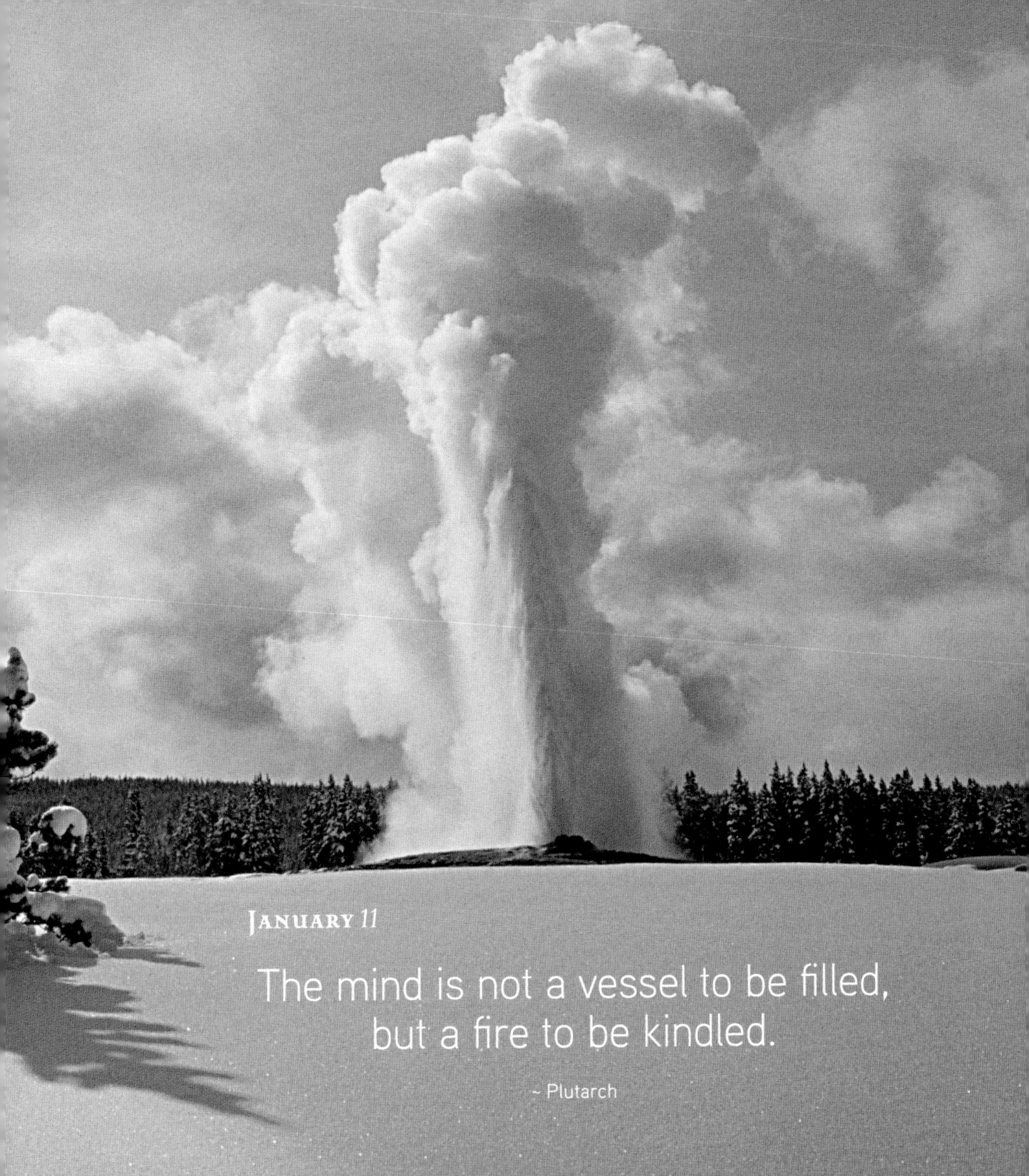

JANUARY 11

The mind is not a vessel to be filled,
but a fire to be kindled.

~ Plutarch

JANUARY 12

There is only one journey:
going inside yourself.

~ Rainer Maria Rilke

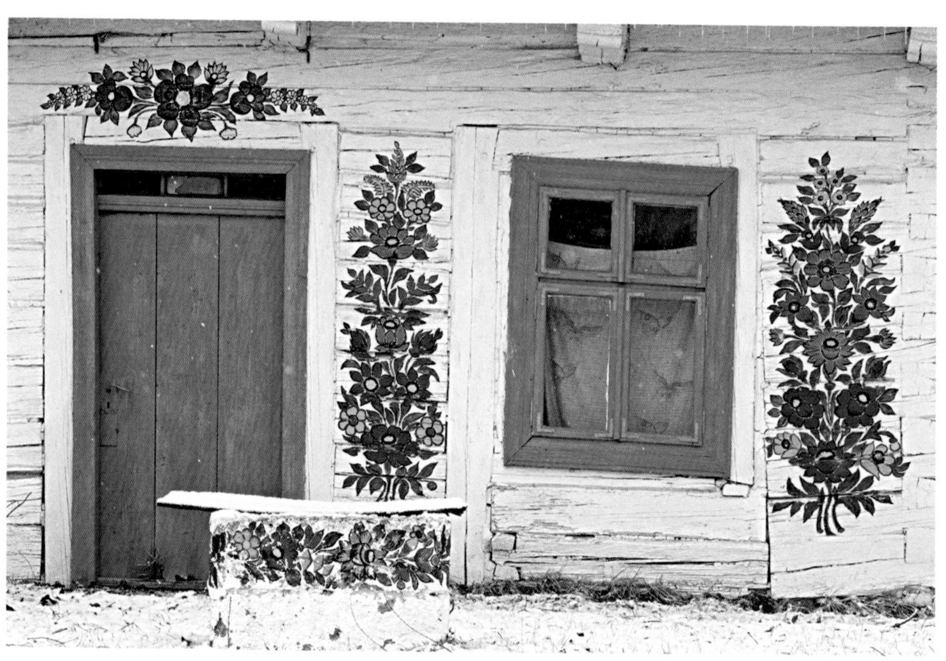

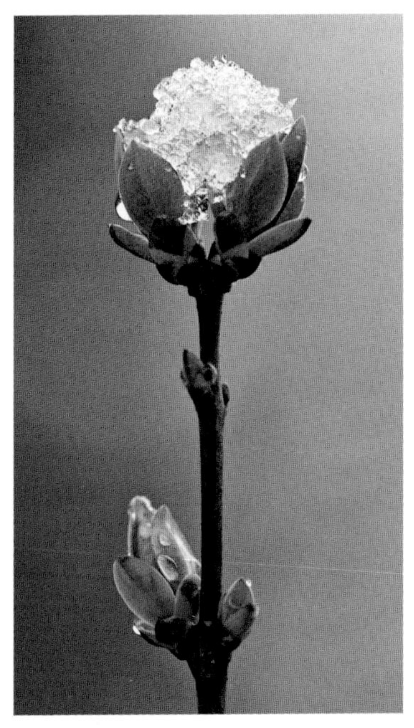

JANUARY 13

Keep your face to the sunshine
and you cannot see the shadows.

~ Helen Keller

January 14

The greatest joy lies not in simply being, but in becoming.

~ Oprah Winfrey

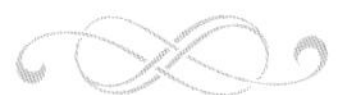

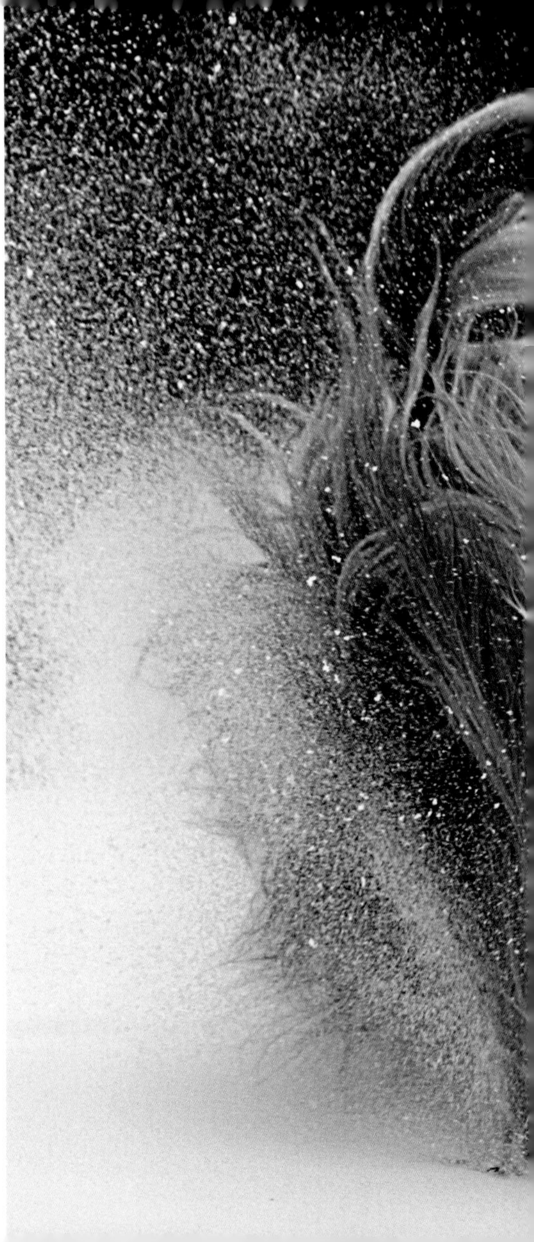

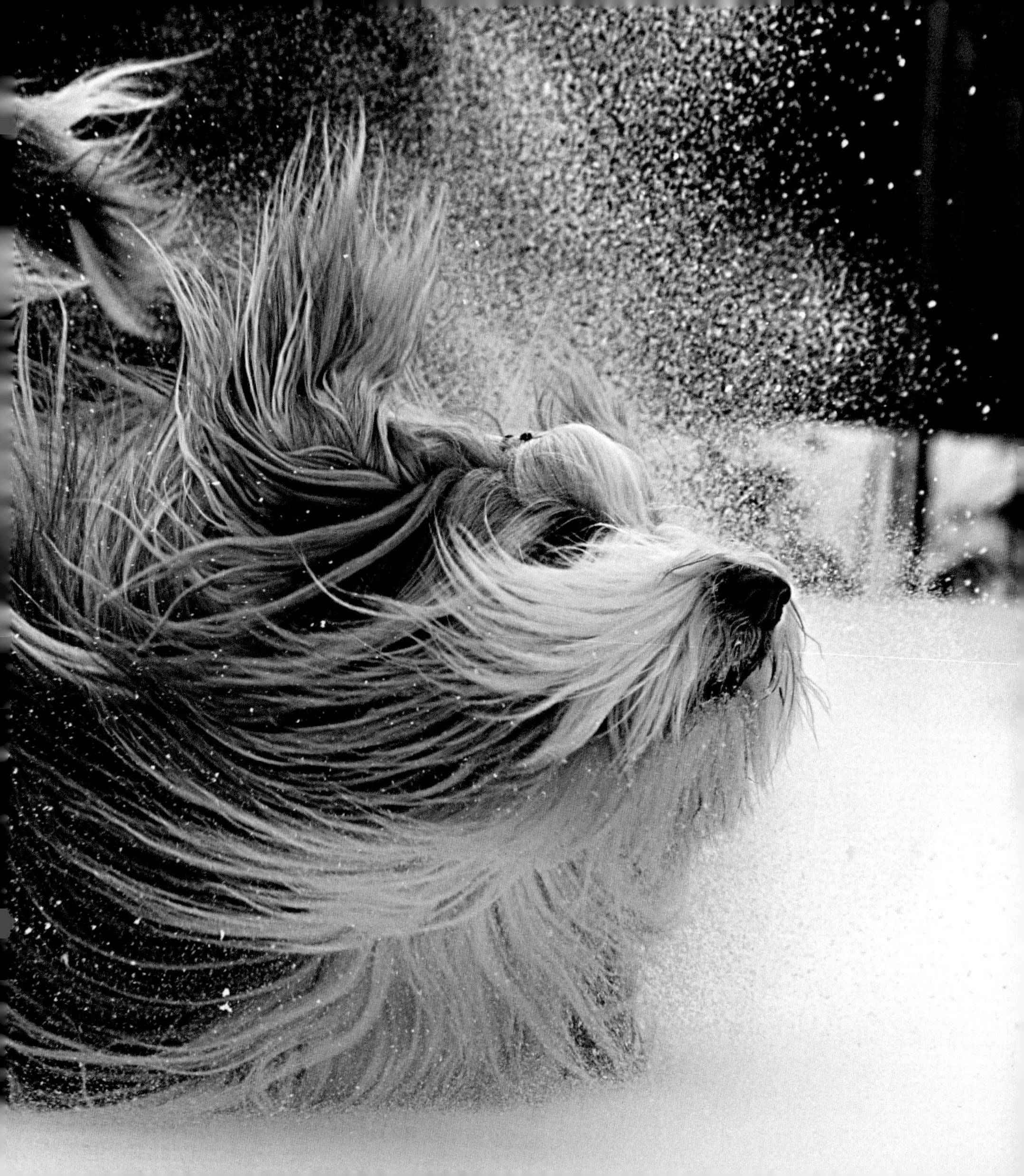

January 15

At some point in life the world's beauty becomes enough. You don't need to photograph, paint, or even remember it. It is enough.

~ Toni Morrison

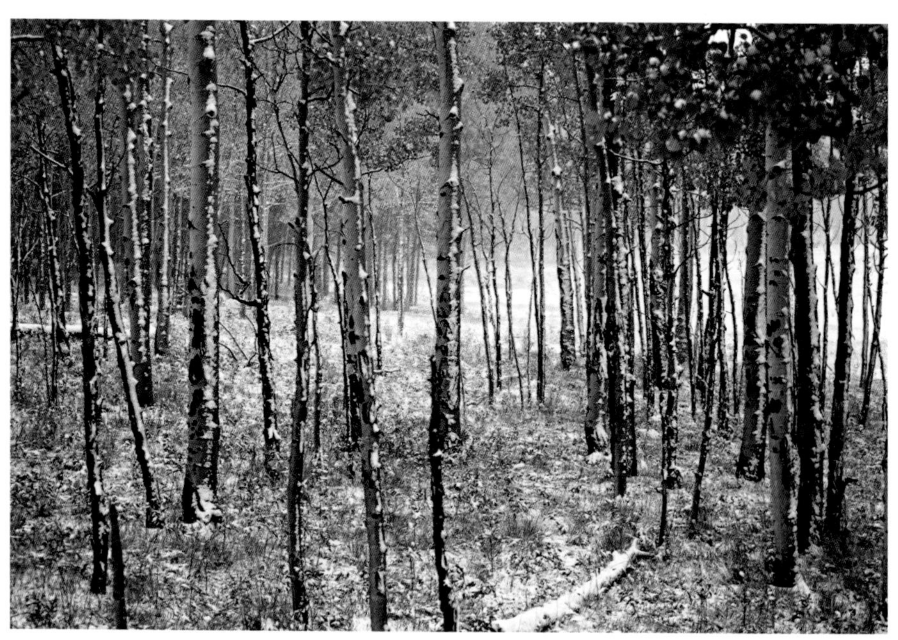

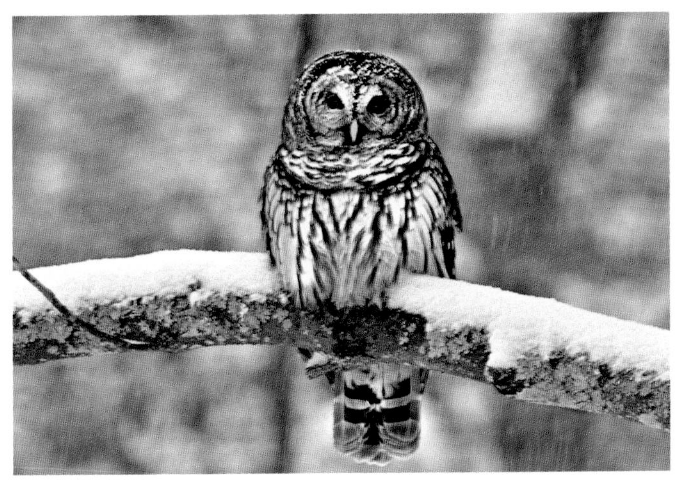

January 16

Nobody gets to live life backward.
Look ahead, that is where
your future lies.

~ Ann Landers

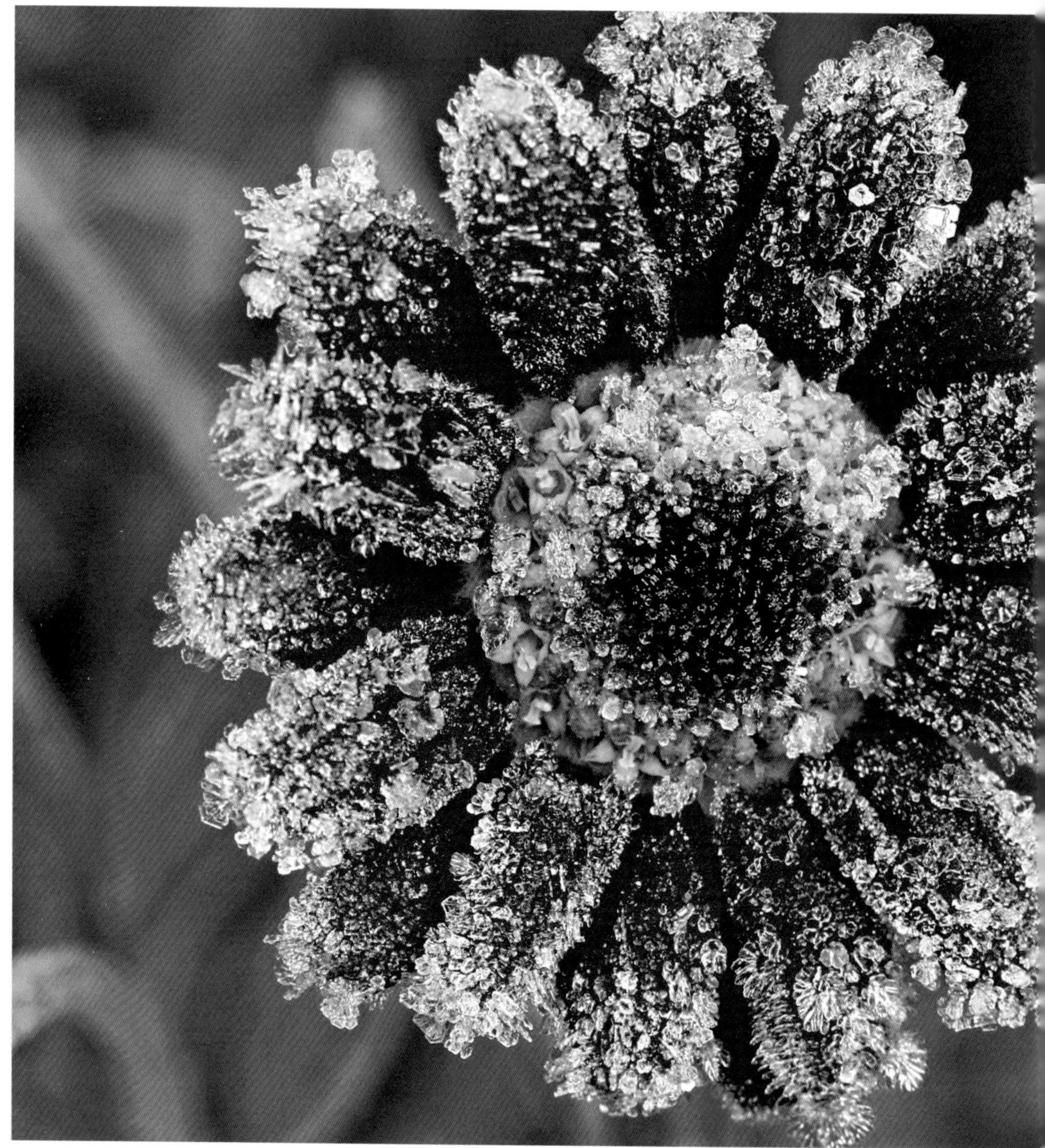

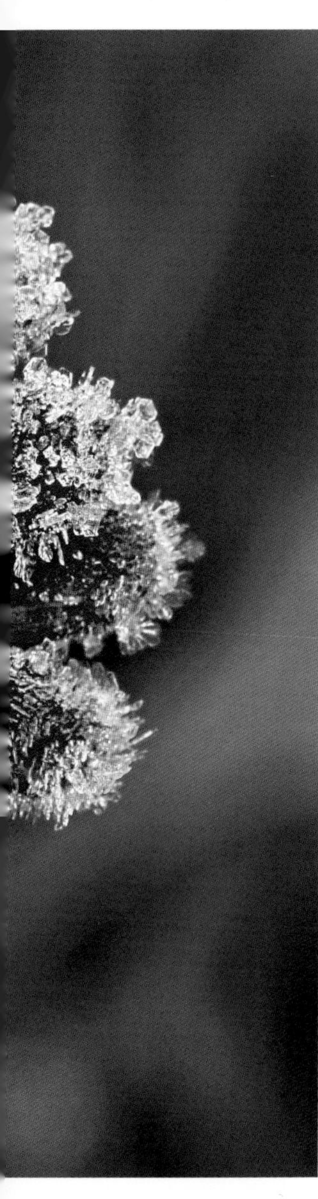

JANUARY 17

Put your ear down close to your soul and listen hard.

~ Anne Sexton

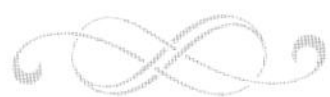

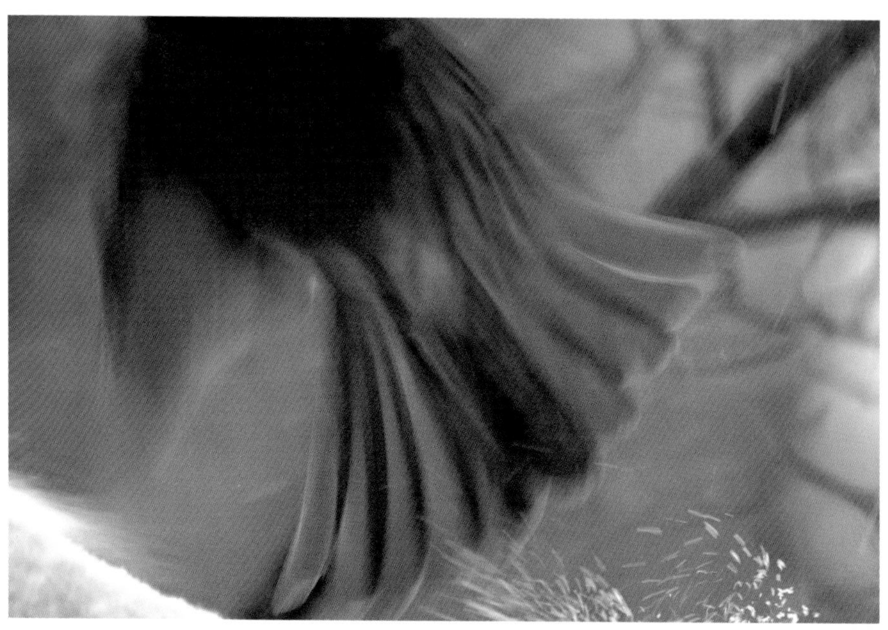

JANUARY *18*

No one saves us but ourselves.
No one can and no one may.
We ourselves must walk the path.

~ Buddha

JANUARY 19

Without forgiveness,
there is no future.

~ Desmond Tutu

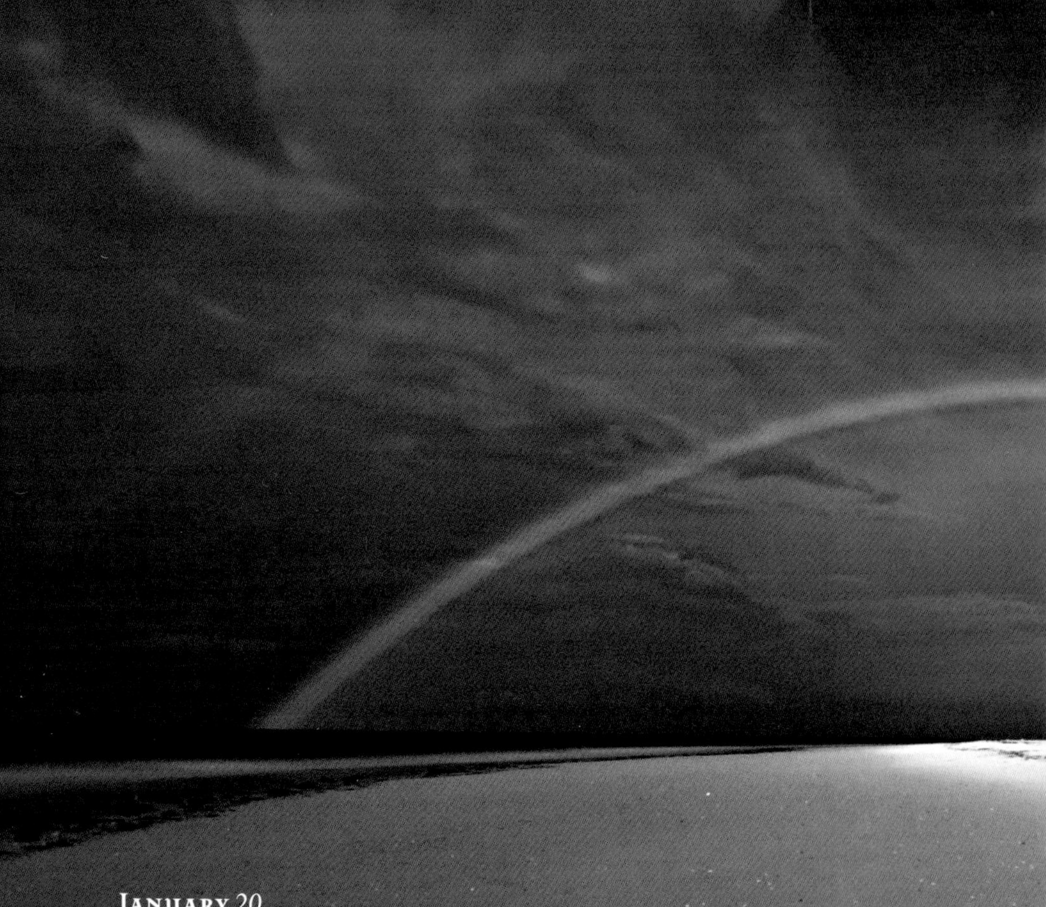

JANUARY 20

Dreams come true; without that possibility, nature would not incite us to have them.

~ John Updike

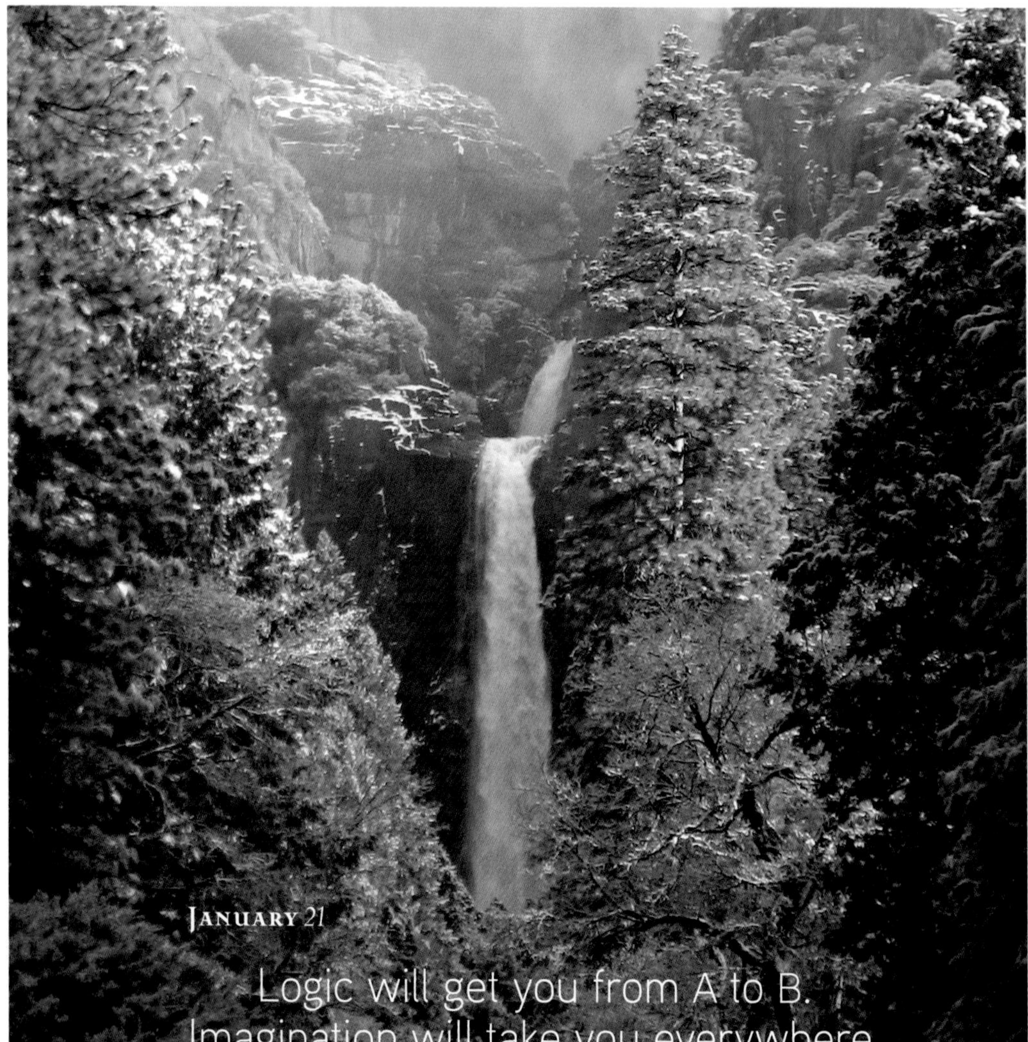

January *21*

Logic will get you from A to B.
Imagination will take you everywhere.

~ Albert Einstein

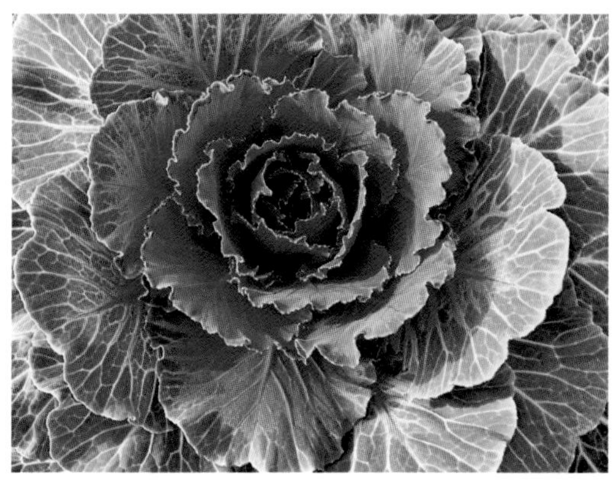

JANUARY 22

Above all, watch with glittering eyes
the whole world around you because
the greatest secrets are always
hidden in the most unlikely places.
Those who don't believe in magic
will never find it.

~ Roald Dahl

JANUARY 23

Joy is what happens to us
when we allow ourselves to recognize
how good things really are.

~ Marianne Williamson

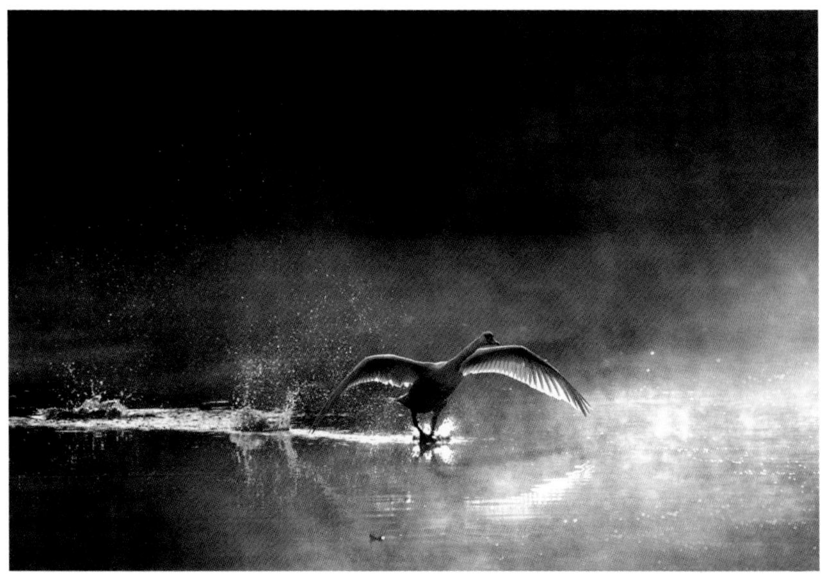

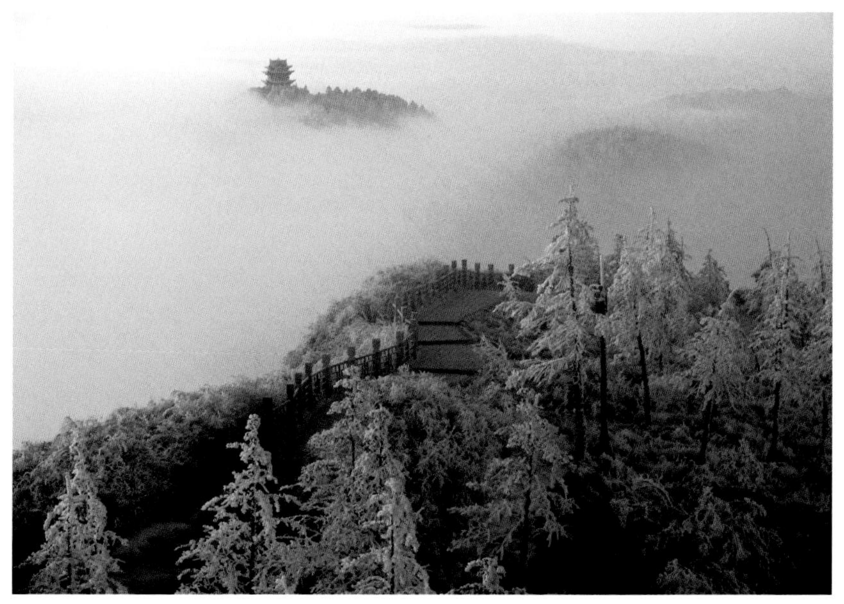

JANUARY *24*

Every great dream begins with a dreamer.
Always remember, you have within you
the strength, the patience, and the passion
to reach for the stars
to change the world.

~ Harriet Tubman

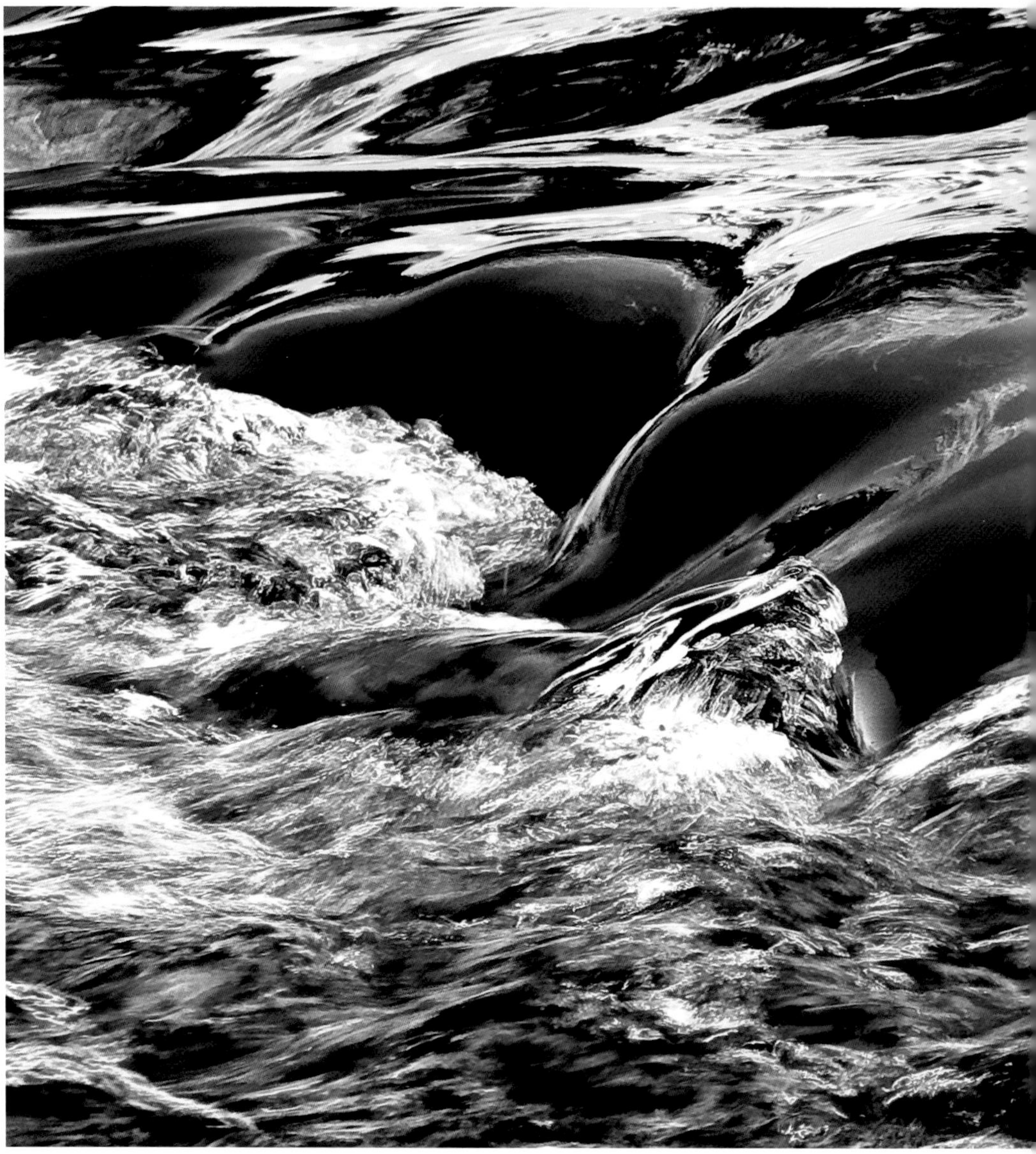

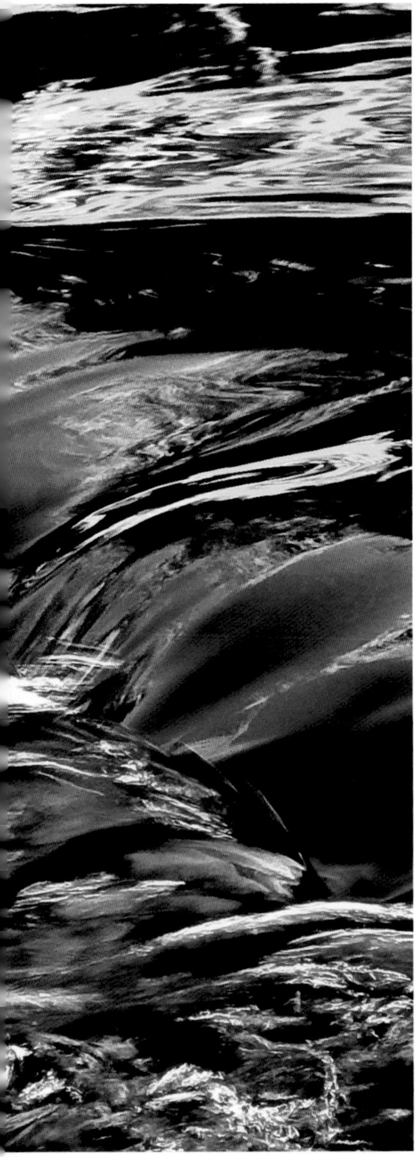

JANUARY 25

Look within.
Within is
the fountain of good,
and it will ever
bubble up,
if thou wilt ever dig.

~ Marcus Aurelius Antoninus

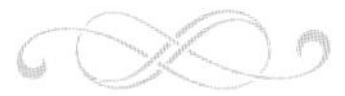

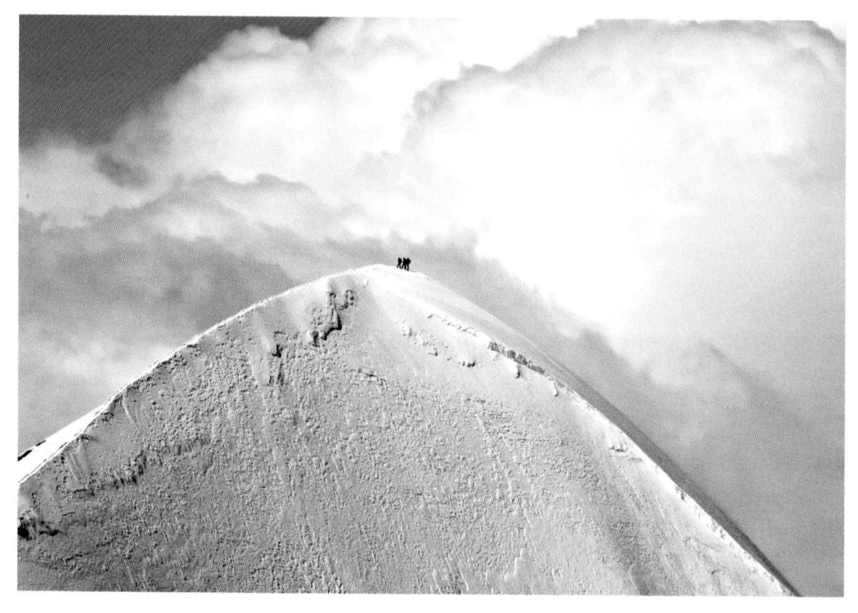

January 26

Only passions, great passions,
can elevate the soul to great things.

~ Denis Diderot

JANUARY 27

March on. Do not tarry. To go forward is to move toward perfection. March on, and fear not the thorns, or the sharp stones on life's path.

~ Kahlil Gibran

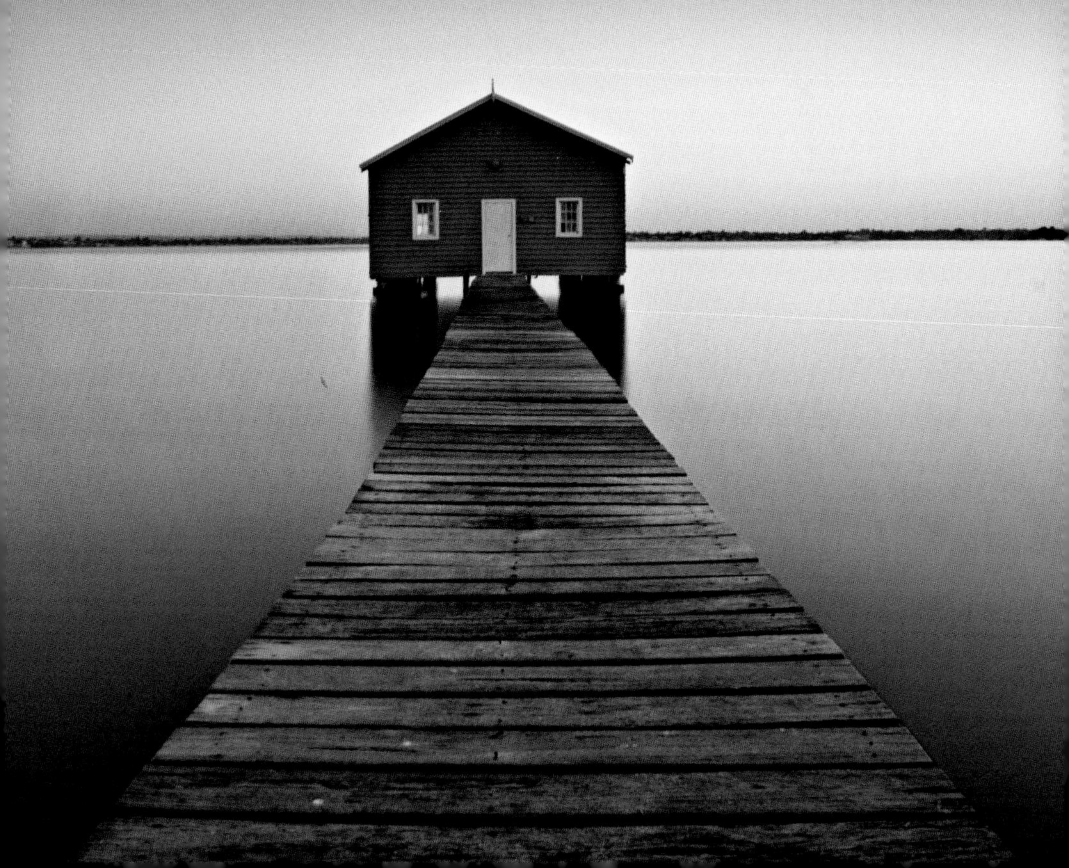

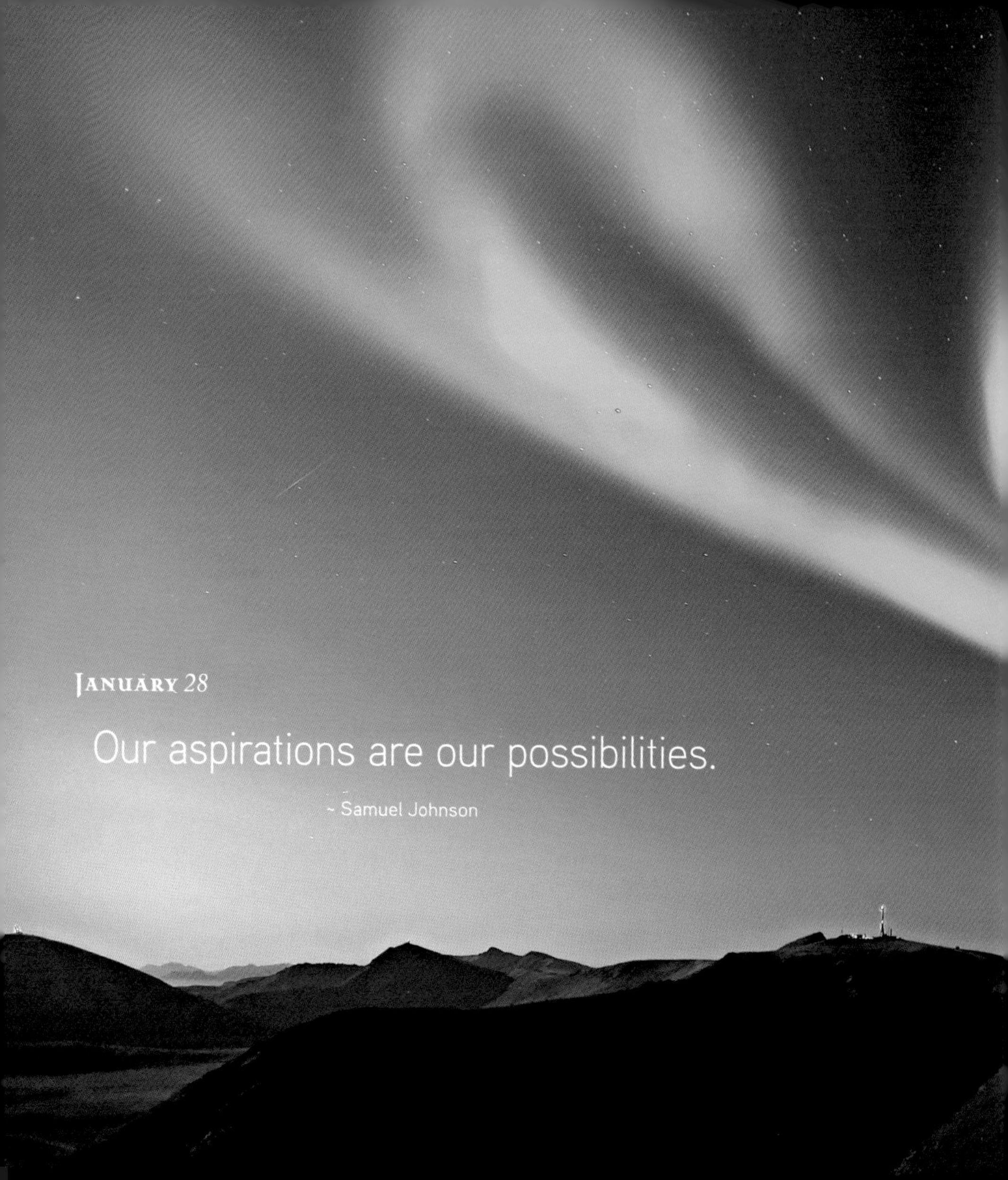

JANUARY 28

Our aspirations are our possibilities.

~ Samuel Johnson

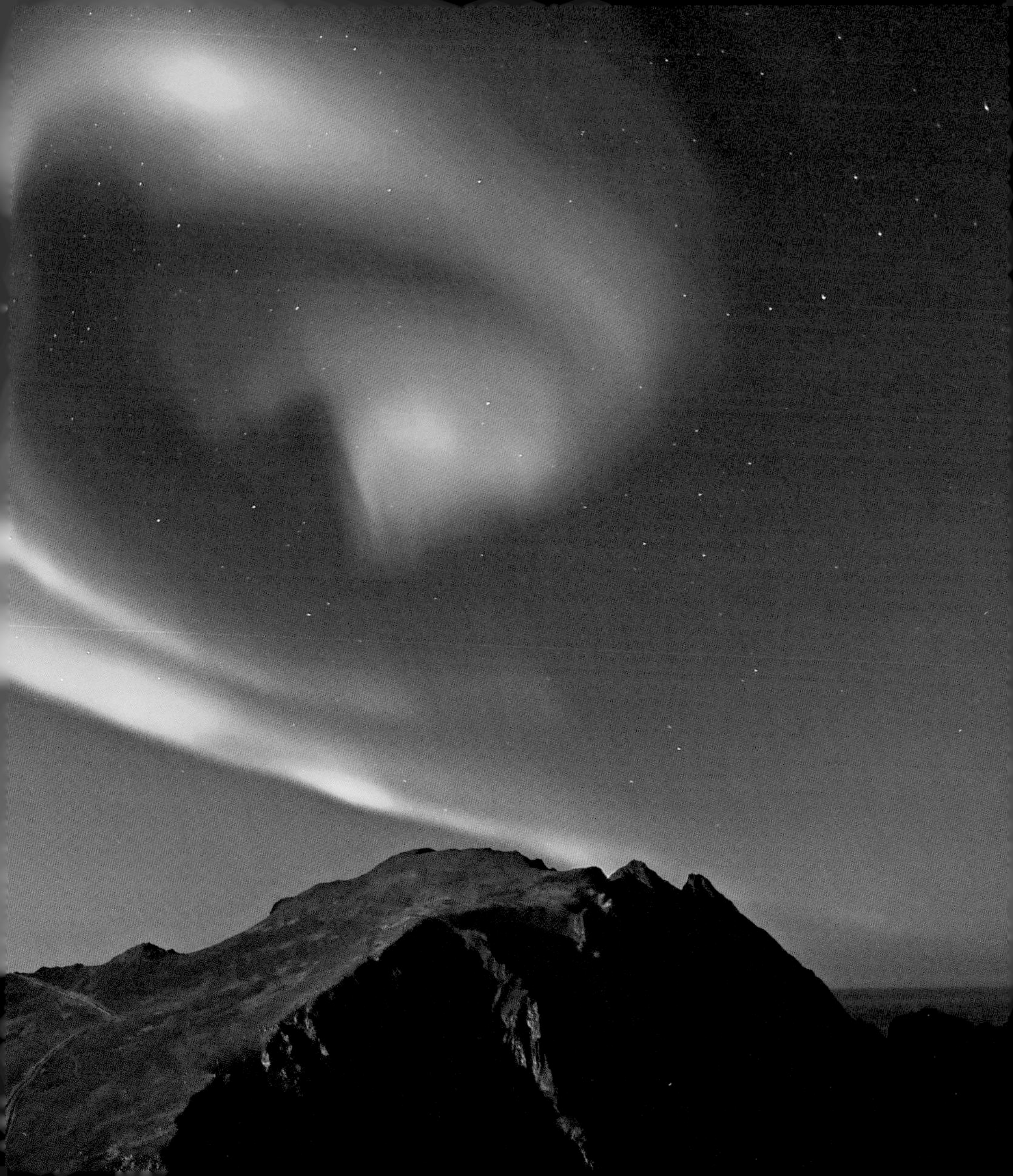

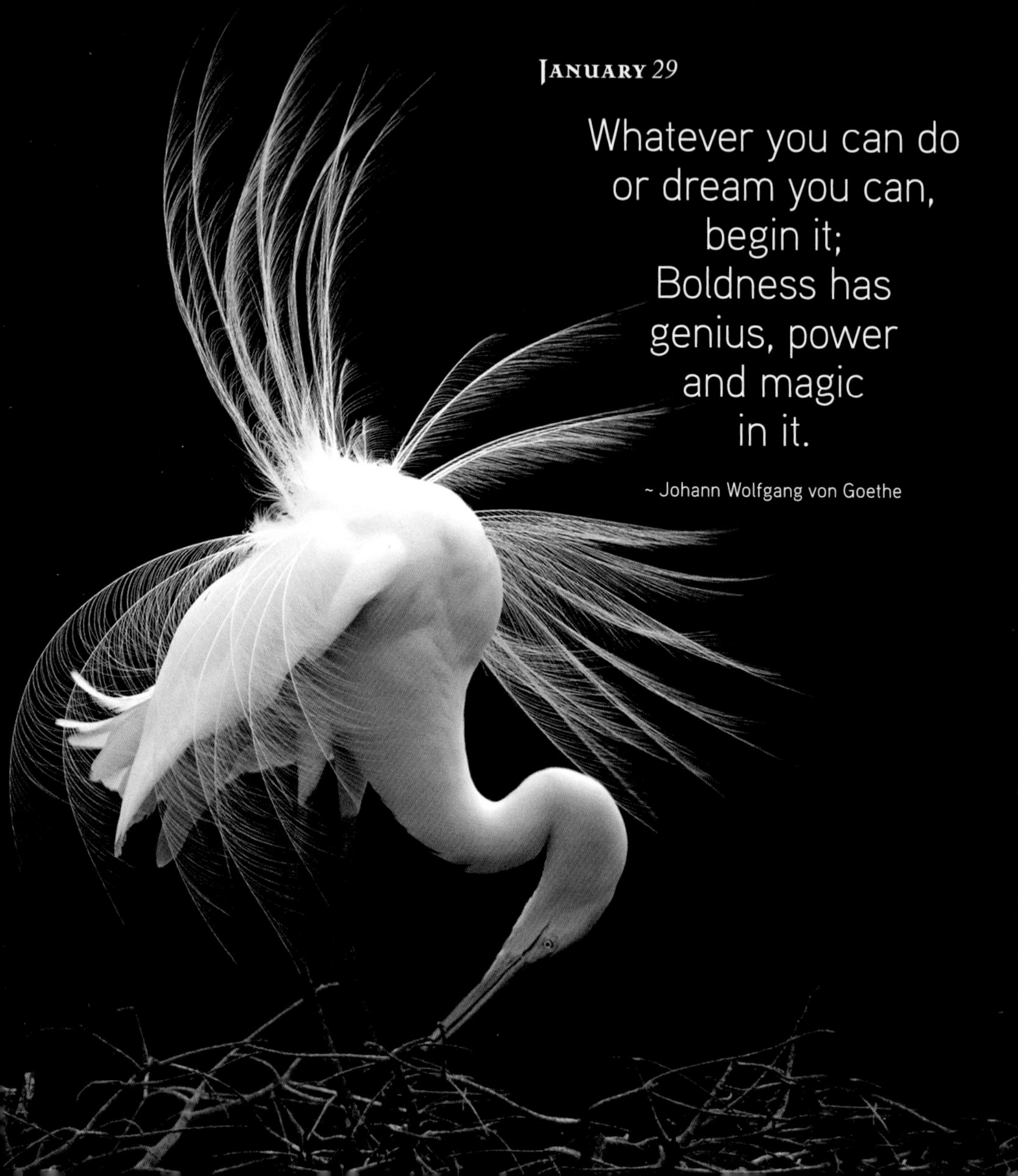

JANUARY 29

Whatever you can do
or dream you can,
begin it;
Boldness has
genius, power
and magic
in it.

~ Johann Wolfgang von Goethe

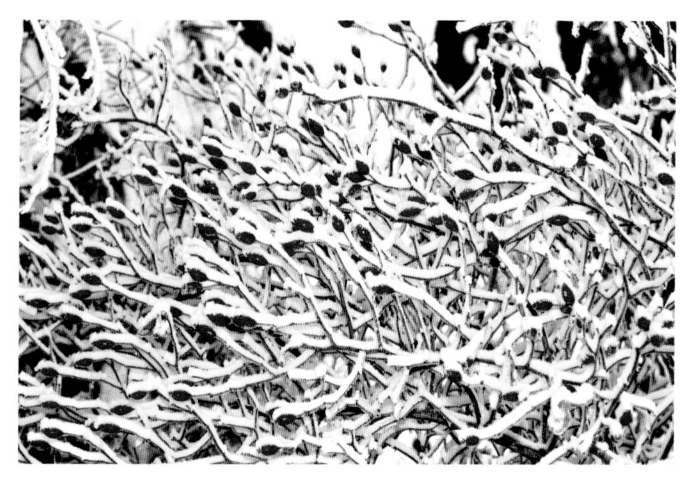

JANUARY 30

Look inside.
That way lies dancing to the melodies
spun out by your own heart.
This is a symphony.
All the rest are jingles.

~ Anna Quindlen

January 31

In the depth of winter
I finally learned
that there was in me
an invincible summer.

~ Albert Camus

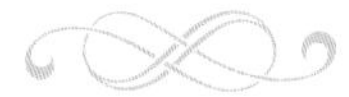

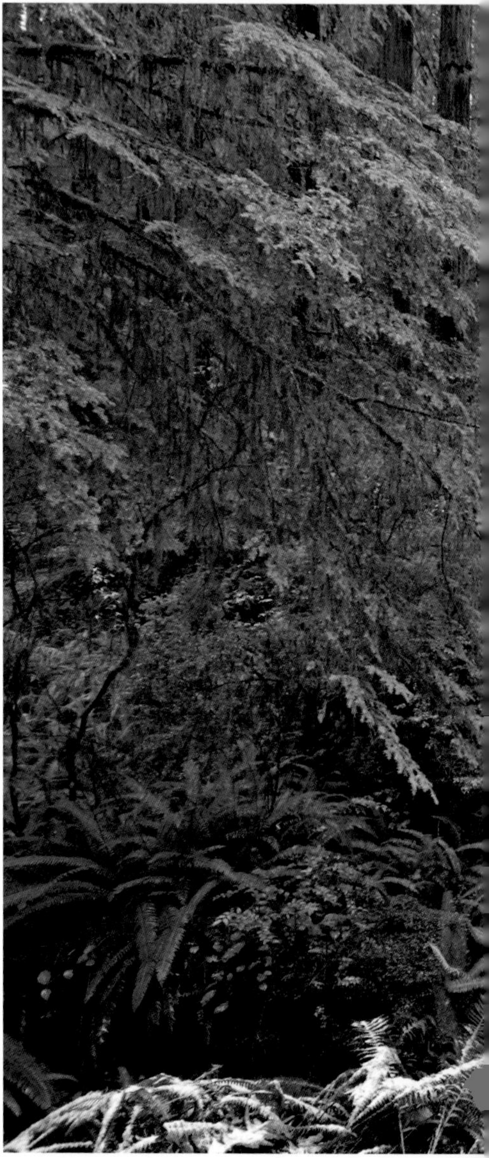

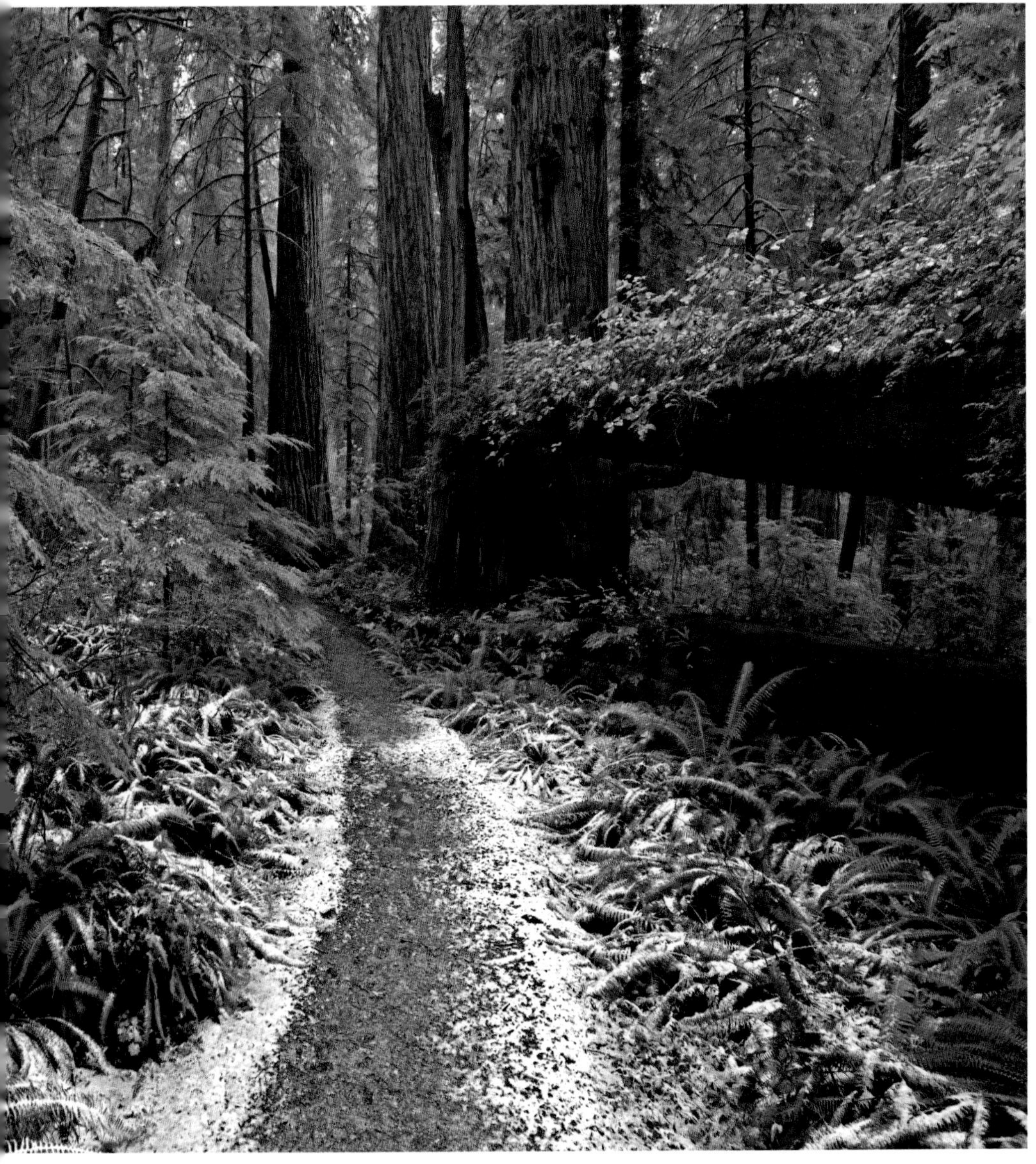

LOVE

February

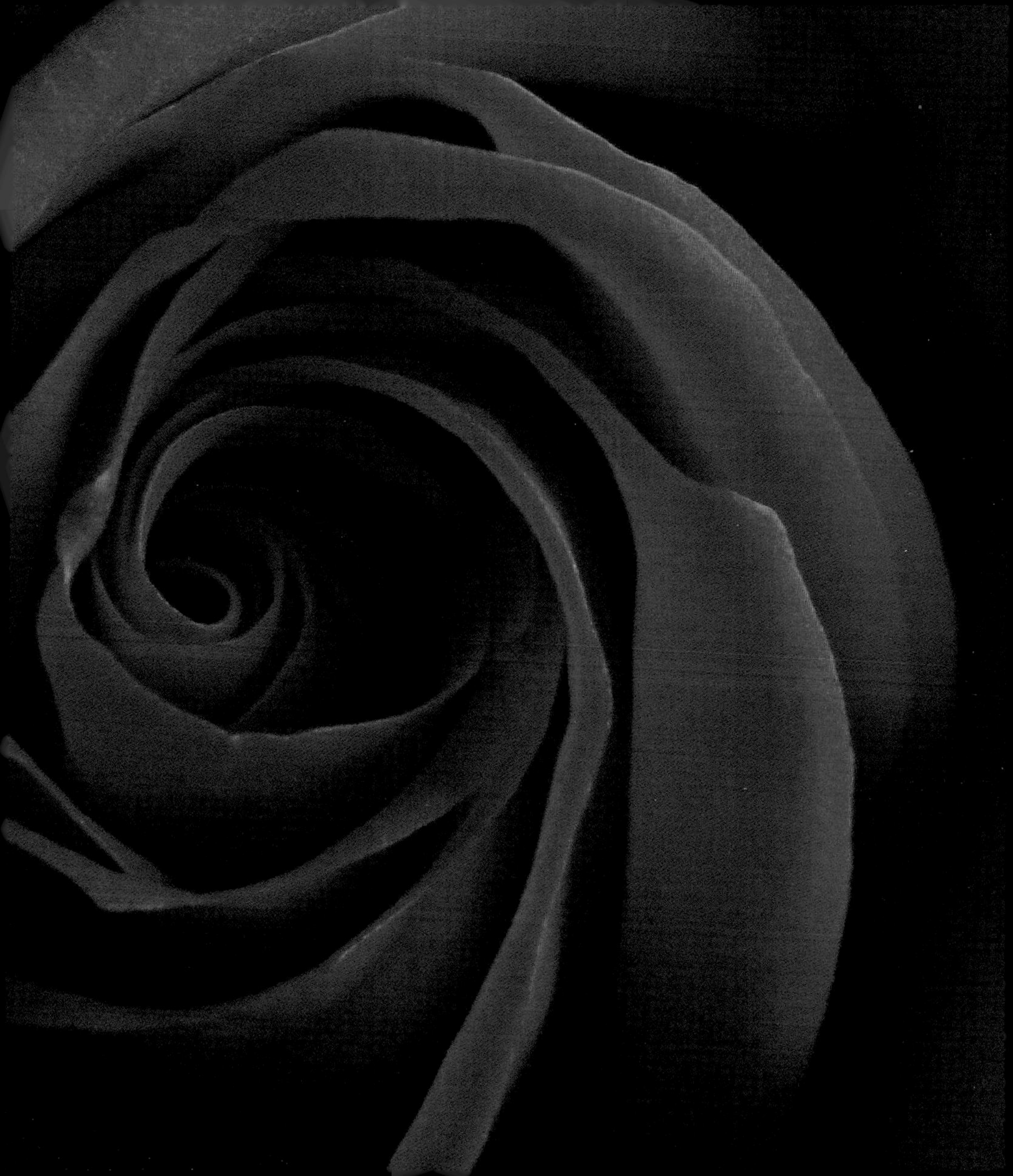

February 1

Nobody has ever measured,
even the poets,
how much a heart can hold.

~ Zelda Fitzgerald

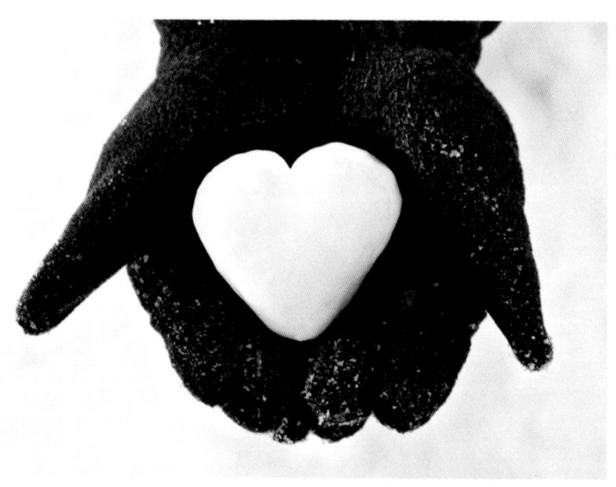

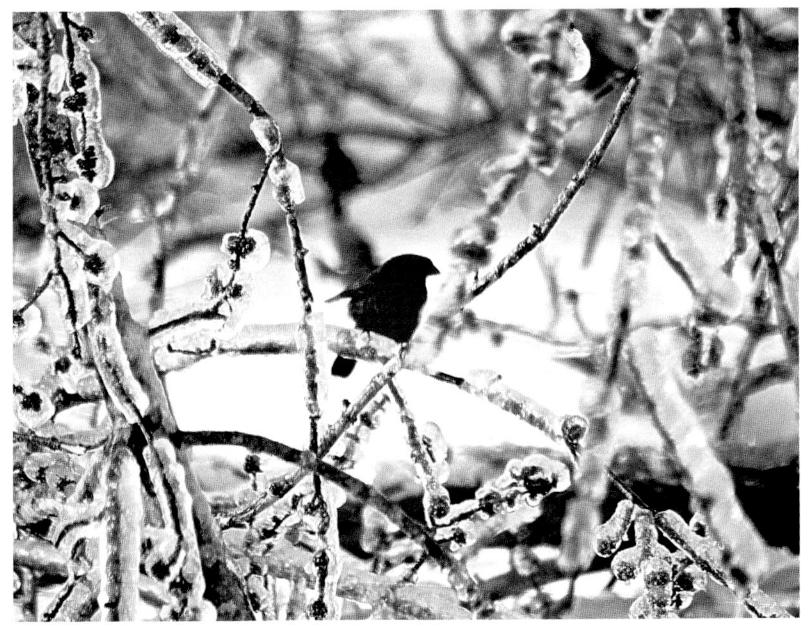

FEBRUARY 2

For one human being to love another—that is perhaps the most difficult of our tasks: the ultimate, the last test and proof, the work for which all other work is but preparation.

~ Rainer Maria Rilke

FEBRUARY 3

Who, being loved, is poor?

~ Oscar Wilde

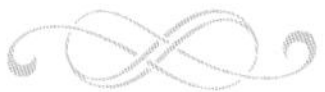

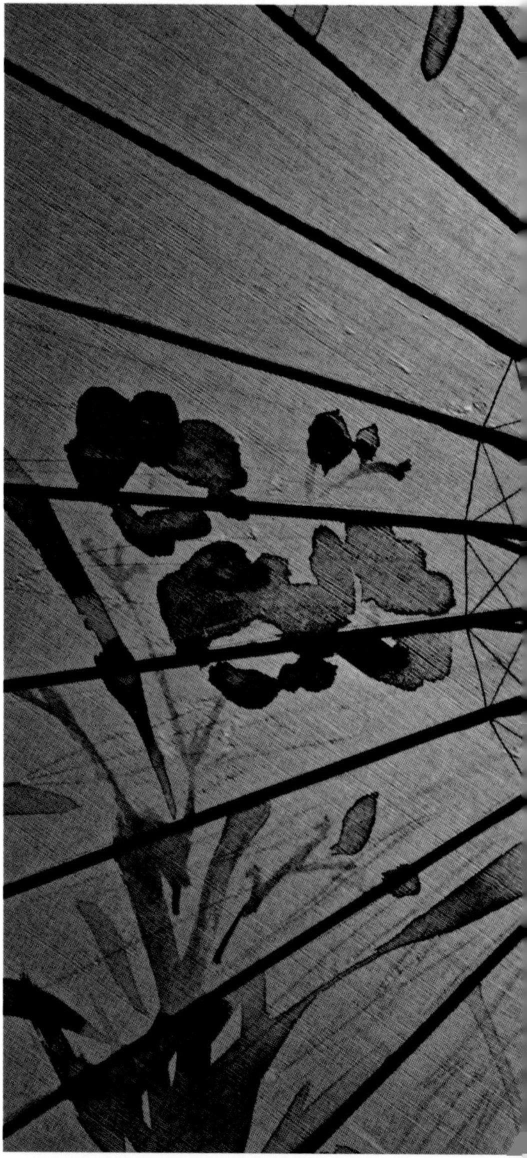

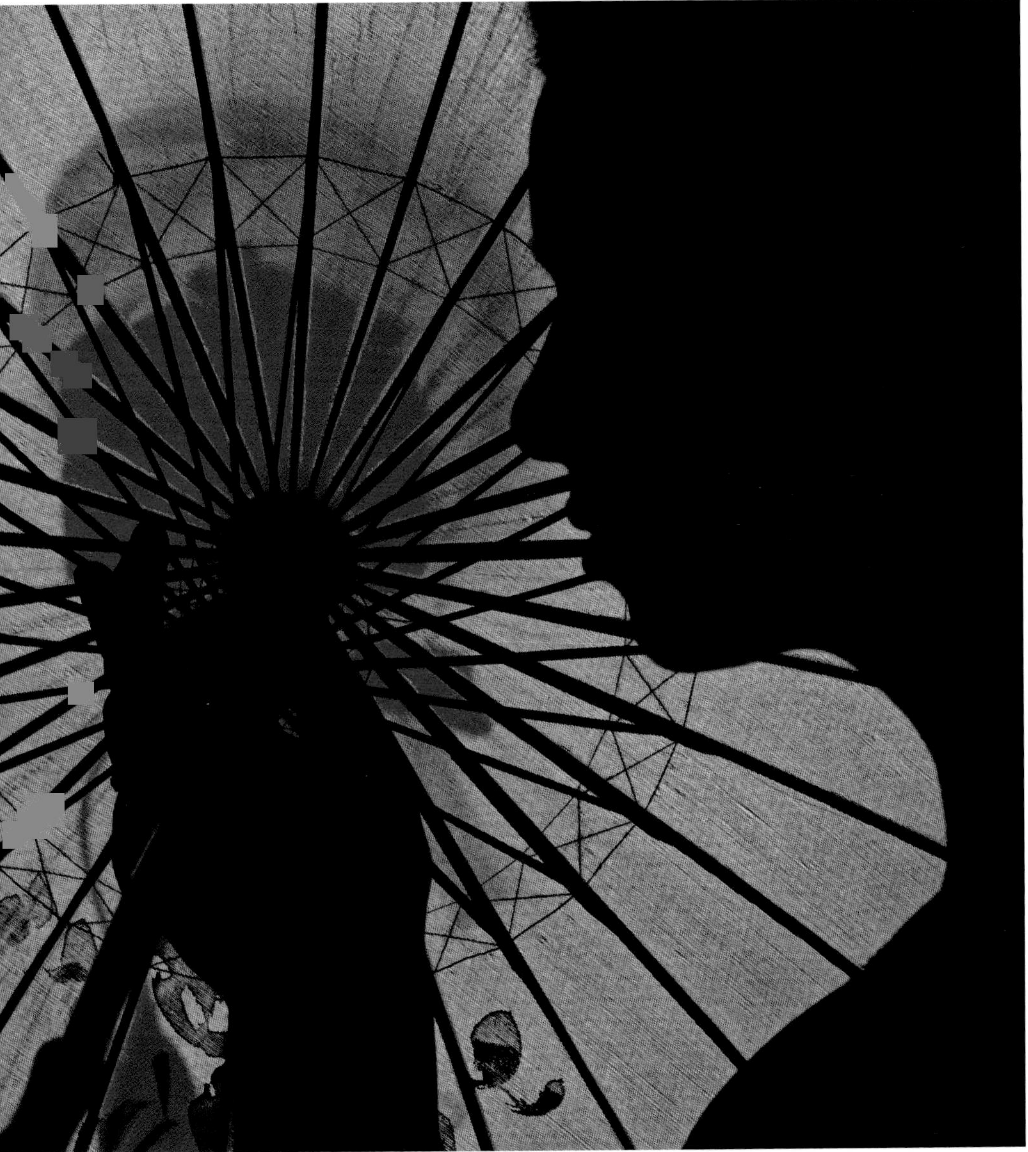

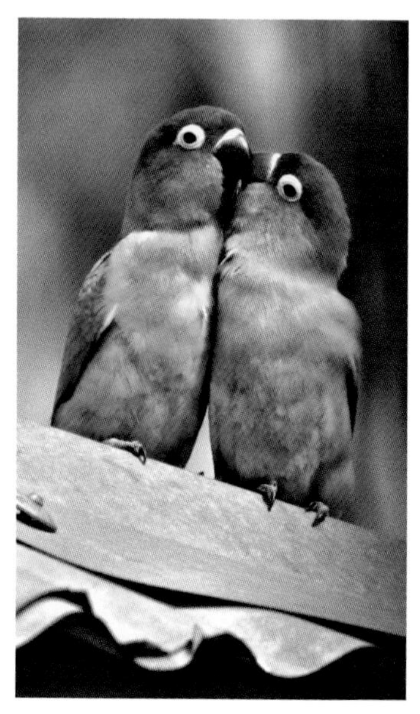

FEBRUARY 4

Being deeply loved by someone
gives you strength,
while loving someone deeply
gives you courage.

~ Lao-tzu

Love does not consist
in gazing at each other,
but in looking outward together
in the same direction.

~ Antoine de Saint-Exupéry

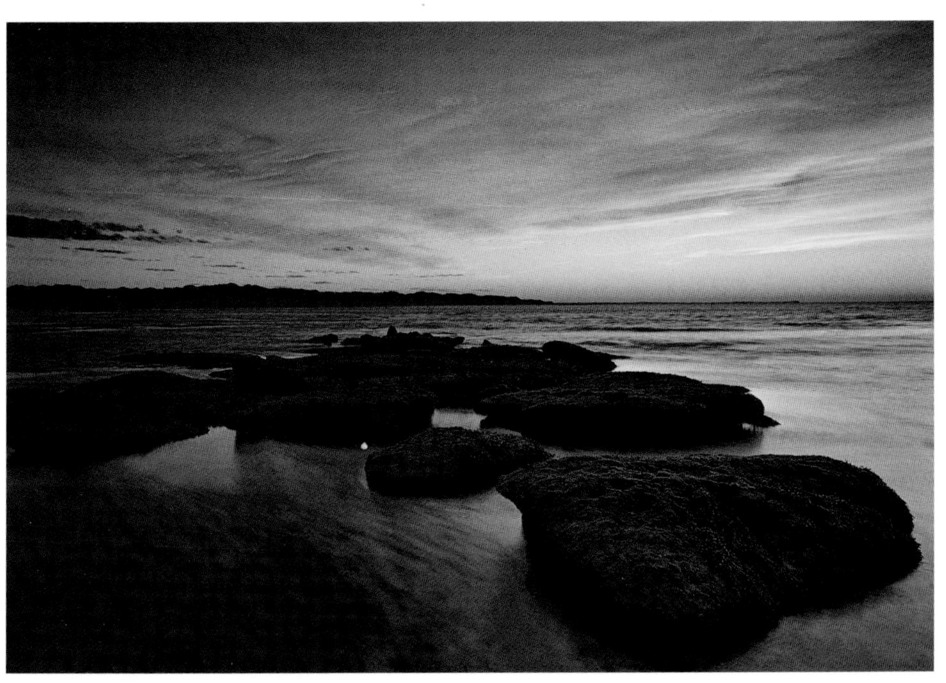

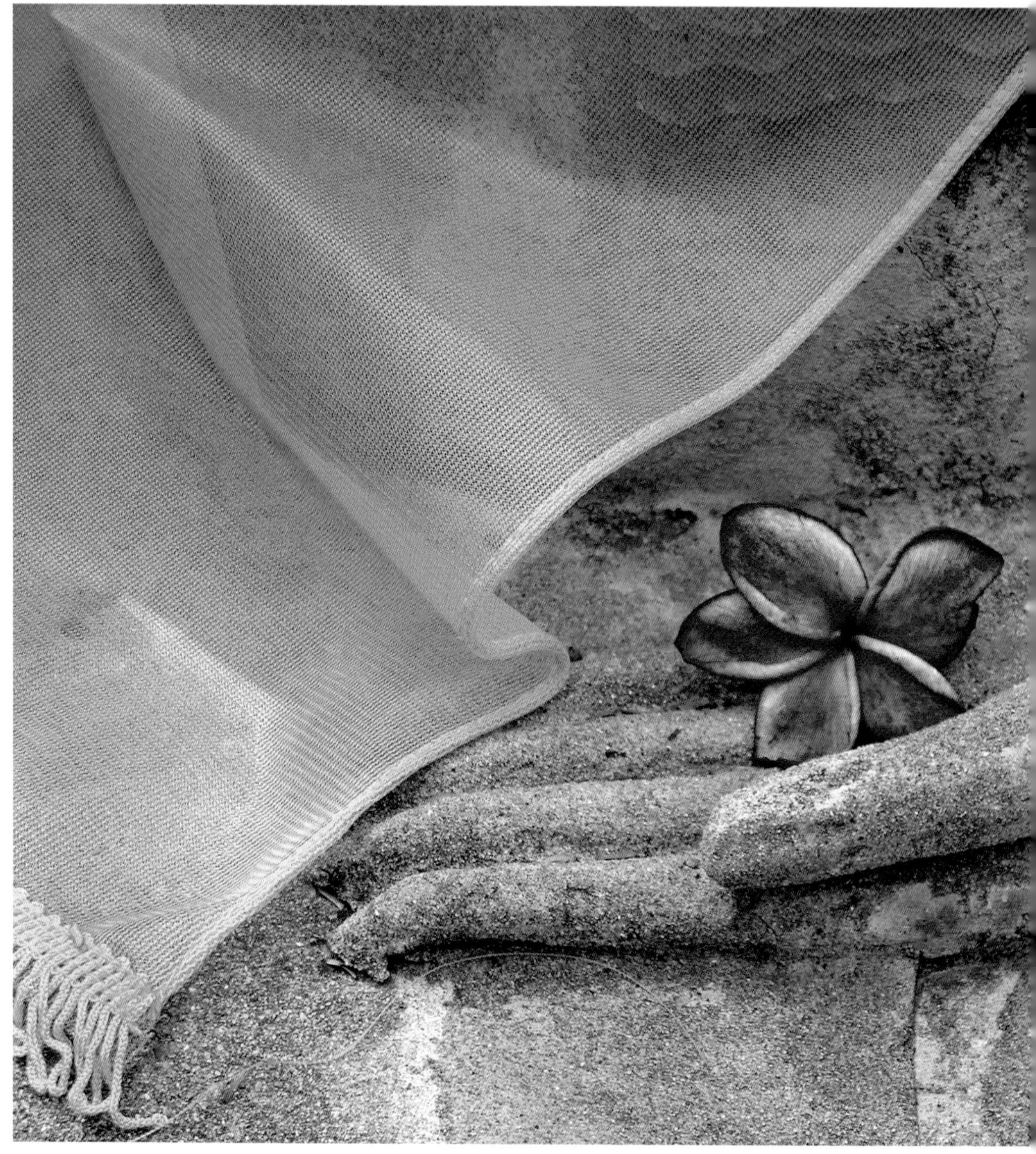

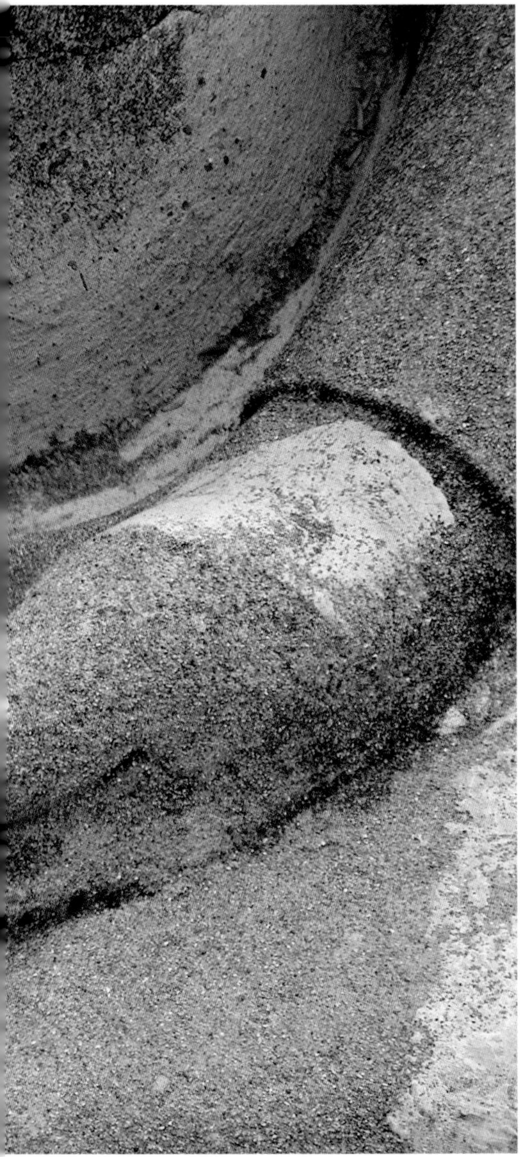

FEBRUARY 6

You yourself,
as much as
anybody
in the entire
universe,
deserve your
love and
affection.

~ Buddha

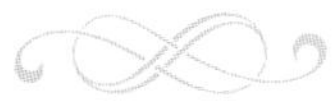

February 7

Age does not
protect you from love.
But love,
to some extent,
protects you from age.

~ Jeanne Moreau

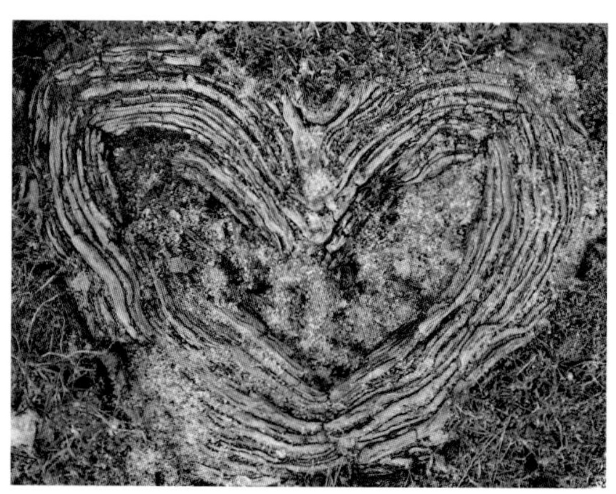

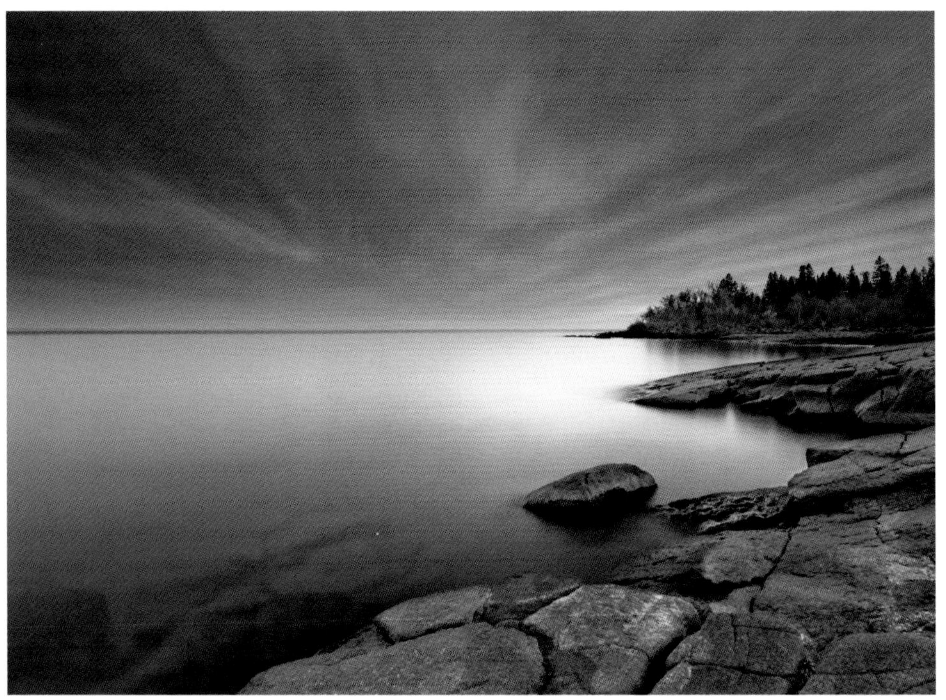

FEBRUARY *8*

To lose balance, sometimes, for love,
is part of living a balanced life.

~ Elizabeth Gilbert

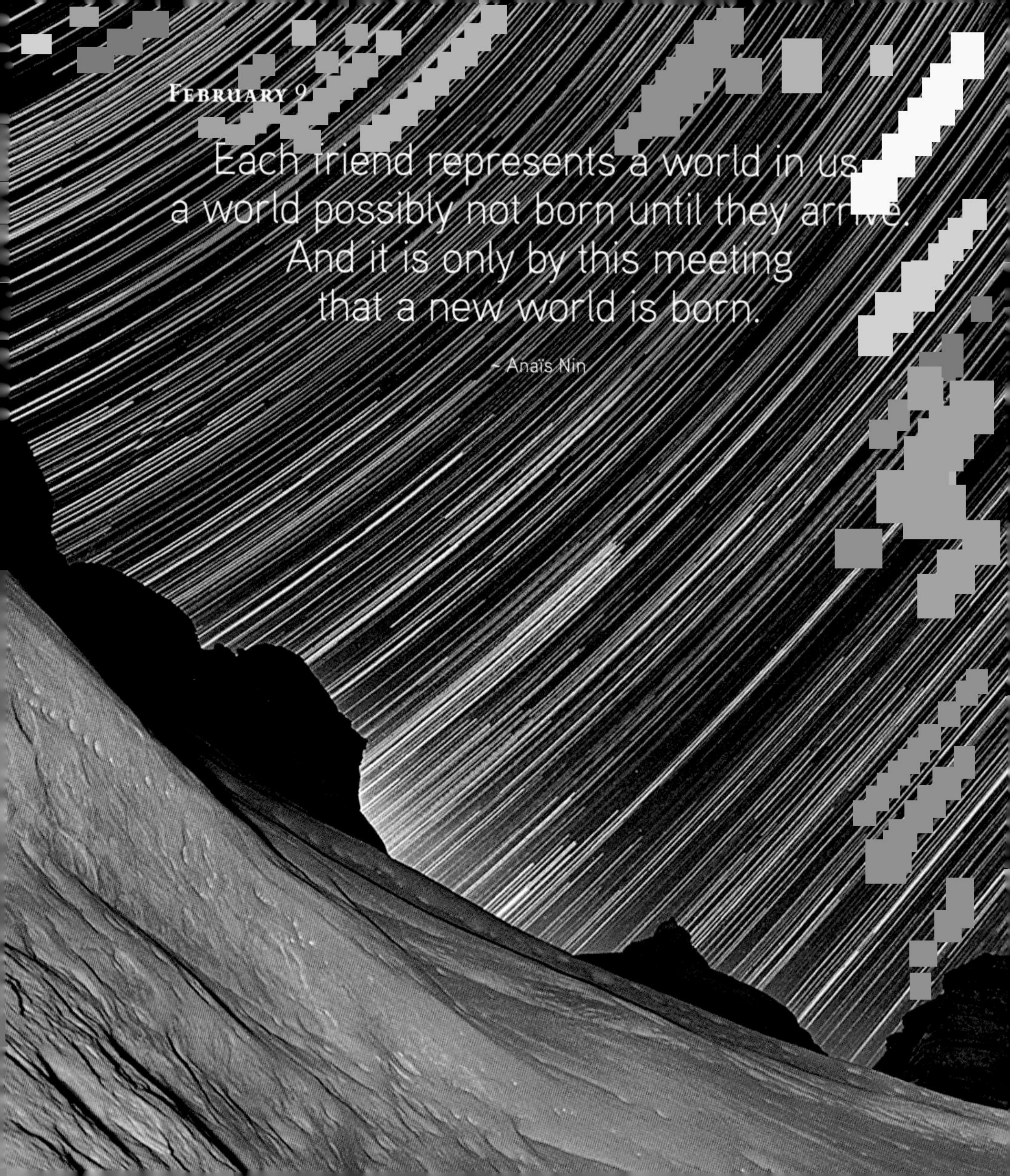

FEBRUARY 9

Each friend represents a world in us,
a world possibly not born until they arrive.
And it is only by this meeting
that a new world is born.

~ Anaïs Nin

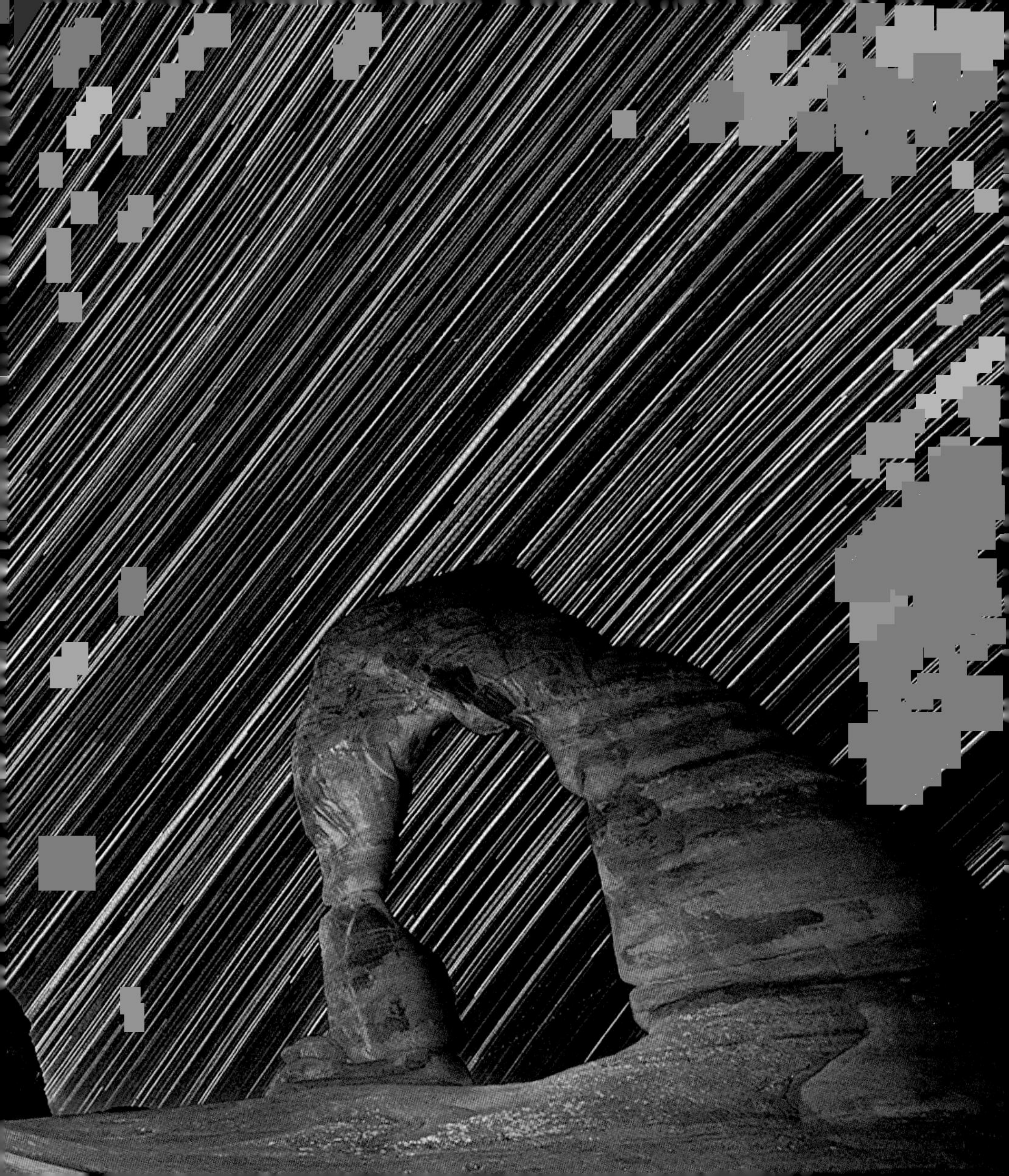

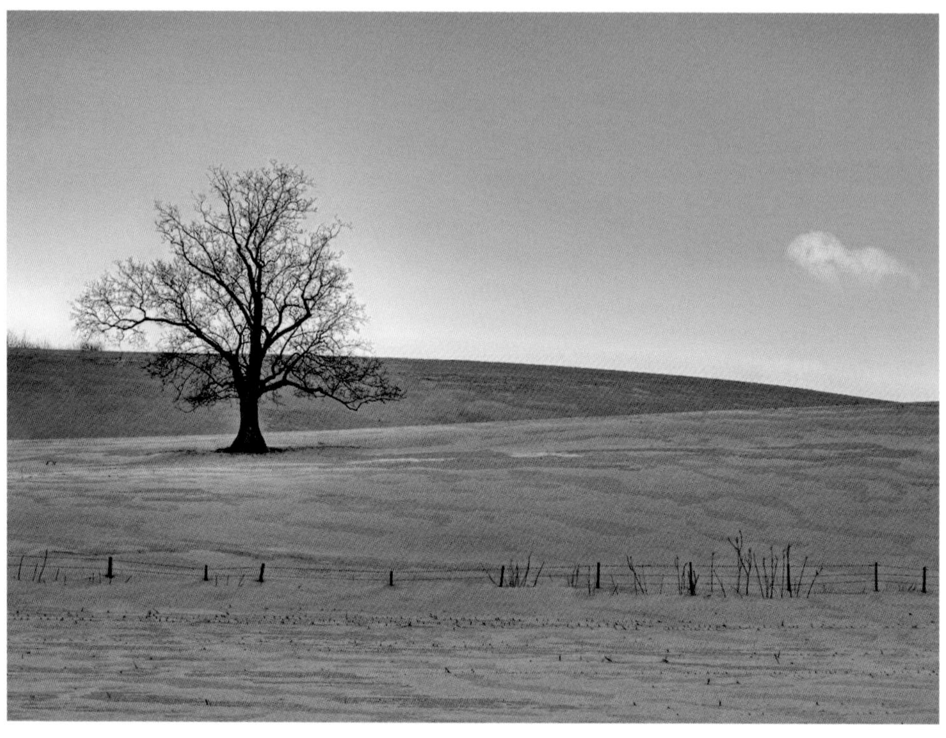

FEBRUARY *10*

Life without love
is like a tree without blossom and fruit.

~ Kahlil Gibran

FEBRUARY 11

Immature love says:
"I love you because I need you."
Mature love says:
"I need you because I love you."

~ Erich Fromm

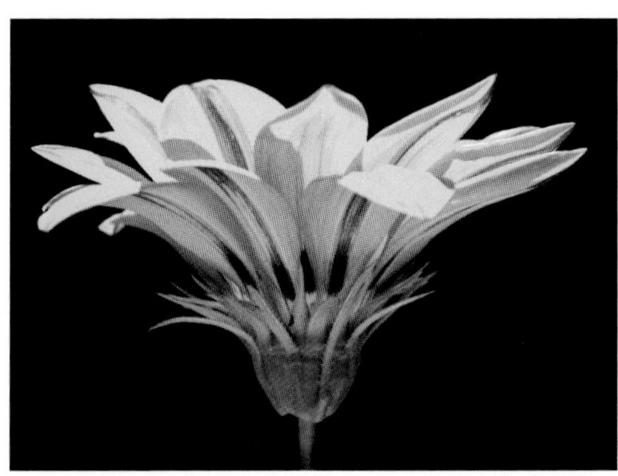

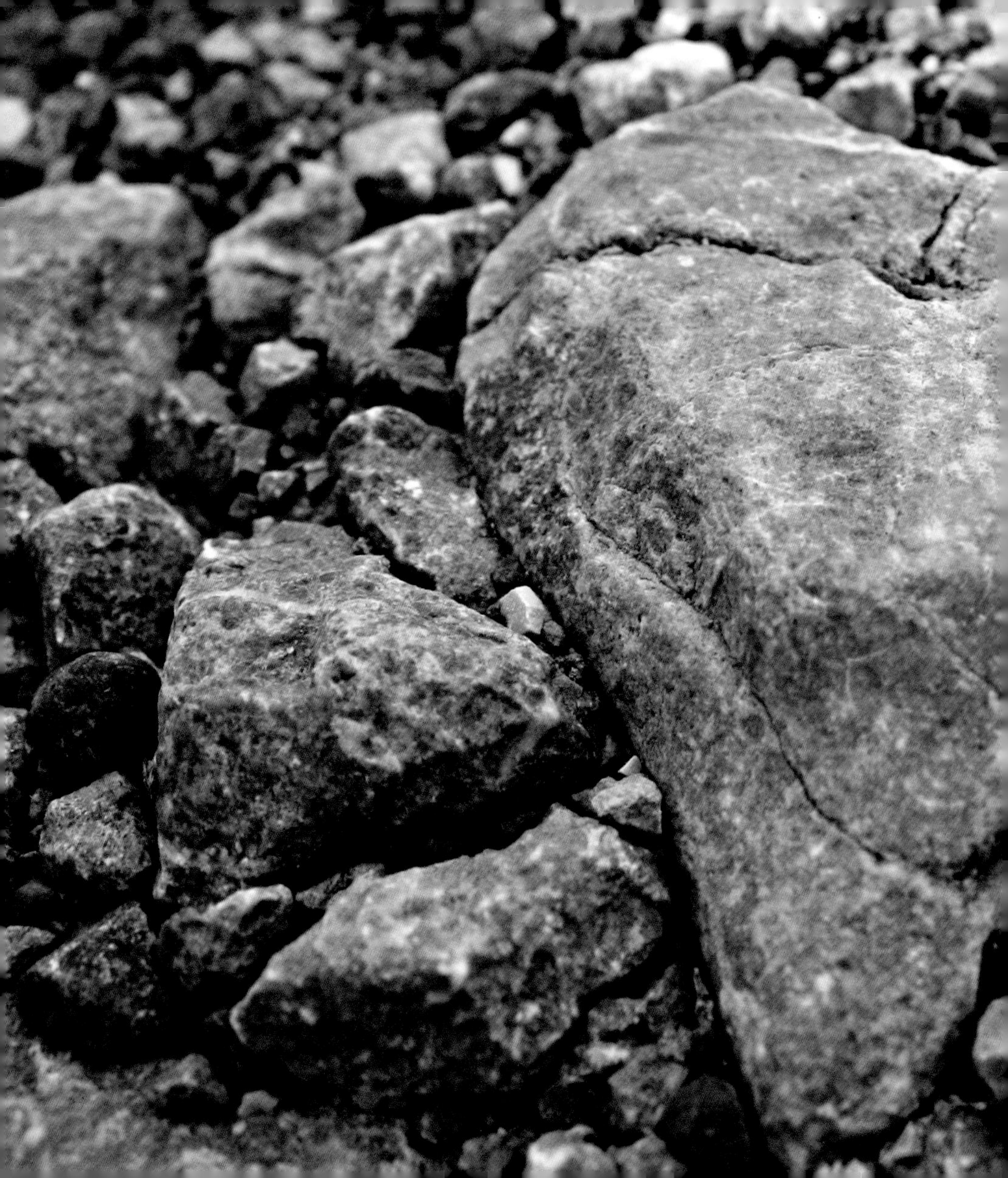

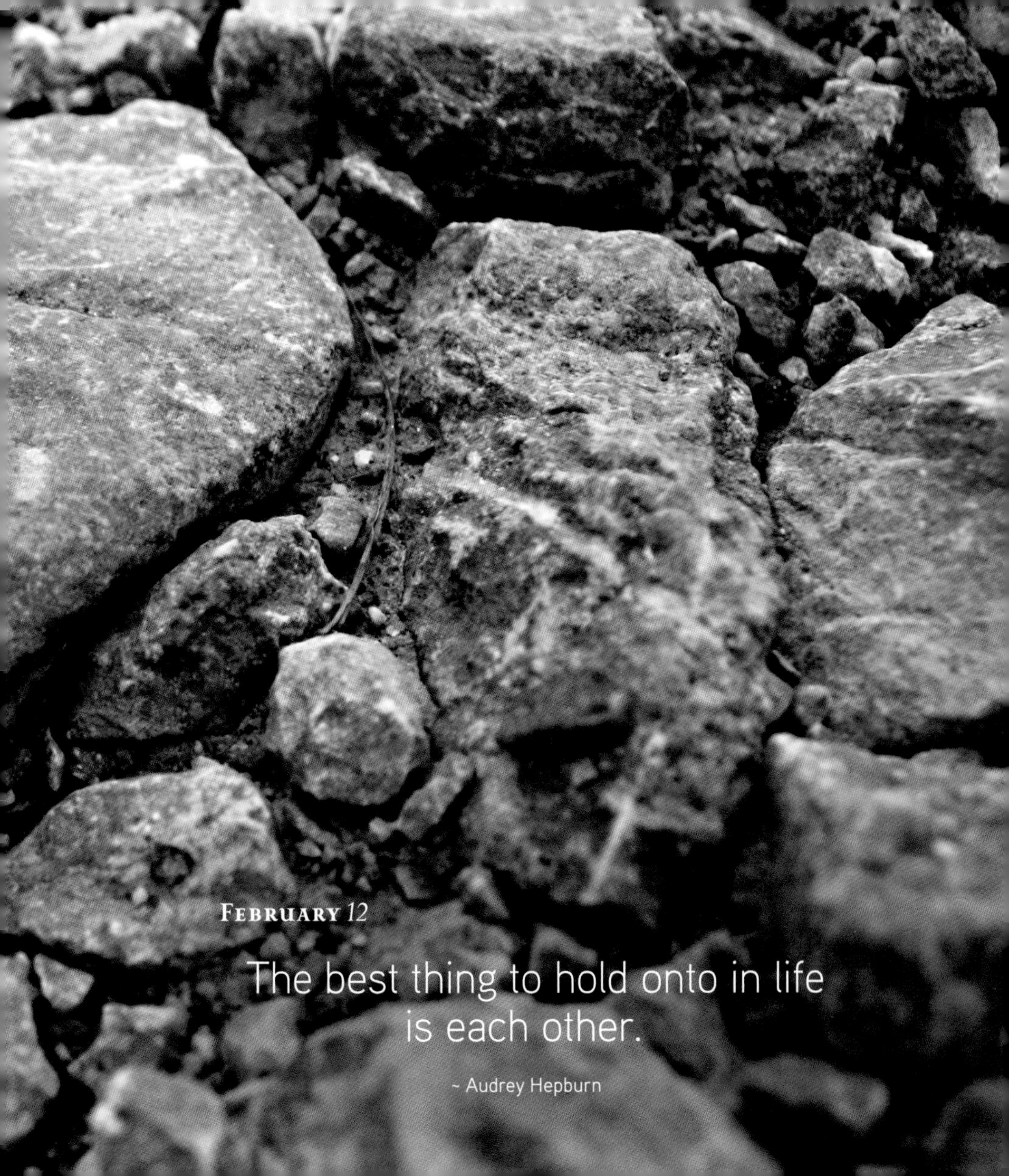

FEBRUARY 12

The best thing to hold onto in life
is each other.

~ Audrey Hepburn

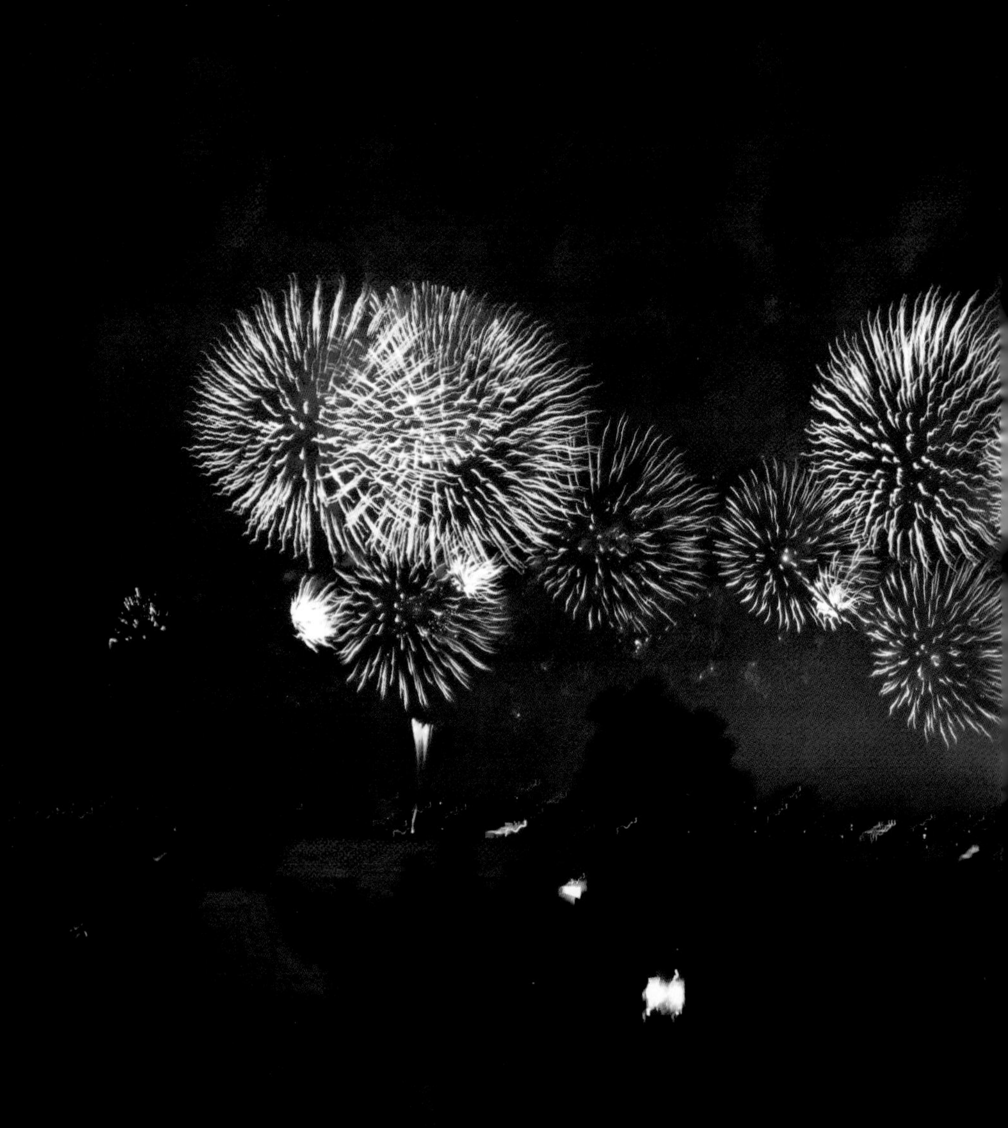

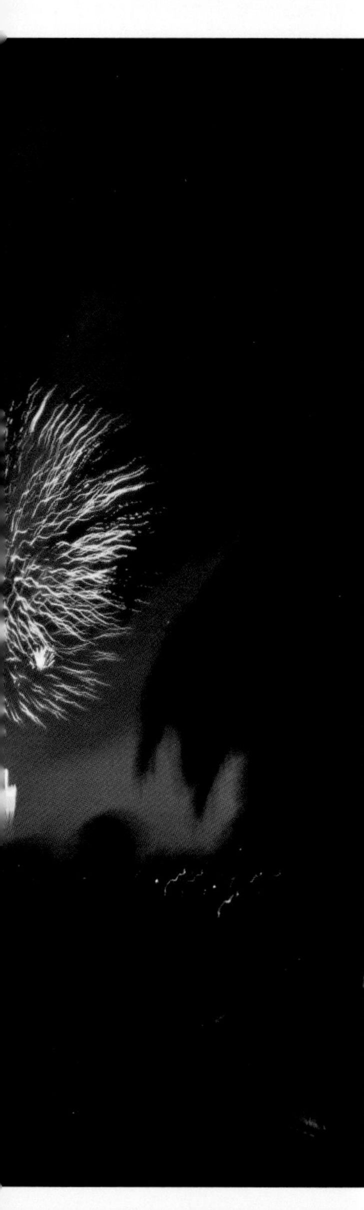

FEBRUARY 13

A very small
degree of hope
is sufficient
to cause
the birth of love.

~ Stendahl

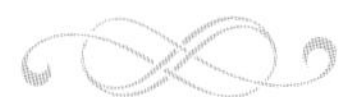

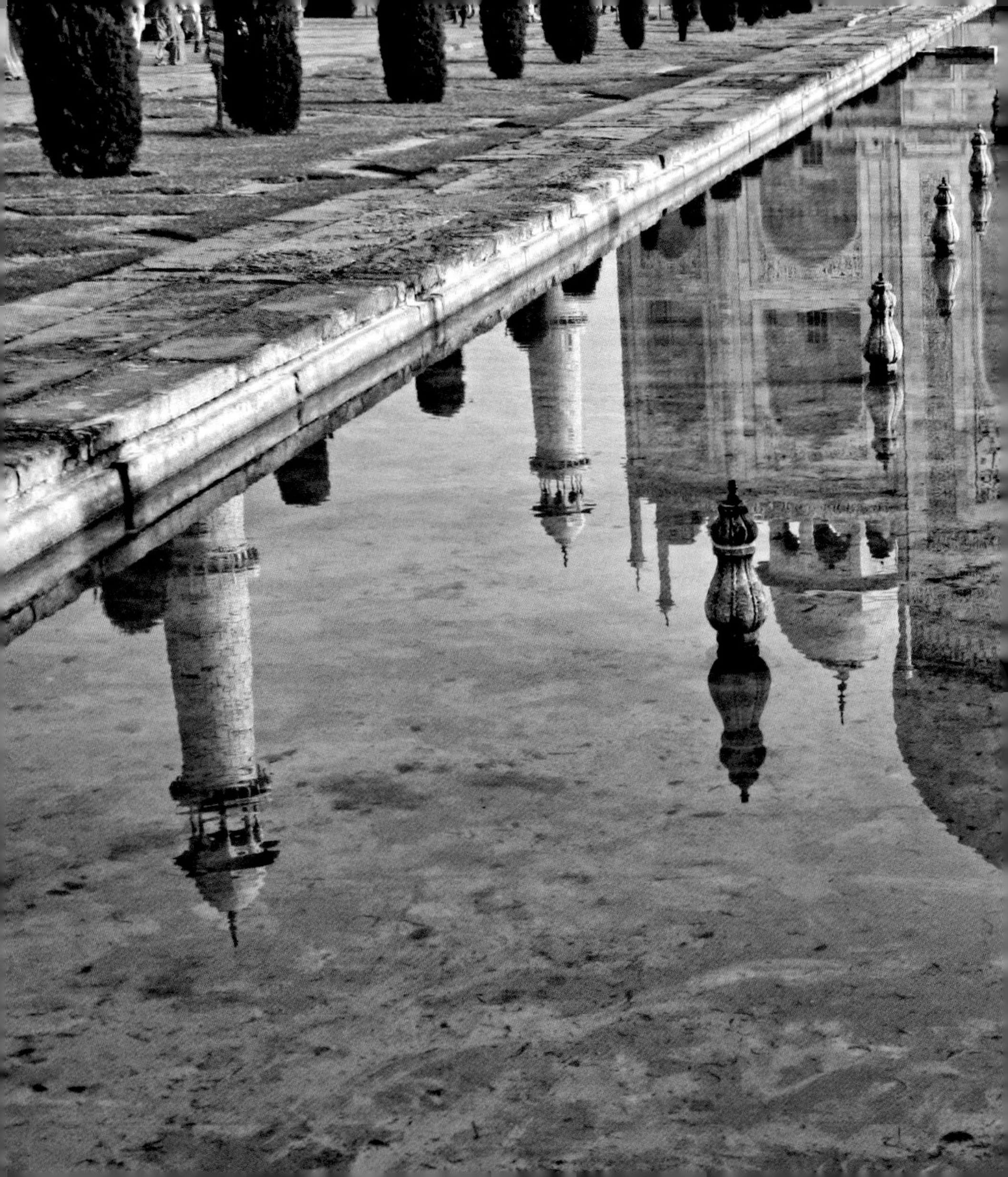

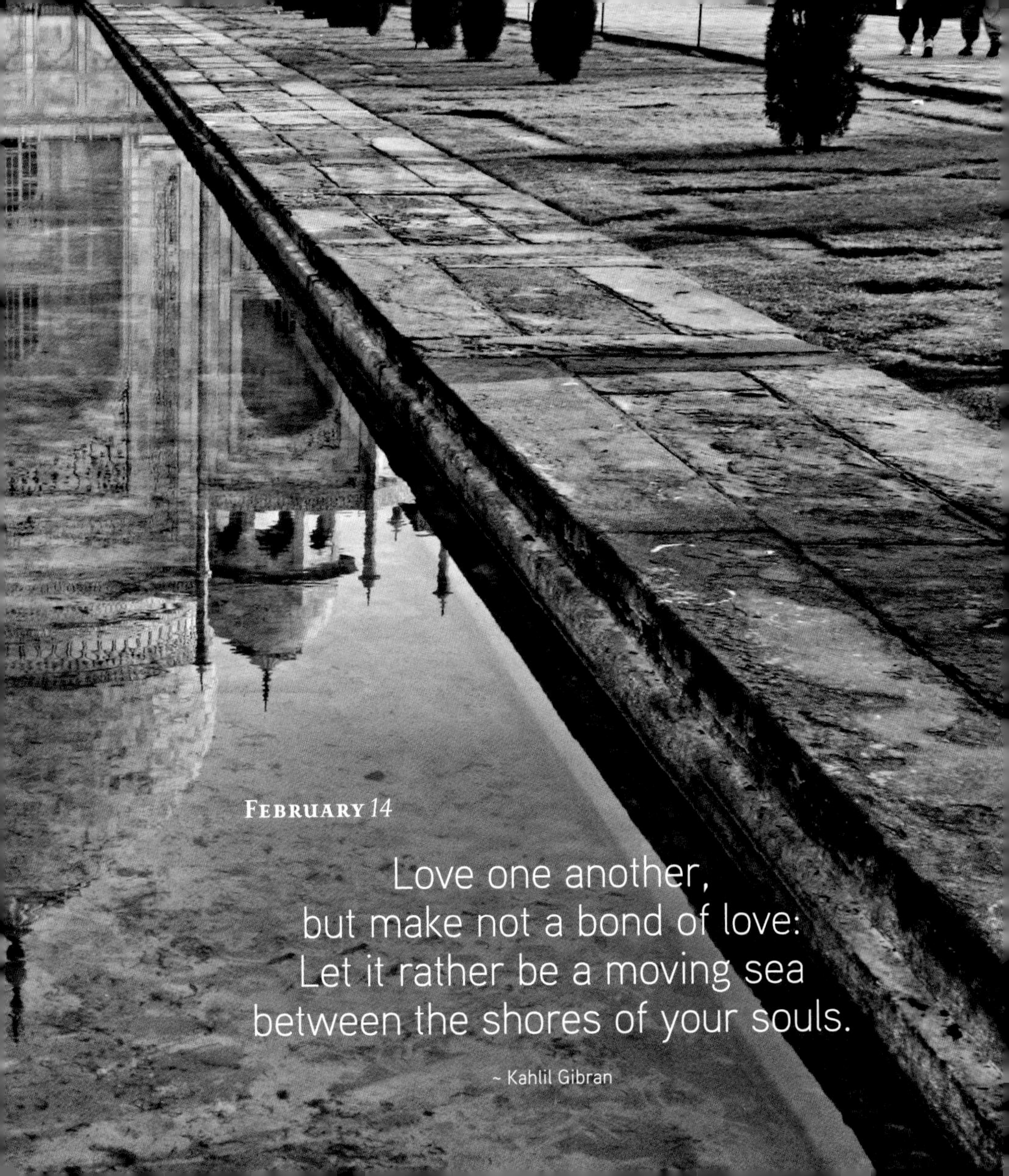

FEBRUARY *14*

Love one another,
but make not a bond of love:
Let it rather be a moving sea
between the shores of your souls.

~ Kahlil Gibran

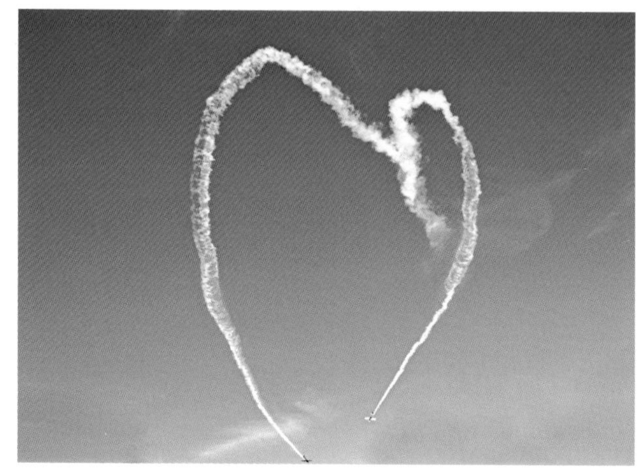

FEBRUARY *15*

We love because
it's the only true adventure.

~ Nikki Giovanni

FEBRUARY 16

When one loves,
one does not calculate.

~ Saint Thérèse of Lisieux

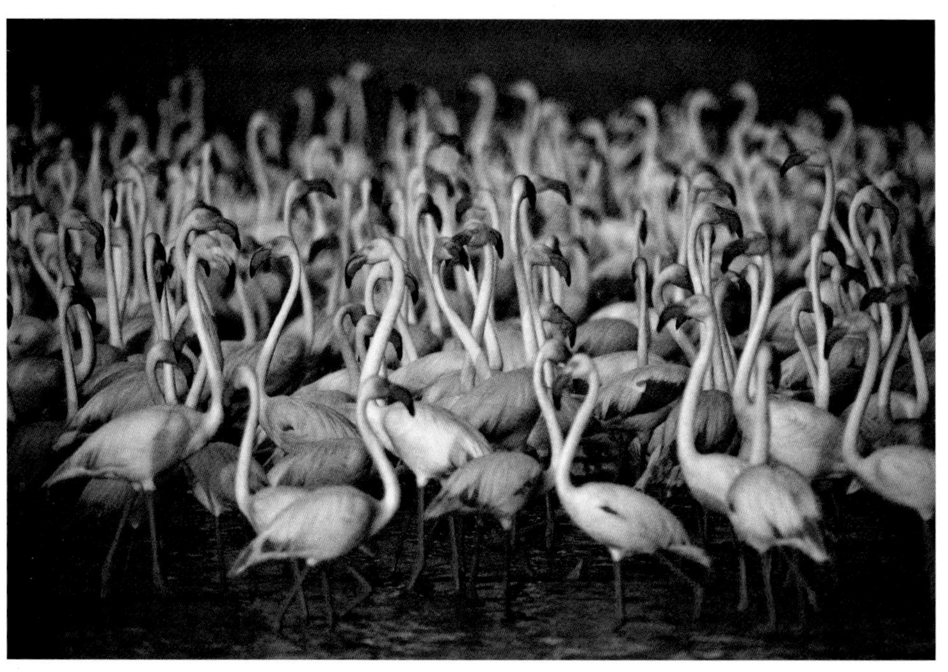

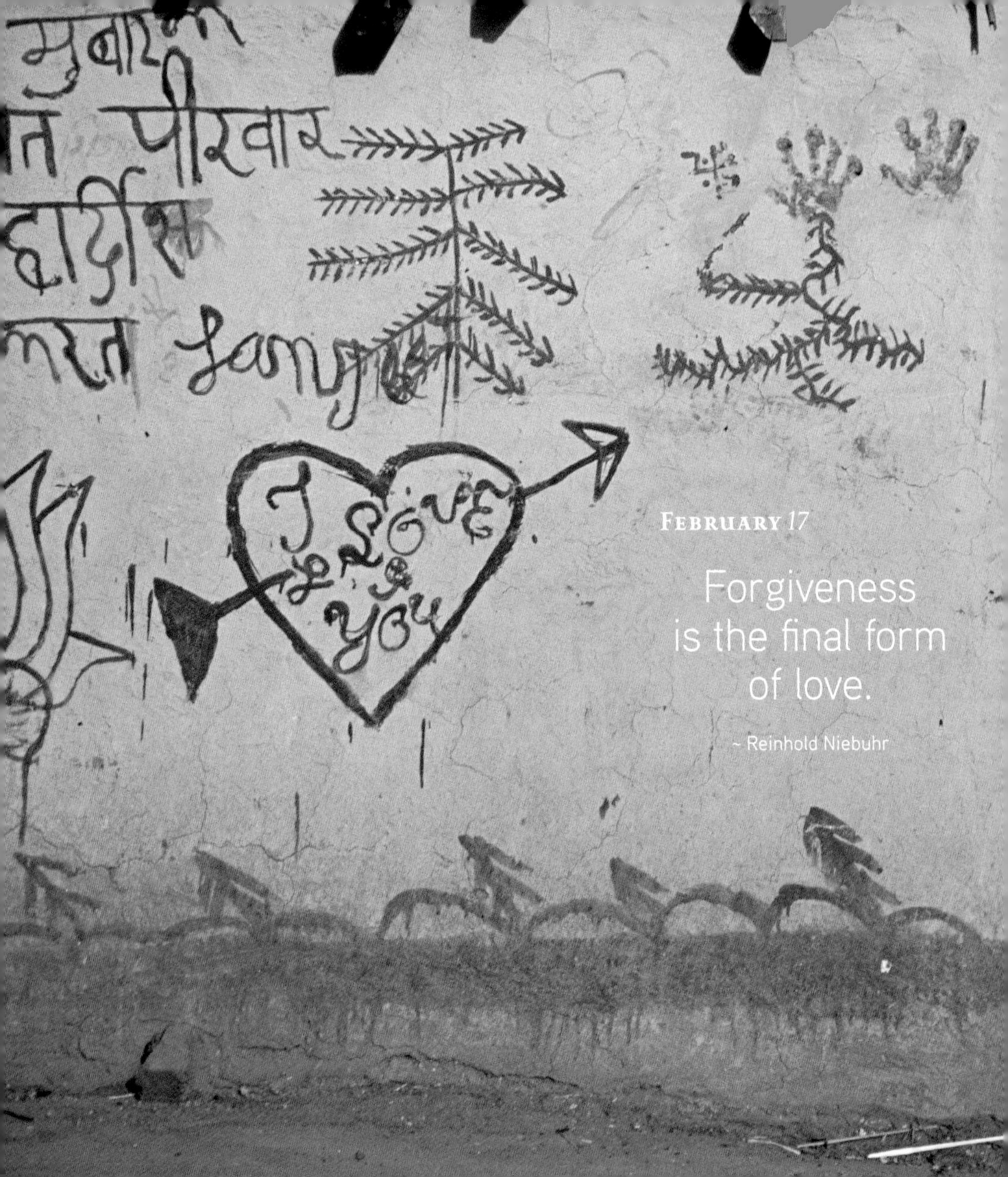

FEBRUARY *17*

Forgiveness
is the final form
of love.

~ Reinhold Niebuhr

FEBRUARY *18*

Talk not of wasted affection; affection never was wasted.

~Henry Wadsworth Longfellow

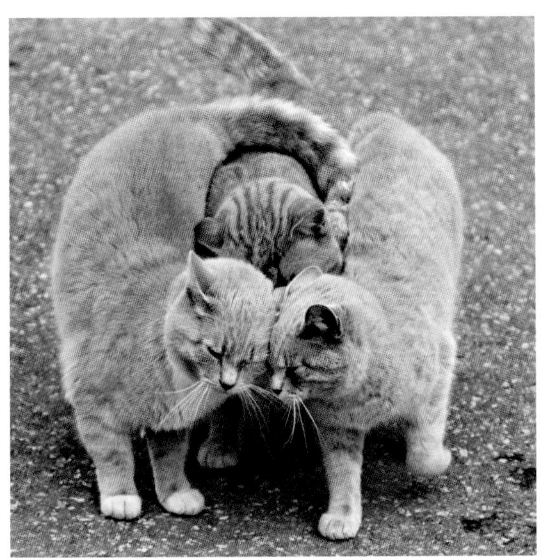

FEBRUARY 19

Love gives not but itself
and takes naught but from itself.
Love possesses not
nor would it be possessed;
For love is sufficient unto love.
And think not you can
direct the course of love,
for love, if it finds you worthy,
directs your course.

~ Kahlil Gibran

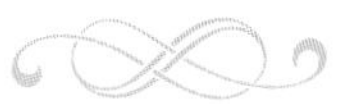

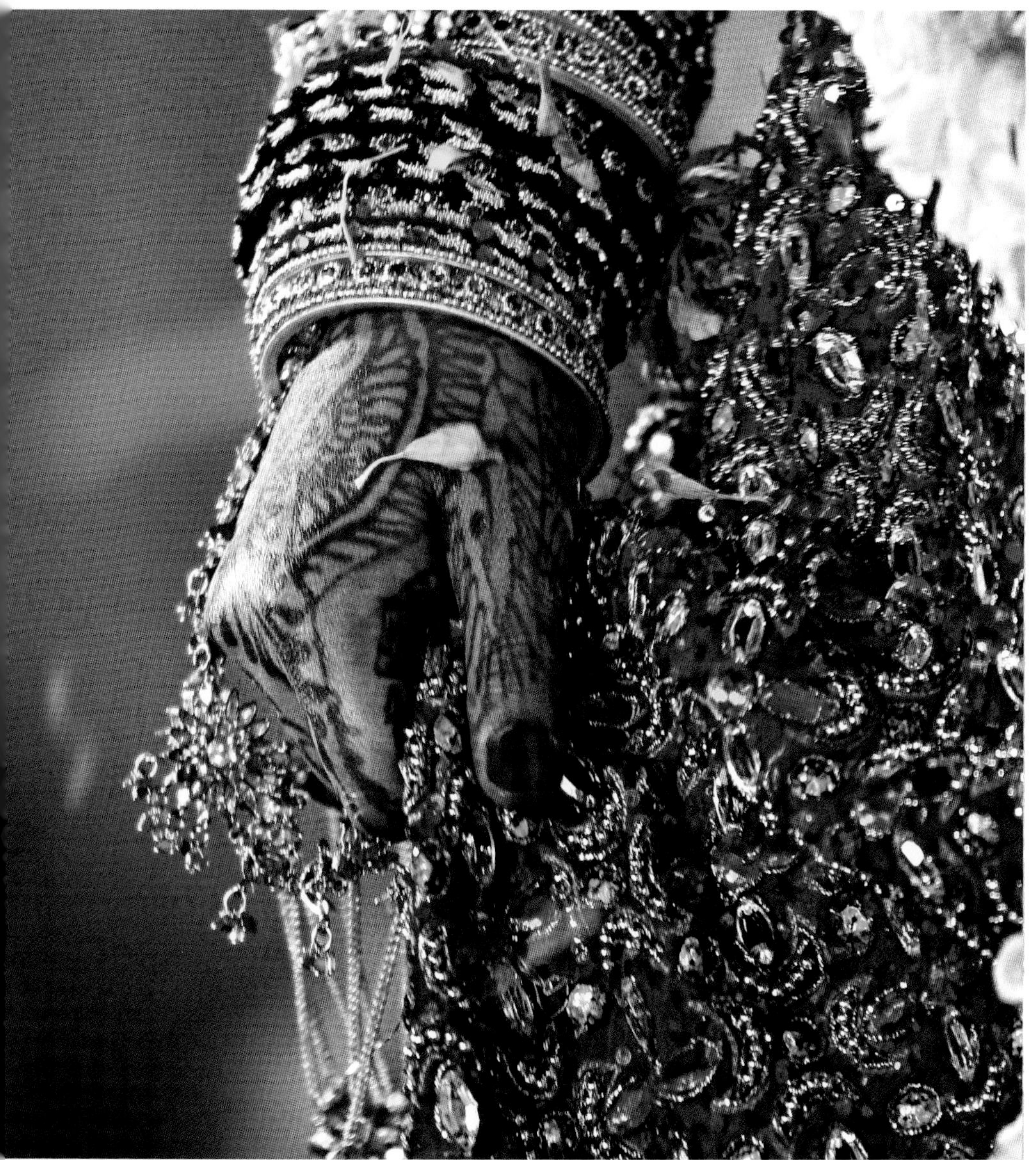

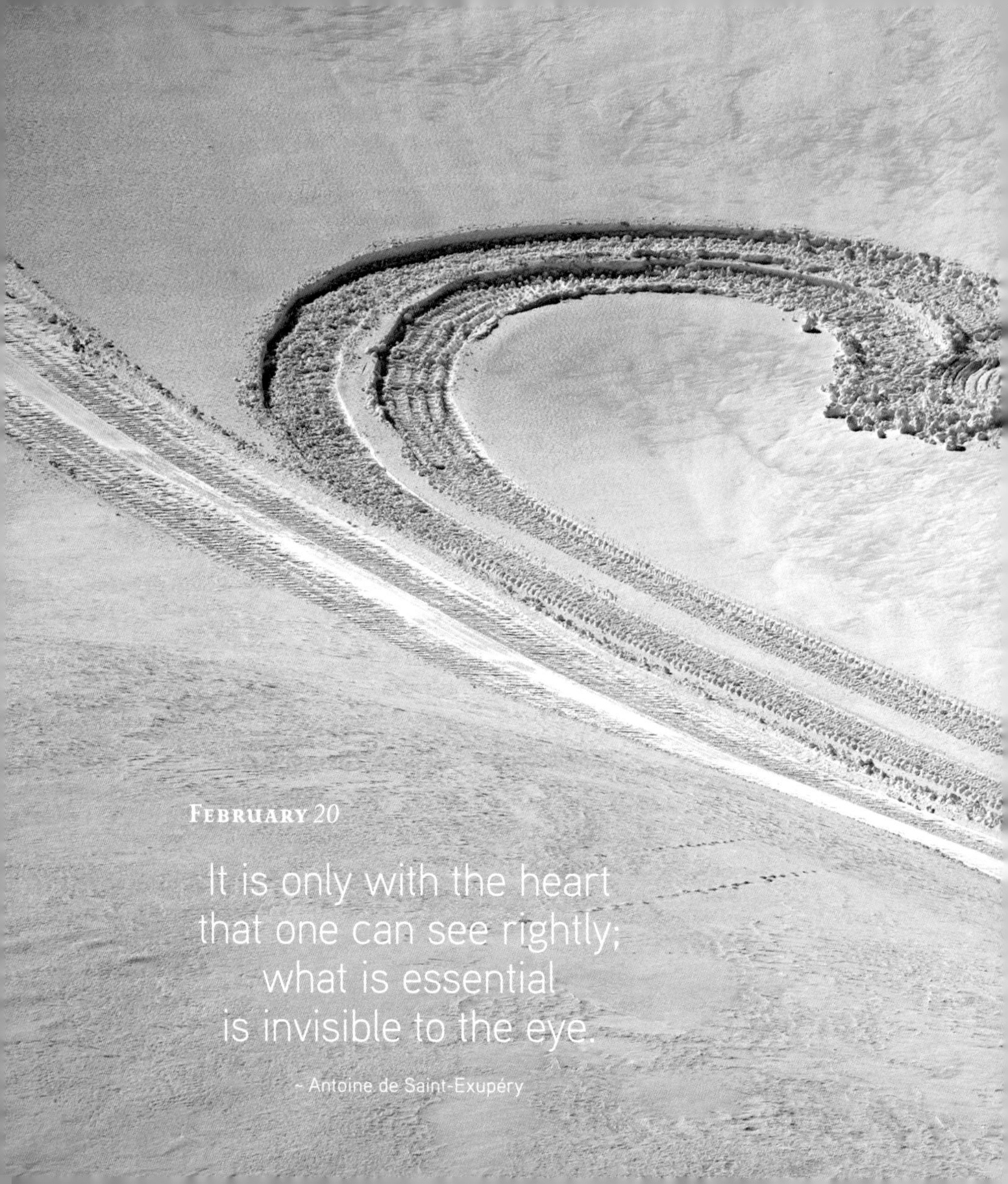

FEBRUARY *20*

It is only with the heart
that one can see rightly;
what is essential
is invisible to the eye.

~ Antoine de Saint-Exupéry

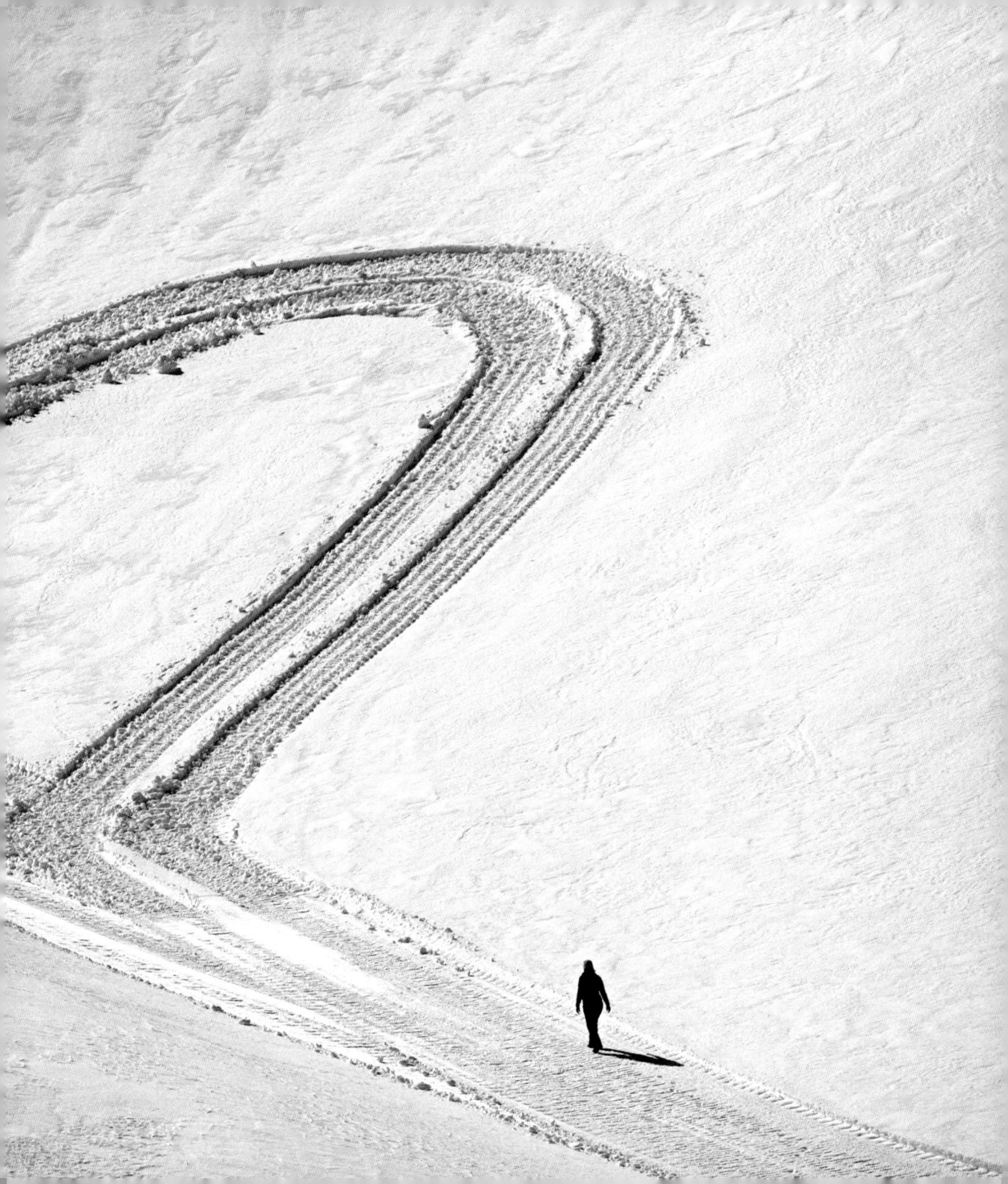

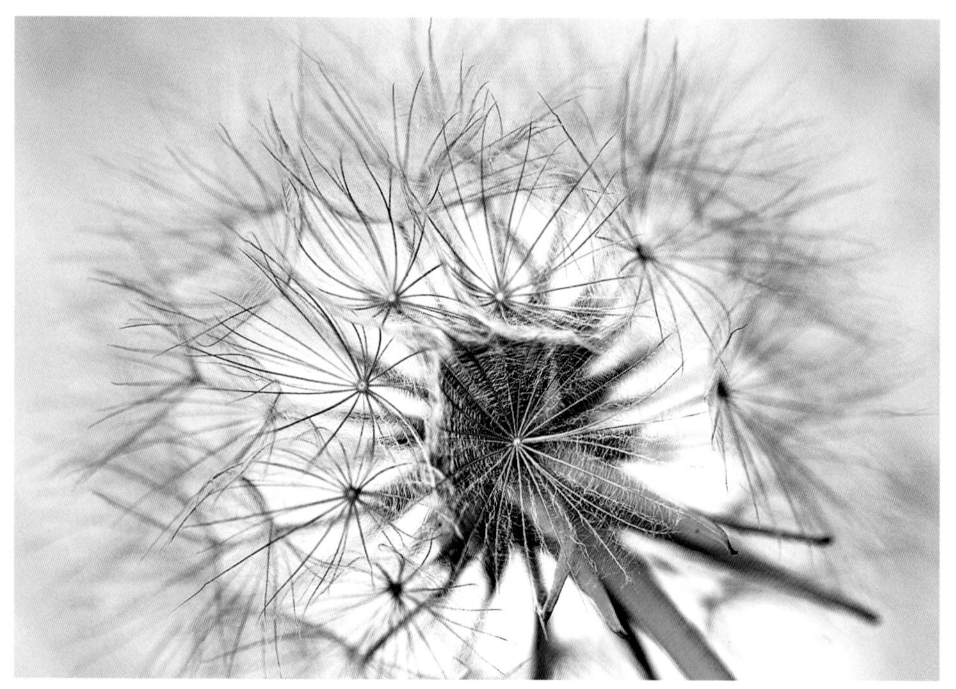

FEBRUARY *21*

Only love can be divided endlessly
and still not diminish.

~ Anne Morrow Lindbergh

FEBRUARY 22

Let the beauty of what you love
be what you do.

~ Rumi

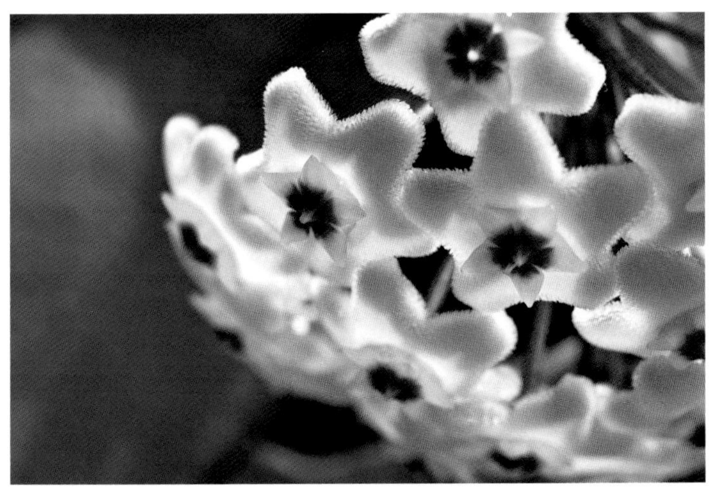

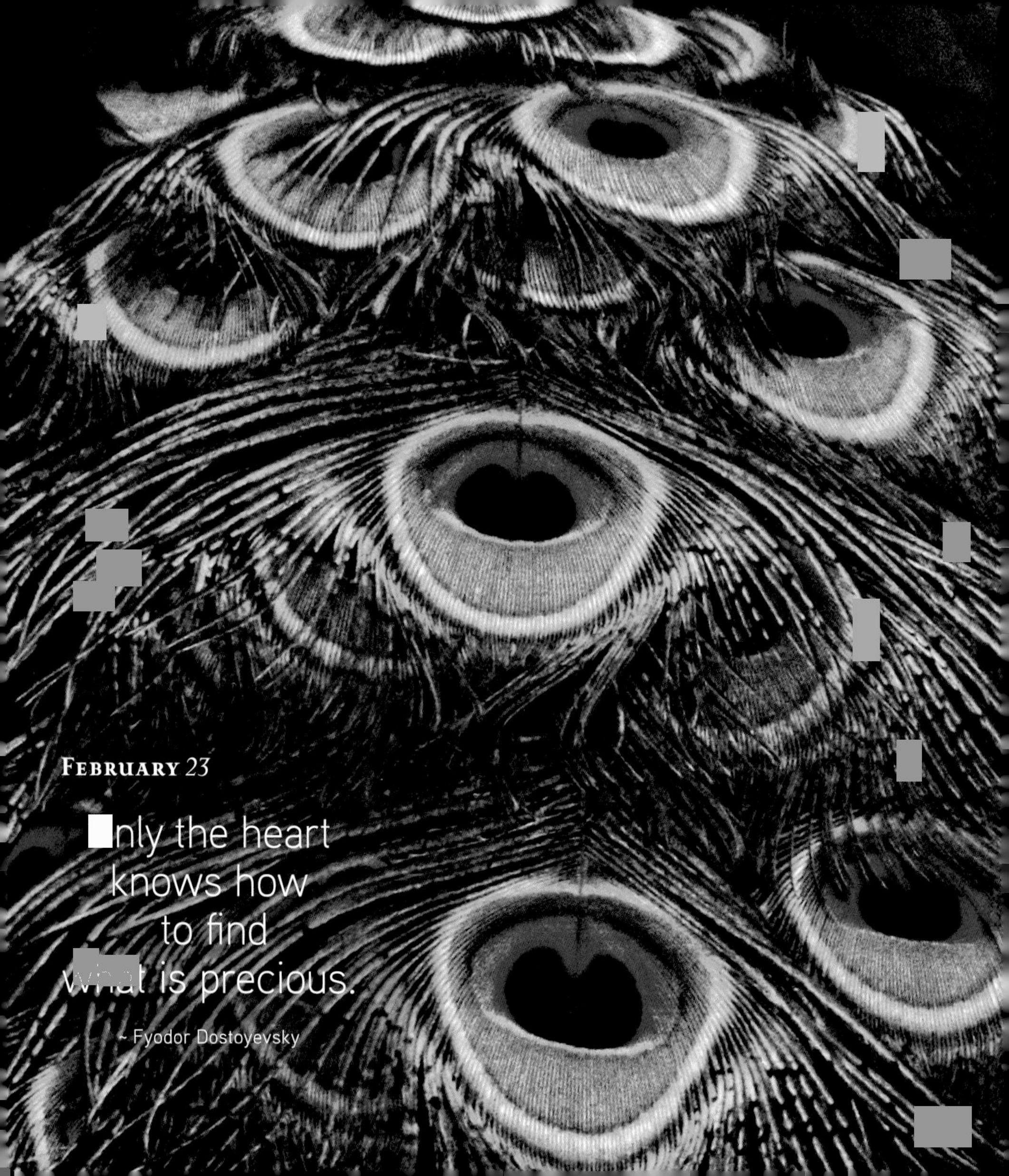
FEBRUARY 23
Only the heart
knows how
to find
what is precious.
~ Fyodor Dostoyevsky

February 24

Love is most nearly itself when the here and now cease to matter.

~ T. S. Eliot

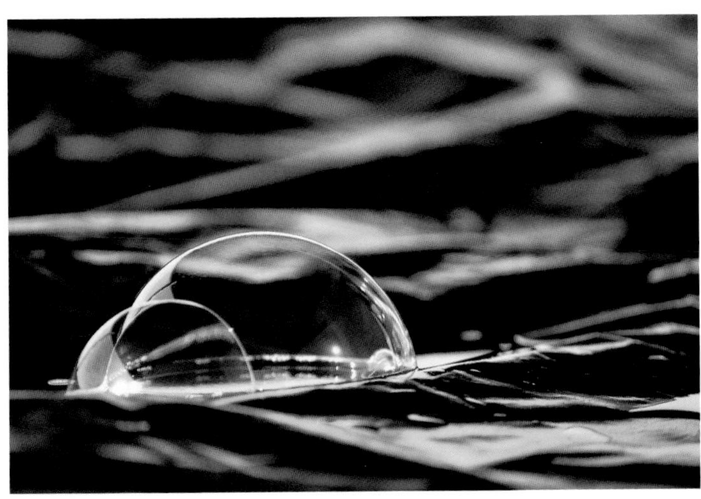

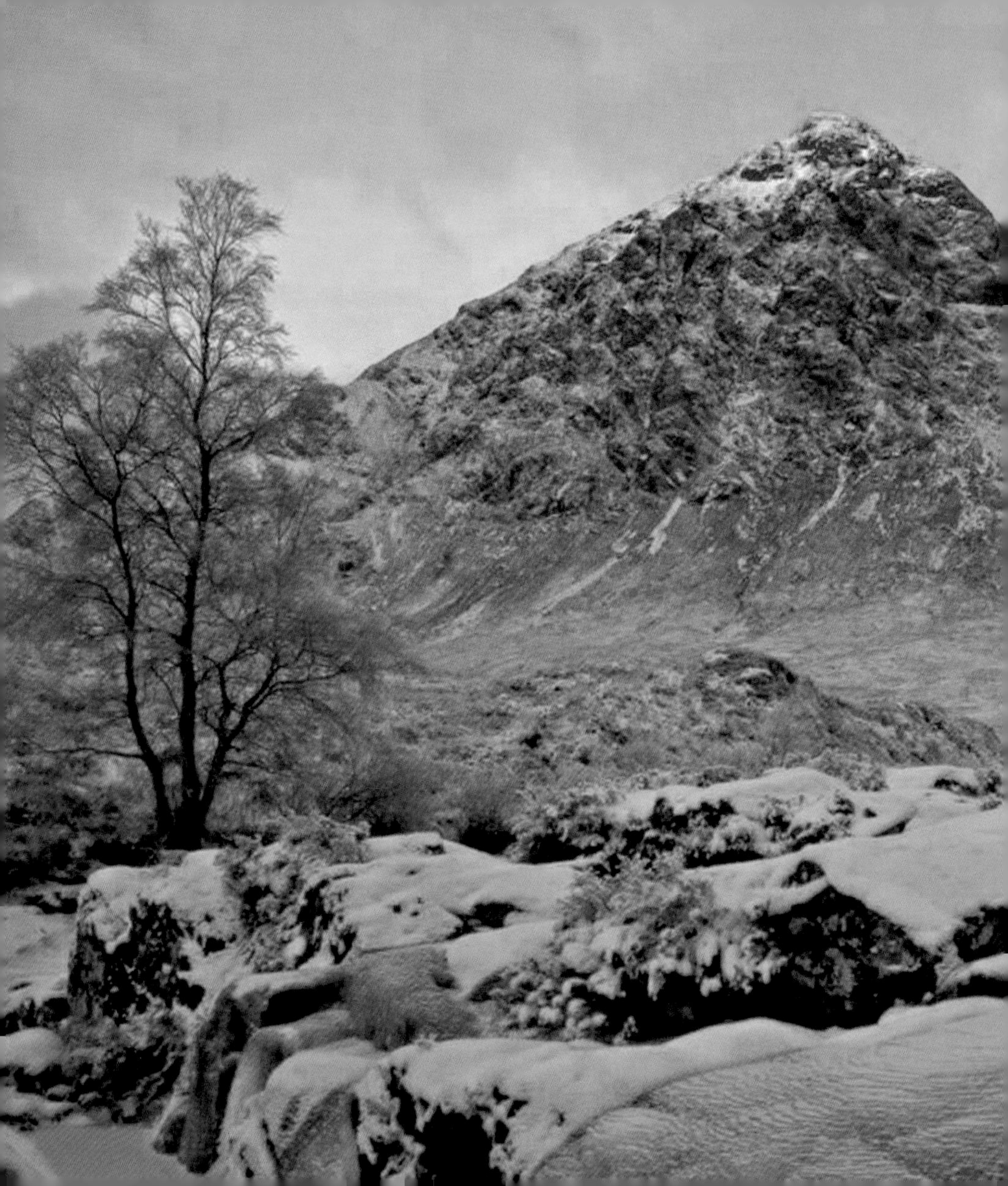

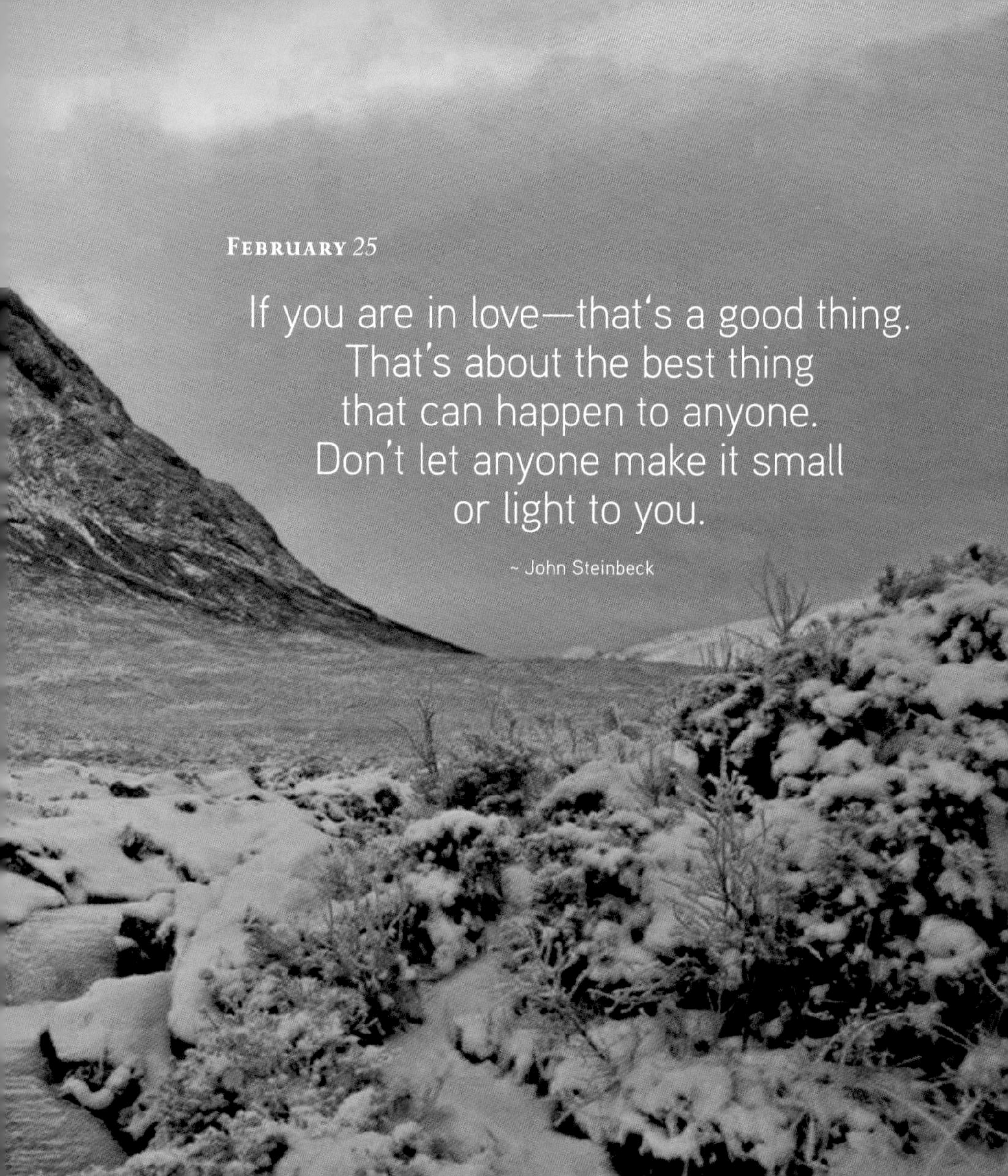

FEBRUARY 25

If you are in love—that's a good thing.
That's about the best thing
that can happen to anyone.
Don't let anyone make it small
or light to you.

~ John Steinbeck

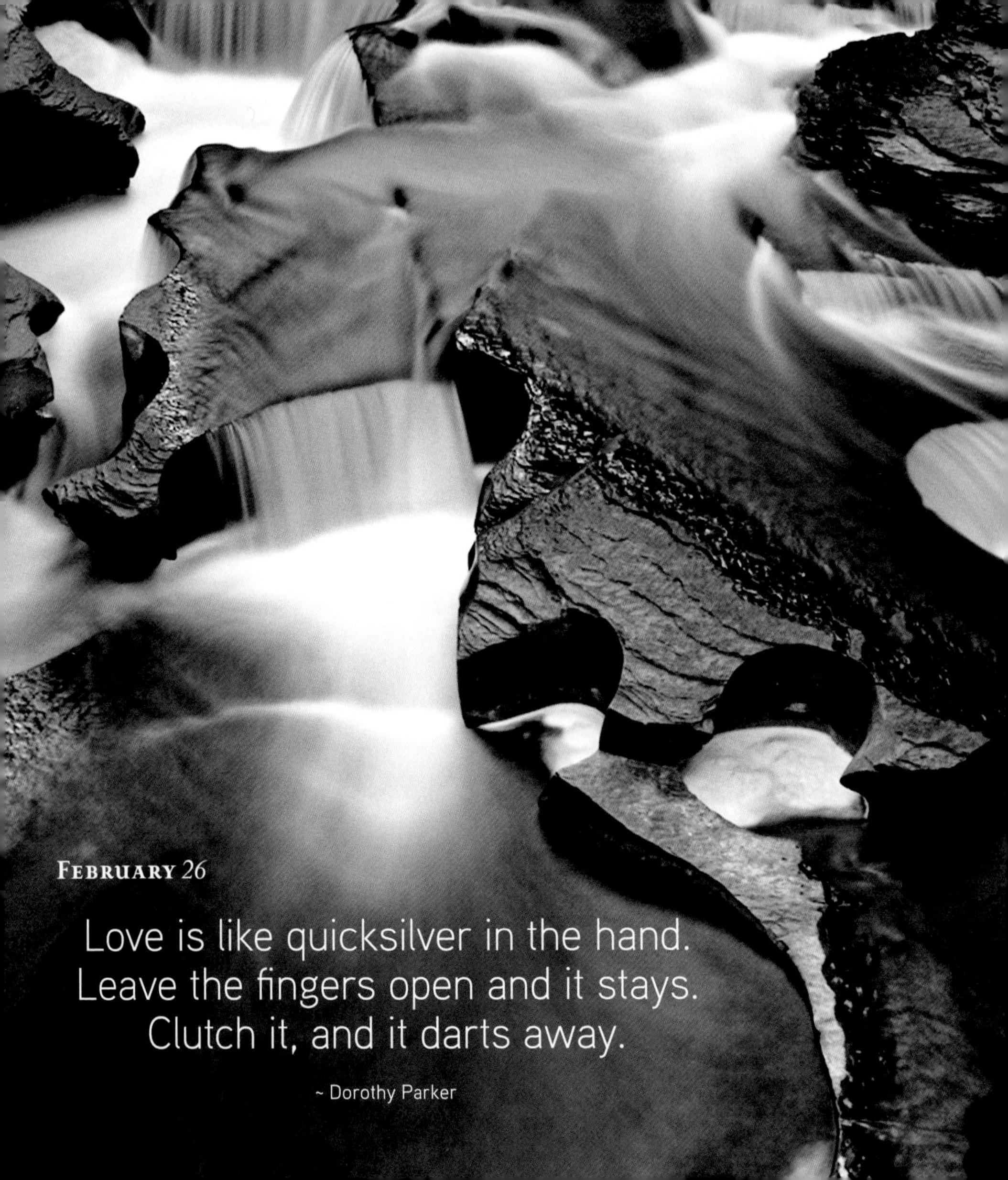

February *26*

Love is like quicksilver in the hand.
Leave the fingers open and it stays.
Clutch it, and it darts away.

~ Dorothy Parker

FEBRUARY 27

Love is what you've been through with somebody.

~ James Thurber

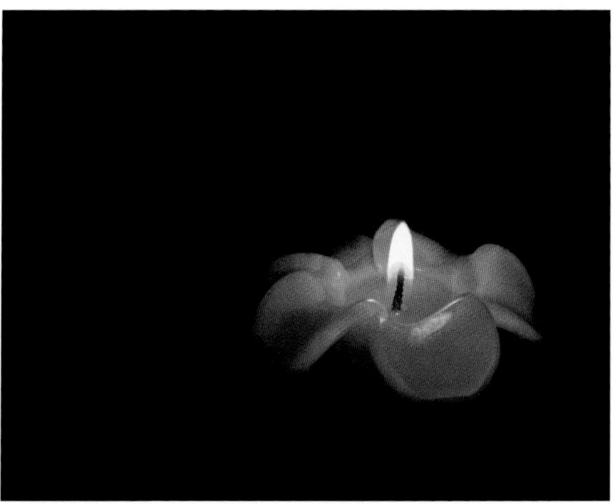

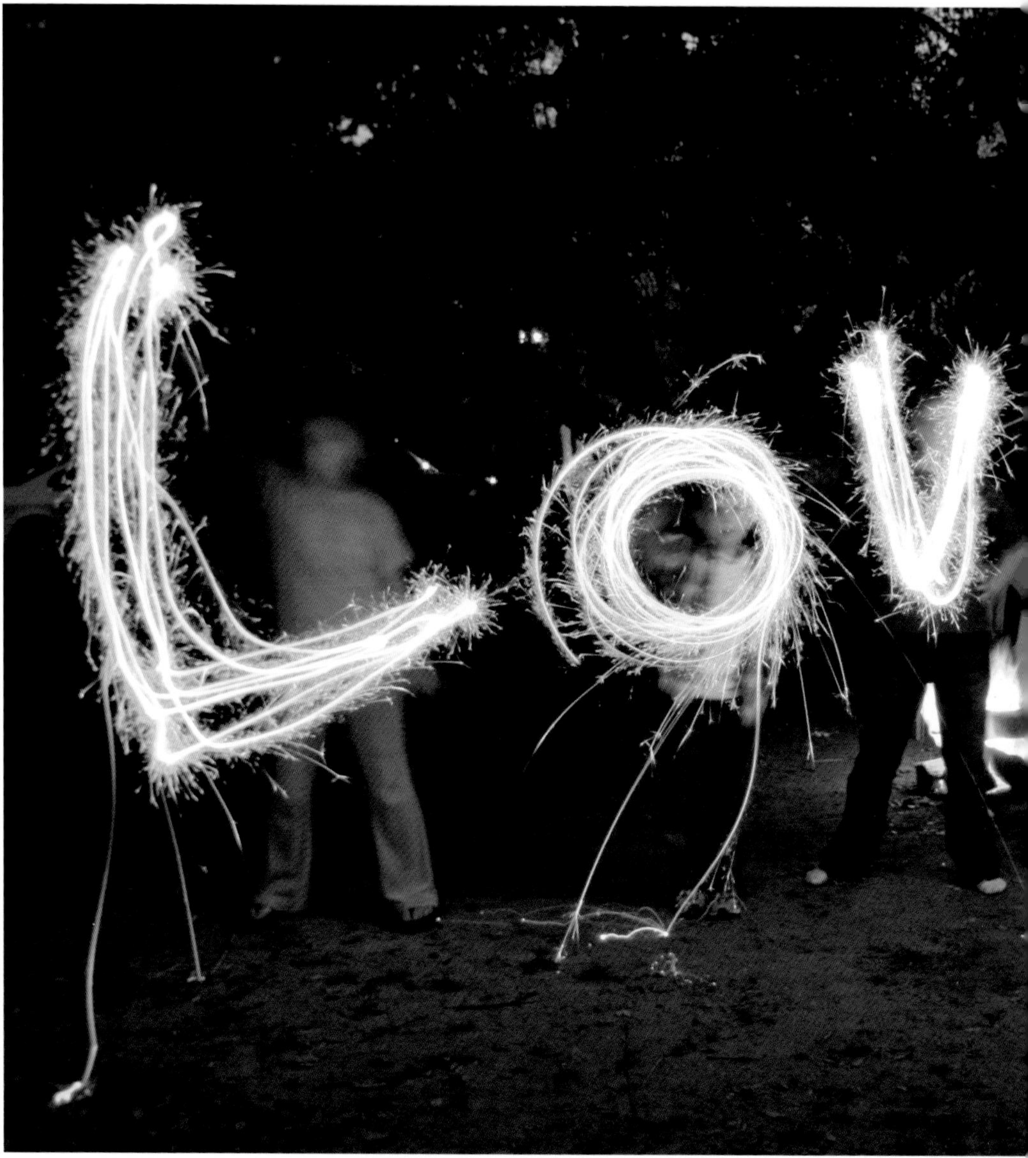
LOV

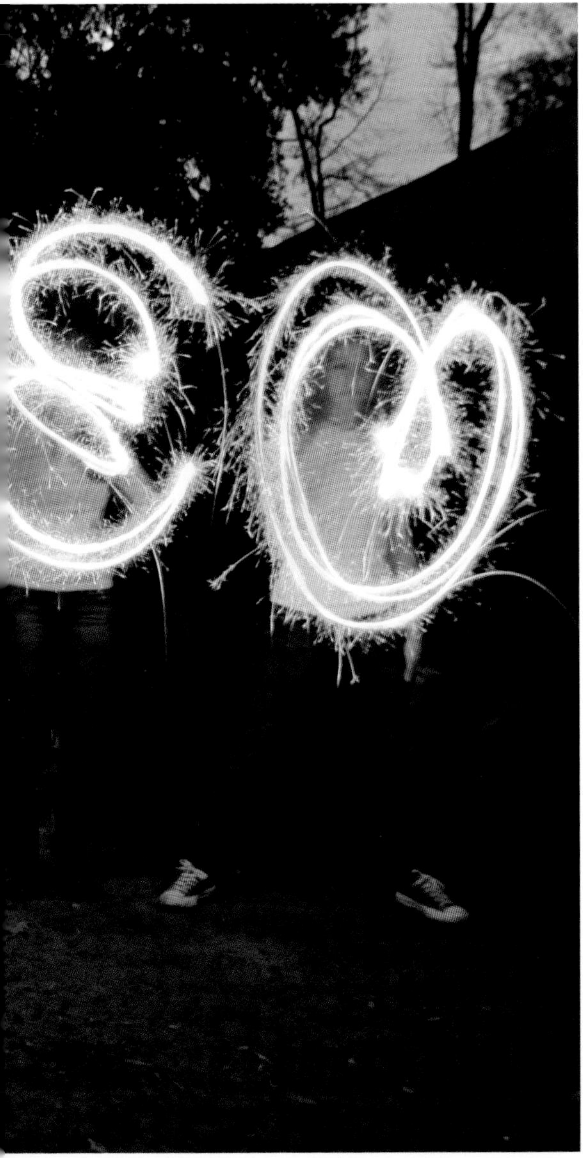

February 28/29

The one thing
we can never get
enough of
is love.
And the one thing
we never give
enough of
is love.

~ Henry Miller

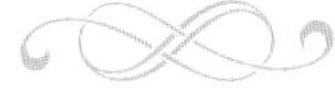

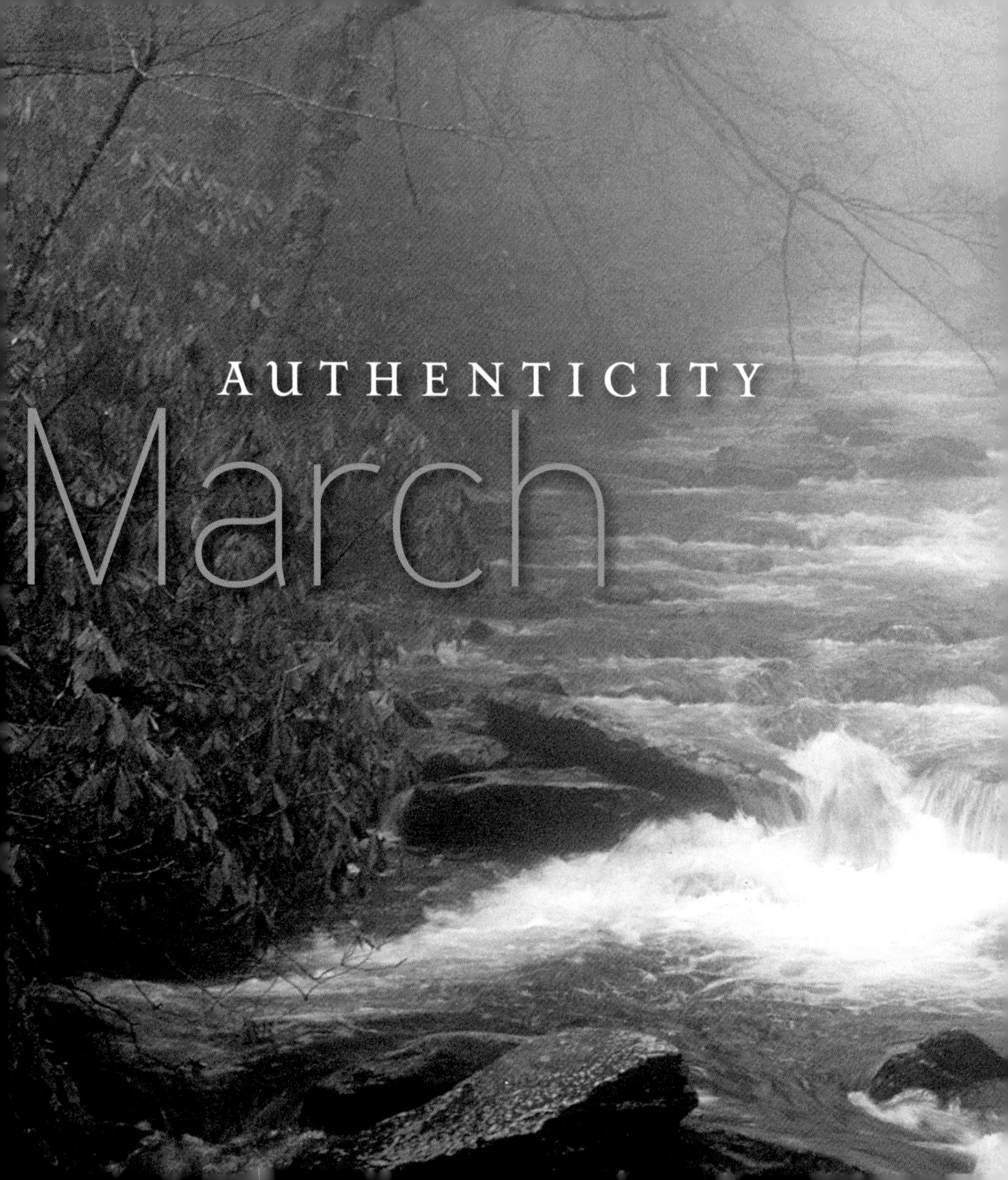
AUTHENTICITY
March

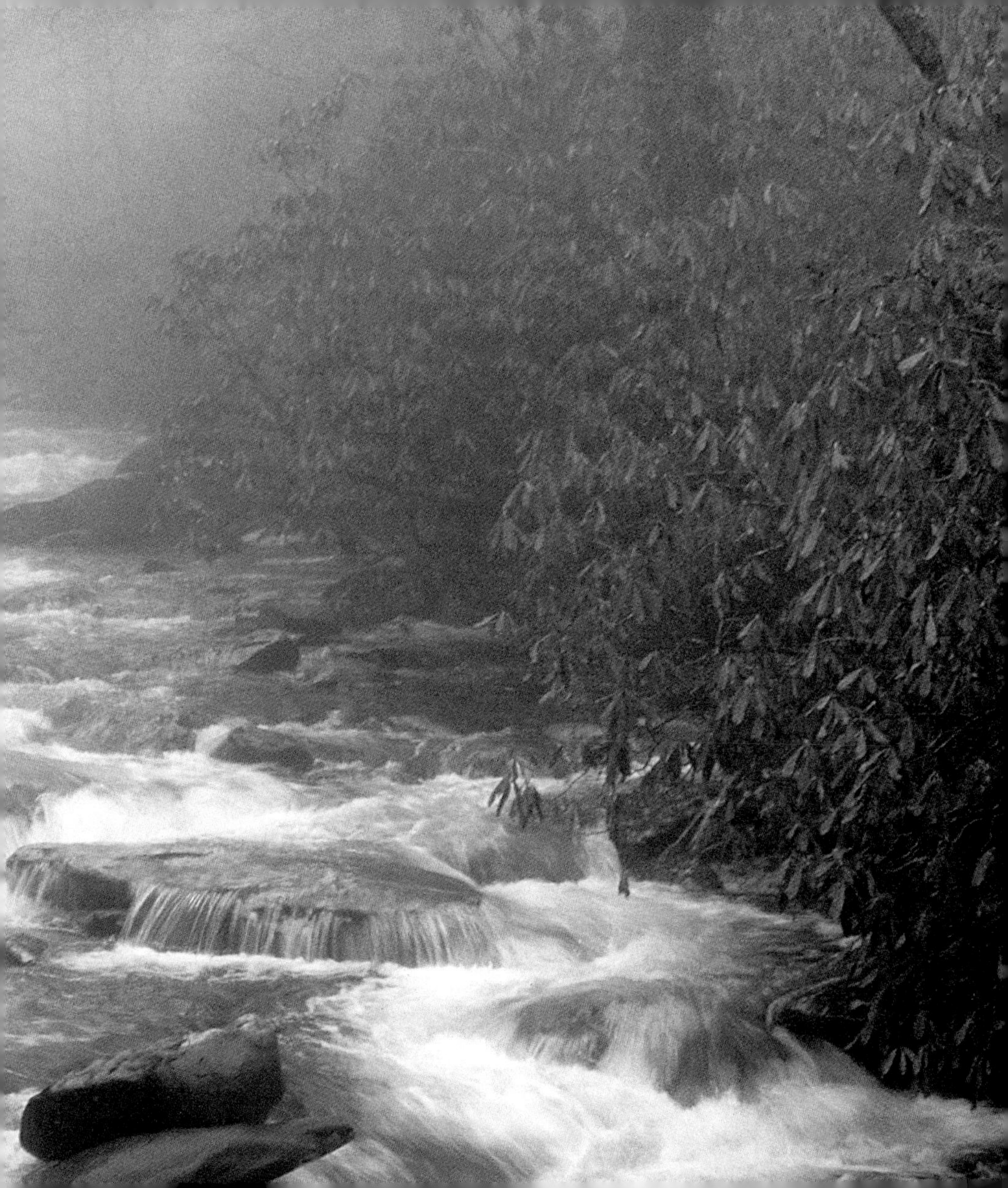

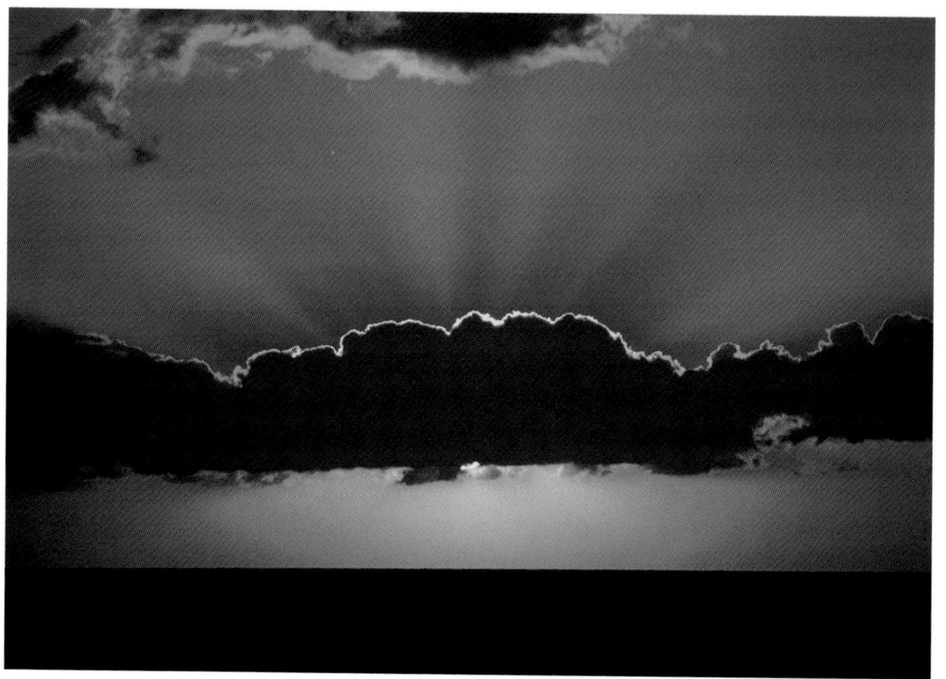

MARCH 1

The summit of happiness is reached when a person is ready to be what he is.

~ Desiderius Erasmus

March 2

Always be a first-rate version of yourself, instead of a second-rate version of somebody else.

~ Judy Garland

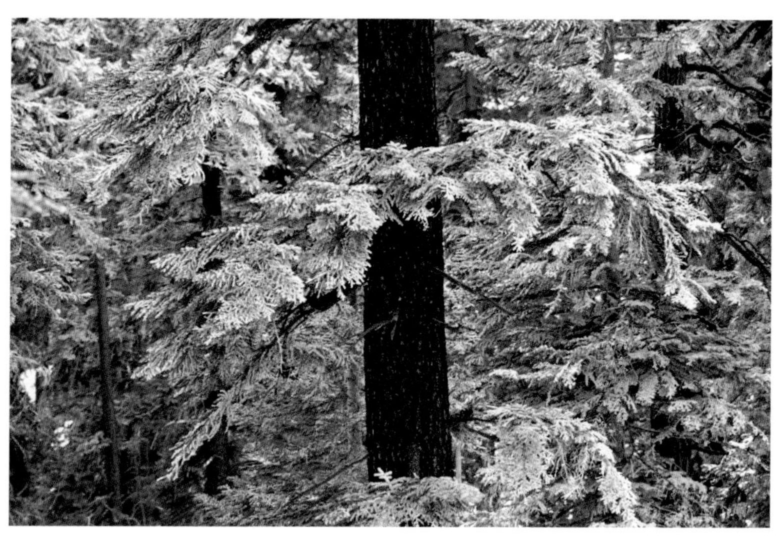

March 3

When a person
cannot deceive himself,
the chances are against
his being able
to deceive other people.

~ Mark Twain

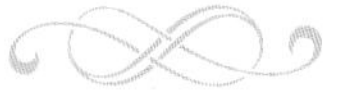

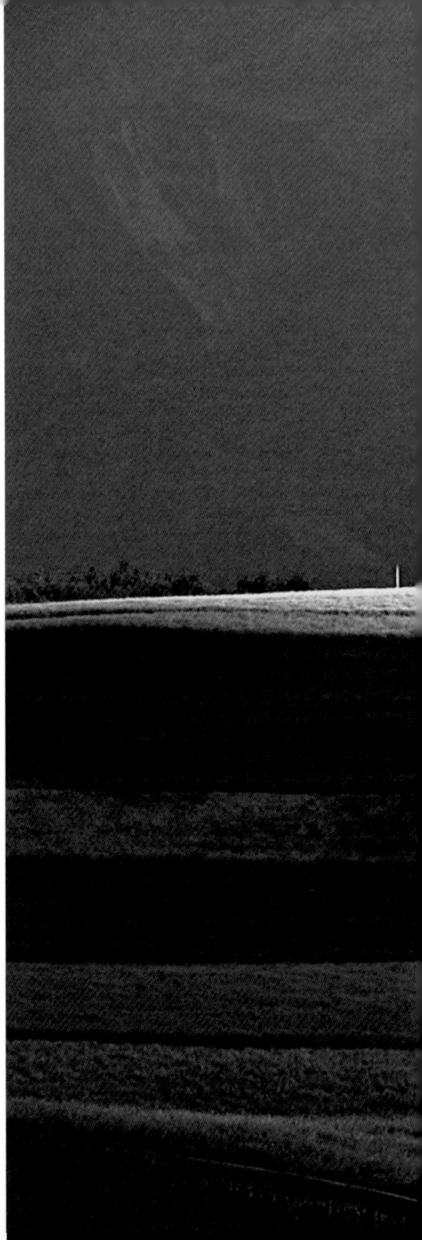

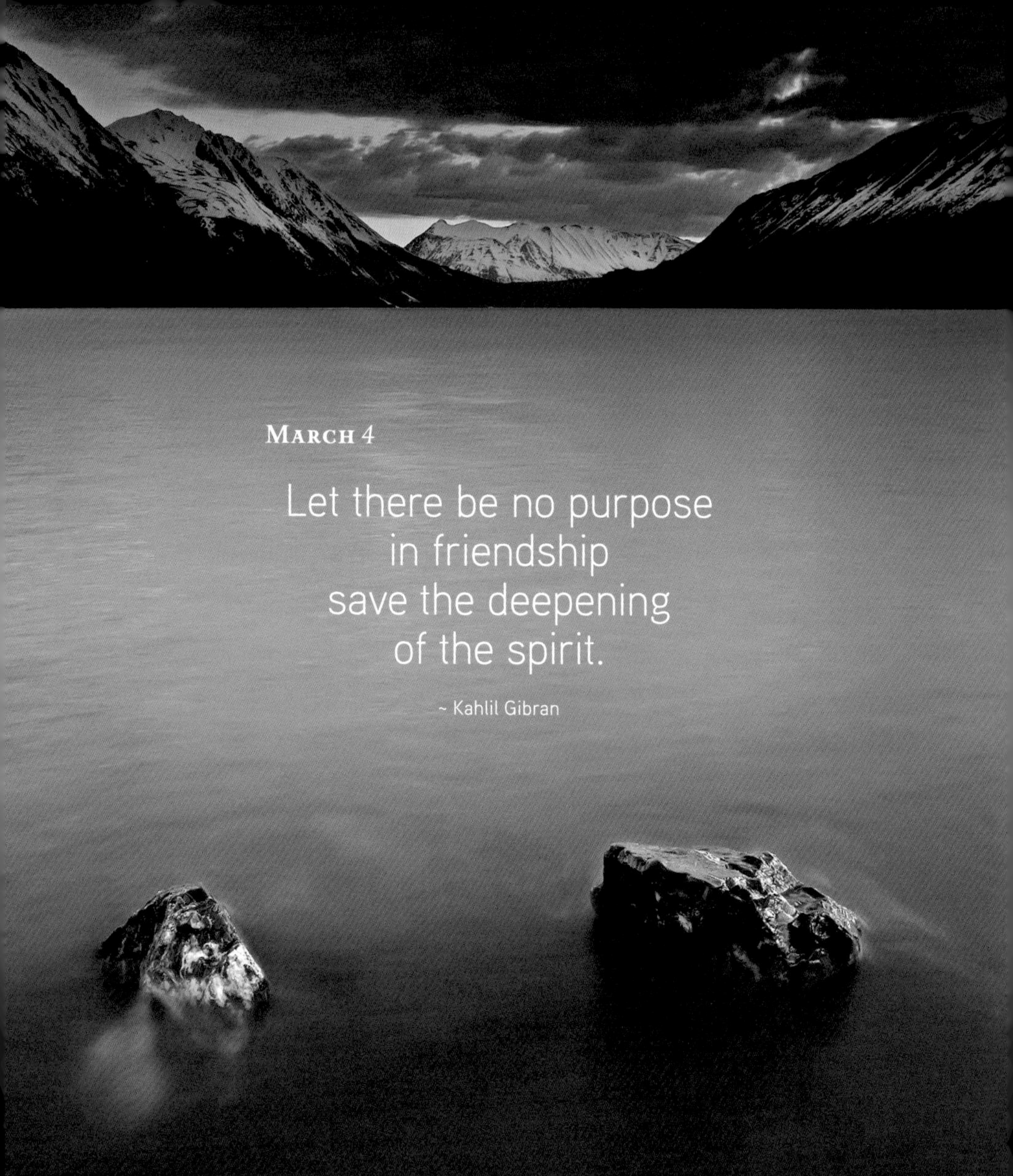

March 4

Let there be no purpose
in friendship
save the deepening
of the spirit.

~ Kahlil Gibran

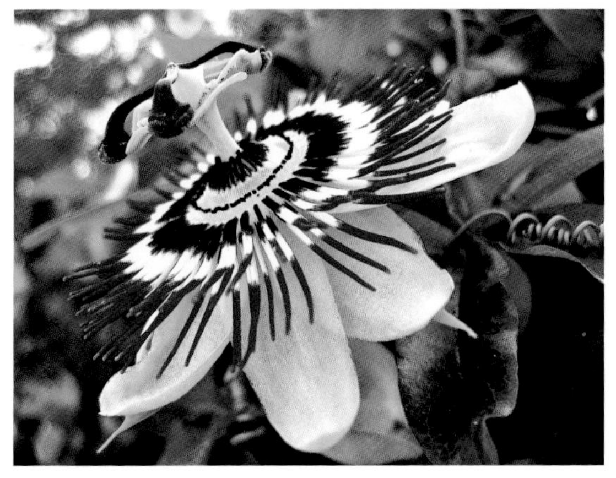

March 5

What is passion?
It is surely
the becoming of a person.

~ John Boorman

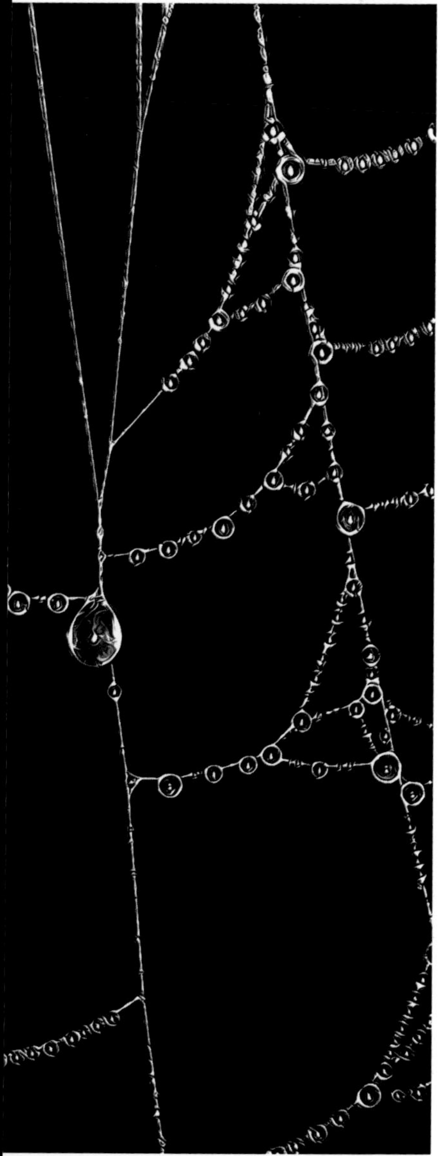

MARCH 6

Our deeds determine us, as much as we determine our deeds.

~ George Eliot

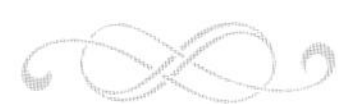

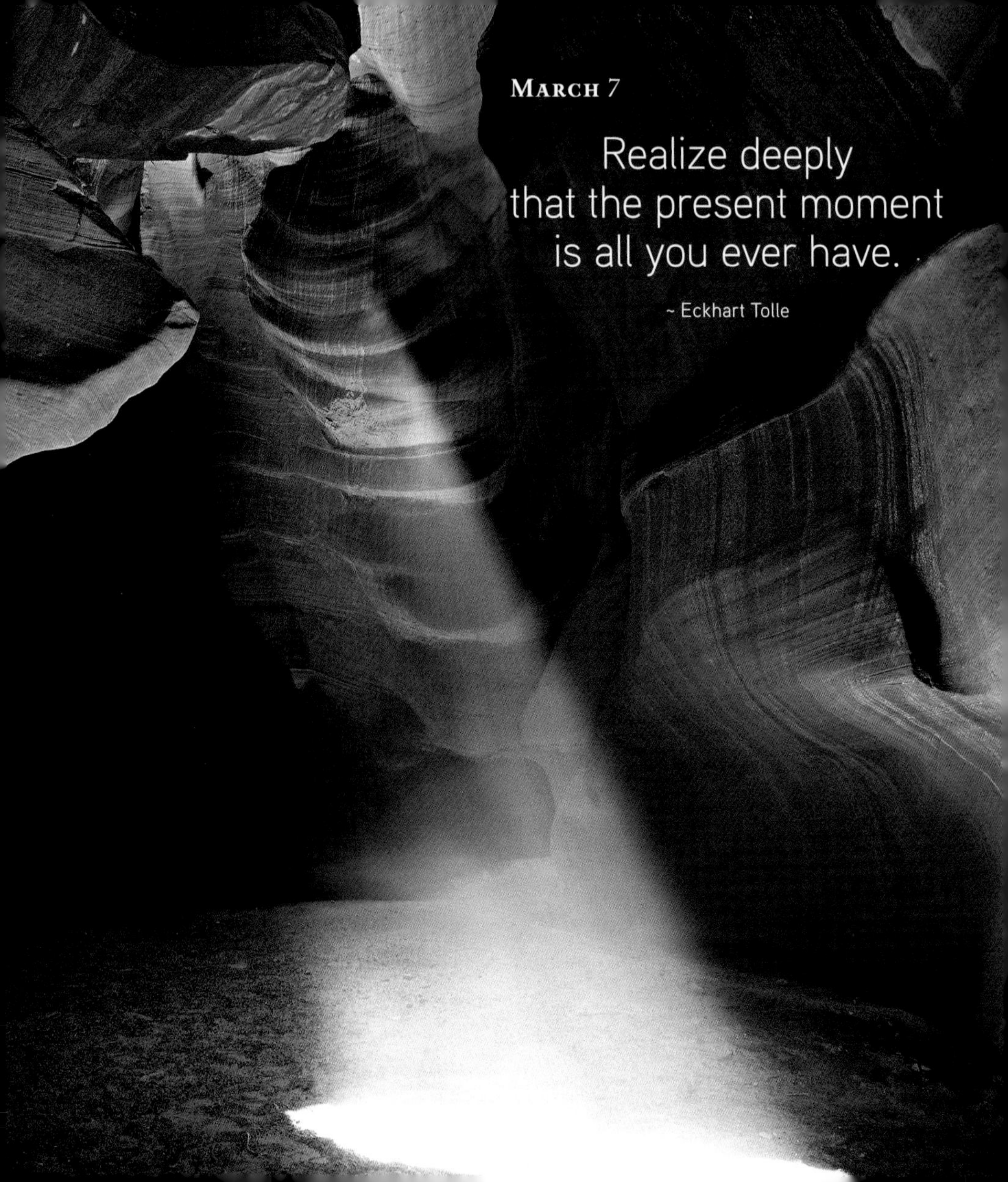

MARCH 7

Realize deeply
that the present moment
is all you ever have.

~ Eckhart Tolle

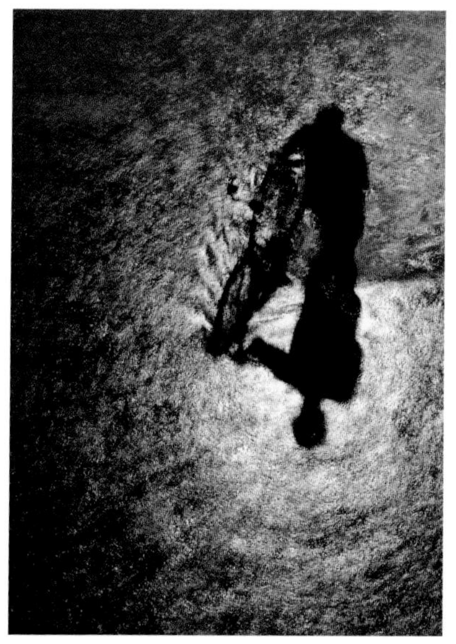

March 8

Hold yourself responsible
for a higher standard
than anybody expects of you.
Never excuse yourself.

~ Henry Ward Beecher

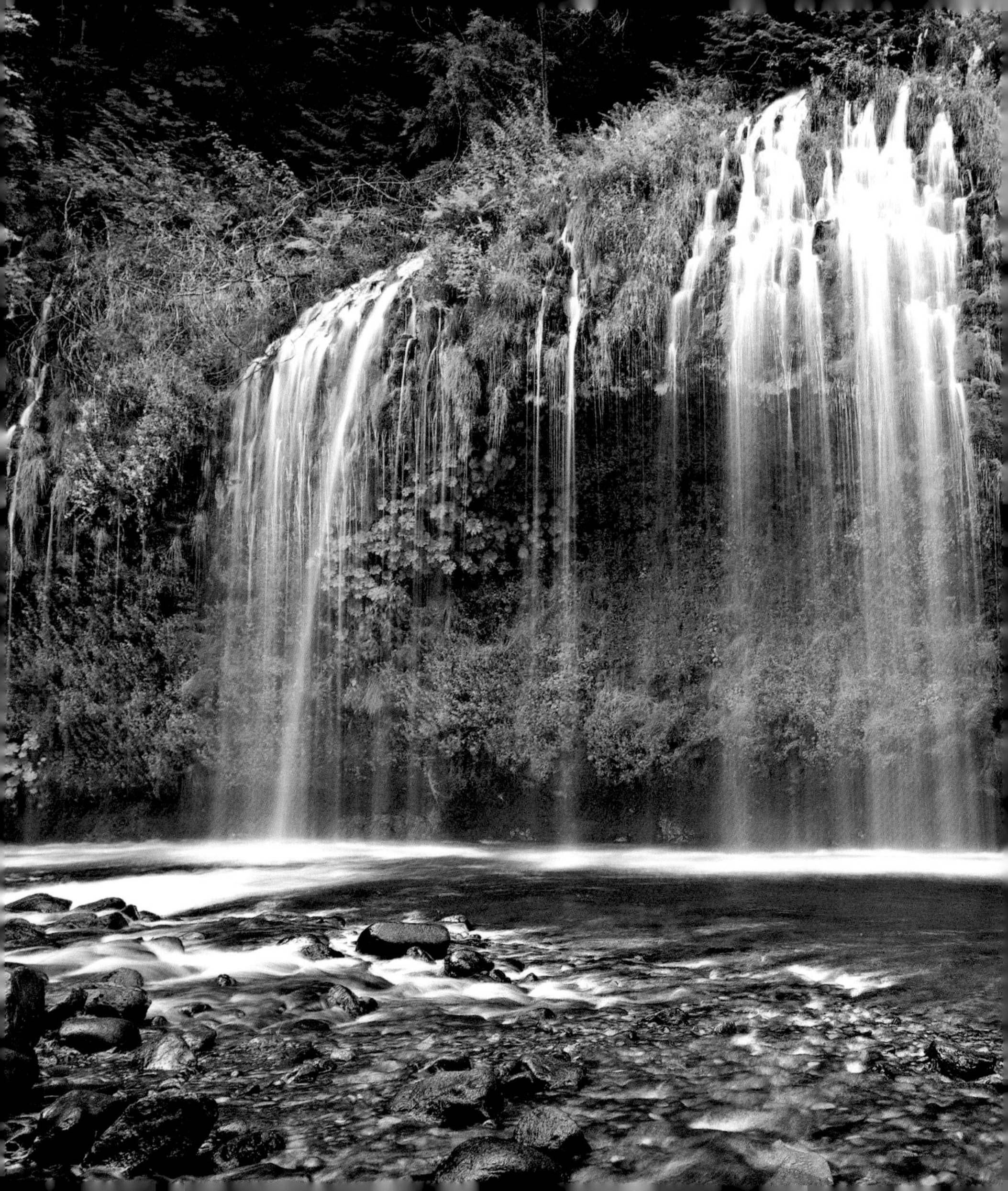

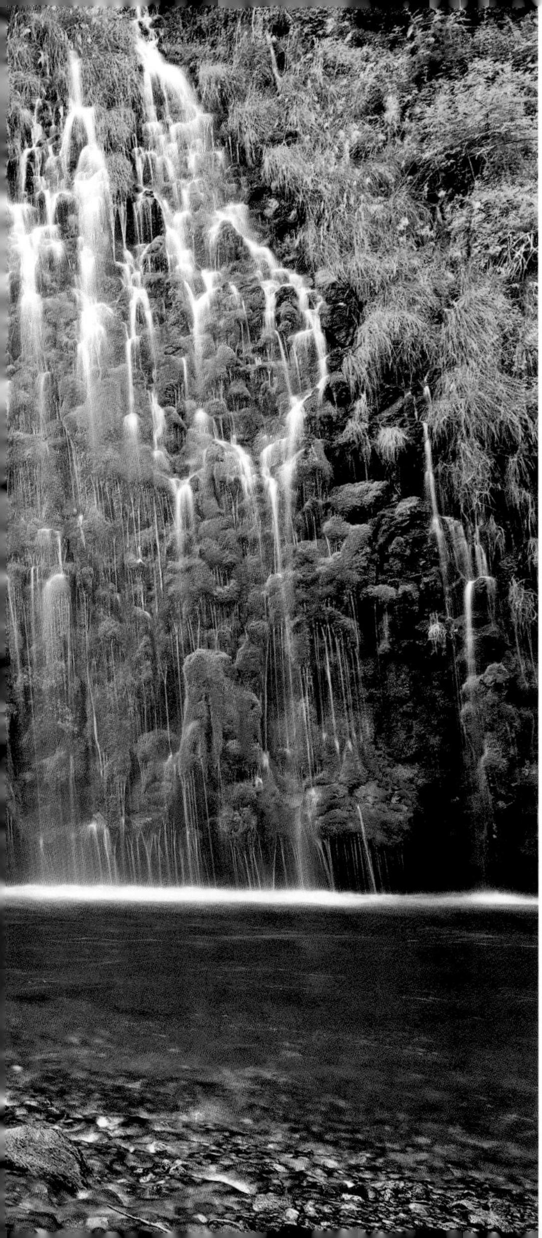

March 9

When you
do things
from your soul,
you feel a river
moving in you,
a joy.

~ Rumi

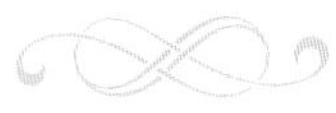

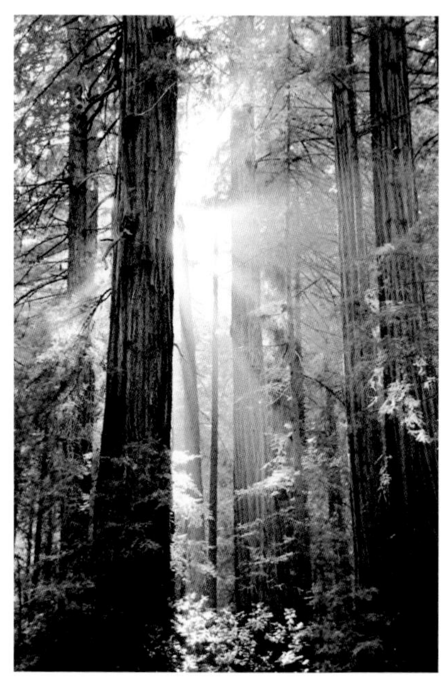

March *10*

It is our choices that show
what we truly are,
far more than our abilities.

~ J. K. Rowling

March 11

Be thine own palace, or the world's thy jail.

~ John Donne

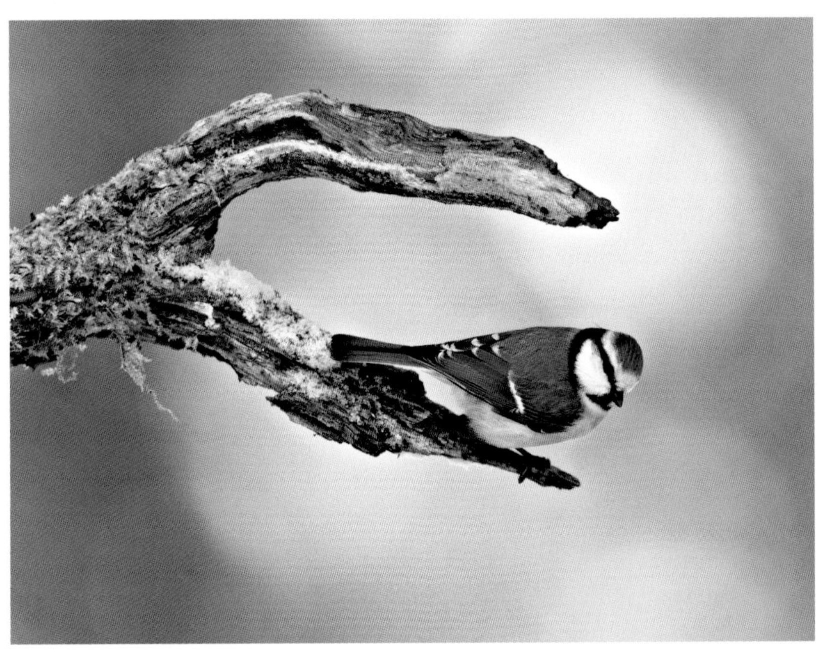

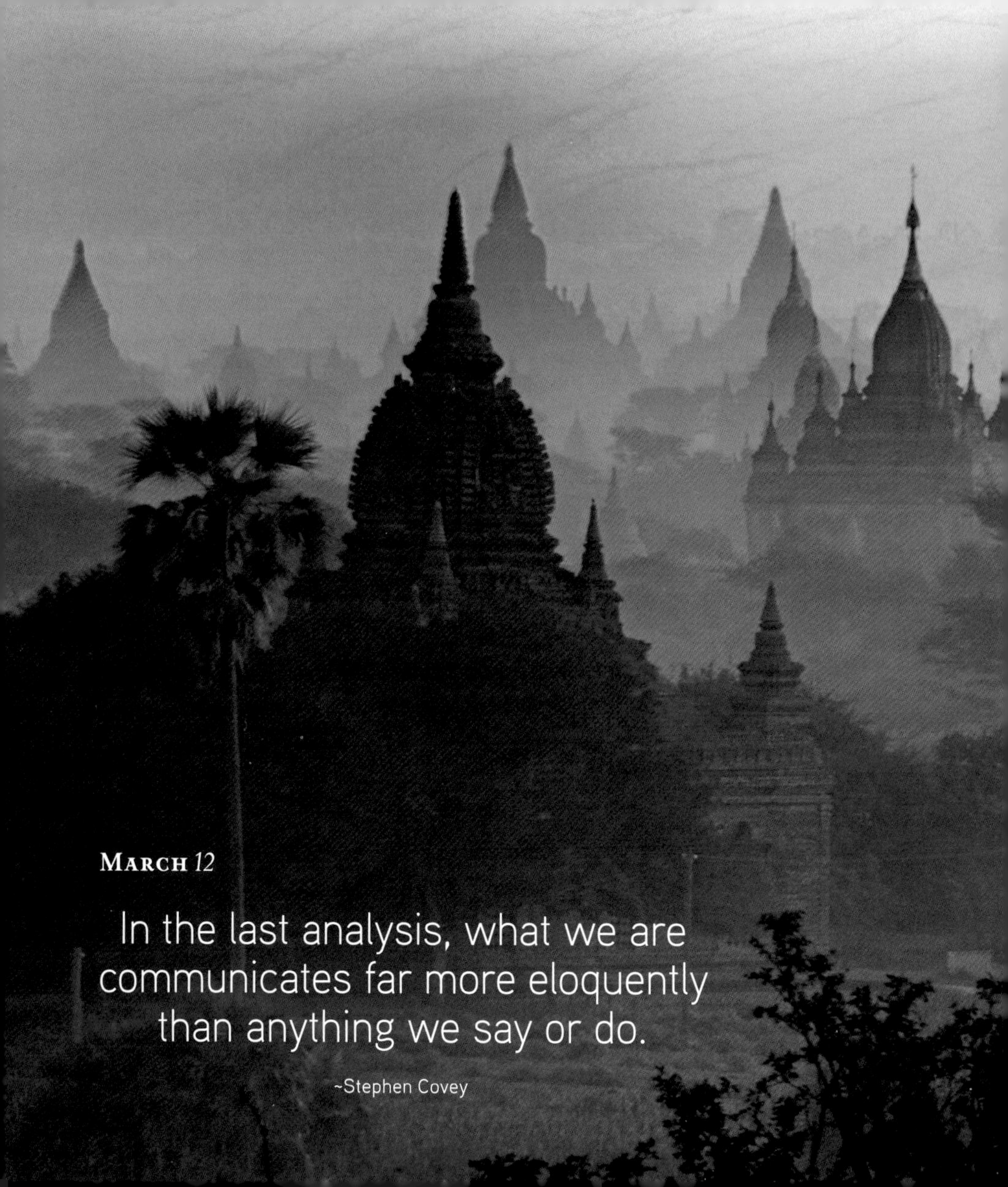

MARCH *12*

In the last analysis, what we are communicates far more eloquently than anything we say or do.

~Stephen Covey

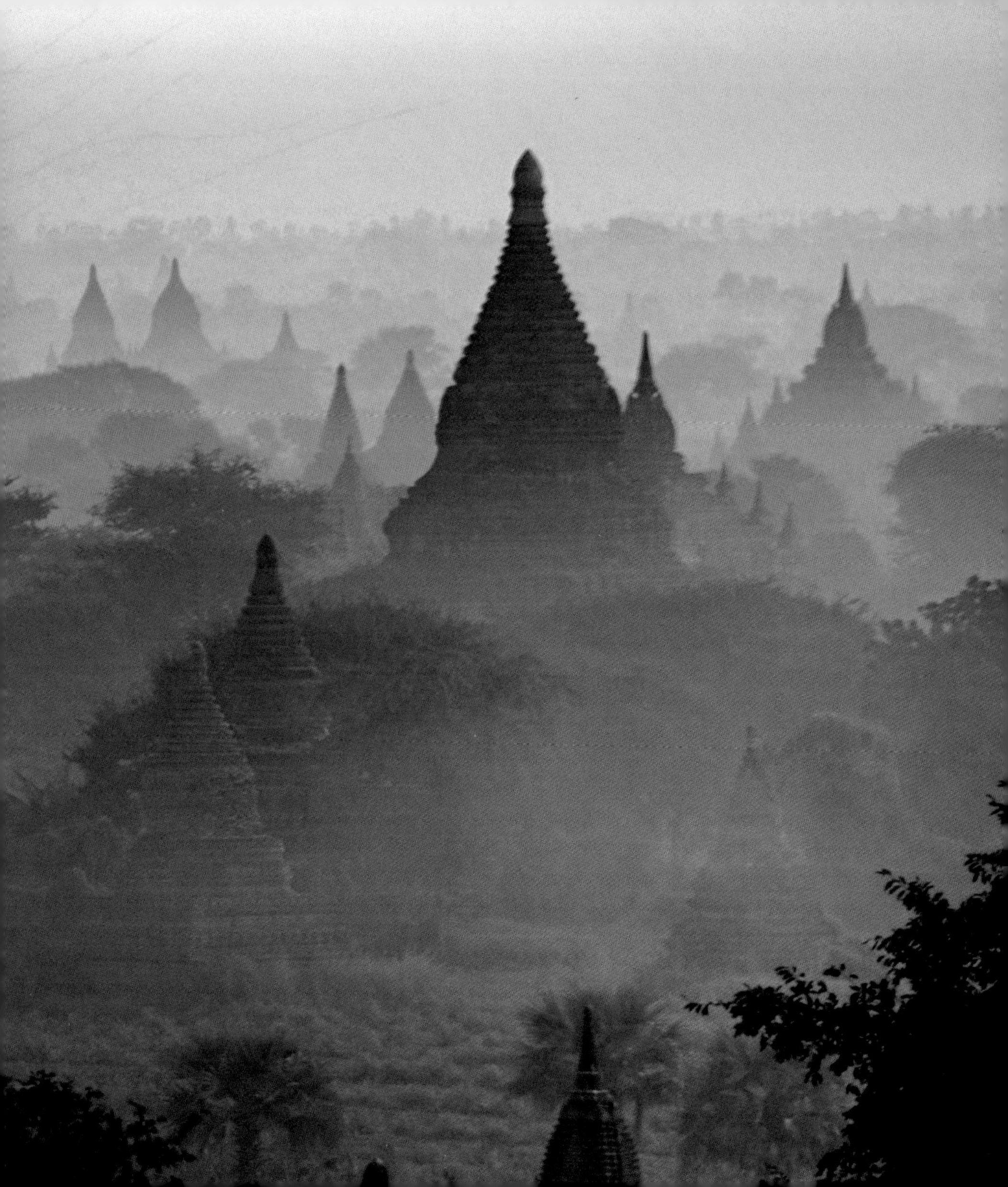

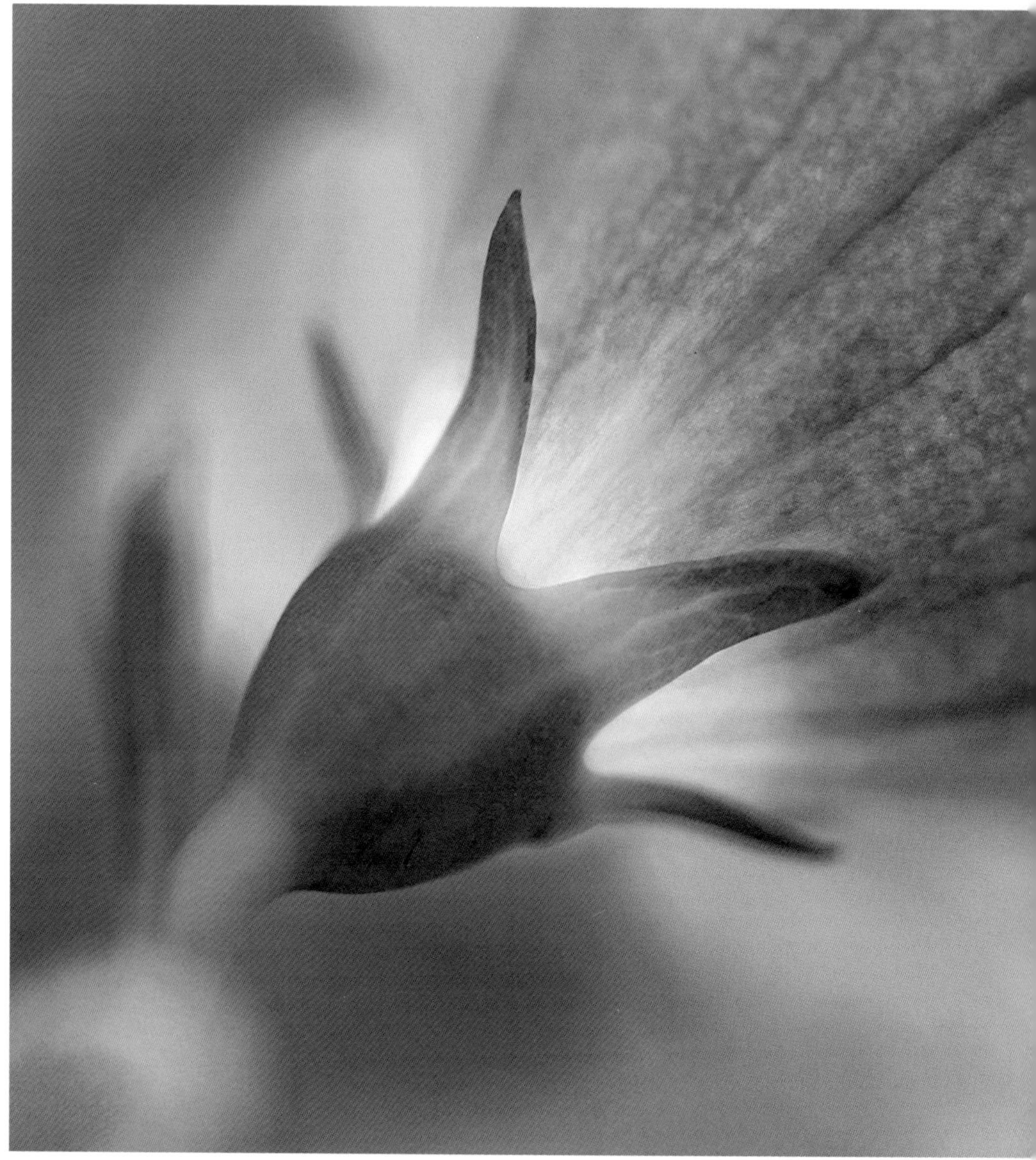

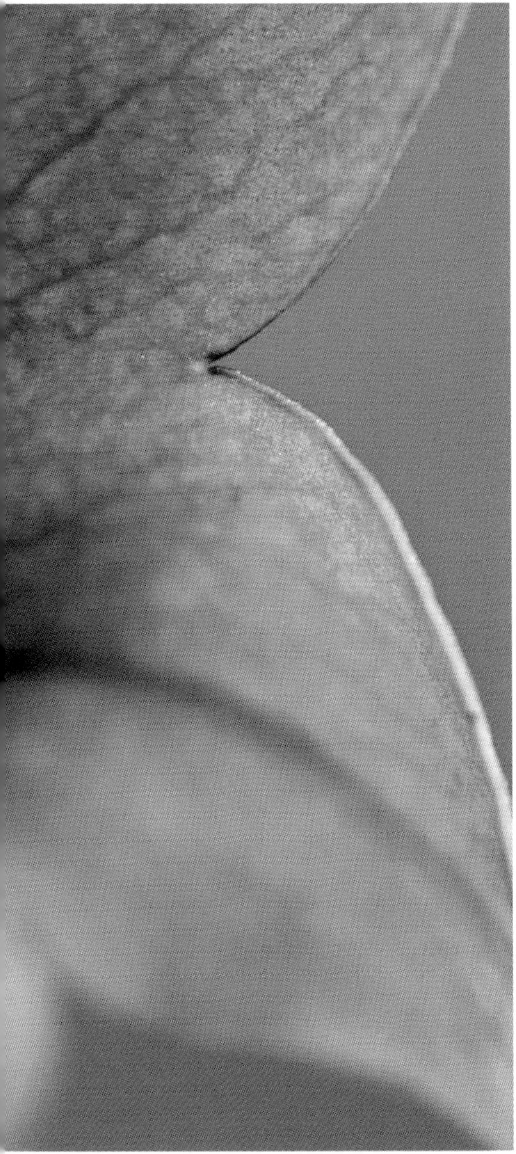

March 13

There is nothing deep down inside us except what we have put there ourselves.

~ Richard Rorty

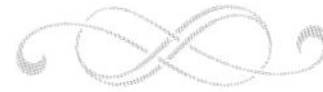

MARCH 14

If we limit ourselves
to the age that we are,
and forget all the ages
that we have been,
we diminish our truth.

~ Madeleine L'Engle

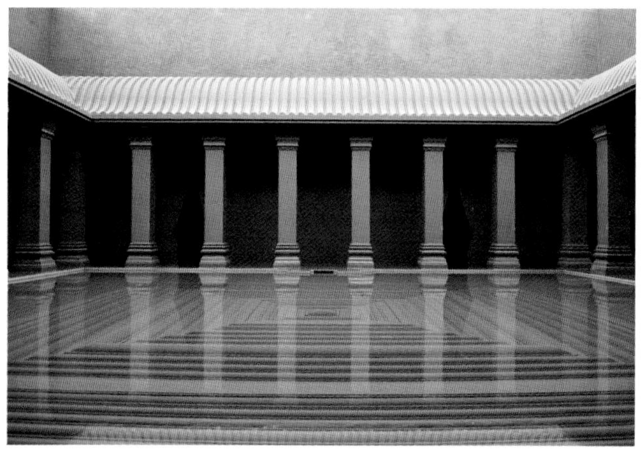

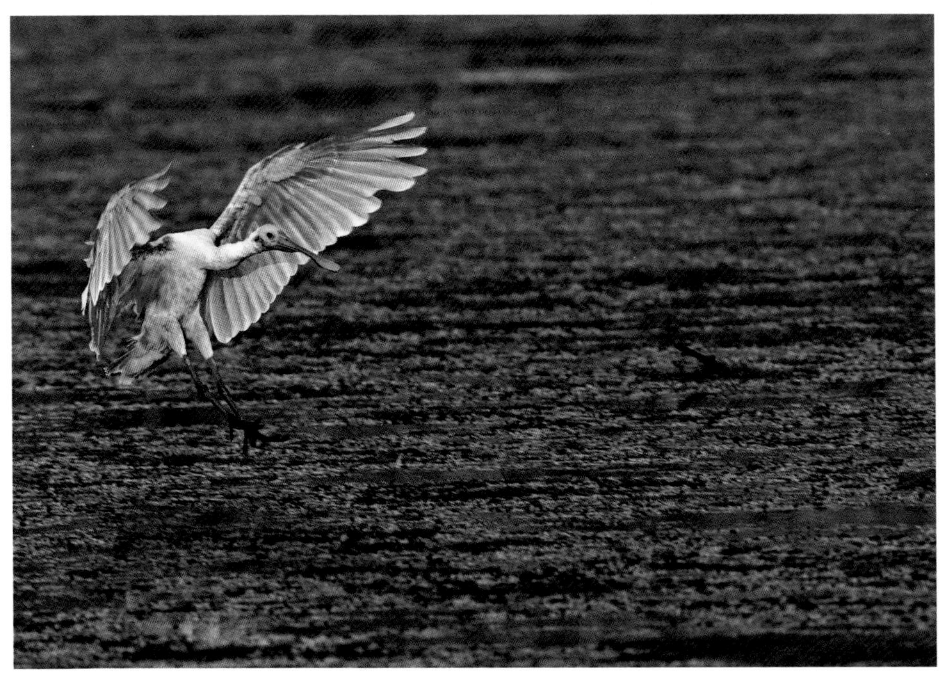

MARCH 15

Things do not change;
we change.

~ Henry David Thoreau

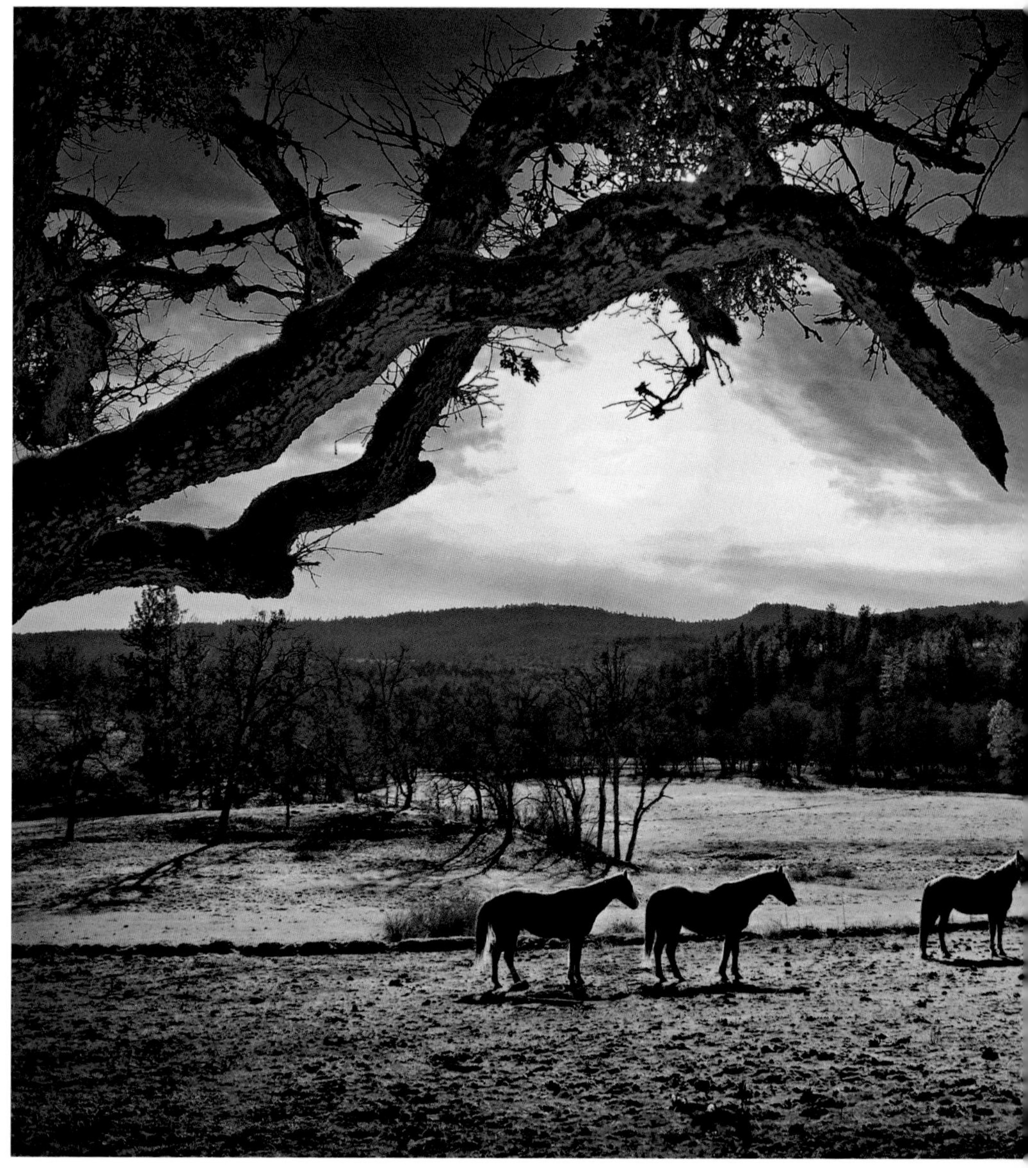

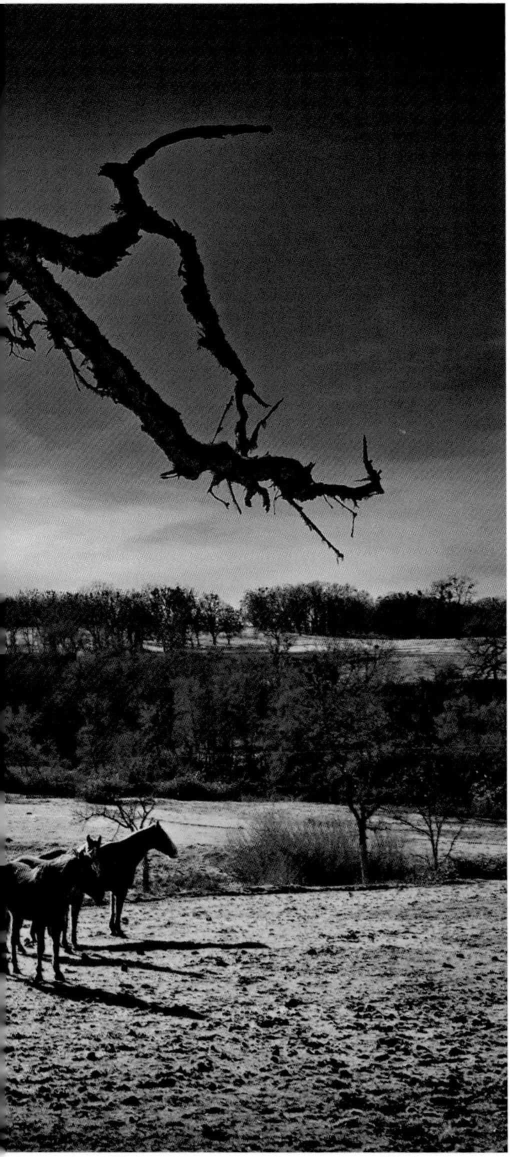

March 16

Happiness is when
what you think,
what you say, and
what you do
are in harmony.

~ Mohandas Gandhi

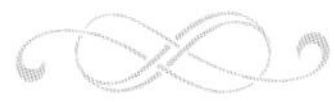

MARCH 17

We make a living by what we get. We make a life by what we give.

~ Sir Winston Churchill

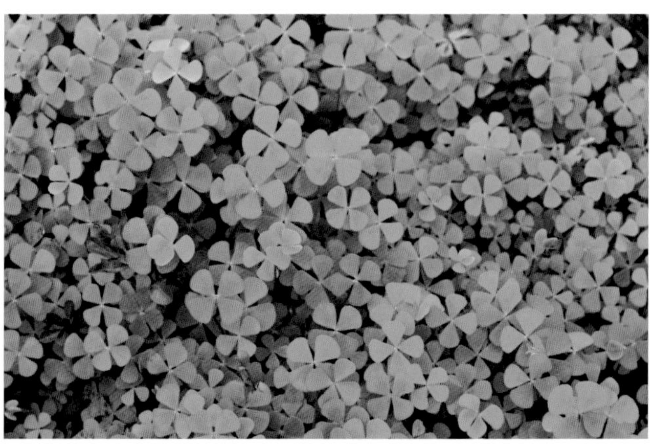

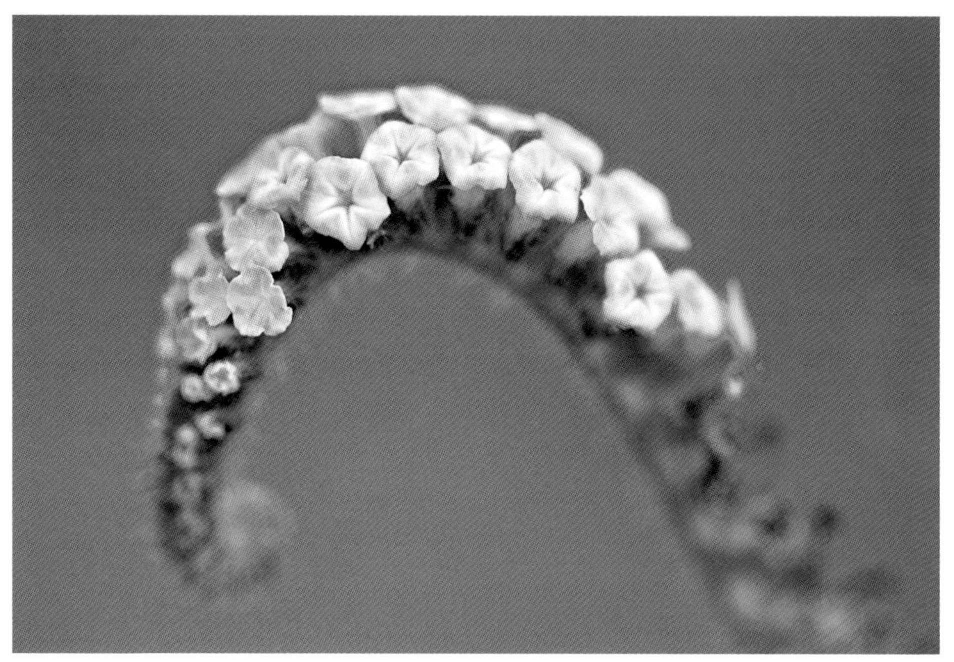

MARCH *18*

Only the truth of who you are,
if realized,
will set you free.

~ Eckhart Tolle

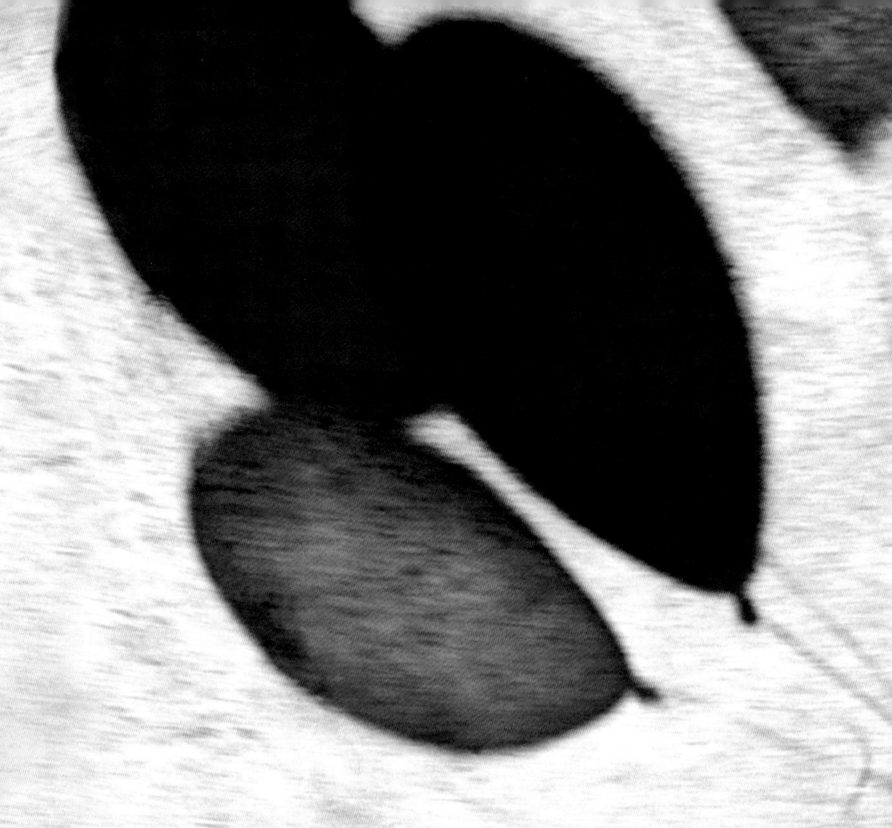

March *19*

If you have nothing at all to create, then perhaps you create yourself.

~ Carl Jung

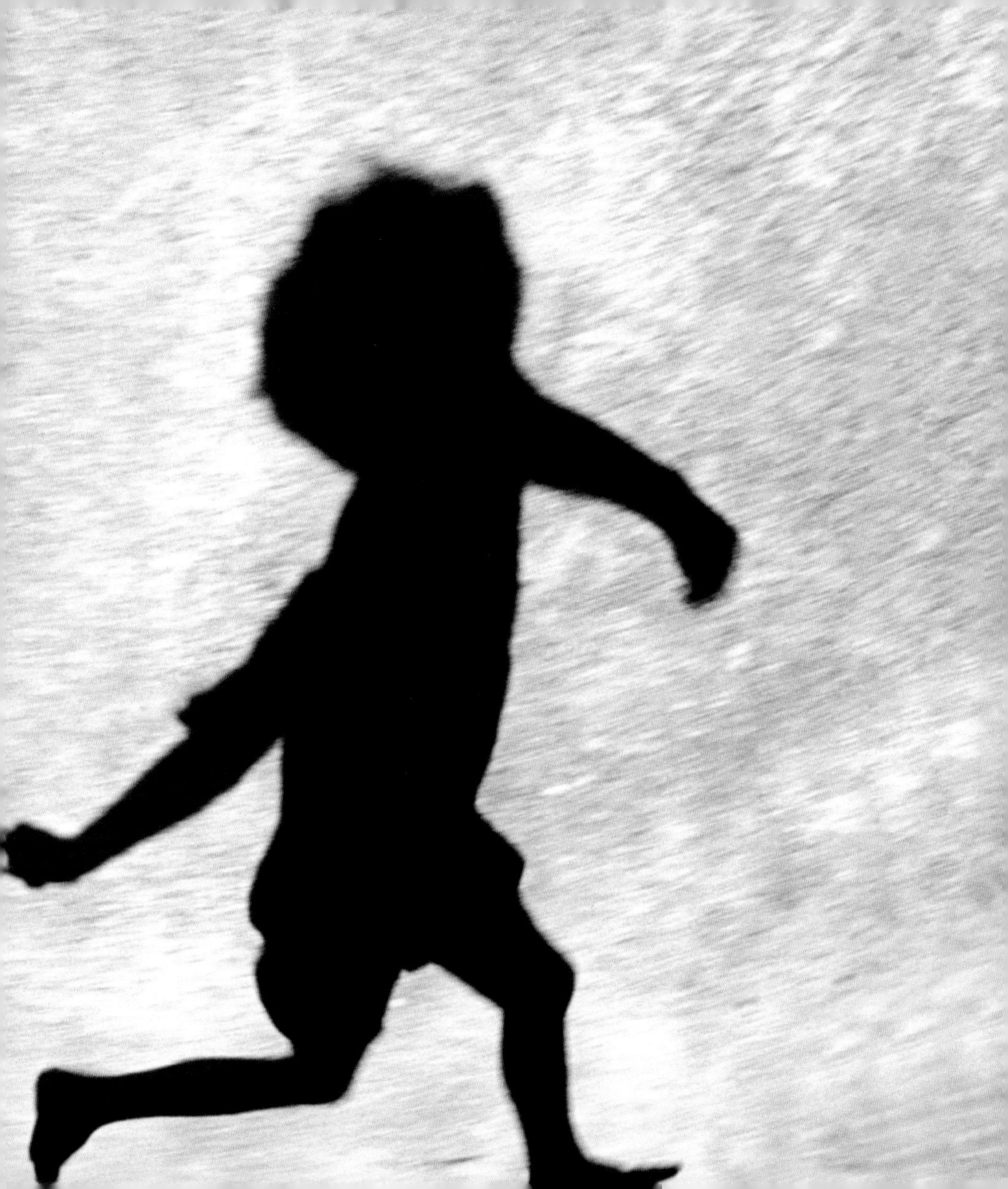

MARCH 20

Just trust yourself,
and then you will know how
to live.

~ Johann Wolfgang von Goethe

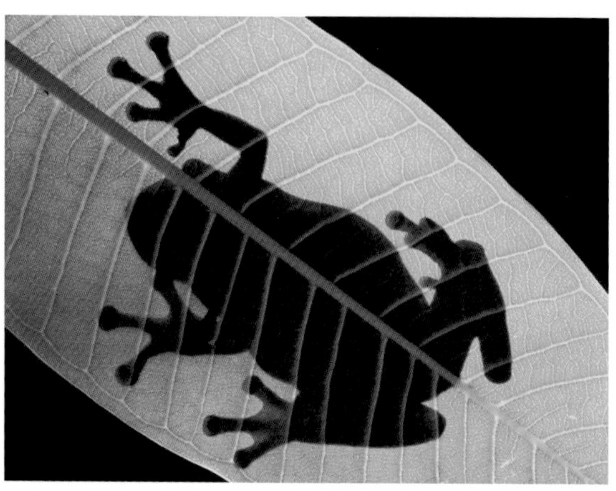

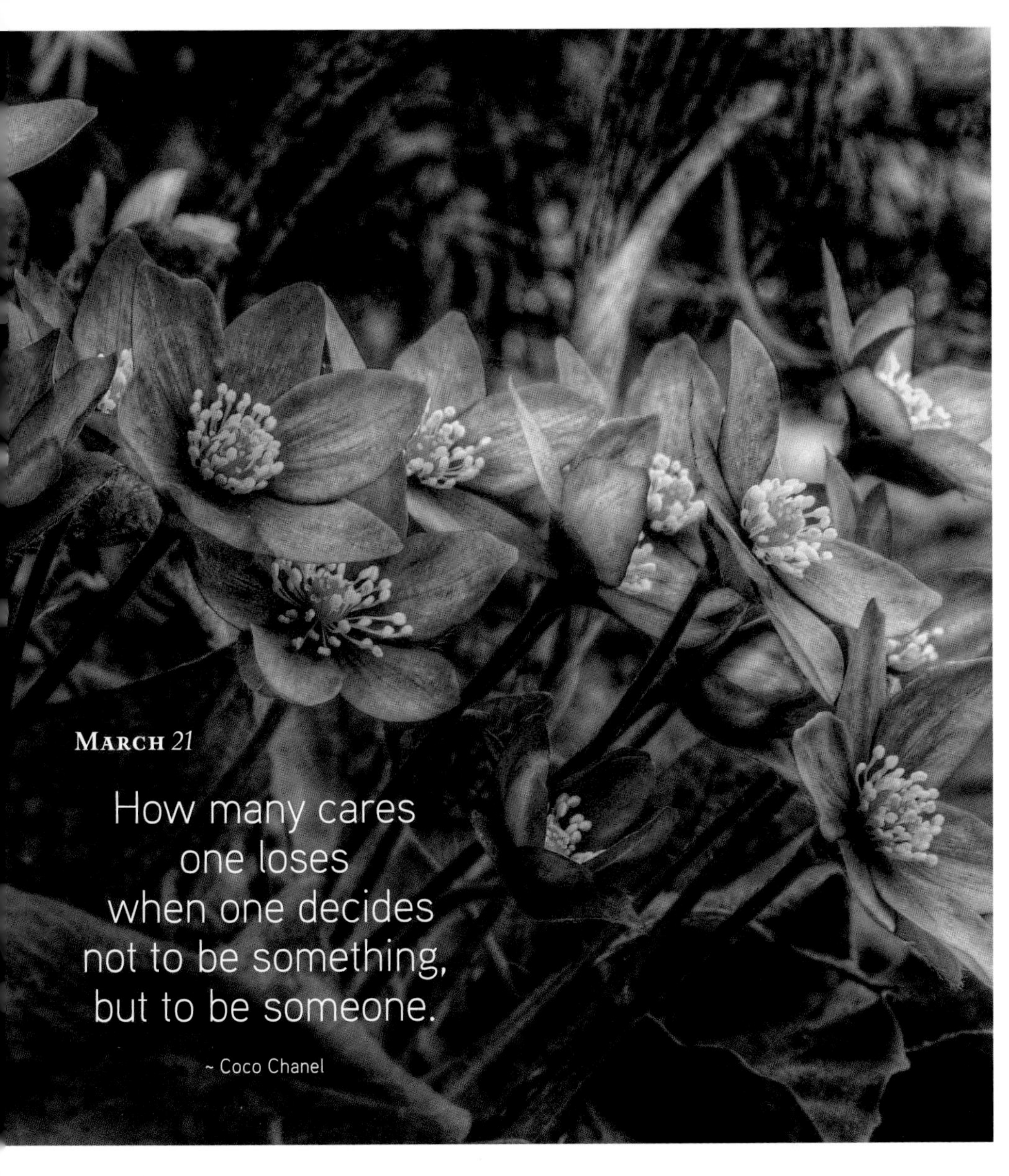
MARCH 21
How many cares
one loses
when one decides
not to be something,
but to be someone.
~ Coco Chanel

MARCH 22

Everything
in the universe
is within you.
Ask all from
yourself.

~ Rumi

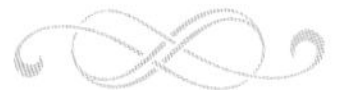

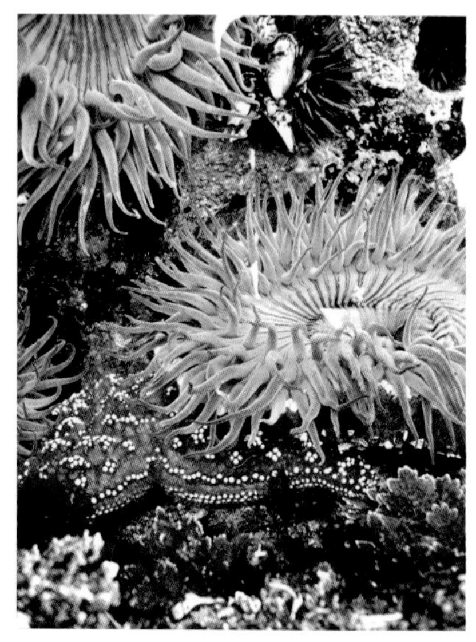

March 23

Everyone thinks
of changing the world,
but no one thinks
of changing himself.

~ Leo Tolstoy

MARCH 24

What we have once enjoyed,
we can never lose.
All that we love deeply
becomes a part of us.

~ Helen Keller

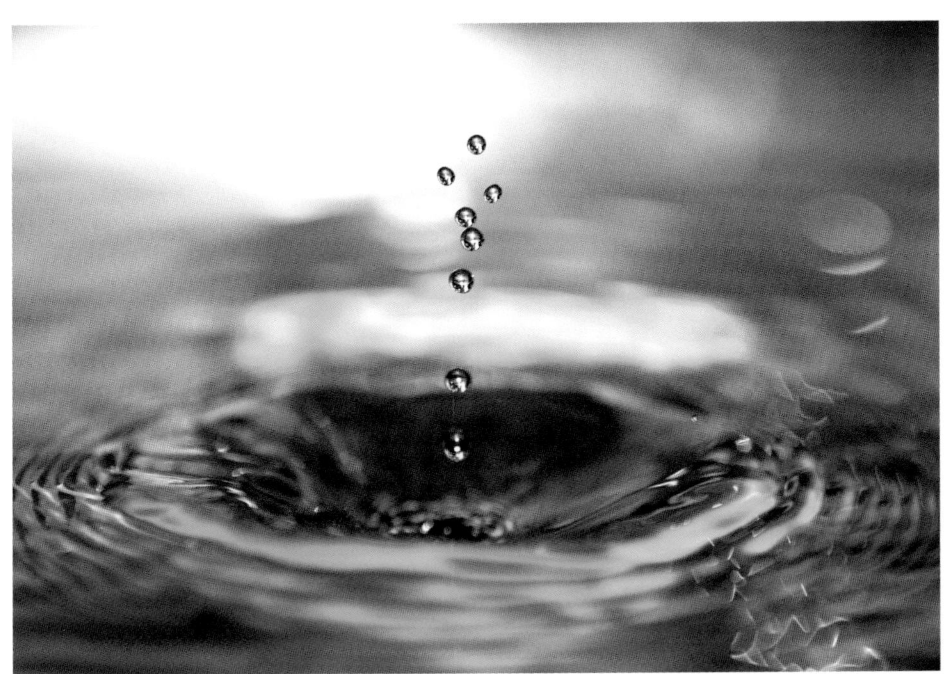

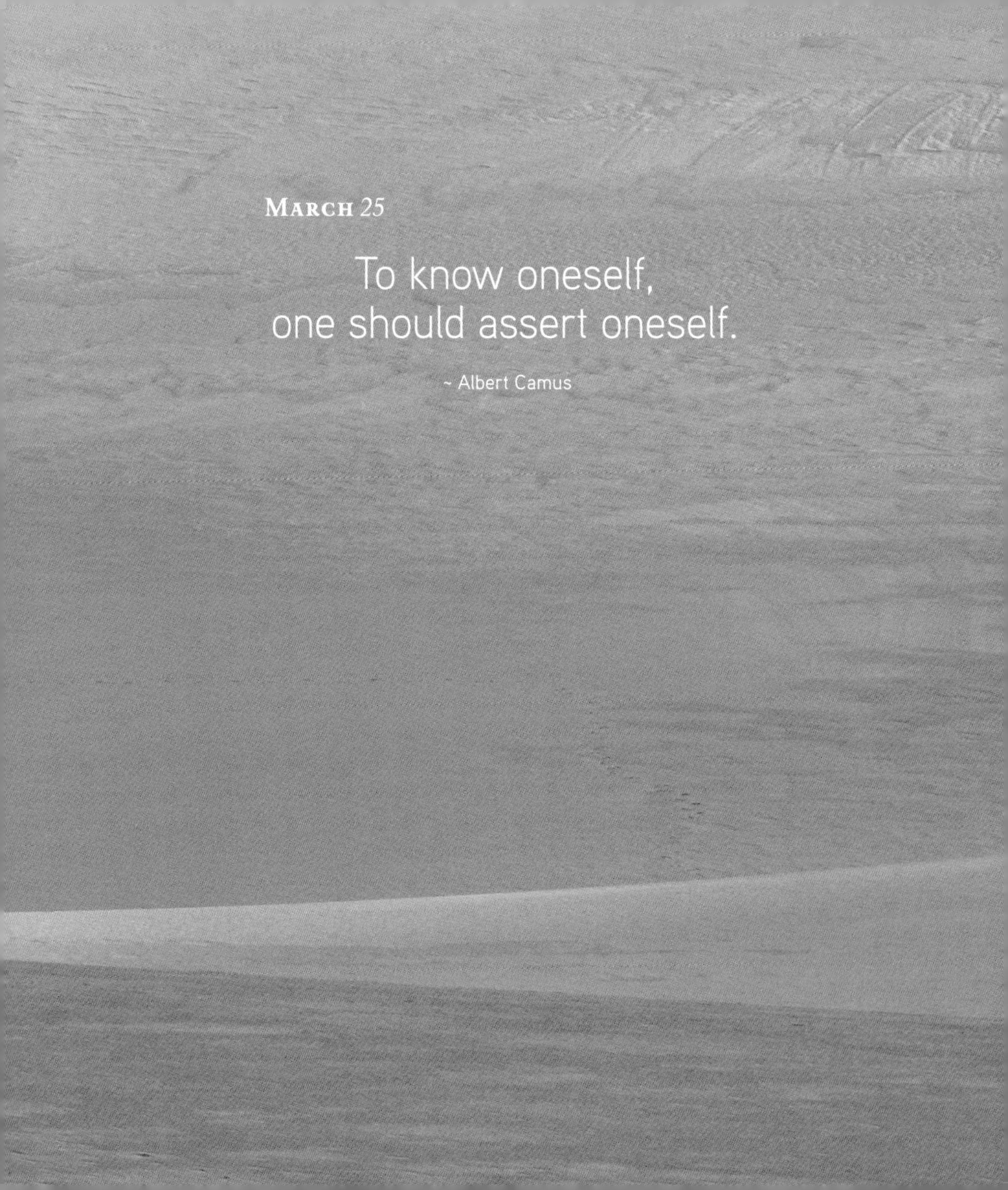

March 25

To know oneself,
one should assert oneself.

~ Albert Camus

March 26

Your time is limited so don't waste it
living someone else's life.
Don't let the noise of others' opinions
drown out your own inner voice.
And most important,
have the courage
to follow your heart and intuition.

~ Steve Jobs

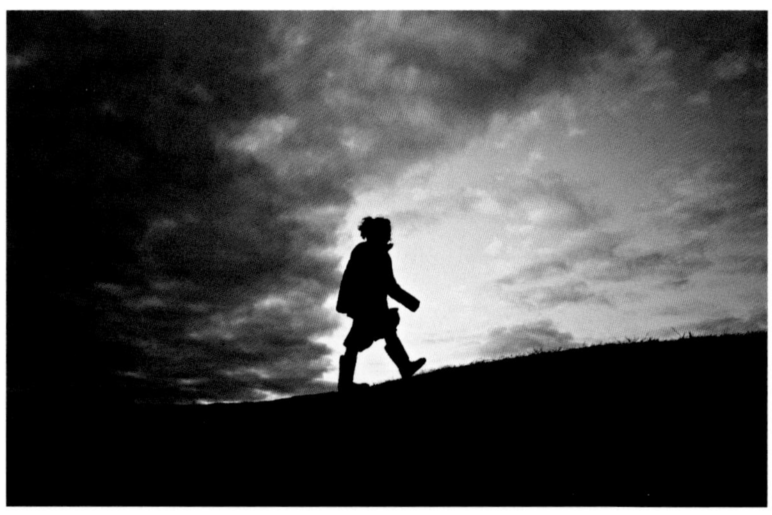

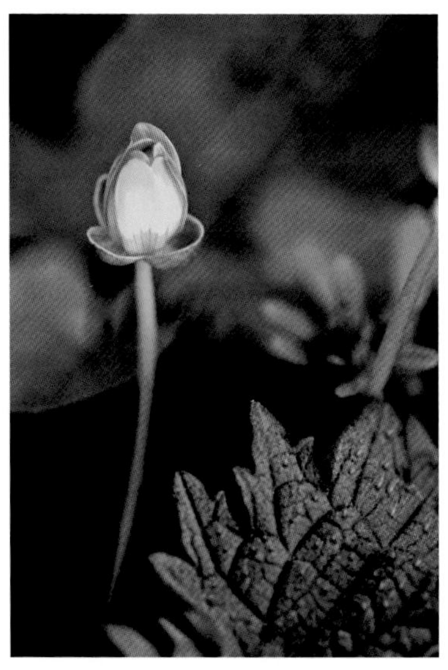

MARCH 27

Friendship with oneself
is all-important,
because without it
one cannot be friends
with anyone else in the world.

~ Eleanor Roosevelt

MARCH 28

The privilege
of a lifetime
is being
who you are.

~ Joseph Campbell

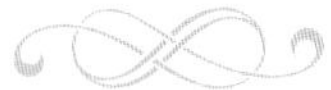

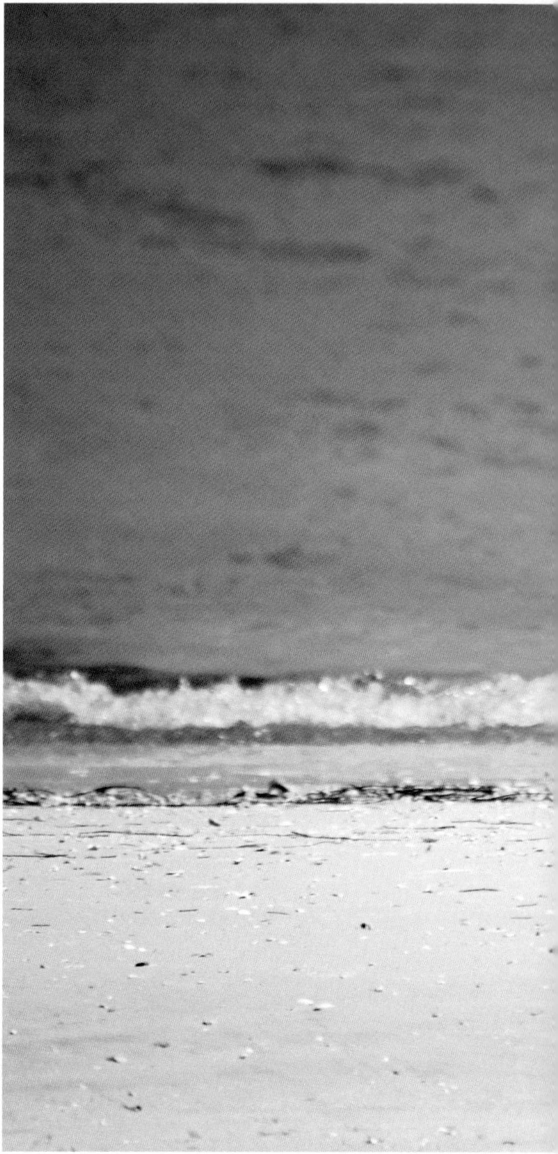

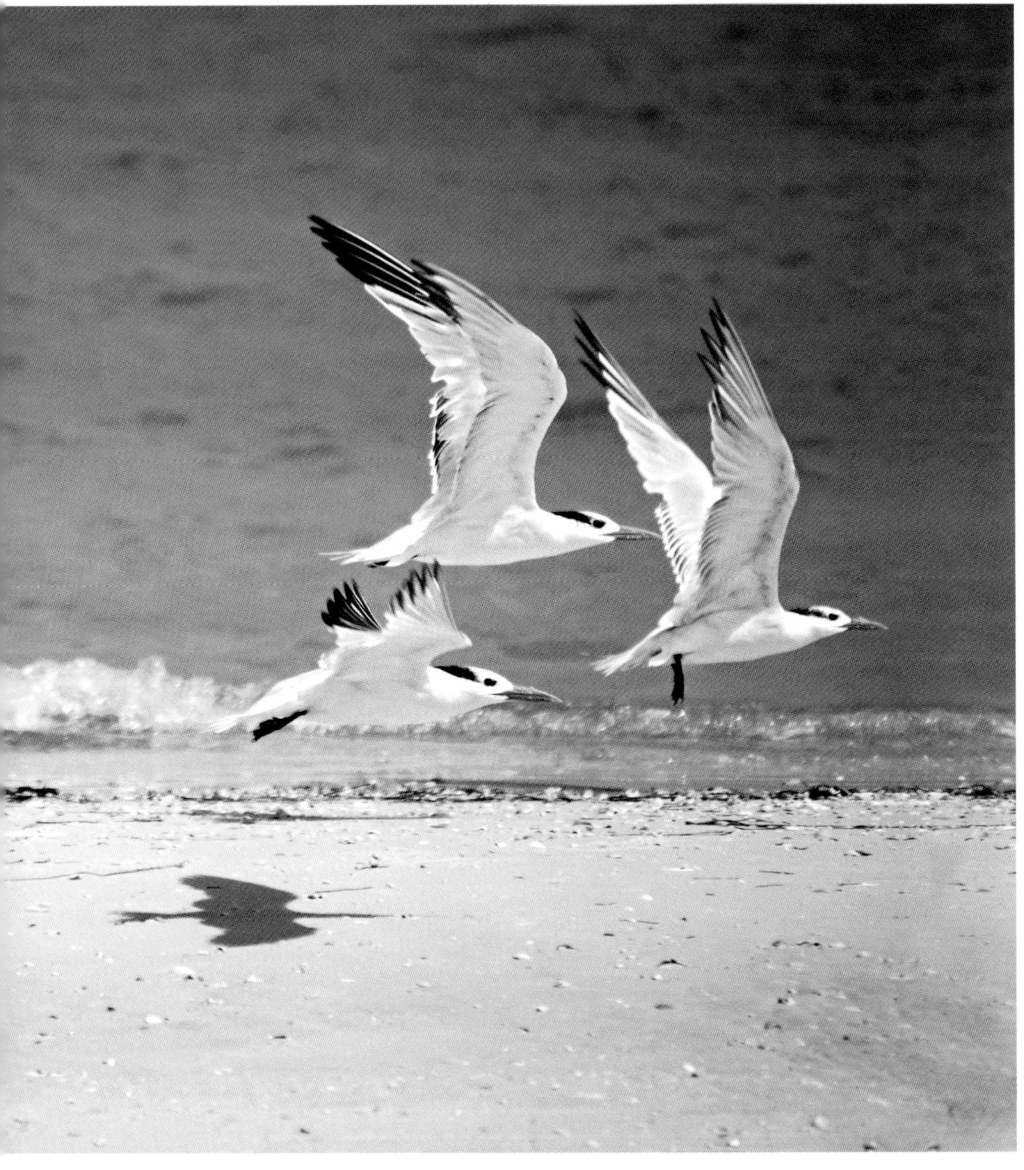

March 29

The shoe that fits one person
pinches another;
there is no recipe for living
that suits all cases.

~ Carl Jung

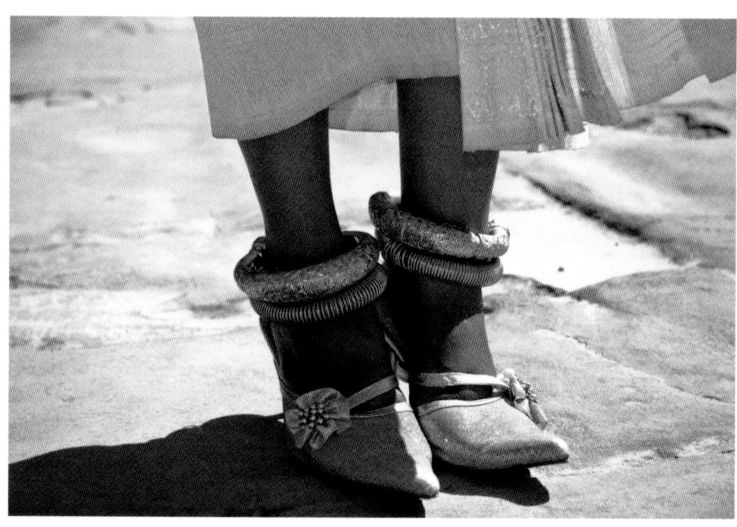

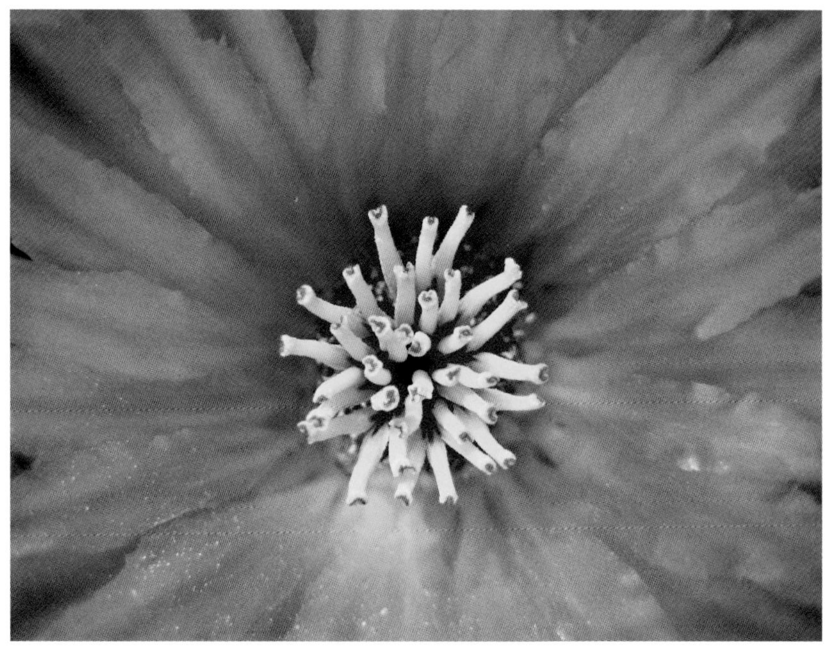

MARCH 30

You give but little
when you give of your possessions.
It is when you give of yourself
that you truly give.

~ Kahlil Gibran

March 31

To be nobody but yourself
in a world
which is doing its best,
night and day,
to make you everybody else
means to fight
the hardest battle
which any human being
can fight.
Never stop fighting.

~ e. e. cummings

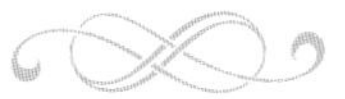

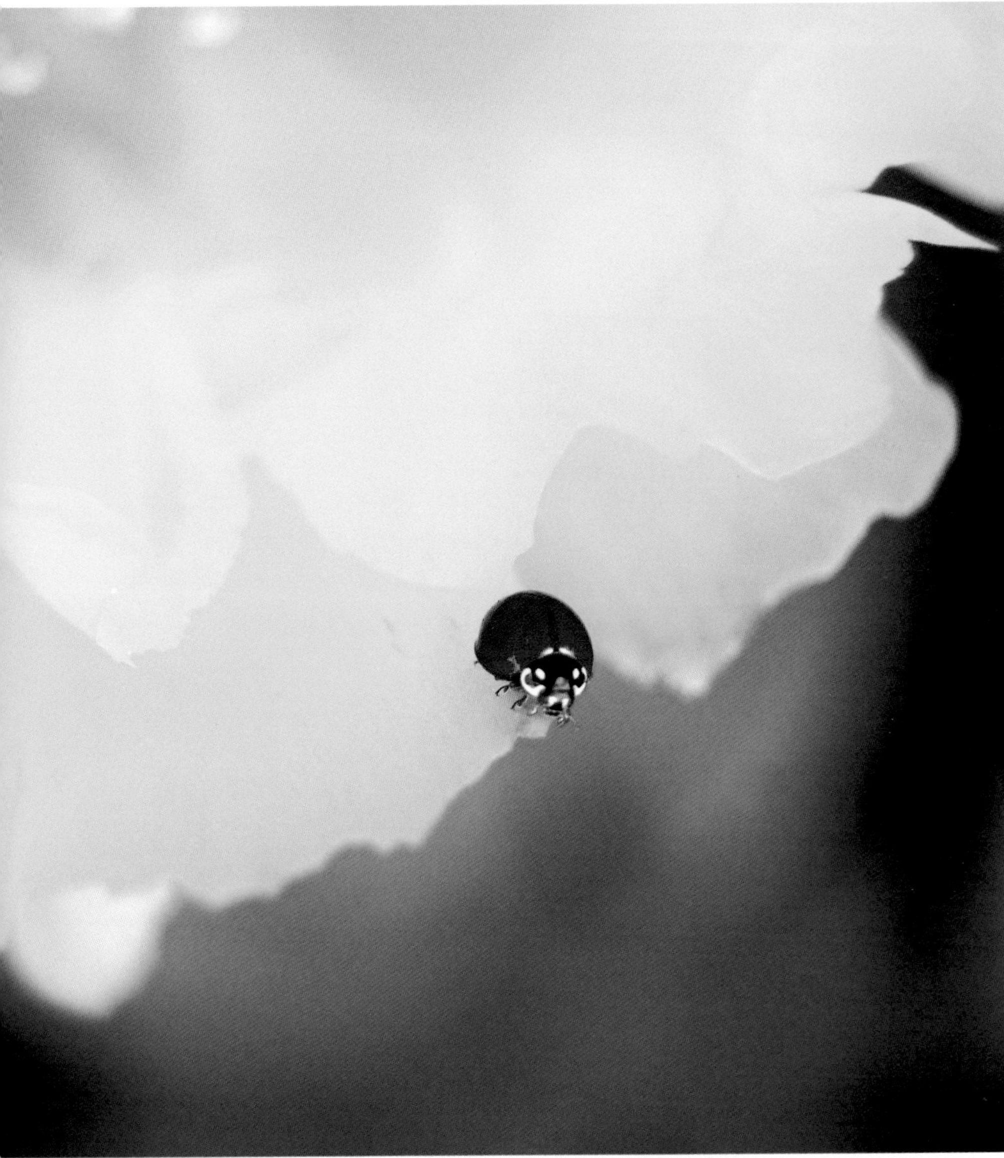

GROWTH

April

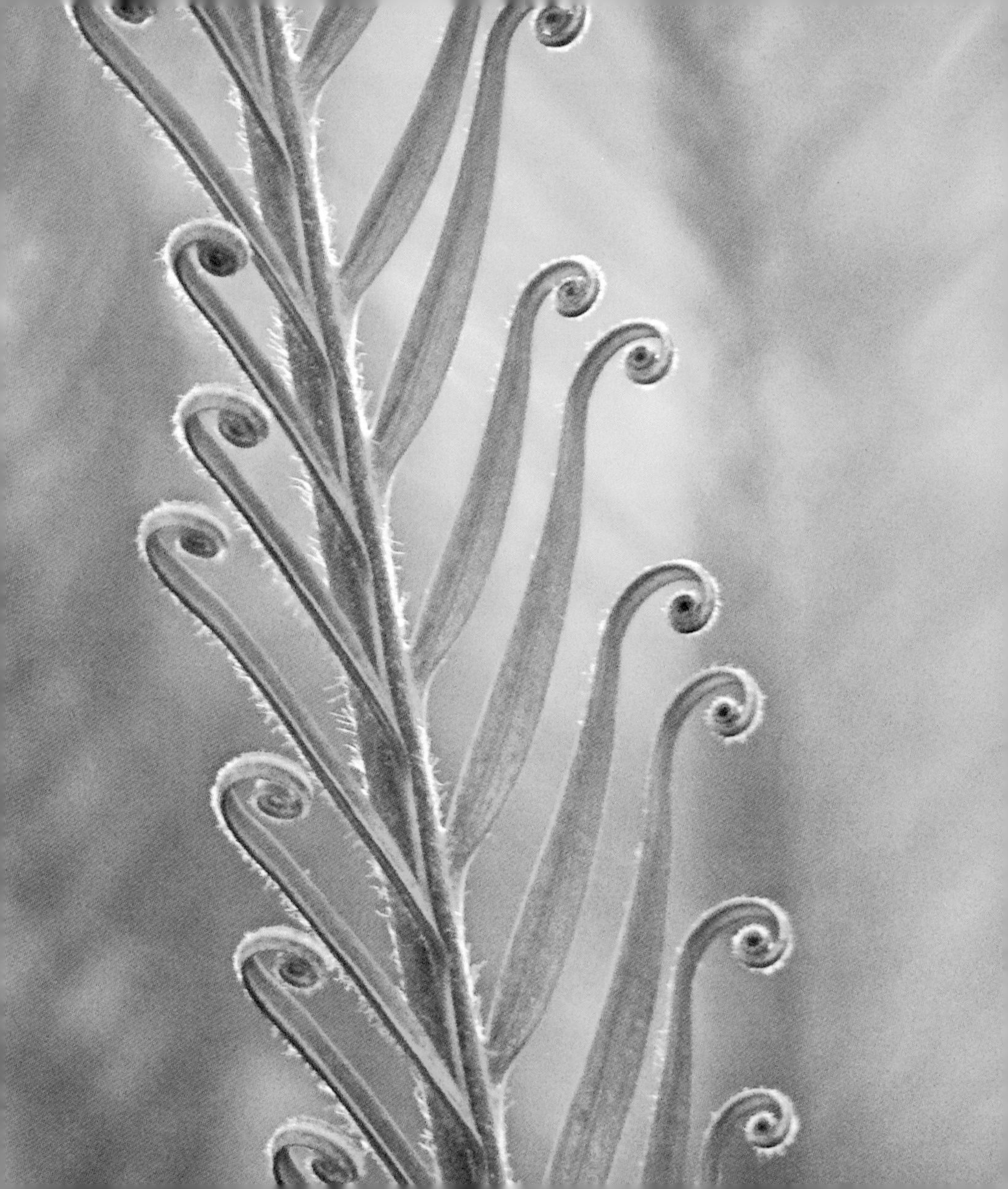

April 1

My favorite thing is to go where I've never been.

~ Diane Arbus

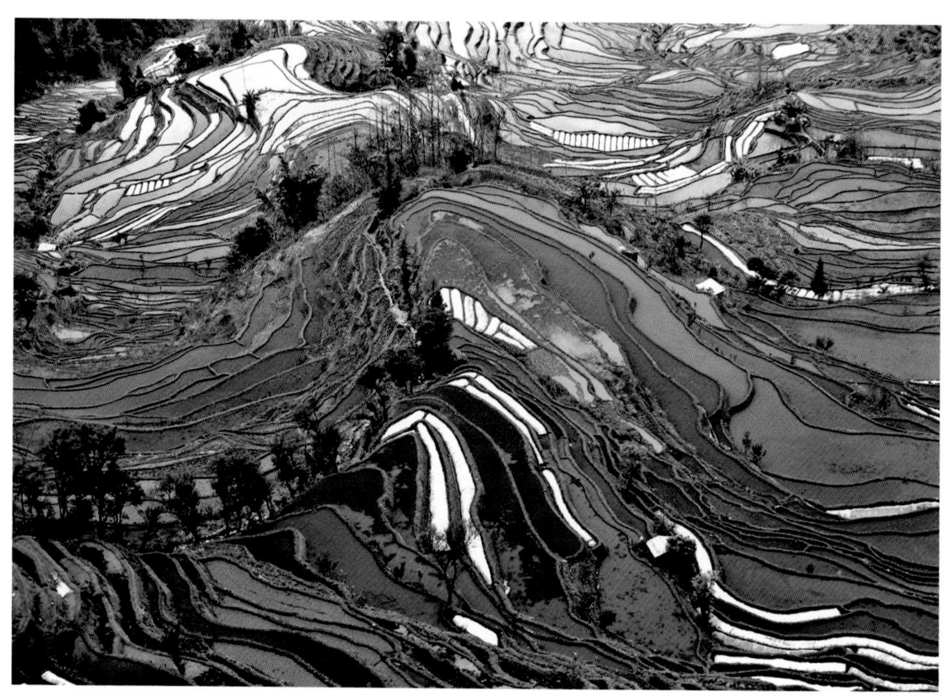

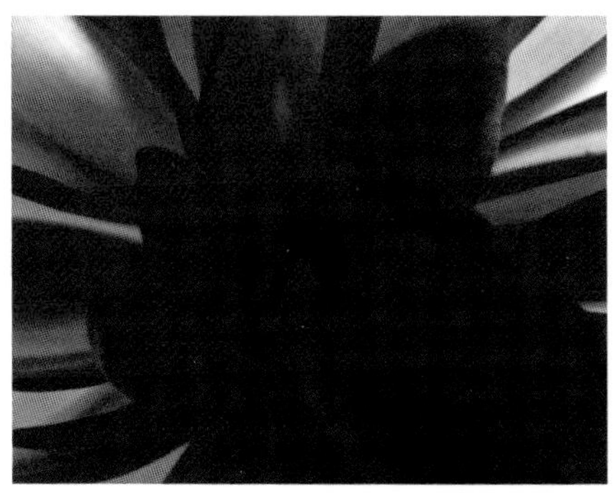

April 2

You are built not to shrink down to less,
but to blossom into more.
To be more splendid.
To be more extraordinary.
To use every moment to fill yourself up.

~ Oprah Winfrey

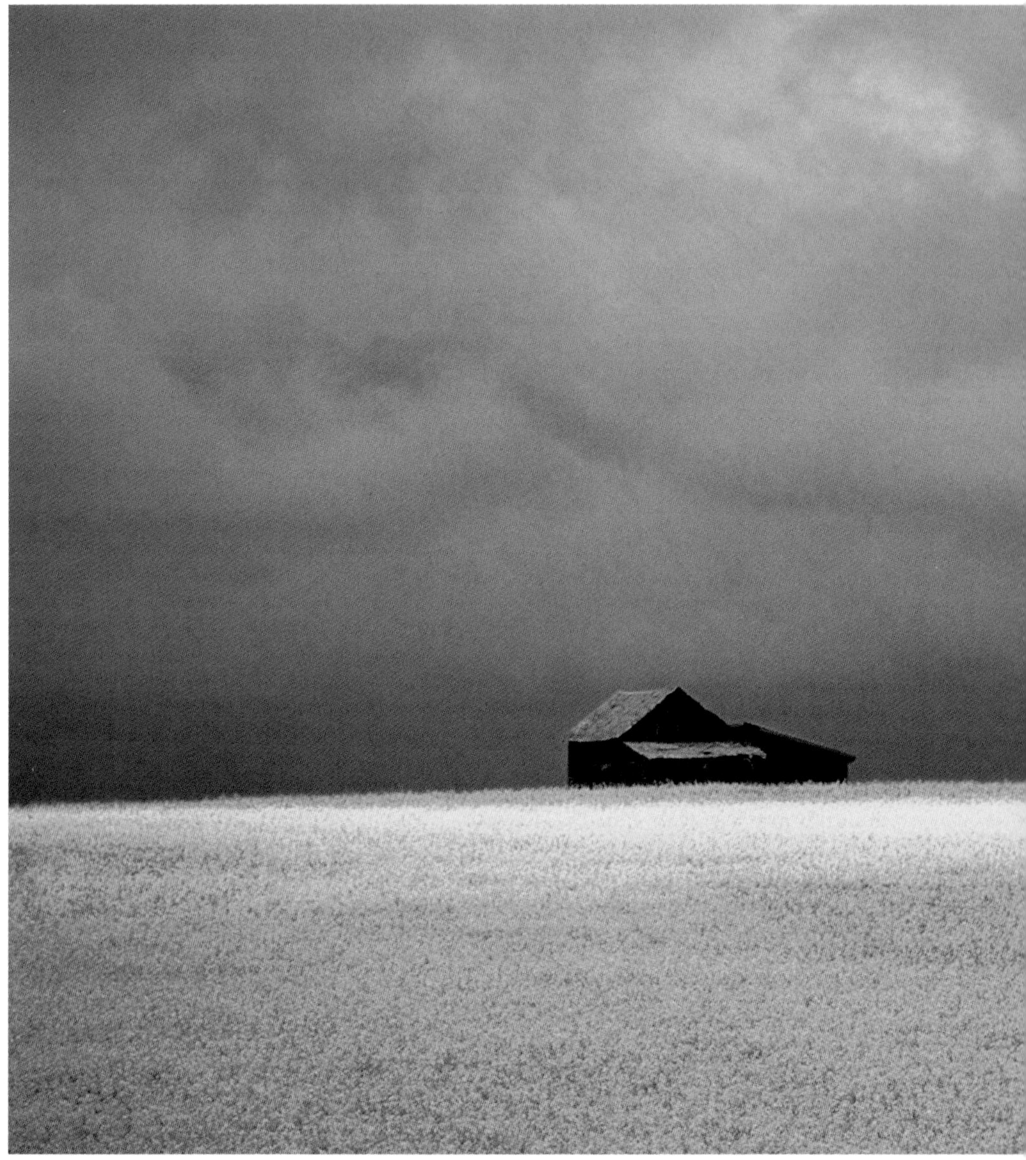

APRIL 3

I have learned that success
is to be measured not so much
by the position that one has reached in life
as by the obstacles which he has overcome
while trying to succeed.

~ Booker T. Washington

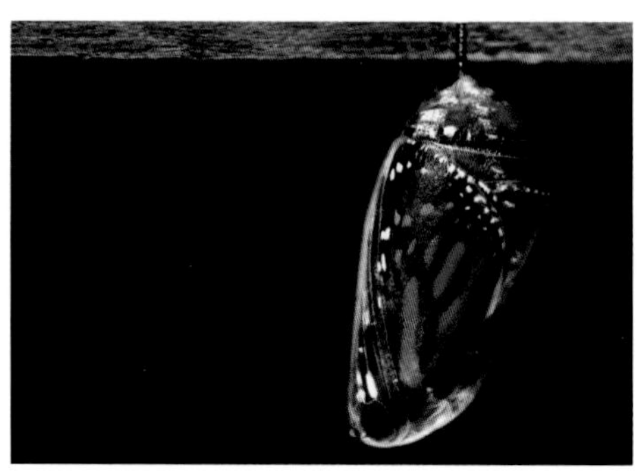

April 4

In the long run,
we shape our lives,
and we shape ourselves.
The process never ends
until we die.
And the choices we make
are ultimately
our own responsibility.

~ Eleanor Roosevelt

April 5

Adopt the pace of nature; her secret is patience.

~ Ralph Waldo Emerson

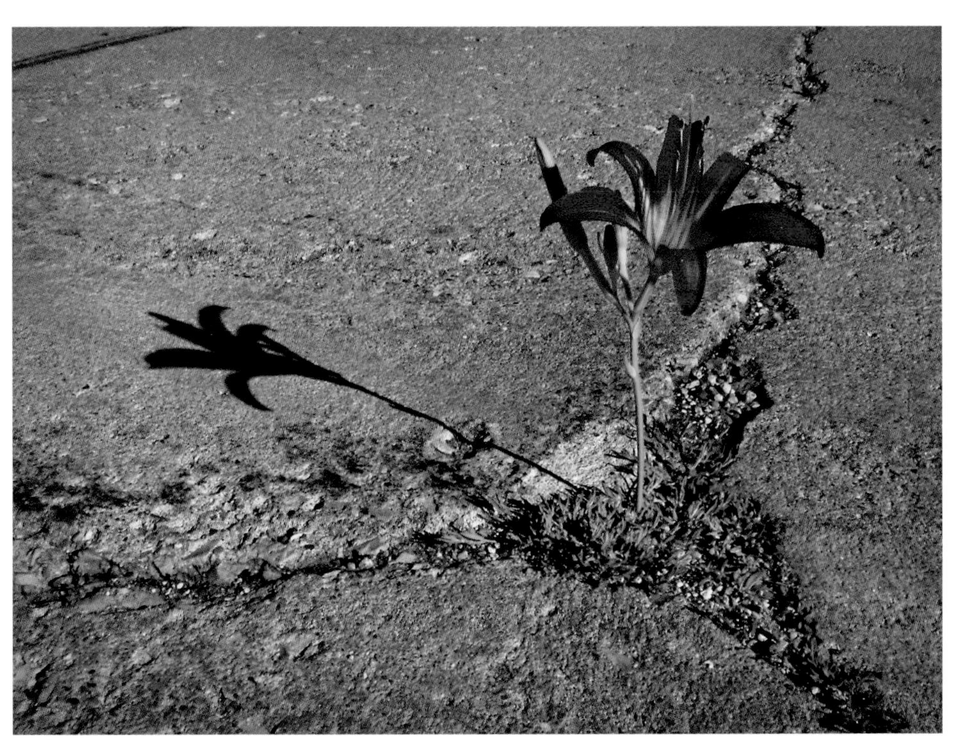

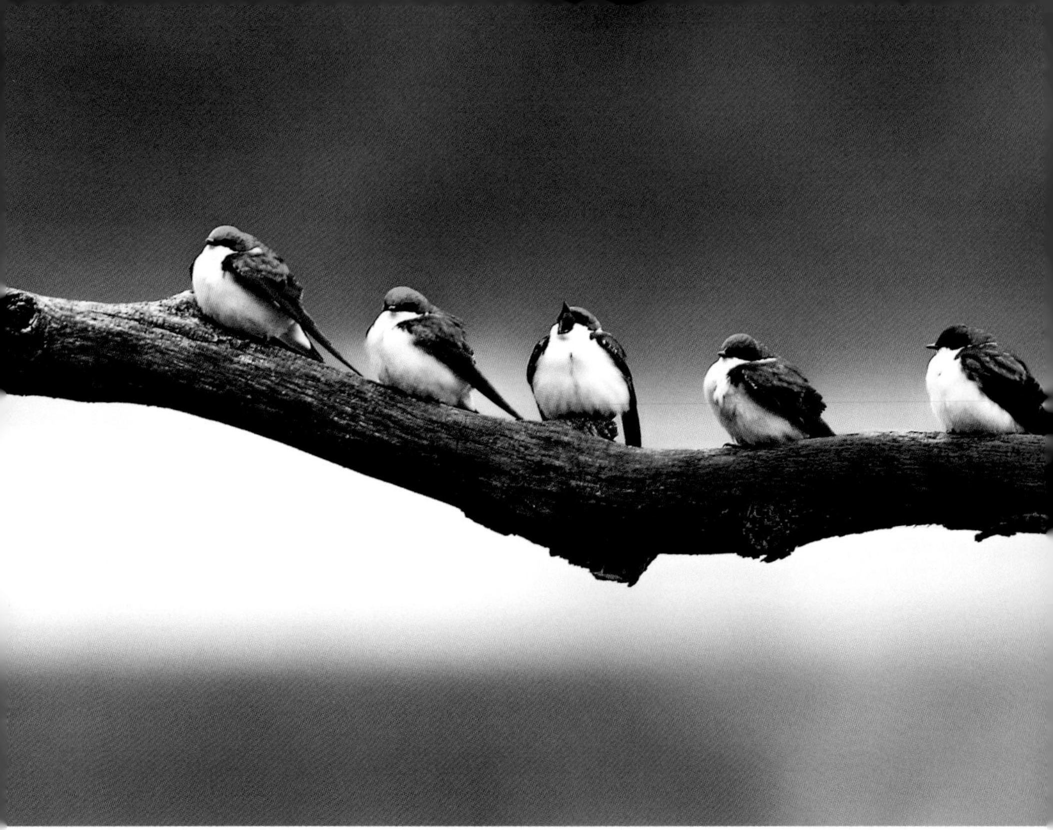

APRIL 6

Arrange whatever pieces come your way.

~ Virginia Woolf

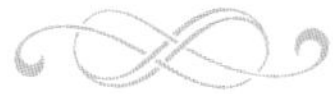

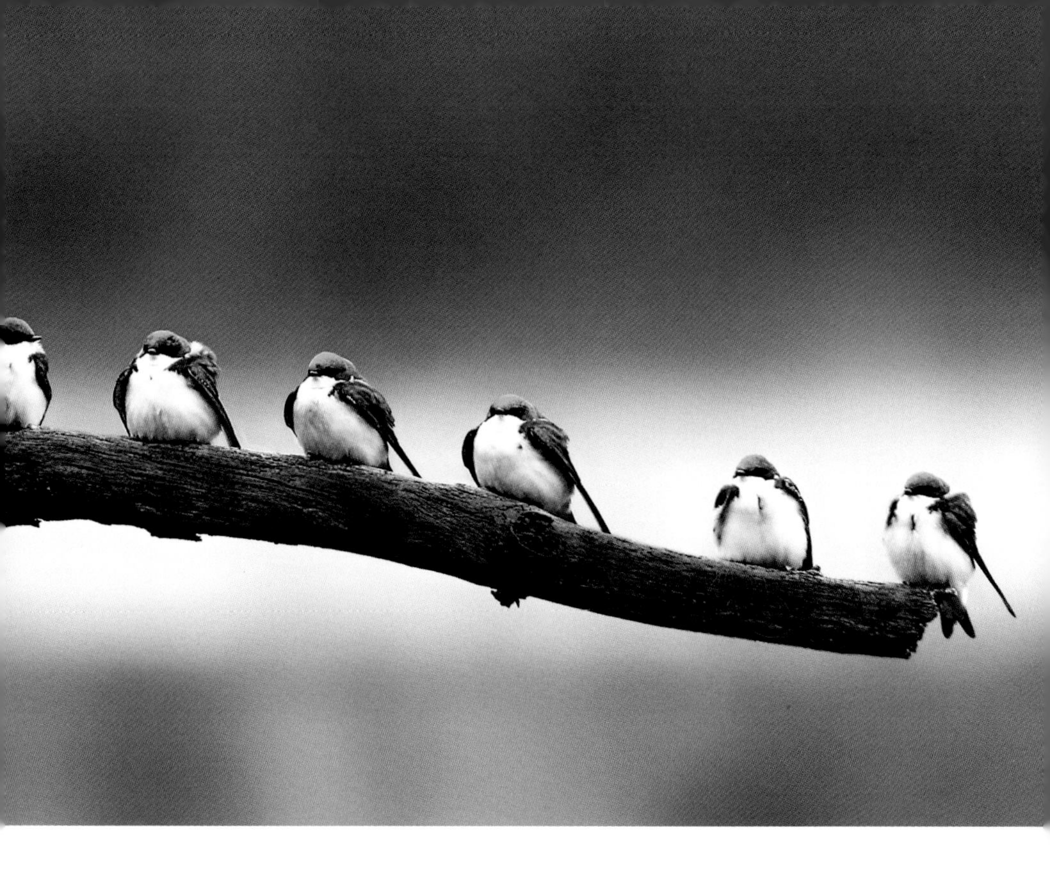

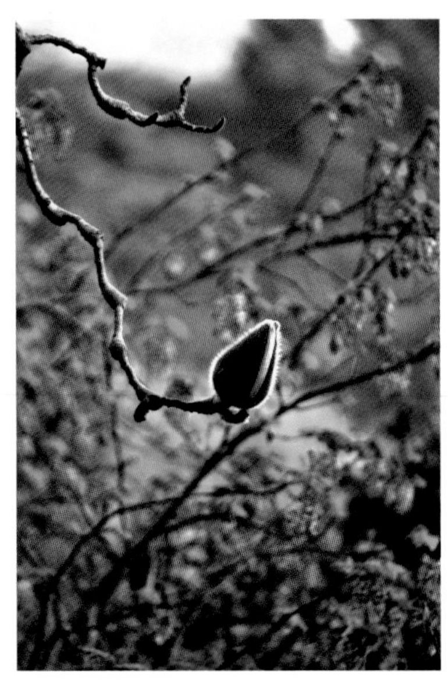

April 7

Life is a process of becoming,
a combination of states
we have to go through.
Where people fail
is that they wish to elect a state
and remain in it.

~ Anaïs Nin

April 8

If you don't like something, change it. If you can't change it, change your attitude.

~ Maya Angelou

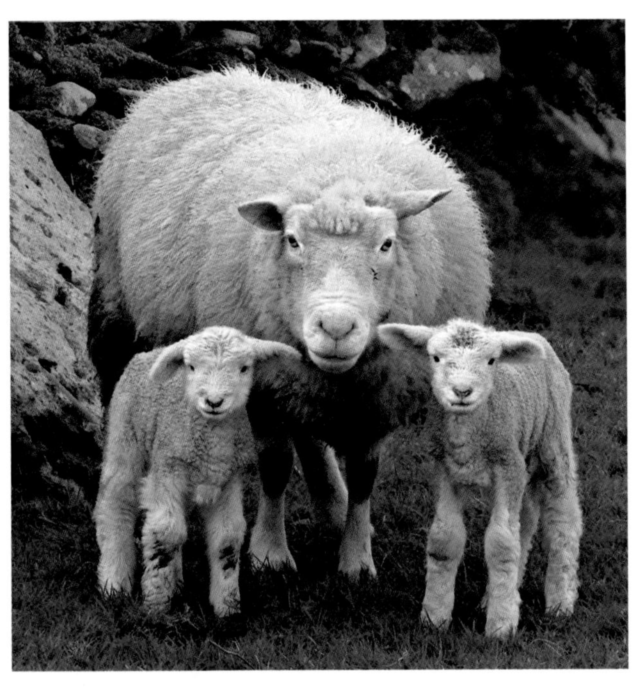

April 9

It is impossible
to live without failing
at something—
unless you live
so cautiously
that you might as well
not have lived at all,
in which case
you have failed
by default.

~ J. K. Rowling

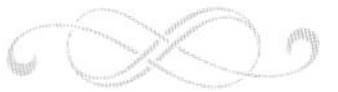

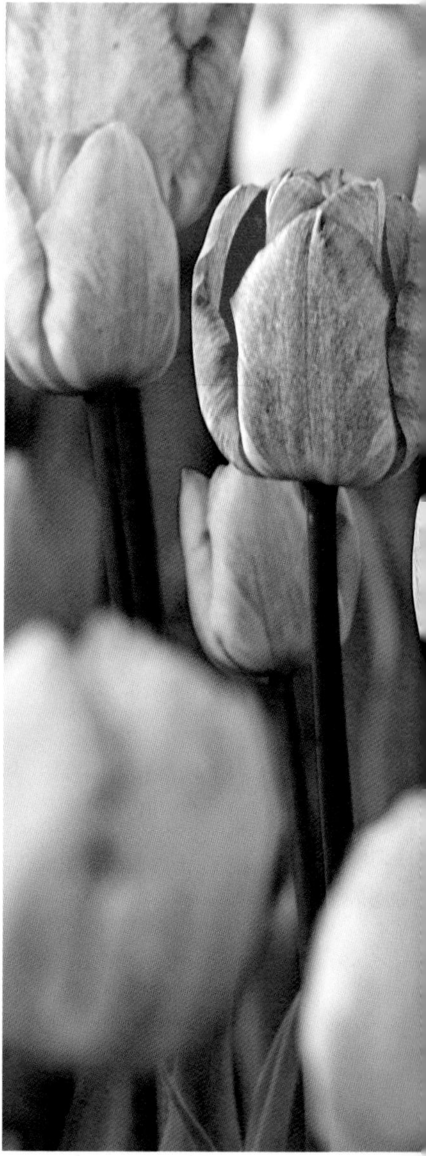

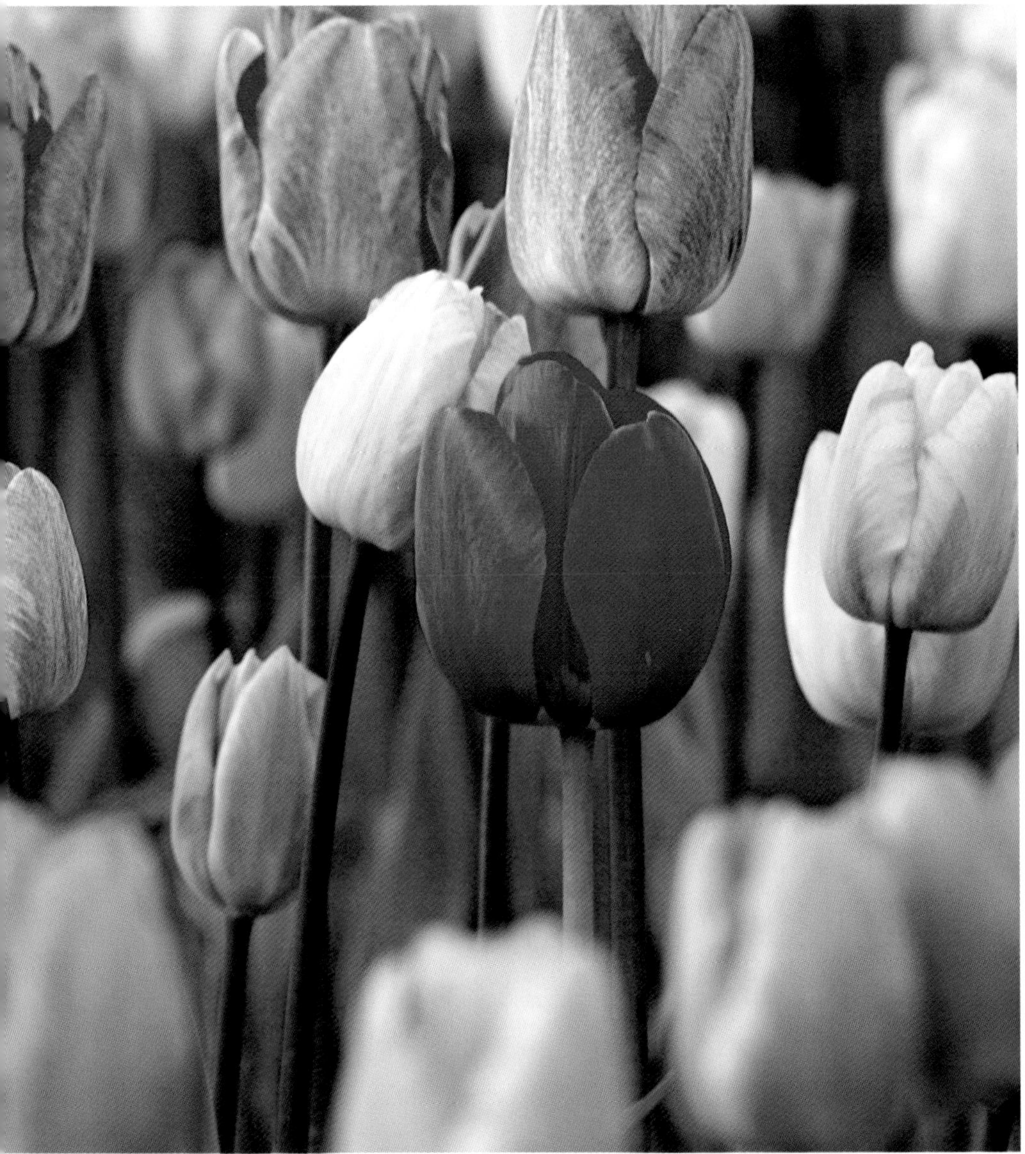

APRIL 10

Trust yourself.
You know more than you think you do.

~ Benjamin Spock

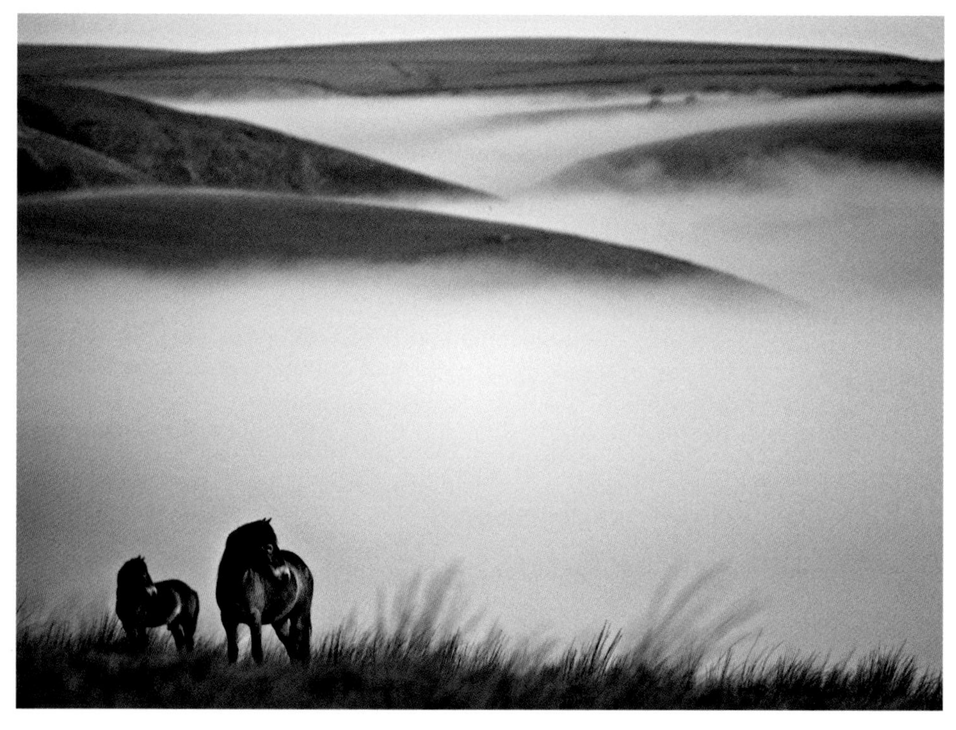

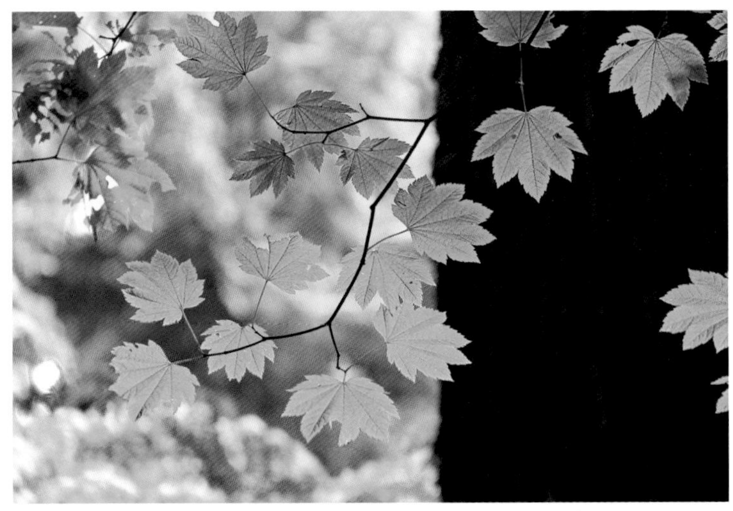

April 11

Because things are
the way they are,
things will not stay
the way they are.

~Bertolt Brecht

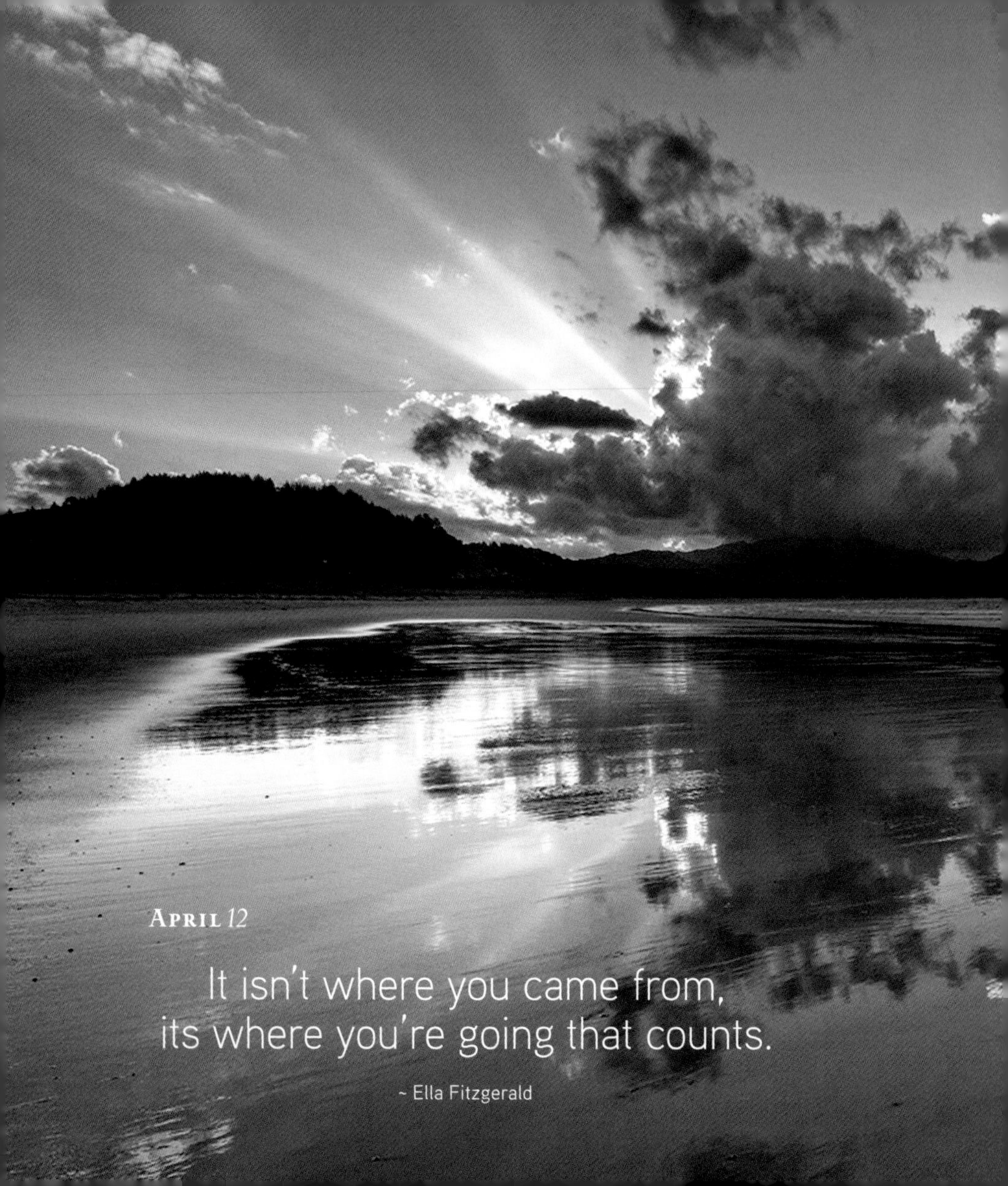

APRIL *12*

It isn't where you came from,
its where you're going that counts.

~ Ella Fitzgerald

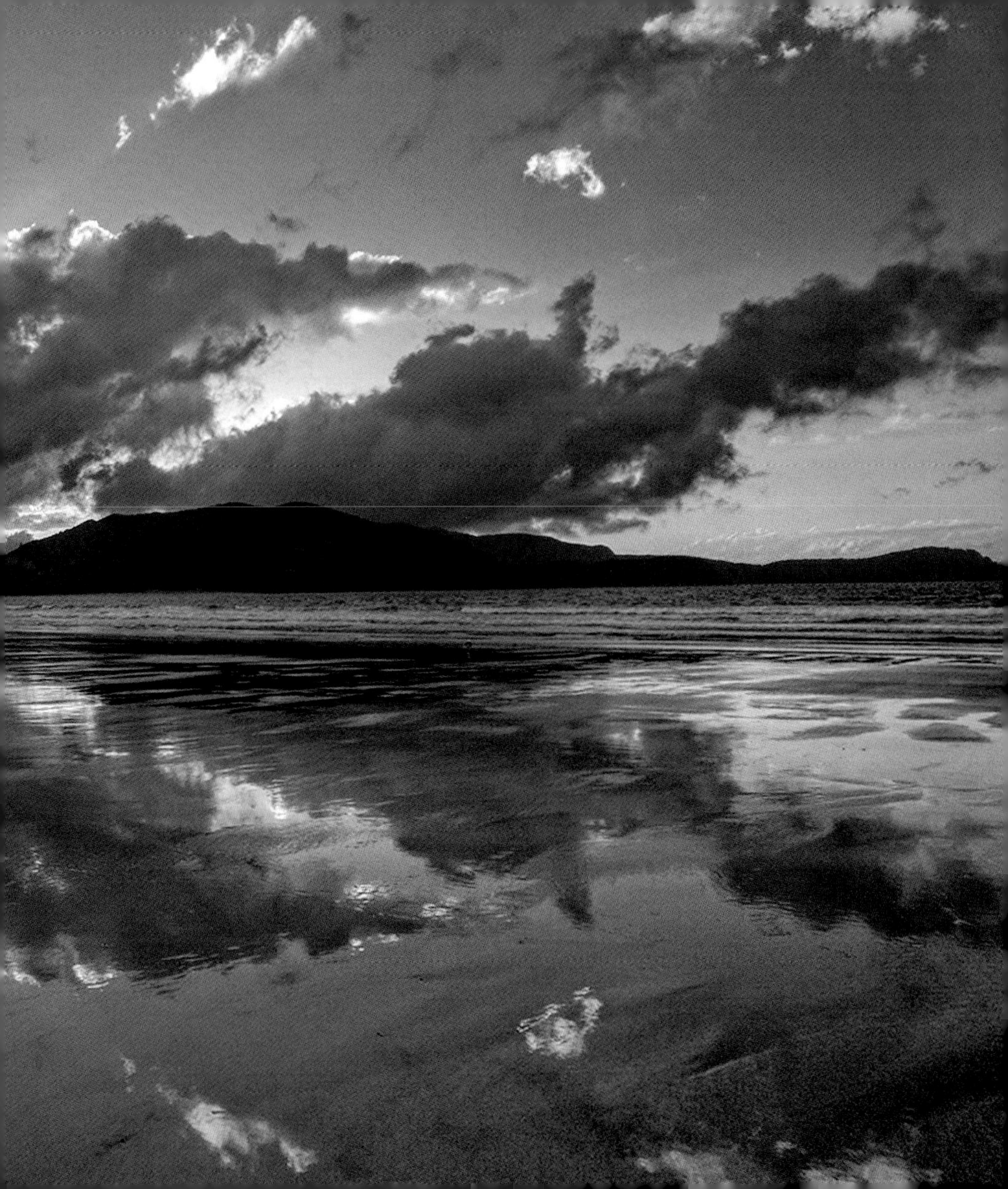

APRIL 13

It's the most unhappy people who most fear change.

~ Mignon McLaughlin

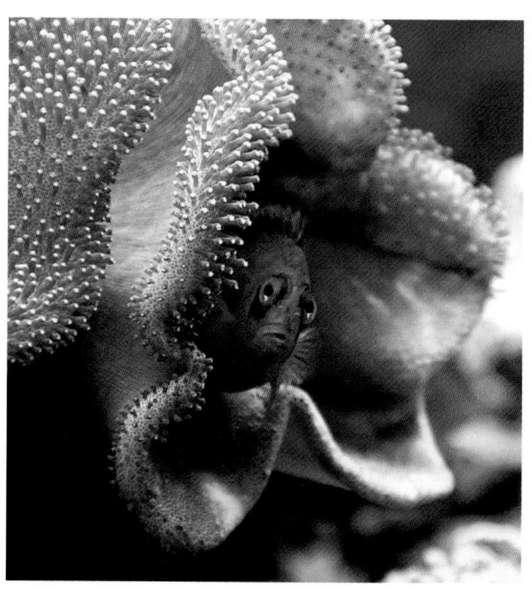

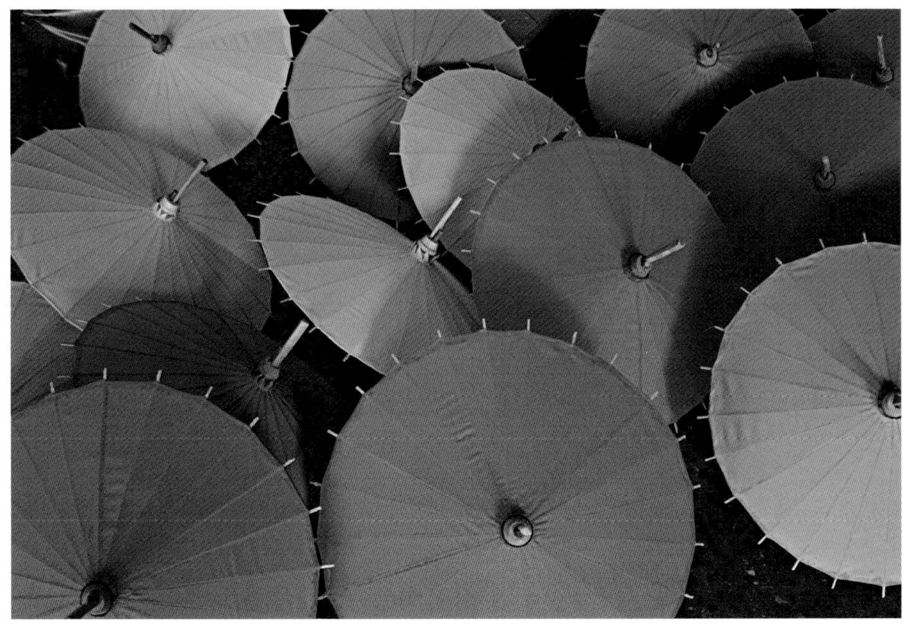

April 14

March on, my friend.
Tarrying is cowardice.
To remain forever gazing
upon the City of the Past is folly.
Behold, the City of the Future beckons.

~ Kahlil Gibran

APRIL 15

When we were children,
we used to think that
when we were grown-up
we would no longer
be vulnerable.
But to grow up is
to accept vulnerability. . .
to be alive
is to be vulnerable.

~ Madeleine L'Engle

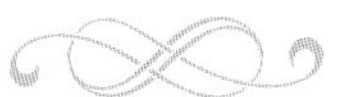

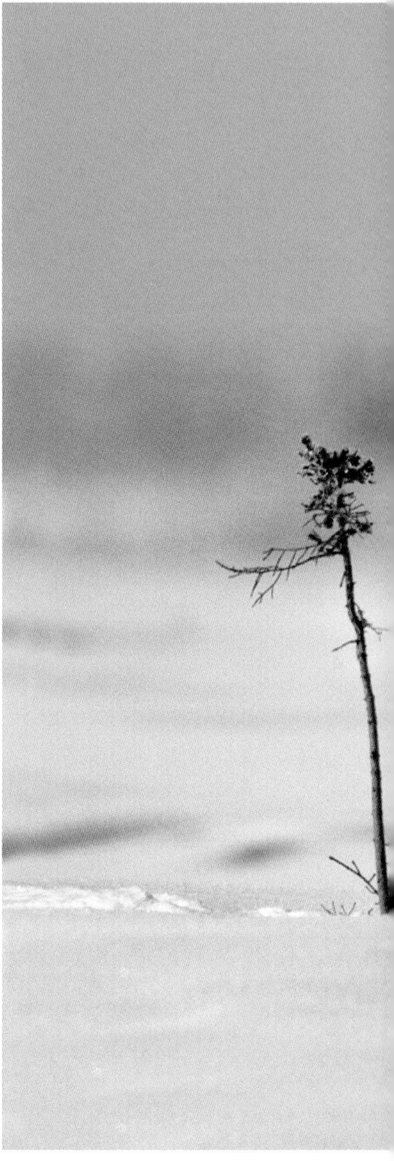

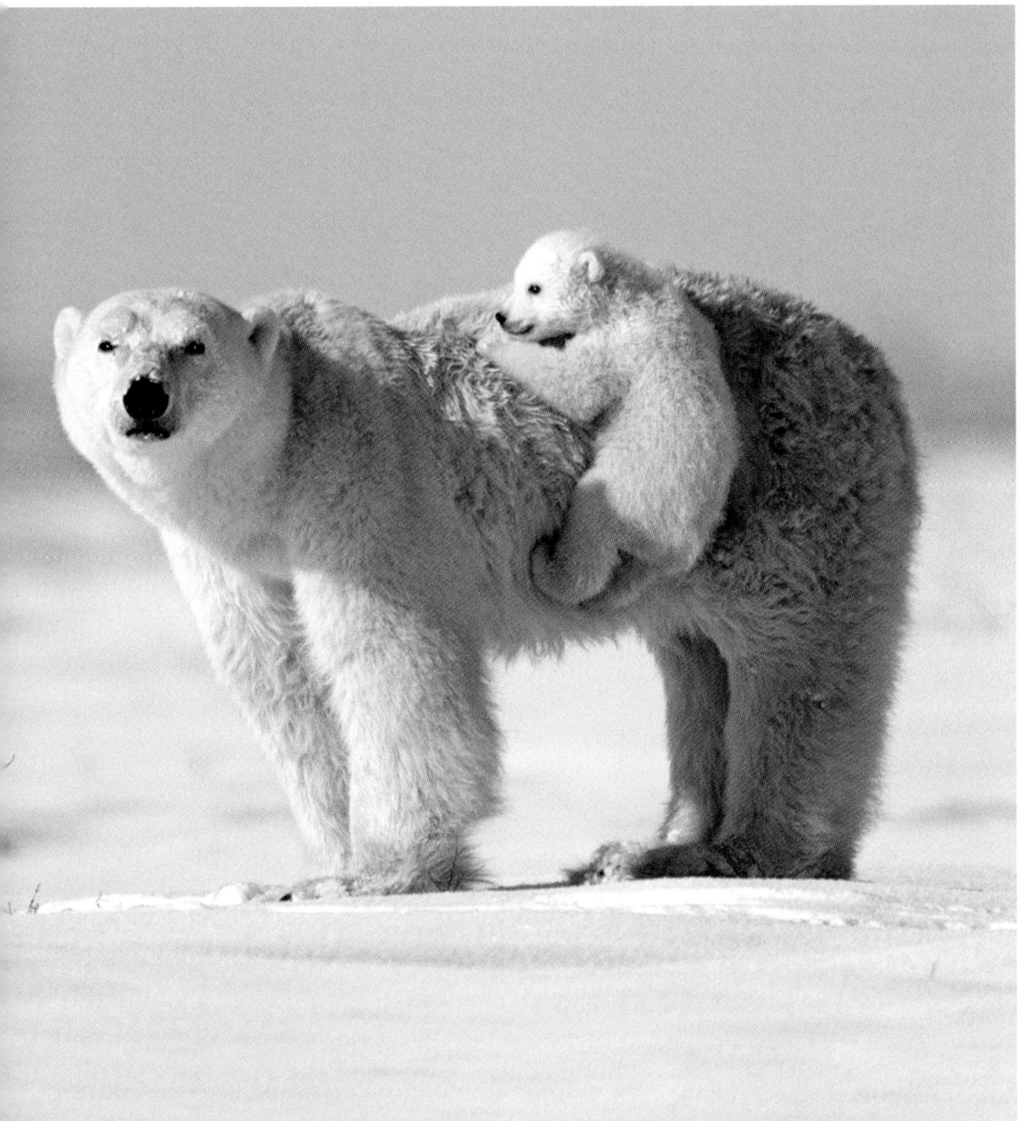

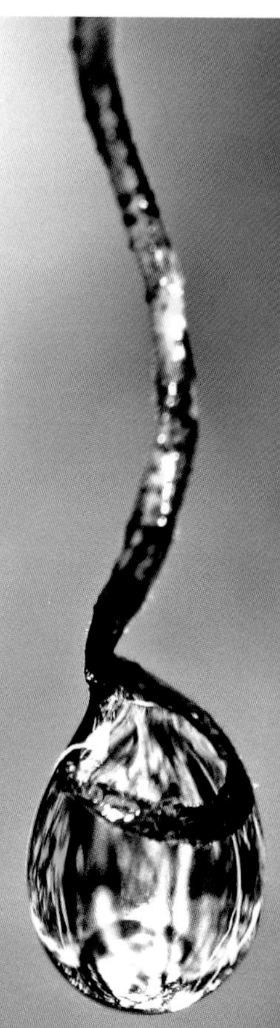

April *16*

A jug fills drop by drop.

~ Buddha

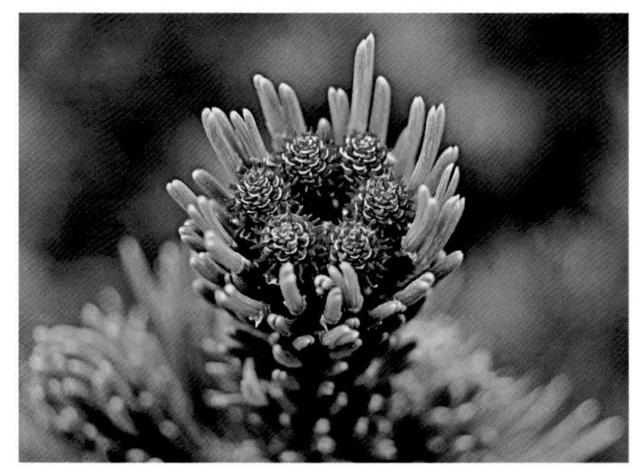

April 17

Things don't have to change the world to be important.

~ Steve Jobs

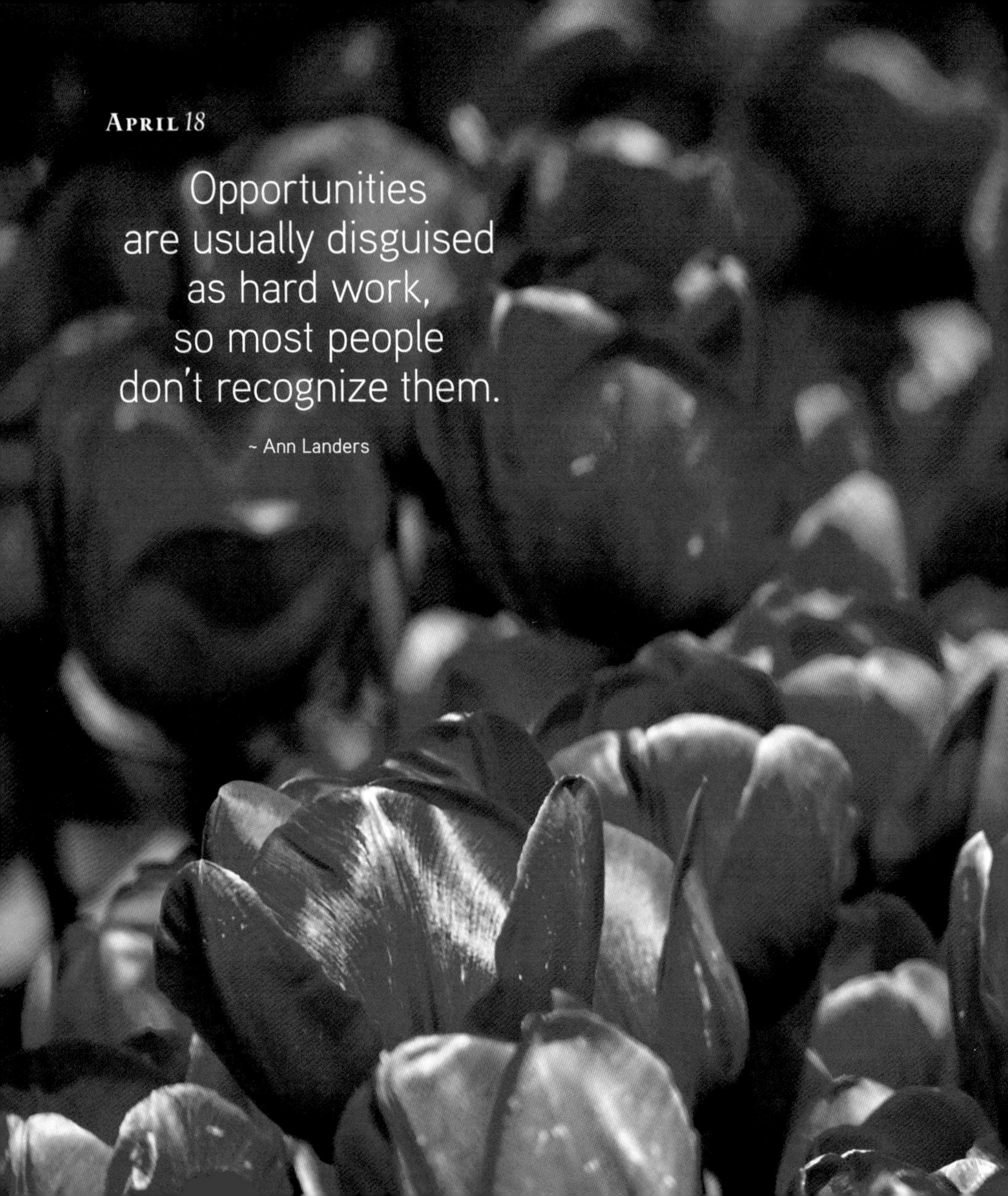
April 18
Opportunities
are usually disguised
as hard work,
so most people
don't recognize them.
~ Ann Landers

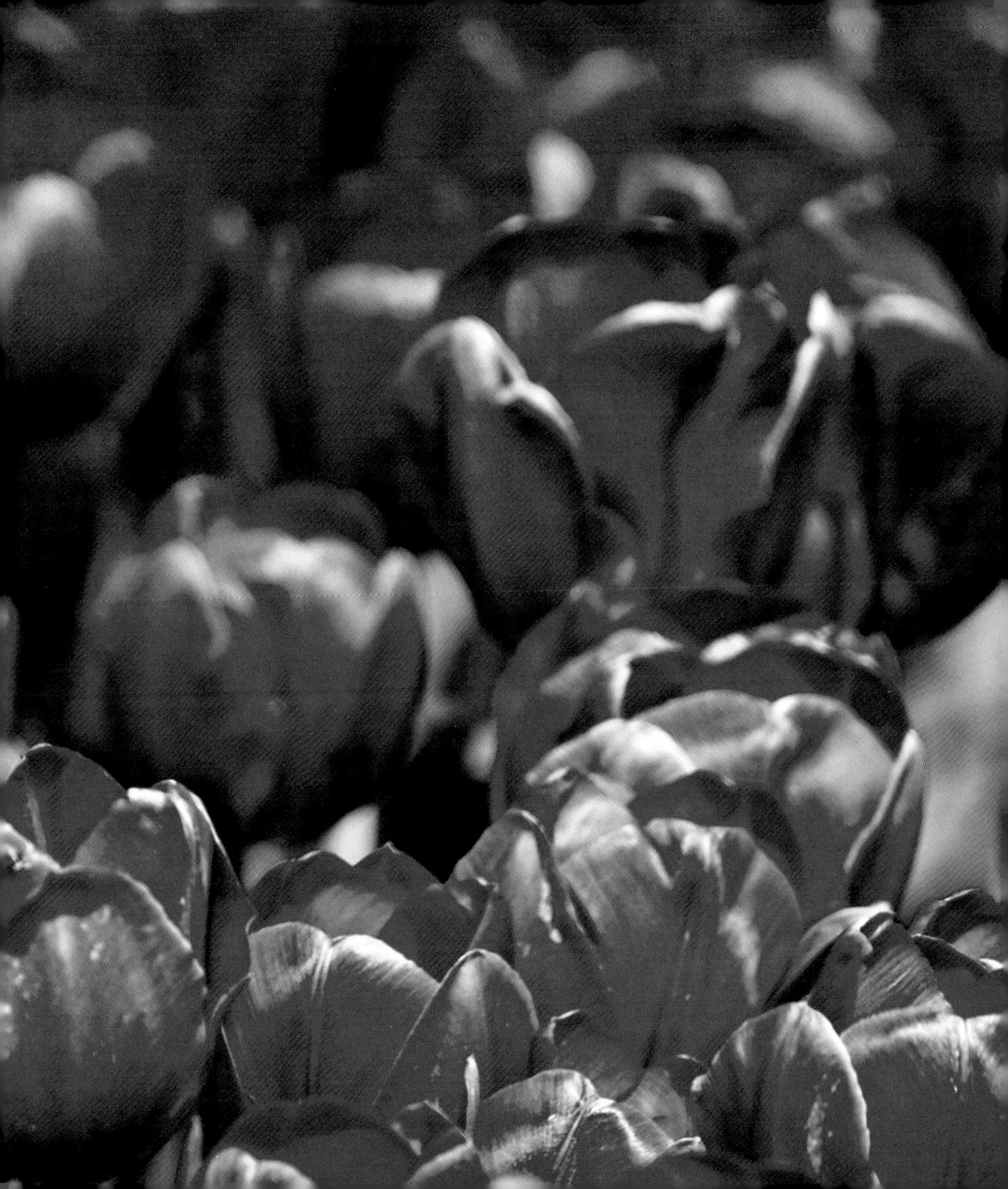

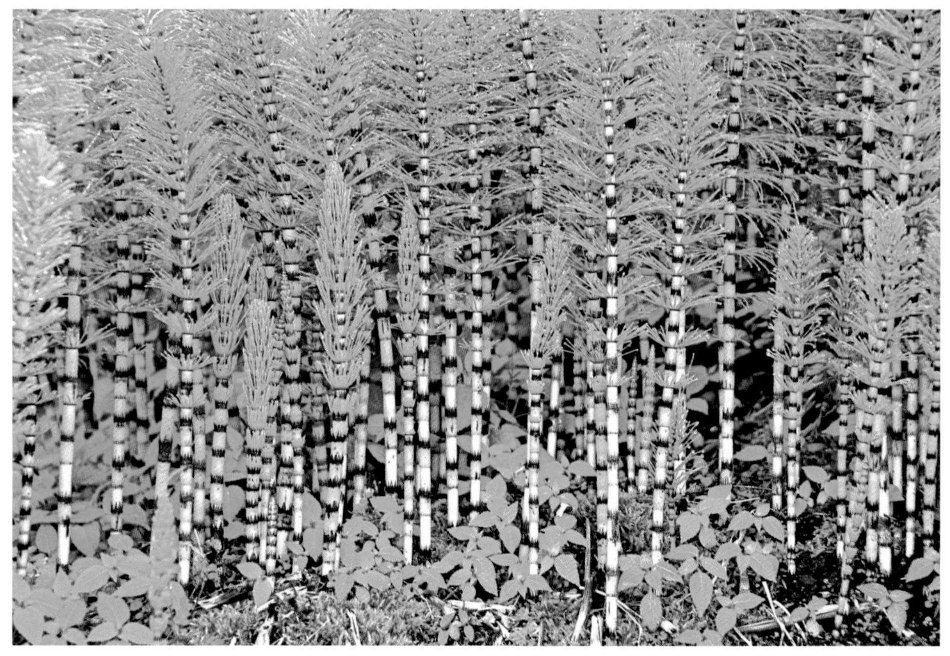

APRIL 19

Action may not always bring happiness; but there is no happiness without action.

~ Benjamin Disraeli

April 20

Growth itself contains the germ of happiness.

~ Pearl S. Buck

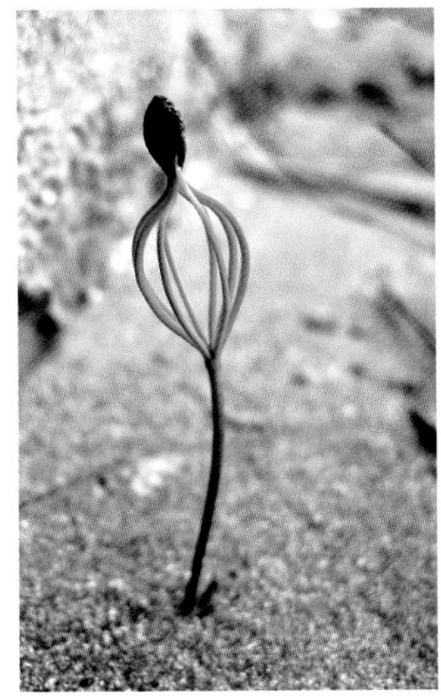

April 21

To look back is to relax one's vigil.

~ Bette Davis

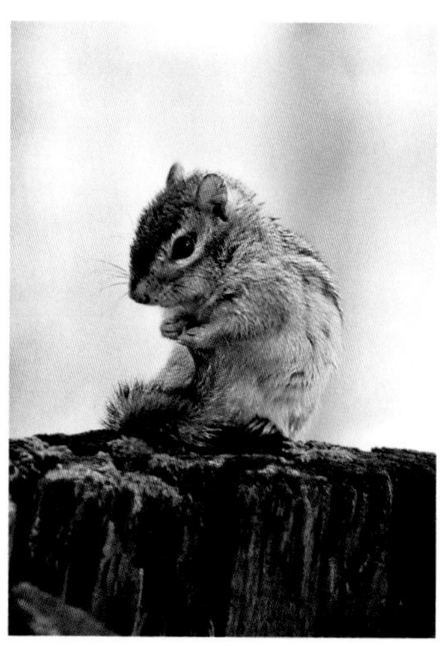

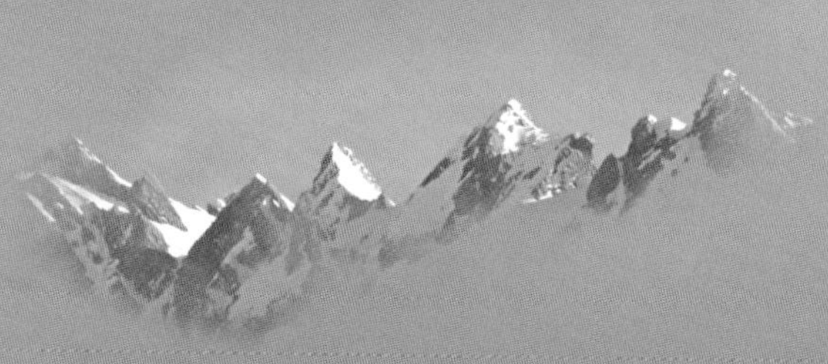

April *22*

All changes, even the most longed for,
have their melancholy;
for what we leave behind us
is a part of ourselves;
we must die to one life
before we can
enter another.

~ Anatole France

APRIL 23

Live out of
your imagination,
not your history.

~ Arthur Bryan

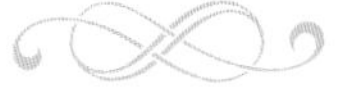

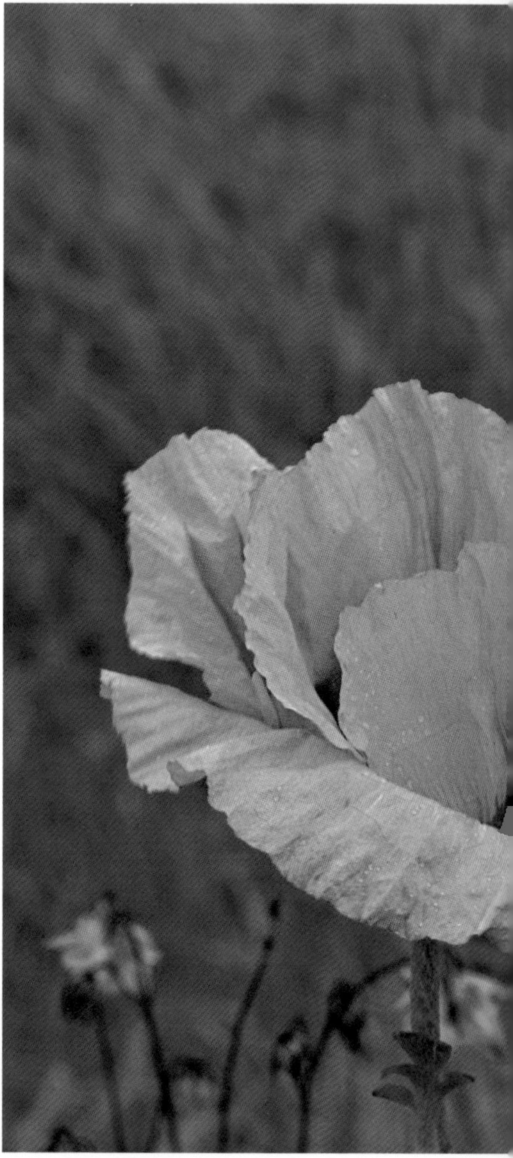

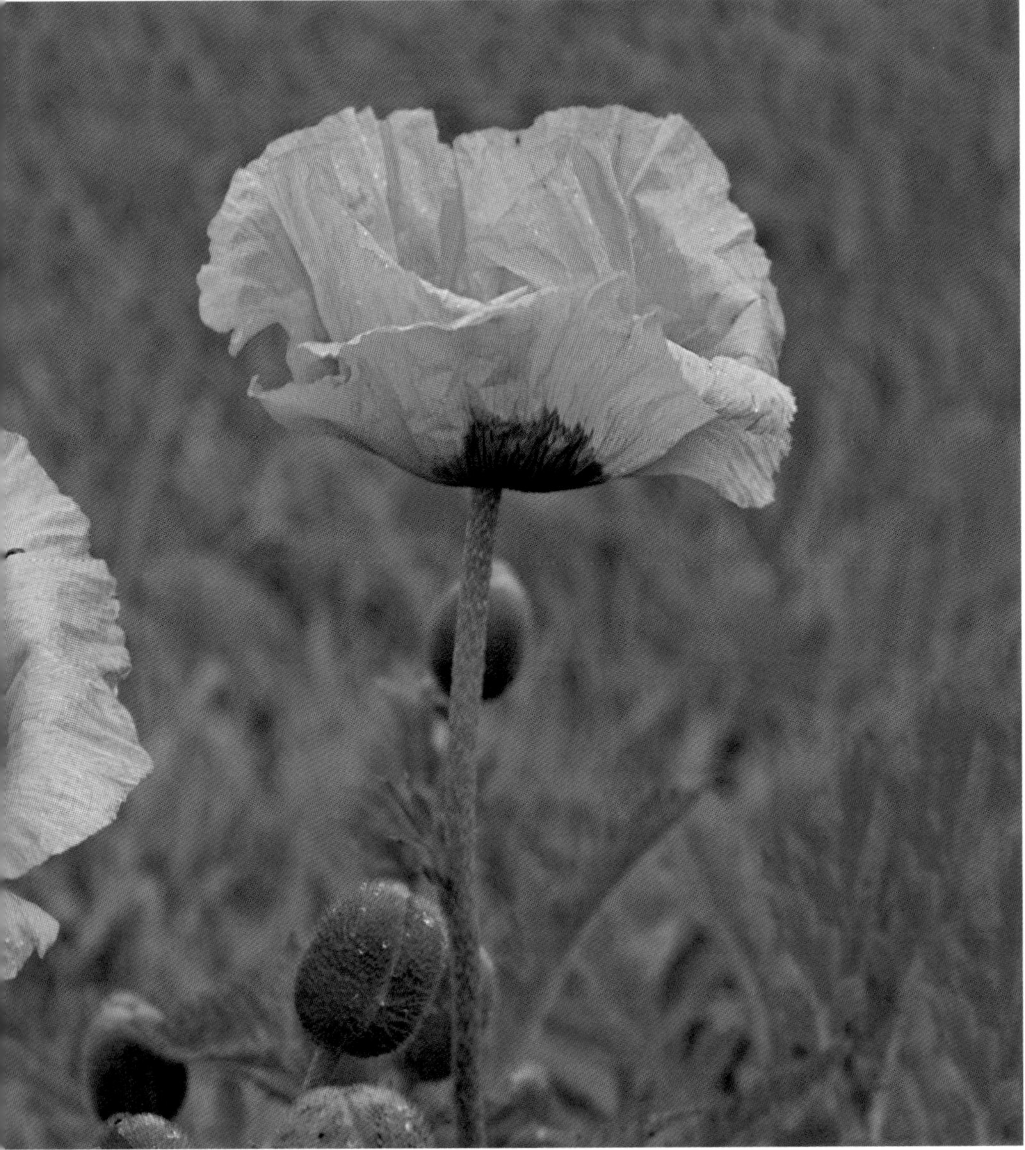

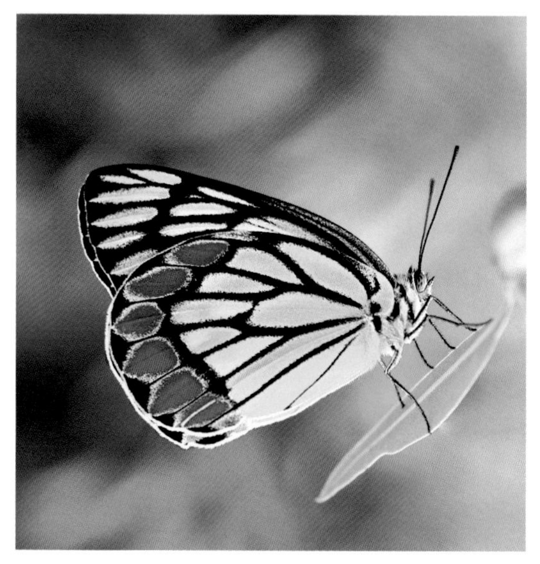

April 24

If we don't change,
we don't grow.
If we don't grow,
we aren't really living.

~ Gail Sheehy

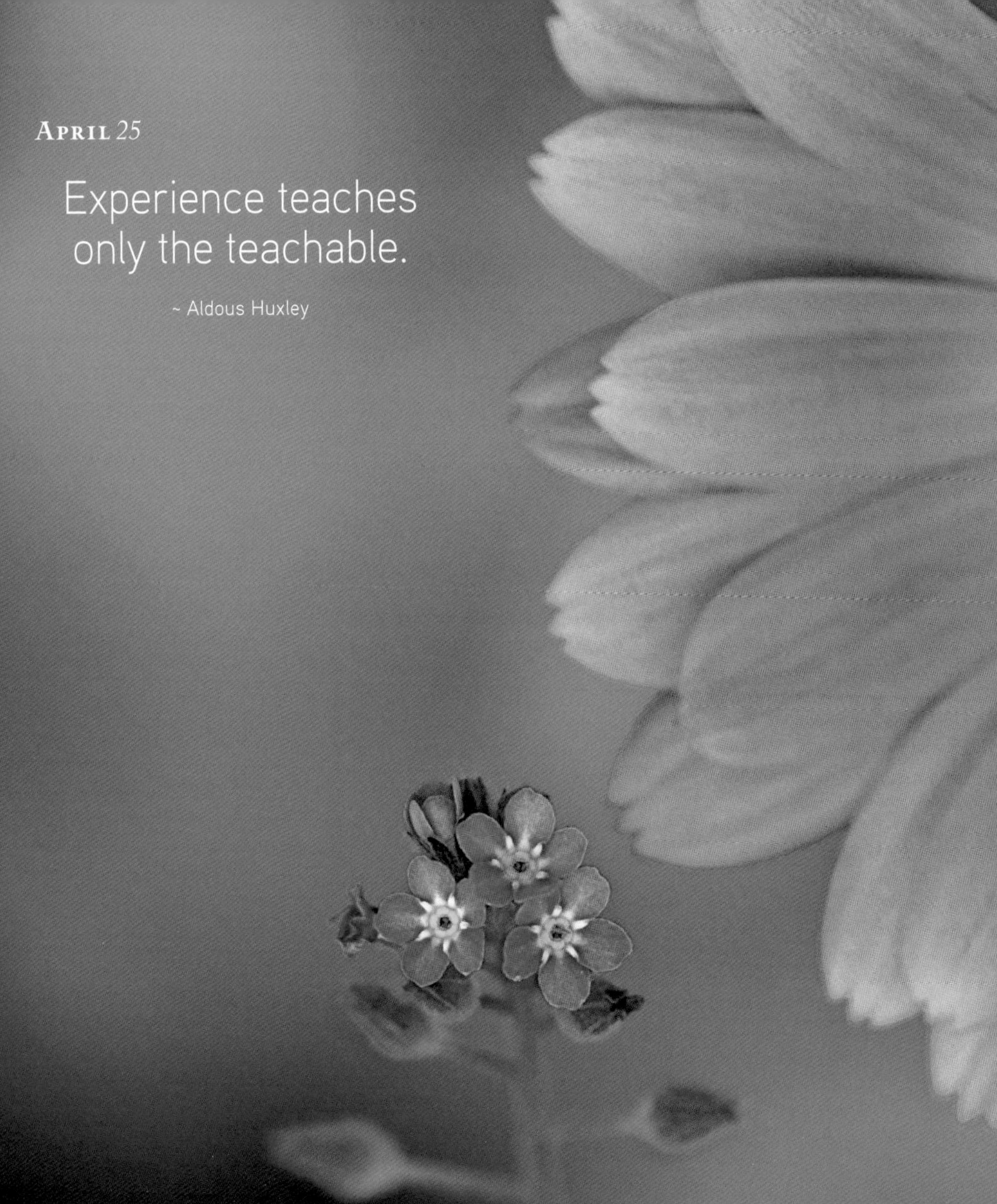

APRIL 25

Experience teaches only the teachable.

~ Aldous Huxley

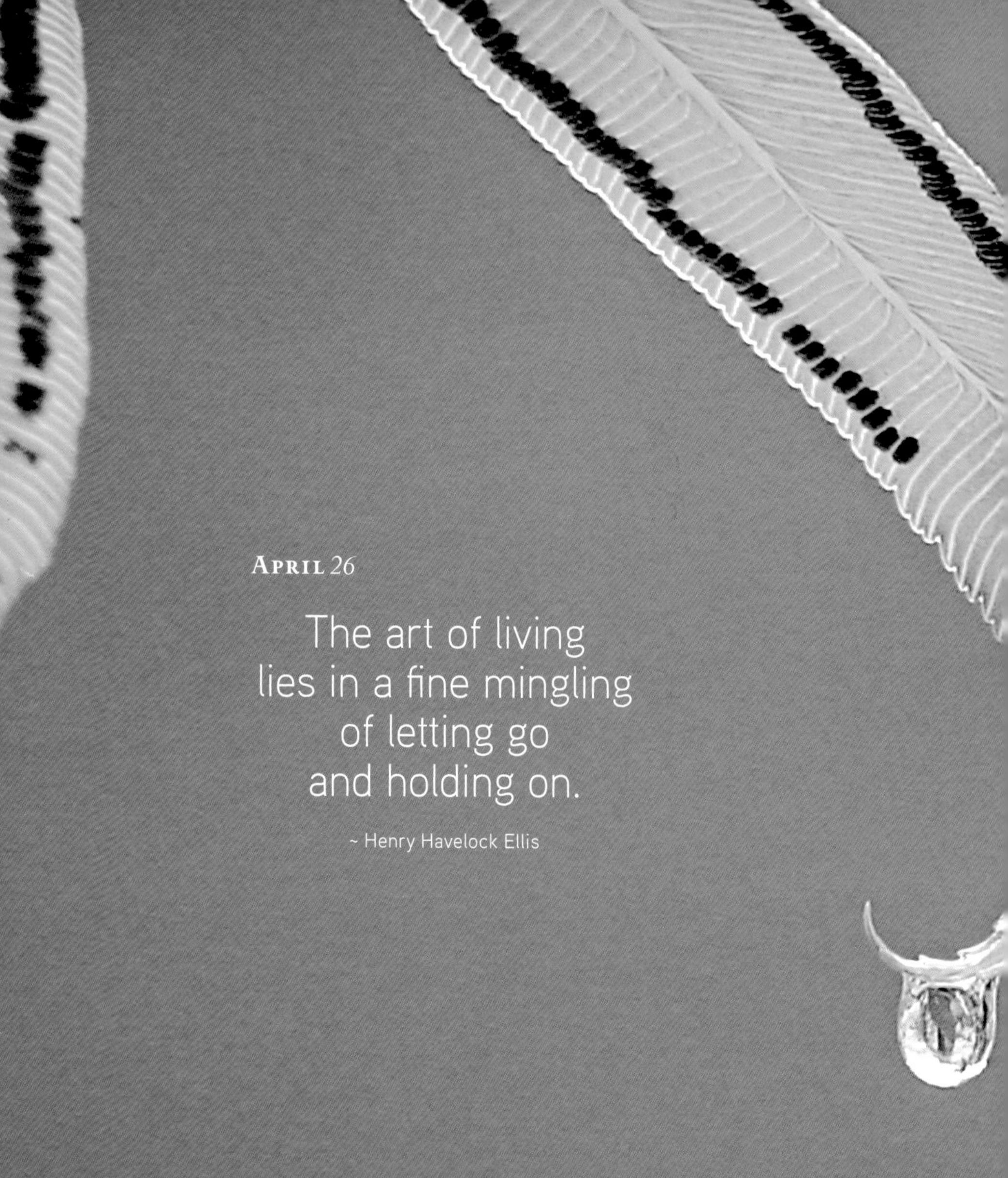

APRIL *26*

The art of living
lies in a fine mingling
of letting go
and holding on.

~ Henry Havelock Ellis

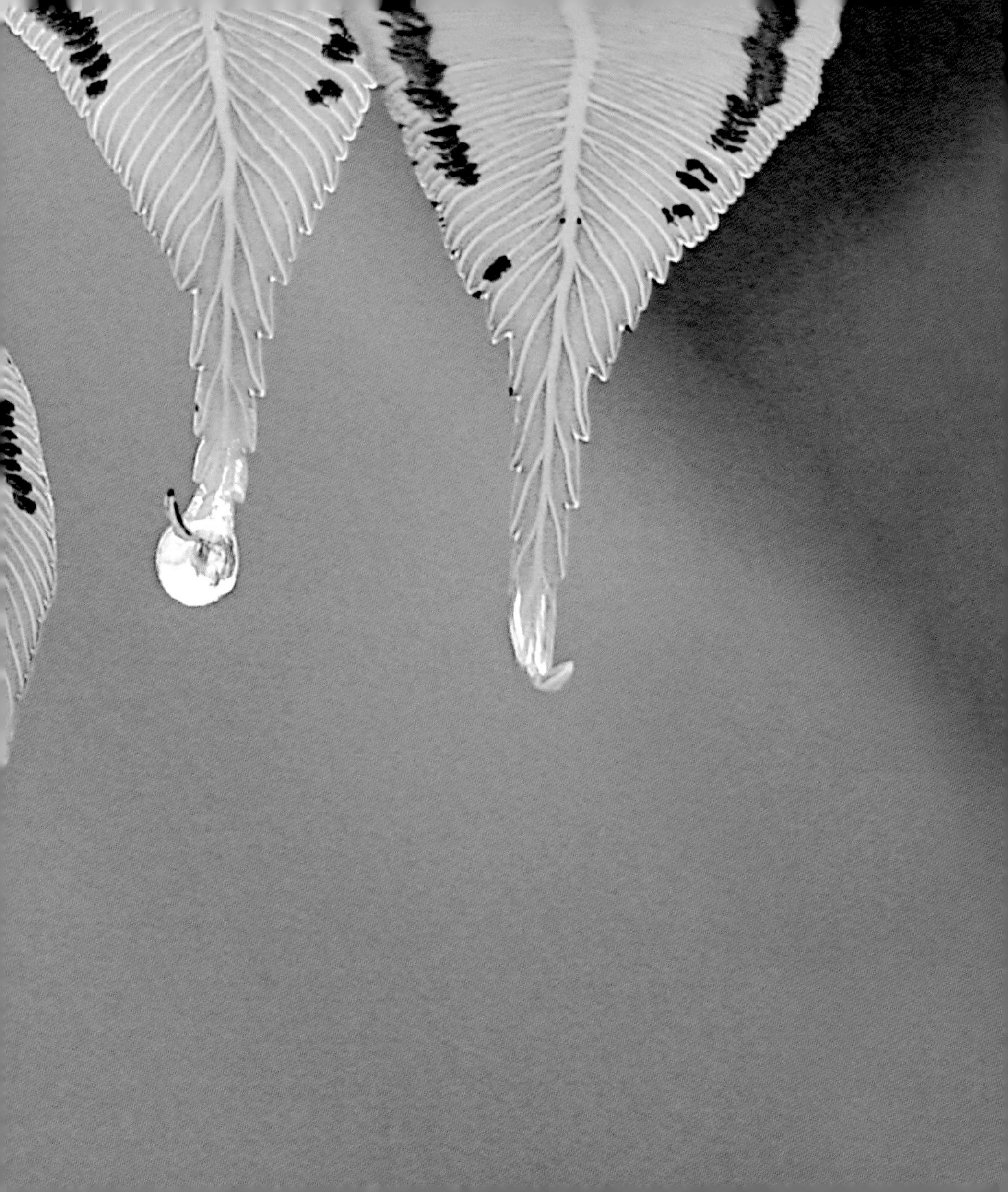

APRIL 27

Nurture your mind
with great thoughts,
for you will never
go any higher
than you think.

~ Benjamin Disraeli

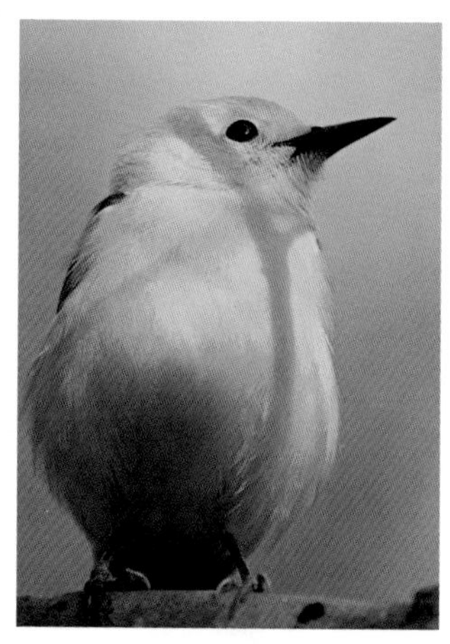

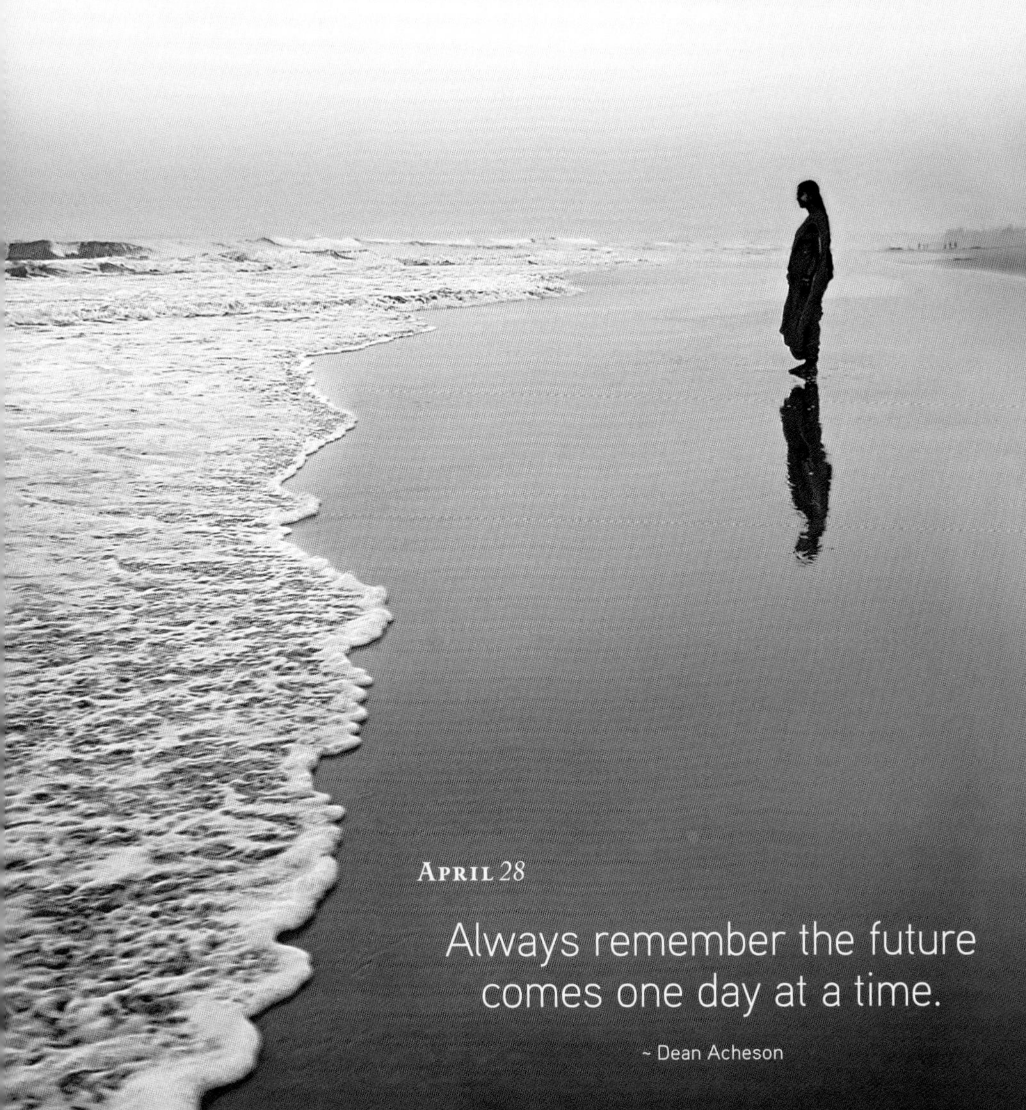

April *28*

Always remember the future
comes one day at a time.

~ Dean Acheson

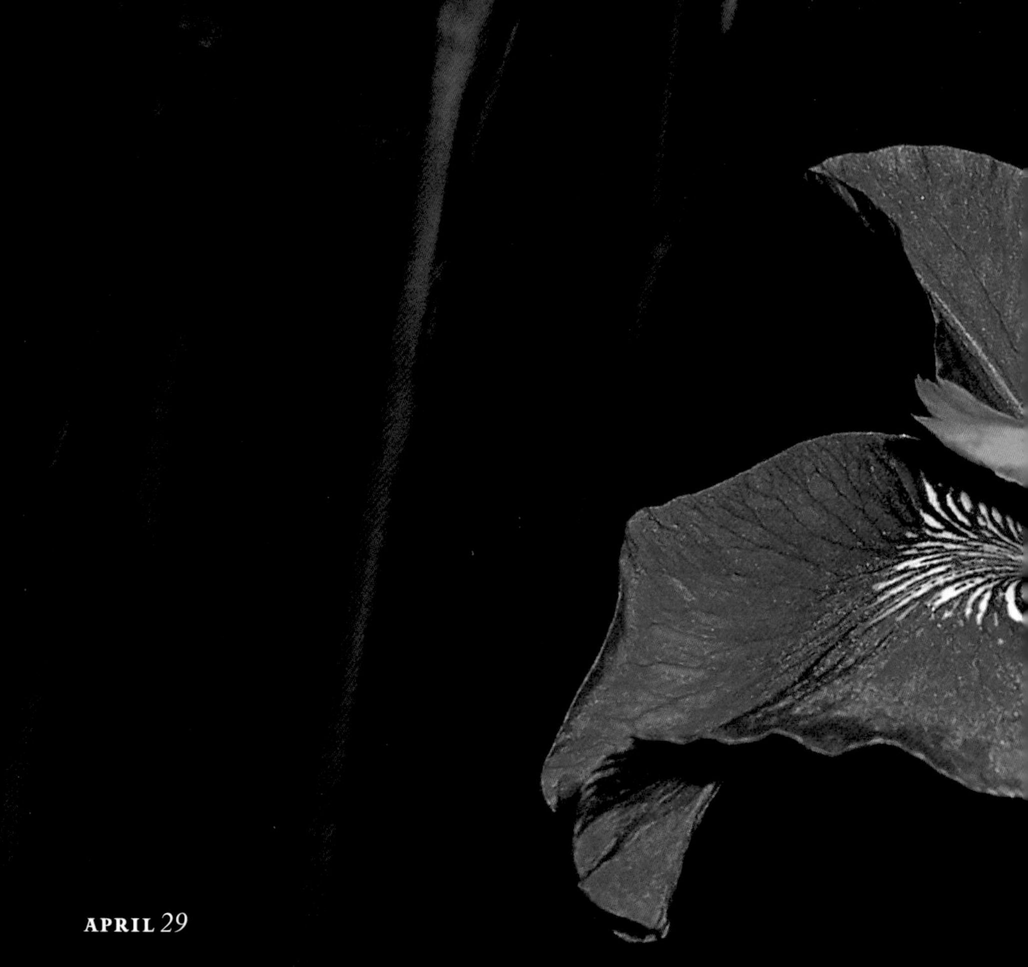

APRIL *29*

The only real progress lies in learning to be wrong all alone.

~ Albert Camus

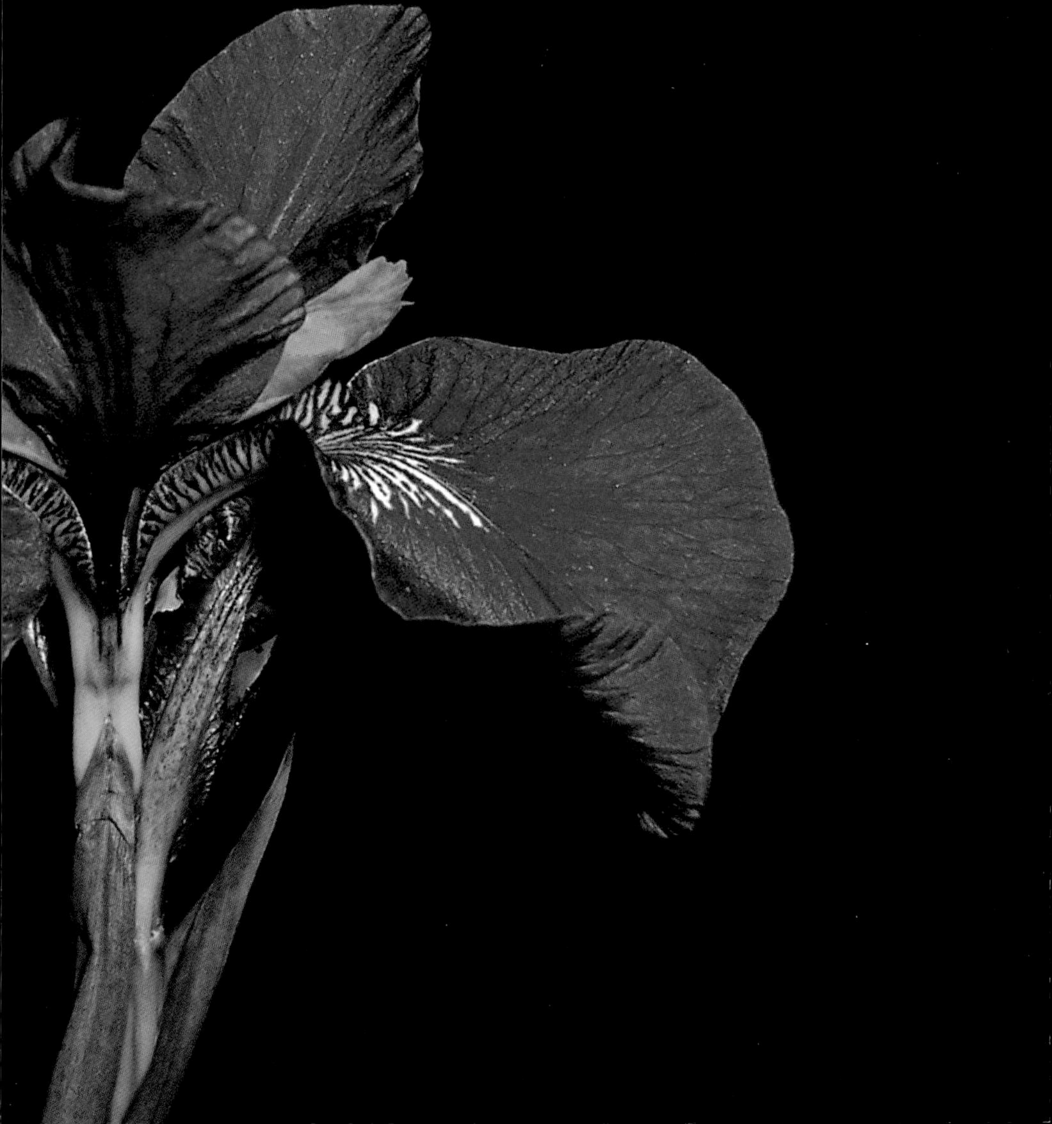

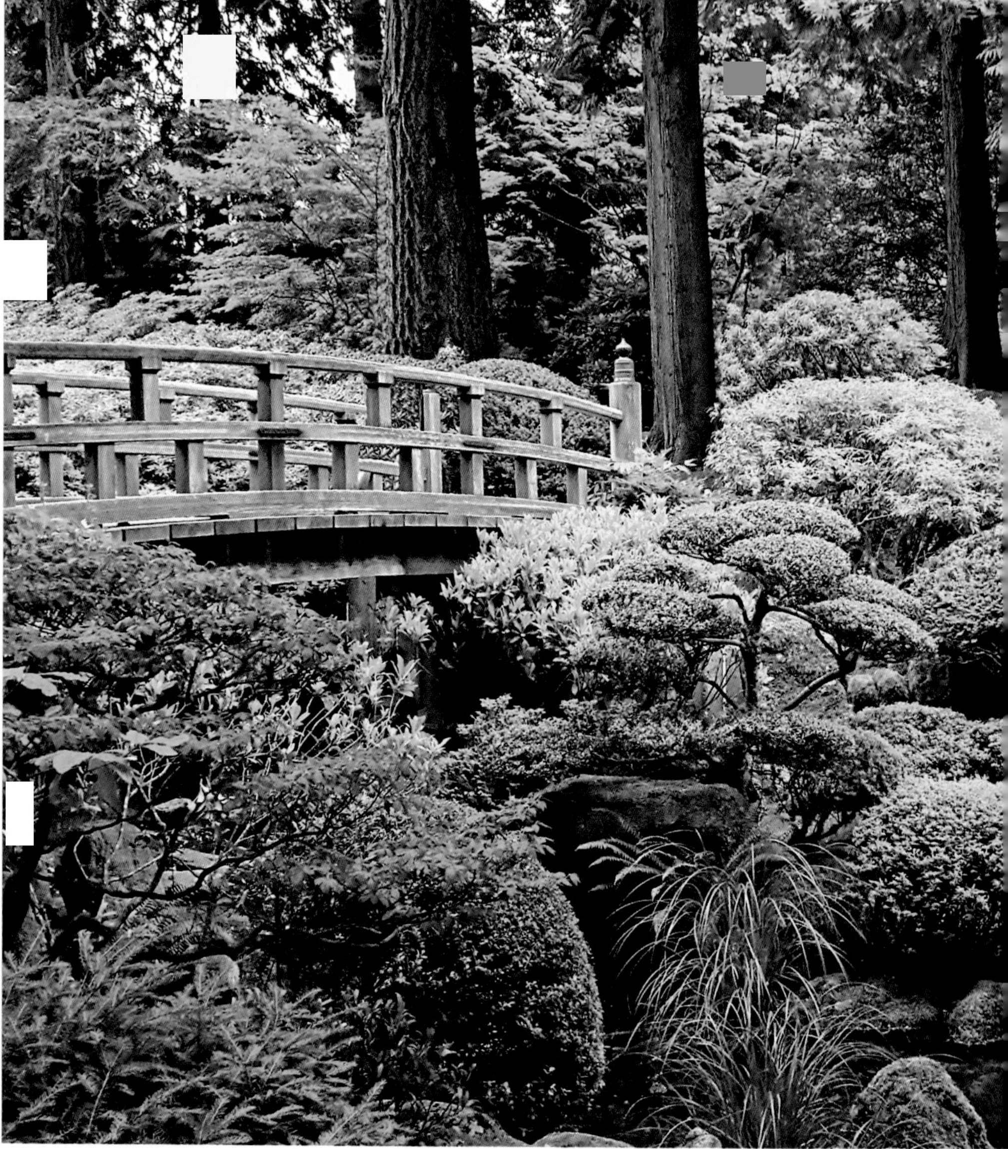

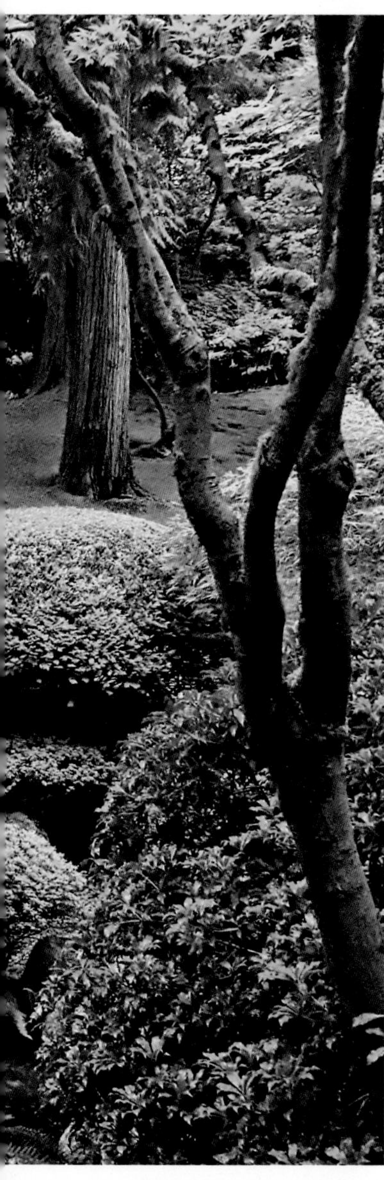

April 30

It is quite true
what philosophy says:
that life must be
understood backwards.
But then one forgets
the other principle:
that it must be
lived forwards.

~ Søren Kierkegaard

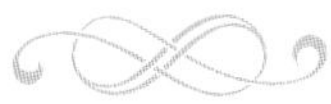

COURAGE

May

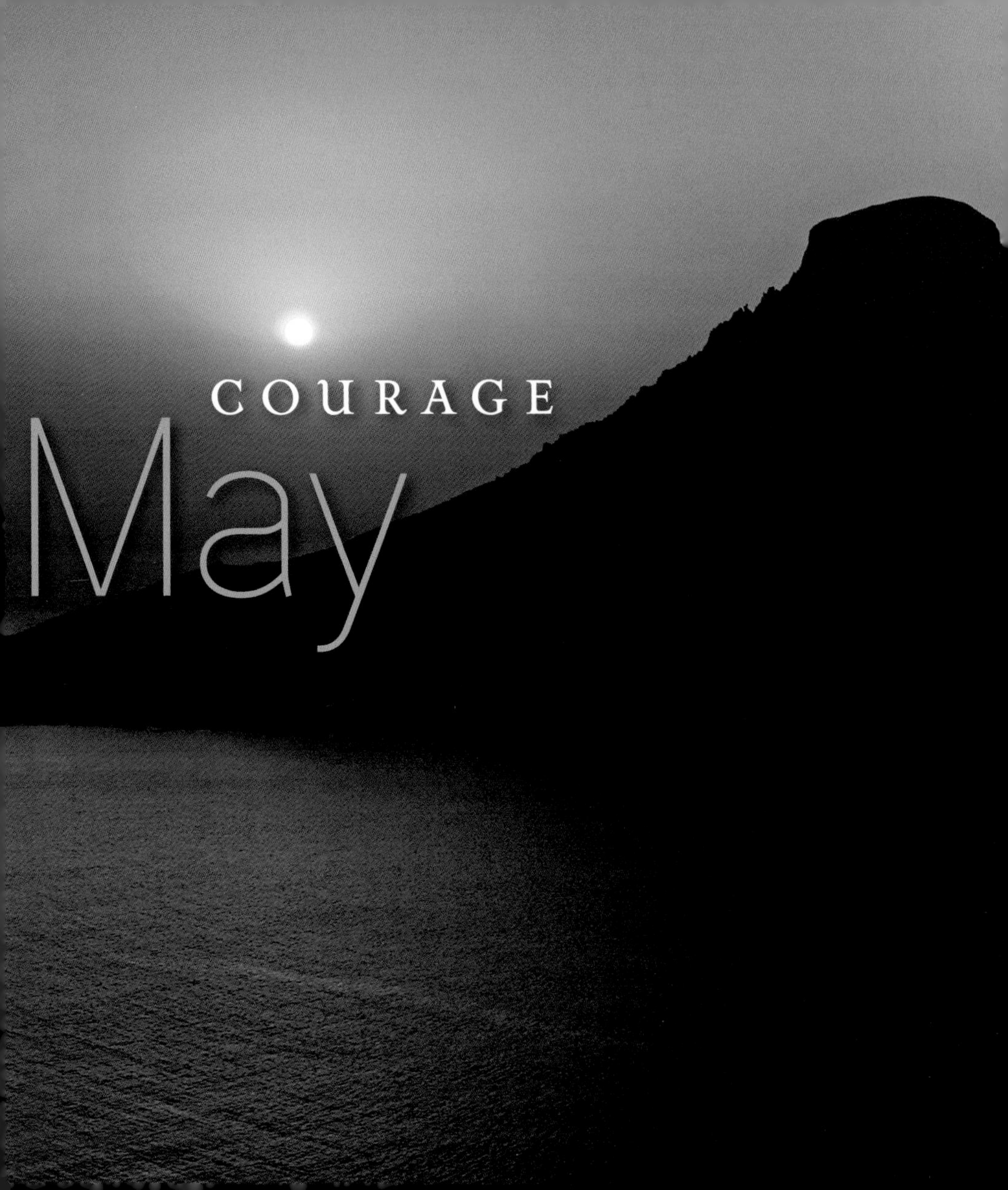

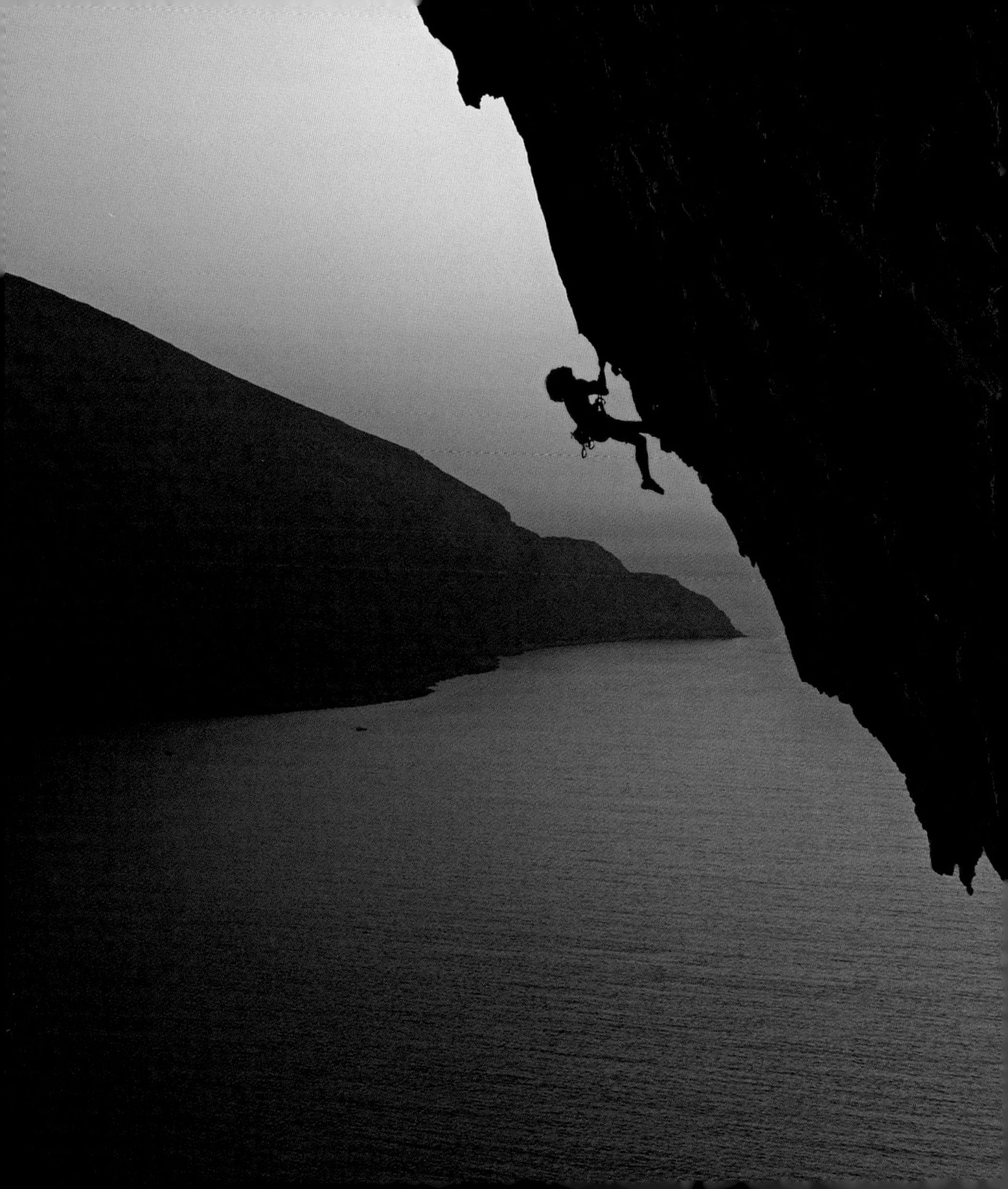

MAY 1

All you need is confidence in yourself.
There is no living thing that
is not afraid when it faces danger.
The true courage is in facing danger
when you are afraid, and that kind
of courage you have in plenty.

~ Frank L. Baum

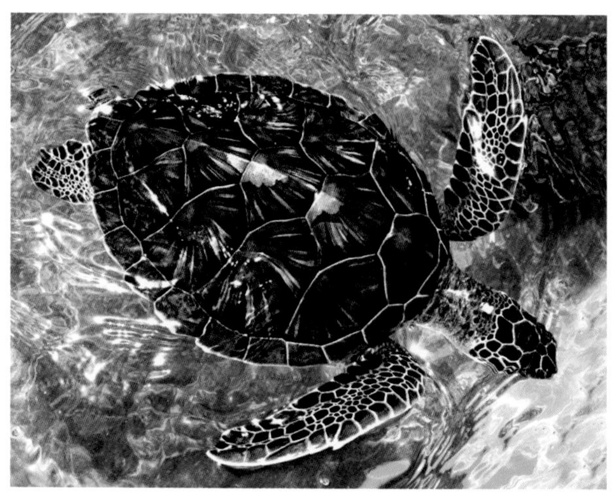

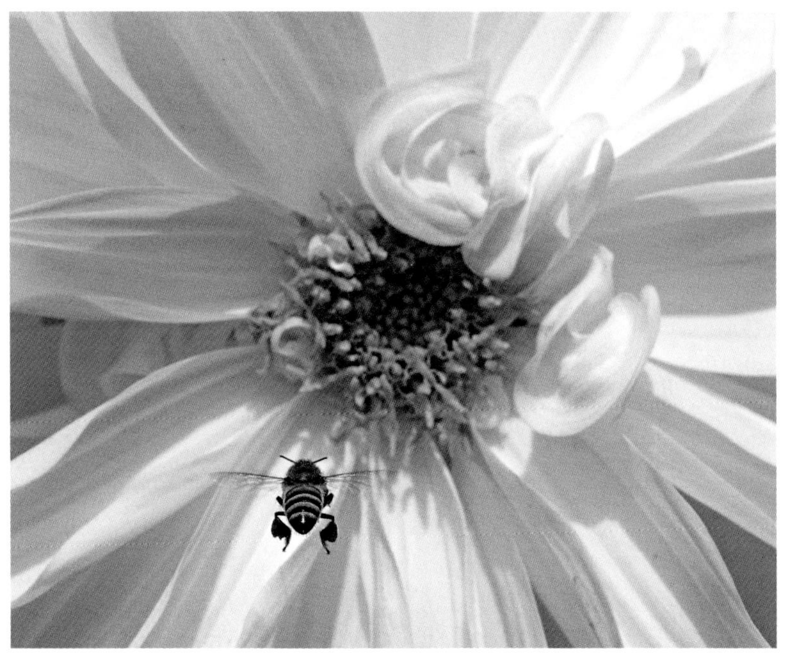

MAY 2

It is not because things are difficult
that we do not dare;
it is because we do not dare
that things are difficult.

~ Lucius Annaeus Seneca

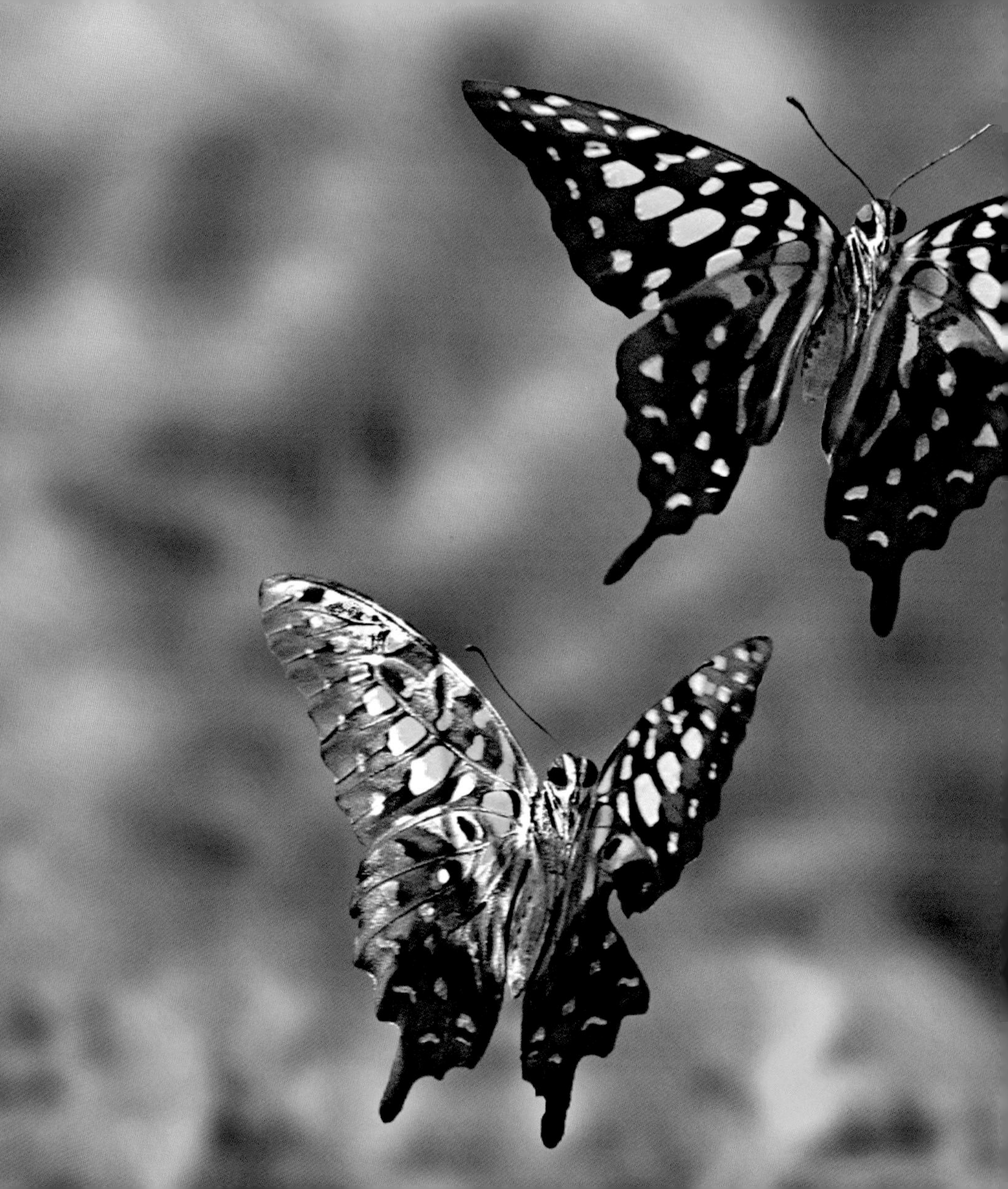

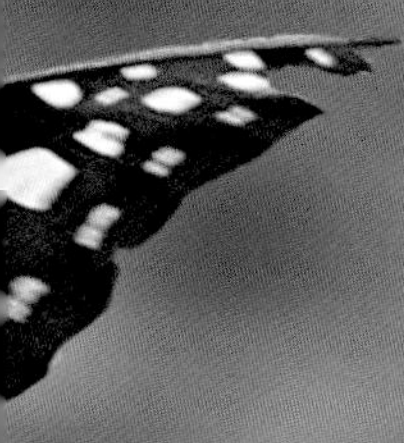

May 3

Avoiding danger
is no safer in the long run
than outright exposure.
Life is either a daring adventure,
or nothing.

~ Helen Keller

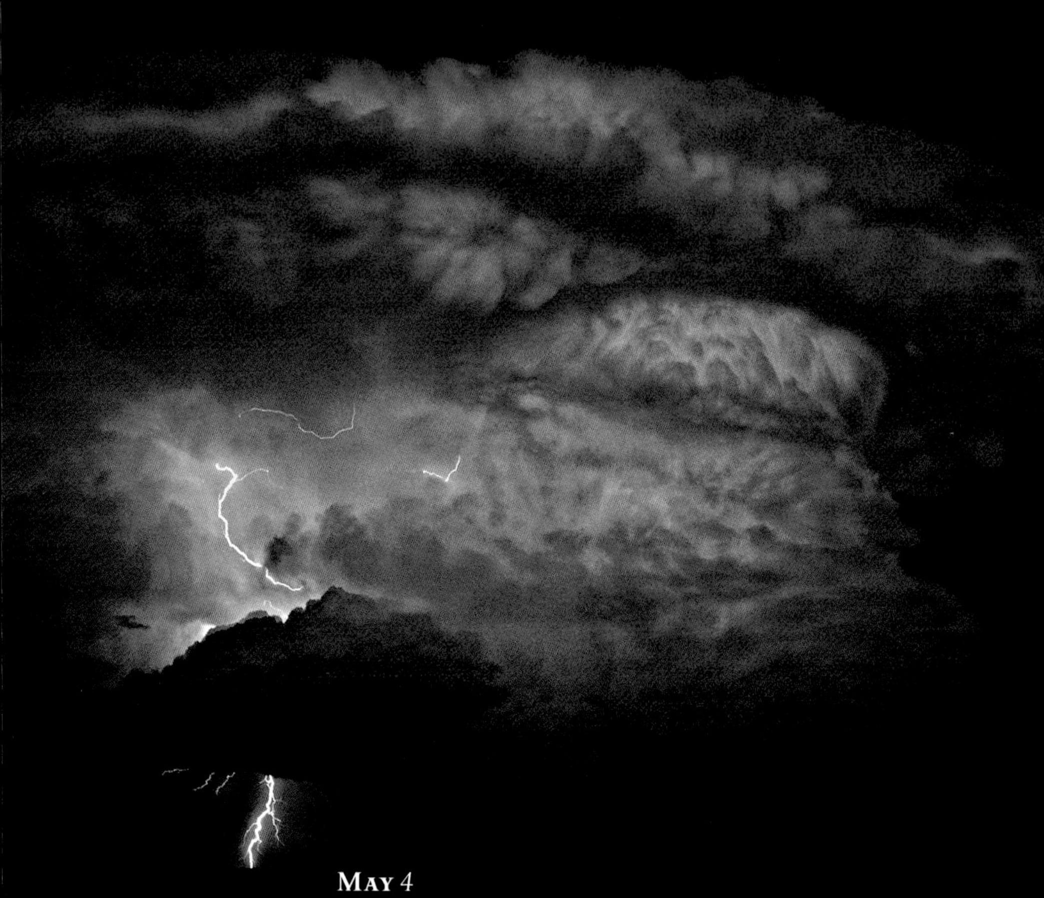

MAY 4

I'm not afraid of storms,
for I'm learning how to sail my ship.

~ Louisa May Alcott

May 5

With enough courage, you can do without a reputation.

~ Margaret Mitchell

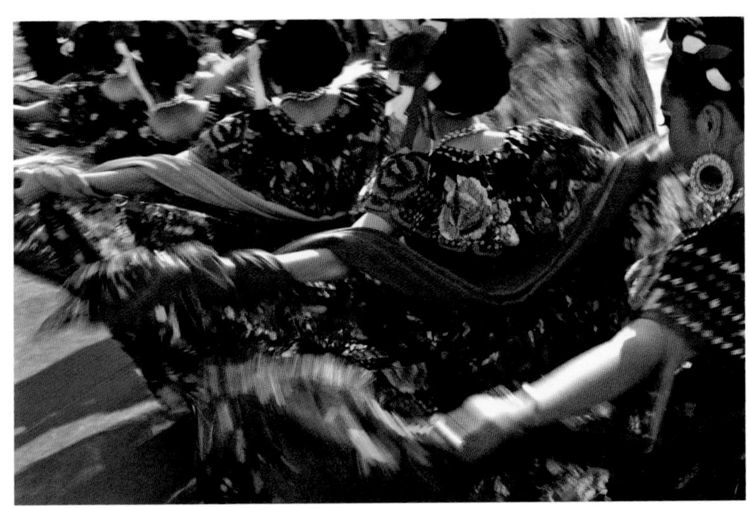

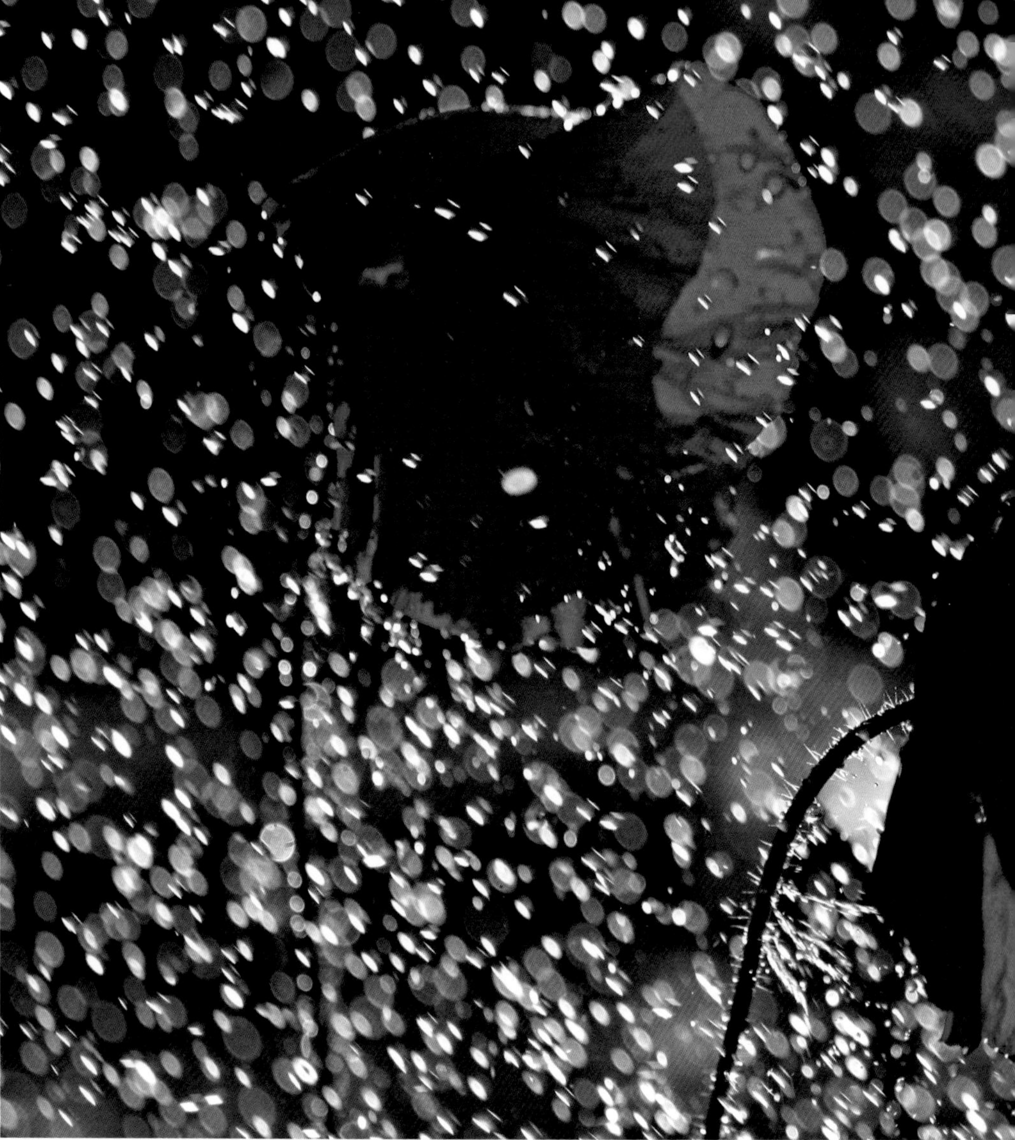

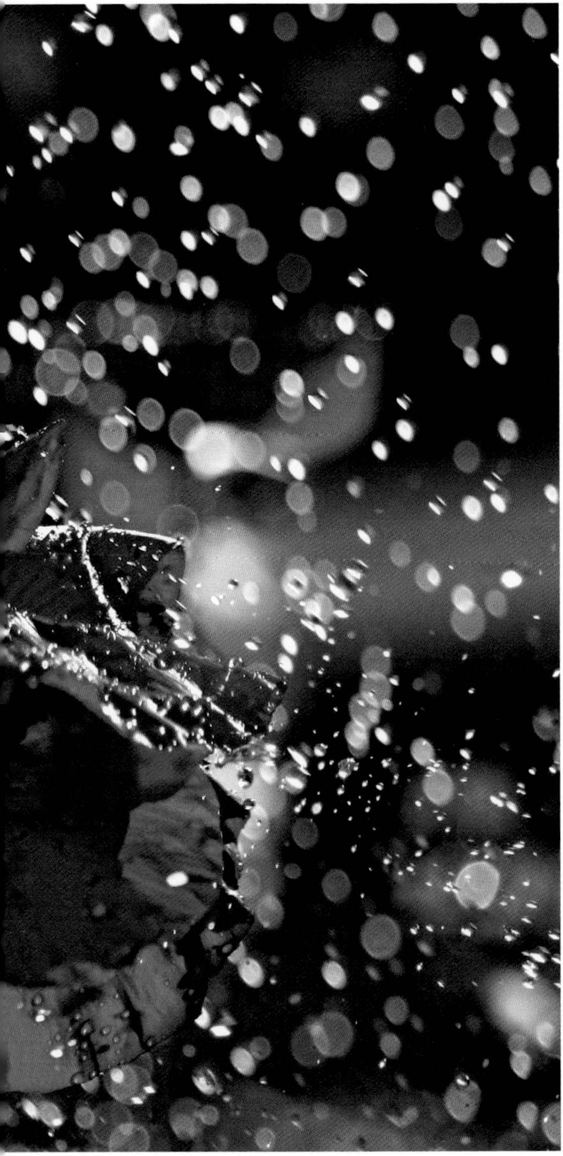

May 6

Courage
is resistance
to fear,
mastery of fear—
but not absence
of fear.

~ Mark Twain

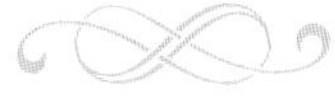

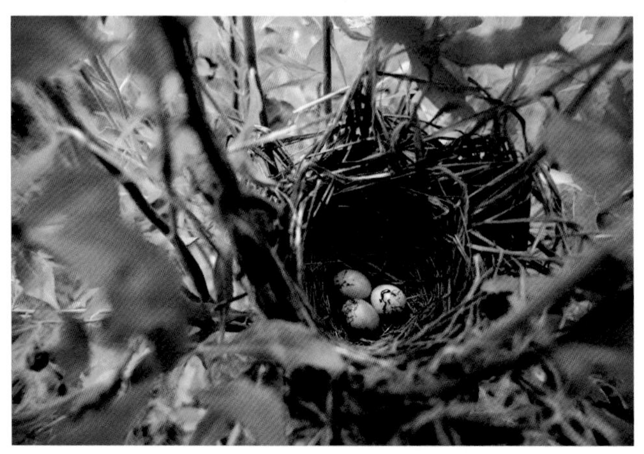

May 7

Inside myself is a place
where I live all alone.
That's where you renew
your springs
that never dry up.

~ Pearl S. Buck

May 8

Life is a series of
collisions with the future.

~ José Ortega y Gasset

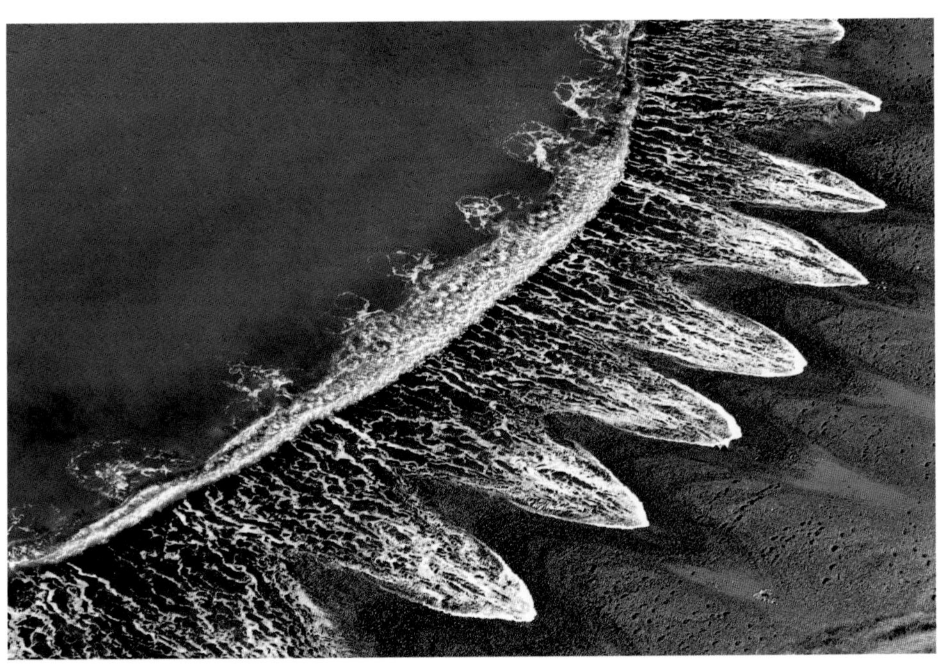

May 9

Courage is what it takes to stand up and speak; courage is also what it takes to sit down and listen.

~ Sir Winston Churchill

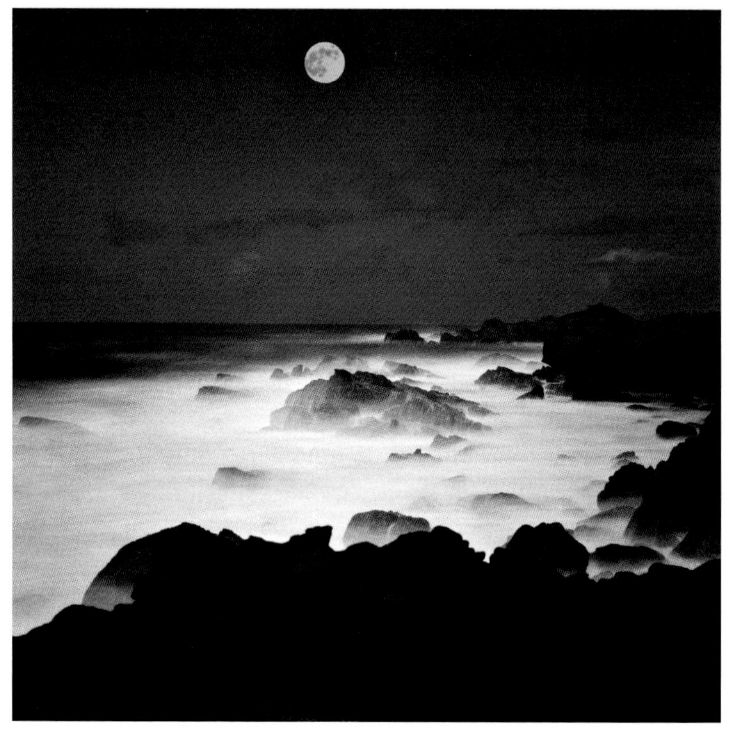

May 10

Everyone has a talent.
What's rare is to follow it
to the dark places where it leads.

~ Erica Jong

May 11

Life shrinks or expands
in proportion to
one's courage.

~ Anaïs Nin

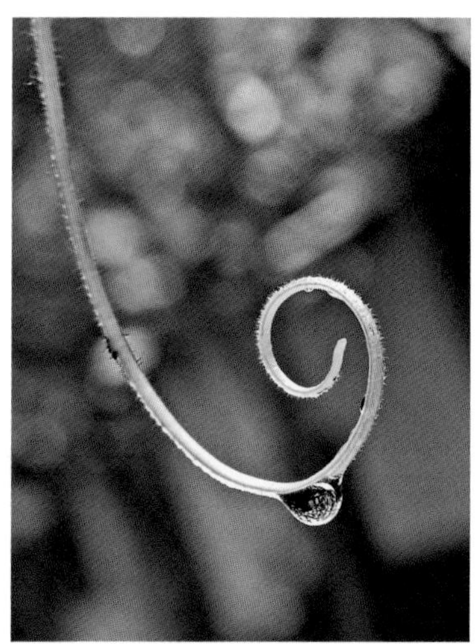

May 12

It takes a great deal
of bravery
to stand up to
our enemies,
but just as much
to stand up to
our friends.

~ J. K. Rowling

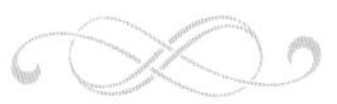

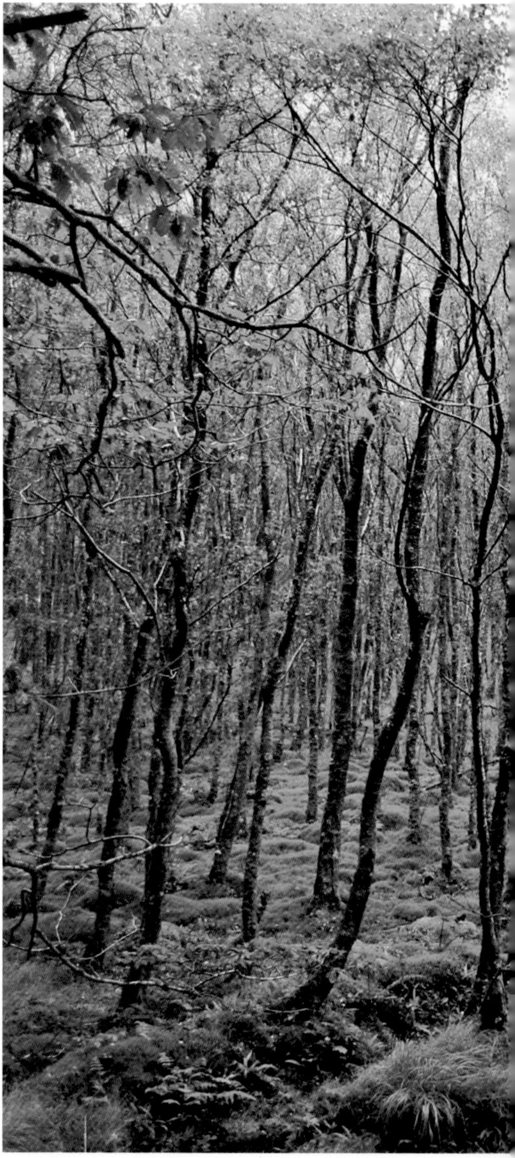

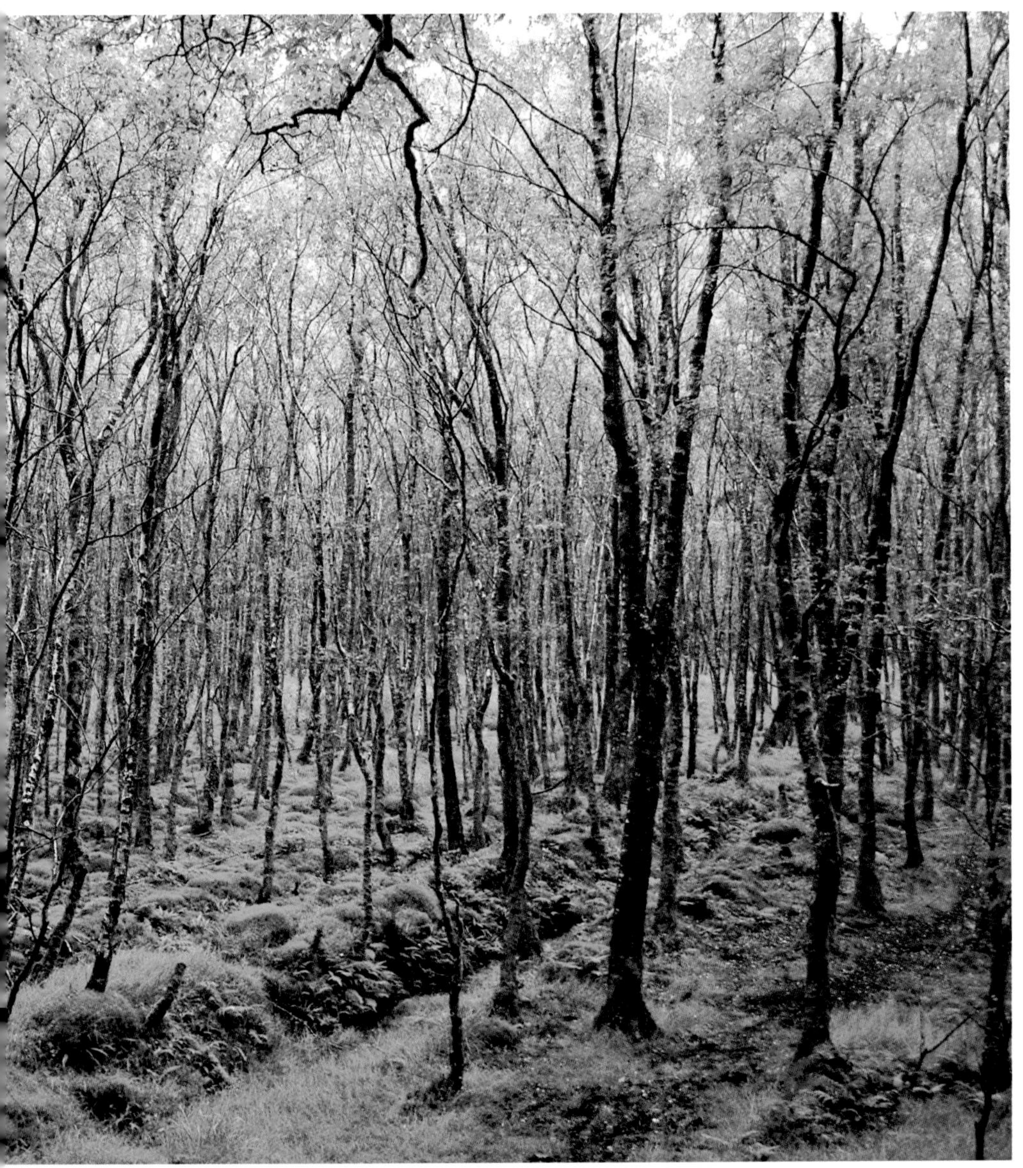

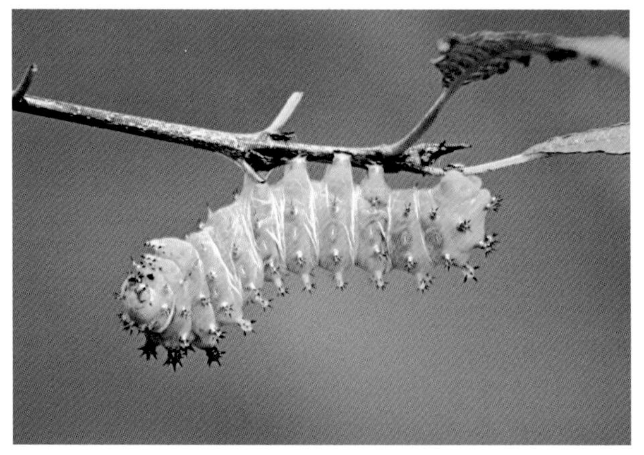

MAY *13*

It takes as much courage to have tried and failed as it does to have tried and succeeded.

~ Anne Morrow Lindbergh

Sooner or later, even the fastest runners have to stand and fight.

~ Stephen King

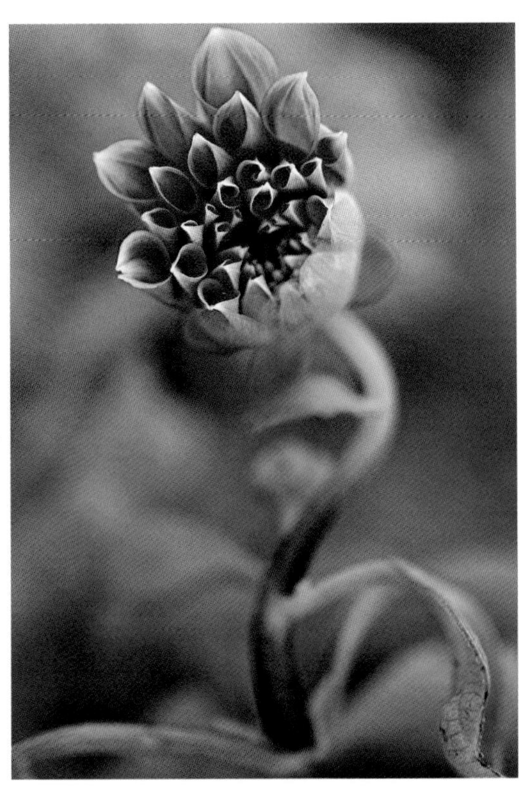

May 15

Confront the dark parts of yourself,
and work to banish them
with illumination or forgiveness.
Your willingness to wrestle with your demons
will cause your angels to sing.

~ August Wilson

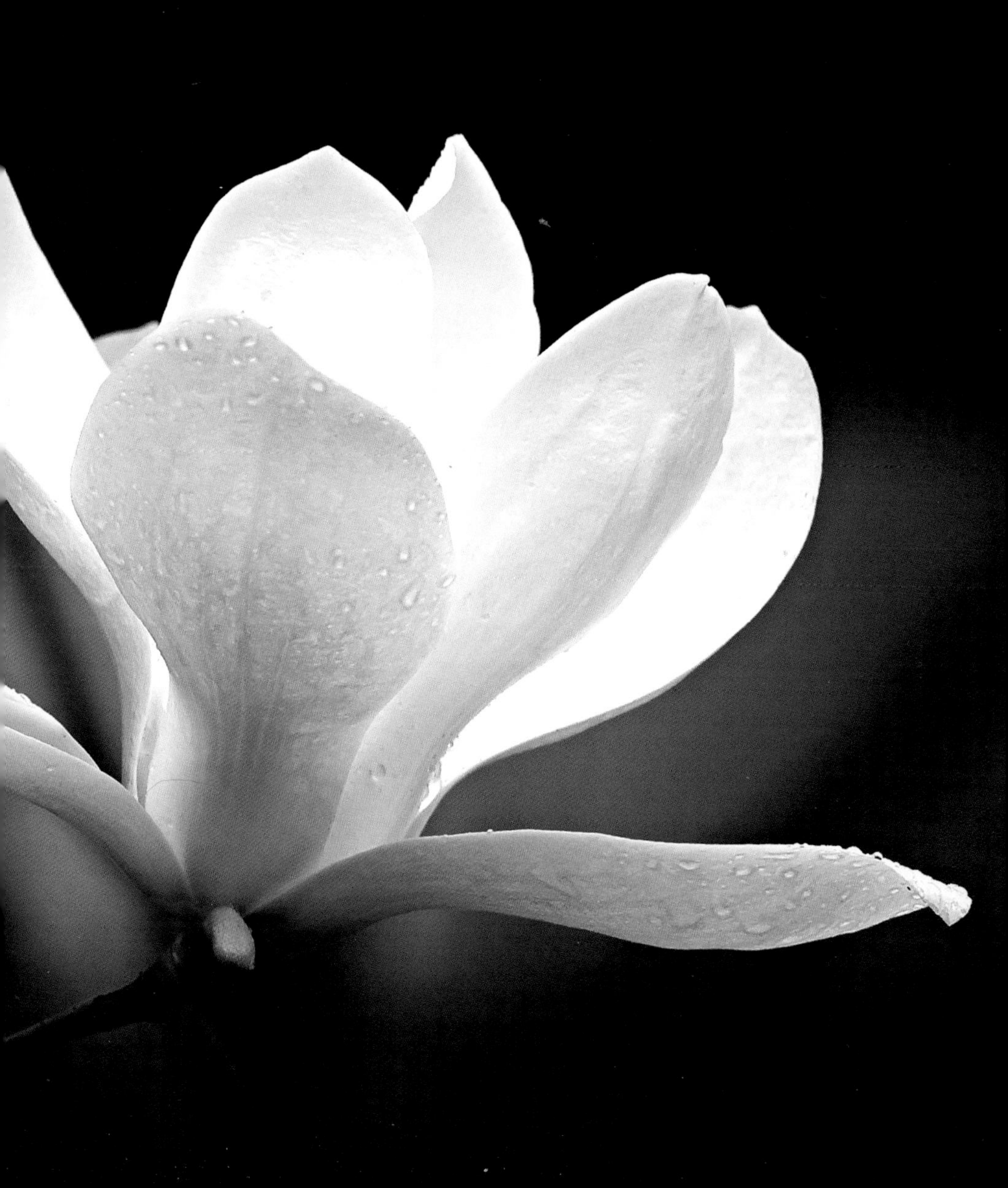

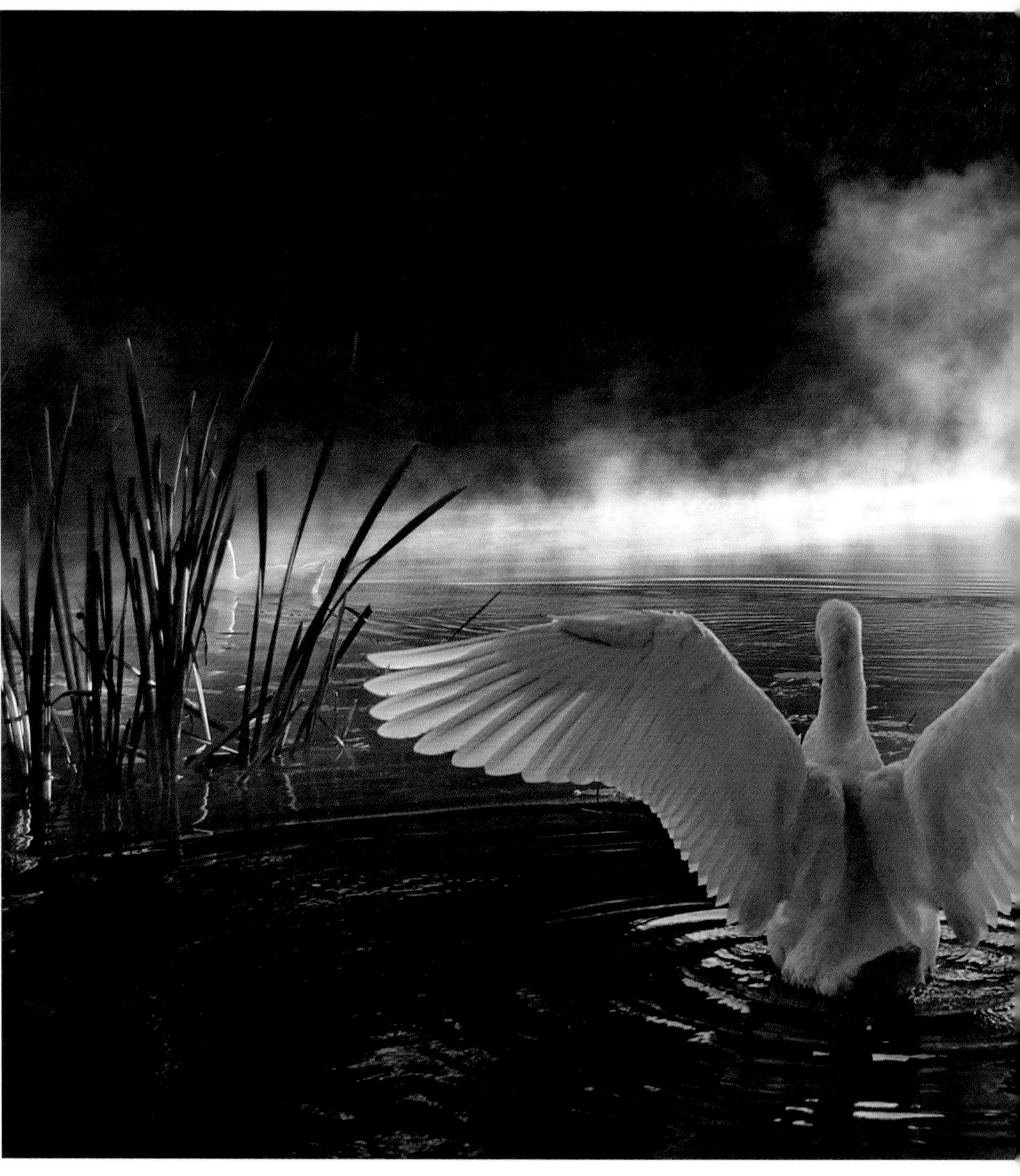

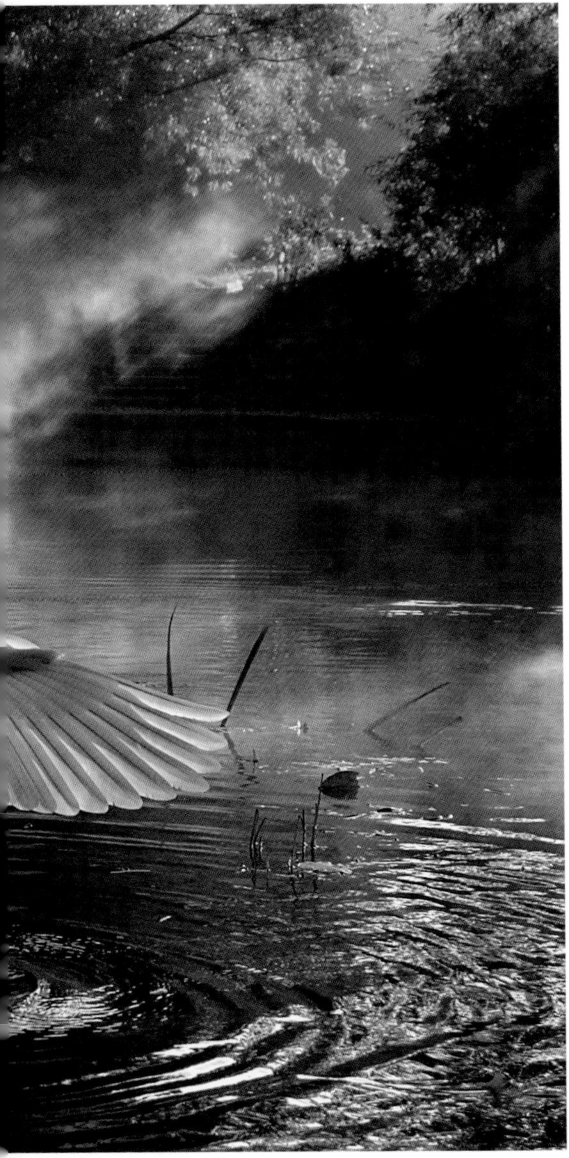

MAY 16

The weak
can never forgive.
Forgiveness is
the attribute of
the strong.

~ Mohandas Gandhi

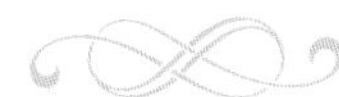

Real courage is when you know
you're licked before you begin—
but you begin anyway
and see it through no matter what.

~ Harper Lee

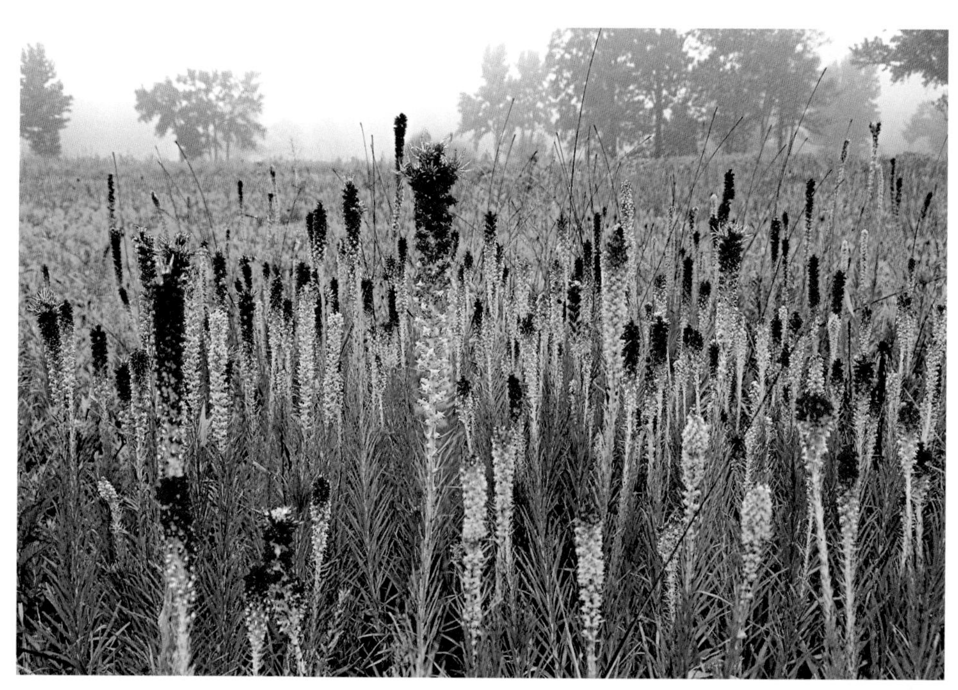

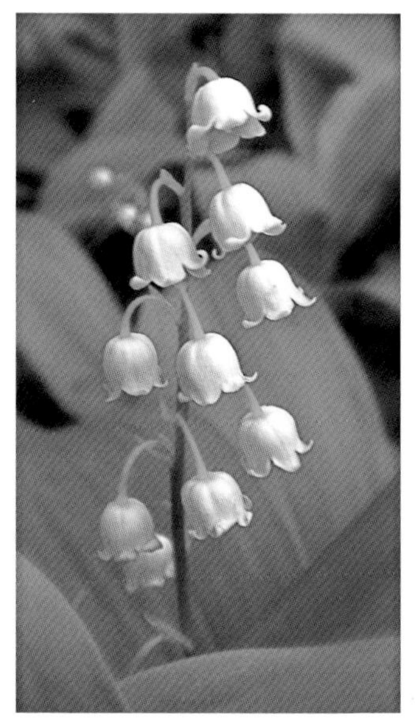

MAY *18*

Class is the sure-footedness
that comes with
having proved
you can meet life.

~ Ann Landers

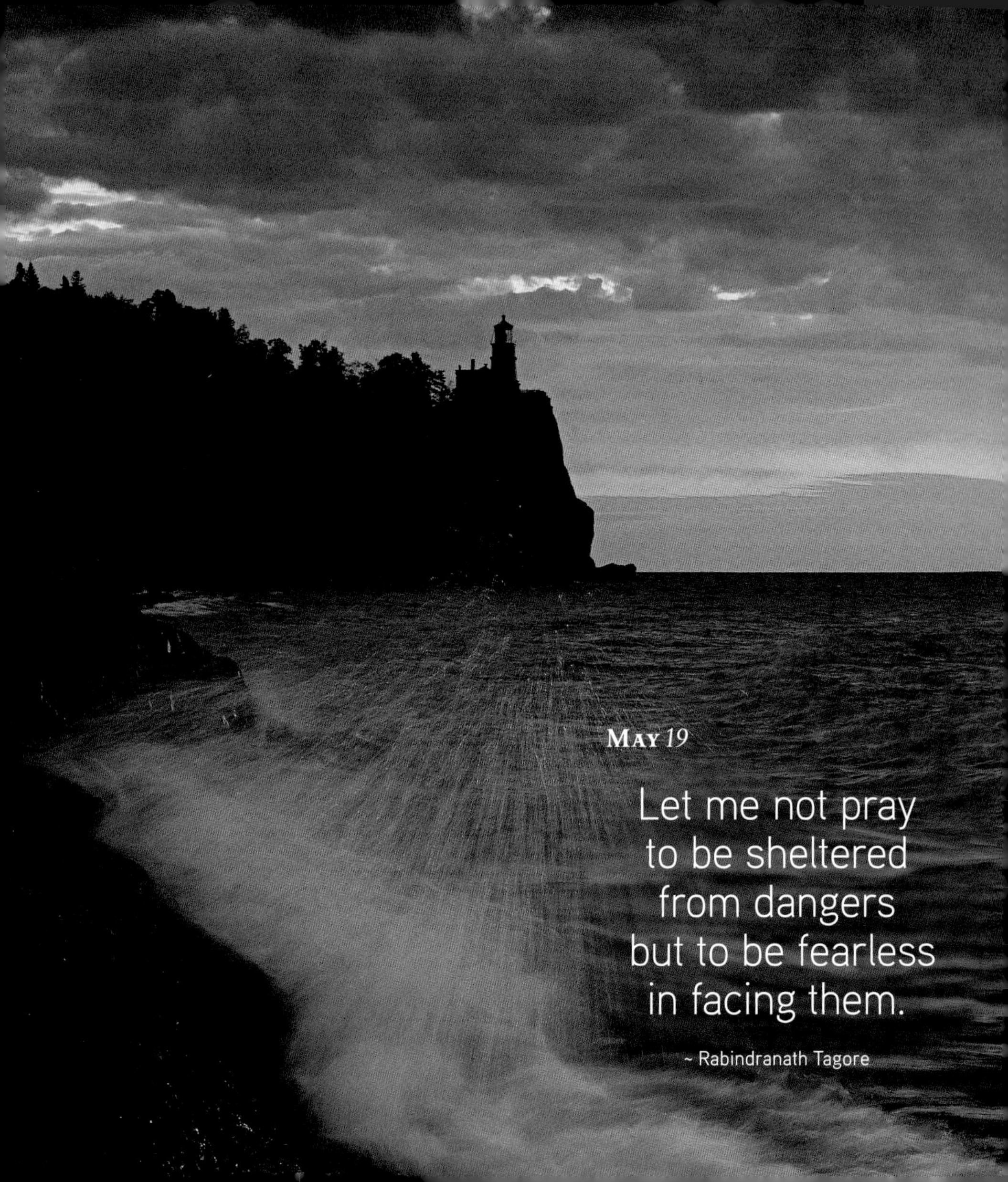

MAY 19

Let me not pray
to be sheltered
from dangers
but to be fearless
in facing them.

~ Rabindranath Tagore

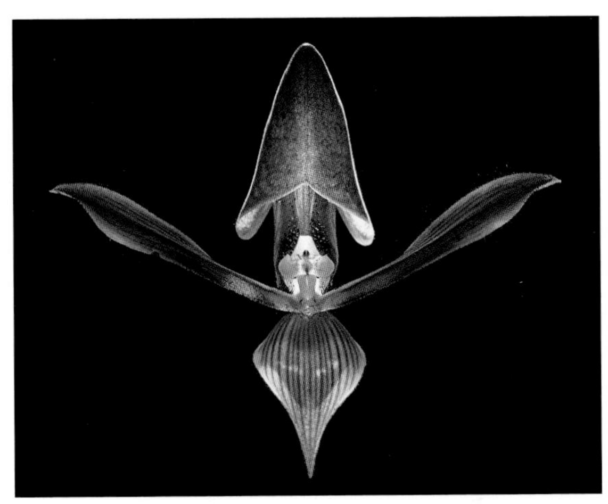

MAY 20

Fortune favors the bold.

~ Virgil

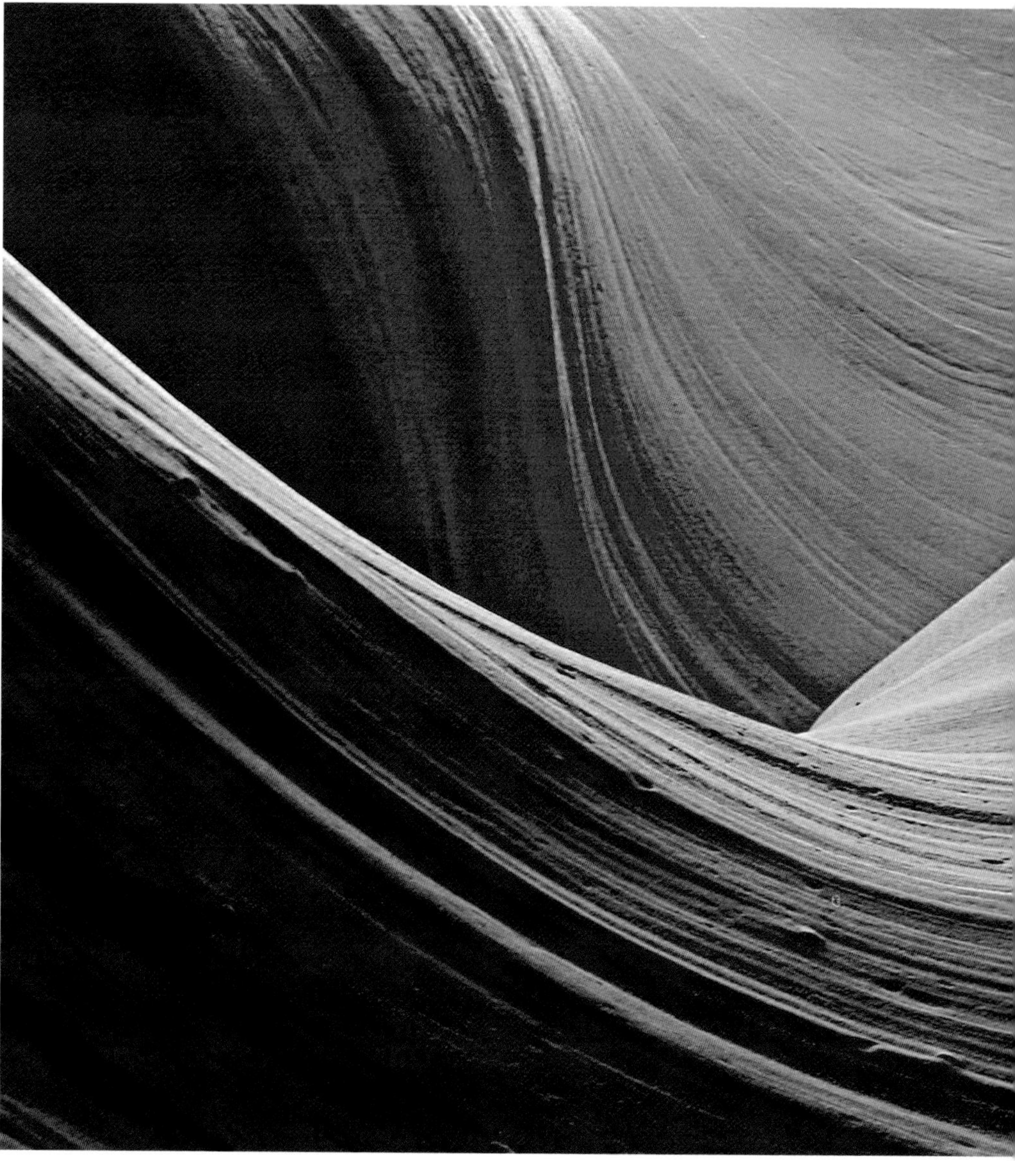

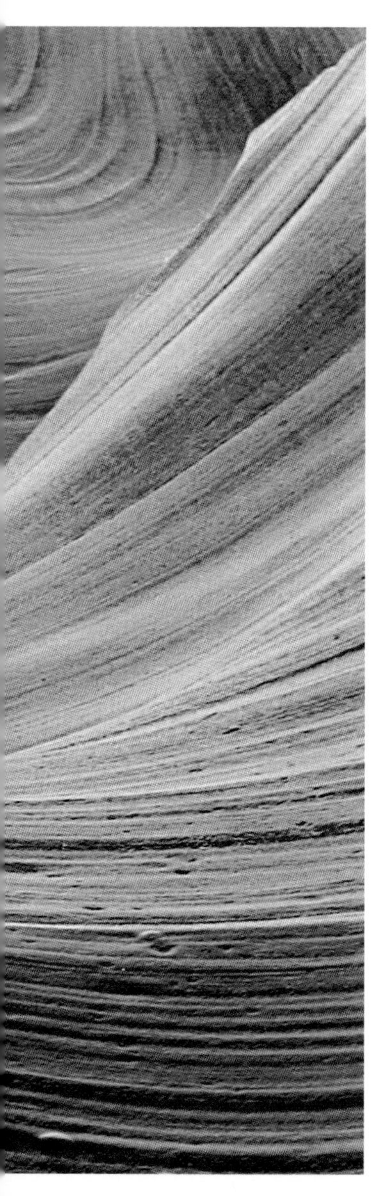

May 21

The marvelous richness
of human experience
would lose something
of rewarding joy
if there were no limitations
to overcome.
The hilltop hour would not
be half so wonderful
if there were no dark valleys
to traverse.

~ Helen Keller

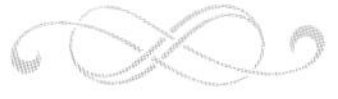

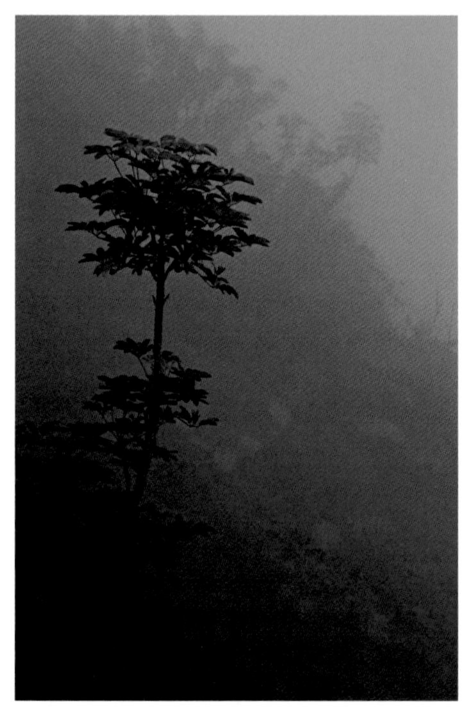

MAY 22

Hardships make
or break people.

~ Margaret Mitchell

MAY 23

The most courageous act
is to think for yourself.
Aloud.

~ Coco Chanel

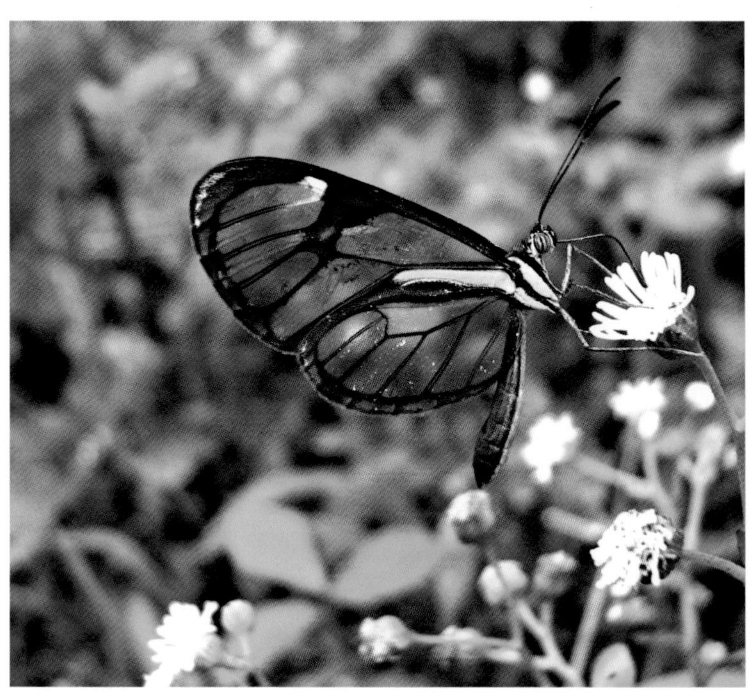

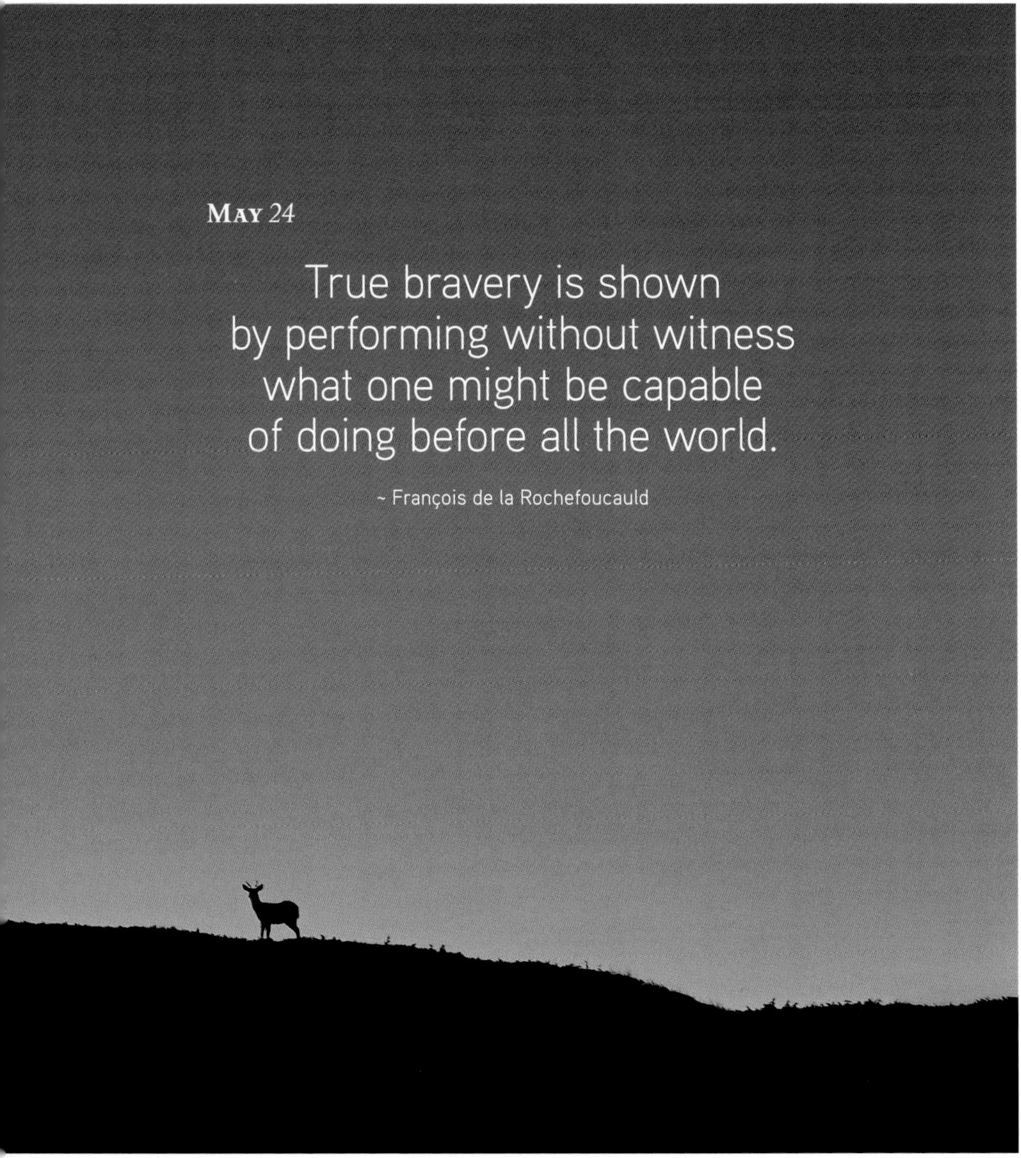

MAY *24*

True bravery is shown
by performing without witness
what one might be capable
of doing before all the world.

~ François de la Rochefoucauld

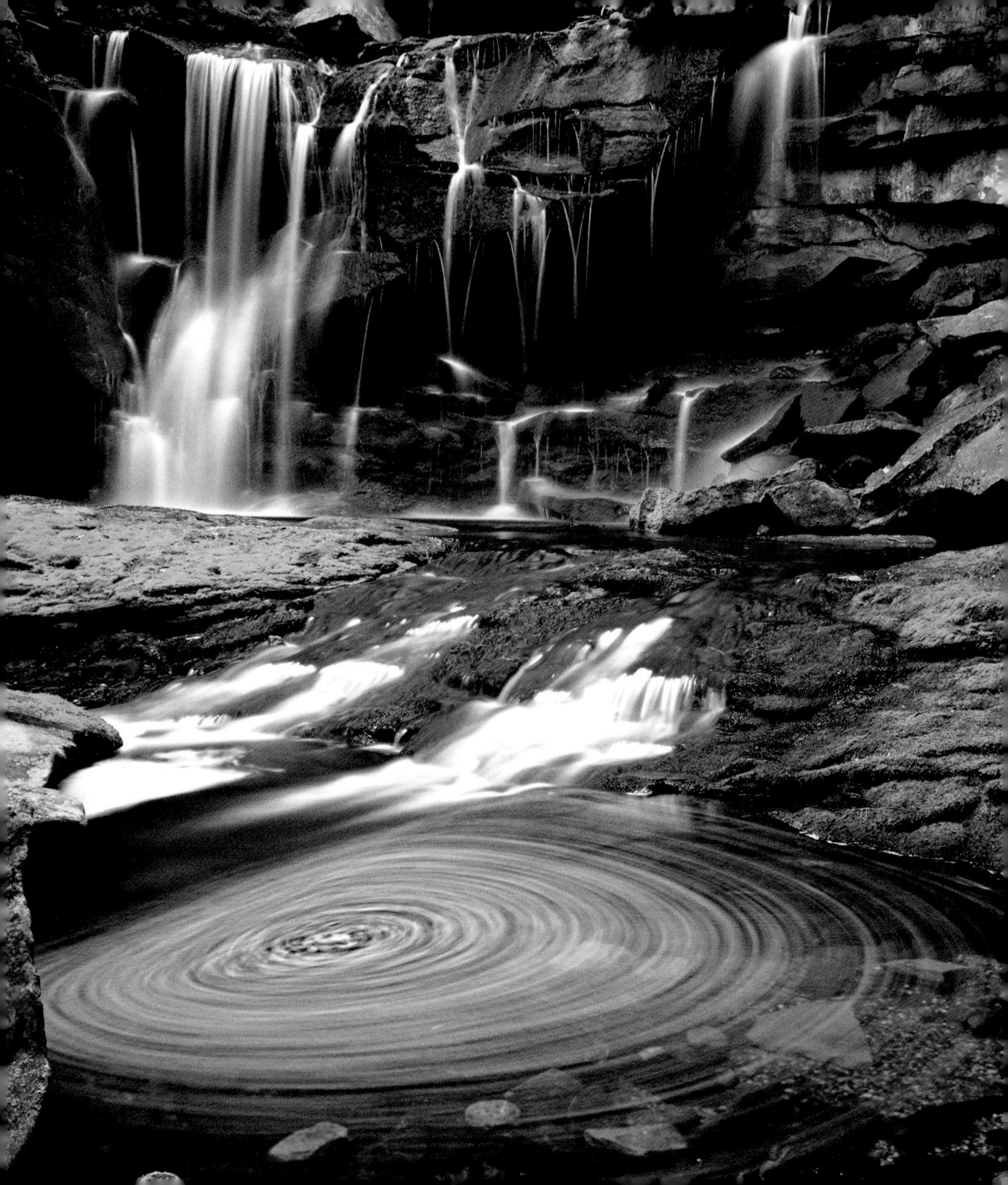

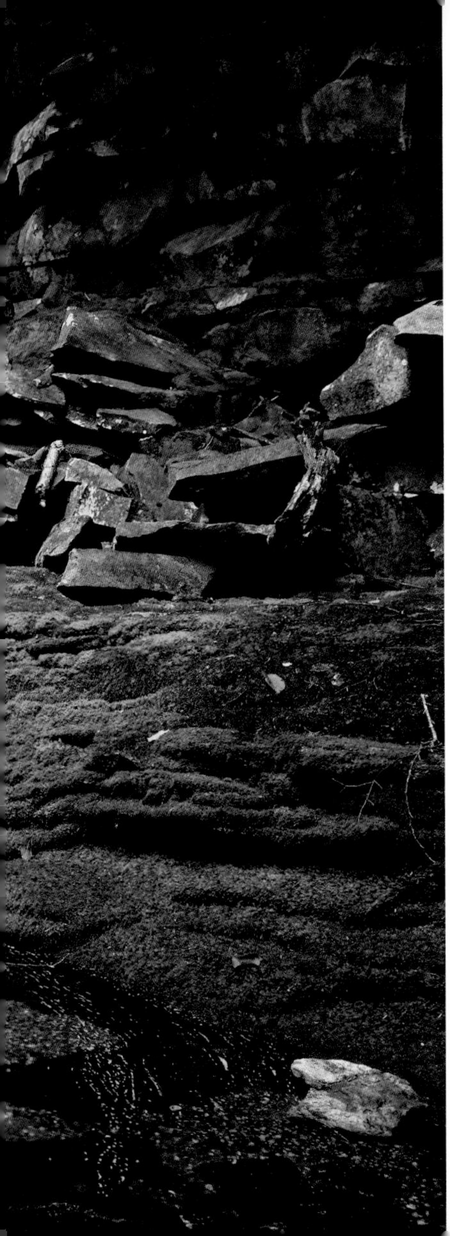

MAY 25

When in doubt,
tell the truth.

~ Mark Twain

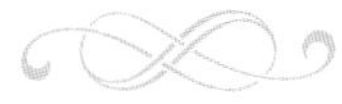

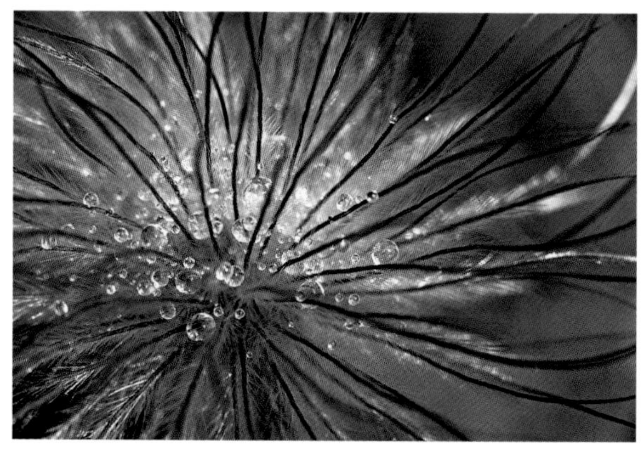

May 26

The knowledge that you have emerged wiser and stronger from setbacks means that you are, ever after, secure in your ability to survive.

~ J. K. Rowling

May 27

The courage of life is often a less dramatic spectacle than the courage of the final moment; but it is no less a magnificent mixture of triumph and tragedy.

~ John F. Kennedy

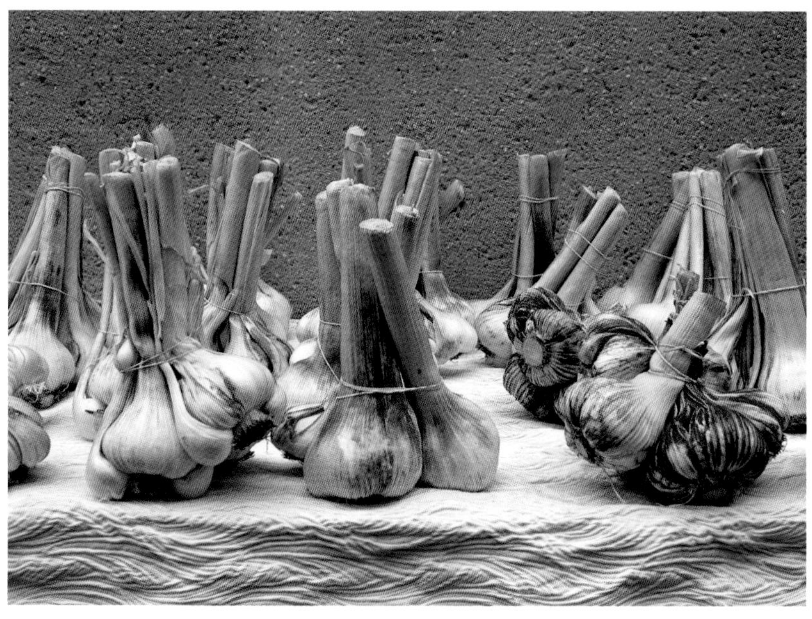

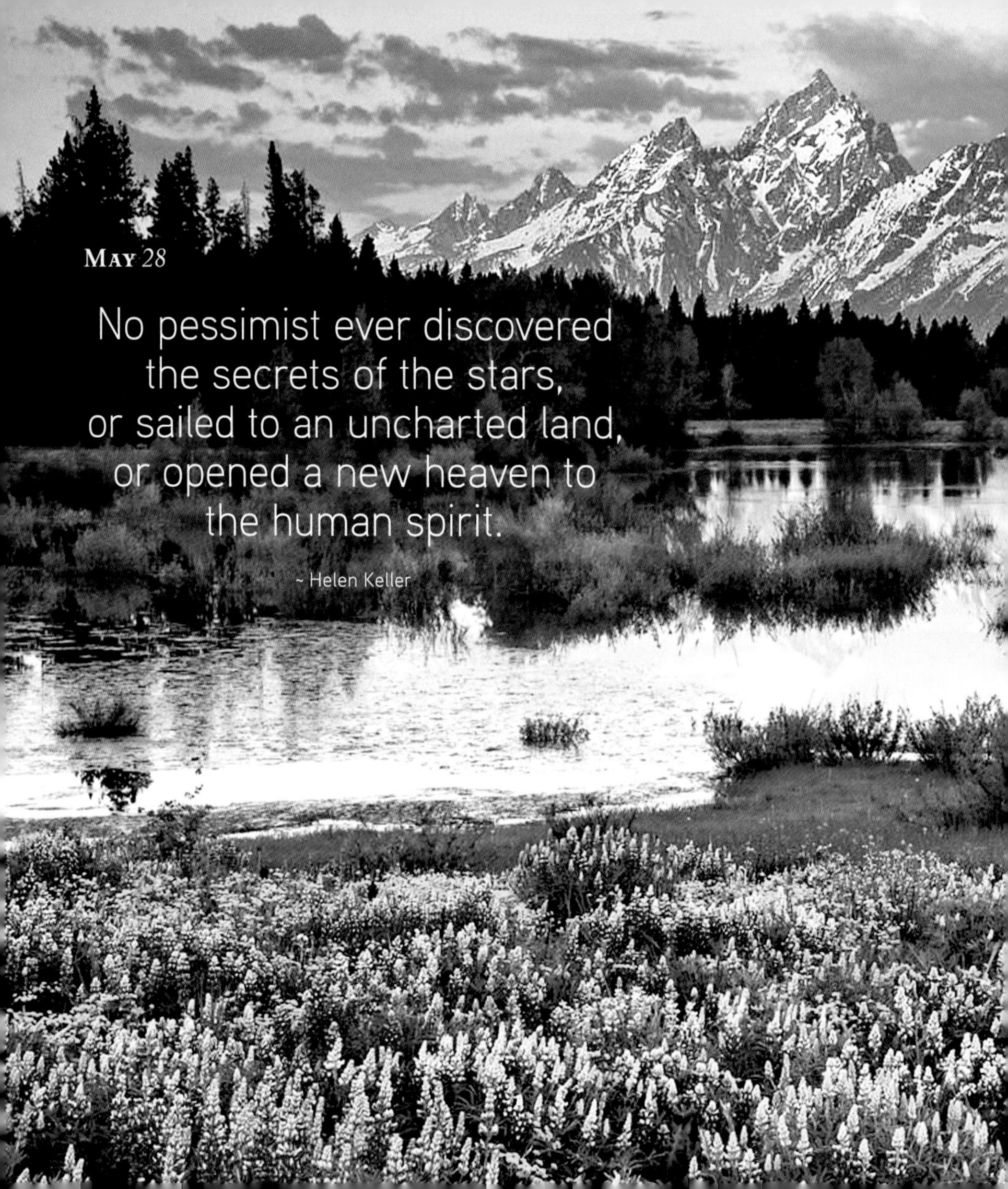
MAY 28
No pessimist ever discovered
the secrets of the stars,
or sailed to an uncharted land,
or opened a new heaven to
the human spirit.
~ Helen Keller

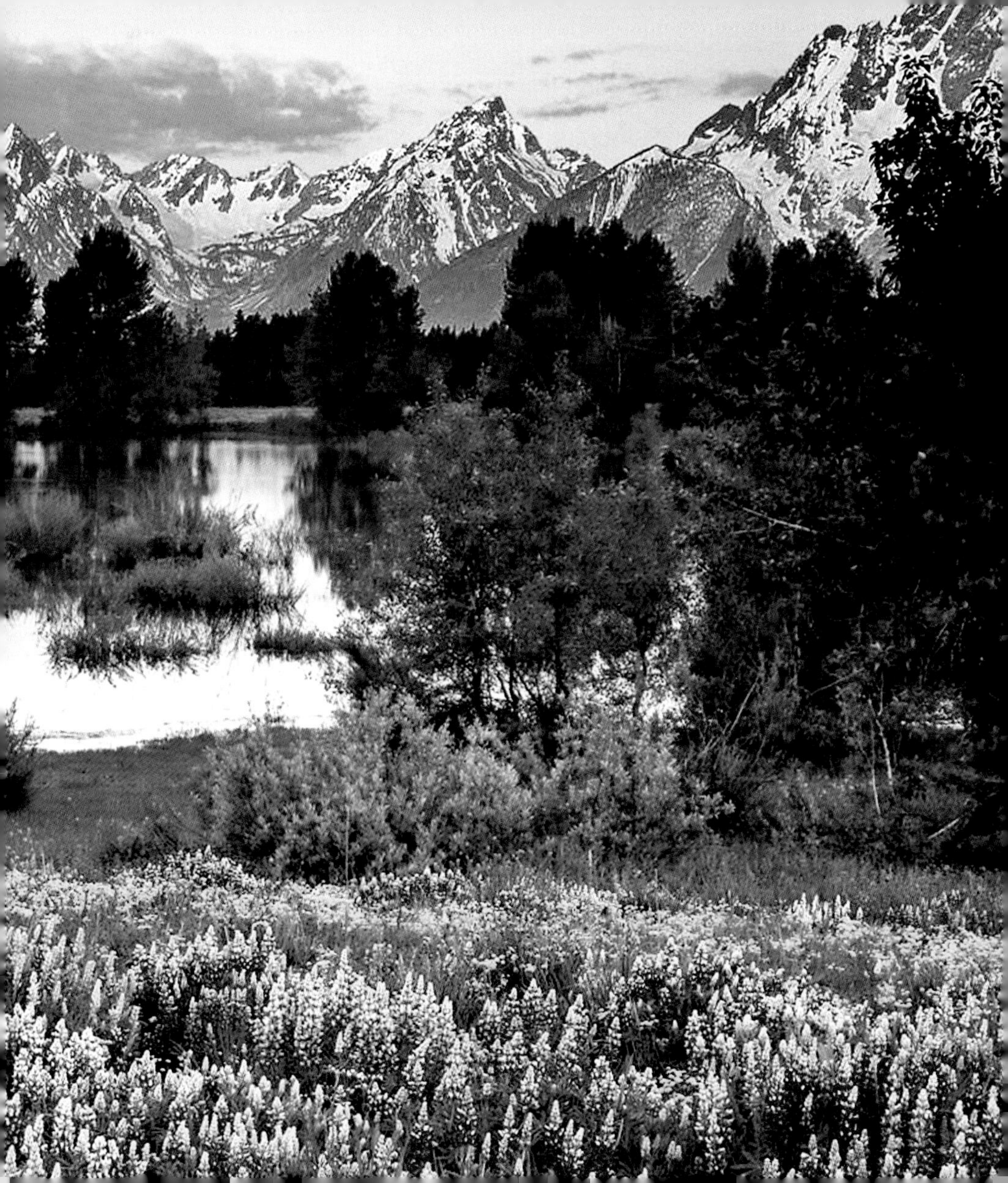

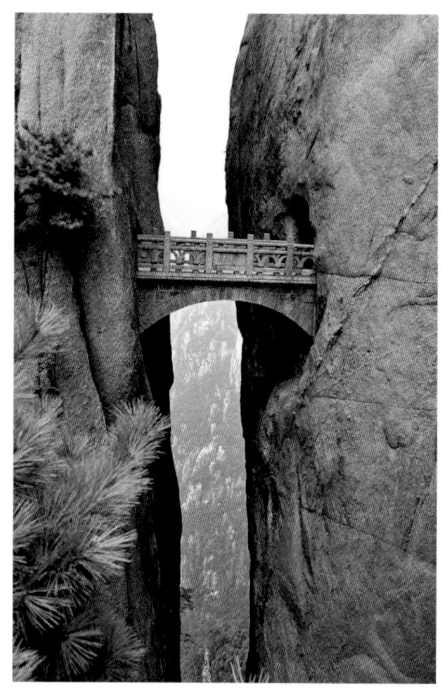

May *29*

Courage is being scared to death—
and saddling up anyway.

~ John Wayne

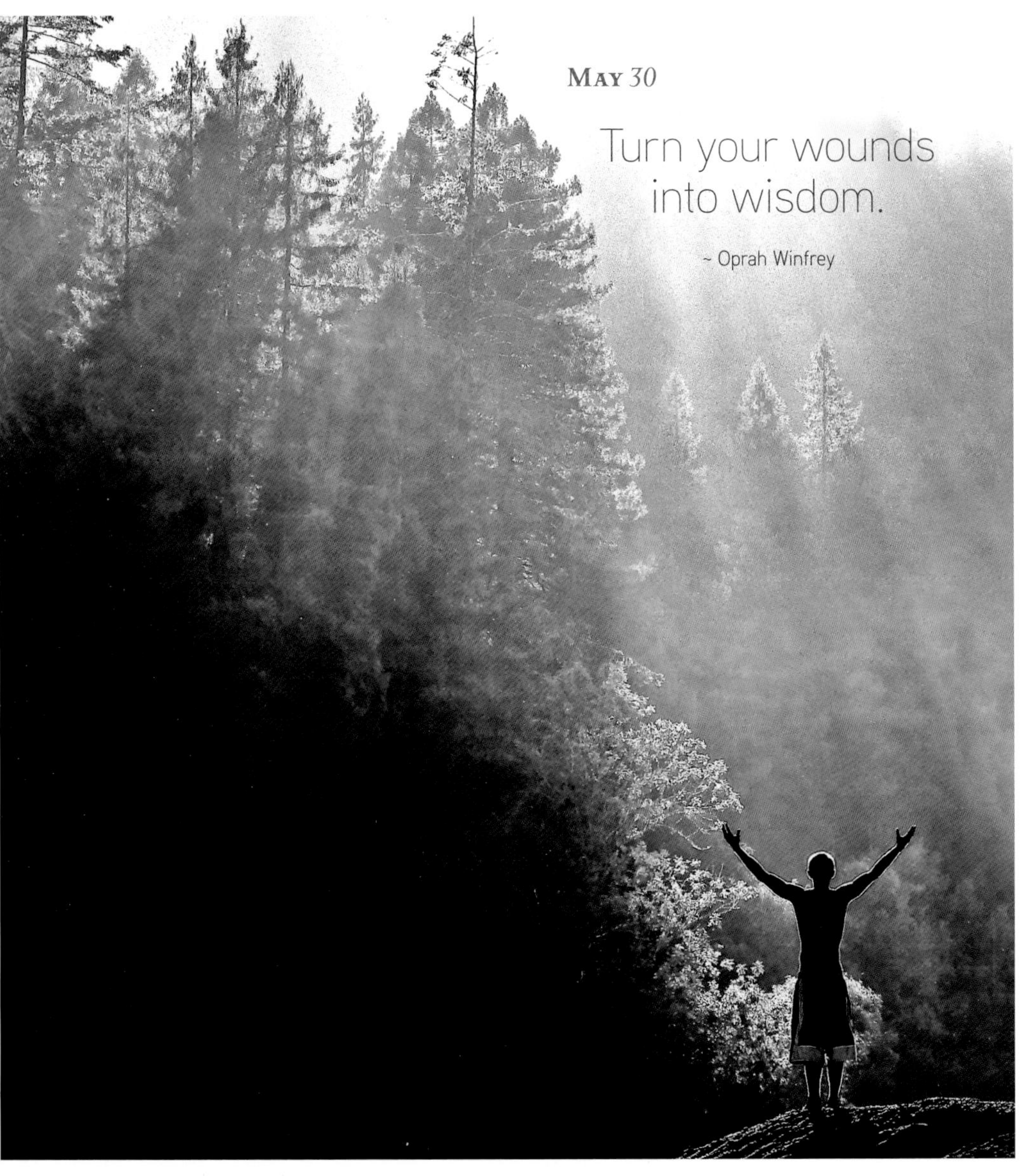

May 30

Turn your wounds into wisdom.

~ Oprah Winfrey

May 31

Courage is not
the towering oak
that sees storms
come and go;
it is the
fragile blossom
that opens
in the snow.

~ Alice Mackenzie Swaim

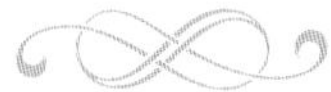

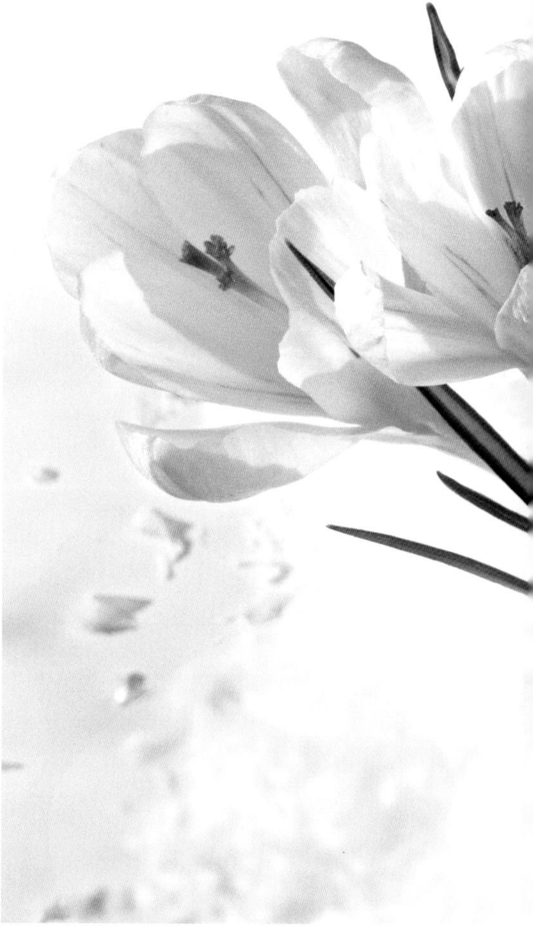

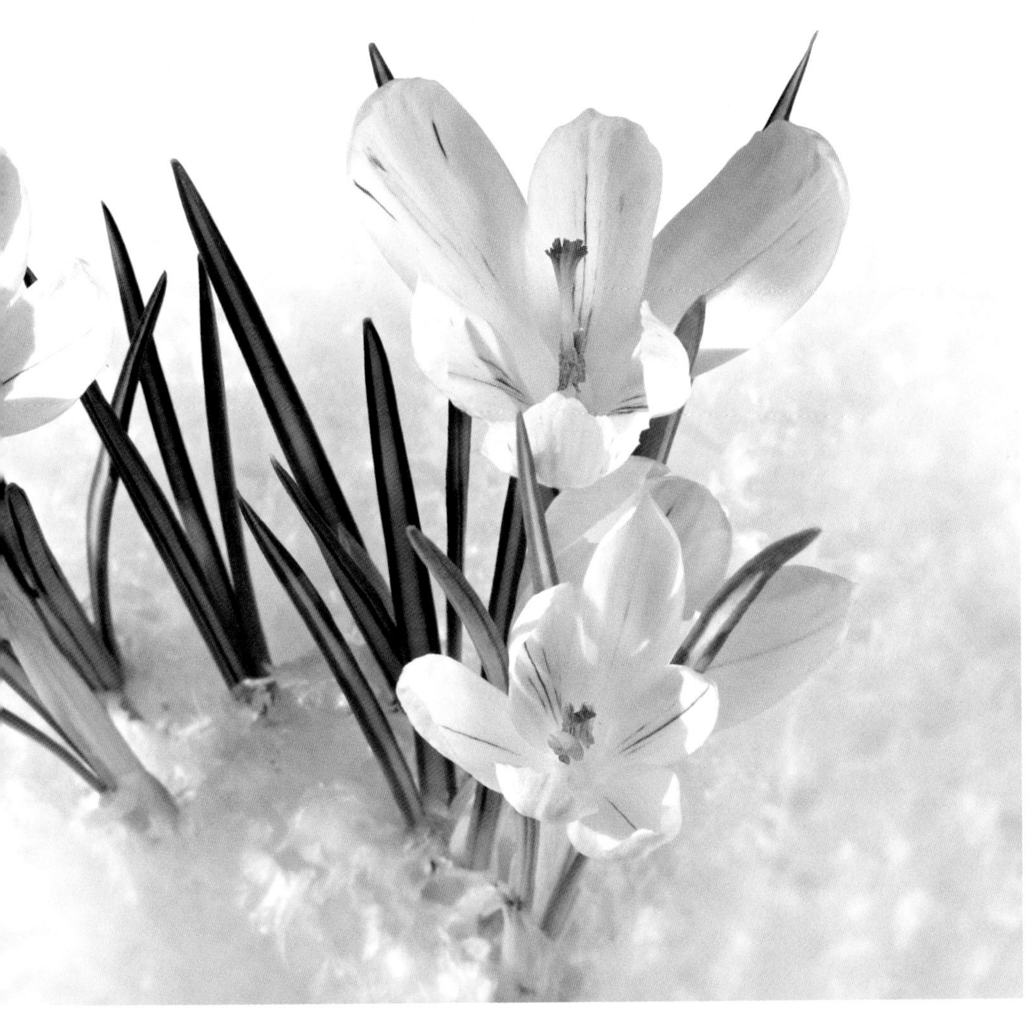

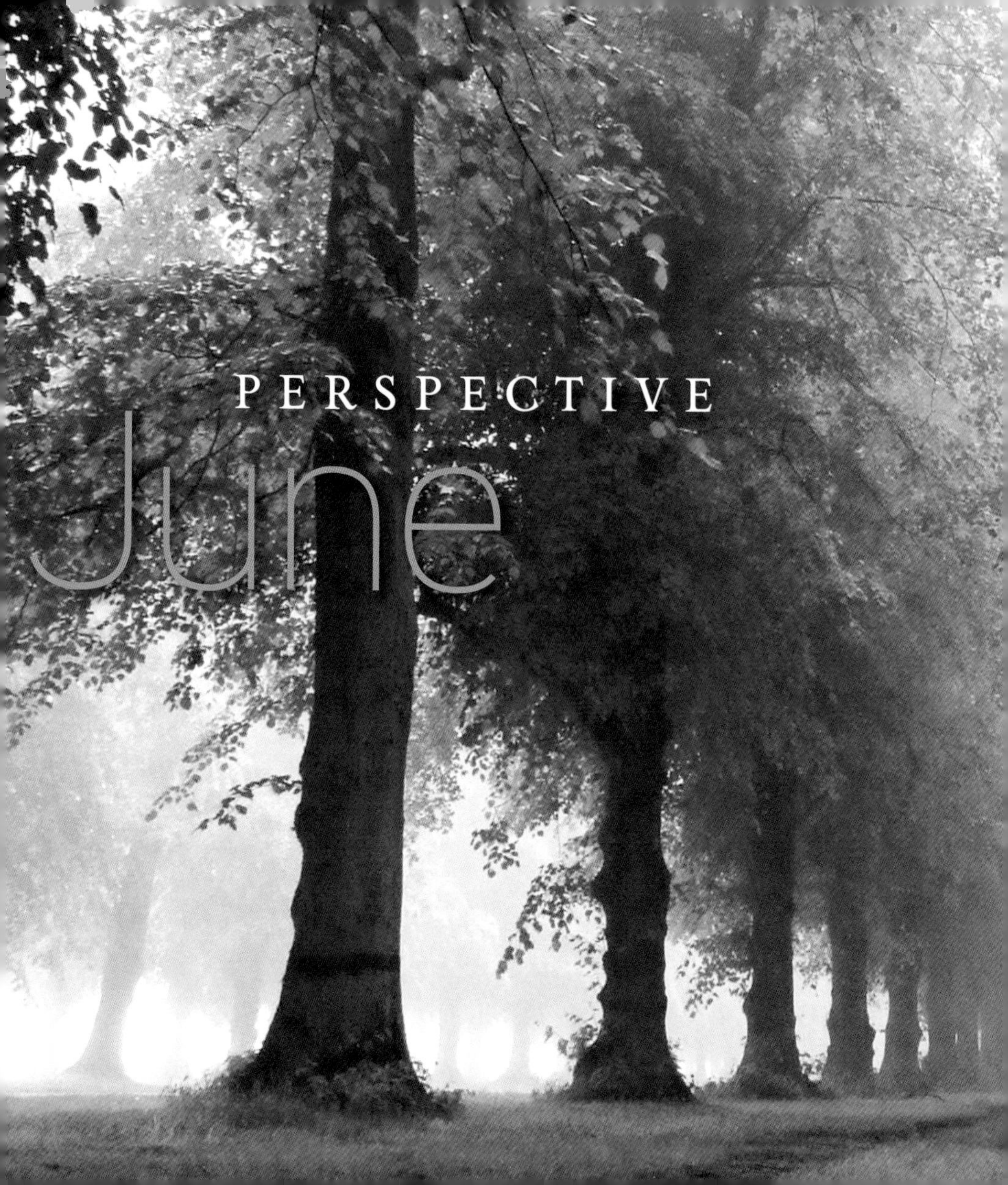

PERSPECTIVE

June

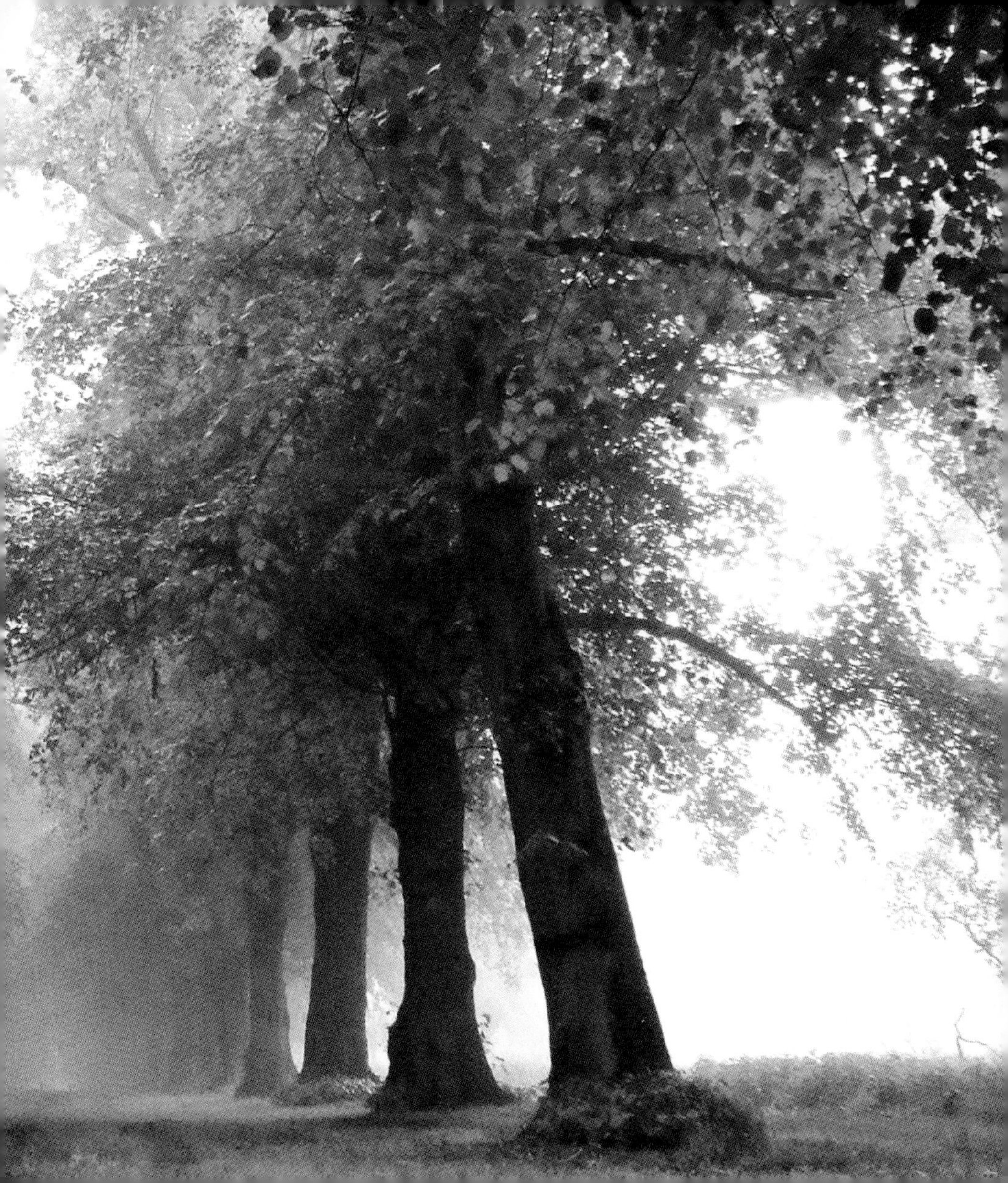

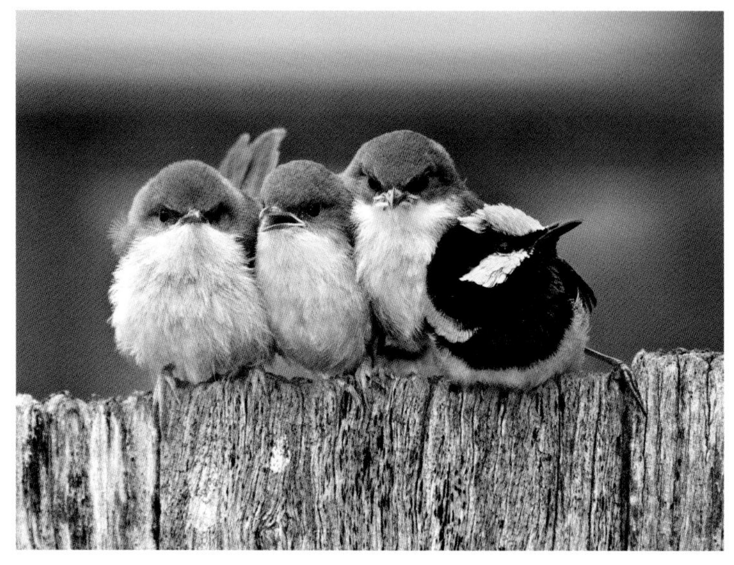

JUNE 1

There are years
that ask questions,
and years that answer.

~ Zora Neale Hurston

JUNE 2

Look at everything
as though you were seeing it
for either the first or last time.
Then your time on earth
will be filled with glory.

~ Betty Smith

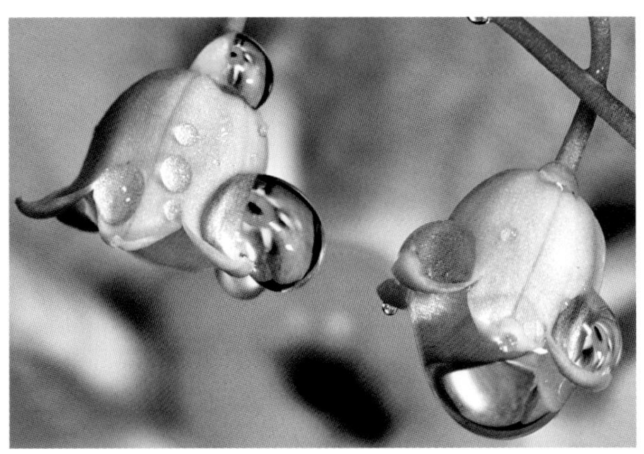

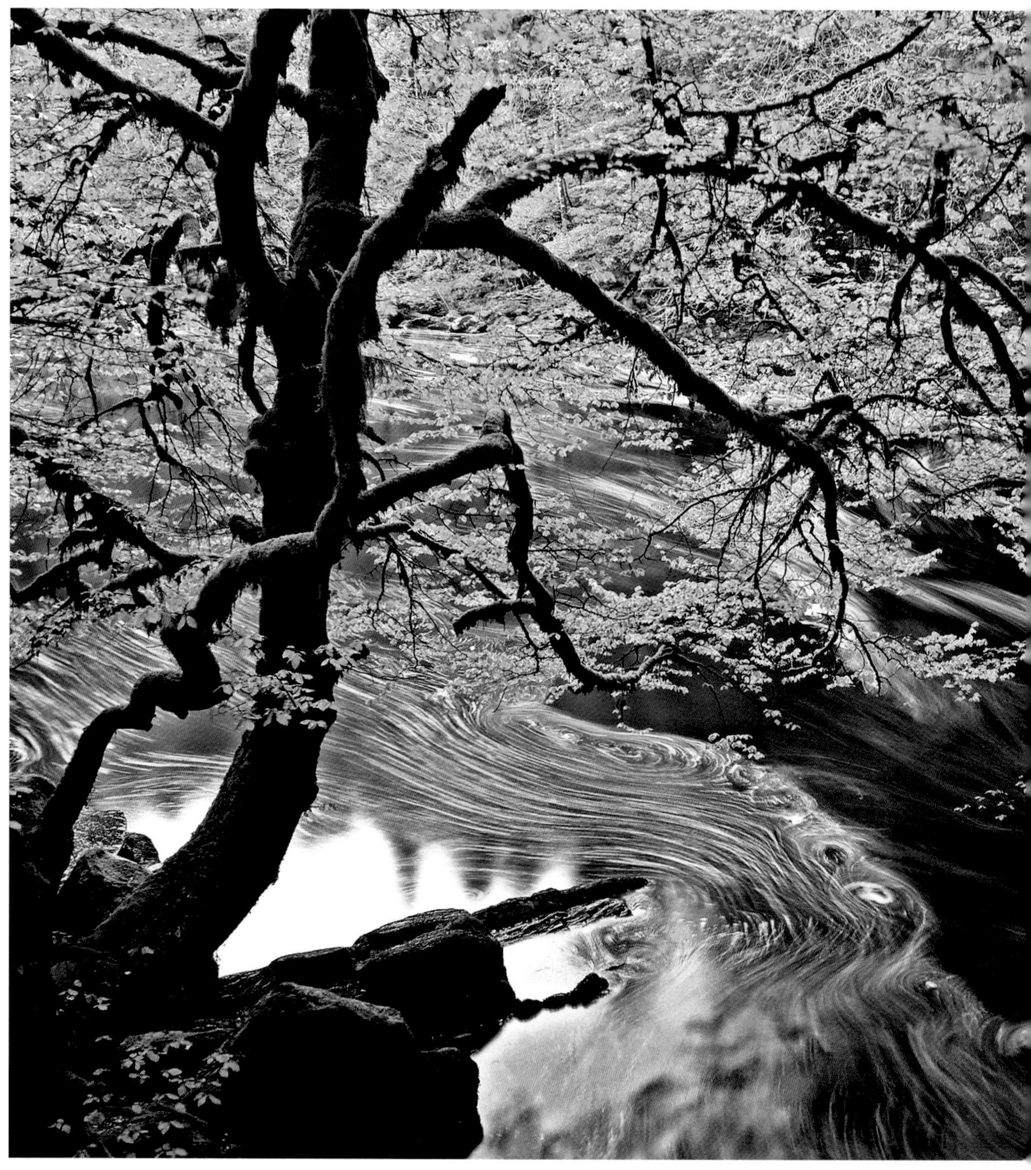

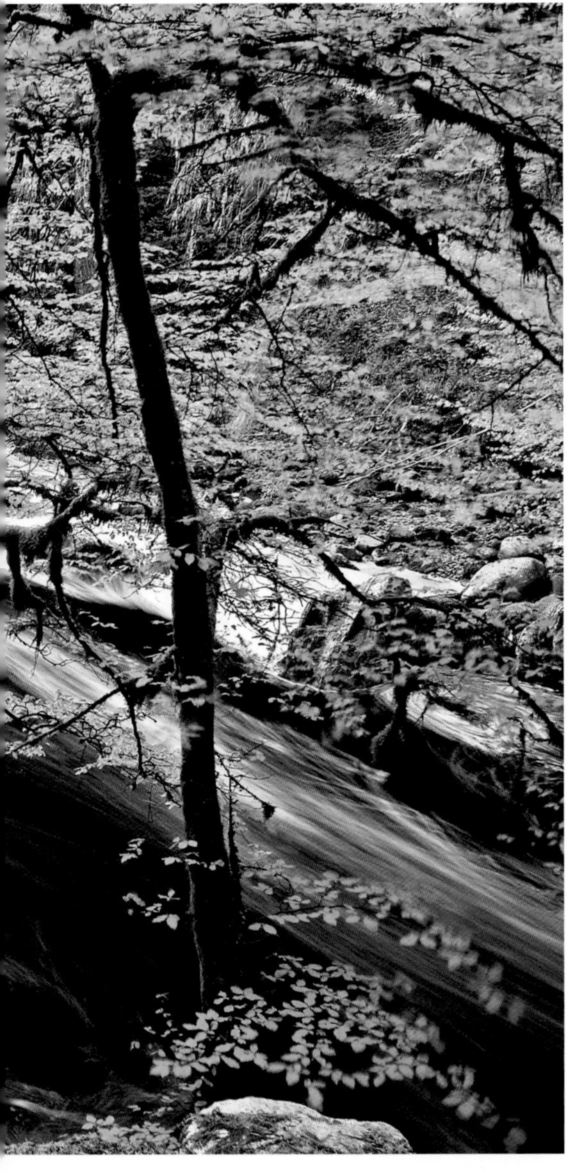

June 3

One is never fortunate or as unfortunate as one imagines.

~ François de la Rochefoucauld

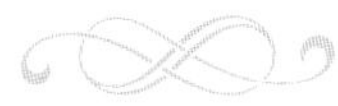

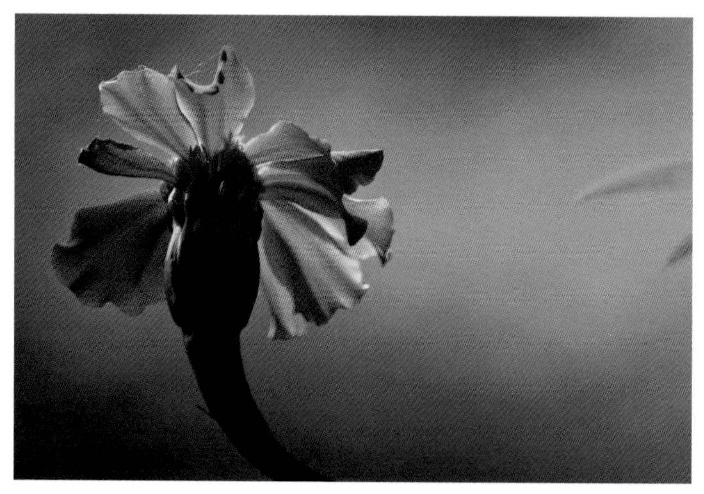

JUNE 4

In order to understand the world, one has to turn away from it on occasion.

~ Albert Camus

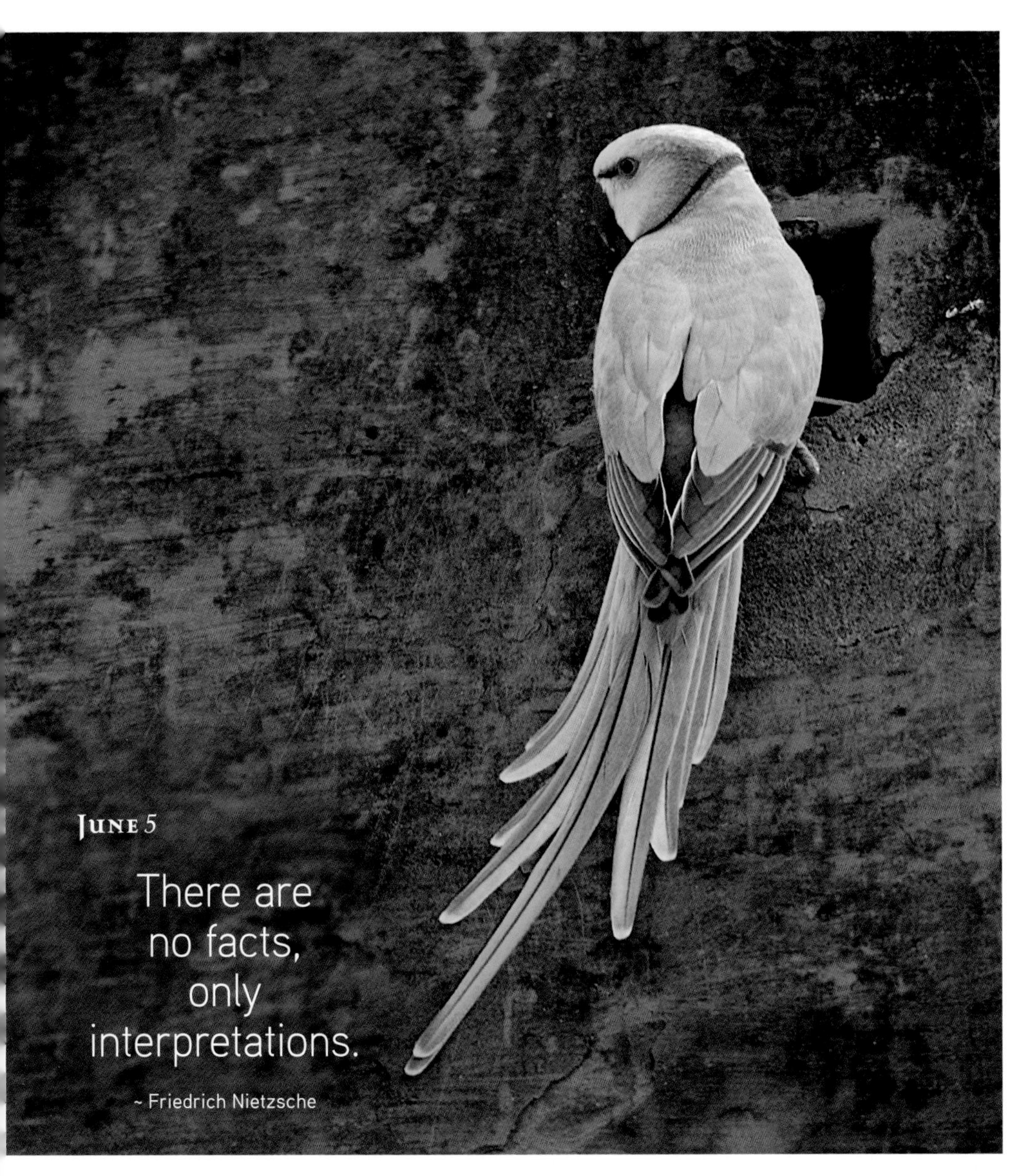
June 5
There are no facts, only interpretations.
~ Friedrich Nietzsche

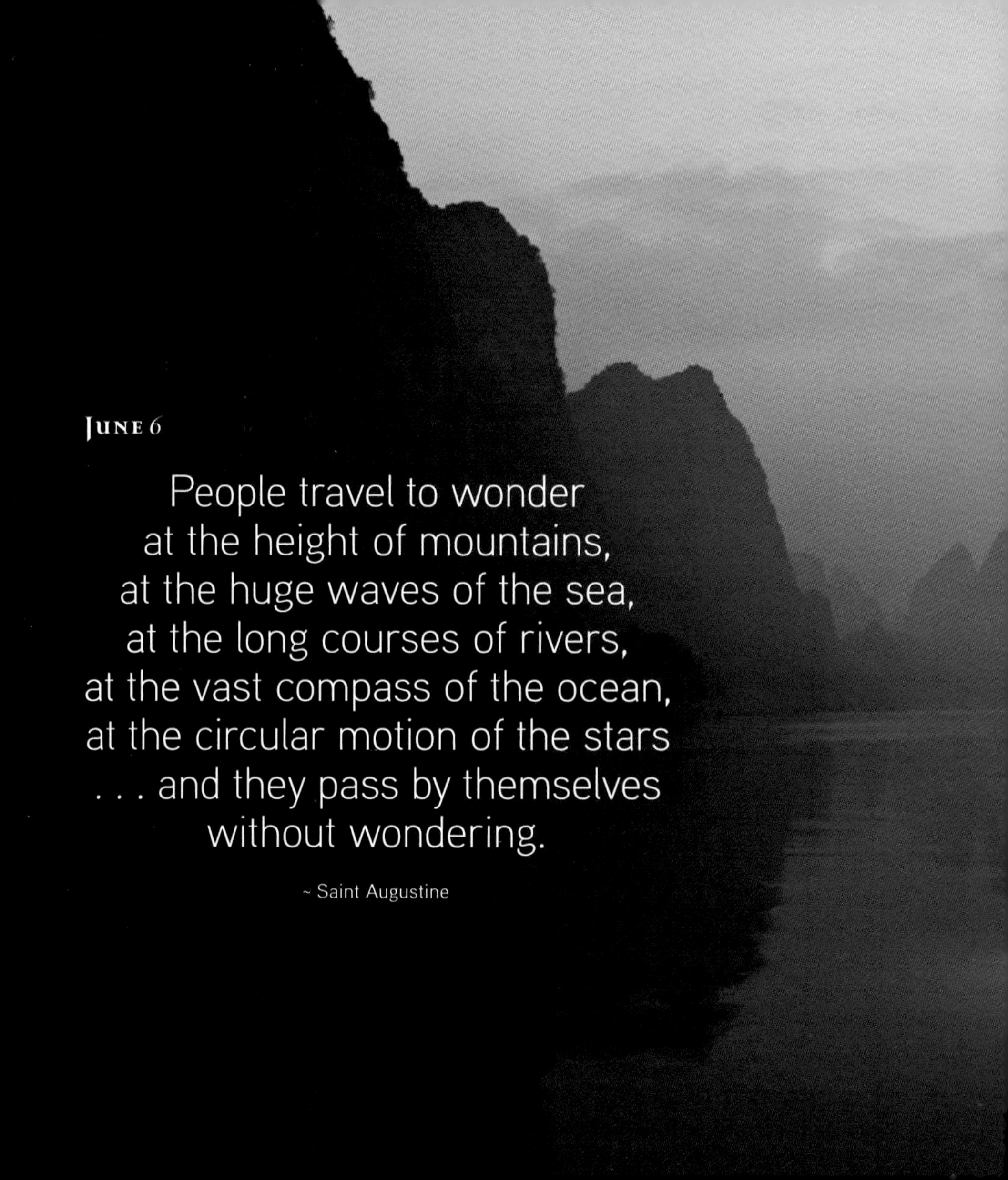

JUNE 6

People travel to wonder
at the height of mountains,
at the huge waves of the sea,
at the long courses of rivers,
at the vast compass of the ocean,
at the circular motion of the stars
. . . and they pass by themselves
without wondering.

~ Saint Augustine

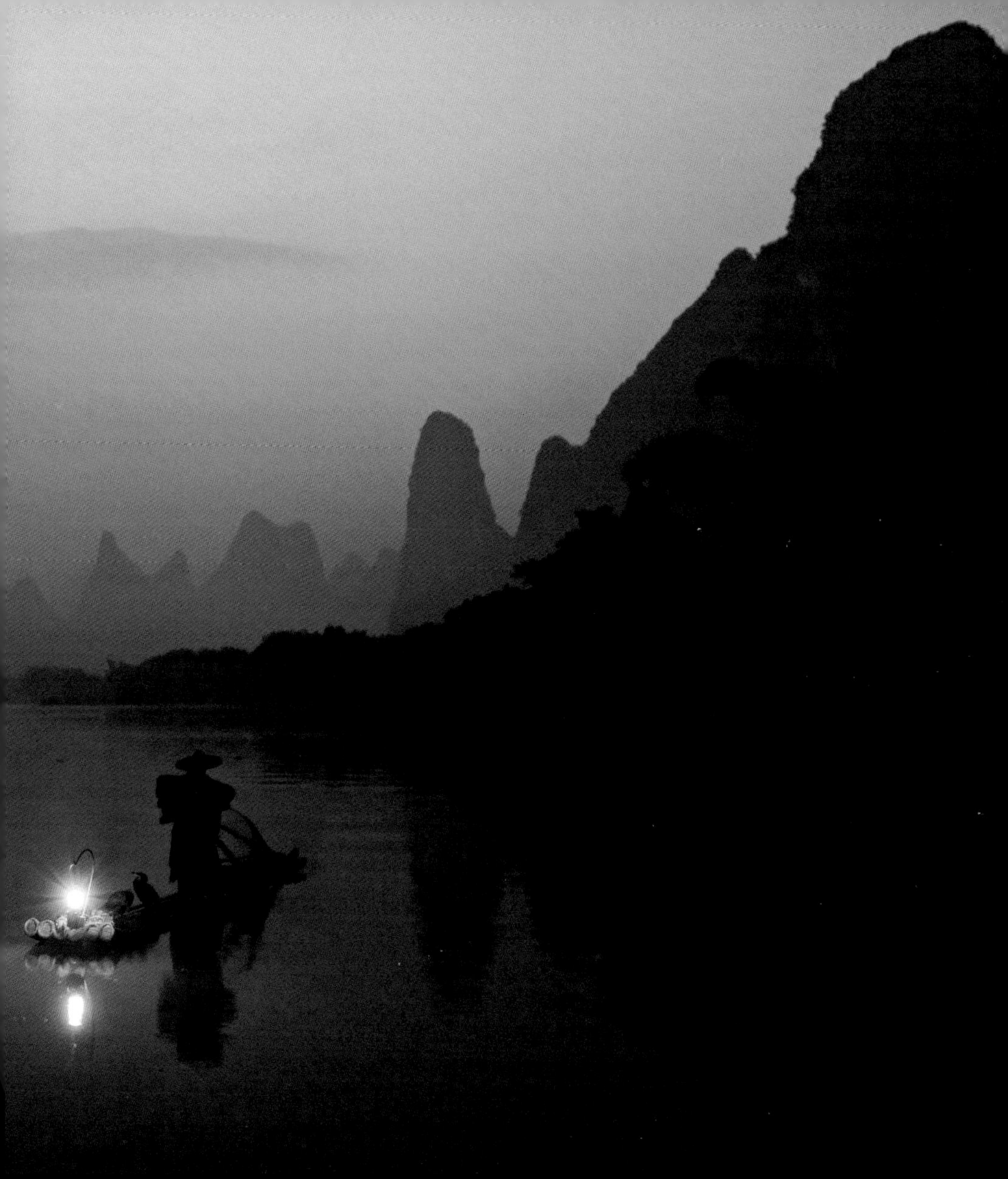

JUNE 7

The question is not
what you look at,
but what you see.

~ Henry David Thoreau

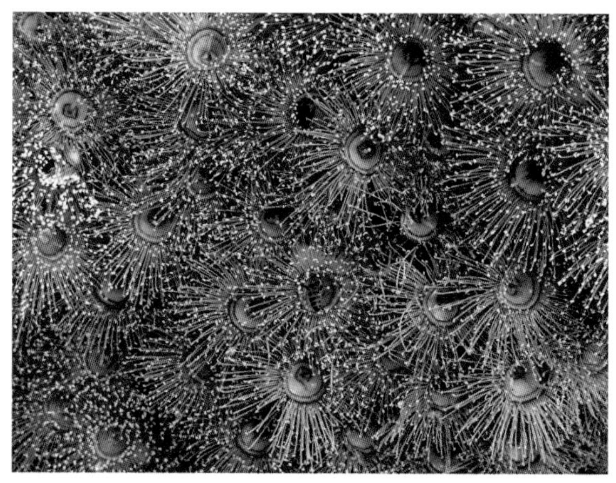

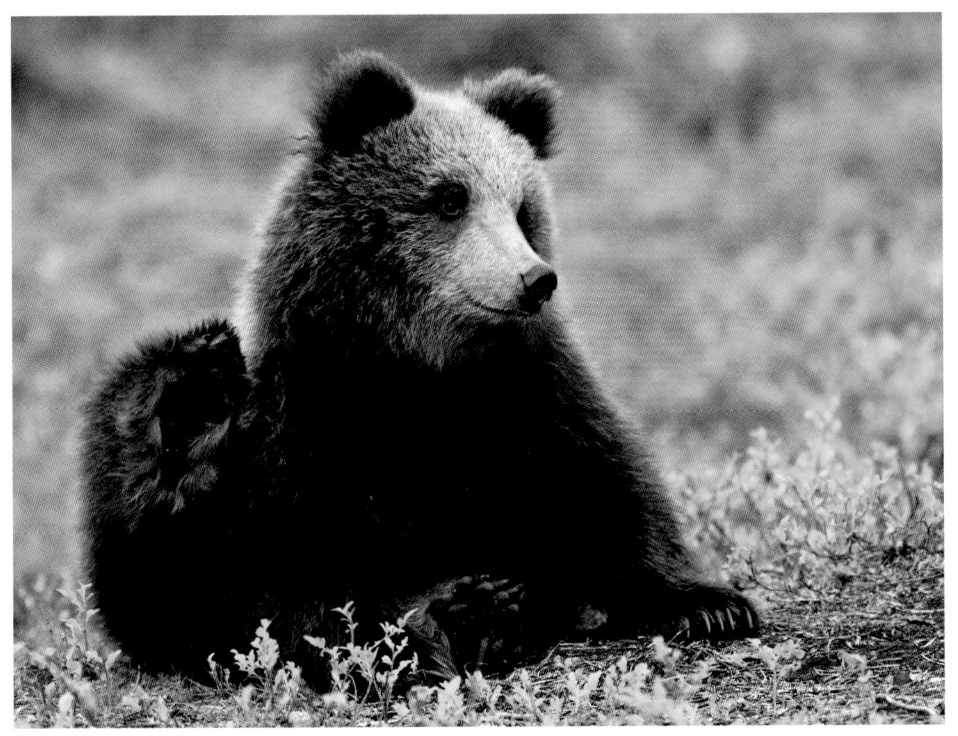

JUNE 8

I never lose sight
of the fact
that just being is fun.

~ Katharine Hepburn

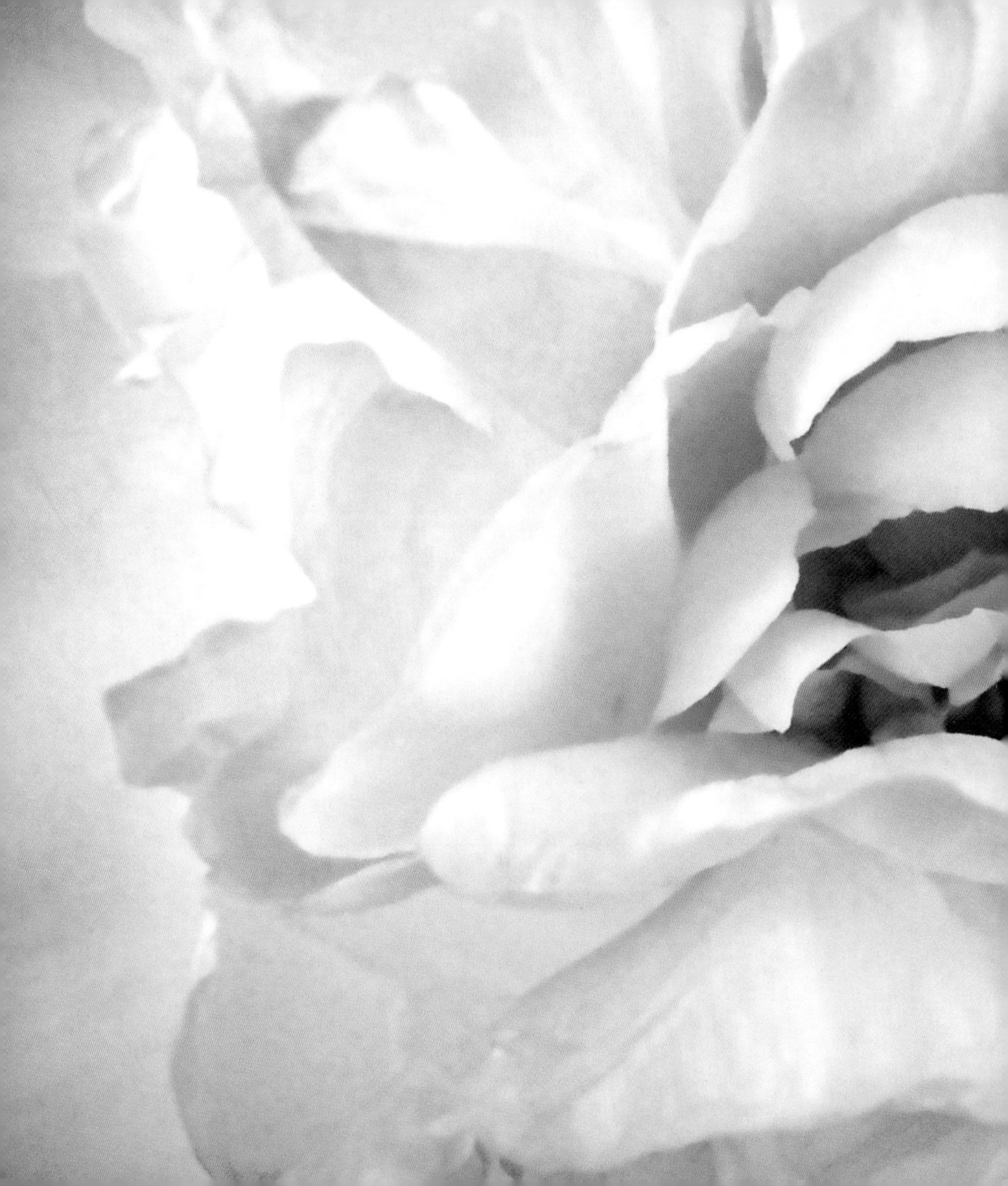

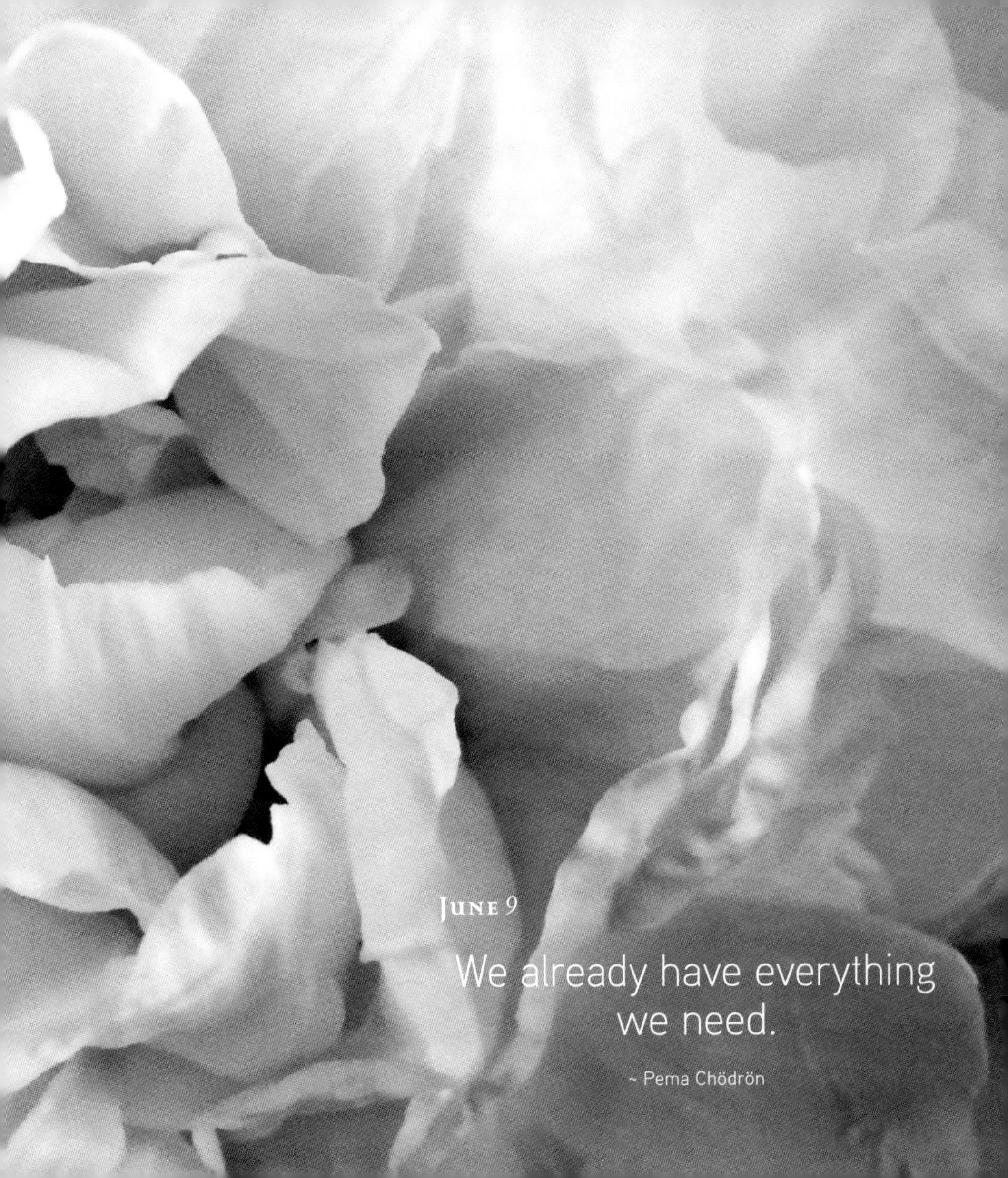

JUNE 9

We already have everything we need.

~ Pema Chödrön

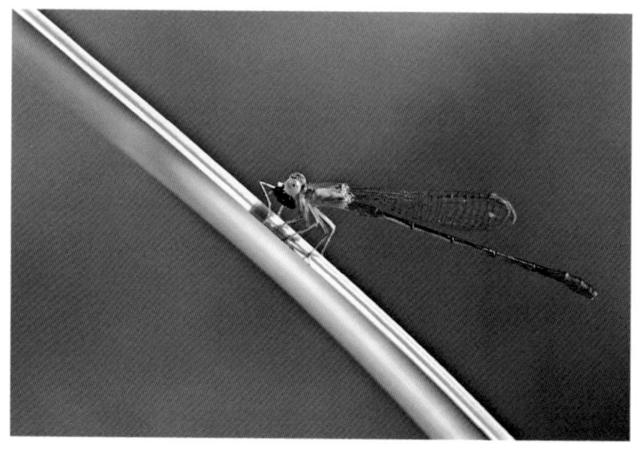

JUNE 10

To understand
the heart and mind
of a person,
look not at what
he has already achieved,
but at what
he aspires to.

~ Kahlil Gibran

God gave us our memories
that we might have roses in December.

~ J. M. Barrie

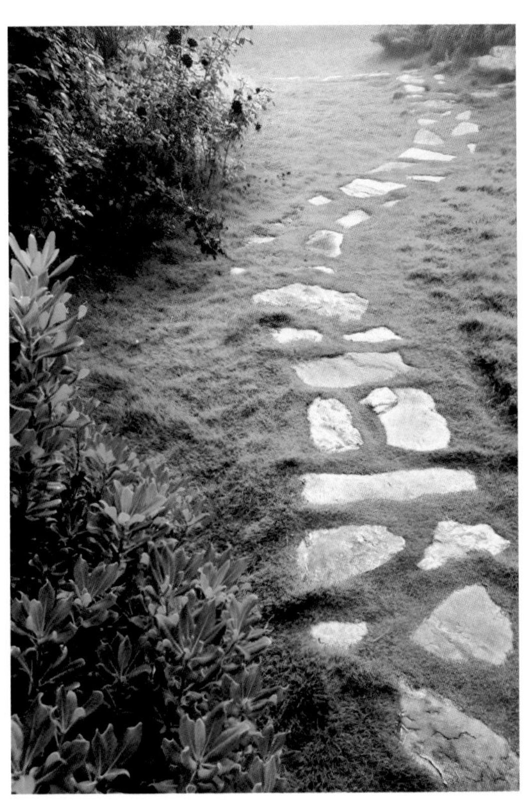

June 12

The voyage of discovery is not in seeking new landscapes, but in having new eyes.

~ Marcel Proust

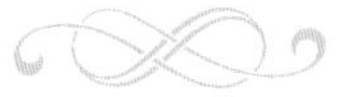

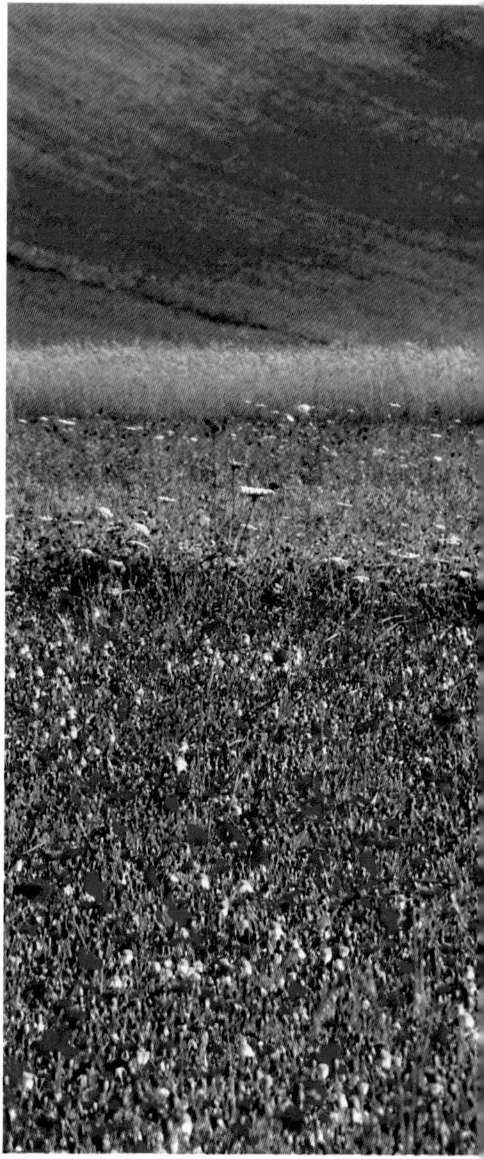

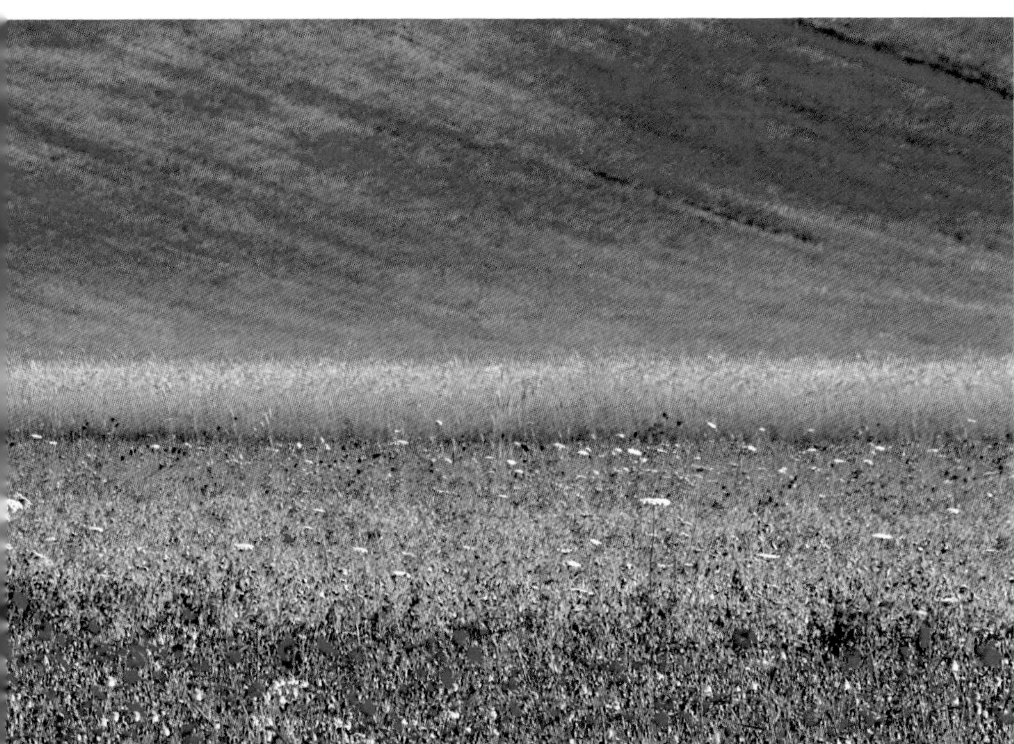

JUNE 13

Happiness depends more on
how life strikes you
than on what happens.

~ Andy Rooney

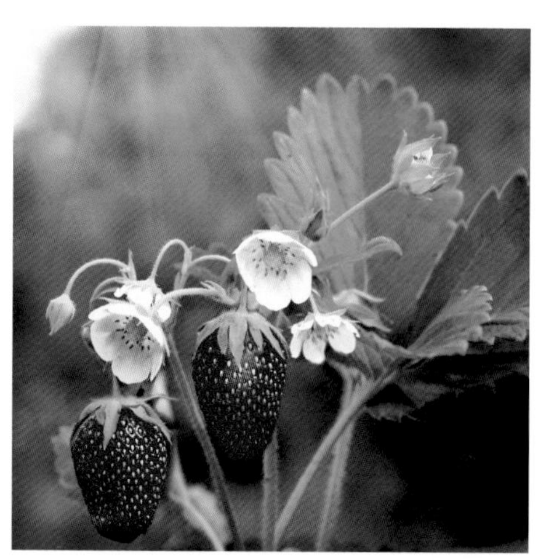

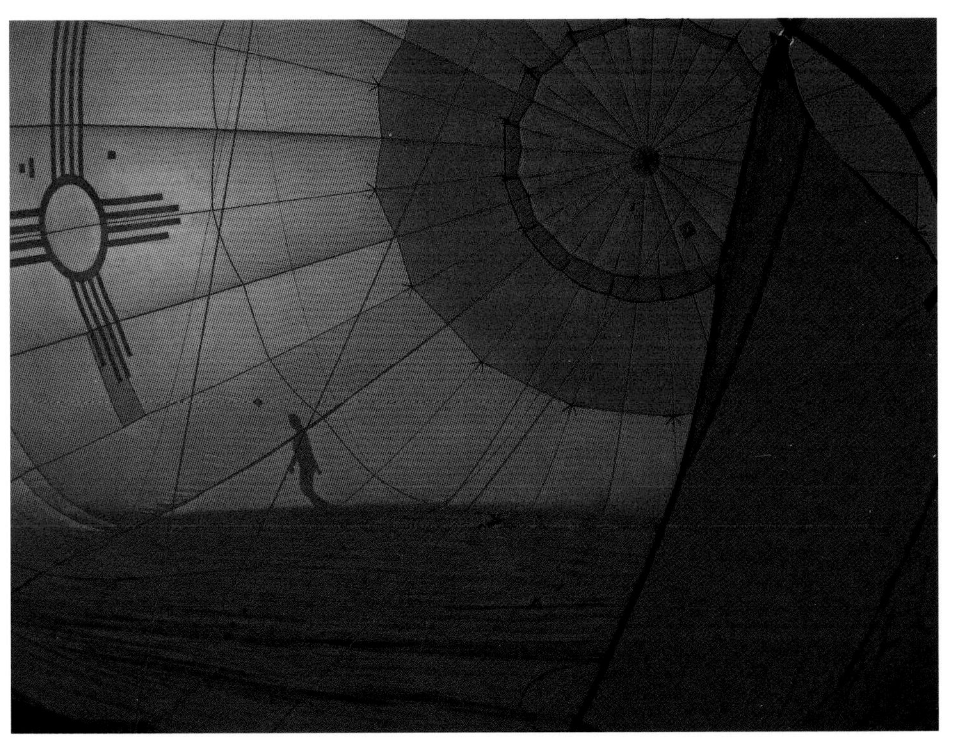

June 14

Since we cannot change reality,
let us change the eyes
which see reality.

~ Nikos Kazantzakis

JUNE *15*

Look deep into nature, and then you will understand everything better.

~ Albert Einstein

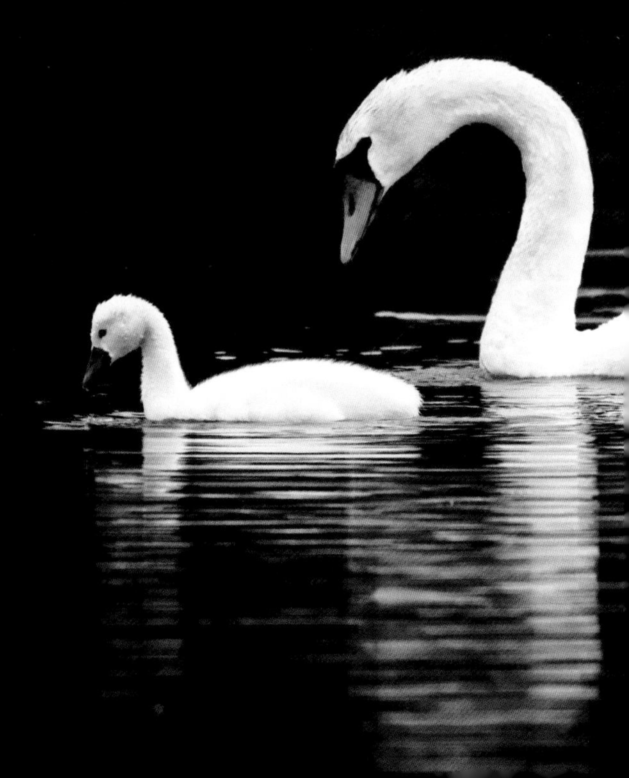

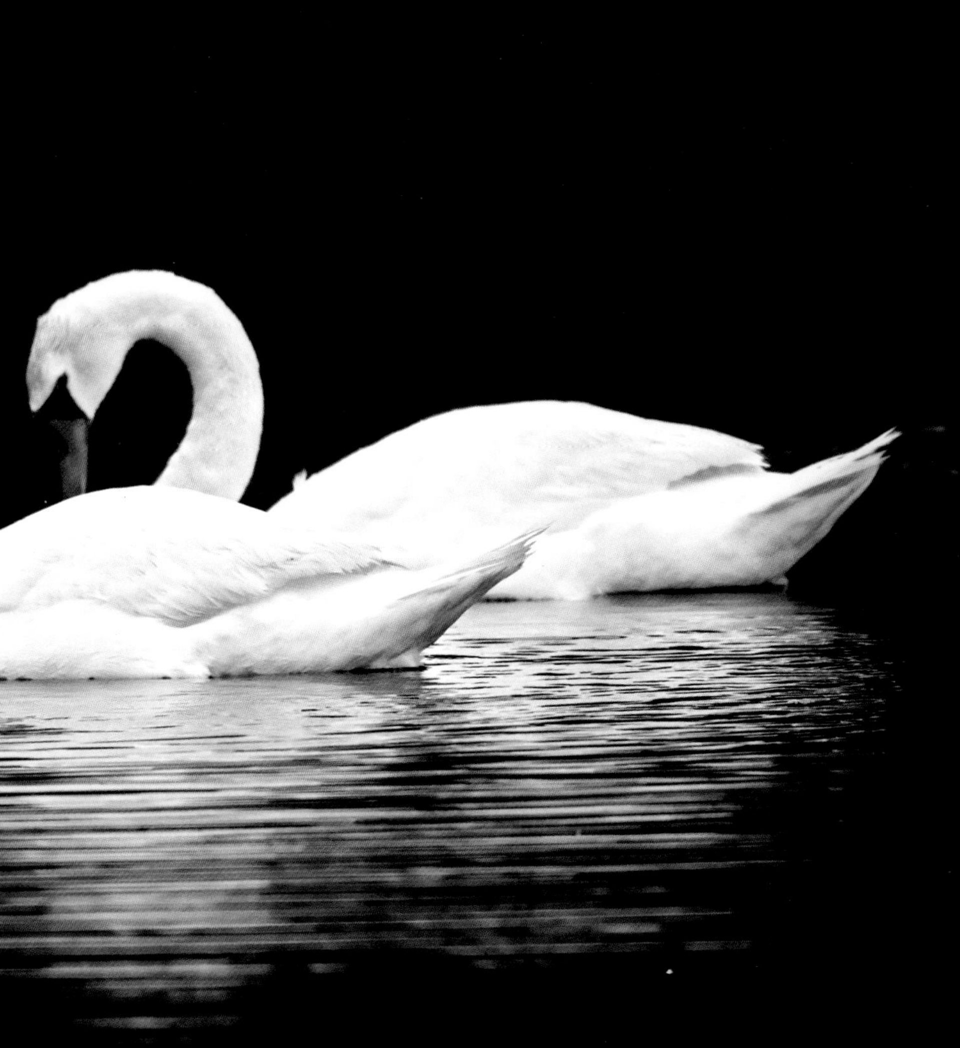

How we spend
our days is, of course,
how we spend our lives.

~ Annie Dillard

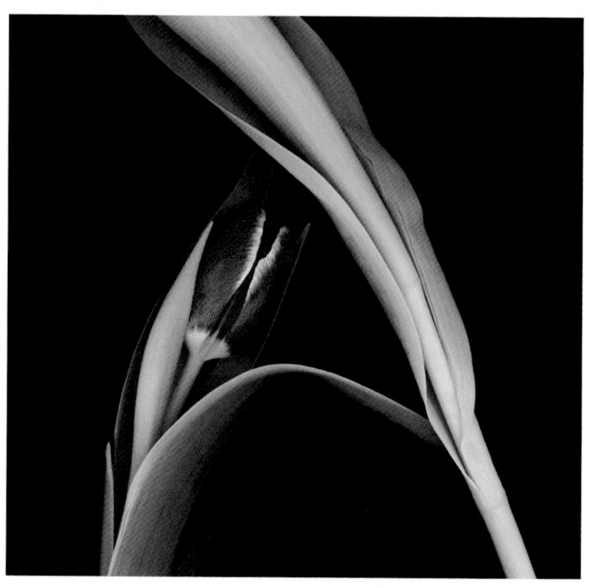

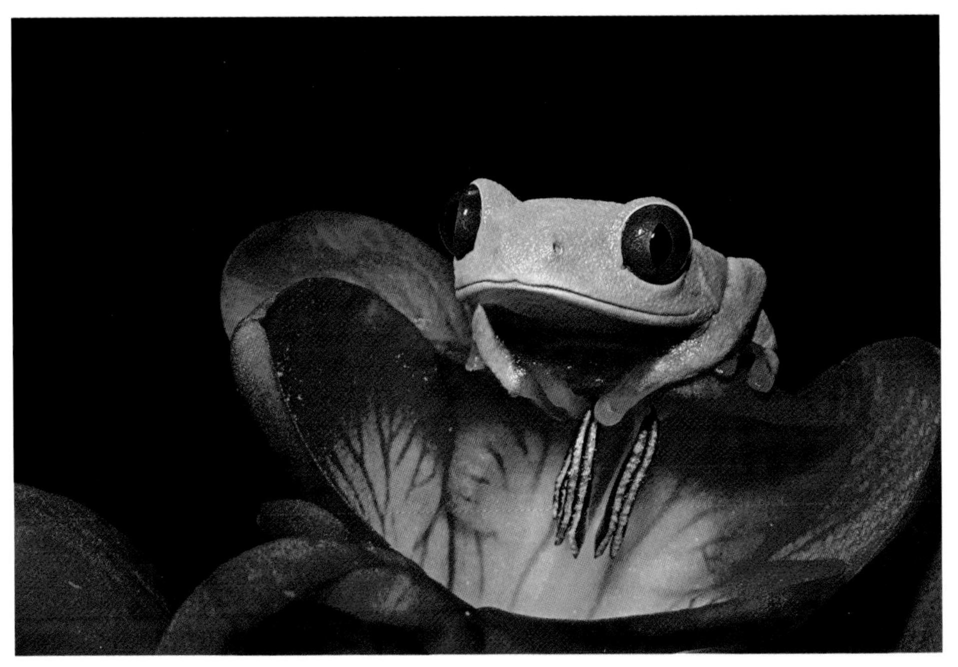

JUNE 17

One's destination
is never a place,
but rather a new way
of looking at things.

~ Henry Miller

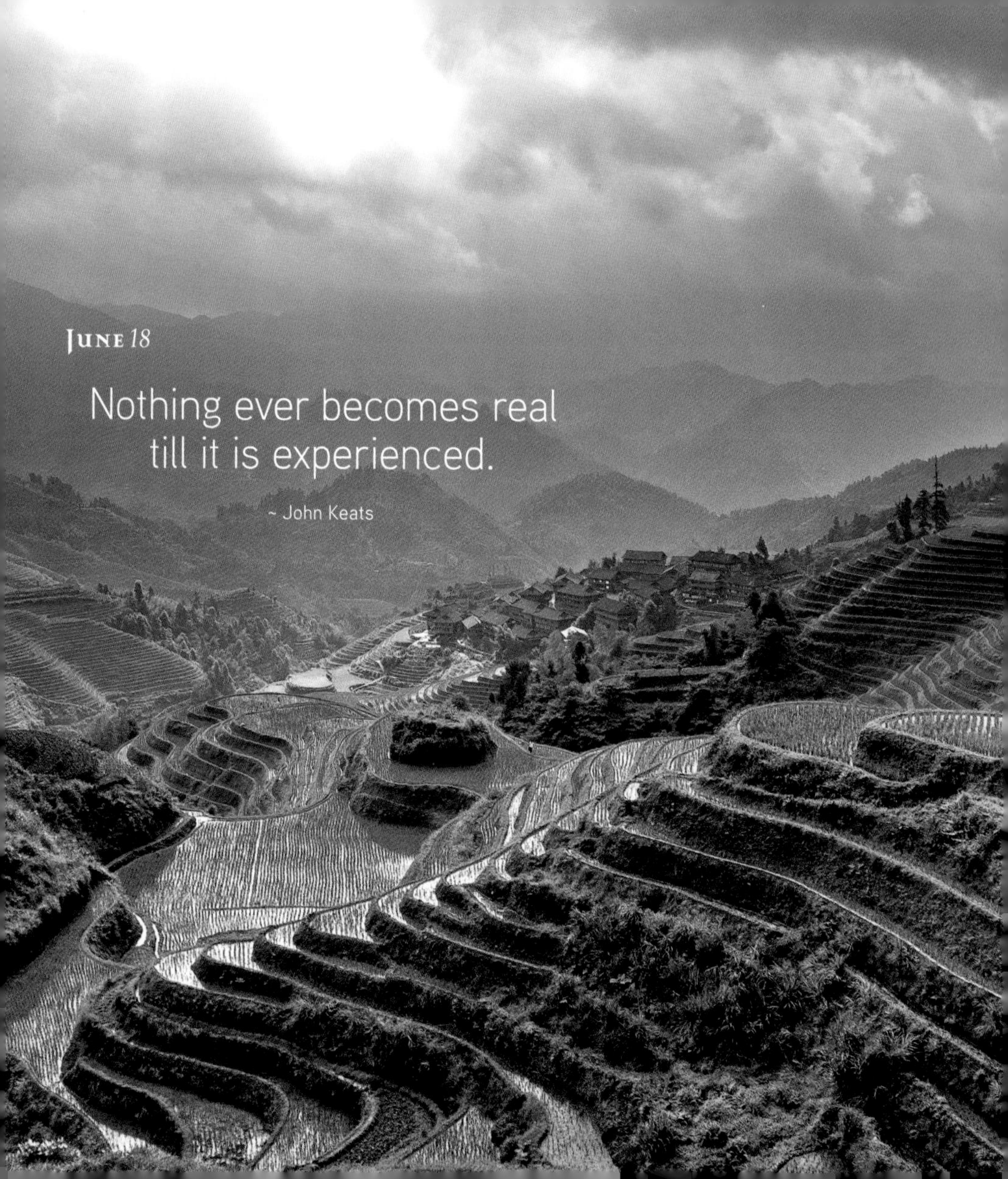
June 18
Nothing ever becomes real
till it is experienced.
~ John Keats

JUNE 19

One of the signs of passing youth
is the birth of a sense of
fellowship with other human beings
as we take our place
among them.

~ Virginia Woolf

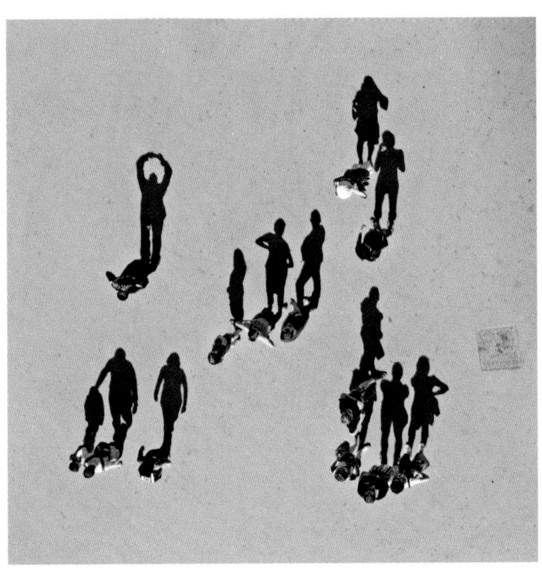

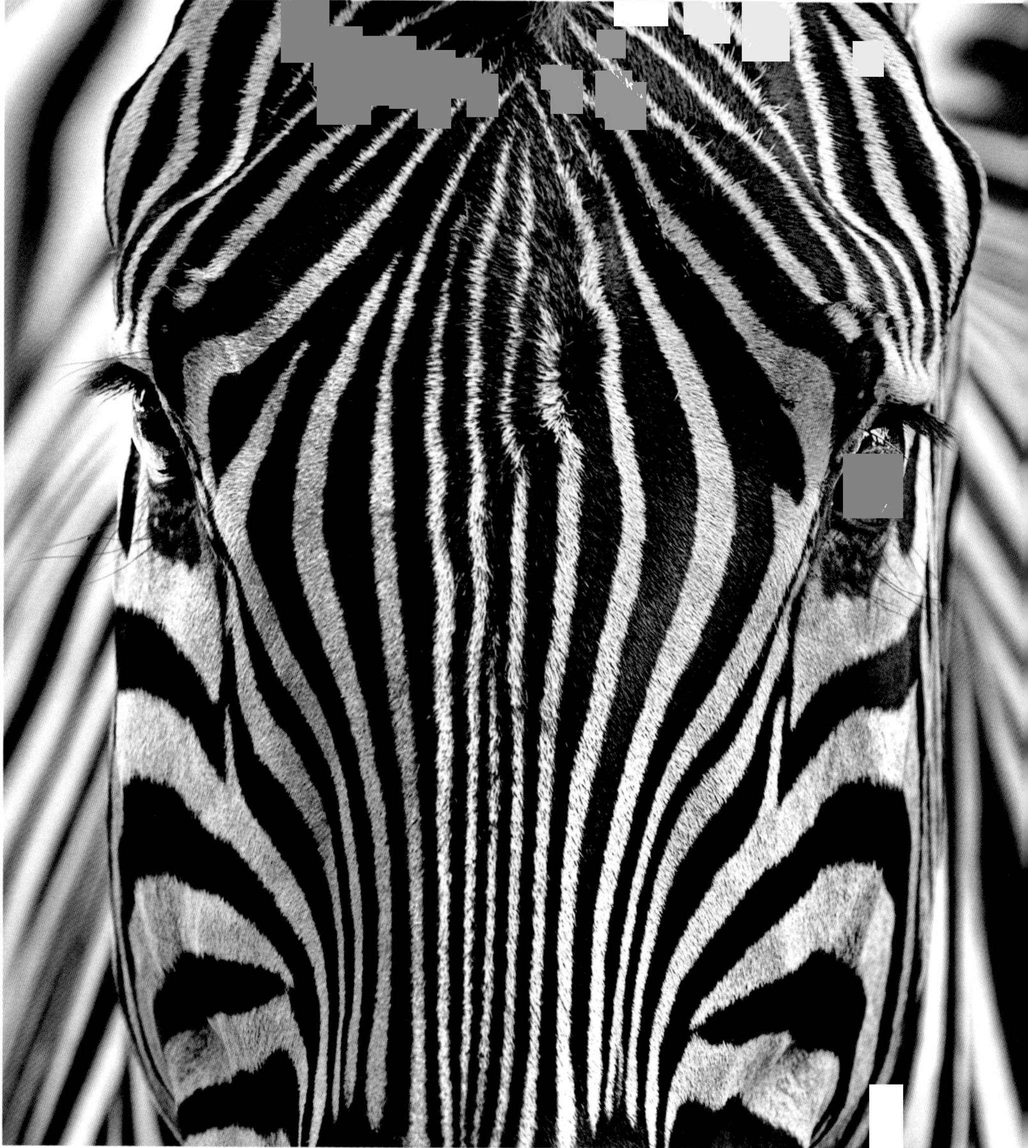

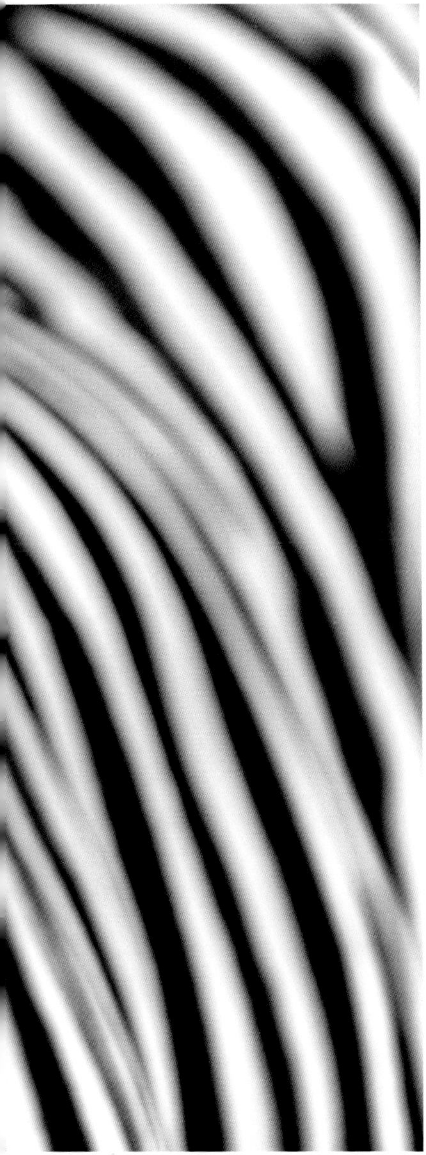

JUNE 20

To see what is
in front of
one's nose needs
a constant struggle.

~ George Orwell

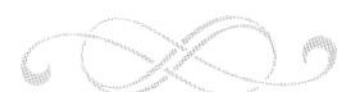

JUNE 21

We always deceive ourselves twice about the people we love—first to their advantage, then to their disadvantage.

~ Albert Camus

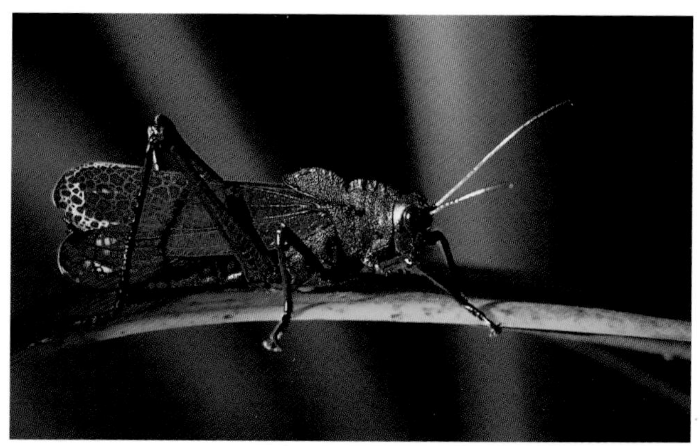

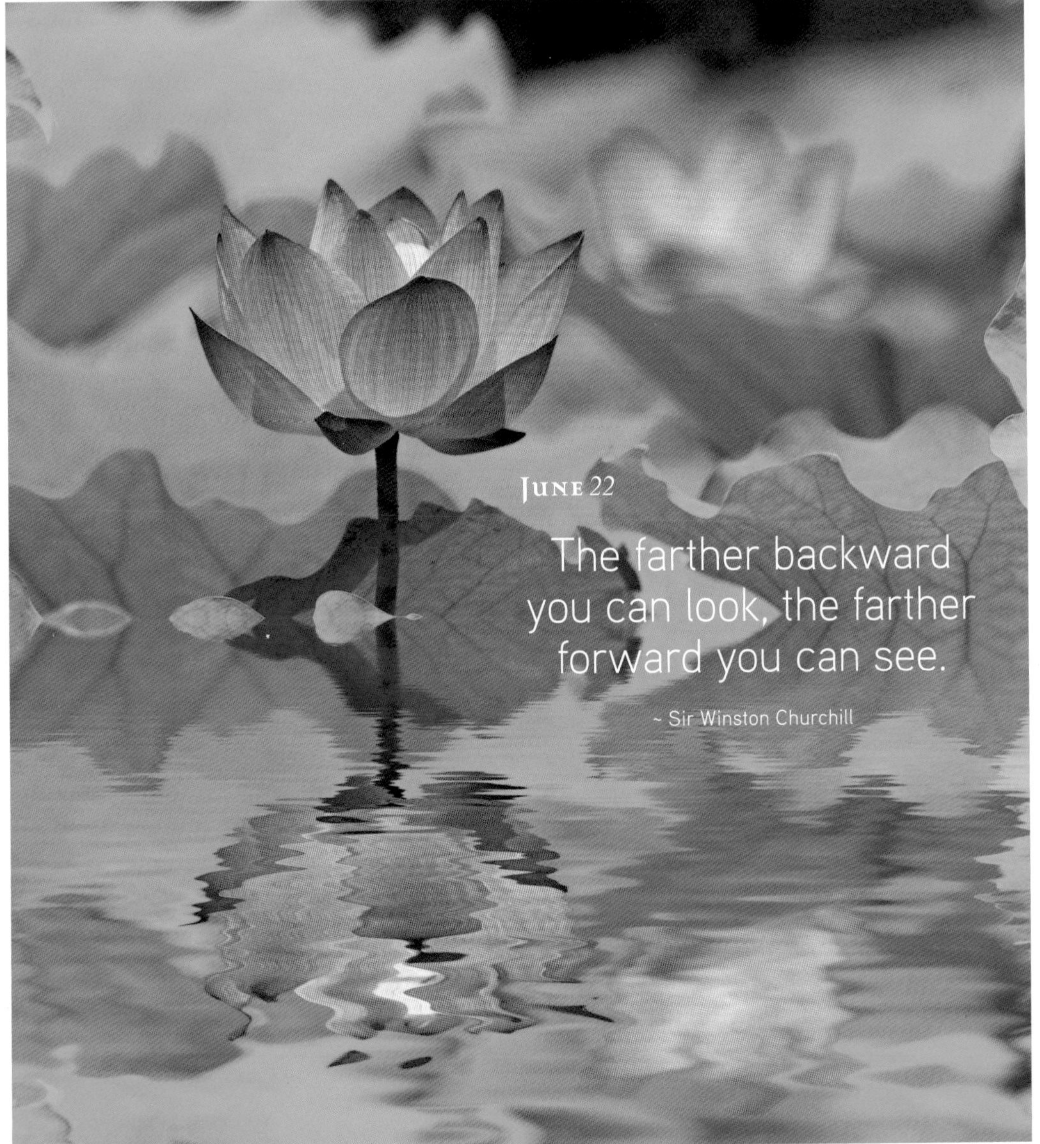
June 22
The farther backward
you can look, the farther
forward you can see.
~ Sir Winston Churchill

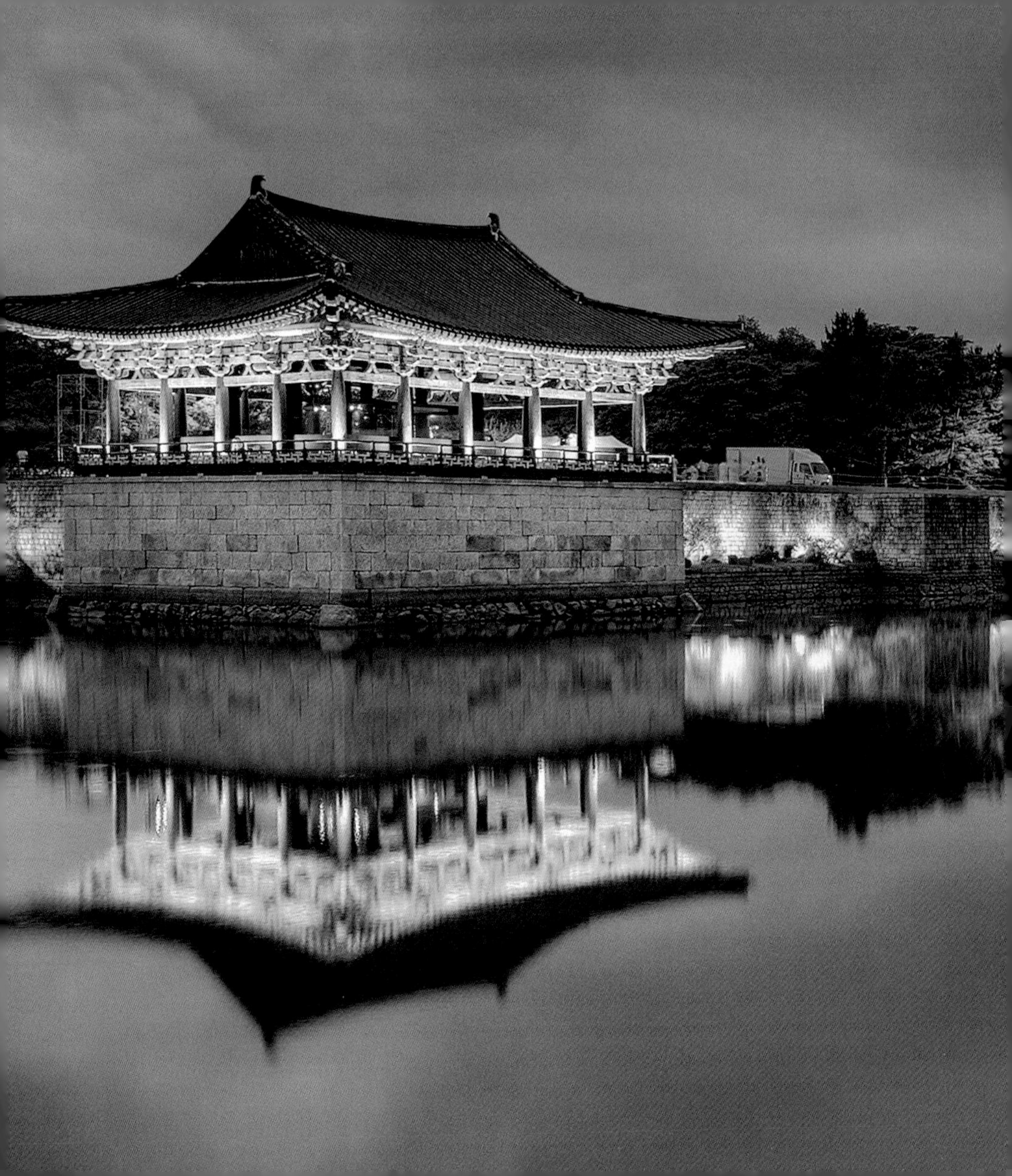

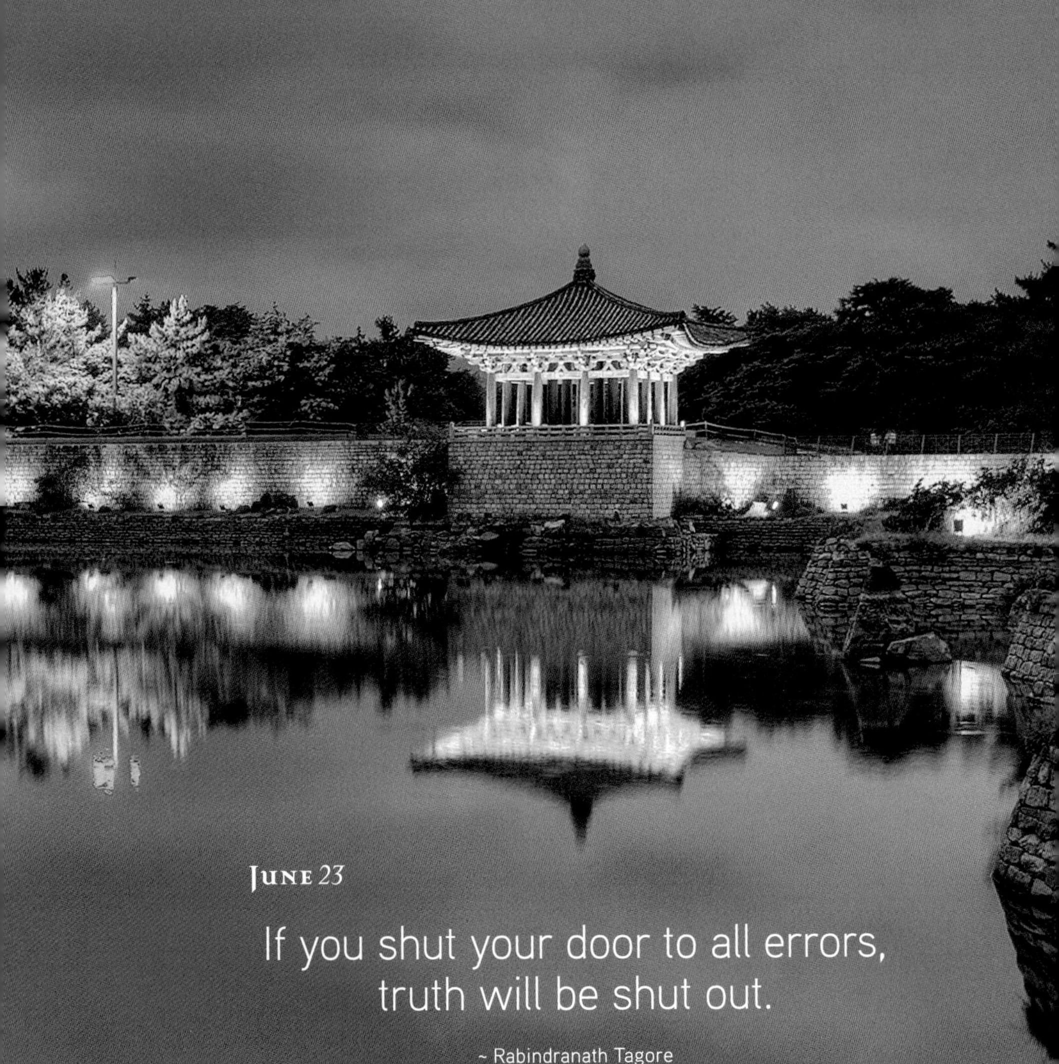

June *23*

If you shut your door to all errors,
truth will be shut out.

~ Rabindranath Tagore

June 24

It does not do
to dwell on dreams
and forget to live.

~ J. K. Rowling

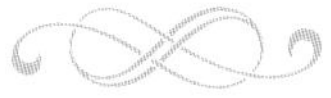

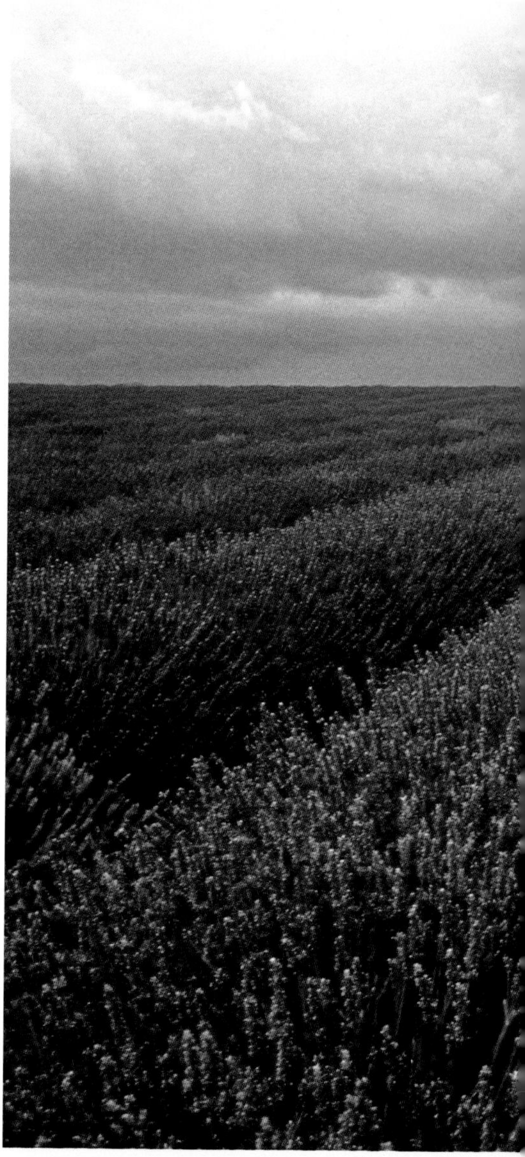

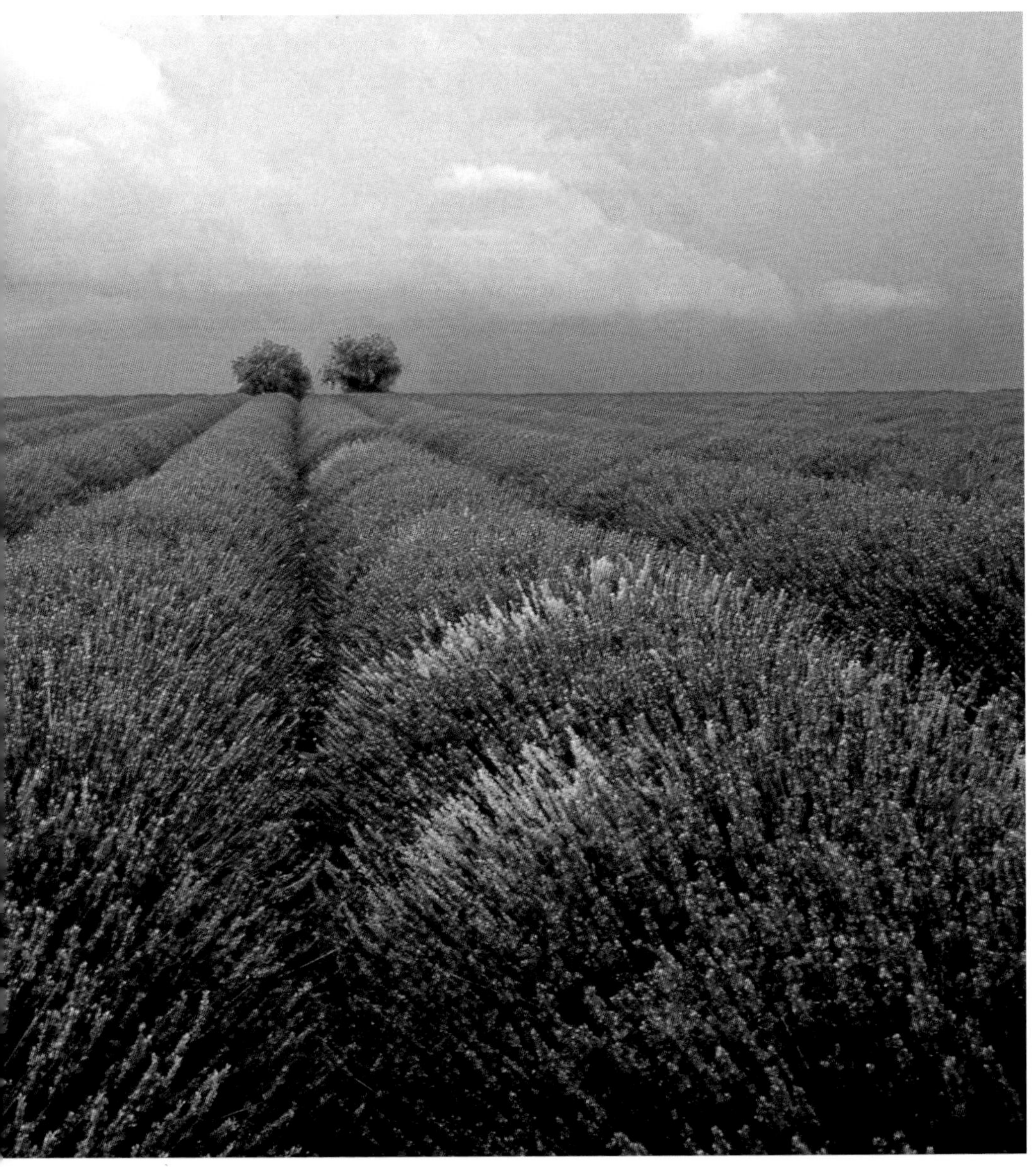

JUNE 25

Distance has the same effect on the mind as on the eye.

~ Samuel Johnson

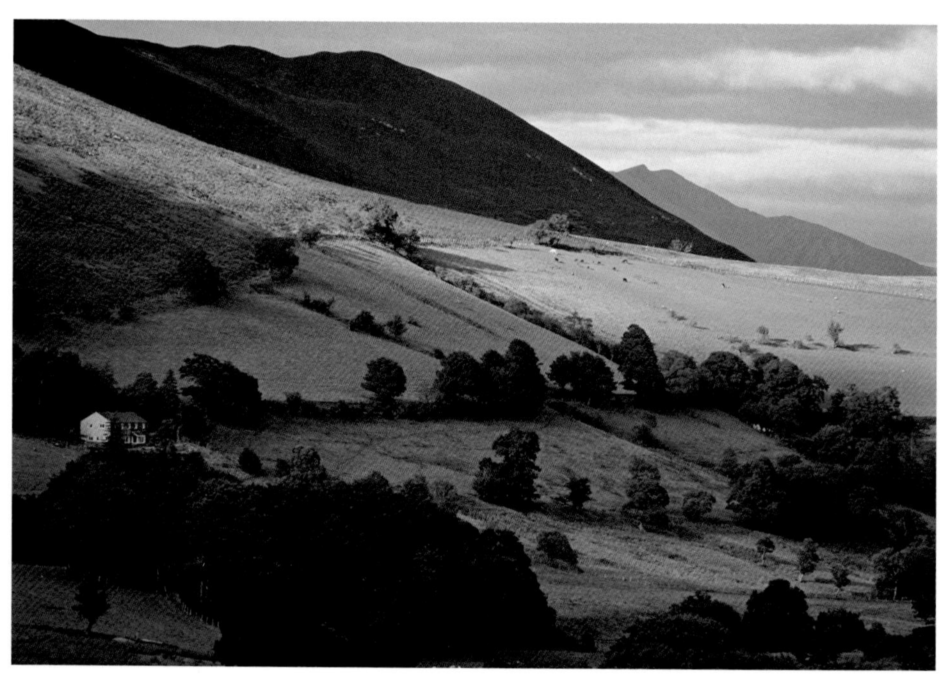

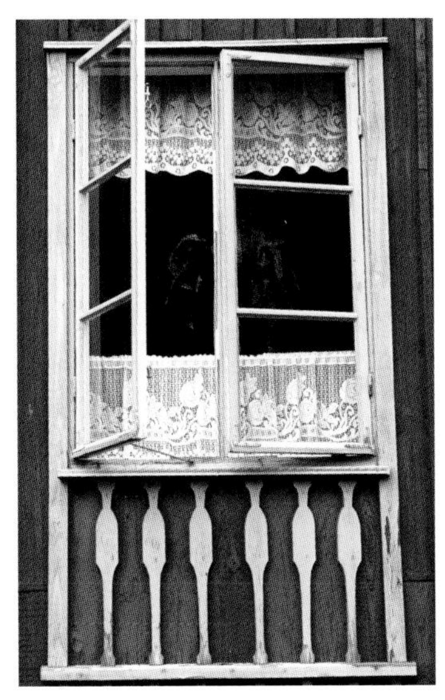

JUNE 26

We can always choose
to perceive things differently.
You can focus on
what's wrong in your life,
or you can focus on
what's right.

~ Marianne Williamson

June *27*

To make the best use of what is in your power, take the rest as it happens.

~ Epictetus

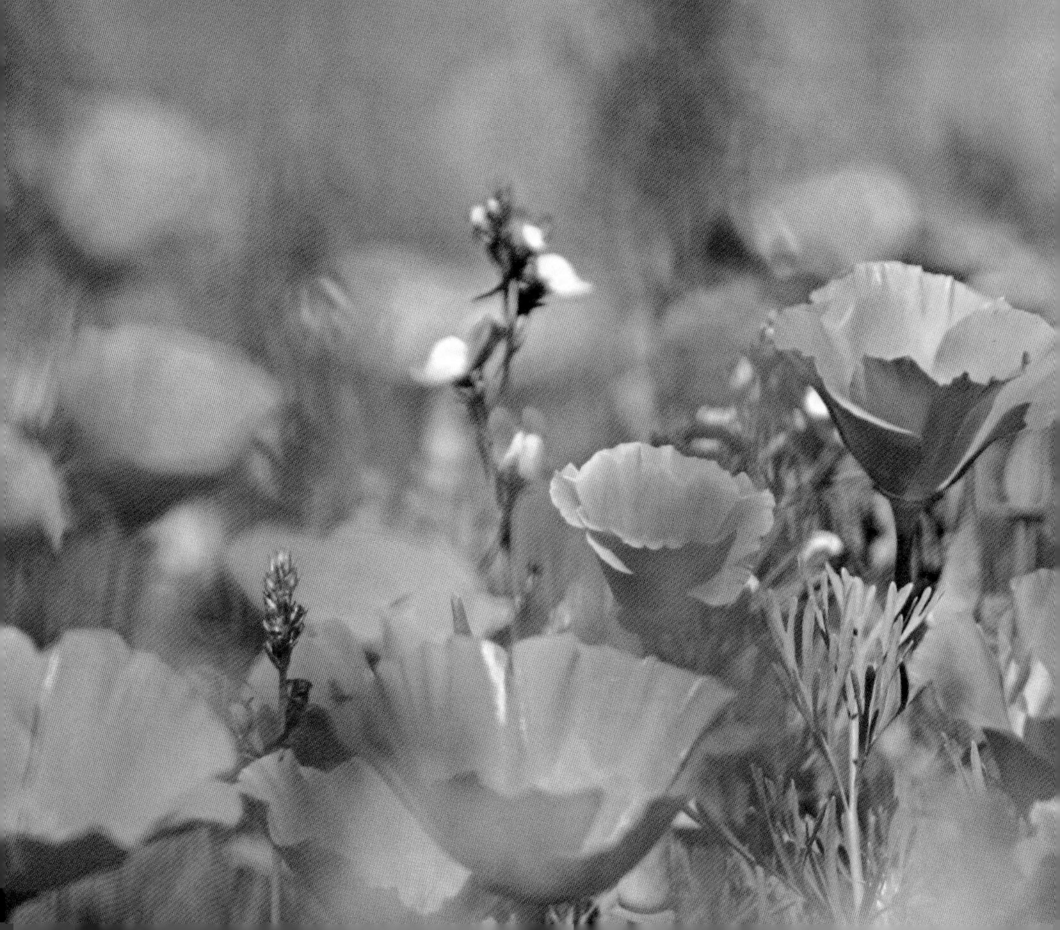

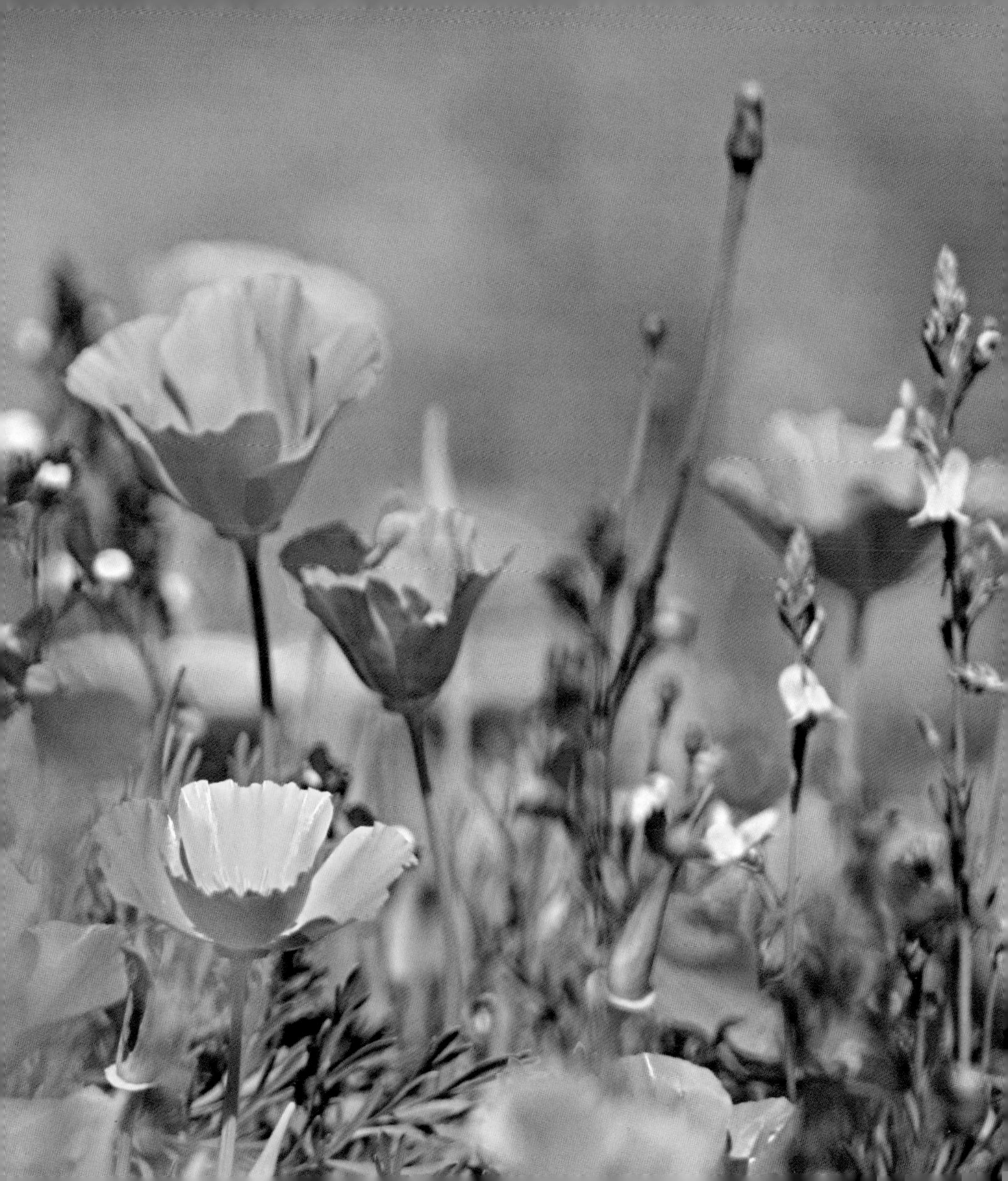

JUNE 28

Happiness is largely
an attitude of mind, of viewing life
from the right angle.

~ Dale Carnegie

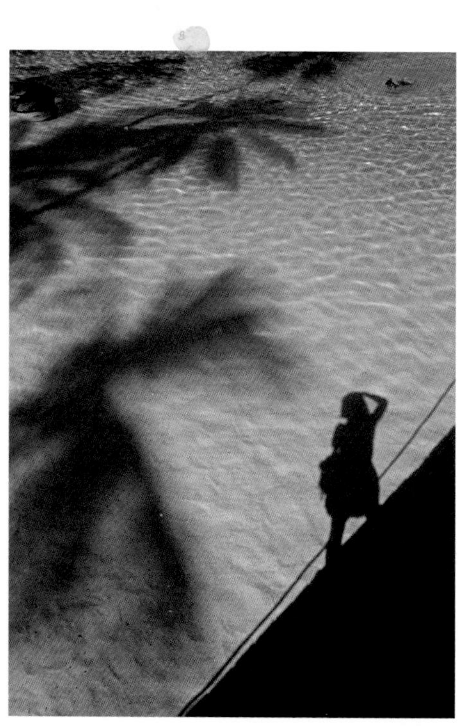

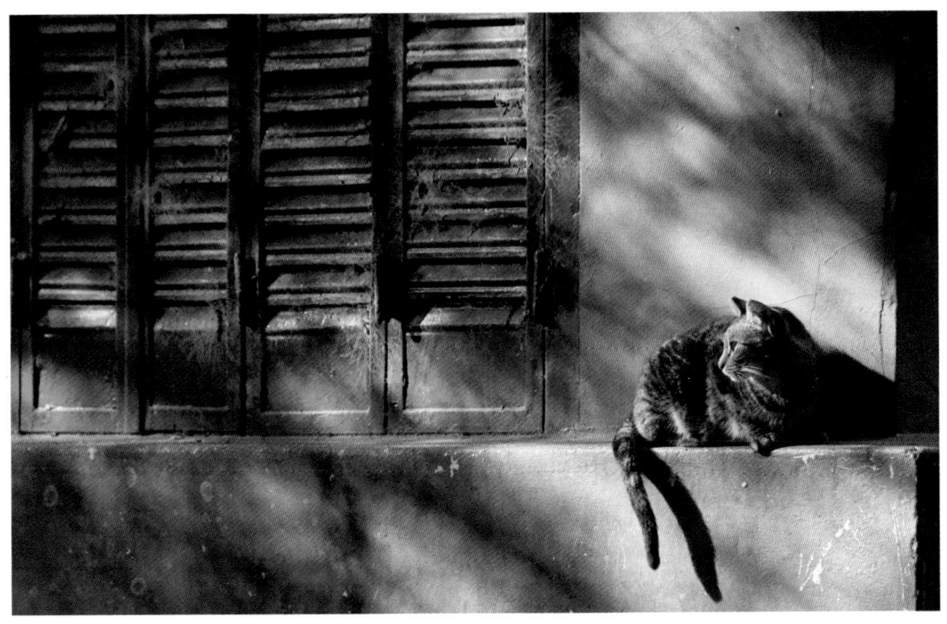

JUNE 29

To be able to look back upon
one's life in satisfaction
is to live twice.

~ Kahlil Gibran

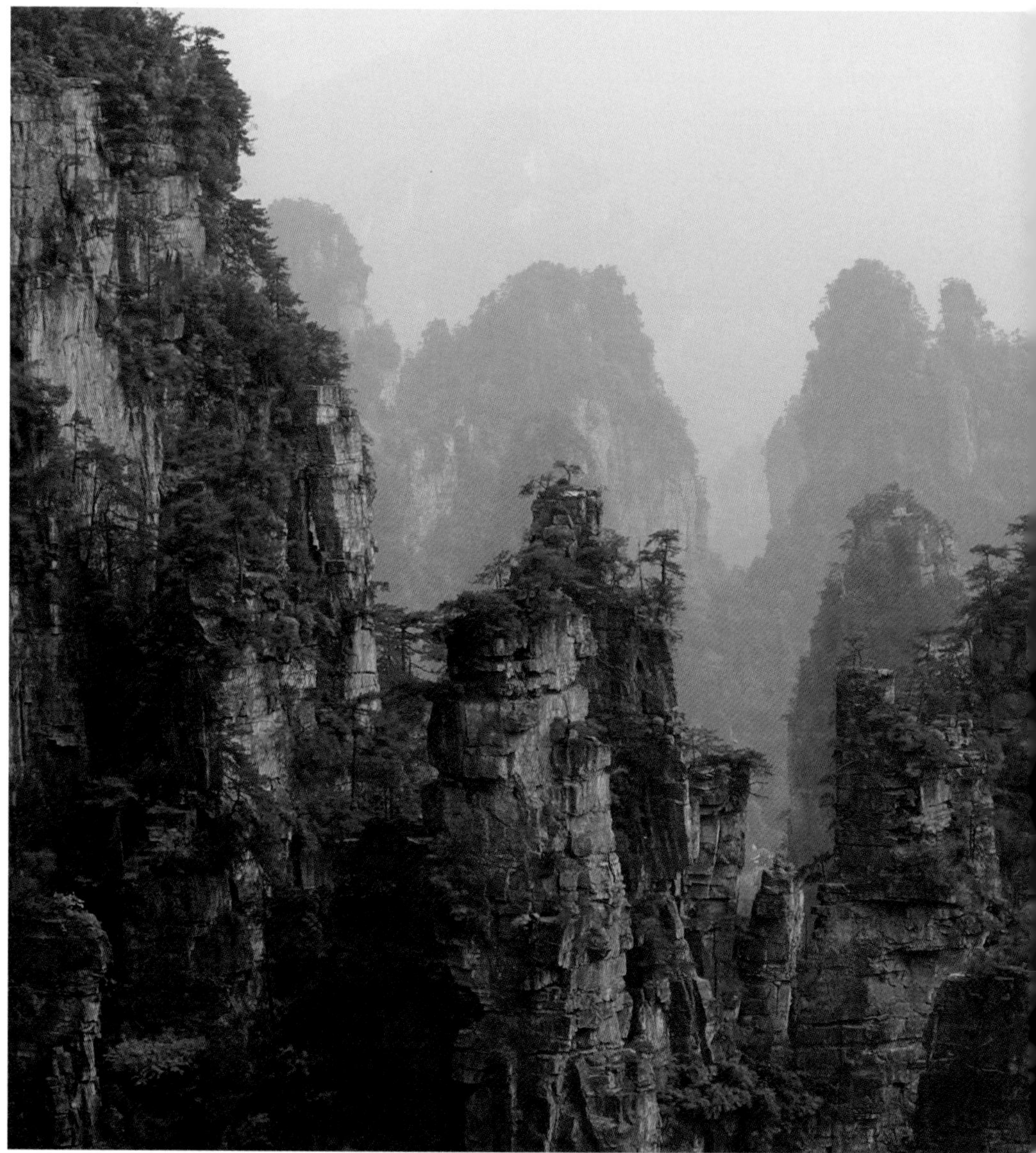

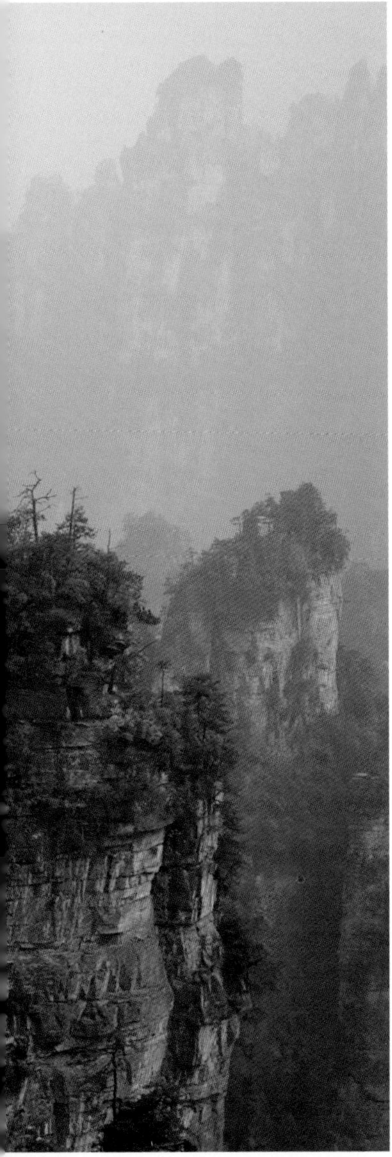

June 30

The years teach much which the days never knew.

~ Ralph Waldo Emerson

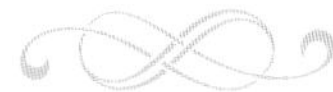

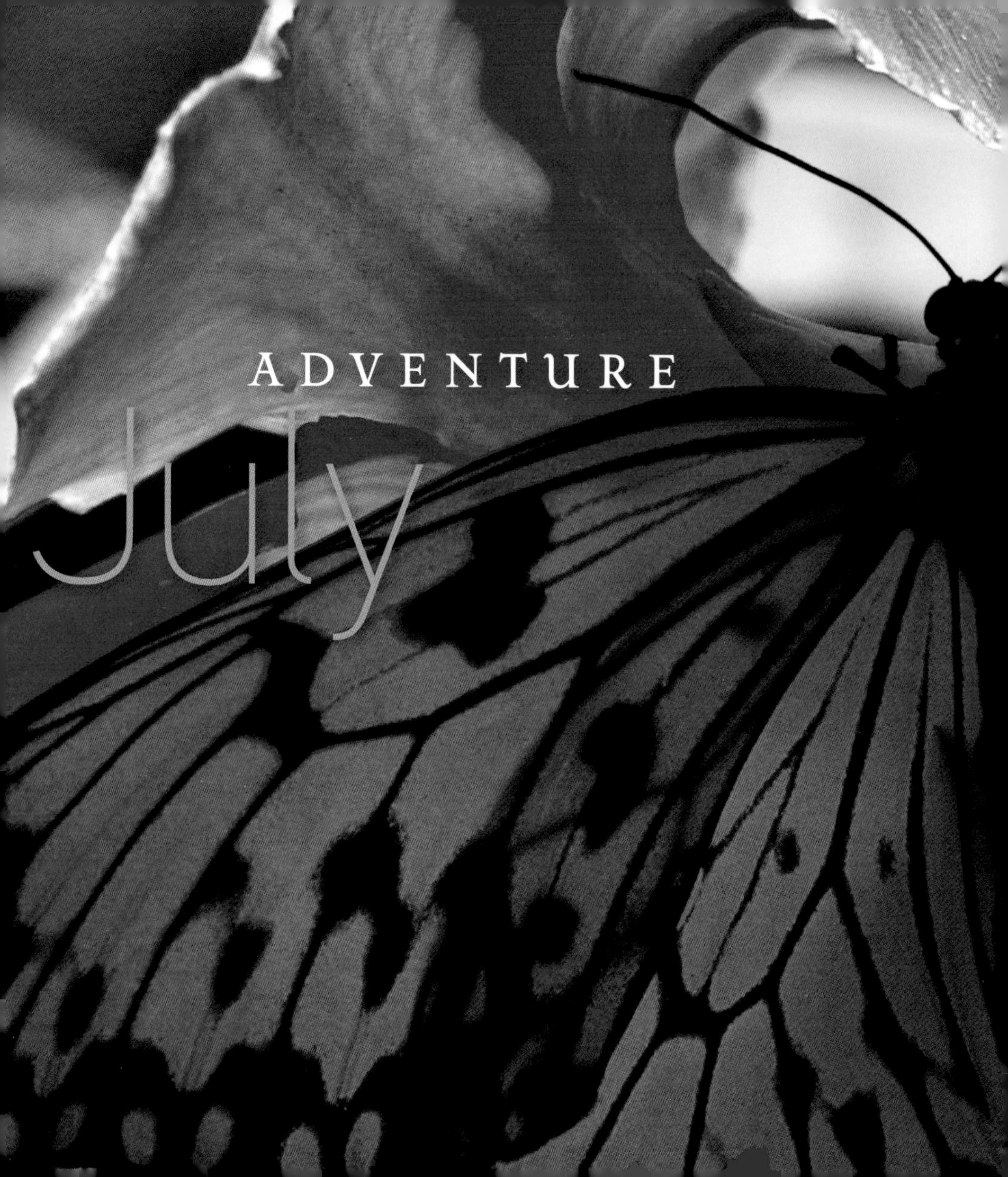

ADVENTURE

July

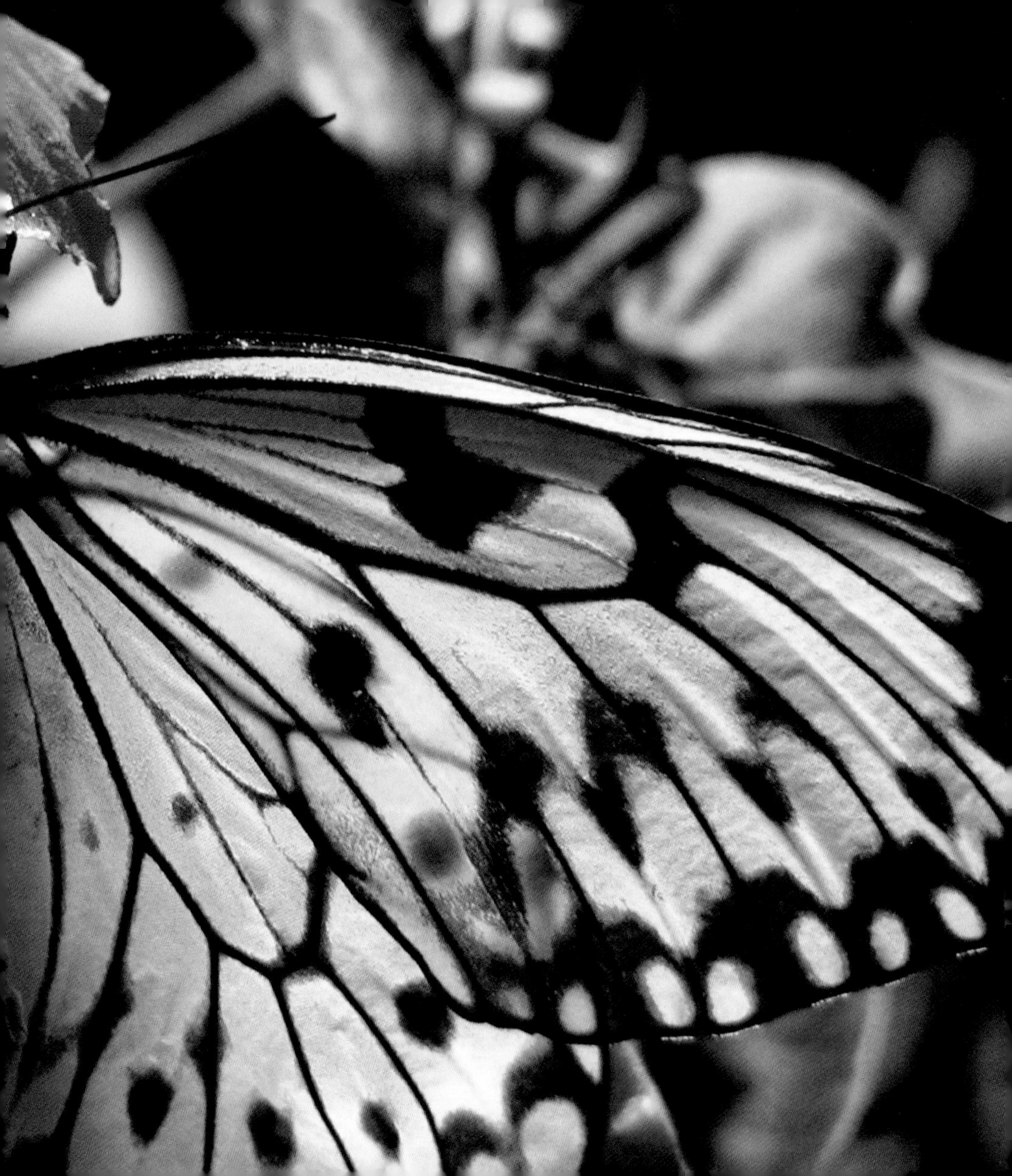

July 1

It is good to love the unknown.

~ Charles Lamb

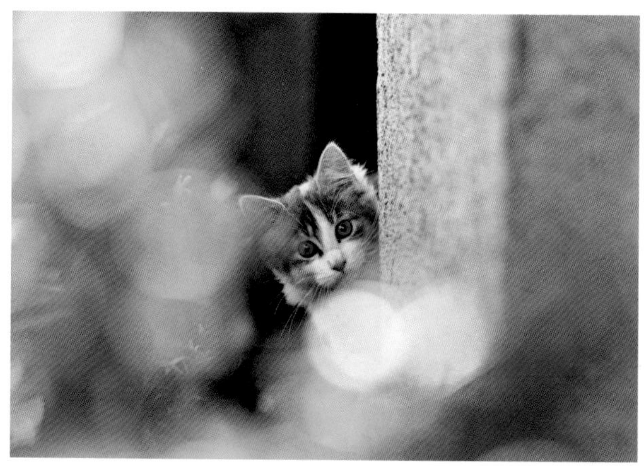

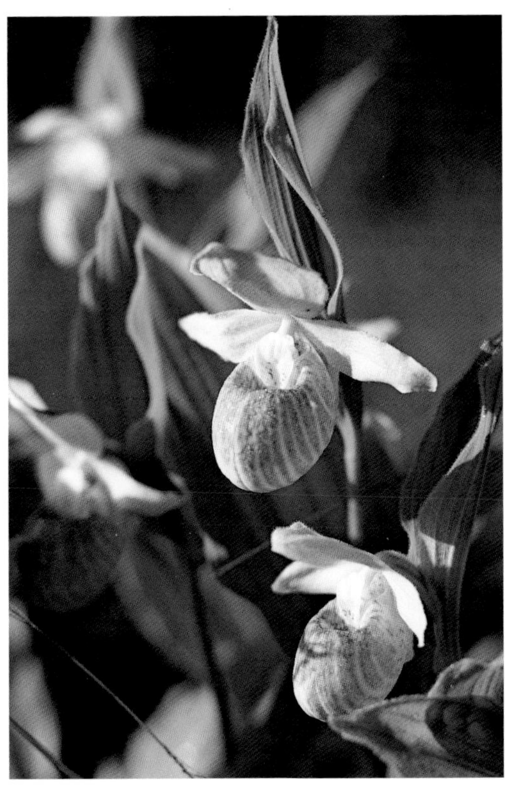

JULY 2

Life was not meant to be easy,
but take courage: it can be delightful.

~ George Bernard Shaw

July 3

If you wait for
the perfect moment
when all is safe
and assured,
it may never arrive.
Mountains will not
be climbed,
races won,
or lasting happiness
achieved.

~ Maurice Chevalier

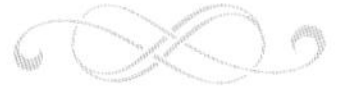

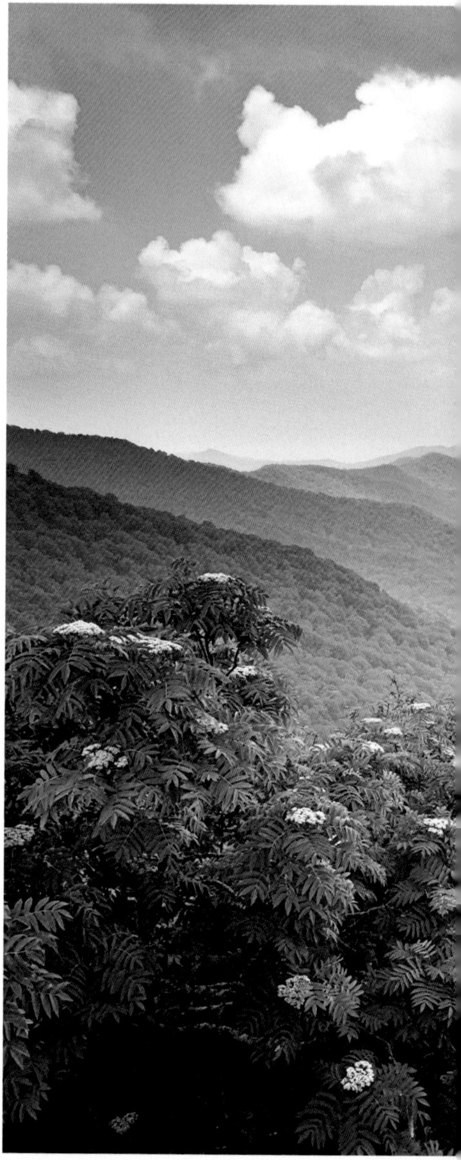

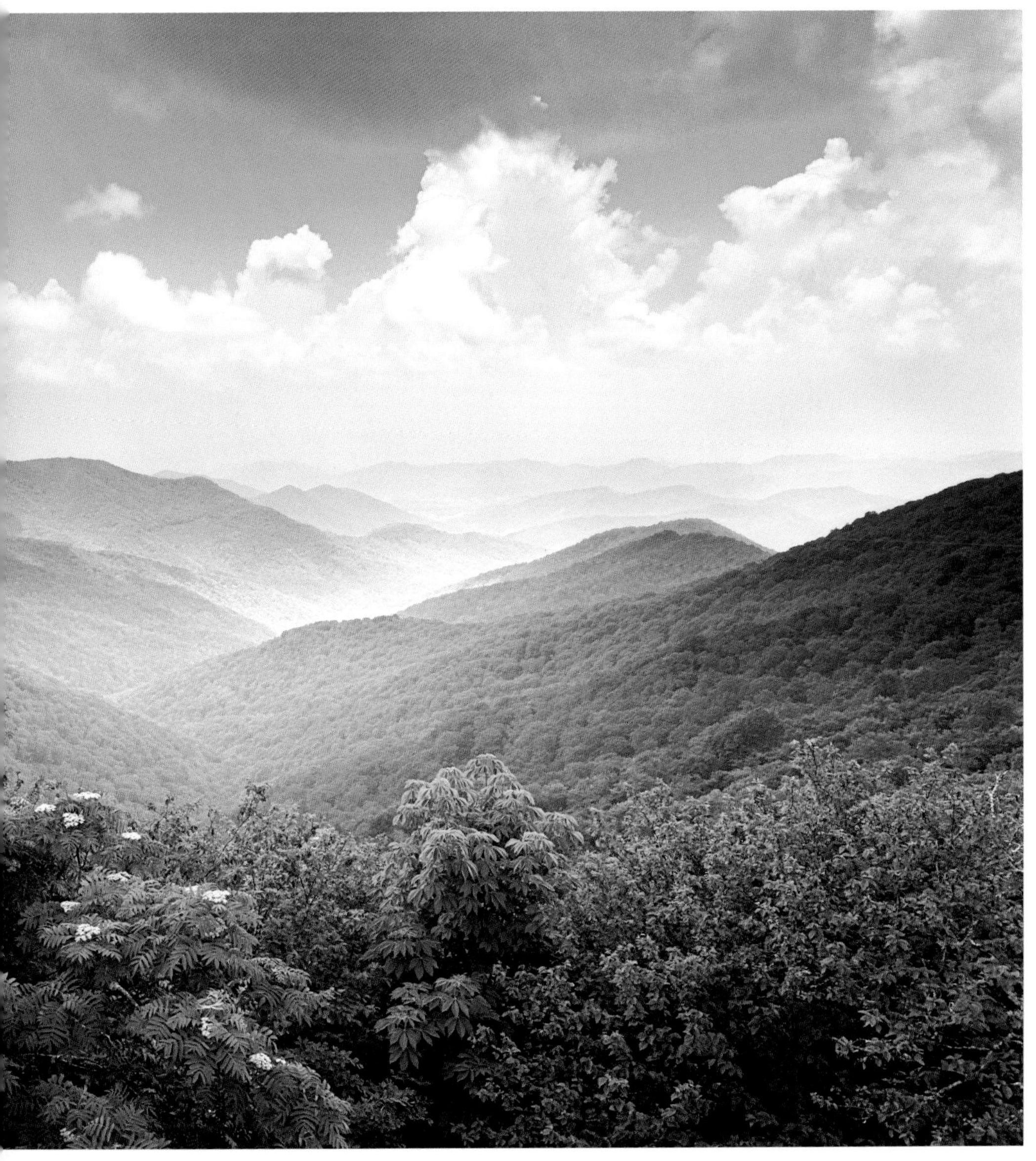

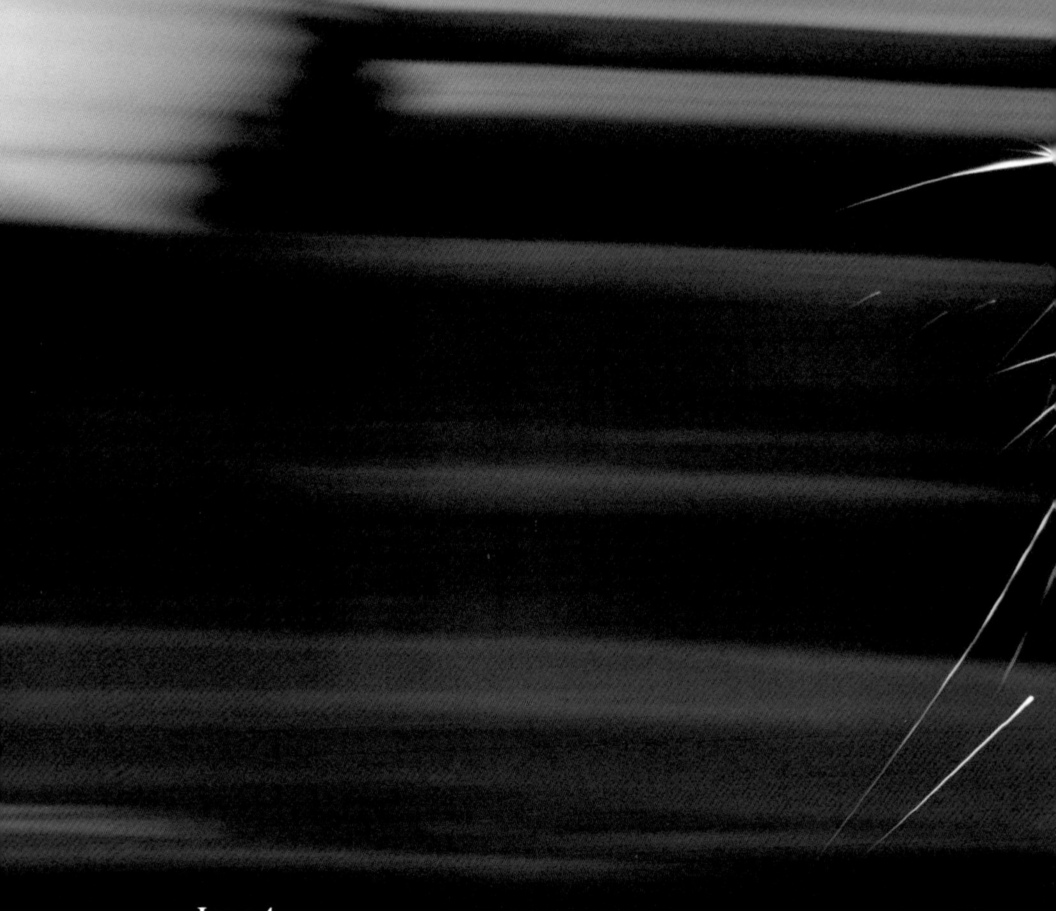

July 4

What we play is life.

~ Louis Armstrong

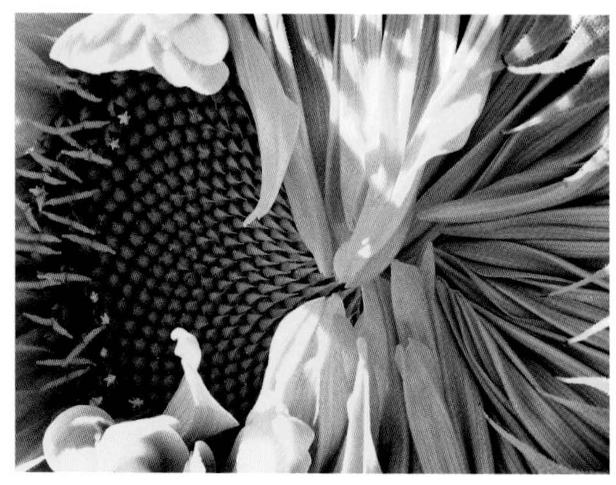

July 5

Pleasure is very seldom found
where it is sought.
Our brightest blazes
are commonly kindled by
unexpected sparks.

~ Samuel Johnson

JULY 6

Make voyages! Attempt them!
There is nothing else.

~ Tennessee Williams

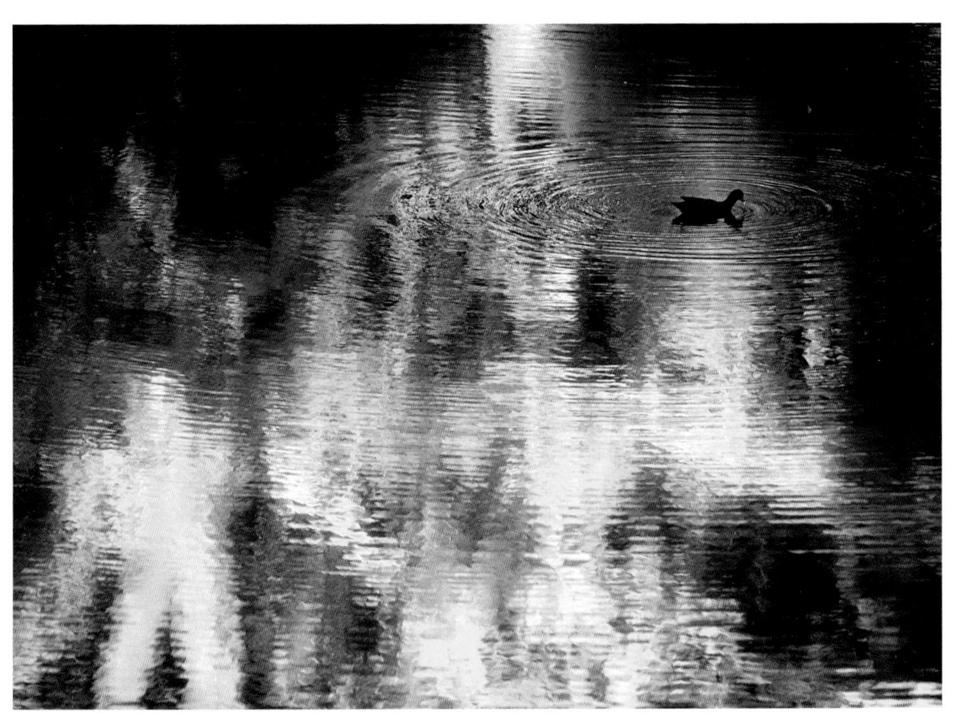

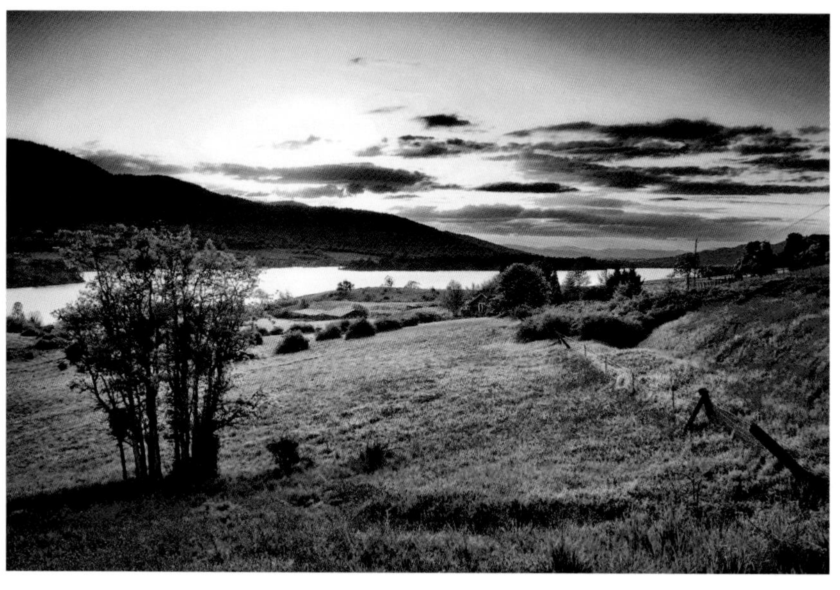

July 7

Today a new sun rises for me;
everything lives,
everything is animated,
everything seems to speak to me
of my passion,
everything invites me to cherish it.

~ Ninon de Lenclos

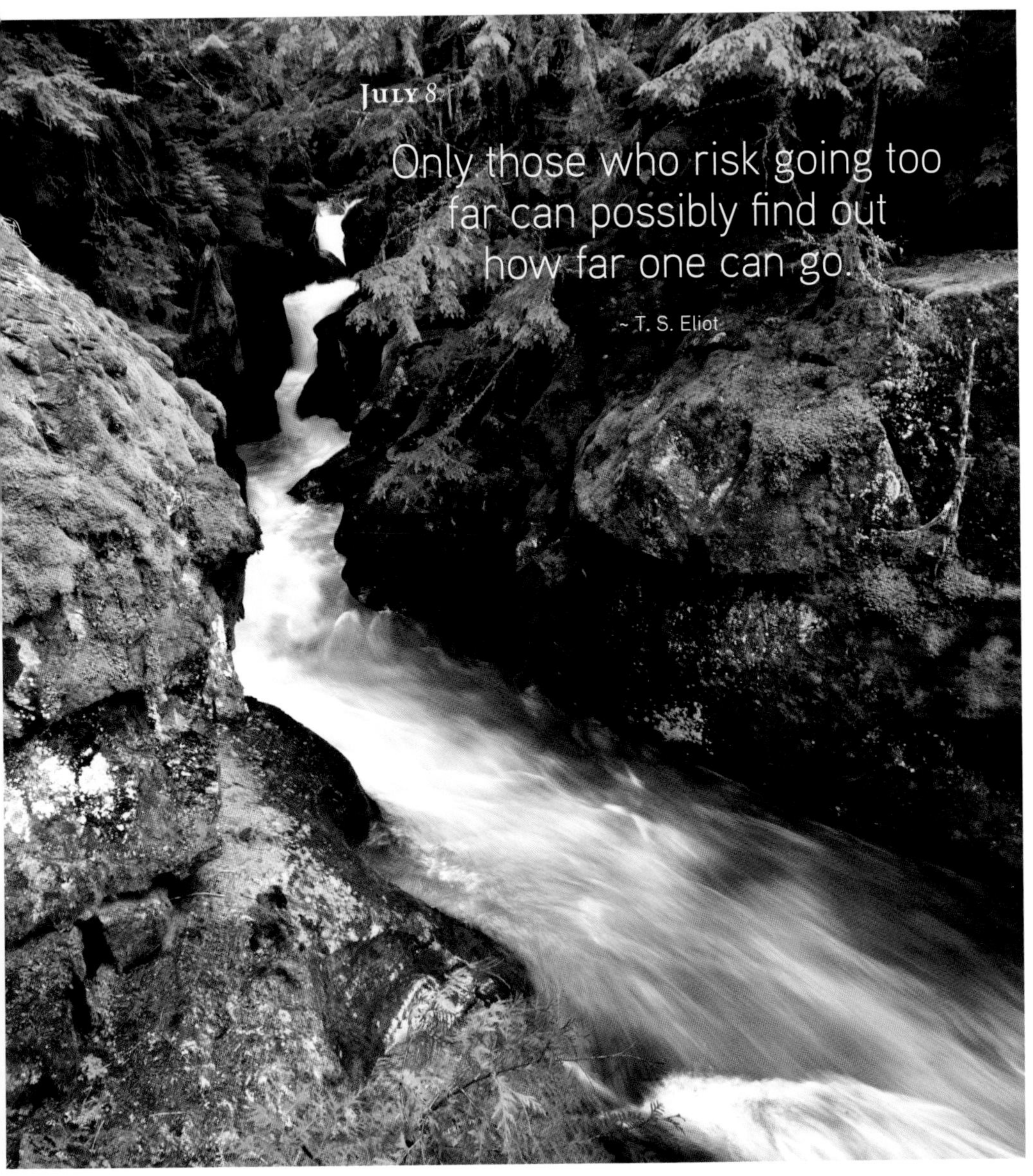

JULY 8

Only those who risk going too far can possibly find out how far one can go.

~ T. S. Eliot

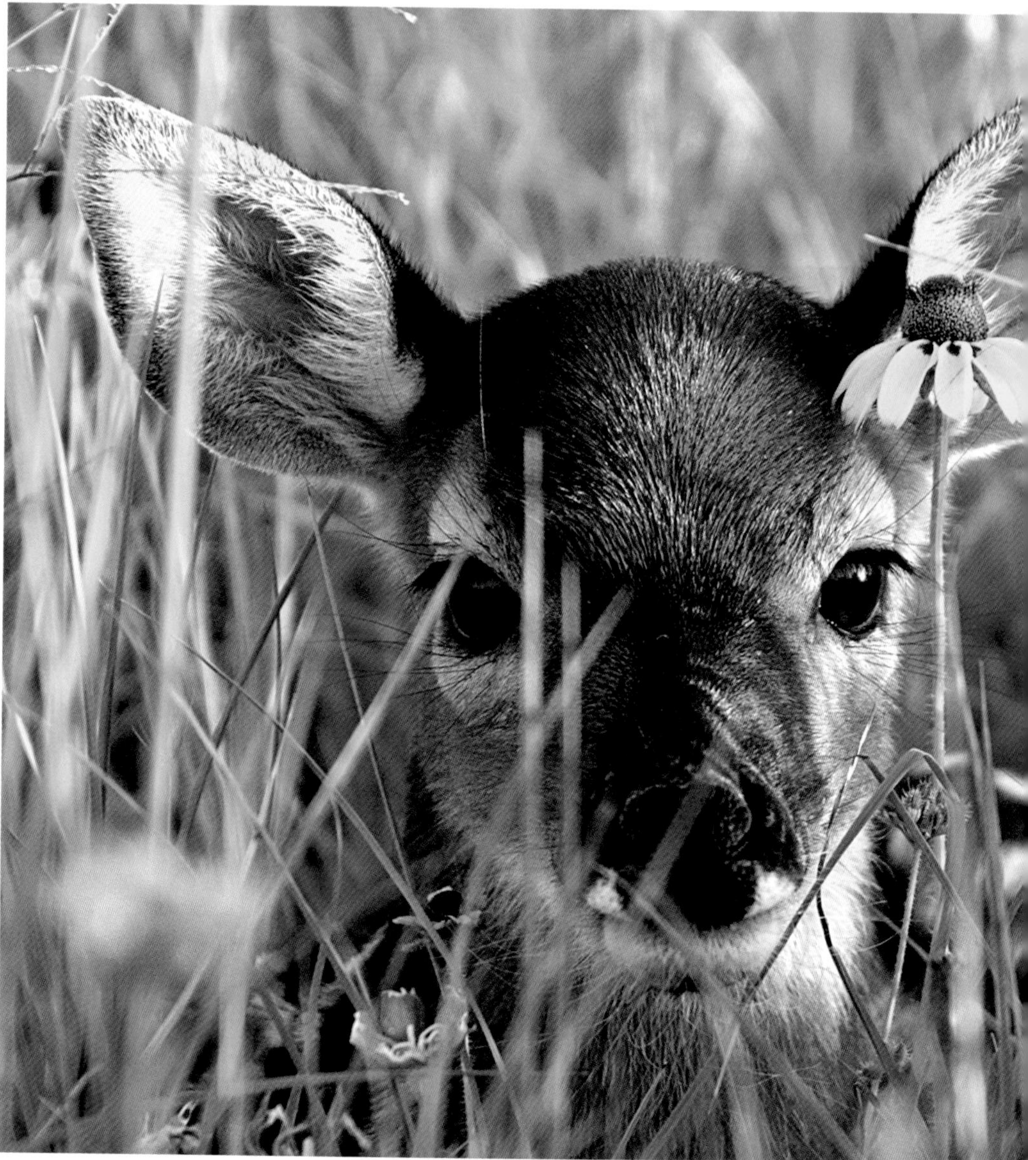

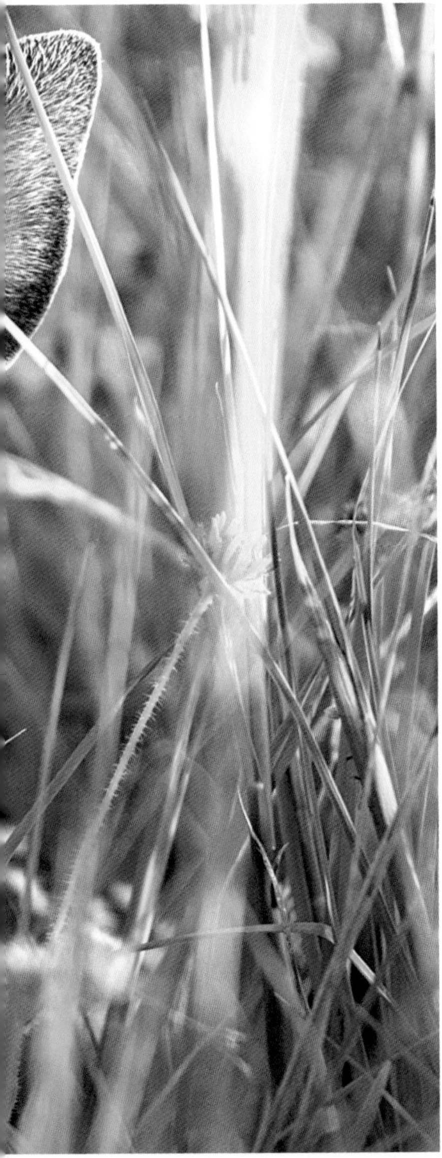

July 9

The young
do not know enough
to be prudent and
therefore they
attempt
the impossible—
and achieve it,
generation after
generation.

~ Pearl S. Buck

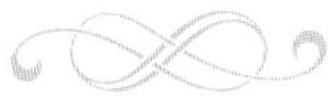

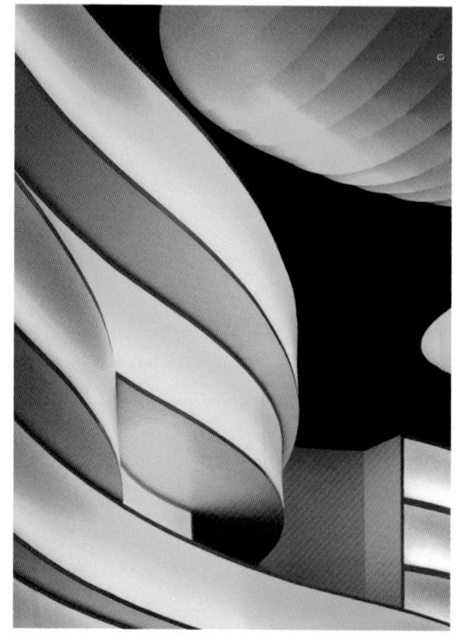

JULY 10

All life is an experiment.
The more experiments you make,
the better.

~ Ralph Waldo Emerson

Remembering that you are going to die
is the best way I know to avoid the trap
of thinking you have something to lose.
You are already naked.
There is no reason not to follow your heart.

~ Steve Jobs

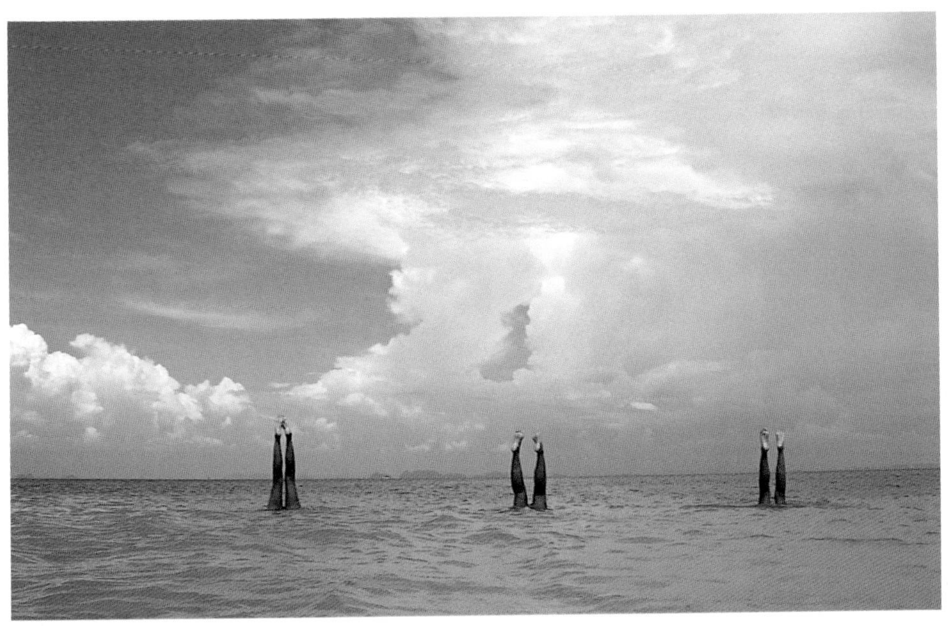

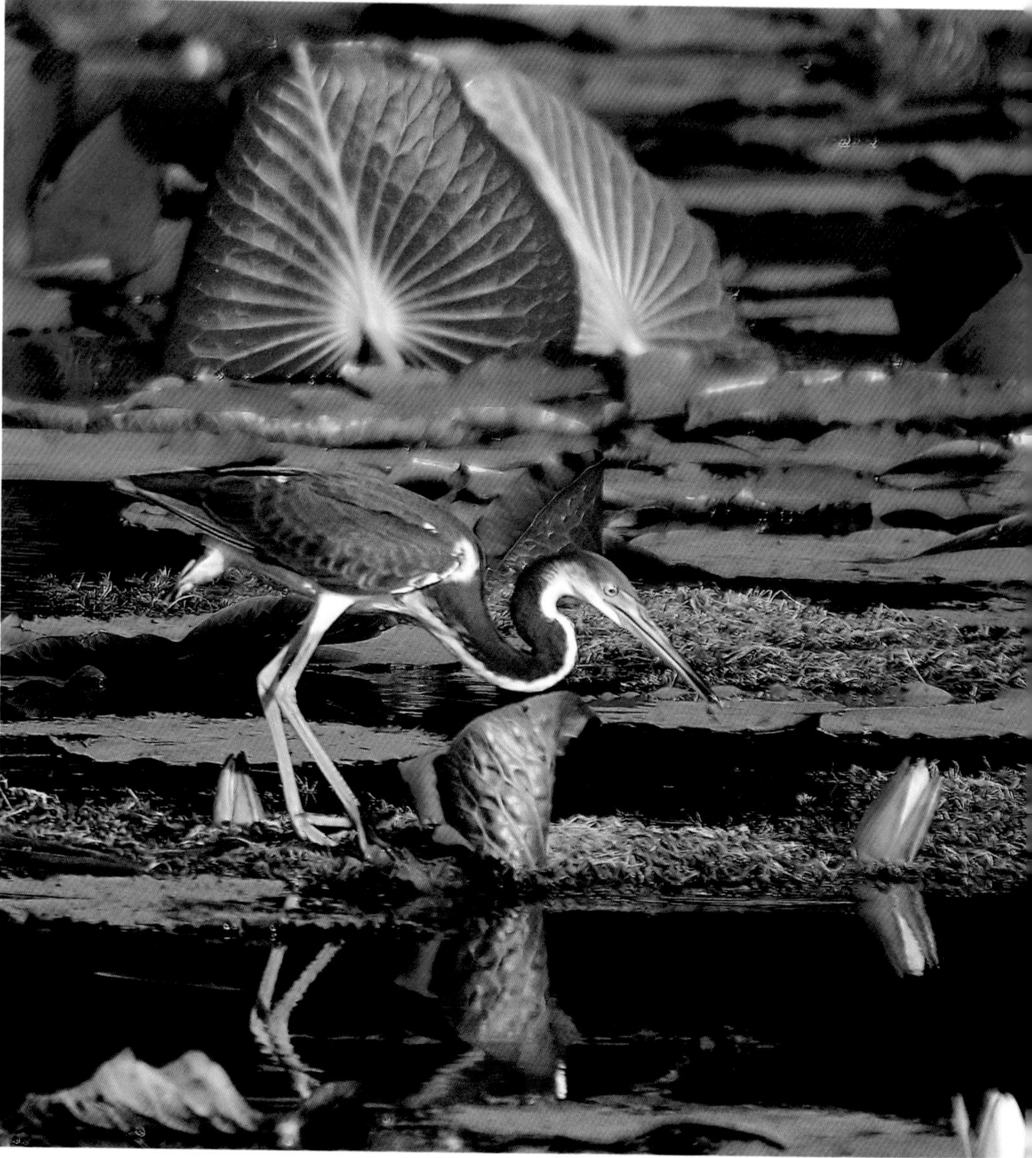

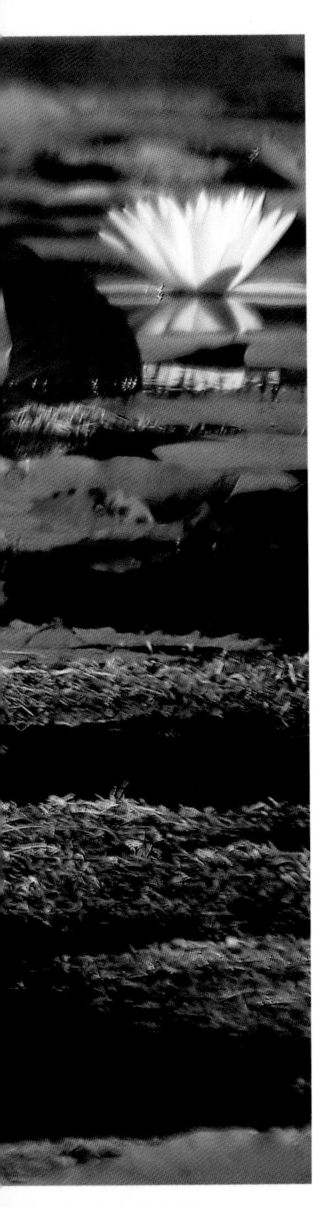

JULY 12

Adventure
is worthwhile in itself.

~ Amelia Earhart

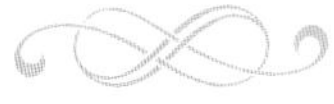

JULY 13

Life was meant to be lived,
and curiosity must be kept alive.
One must never, for whatever reason,
turn his back on life.

~ Eleanor Roosevelt

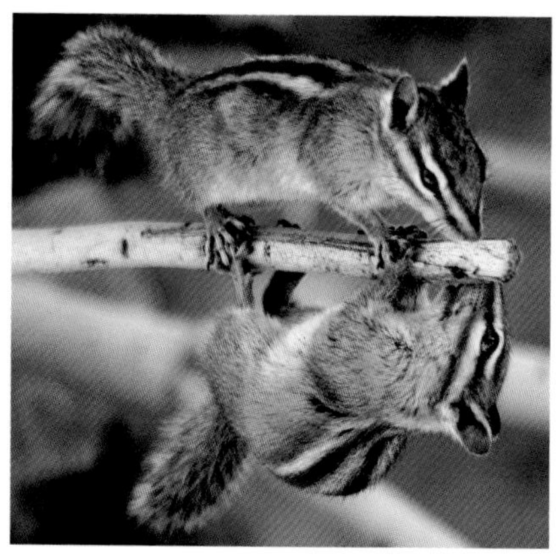

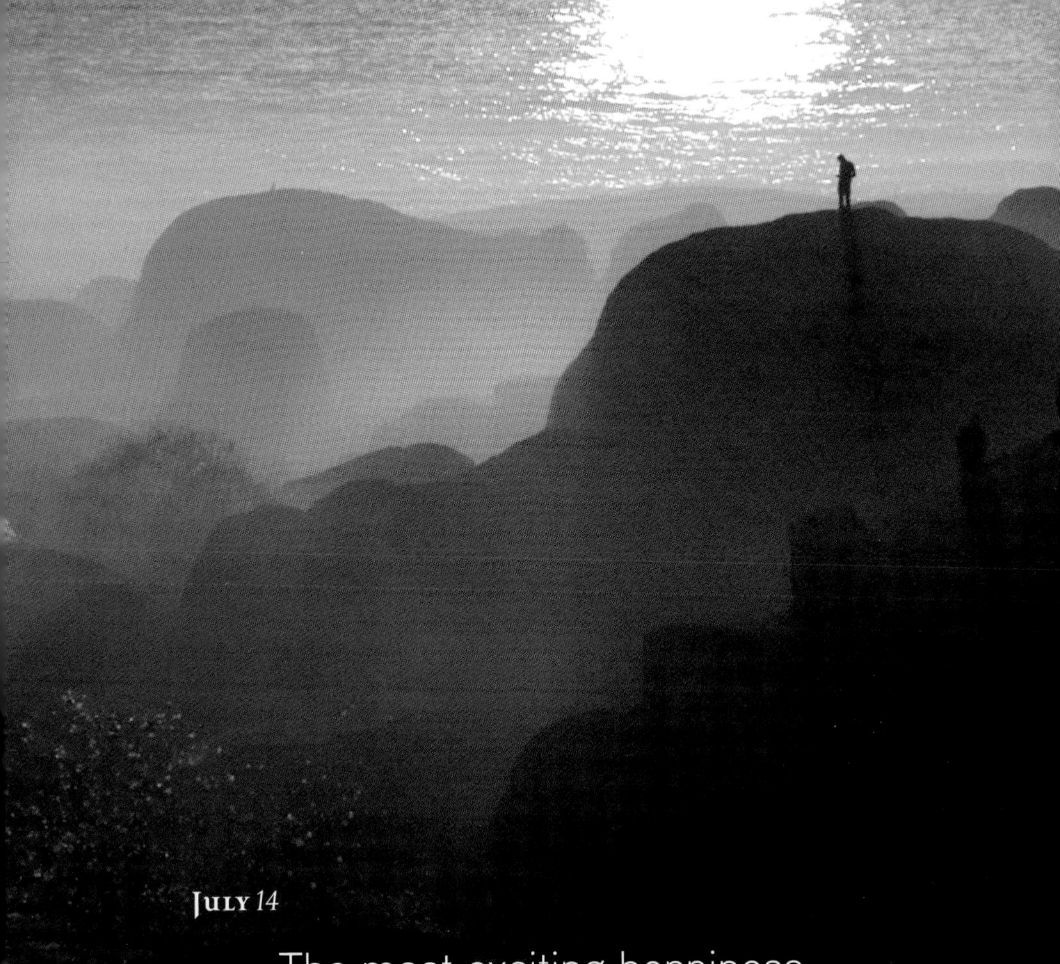

JULY 14

The most exciting happiness
is happiness generated by forces
beyond your control.

~ Ogden Nash

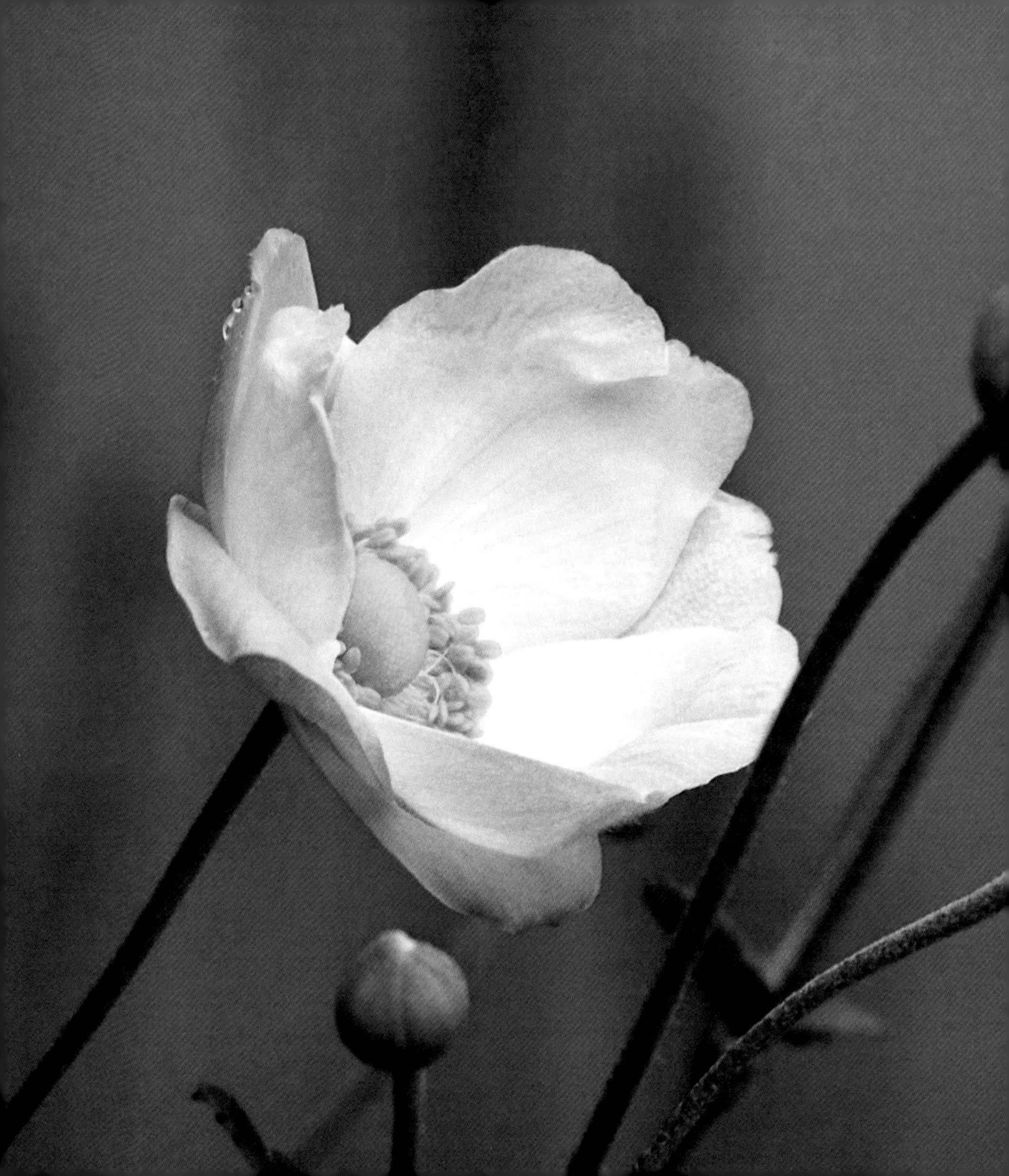

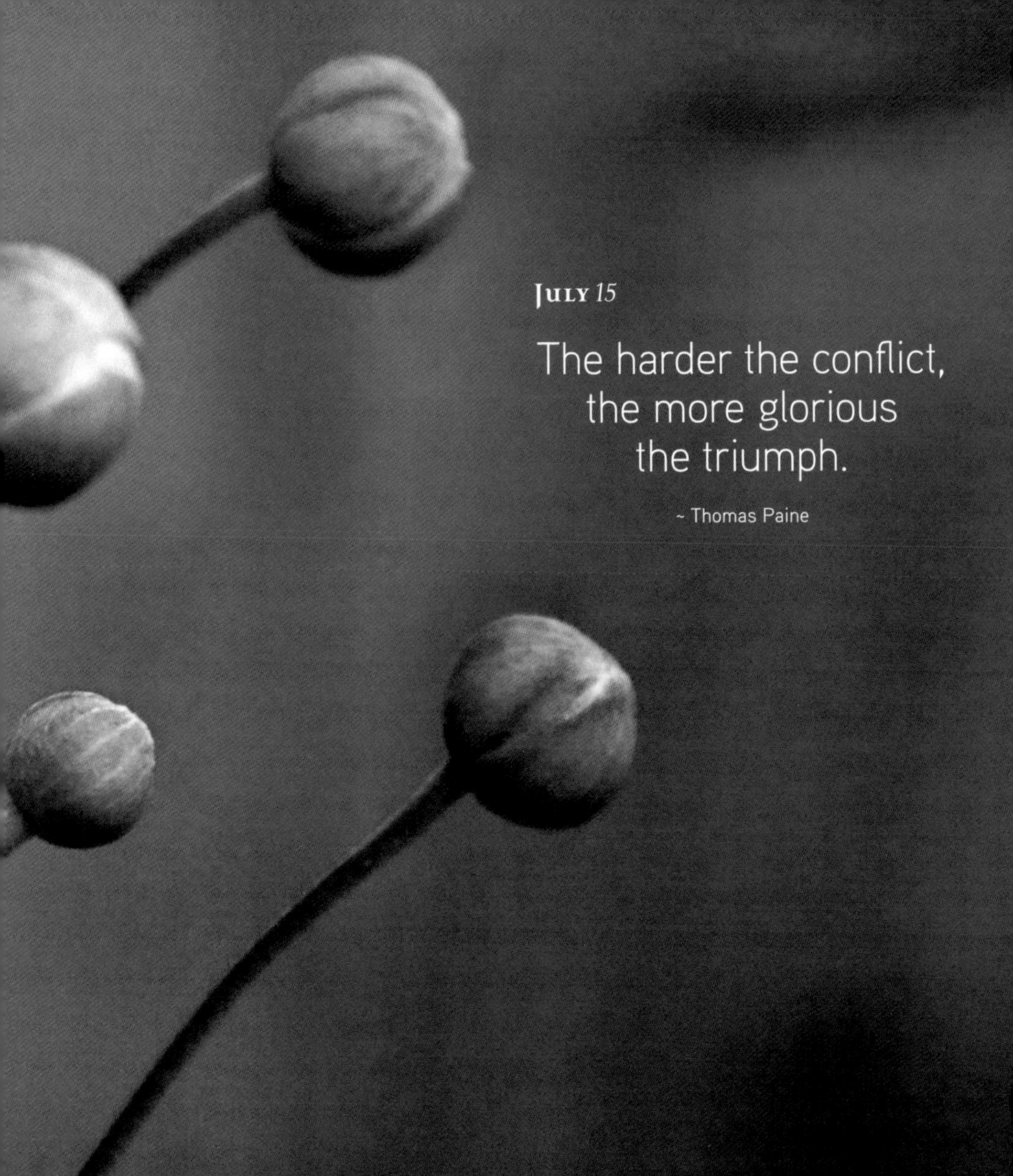
July 15
The harder the conflict,
the more glorious
the triumph.
~ Thomas Paine

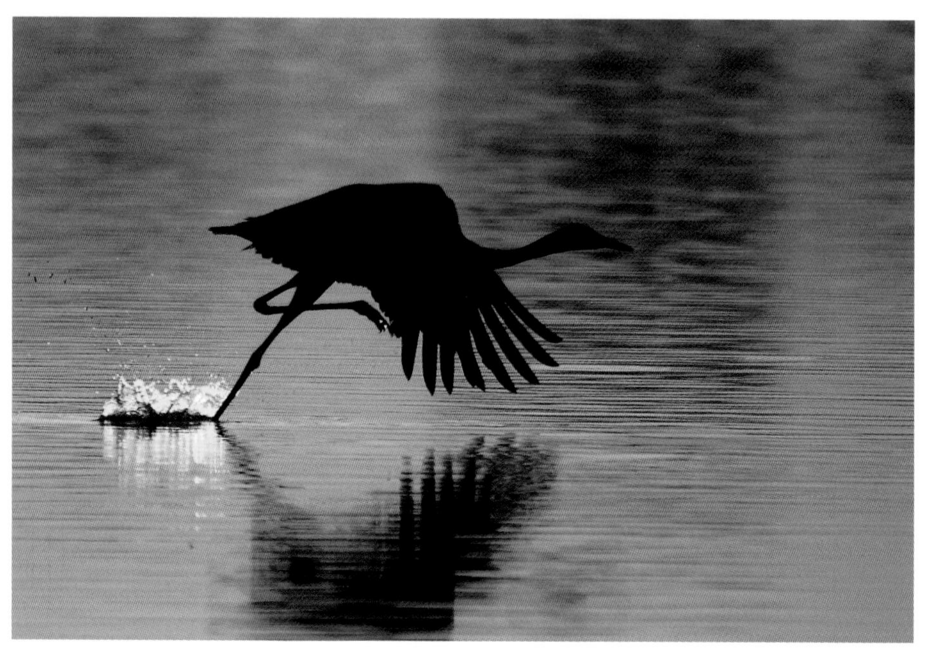

July 16

Living is a form of not being sure,
not knowing what next or how. . .
We guess.
We may be wrong,
but we take leap after leap in the dark.

~ Agnes de Mille

JULY 17

Nobody can conceive
or imagine all the wonders
there are unseen and
unseeable in the world.

~ Francis P. Church

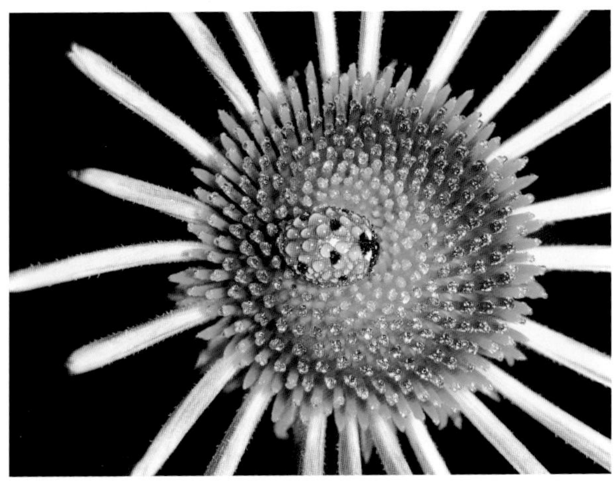

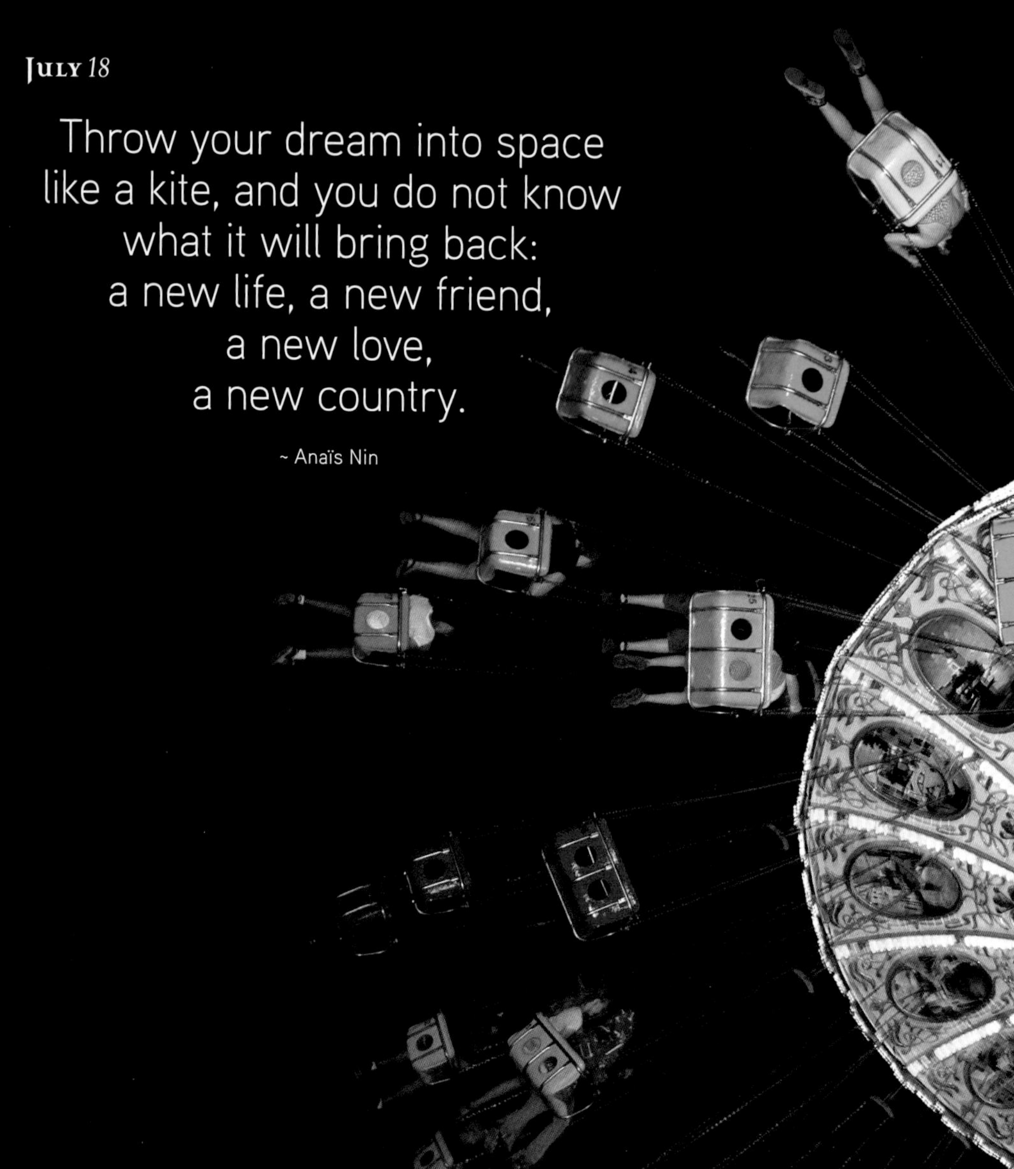

July 18

Throw your dream into space
like a kite, and you do not know
what it will bring back:
a new life, a new friend,
a new love,
a new country.

~ Anaïs Nin

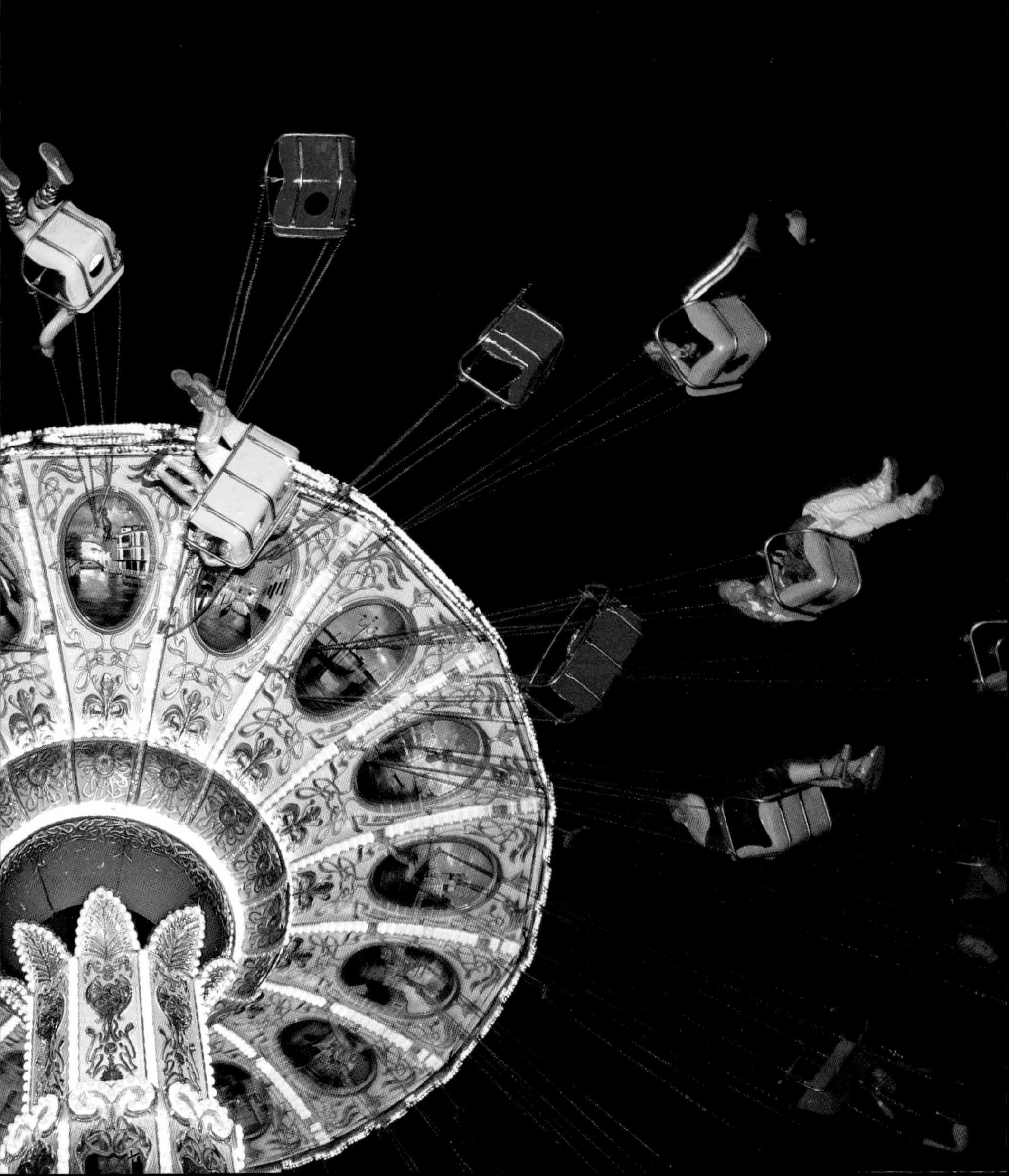

JULY 19

Develop interest in life as you see it; in people, things, literature, music—the world is so rich, simply throbbing with rich treasures, beautiful souls and interesting people. Forget yourself.

~ Henry Miller

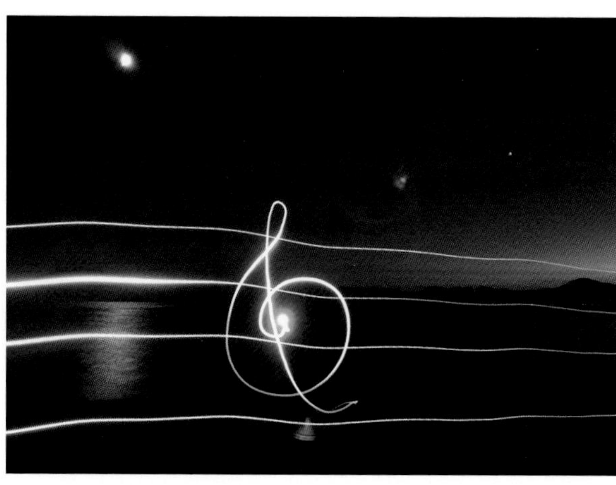

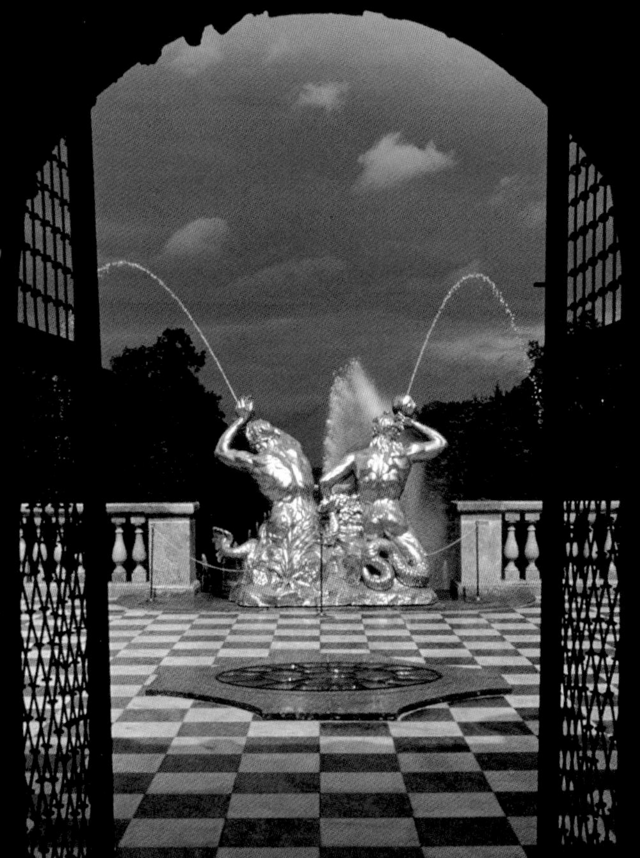

JULY 20

Destiny is not a *matter* of chance; it is a matter of choice. It is not a thing to be waited for; it is a thing to be achieved.

~ William Jennings Bryan

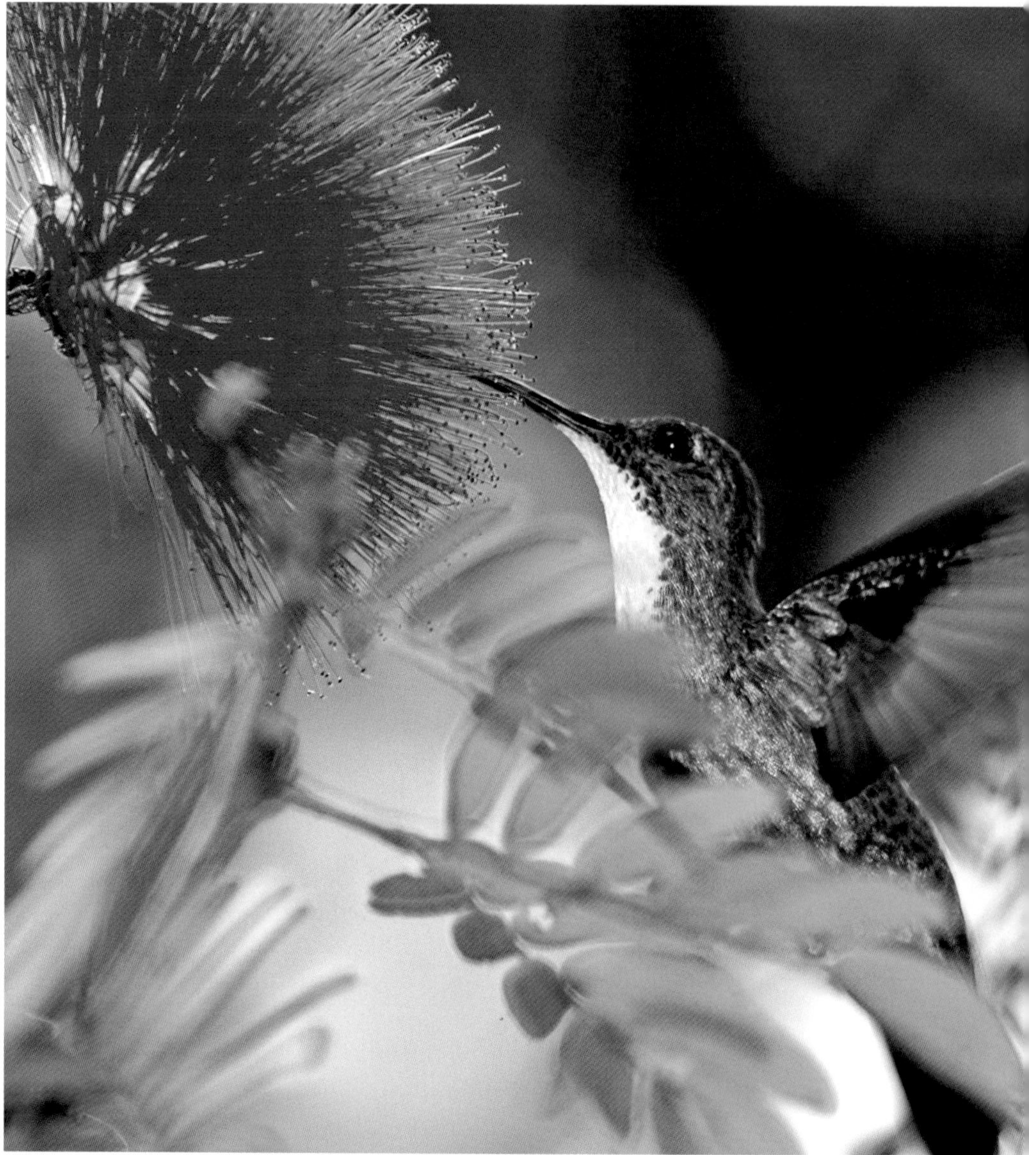

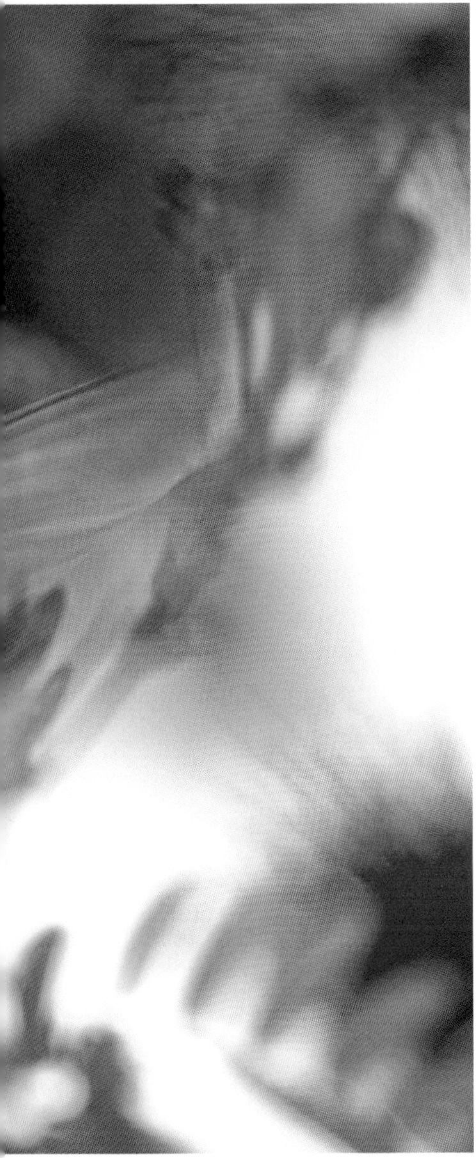

JULY 21

Life itself
is the proper binge.

~ Julia Child

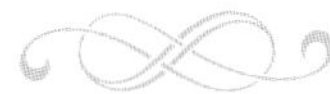

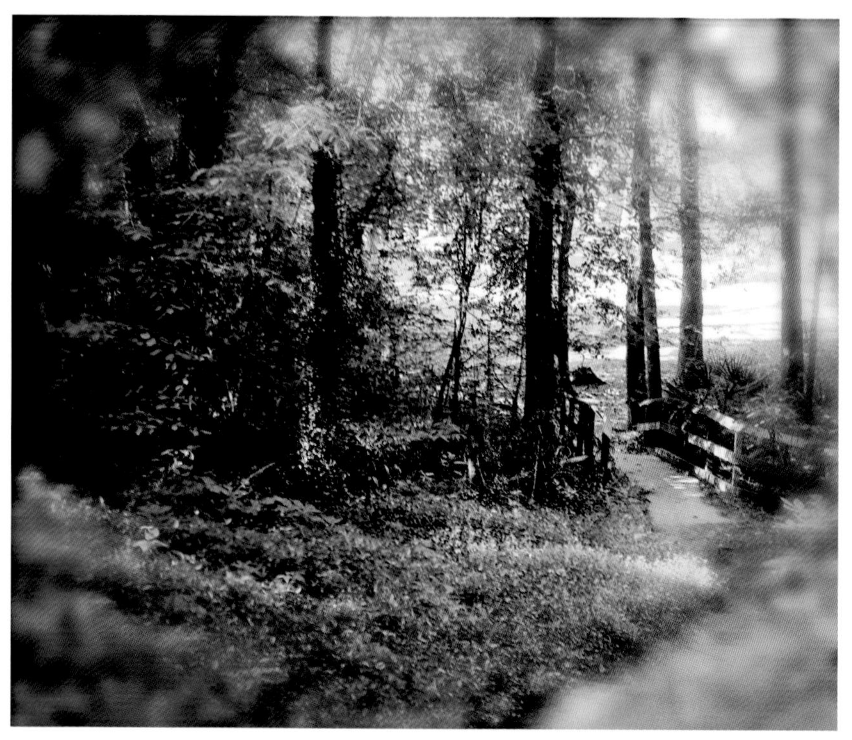

July 22

Imagination will often carry us
to worlds that never were.
But without it, we go nowhere.

~ Carl Sagan

July 23

Life itself
is the most wonderful fairy tale.

~ Hans Christian Andersen

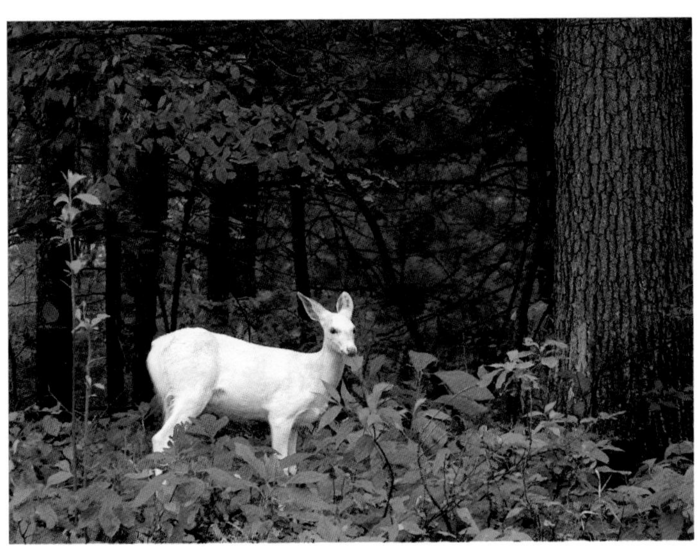

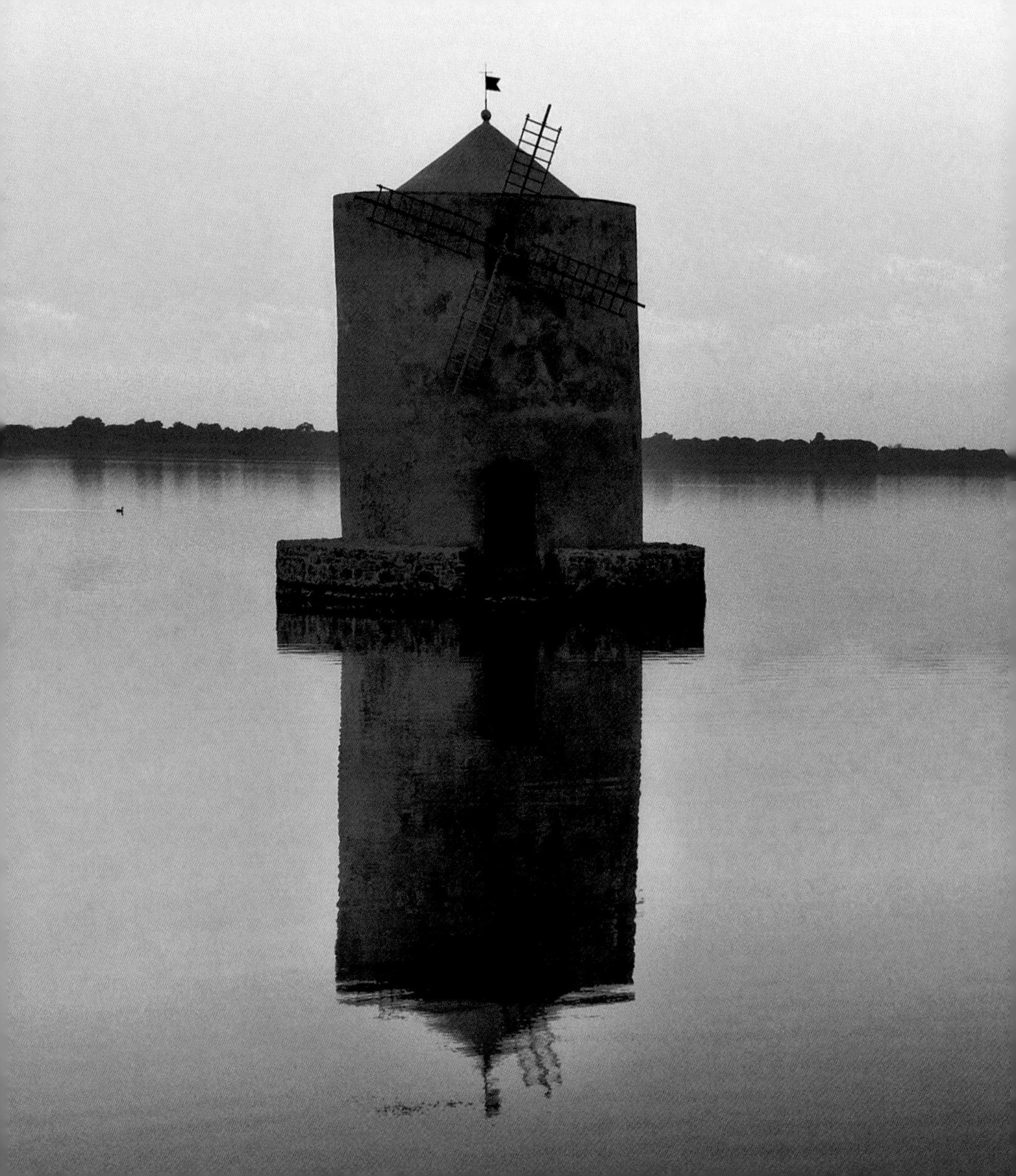

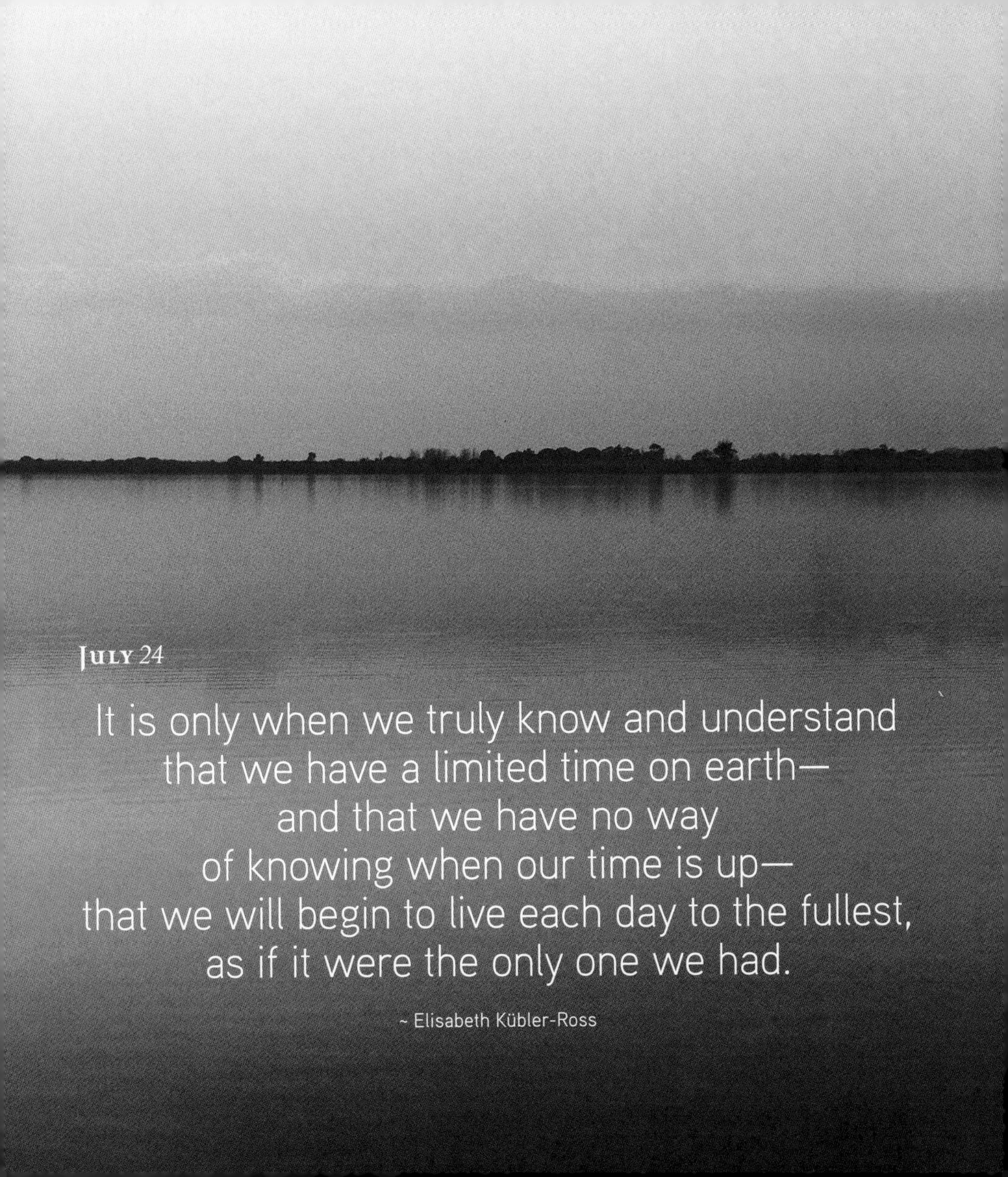

July 24

It is only when we truly know and understand
that we have a limited time on earth—
and that we have no way
of knowing when our time is up—
that we will begin to live each day to the fullest,
as if it were the only one we had.

~ Elisabeth Kübler-Ross

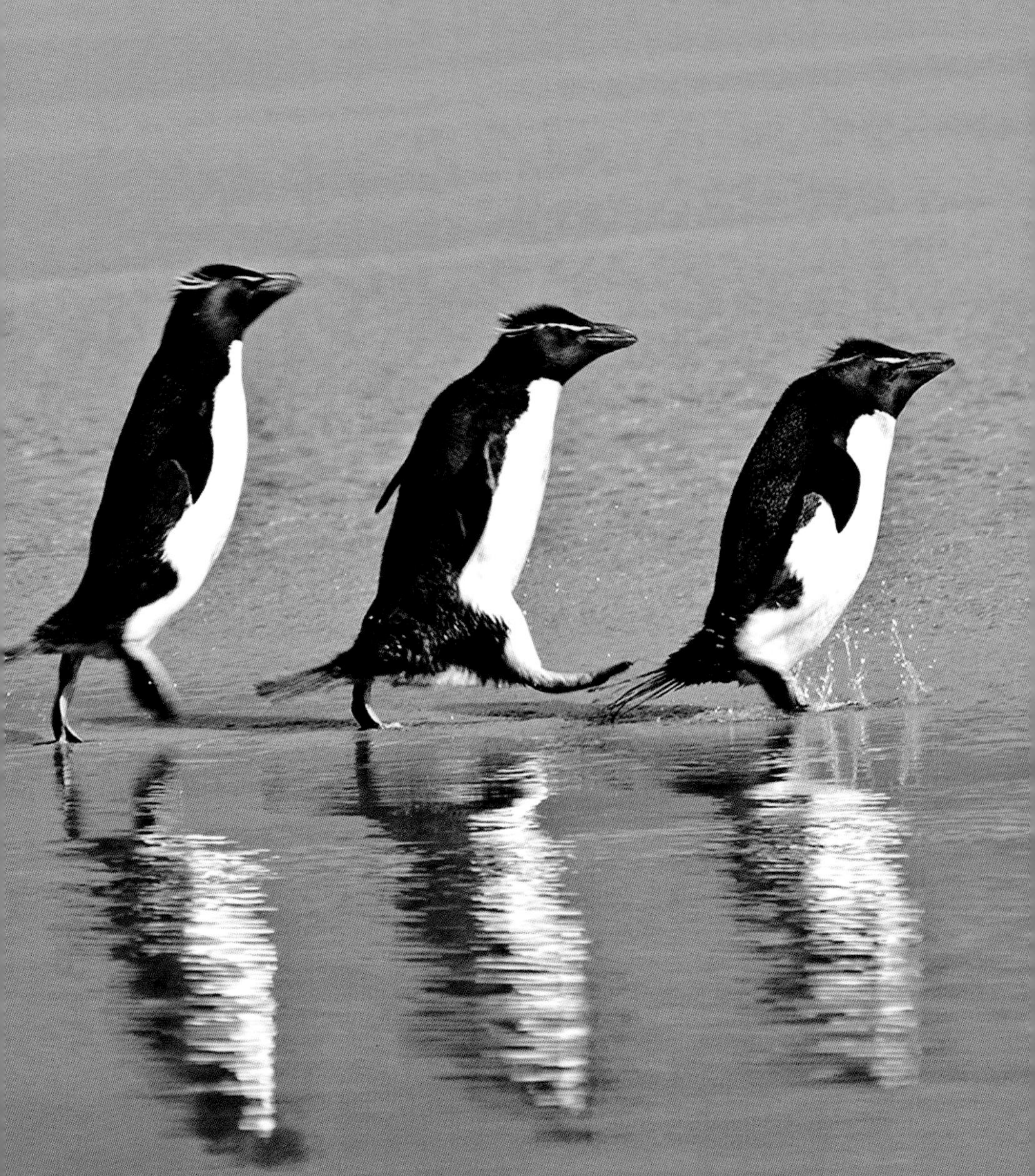

JULY 25

Be bold . . .
When you embark
for strange places,
don't leave
any of yourself
safely on shore.

~ Alan Alda

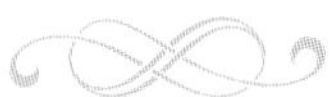

July 26

Though we travel the world over to find the beautiful, we must carry it with us or we find it not.

~ Ralph Waldo Emerson

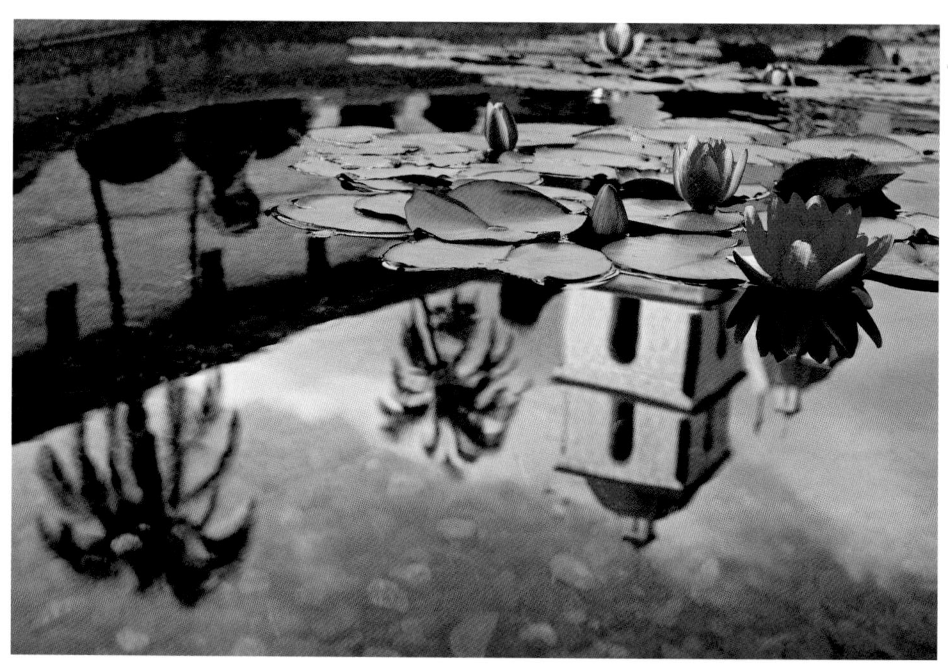

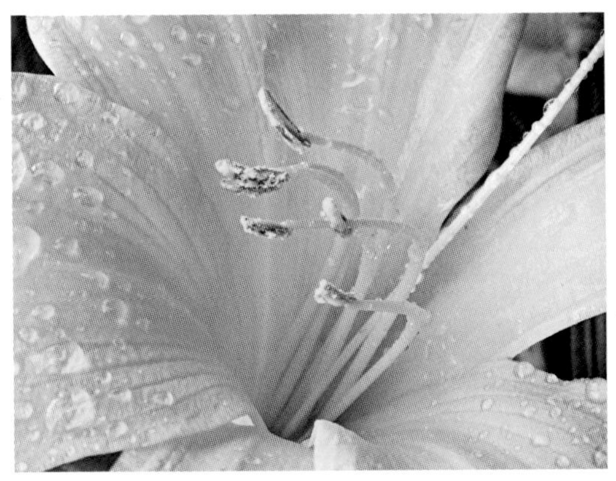

July 27

The soul should always
stand ajar,
ready to welcome
the ecstatic experience.

~ Emily Dickinson

July 28

Life calls the tune, we dance.

~ John Galsworthy

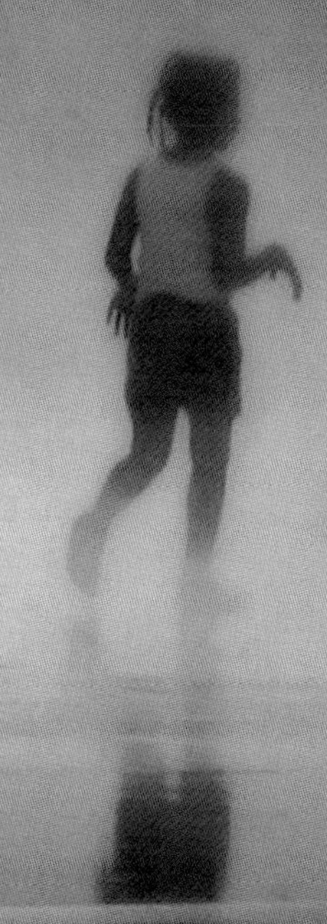

July 29

Stay hungry. Stay foolish.

~ Steve Jobs

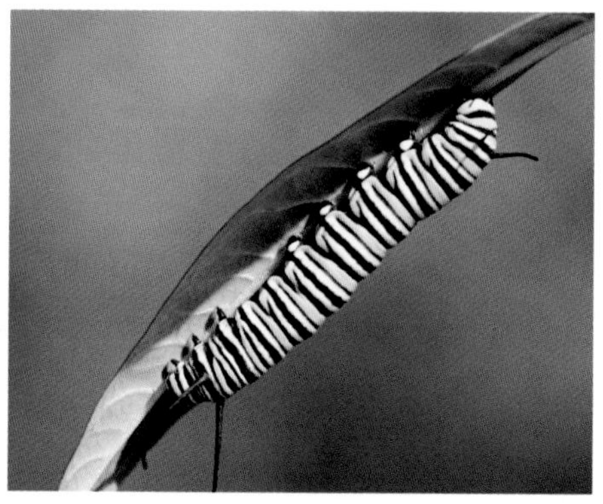

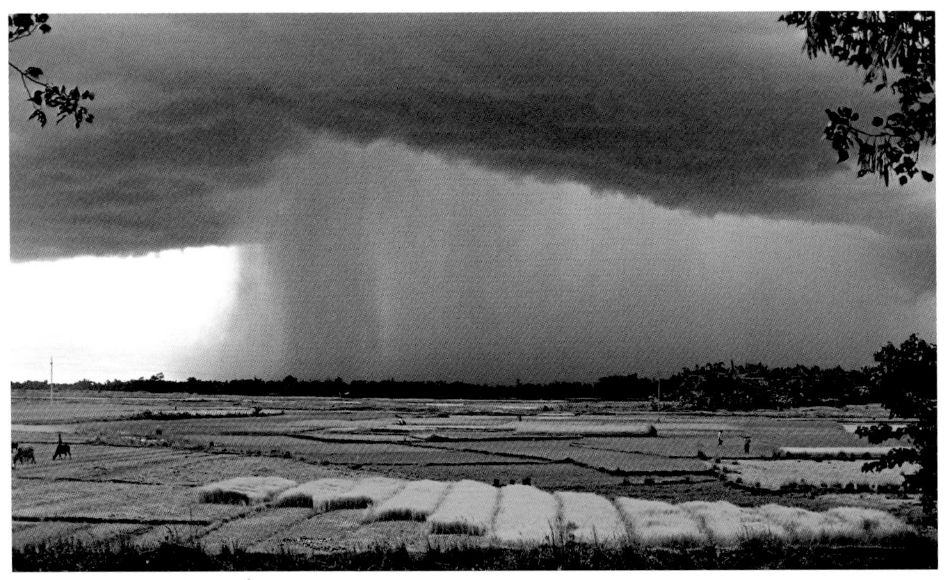

JULY 30

Stuff your eyes with wonder;
live as if you'd drop dead in ten seconds.
See the world. It's more fantastic than
any dream made or paid for in factories.

~ Ray Bradbury

July 31

There are only two ways
to live your life.
One is as though
nothing is a miracle.
The other
is as though everything
is a miracle.

~ Albert Einstein

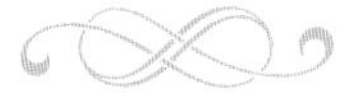

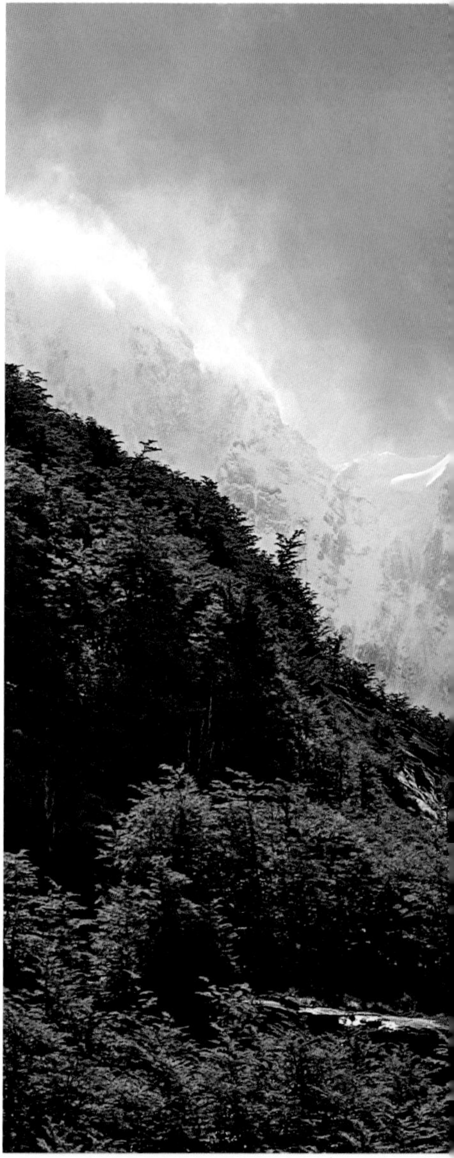

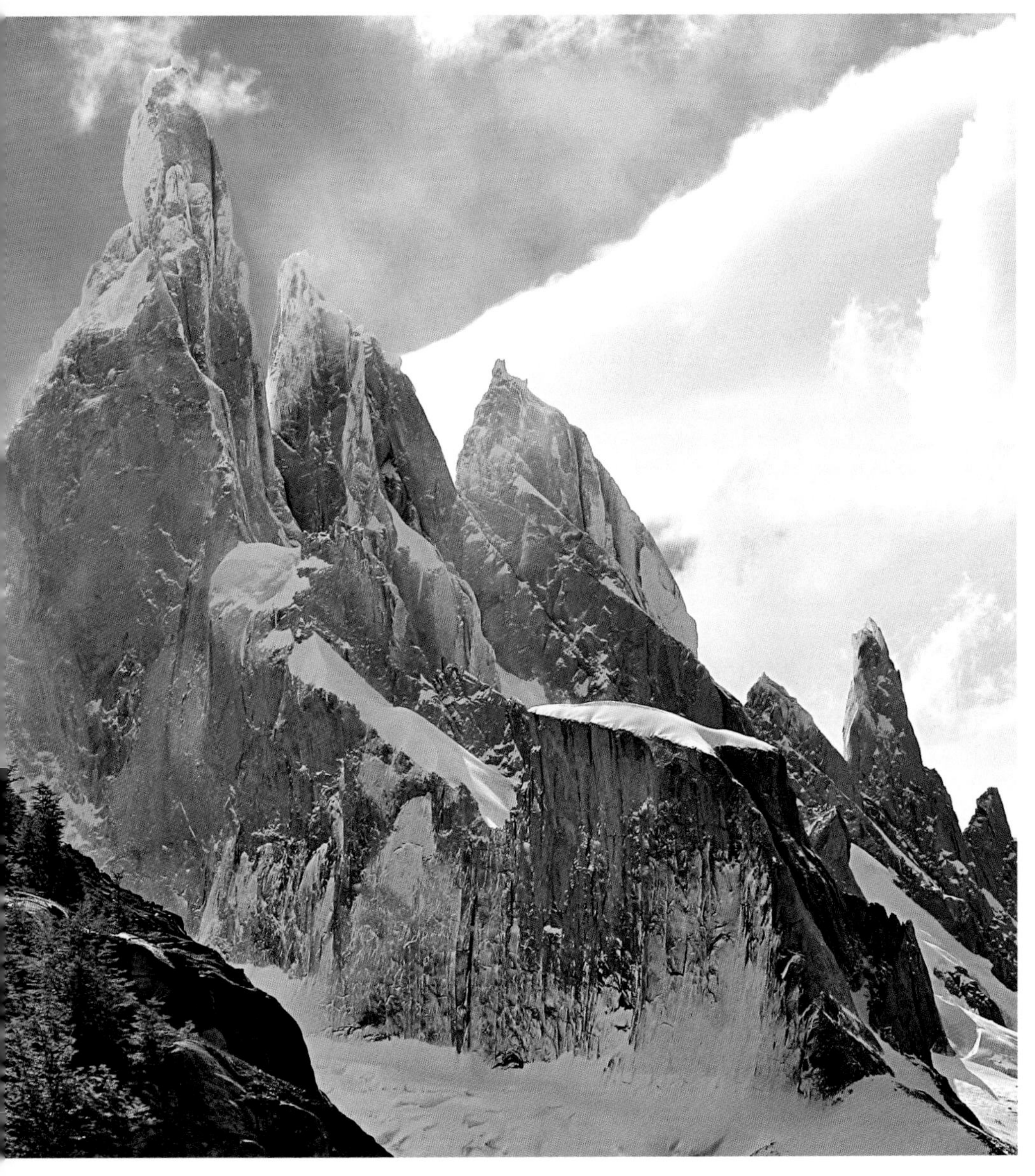

FREEDOM

August

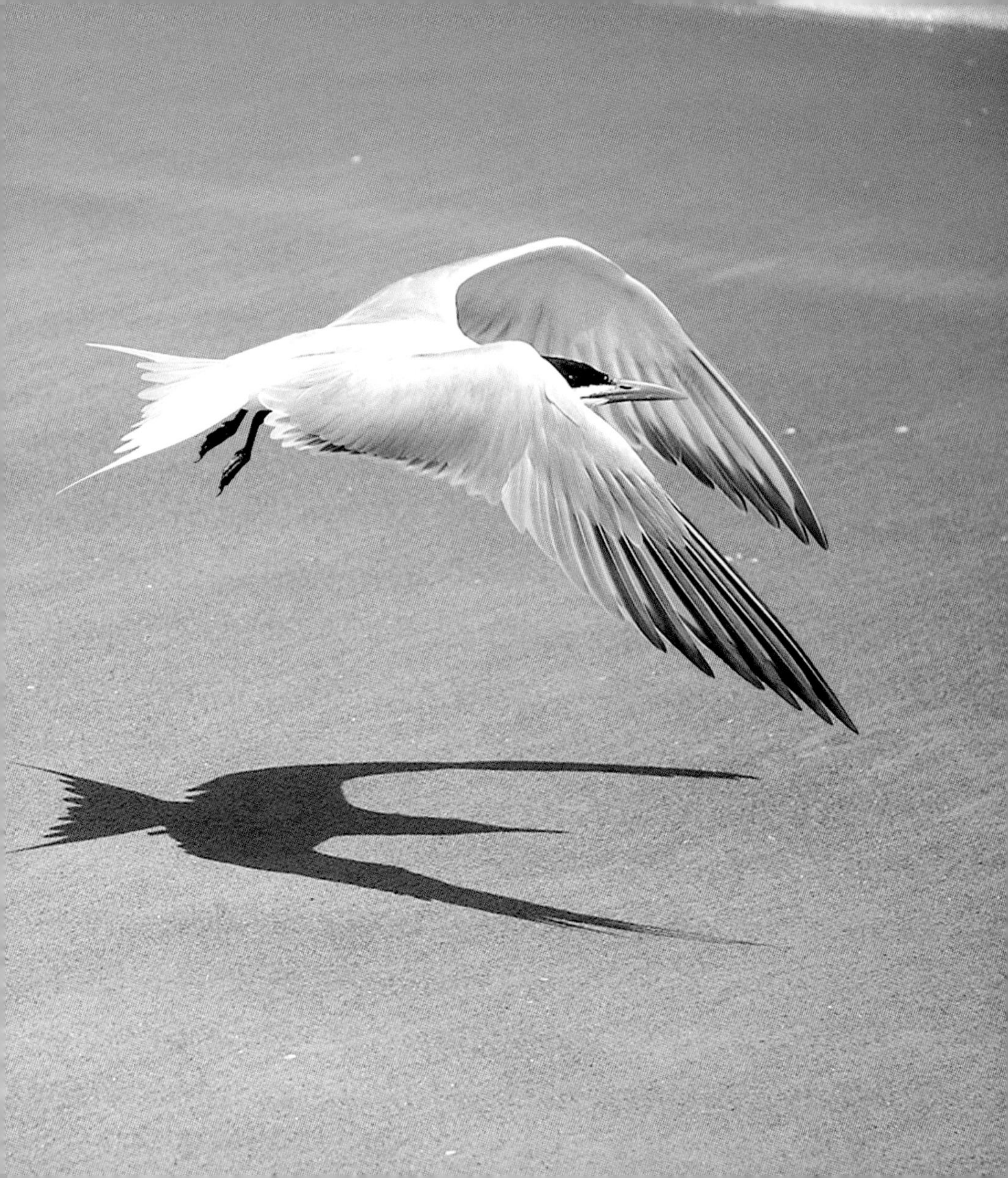

AUGUST 1

Freedom is nothing else but a chance to be better.

~ Albert Camus

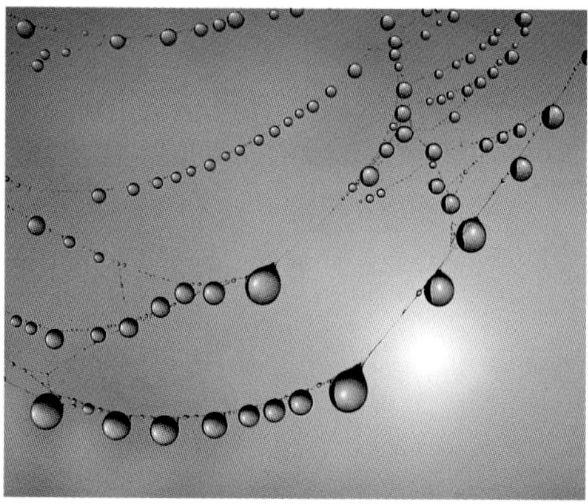

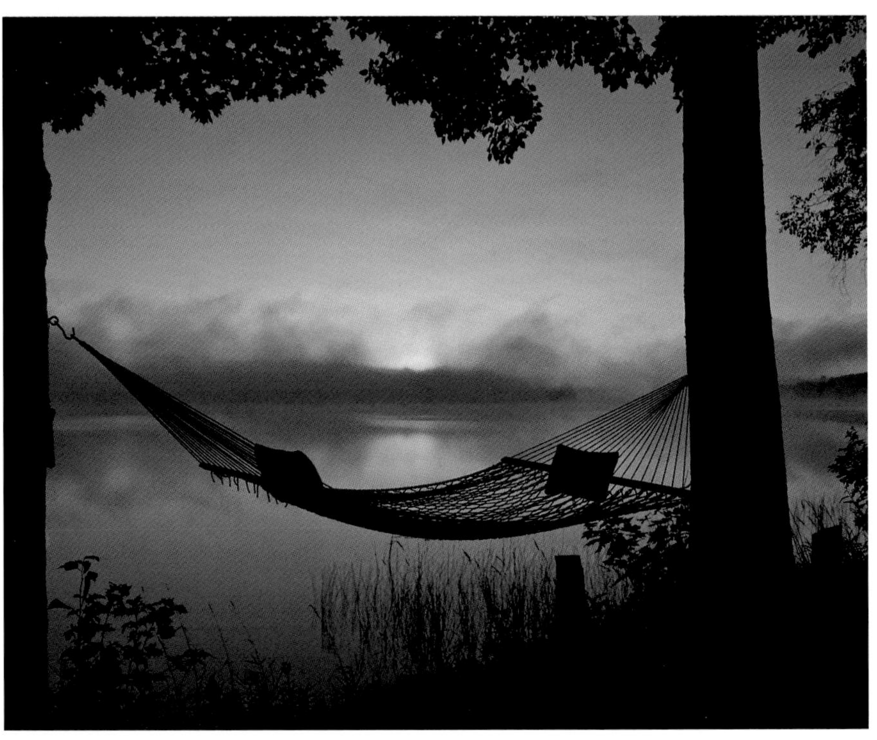

AUGUST 2

If you can spend a perfectly useless afternoon in a perfectly useless manner, you have learned how to live.

~ Lin Yutang

August 3

It is the ability to choose which makes us human.

~ Madeleine L'Engle

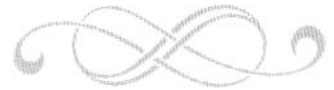

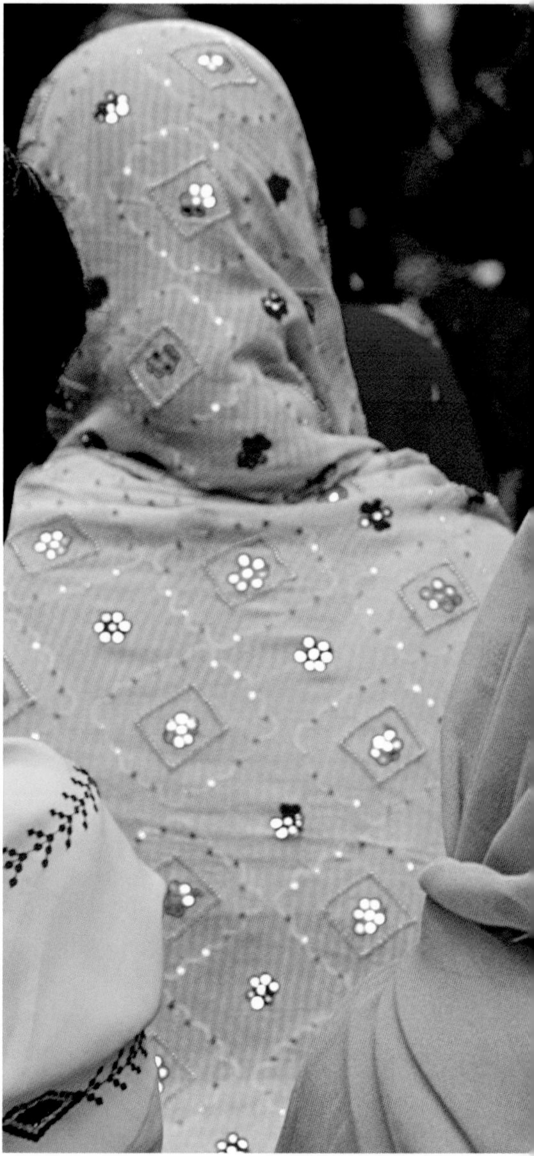

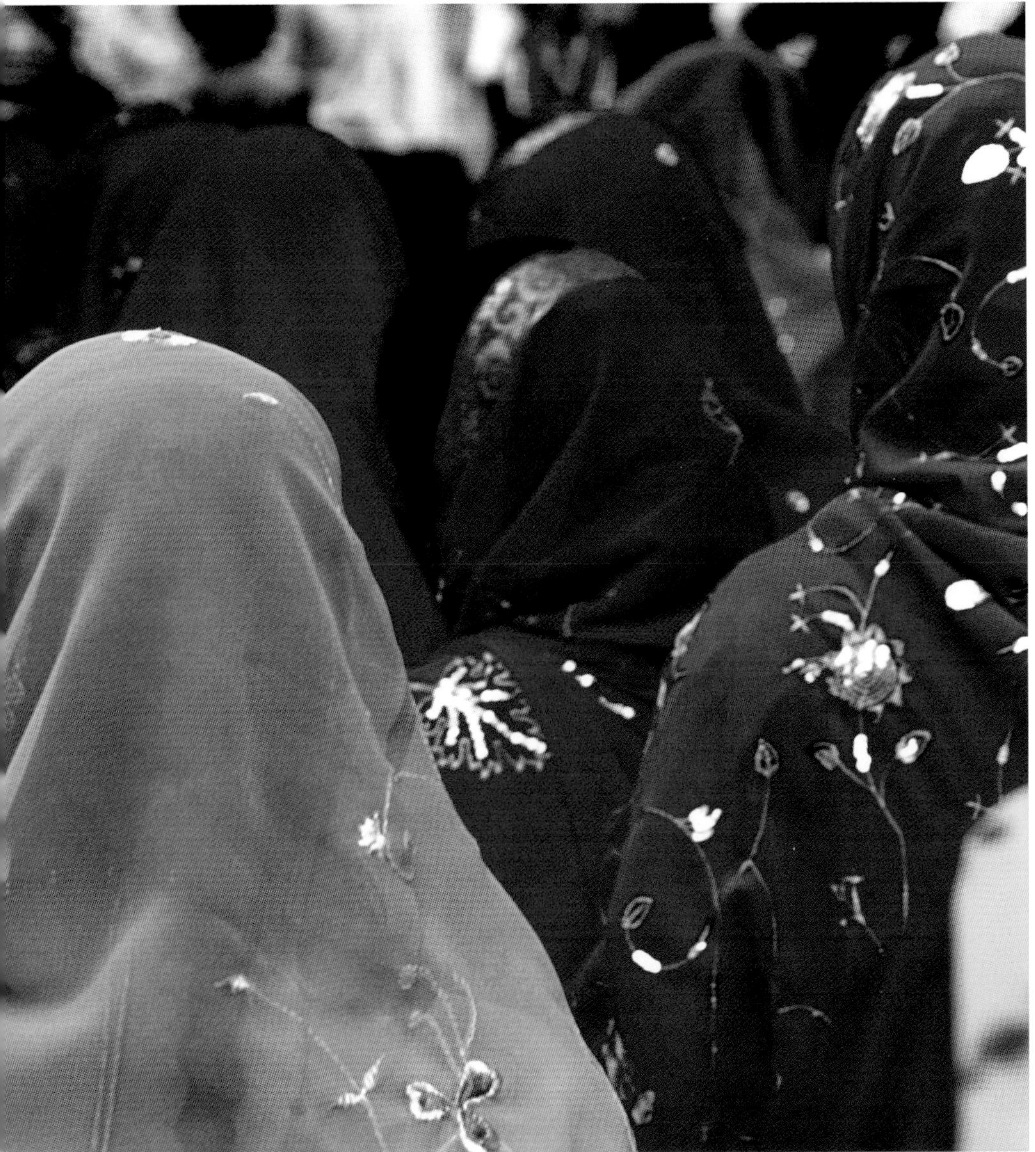

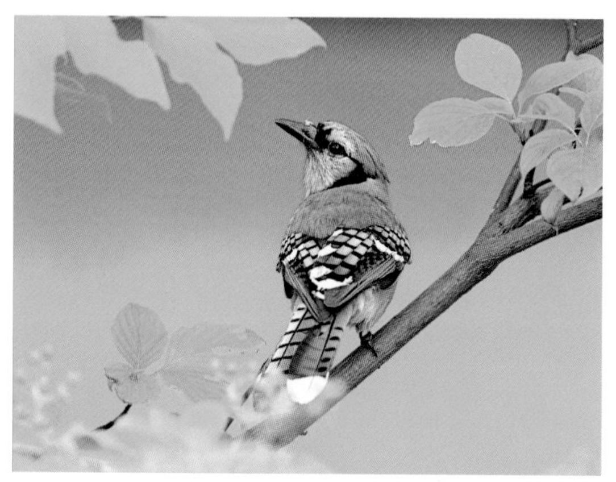

August 4

You can muffle the drum,
and you can loosen
the strings of the lyre—
but who shall command
the skylark not to sing?

~ Kahlil Gibran

August 5

The real happiness of life is to enjoy the present, without any anxious dependence upon the future.

~ Lucius Annaeus Seneca

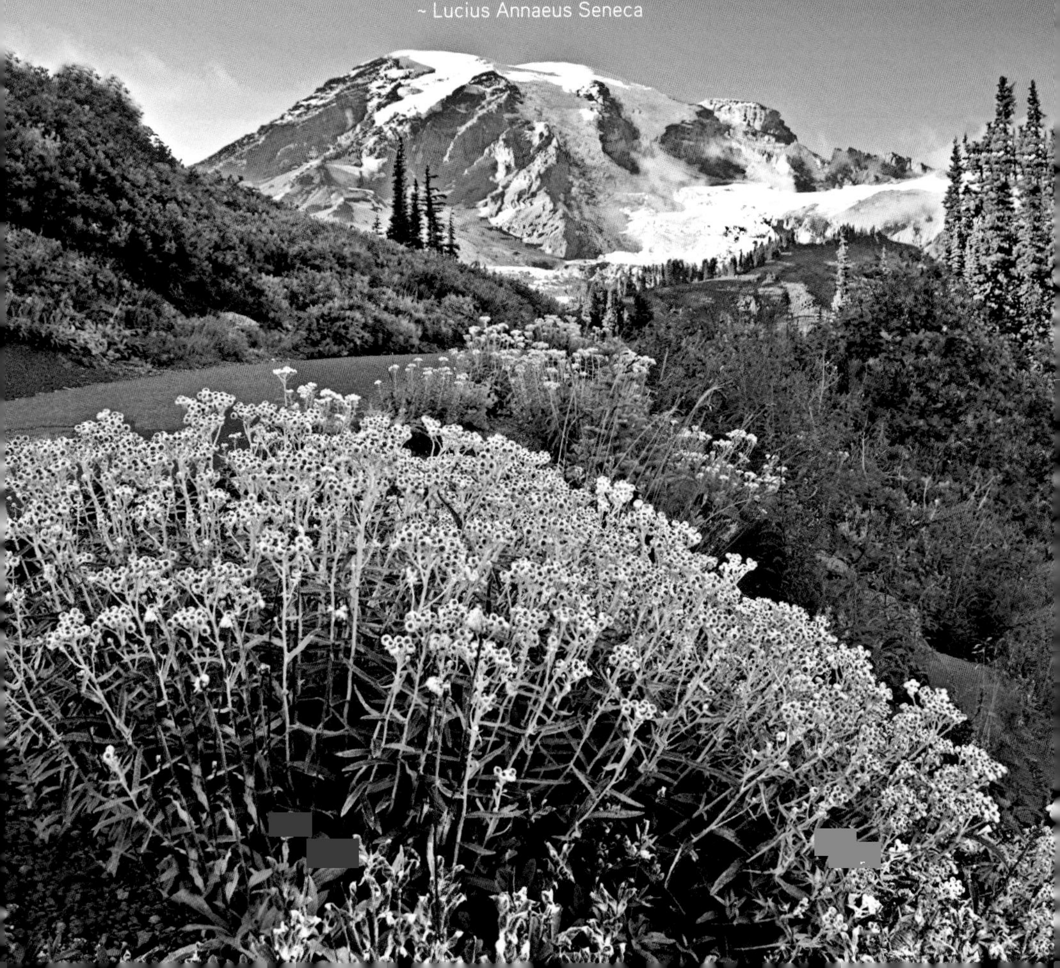

August 6

If you obey
all the rules
you miss
all the fun.

~ Katharine Hepburn

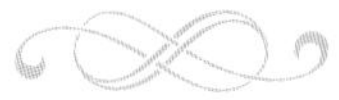

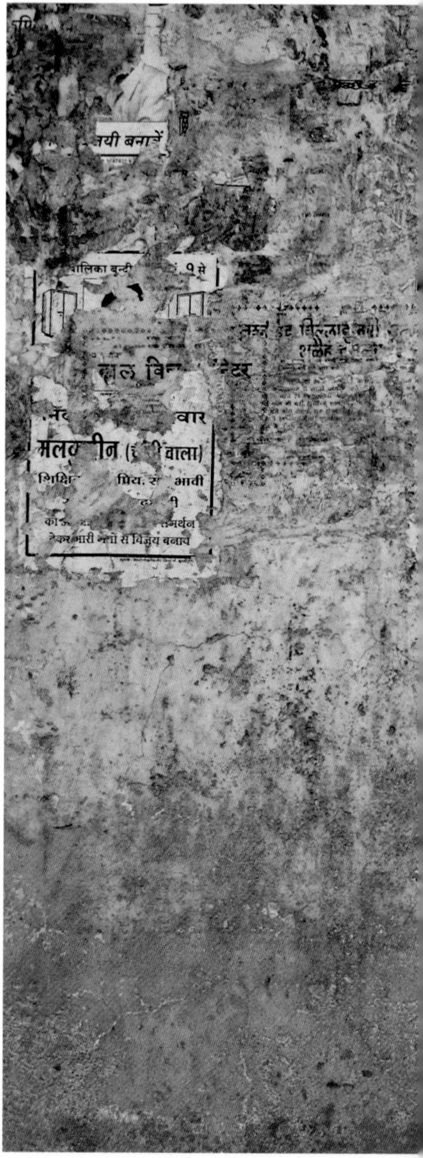

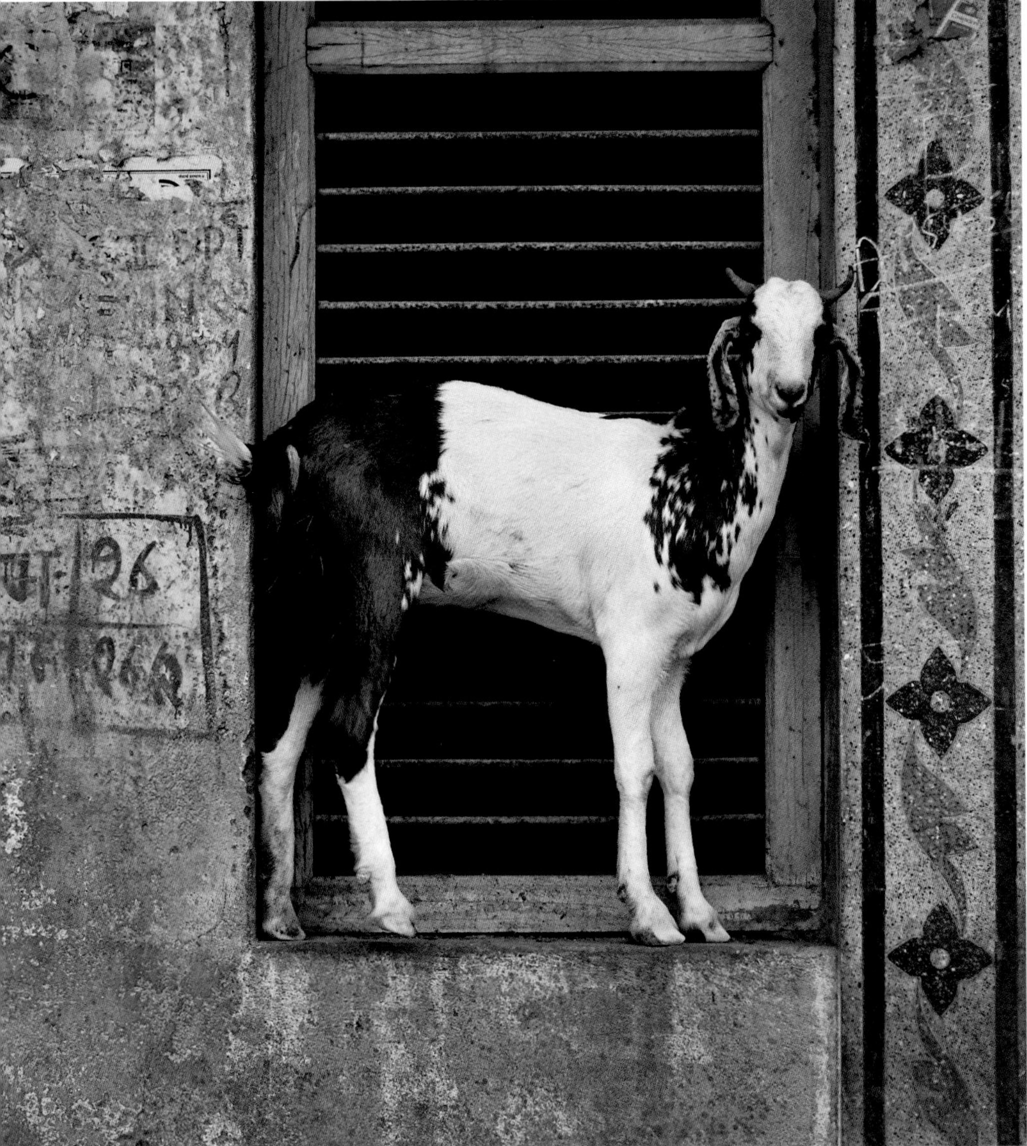

August 7

We travel, some of us forever, to seek other states, other lives, other souls.

~ Anaïs Nin

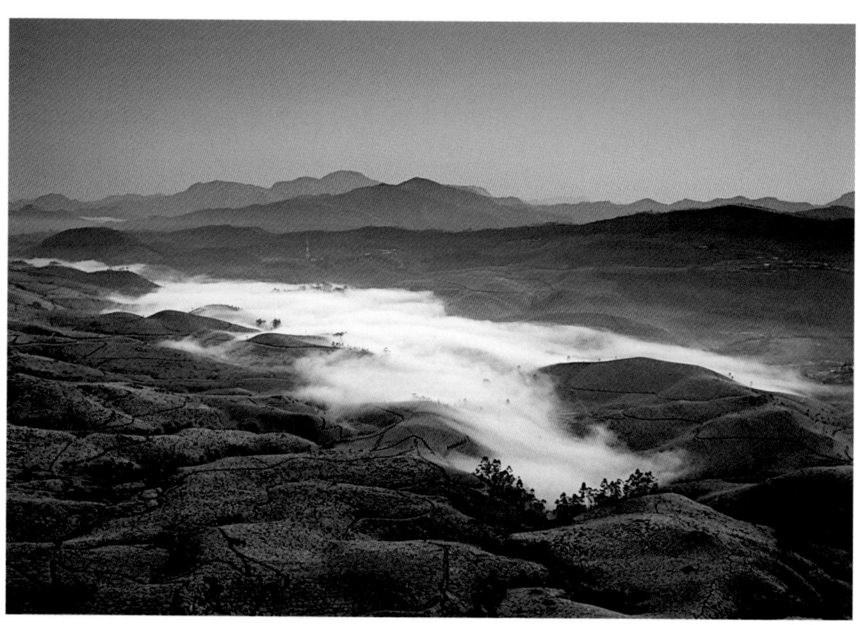

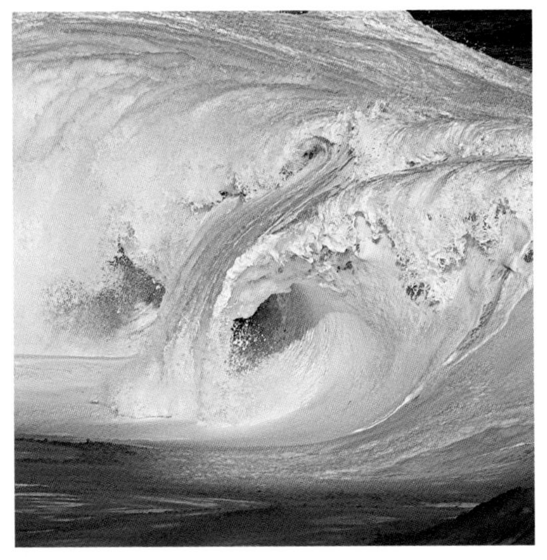

August 8

I know but one freedom, and that is the freedom of the mind.

~ Antoine de Saint-Exupéry

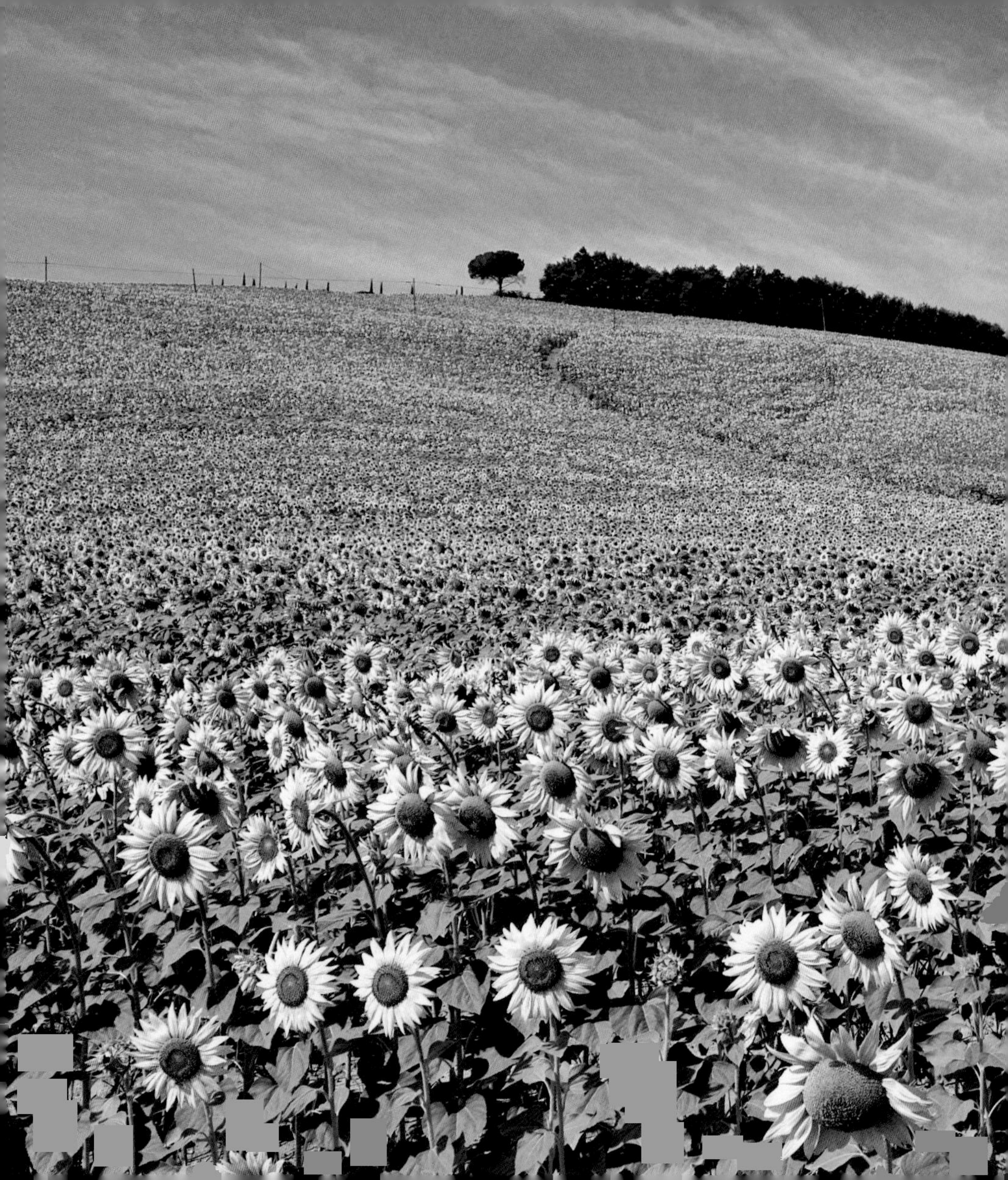

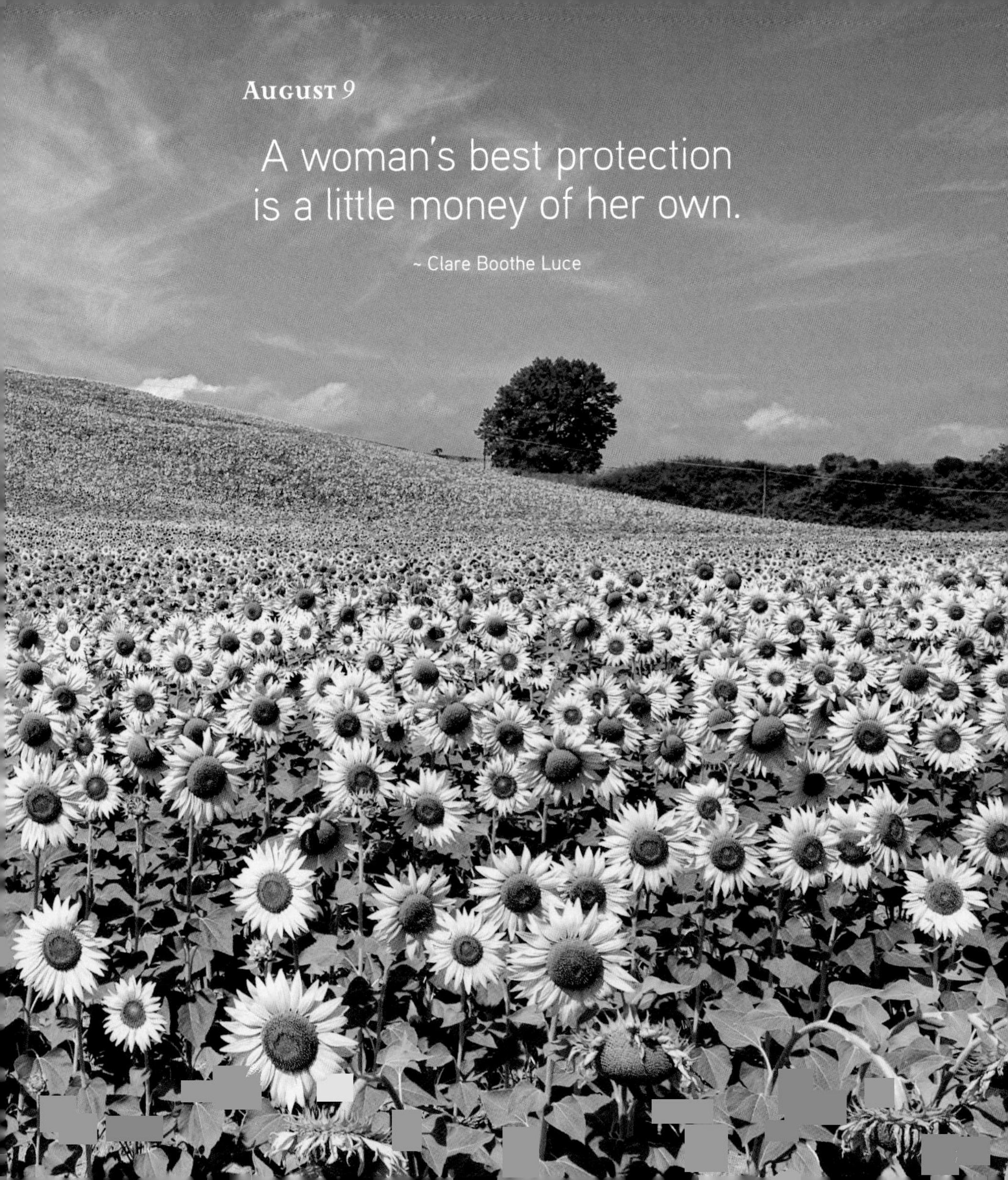
AUGUST 9
A woman's best protection
is a little money of her own.
~ Clare Boothe Luce

AUGUST *10*

Nothing is more difficult,
and therefore more precious,
than to be able to decide.

~ Napoleon Bonaparte

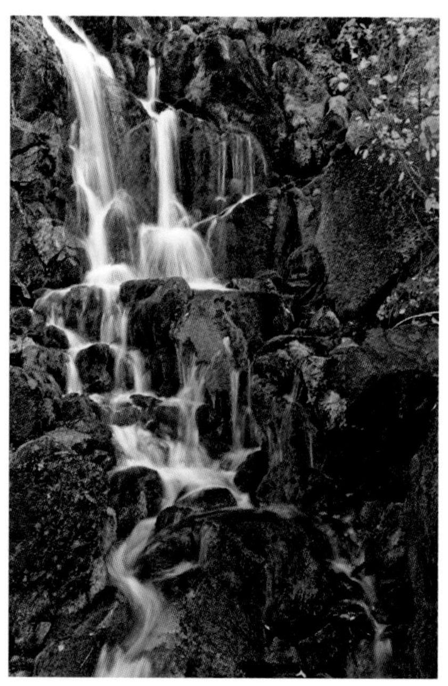

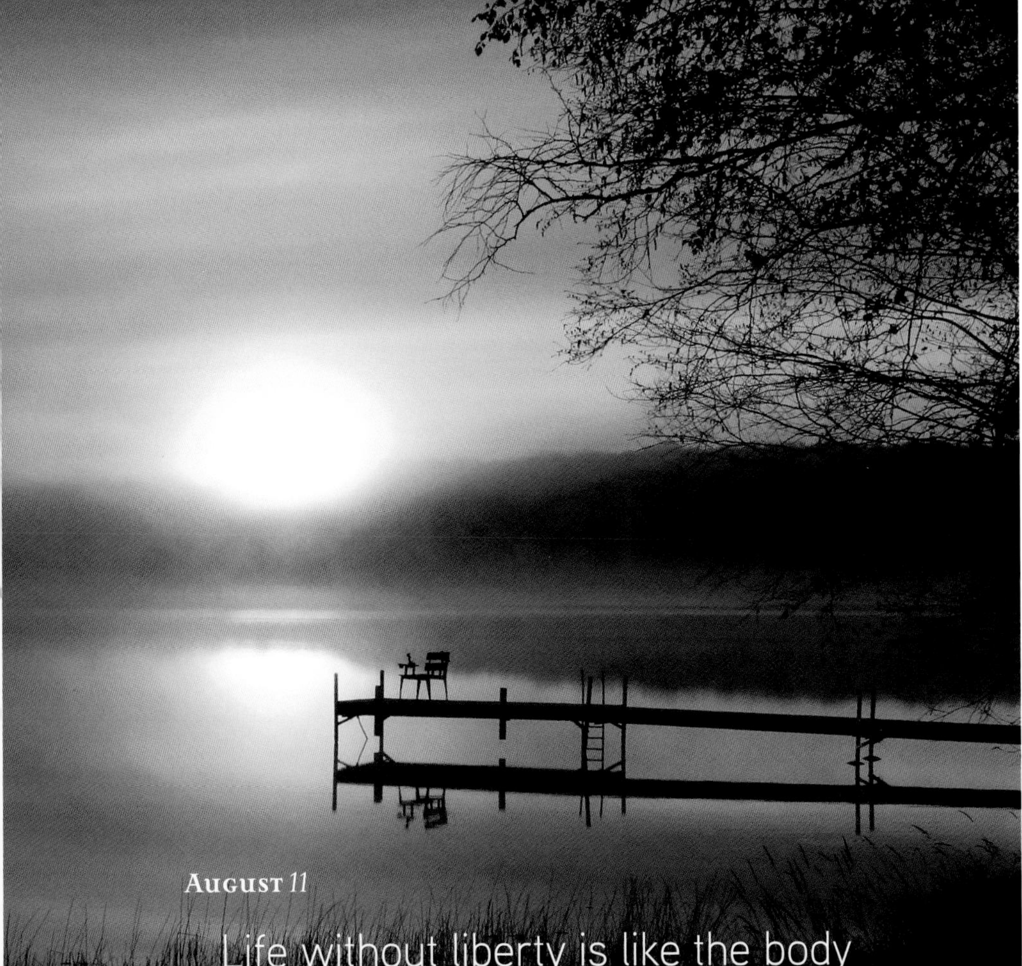

AUGUST *11*

Life without liberty is like the body without spirit.

~ Kahlil Gibran

August *12*

For in the end,
freedom is a personal
and lonely battle;
and one faces down
the fears of today
so that those
of tomorrow
might be engaged.

~ Alice Walker

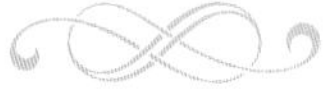

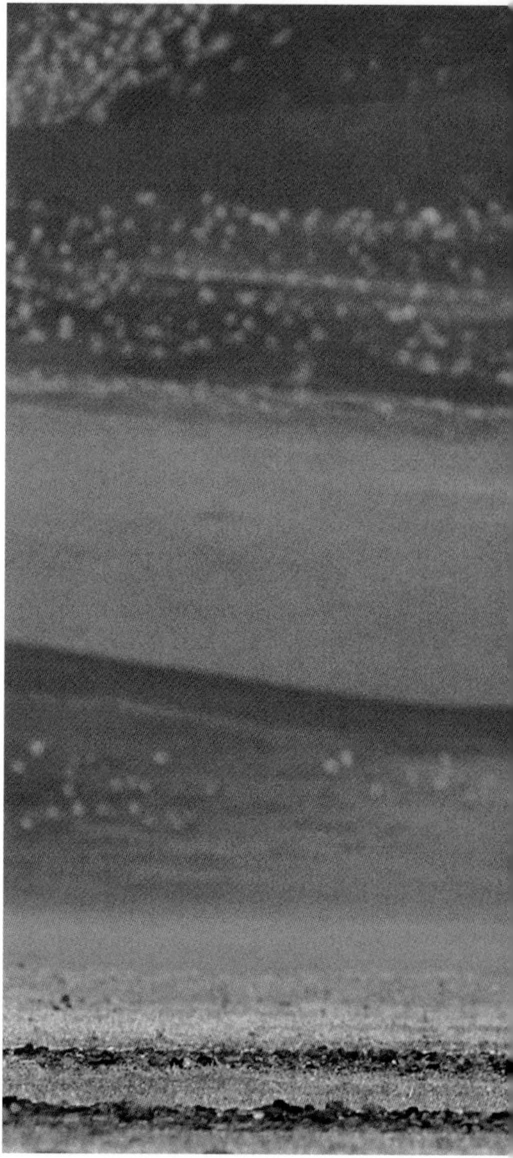

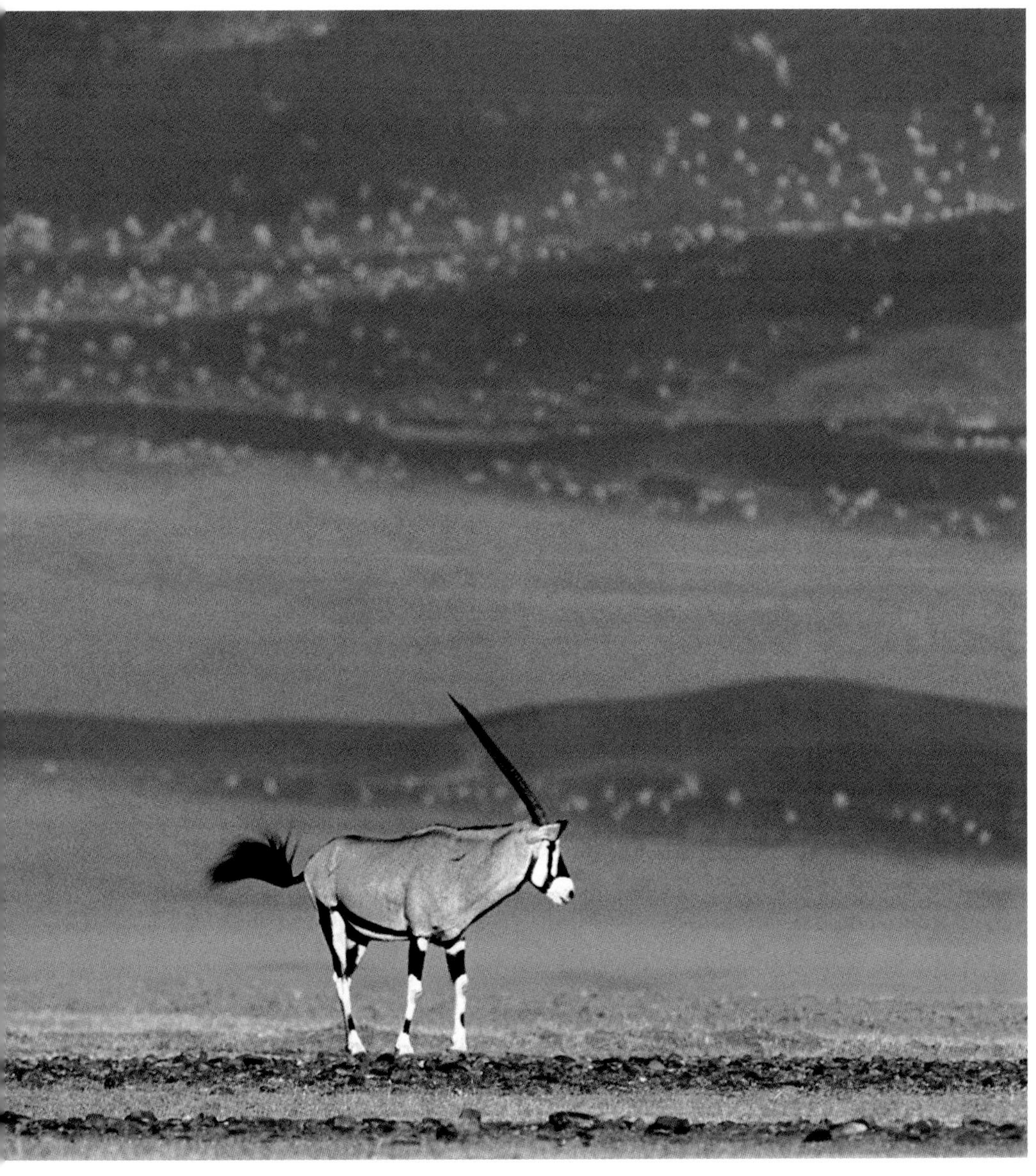

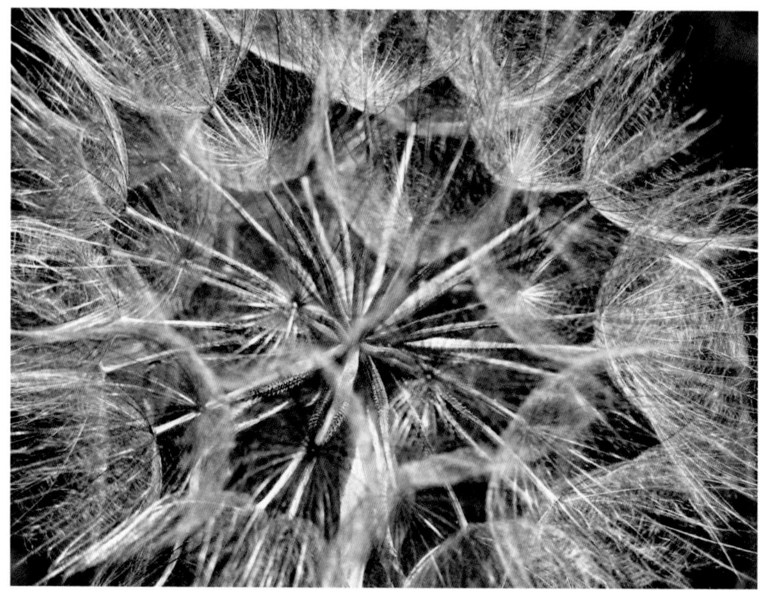

AUGUST 13

The power of imagination
makes us infinite.

~ John Muir

Letting go gives us freedom,
and freedom is the only condition
for happiness. If, in our heart, we still
cling to anything—anger, anxiety, or
possessions—we cannot be free.

~ Thich Nhat Hanh

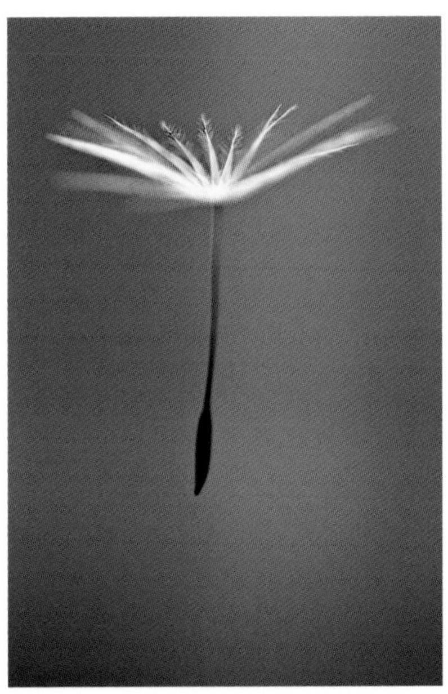

Puttering is really a time to be alone, to dream and to get in touch with yourself . . . To putter is to discover.

~ Alexandra Stoddard

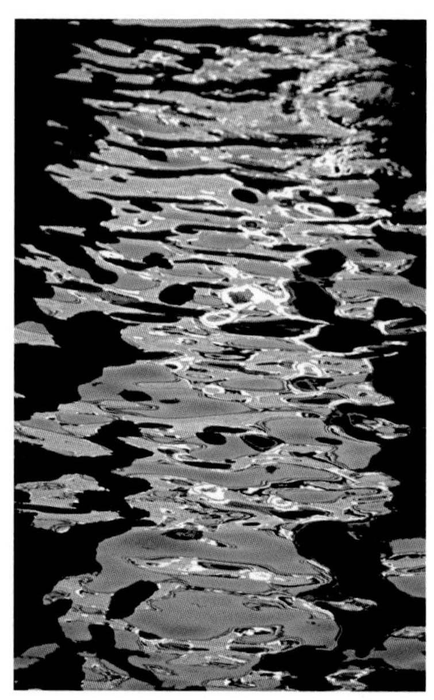

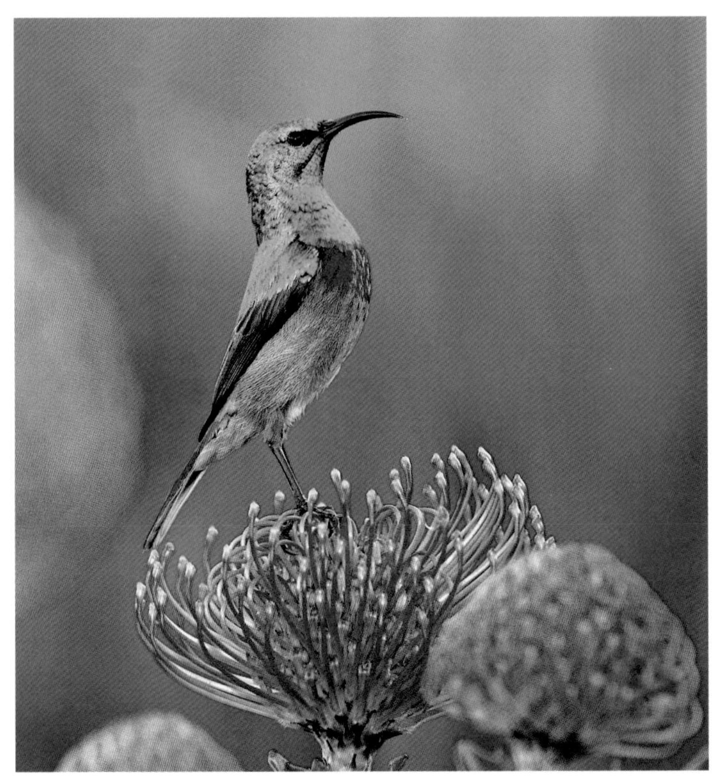

AUGUST *16*

Freedom lies in being bold.

~ Robert Frost

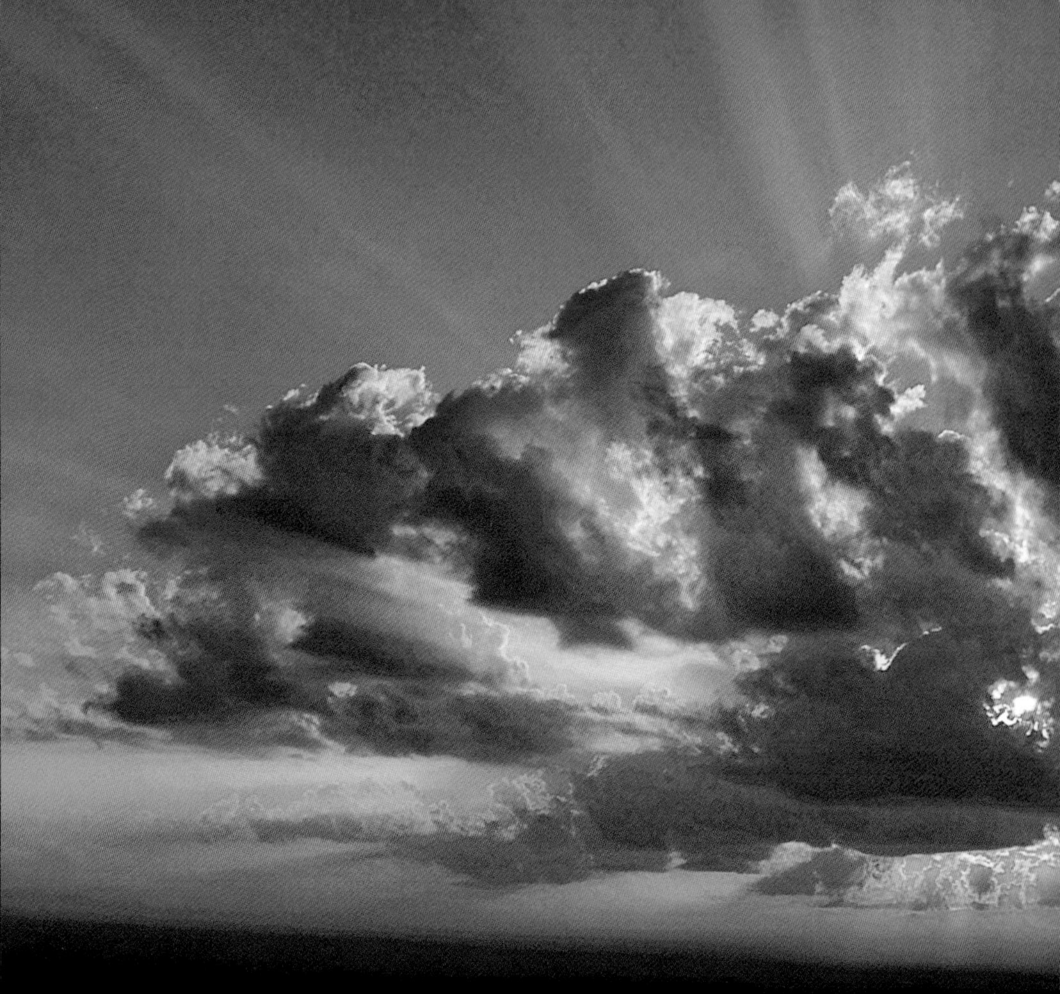

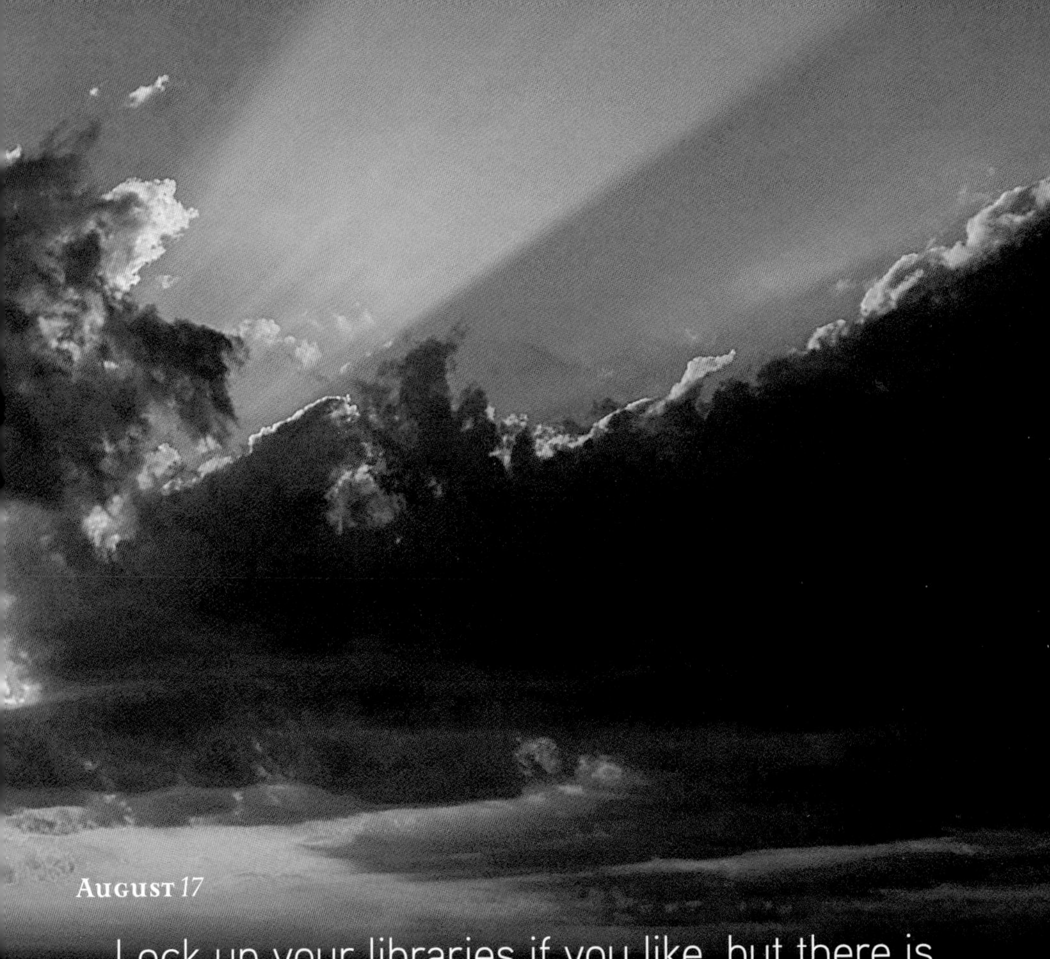

August 17

Lock up your libraries if you like, but there is no gate, no lock, no bolt, that you can set upon the freedom of my mind.

~ Virginia Woolf

August 18

To have
what we want
is riches;
but to be able to
do without
is power.

~ George Macdonald

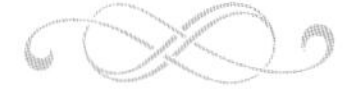

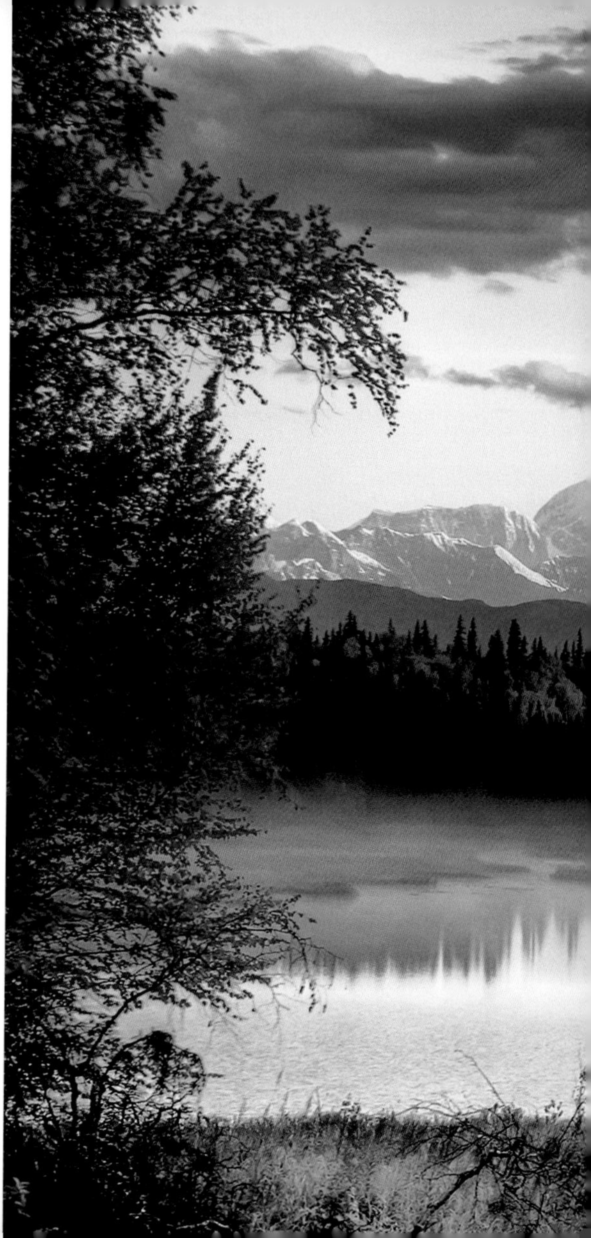

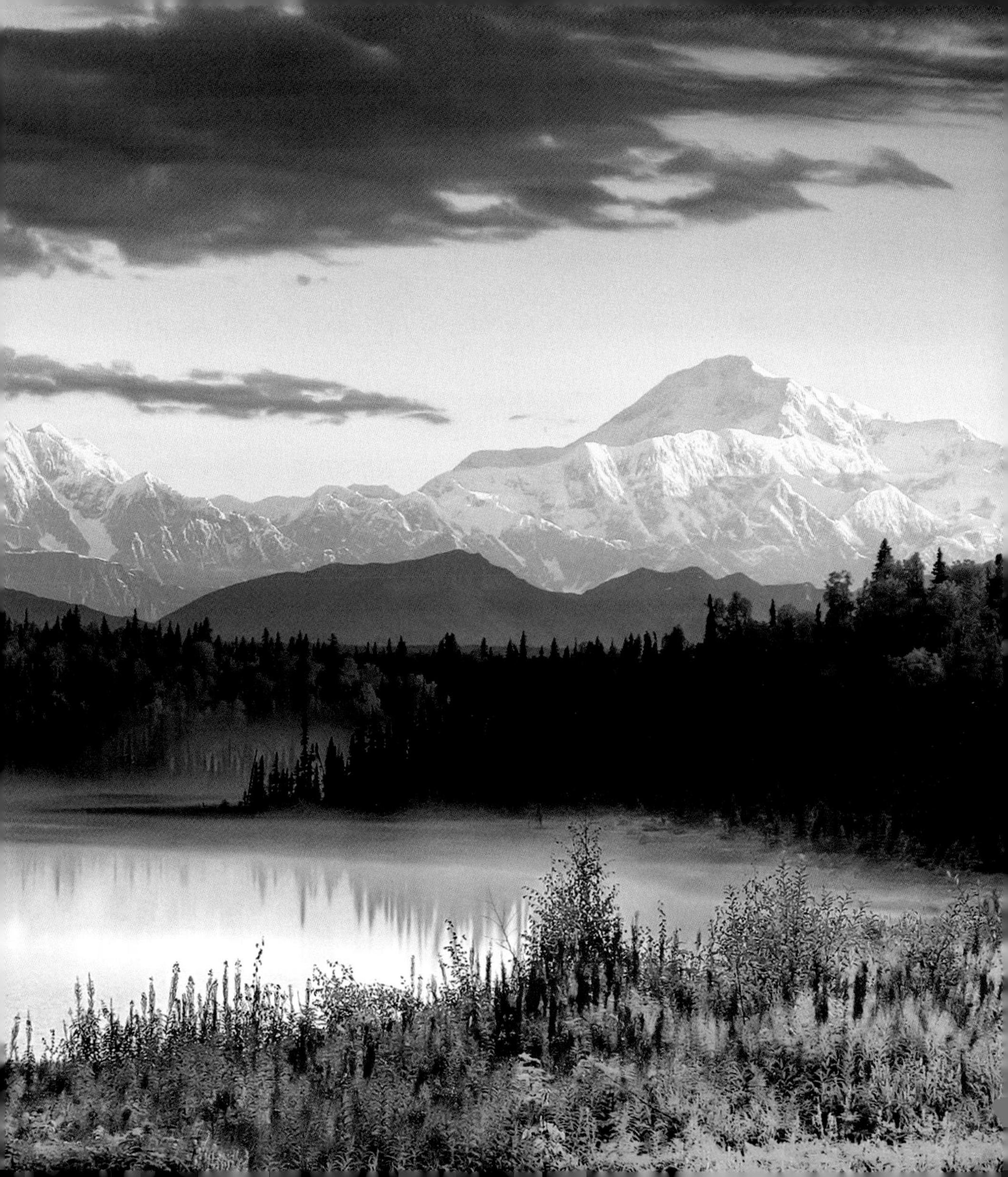

August 19

We do not need magic
to change the world,
we carry all the power we need
inside ourselves already:
we have the power
to imagine better.

~ J. K. Rowling

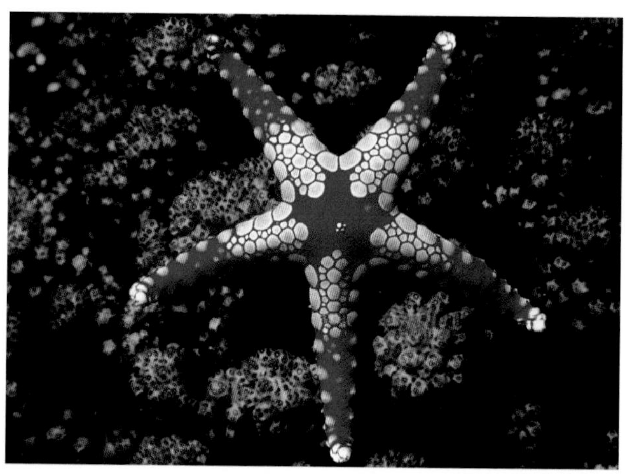

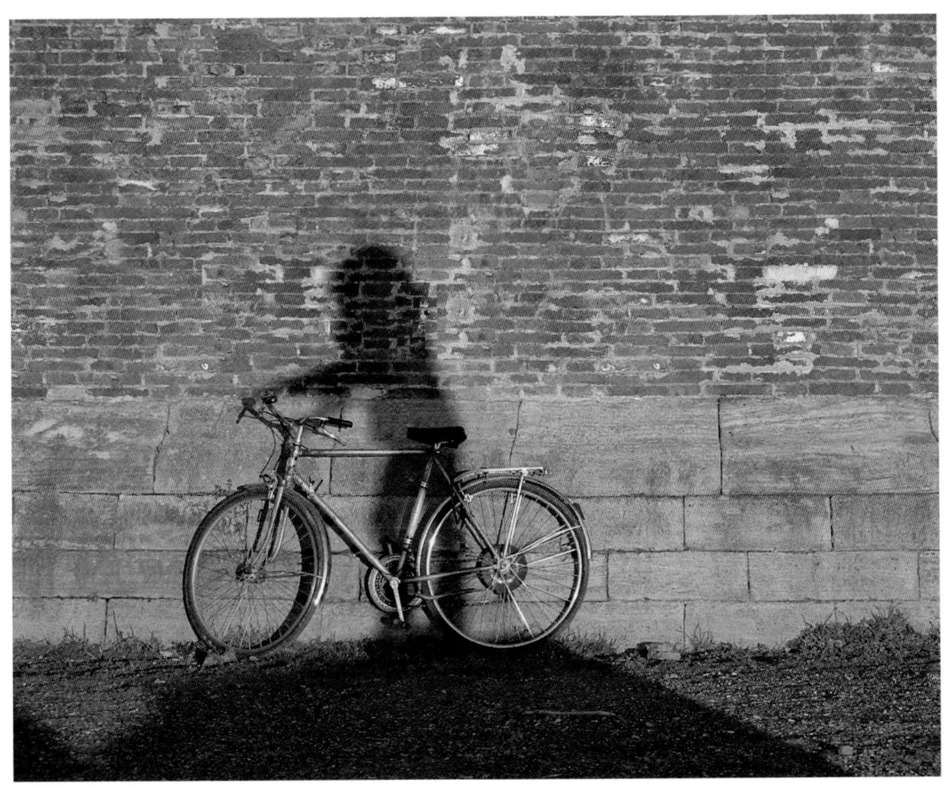

AUGUST 20

The woman who can create her own job
is the woman who will win fame and fortune.

~ Amelia Earhart

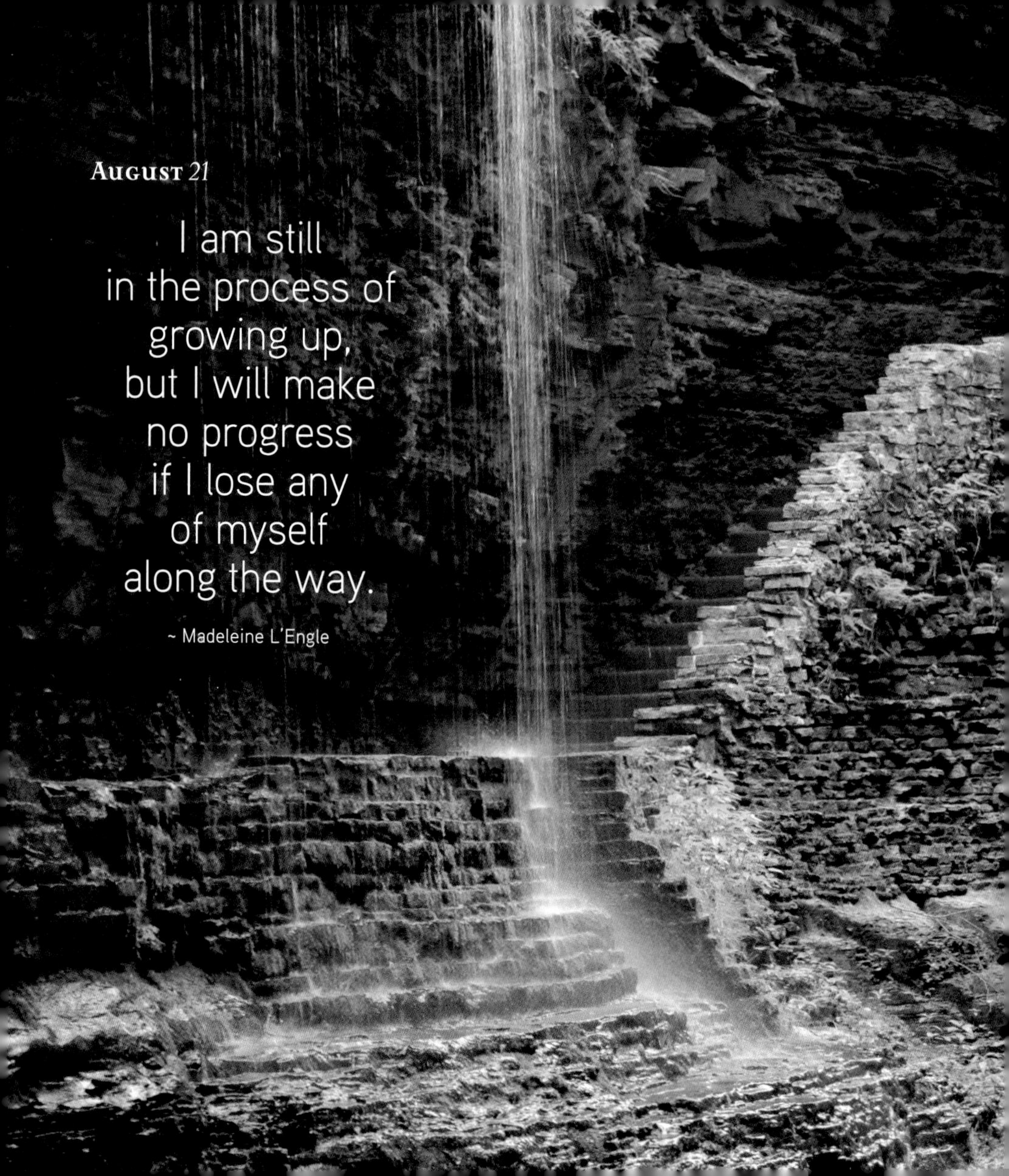
August 21
I am still
in the process of
growing up,
but I will make
no progress
if I lose any
of myself
along the way.
~ Madeleine L'Engle

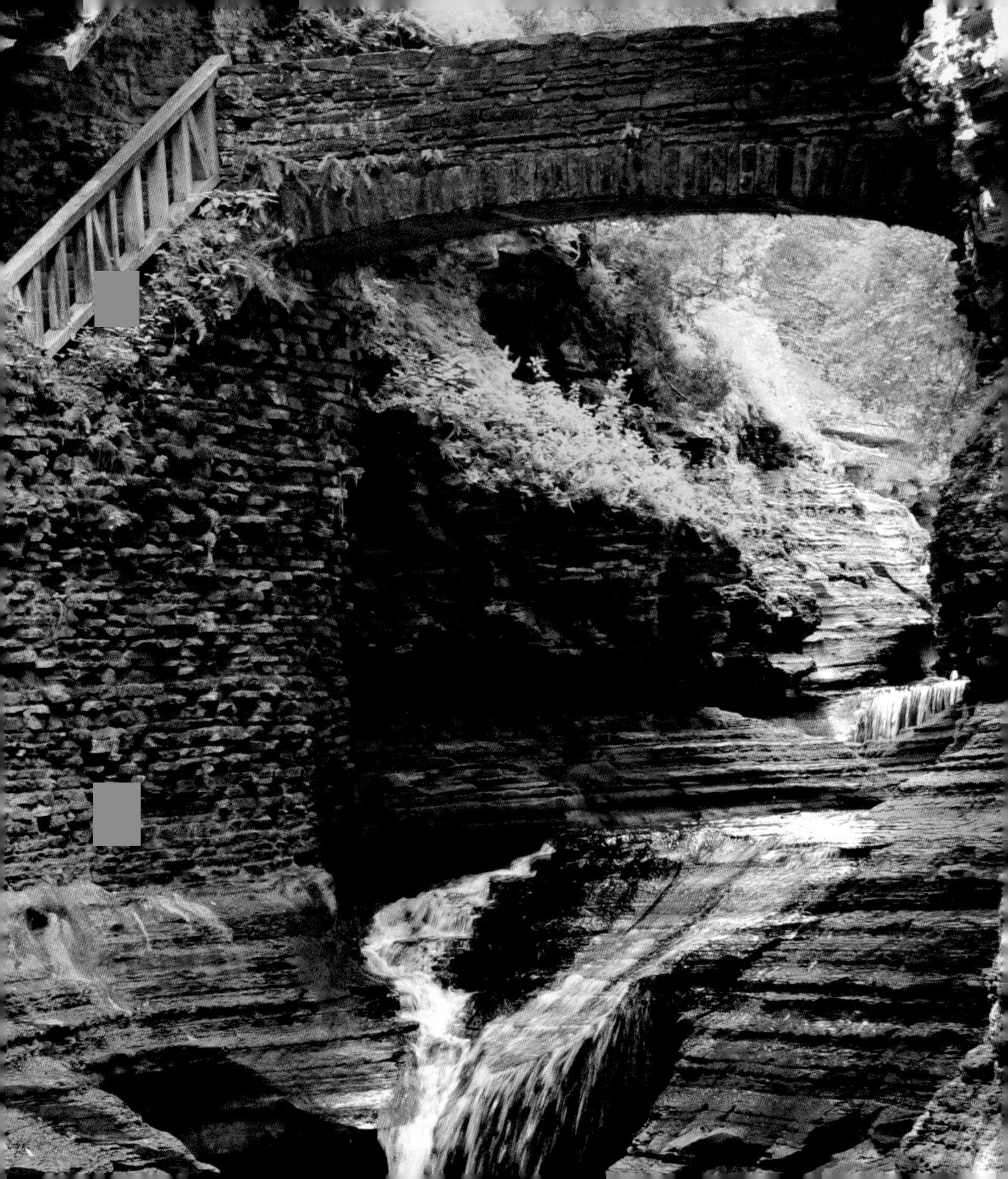

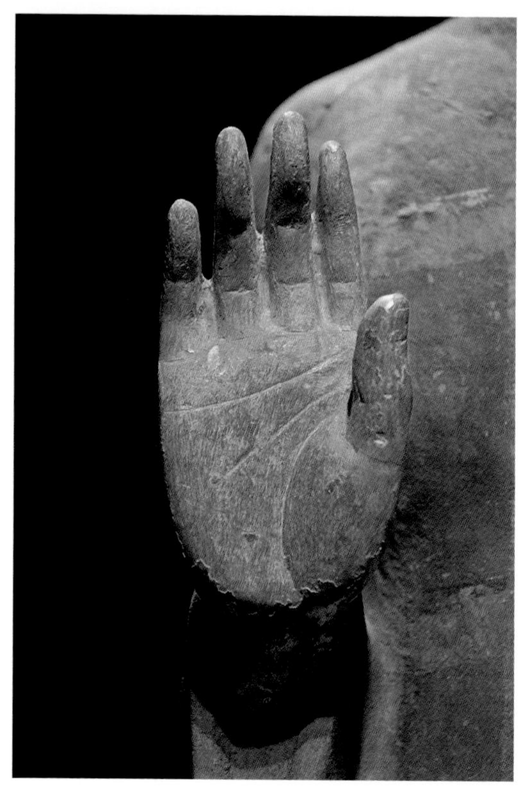

AUGUST 22

Those who are free of resentful thoughts
surely find peace.

~ Buddha

AUGUST 23

Without leaps of imagination, or dreaming, we lose the excitement of possibilities. Dreaming, after all, is a form of planning.

~ Gloria Steinem

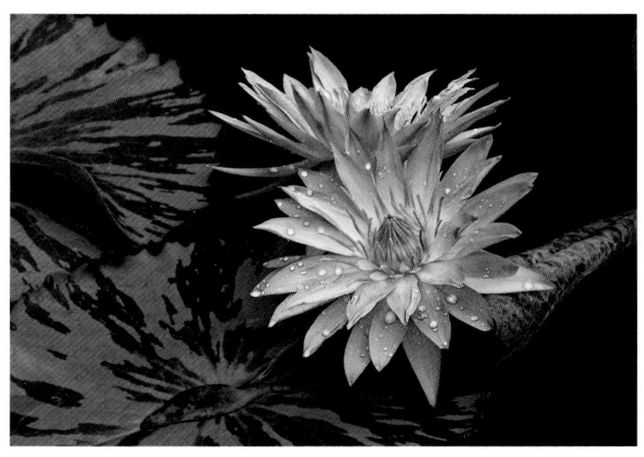

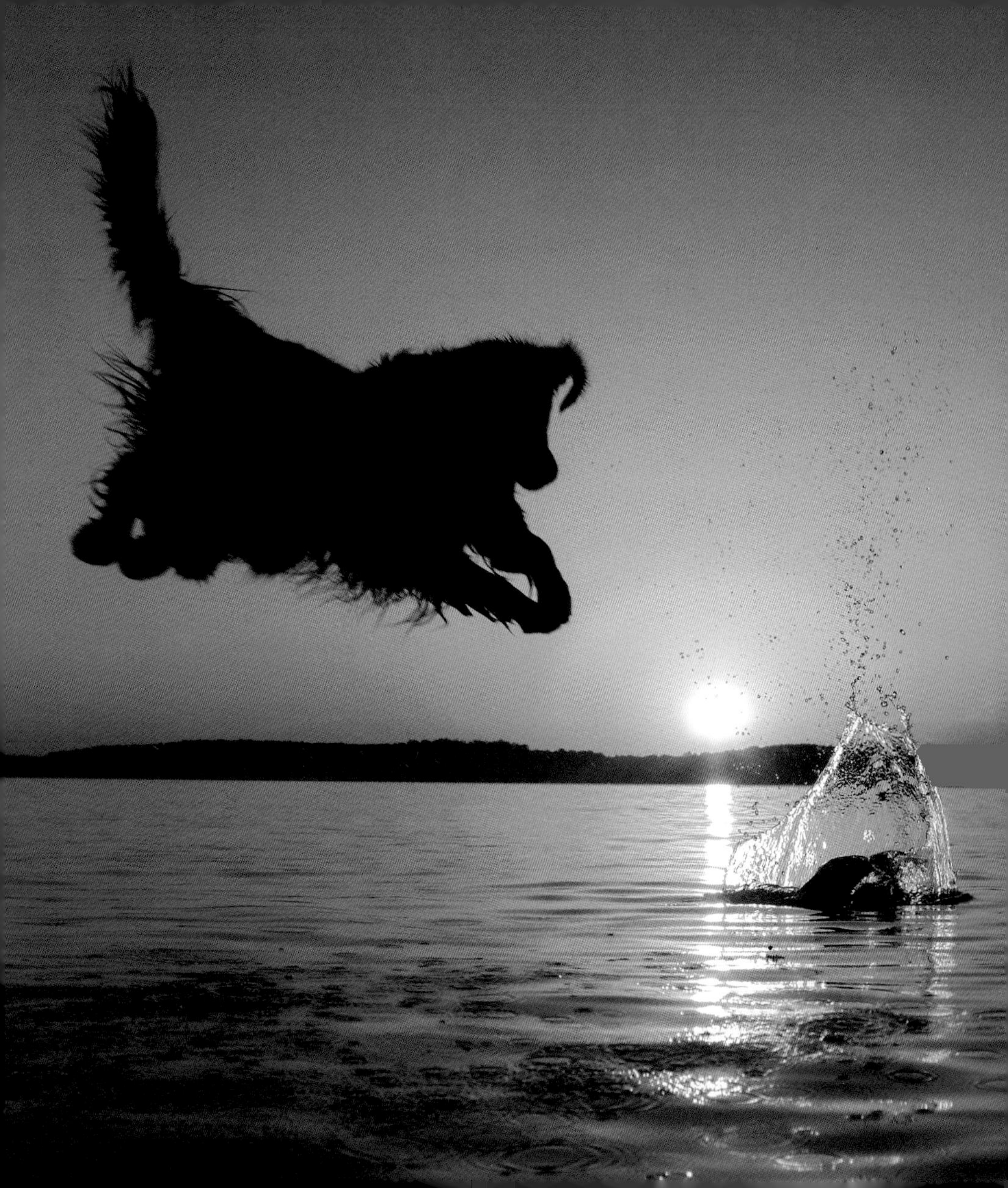

AUGUST 24

Perhaps
loving something
is the only
starting place there is
for making your life
your own.

~ Alice Koller

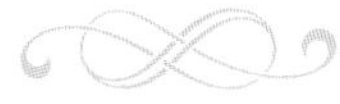

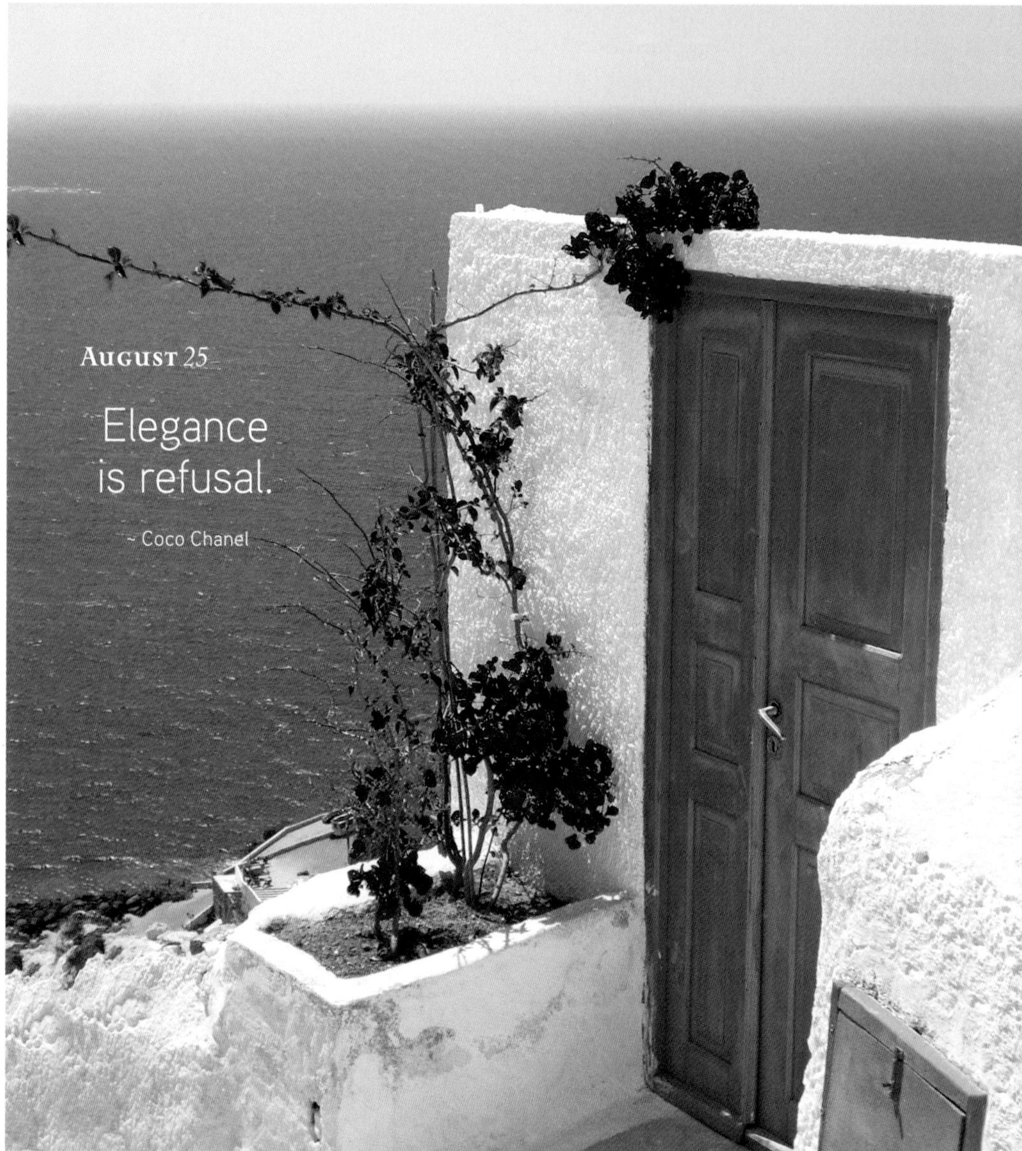

AUGUST 25

Elegance is refusal.

~ Coco Chanel

August 26

Forgetfulness is a form of freedom.

~ Kahlil Gibran

AUGUST 27

I have made my world,
and it is a
much better world
than I ever saw
outside.

~ Louise Nevelson

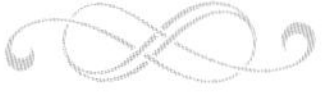

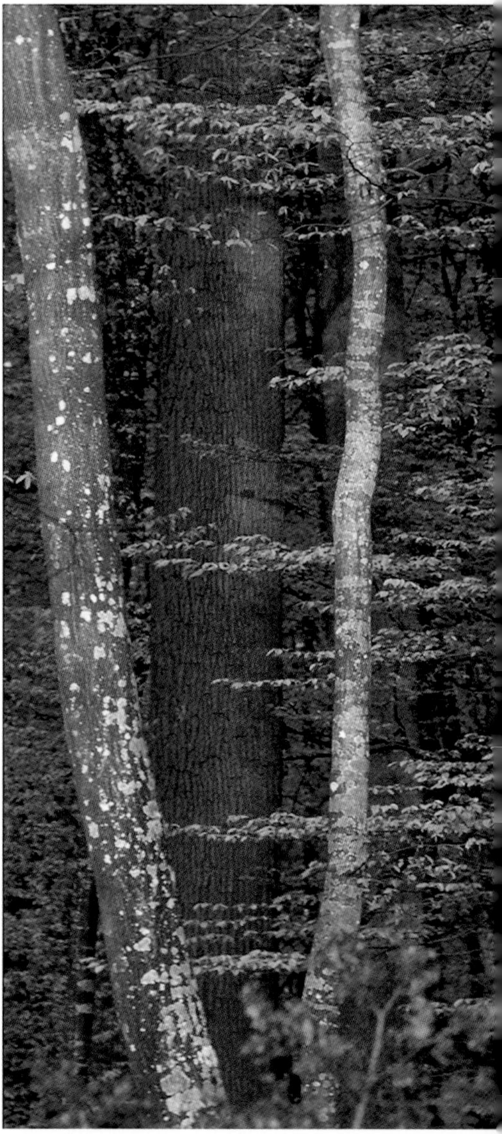

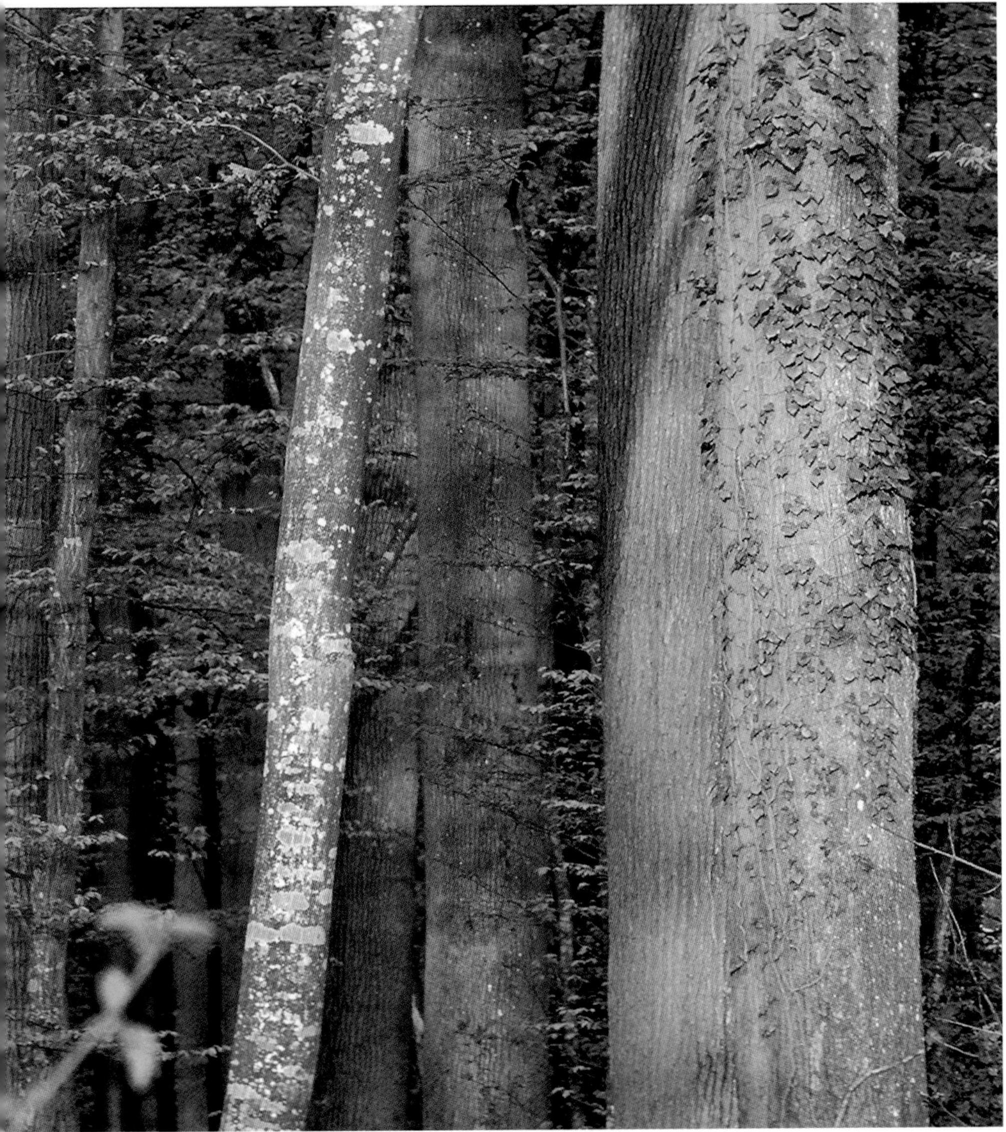

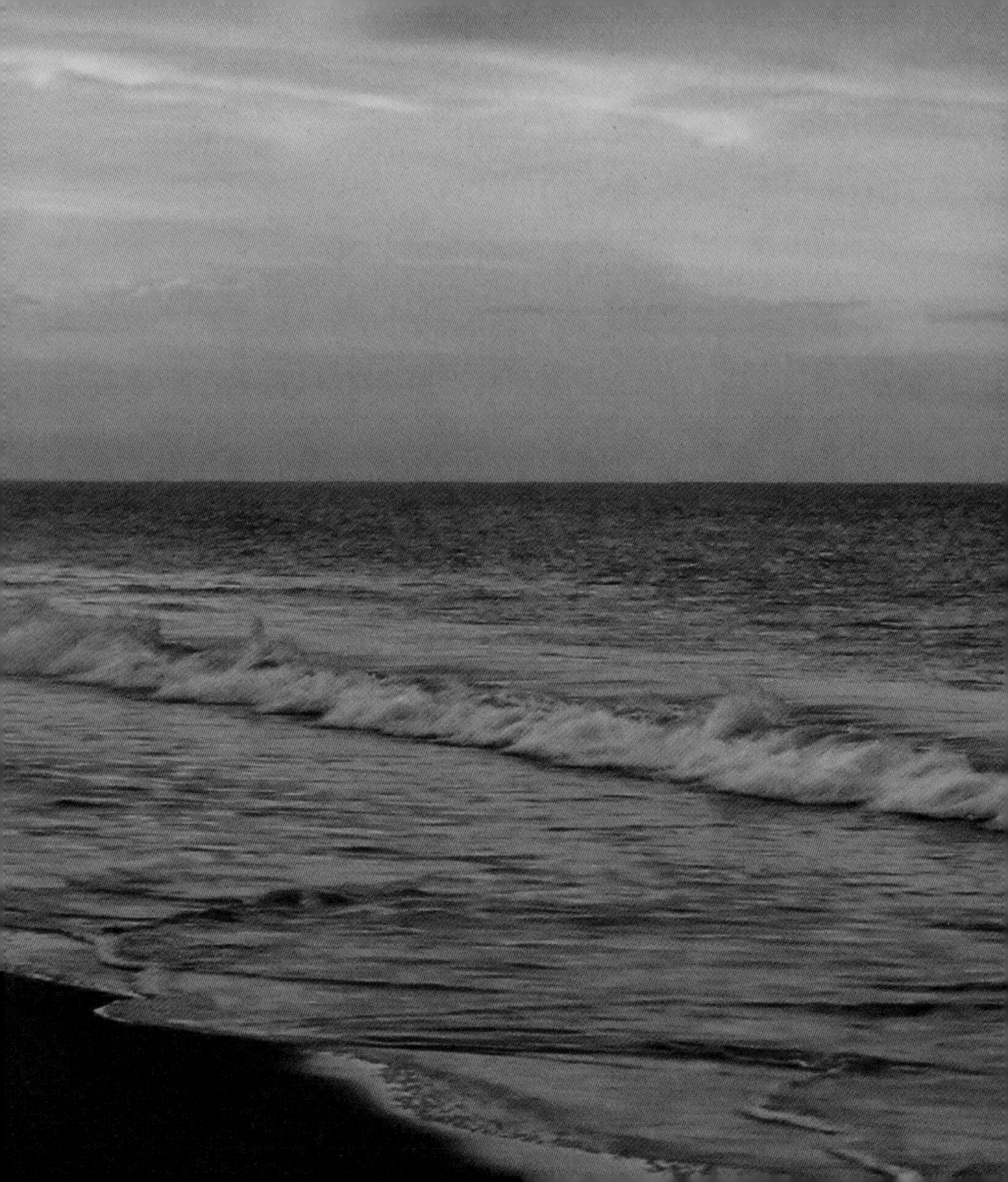

Be daring, be different, be impractical,
be anything that will assert integrity of purpose
and imaginative vision against the play-it-safers,
the creatures of the commonplace,
the slaves of the ordinary.

~ Cecil Beaton

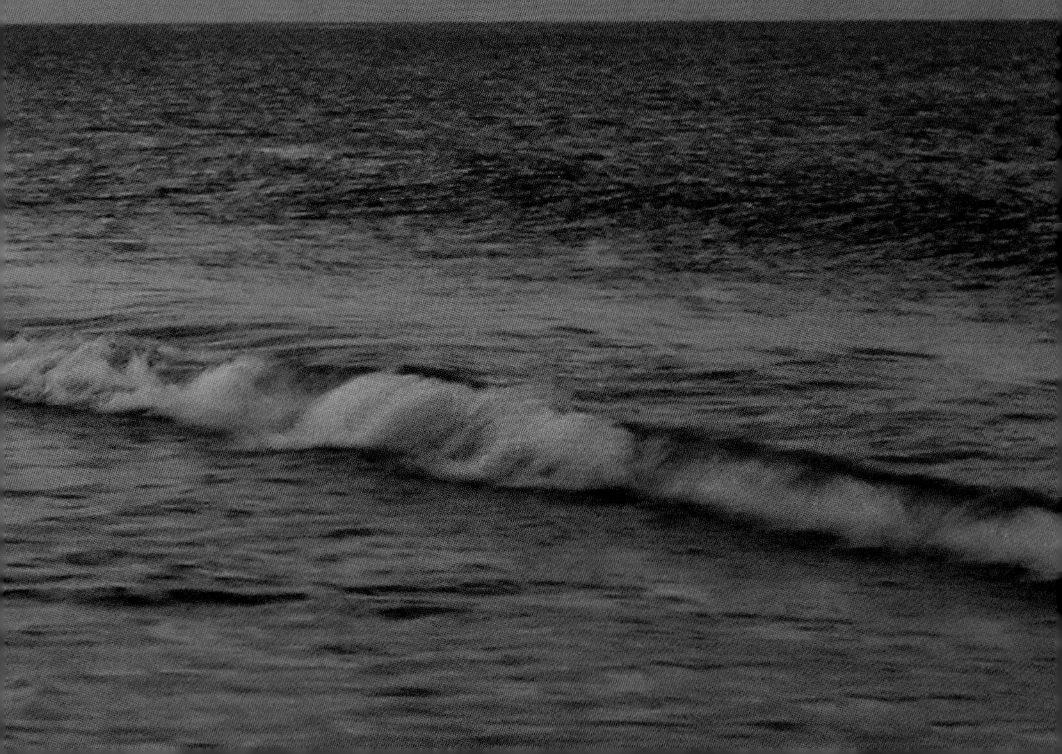

AUGUST 29

In solitude we give
passionate attention
to our lives,
to our memories,
to the details around us.

~ Virginia Woolf

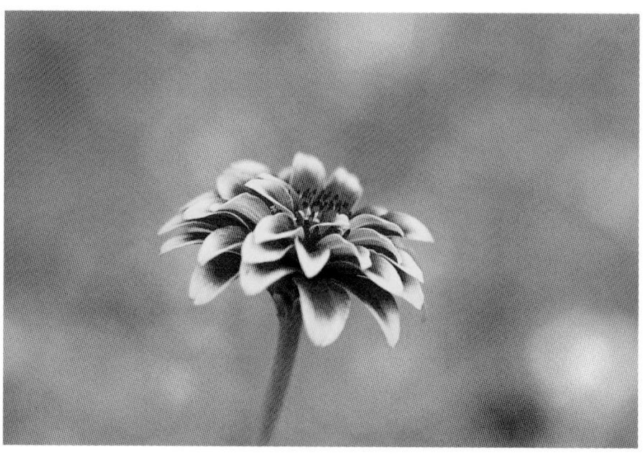

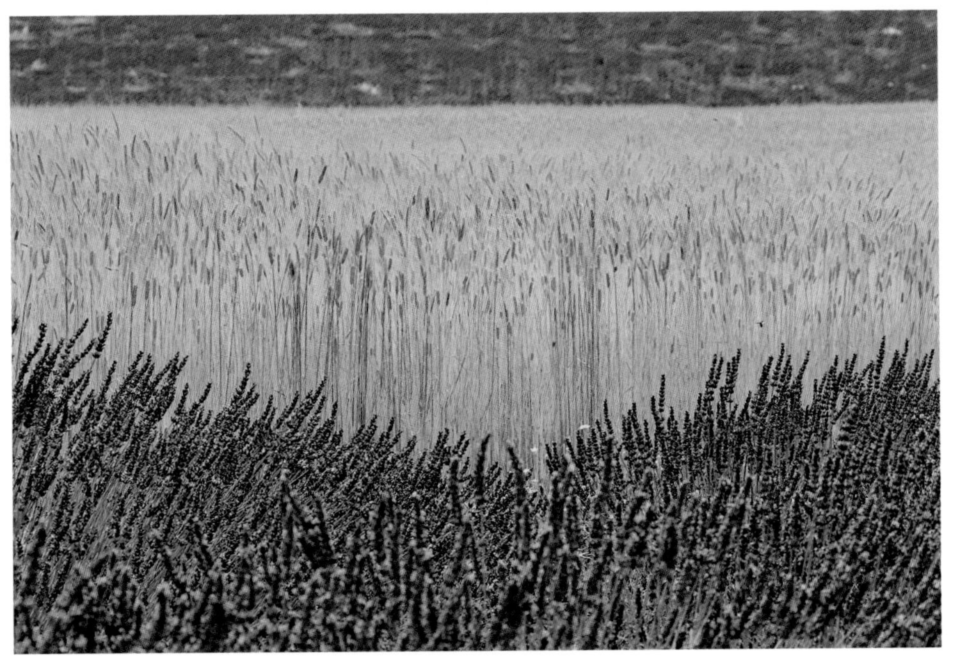

AUGUST 30

In the last analysis,
our only freedom is the freedom
to discipline ourselves.

~ Bernard Baruch

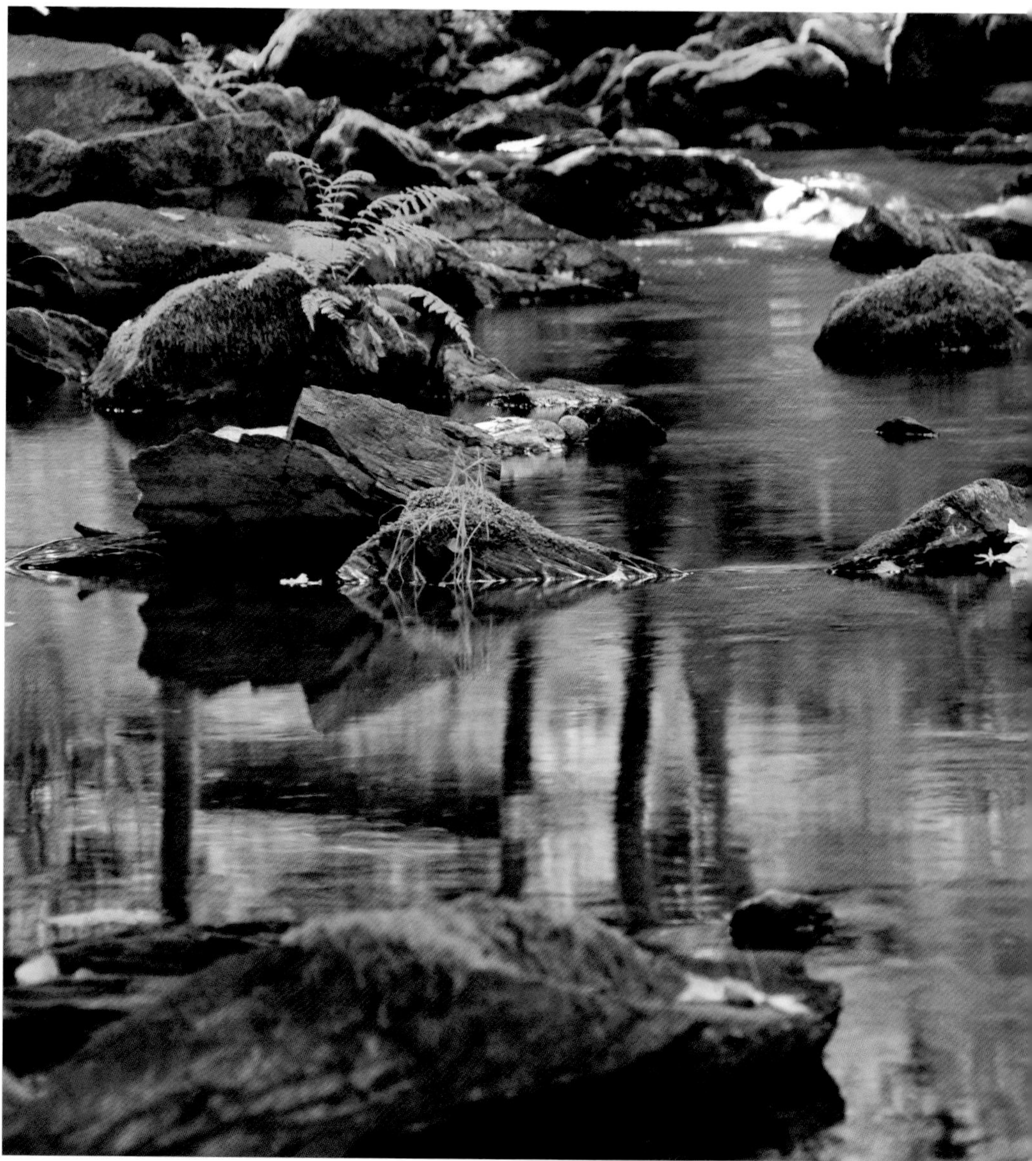

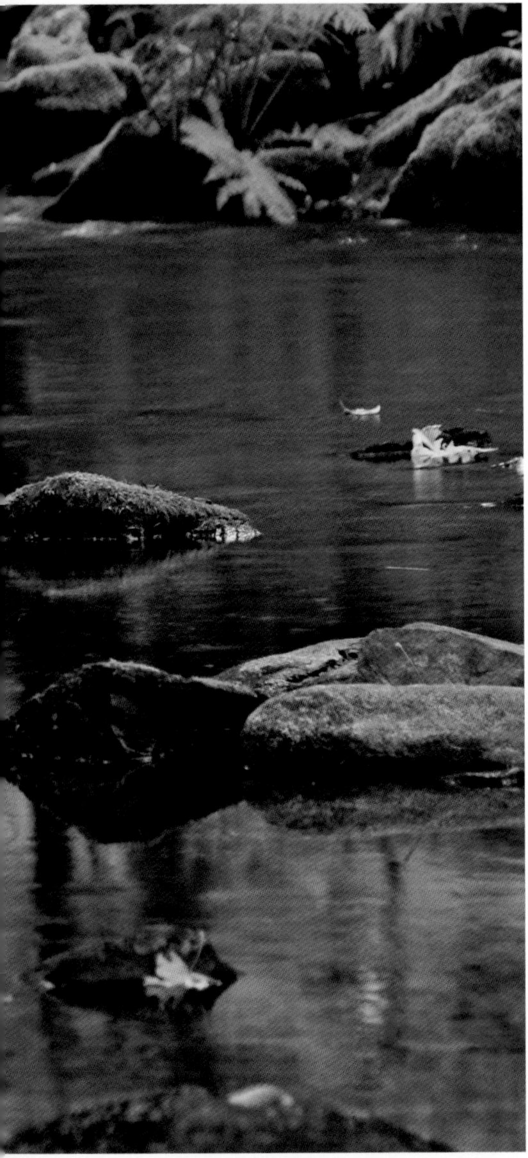

AUGUST 31

Freedom
is from within.

~ Frank Lloyd Wright

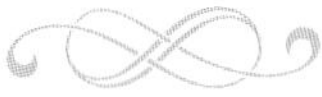

PURPOSE

September

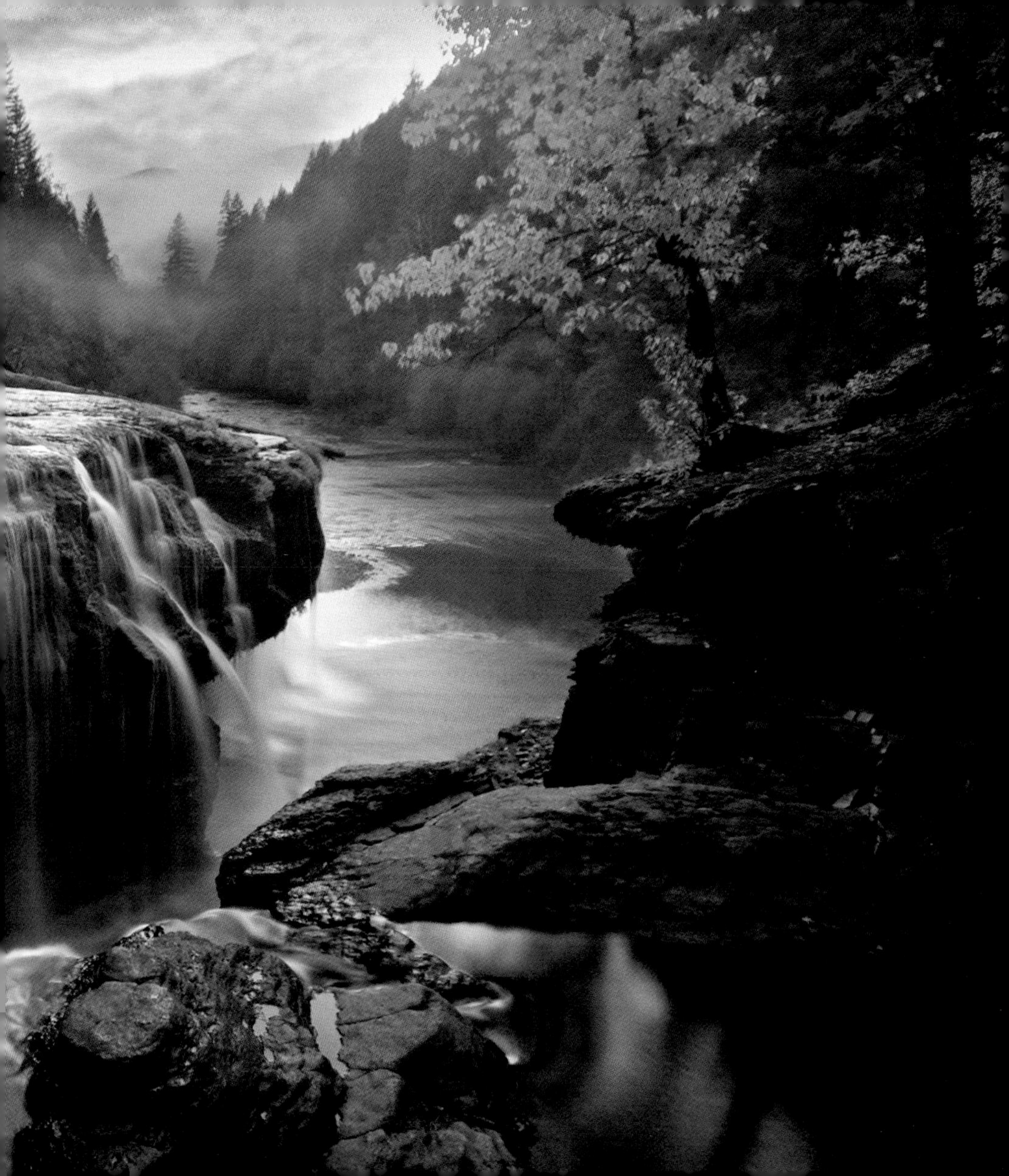

SEPTEMBER 1

Try again. Fail again. Fail better.

~ Samuel Beckett

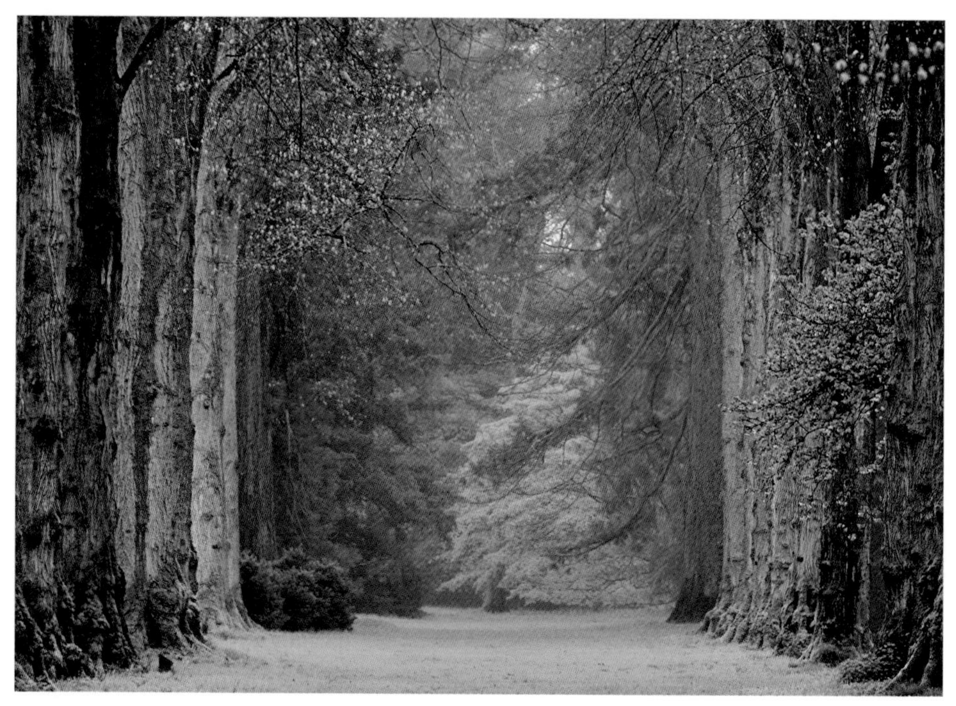

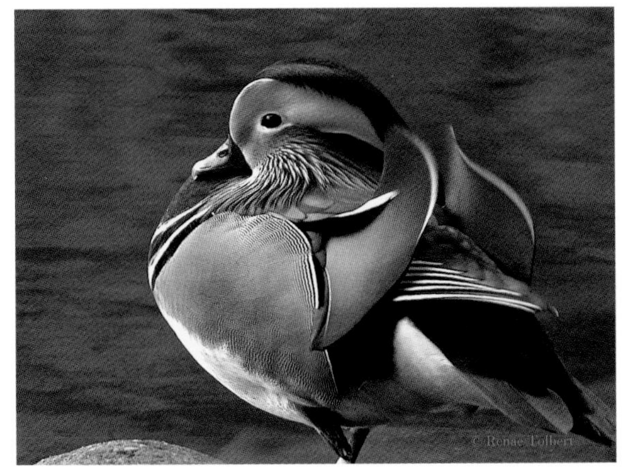

SEPTEMBER 2

Perplexity is the beginning of knowledge.

~ Kahlil Gibran

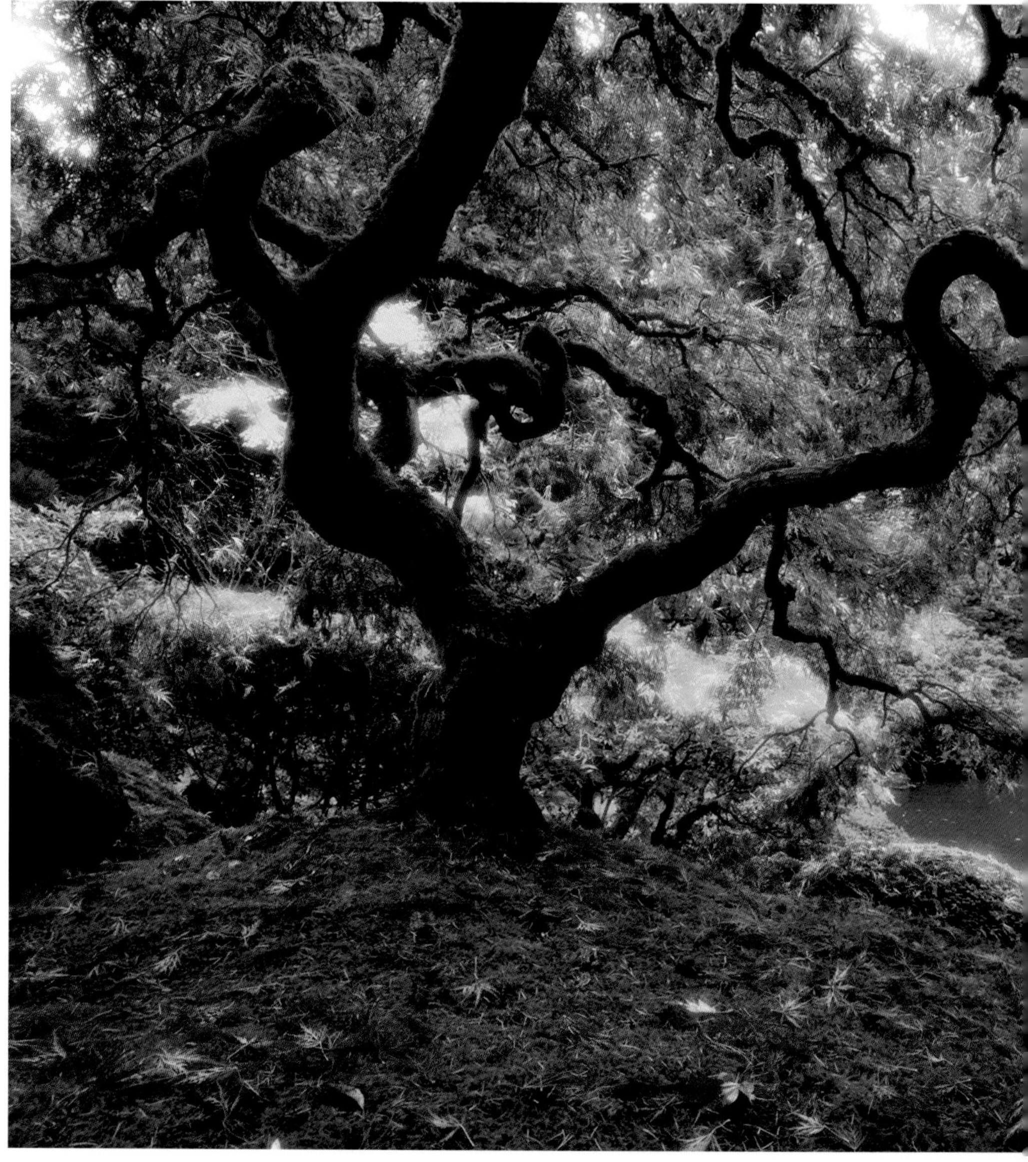

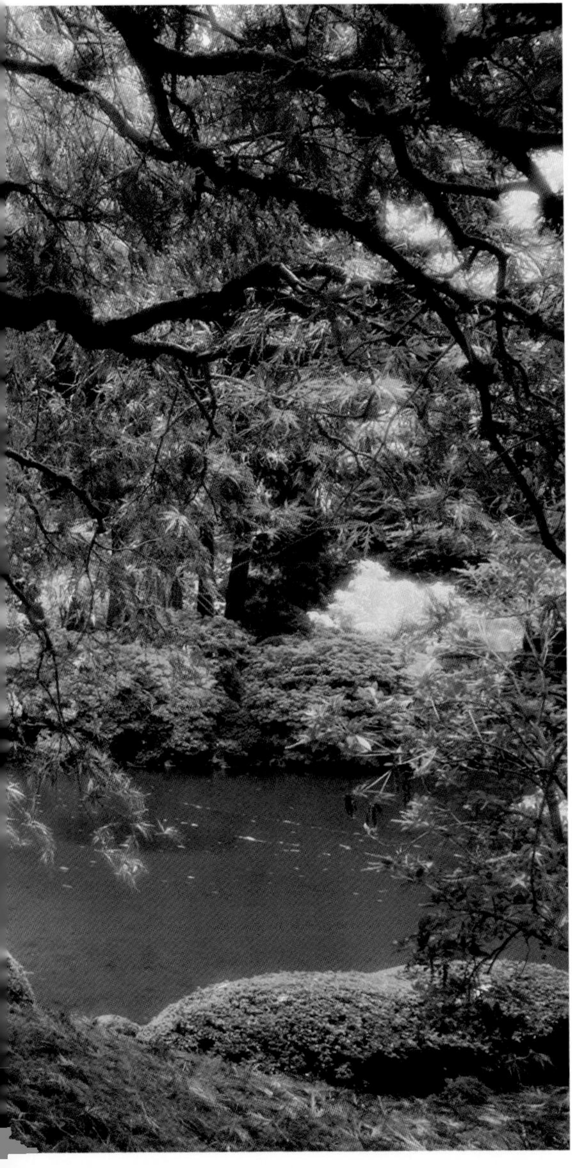

SEPTEMBER 3

Do not weep;
do not wax
indignant.
Understand.

~ Baruch Spinoza

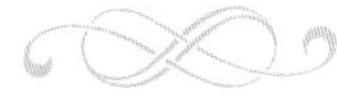

September 4

Dream big—dream very big.
Work hard—work very hard.
And after you've done all
you can, you stand, wait,
and fully surrender.

~ Oprah Winfrey

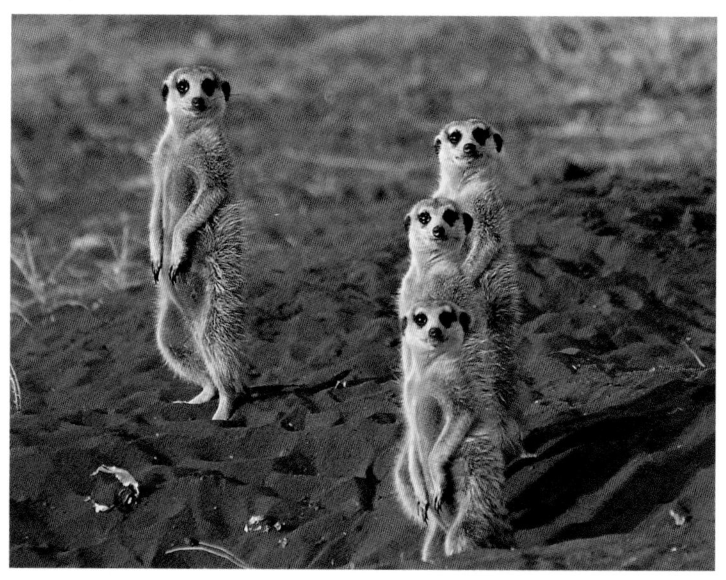

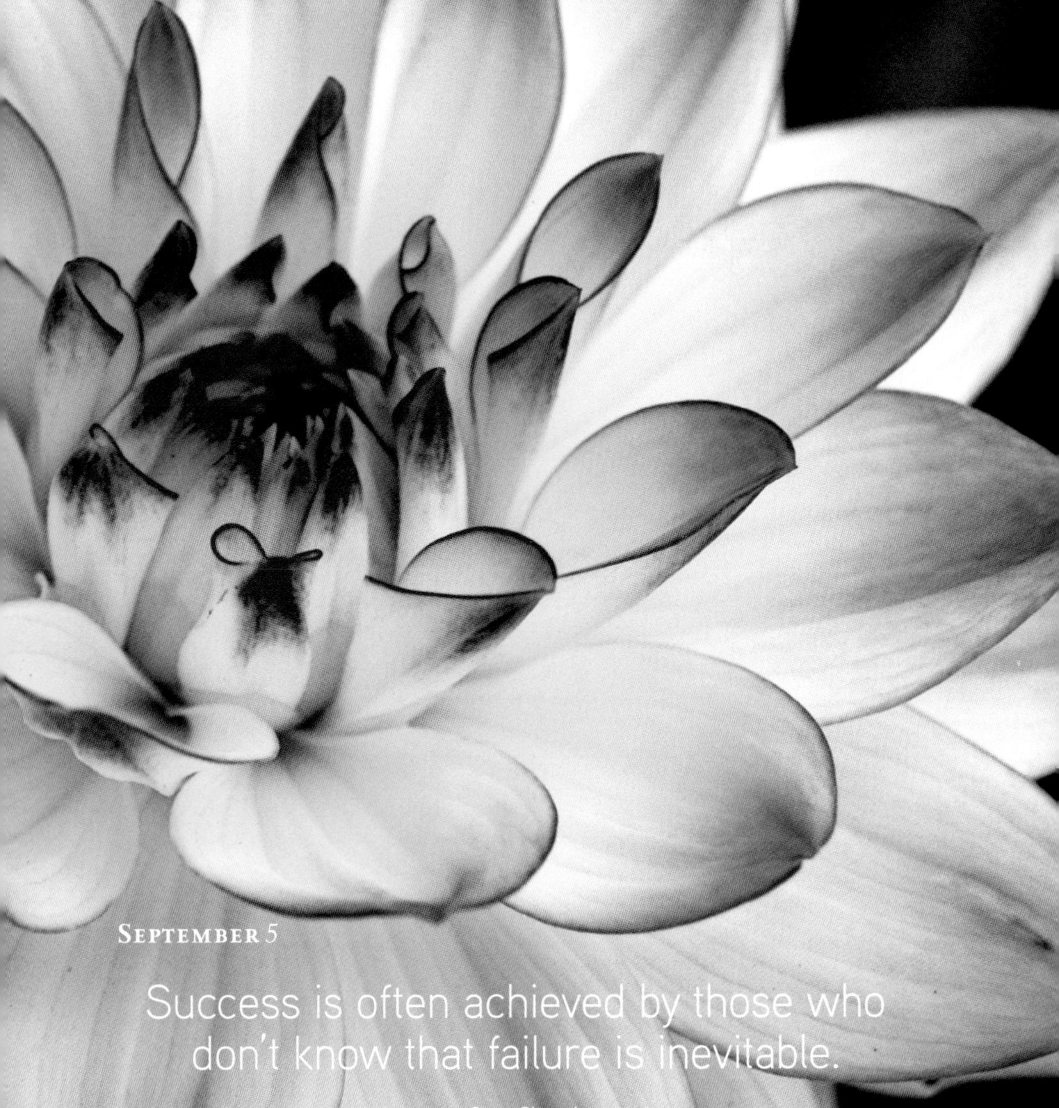

SEPTEMBER *5*

Success is often achieved by those who don't know that failure is inevitable.

~ Coco Chanel

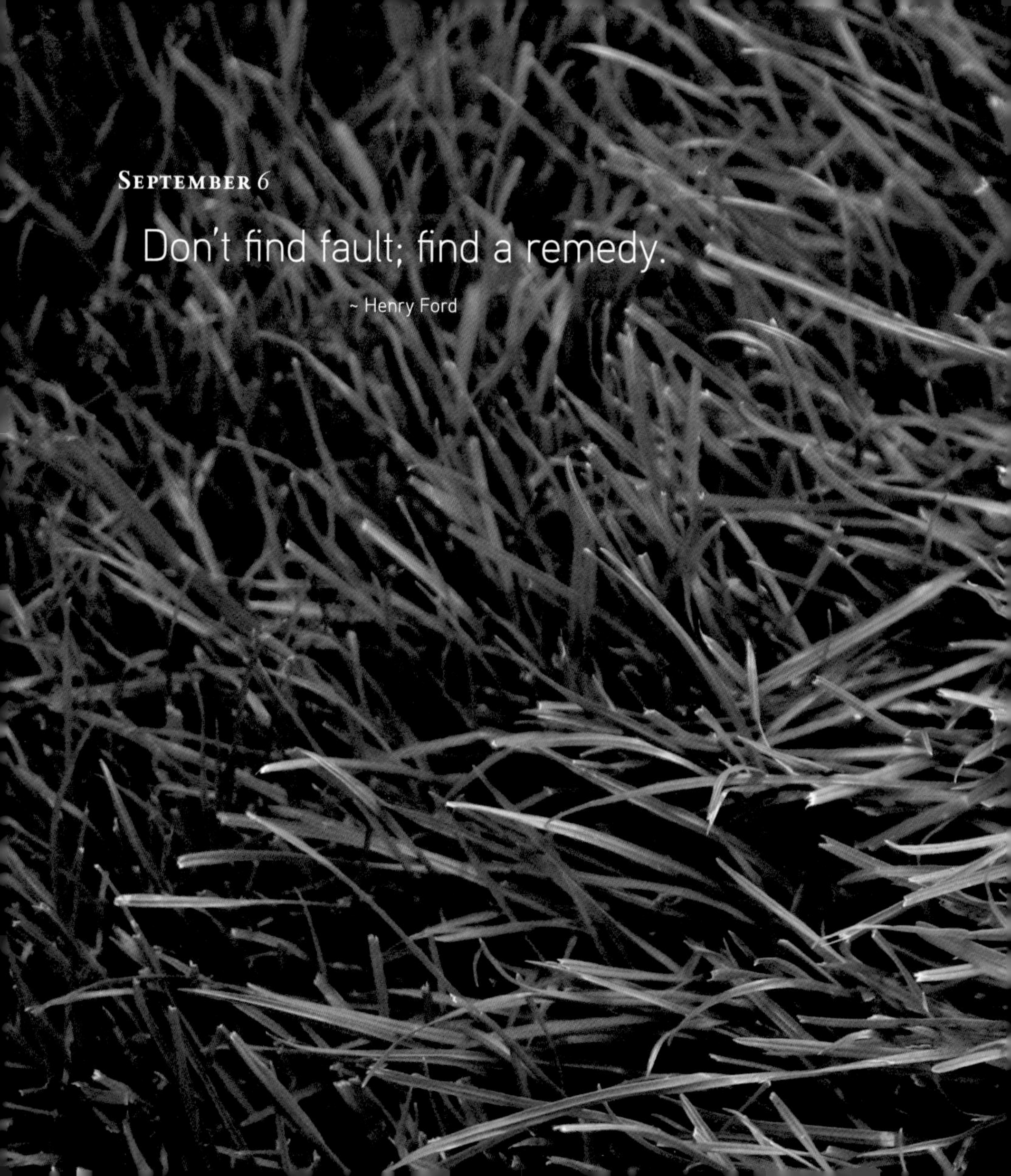
SEPTEMBER 6
Don't find fault; find a remedy.
~ Henry Ford

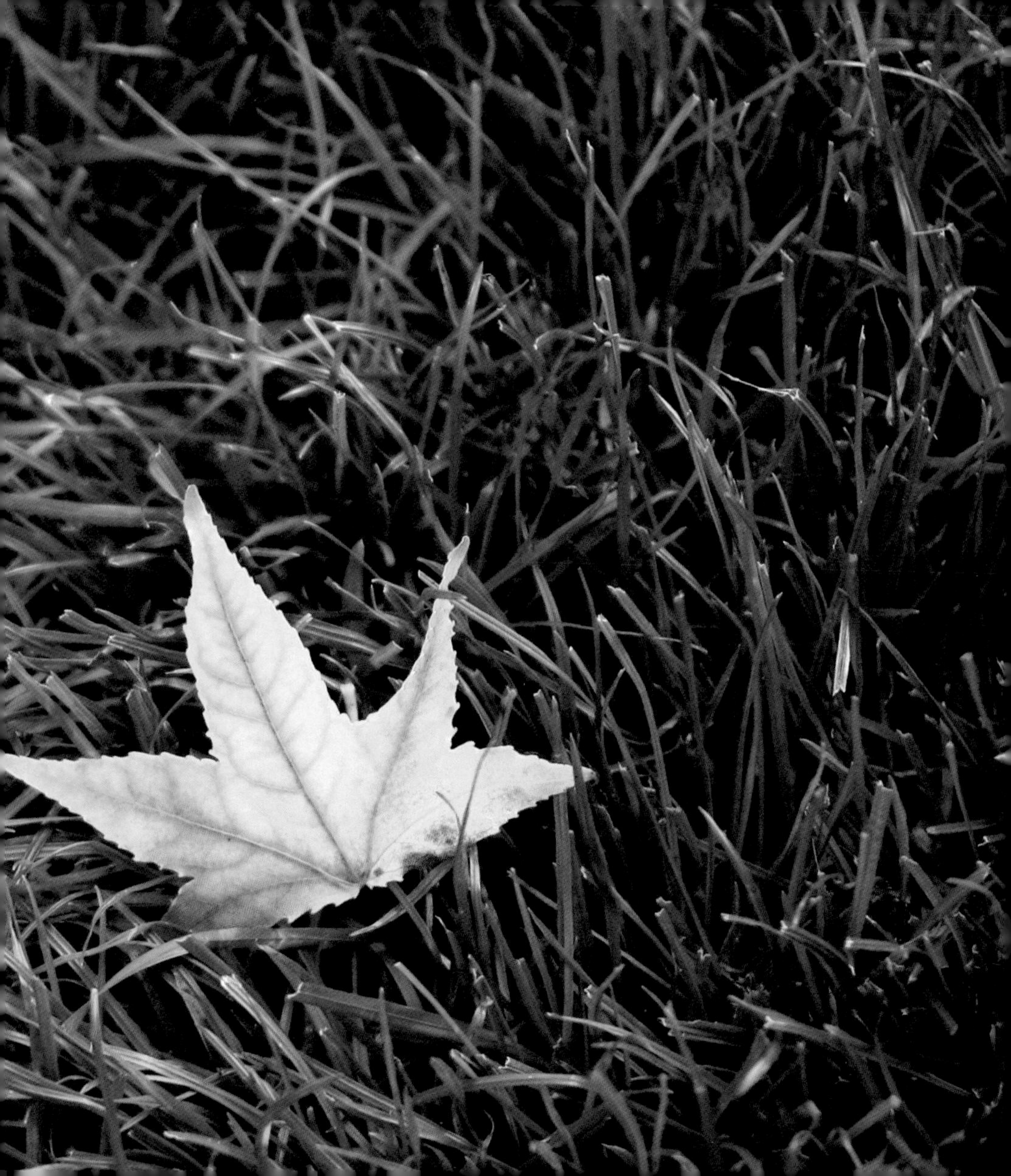

SEPTEMBER 7

The right word may be effective, but no word was ever as effective as a rightly timed pause.

~ Mark Twain

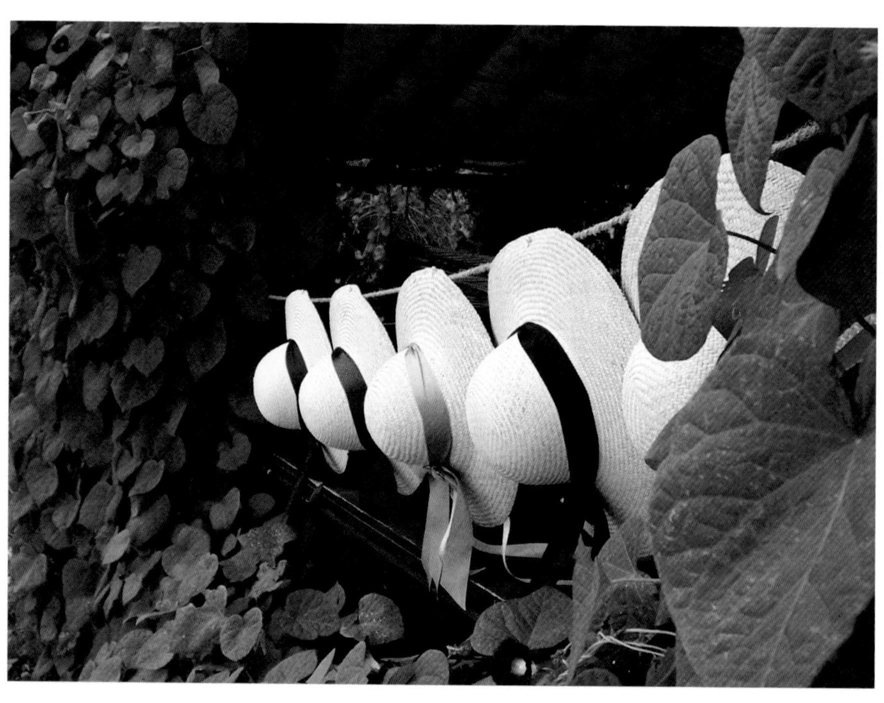

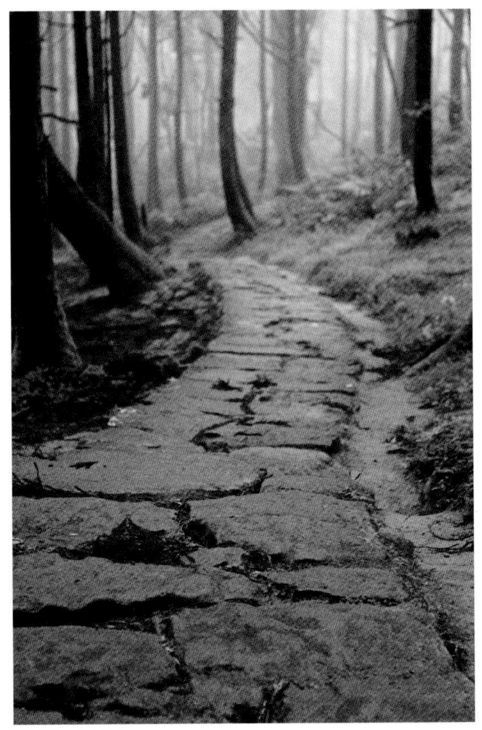

SEPTEMBER 8

Learn to get in touch with the silence within yourself and know that everything in this life has a purpose.

~ Elisabeth Kübler-Ross

September 9

Inspiration usually comes during work, rather than before it.

~ Madeleine L'Engle

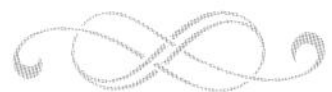

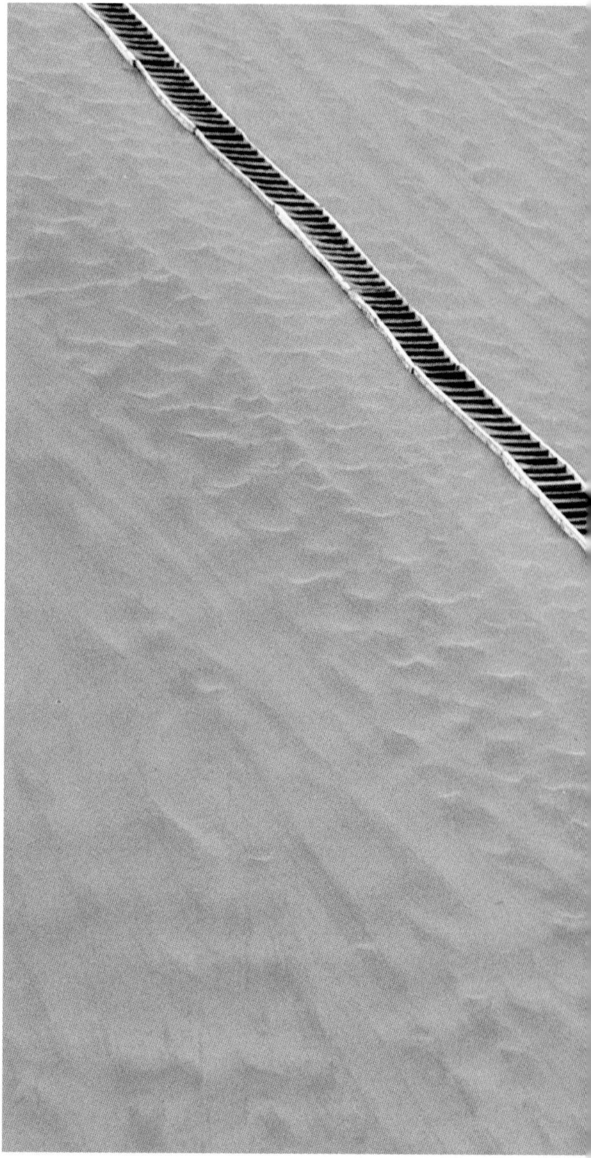

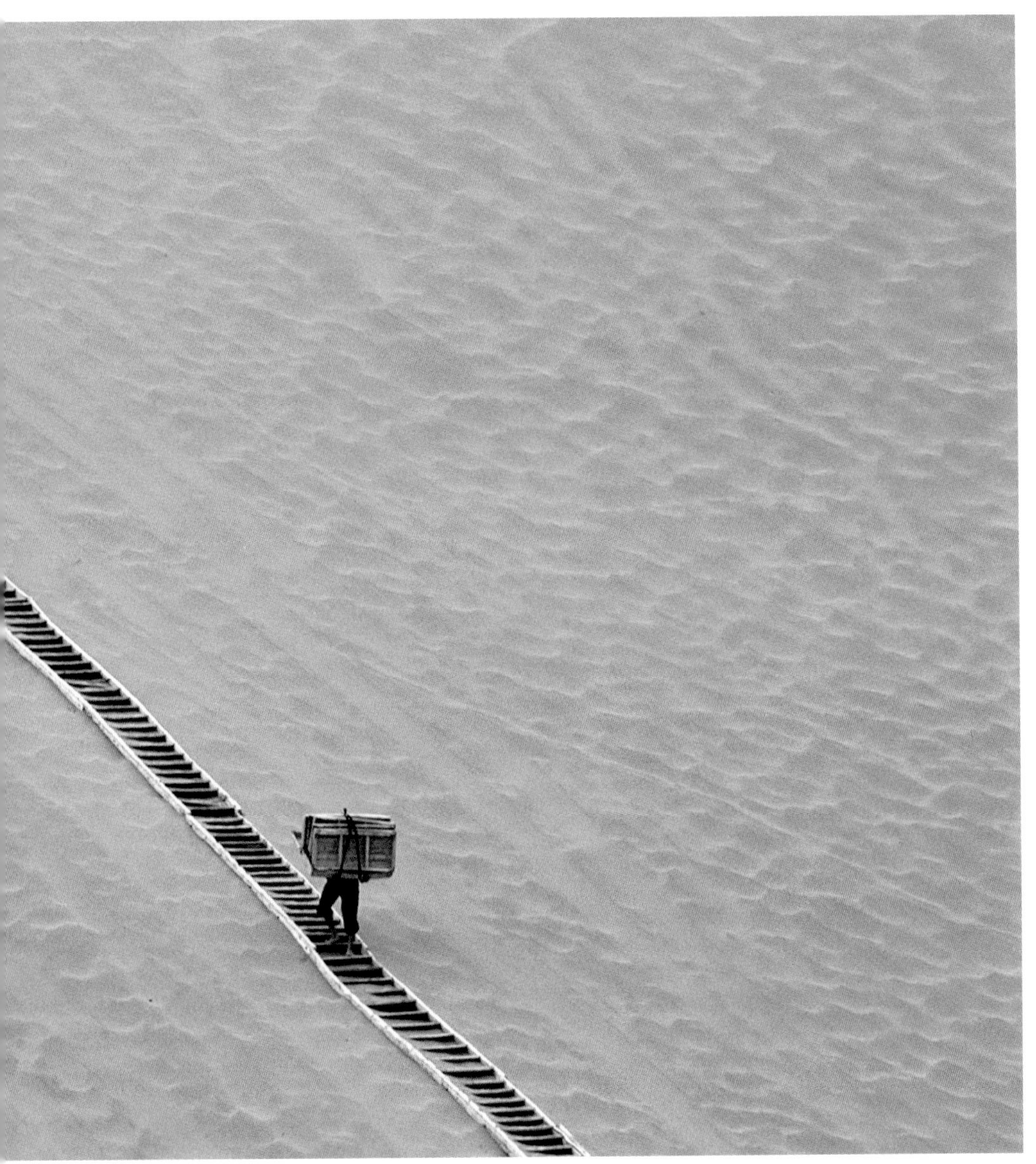

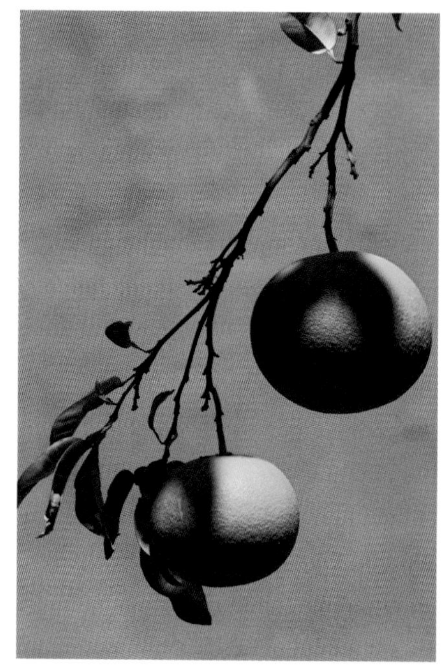

SEPTEMBER *10*

The only source
of knowledge
is experience.

~ Albert Einstein

September 11

Pleasure and action make the hours seem short.

~ William Shakespeare

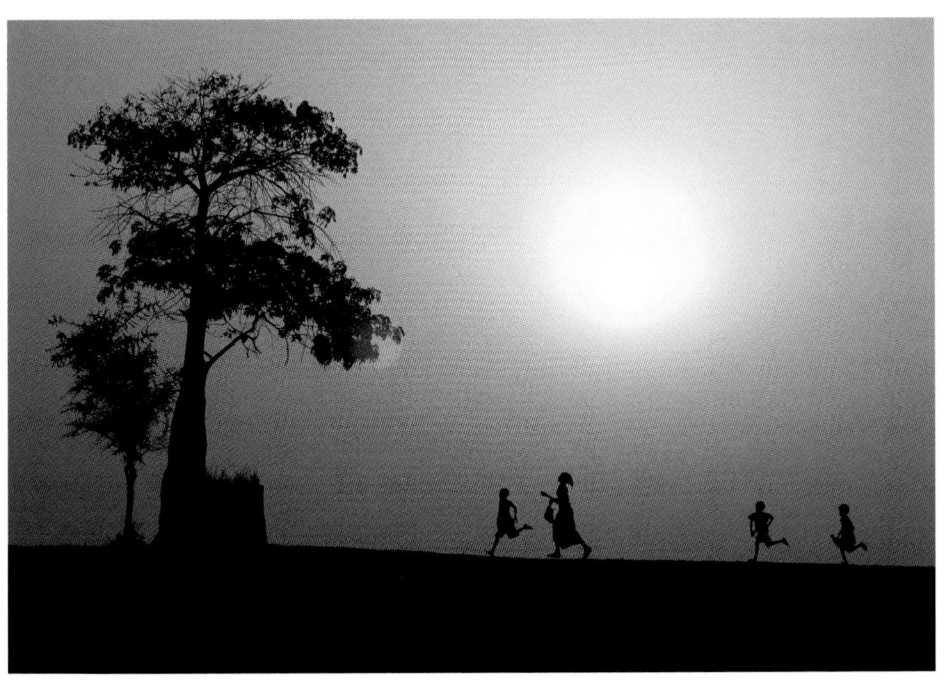

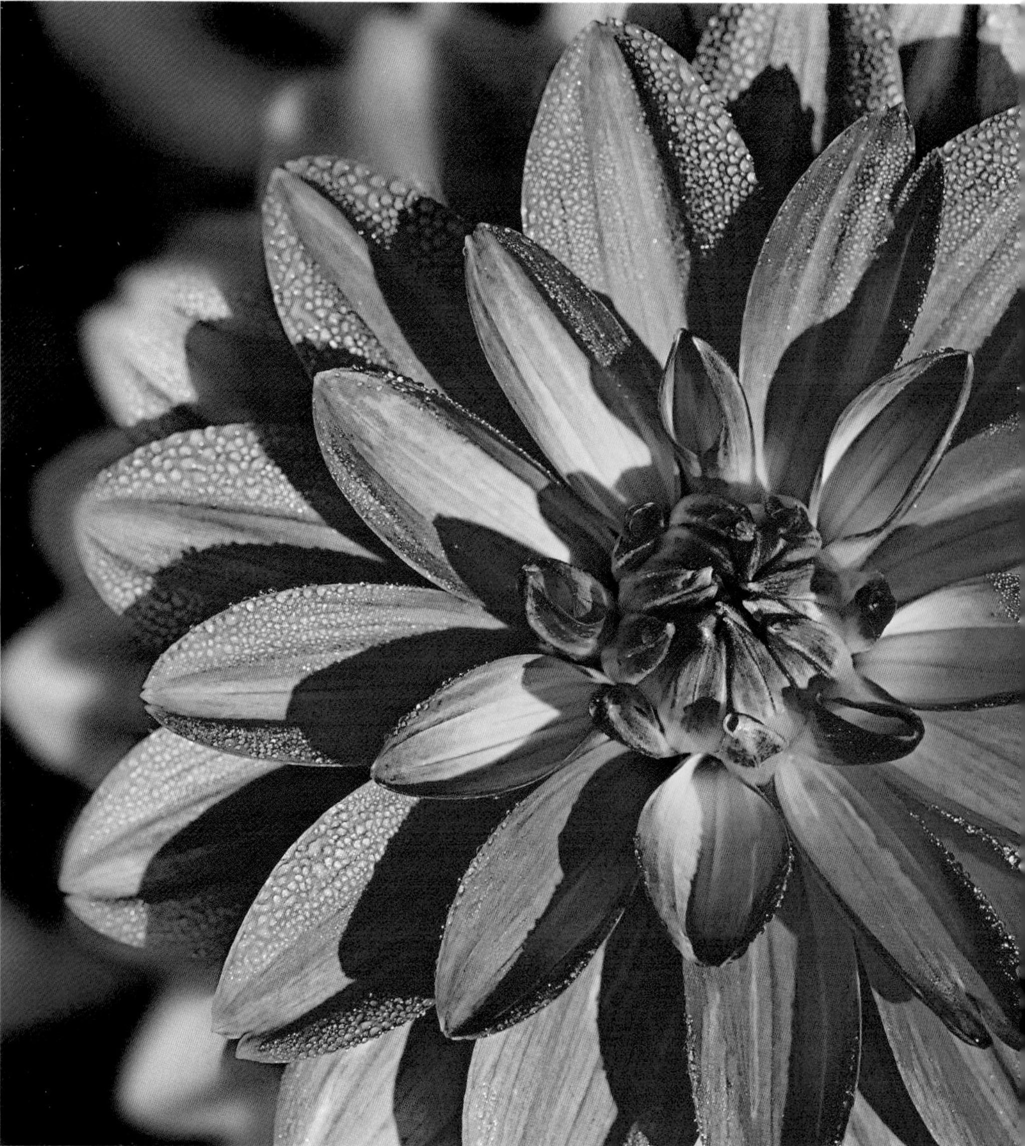

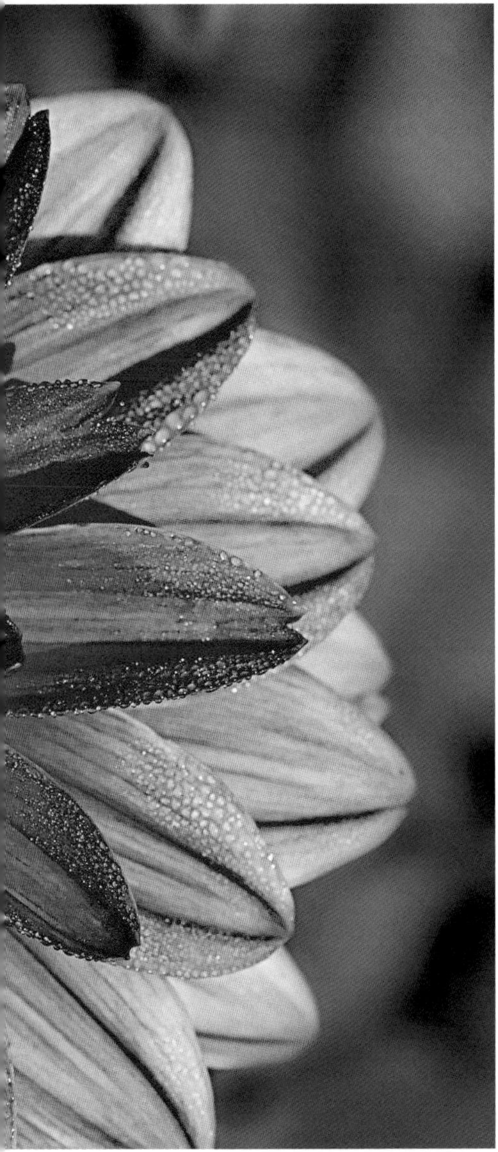

SEPTEMBER 12

You have to participate relentlessly in the manifestation of your own blessings.

~ Elizabeth Gilbert

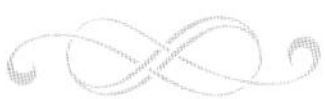

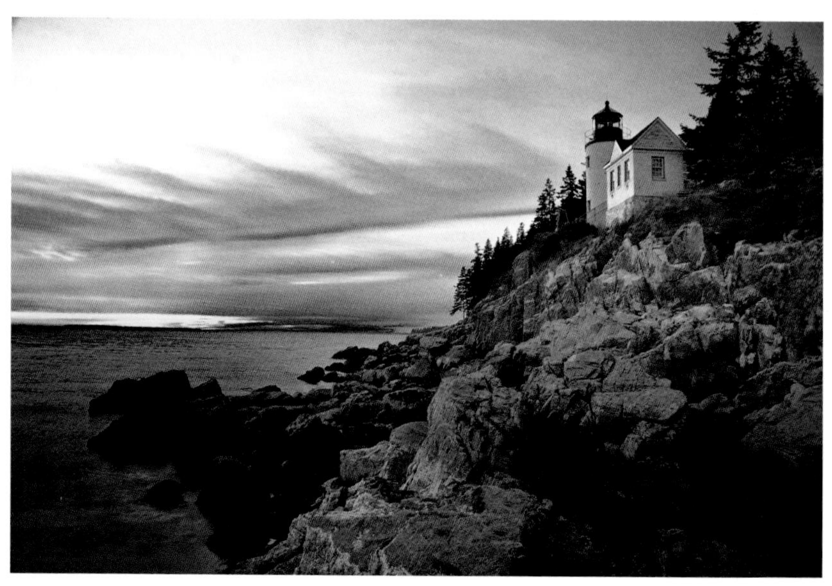

SEPTEMBER 13

Don't aim for success if you want it; just do what you love and believe in, and it will come naturally.

~ David Frost

SEPTEMBER *14*

Nothing is a waste of time if you use the experience wisely.

~ Auguste Rodin

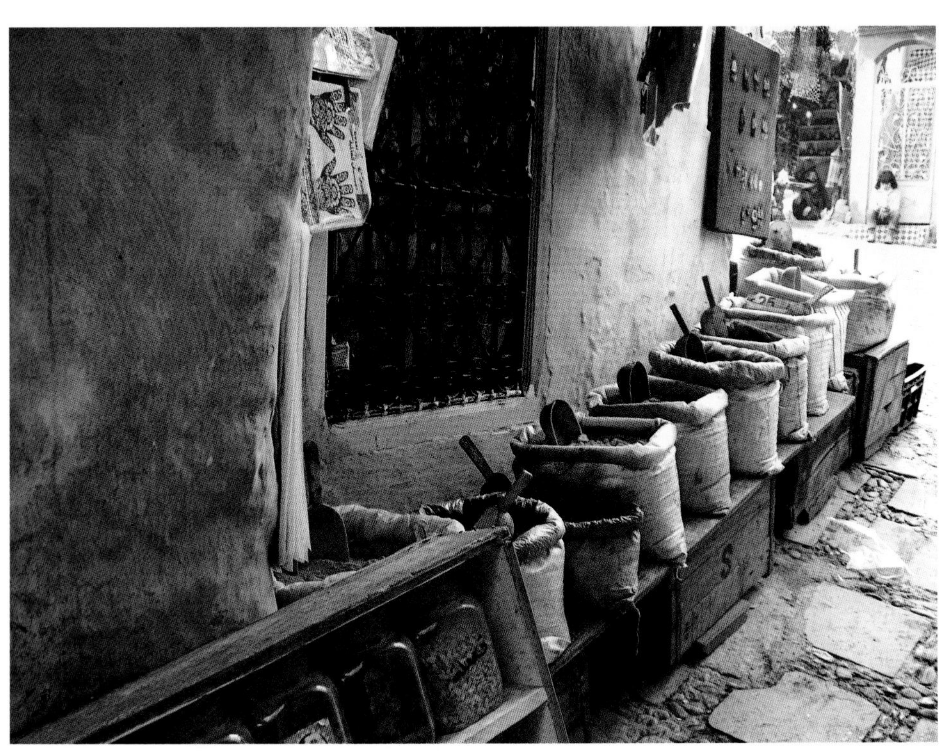

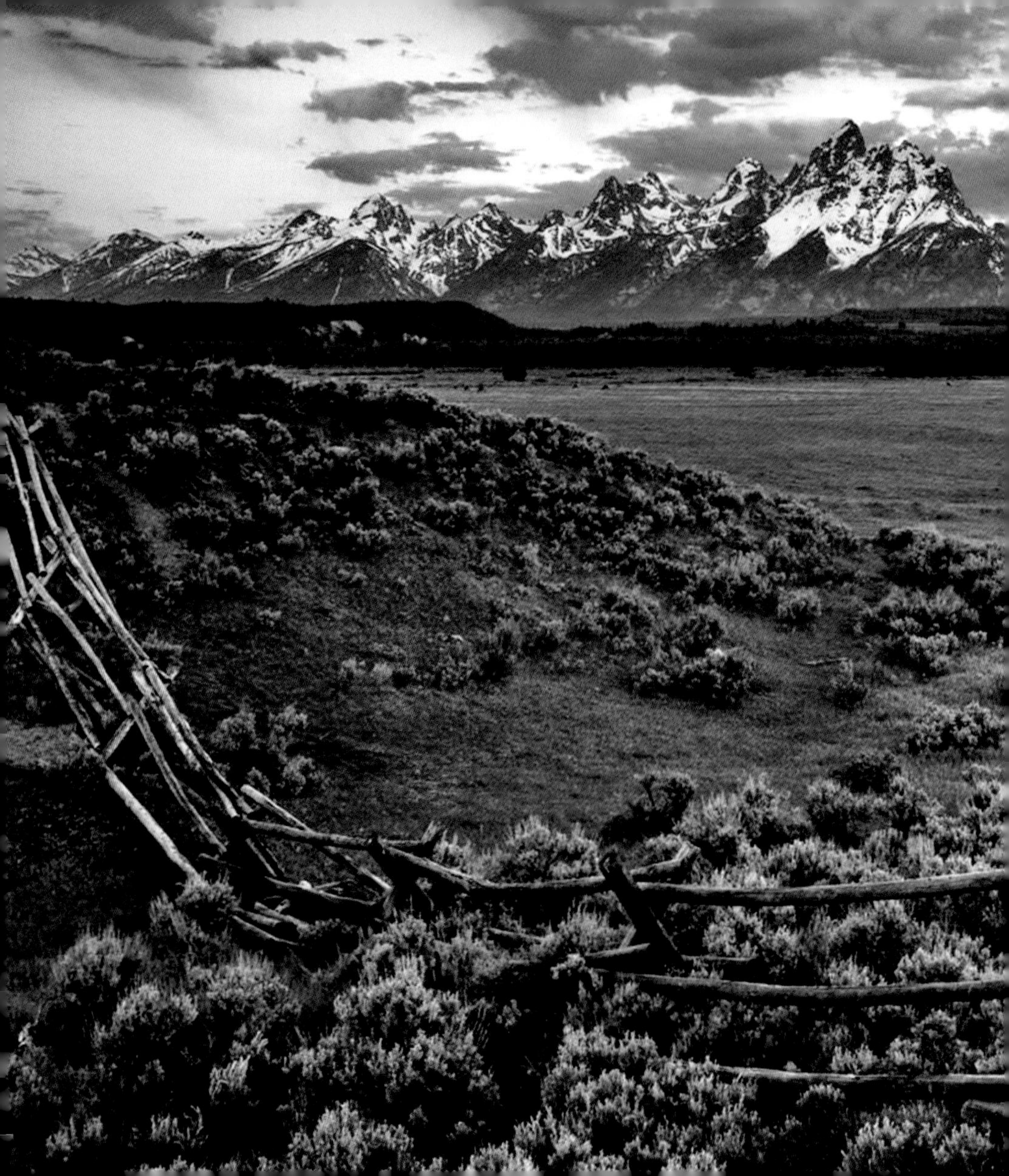

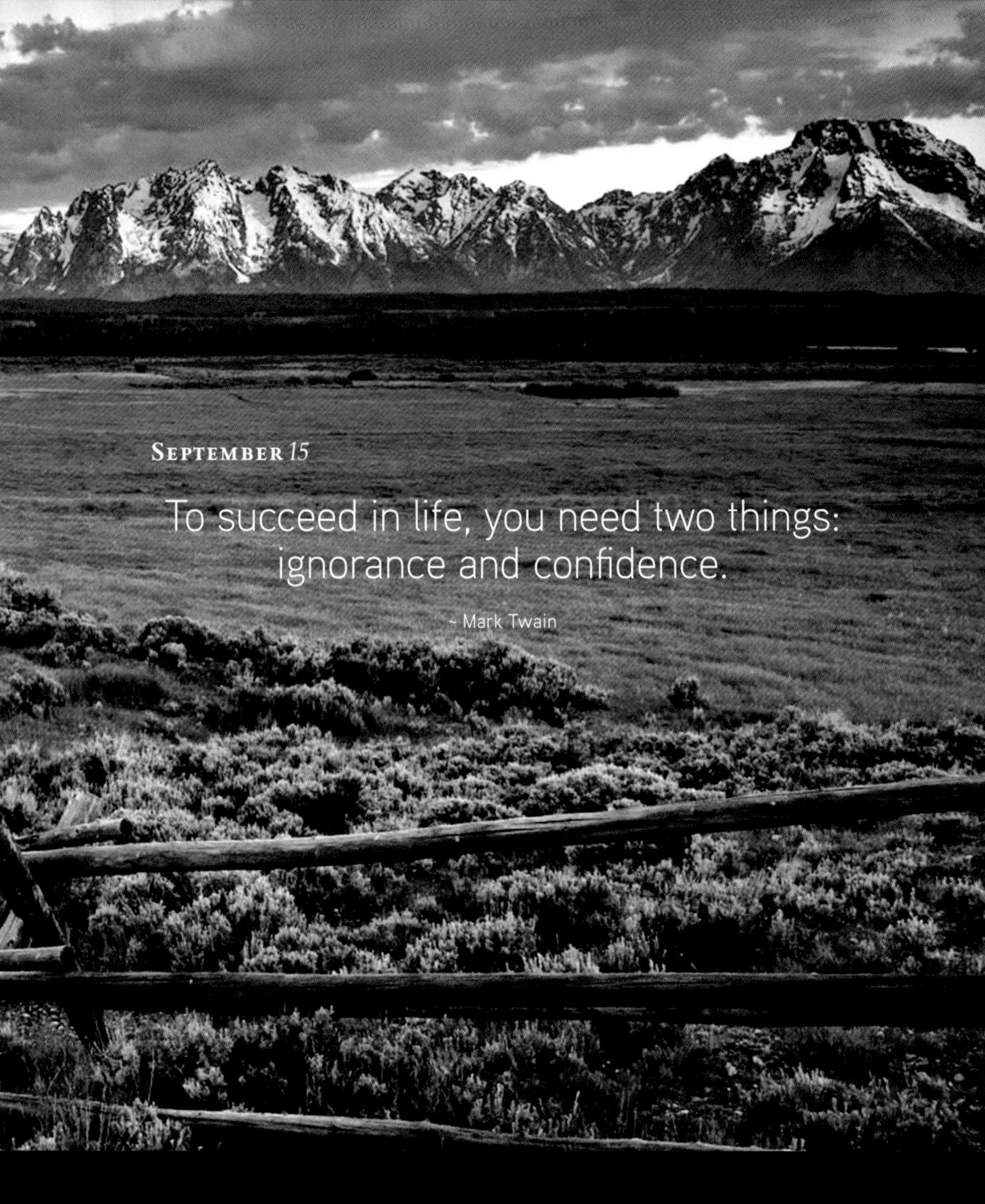

SEPTEMBER *15*

To succeed in life, you need two things: ignorance and confidence.

~ Mark Twain

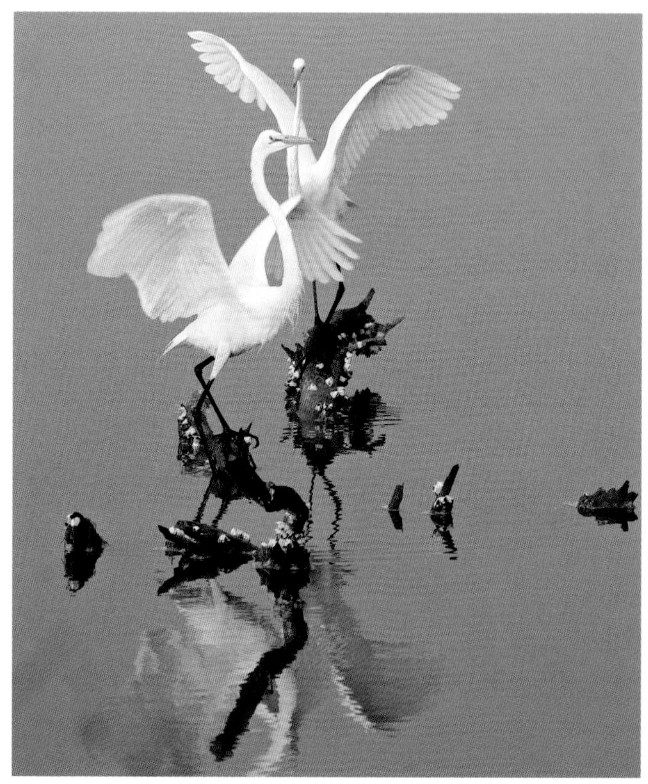

September *16*

Nothing great was ever achieved without enthusiasm.

~ Ralph Waldo Emerson

September 17

What one has to do usually can be done.

~ Eleanor Roosevelt

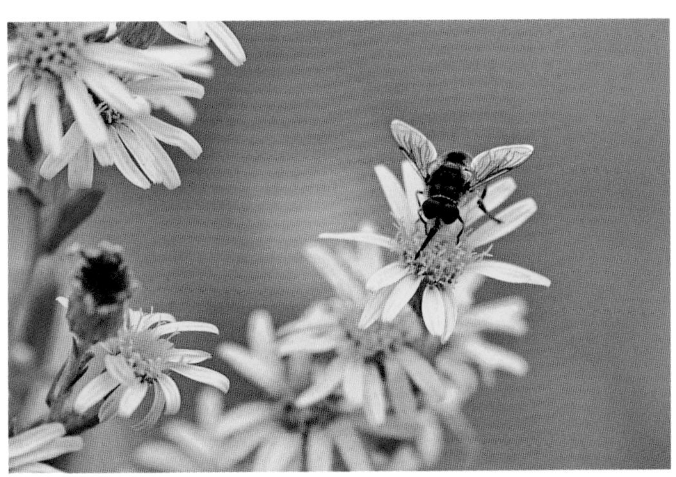

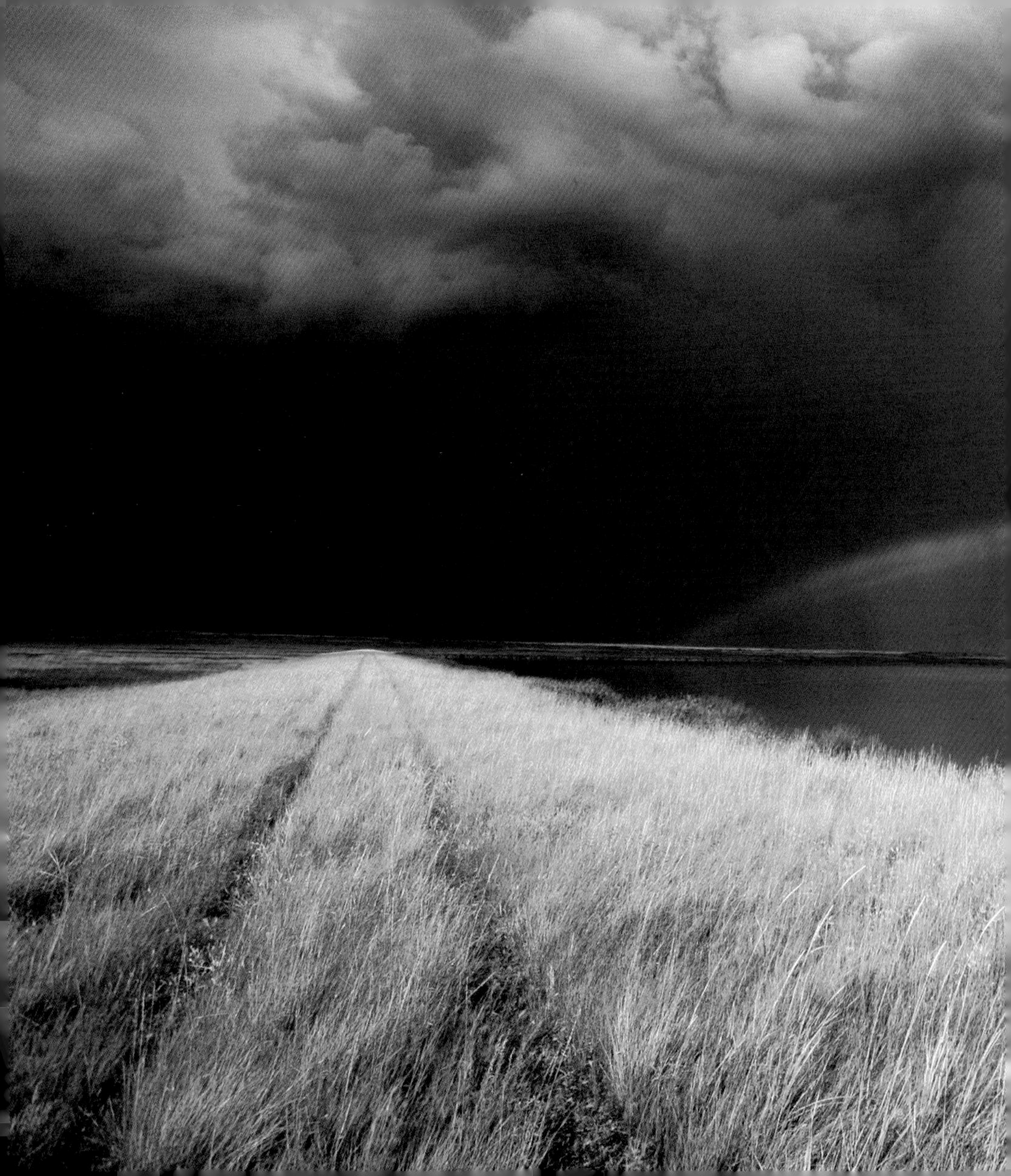

September 18

Failure is only the opportunity to begin again more intelligently.

~ Henry Ford

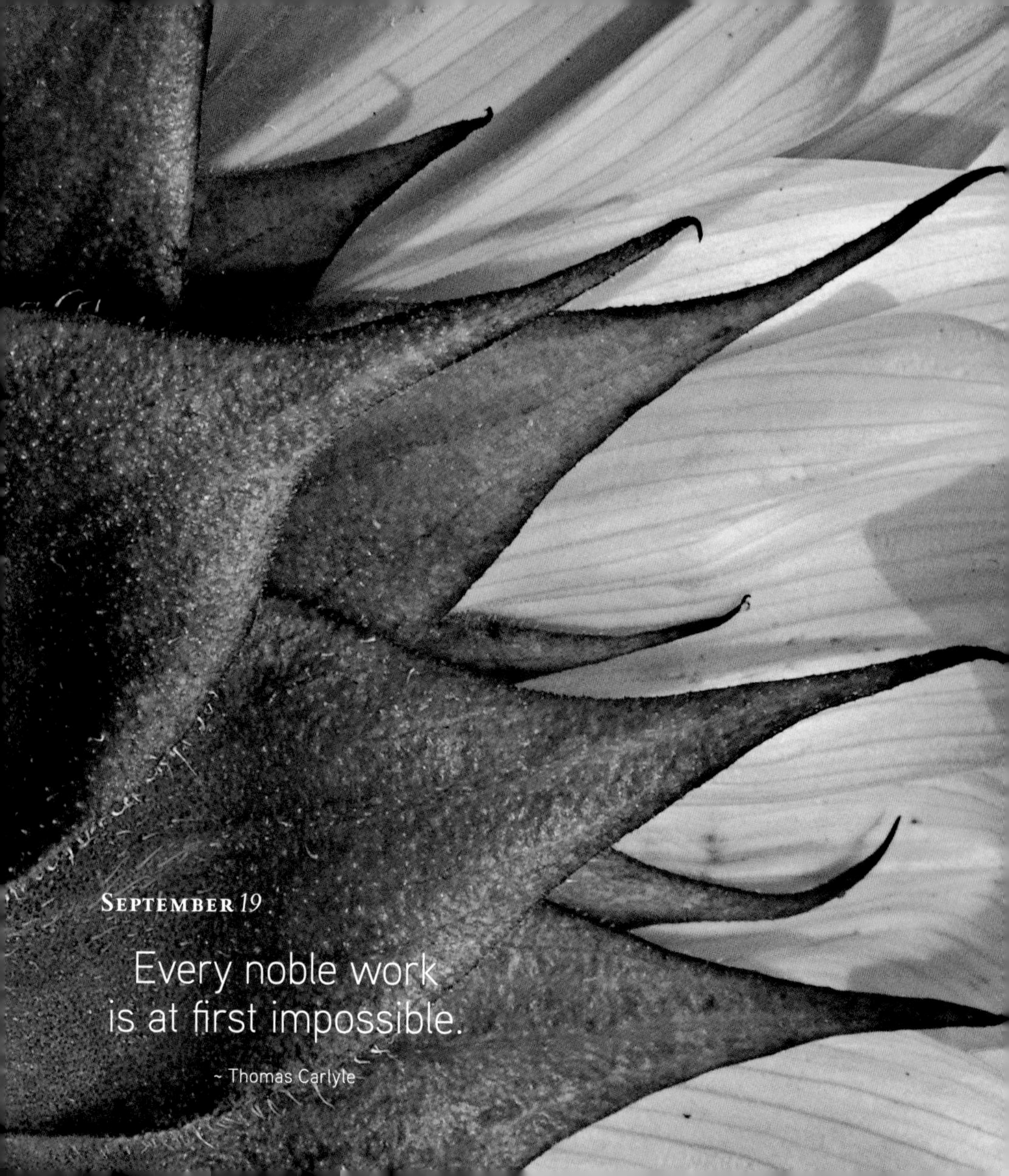

SEPTEMBER *19*

Every noble work
is at first impossible.

~ Thomas Carlyle

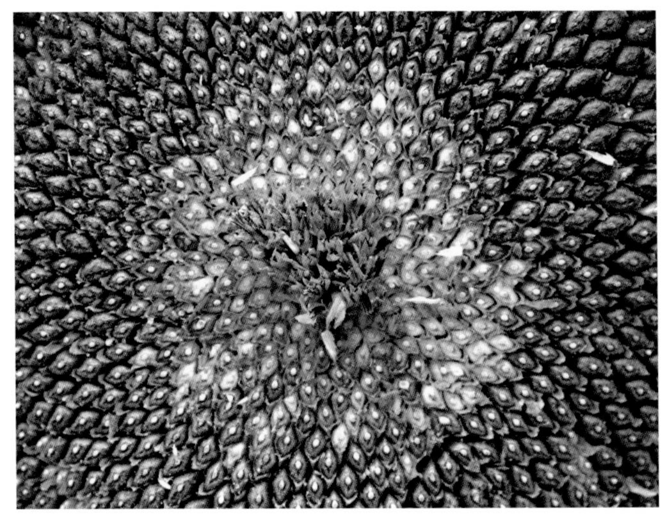

SEPTEMBER 20

Success is blocked
by concentrating on it
and planning for it.
Success is shy;
it won't come out
while you're watching.

~ Tennessee Williams

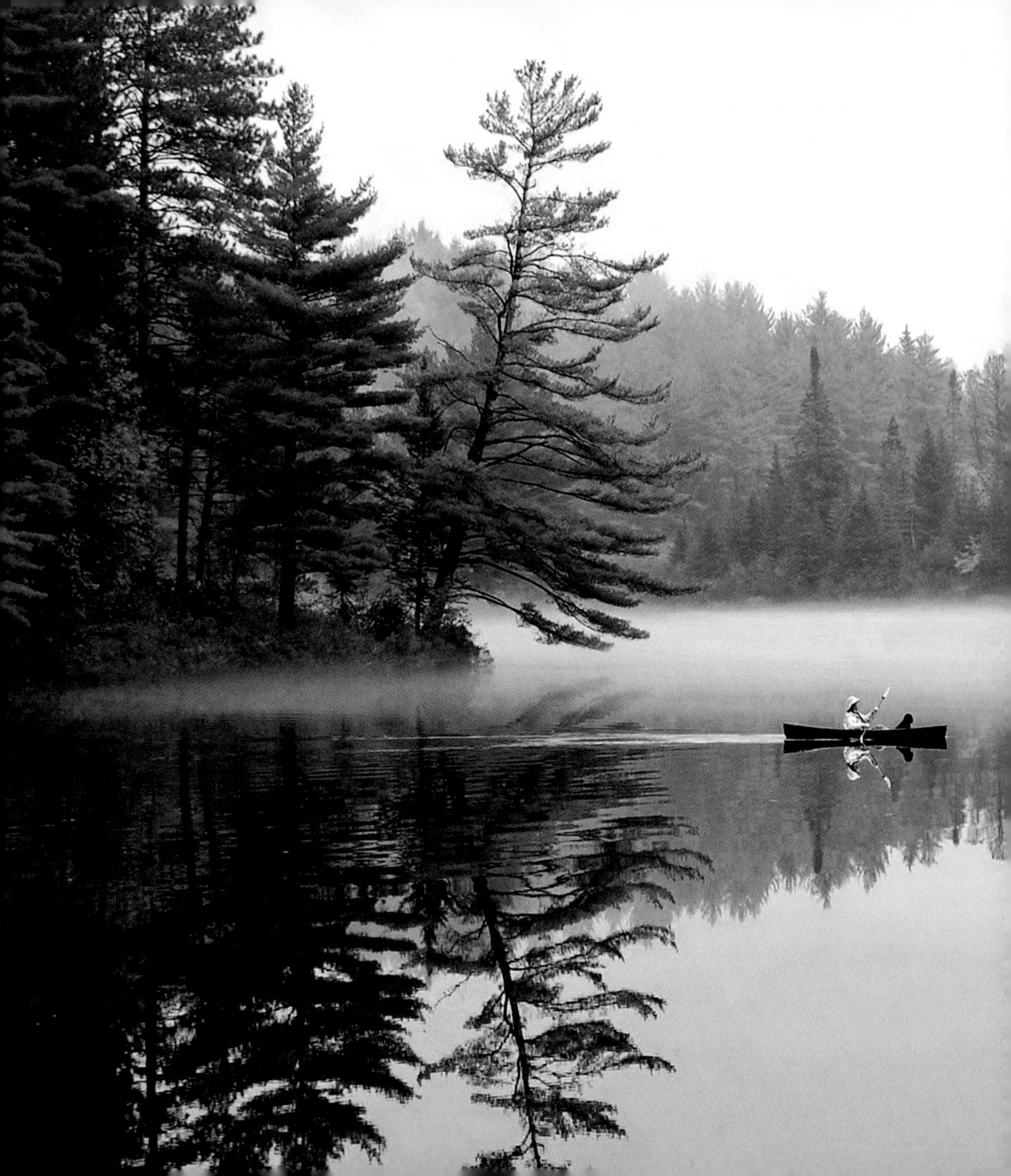

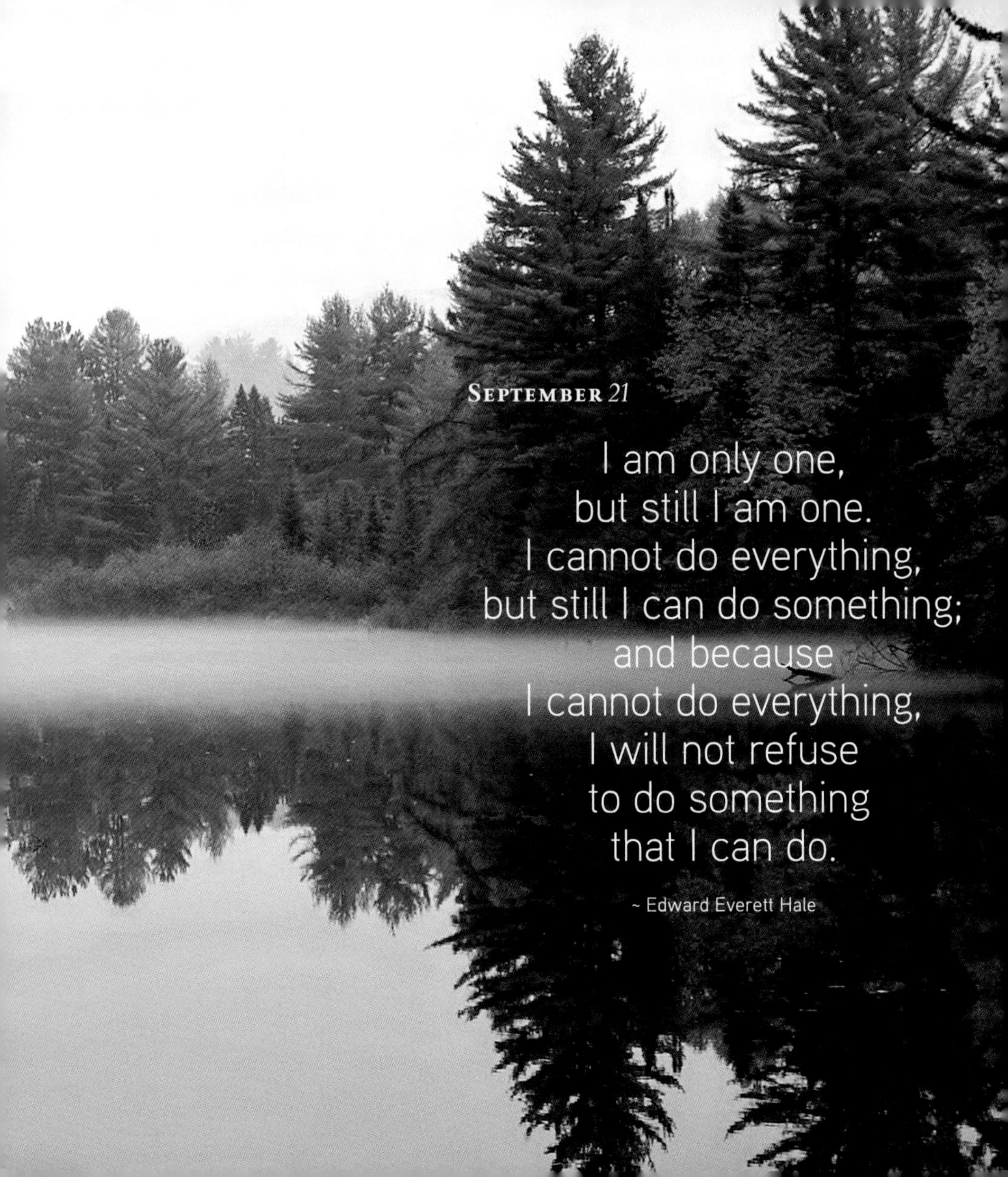

SEPTEMBER *21*

I am only one,
but still I am one.
I cannot do everything,
but still I can do something;
and because
I cannot do everything,
I will not refuse
to do something
that I can do.

~ Edward Everett Hale

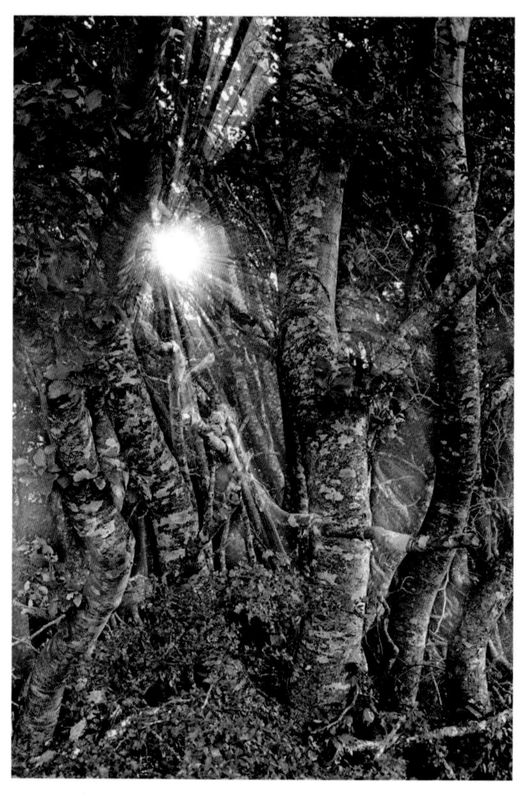

SEPTEMBER 22

Always bear in mind that your own resolution to succeed is more important than any other.

~ Abraham Lincoln

September 23

Although the world is full of suffering, it is also full of overcoming it.

~ Helen Keller

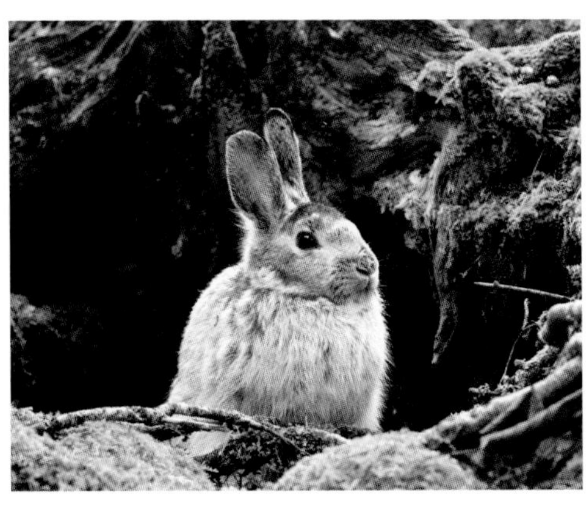

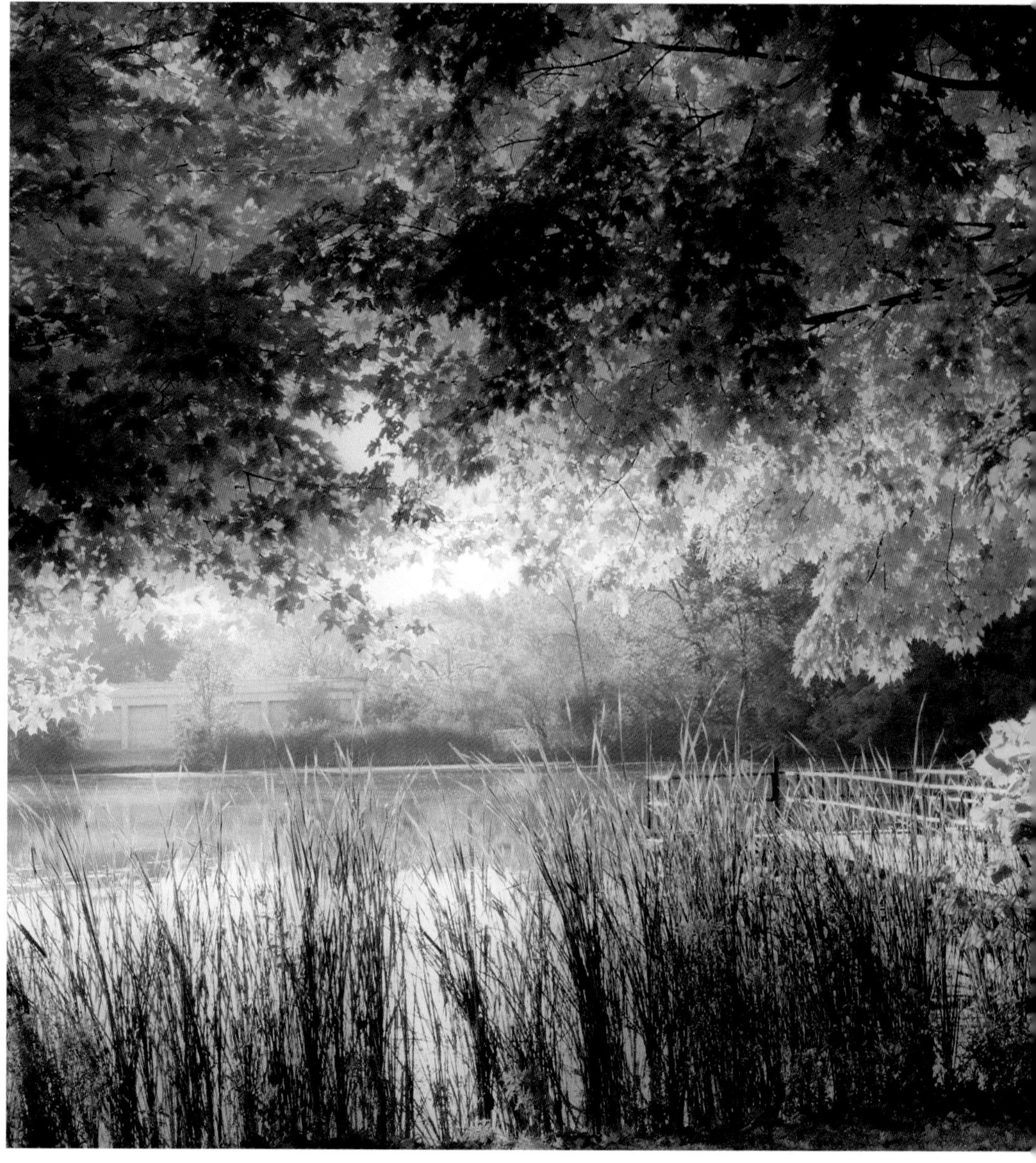

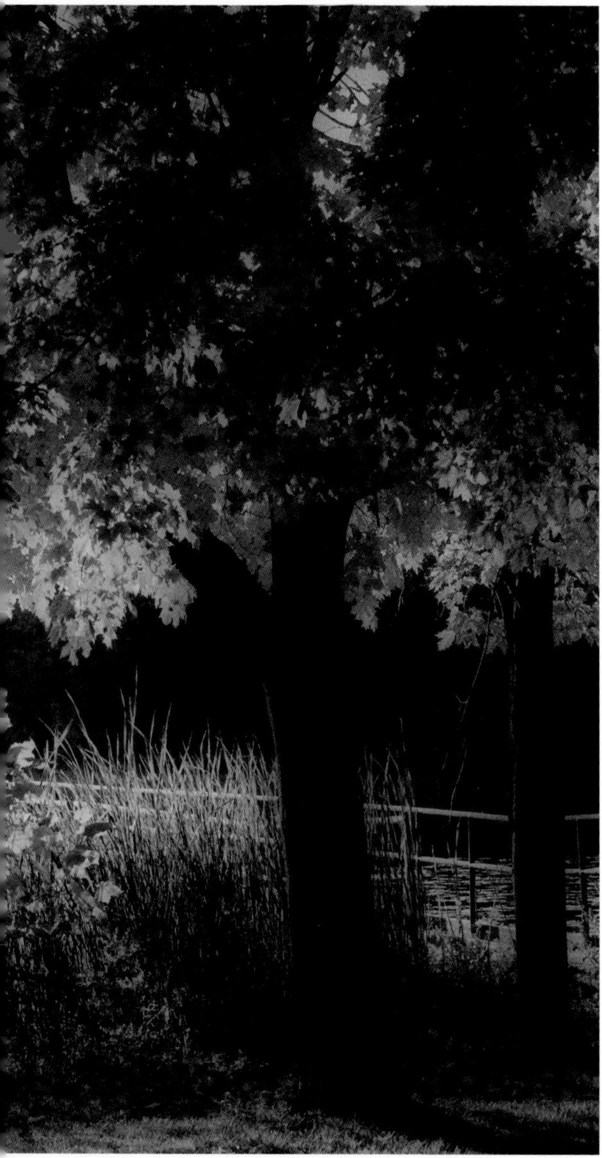

SEPTEMBER 24

Out of clutter,
find simplicity.

~ Albert Einstein

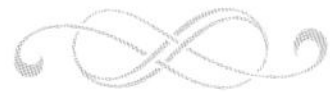

SEPTEMBER 25

Great minds have purposes;
others have wishes.

~ Washington Irving

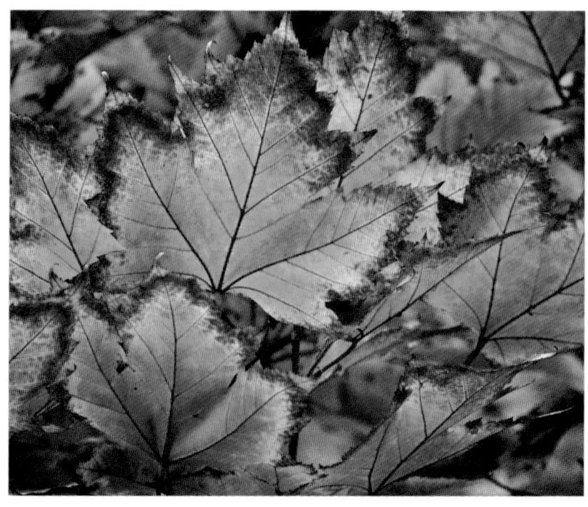

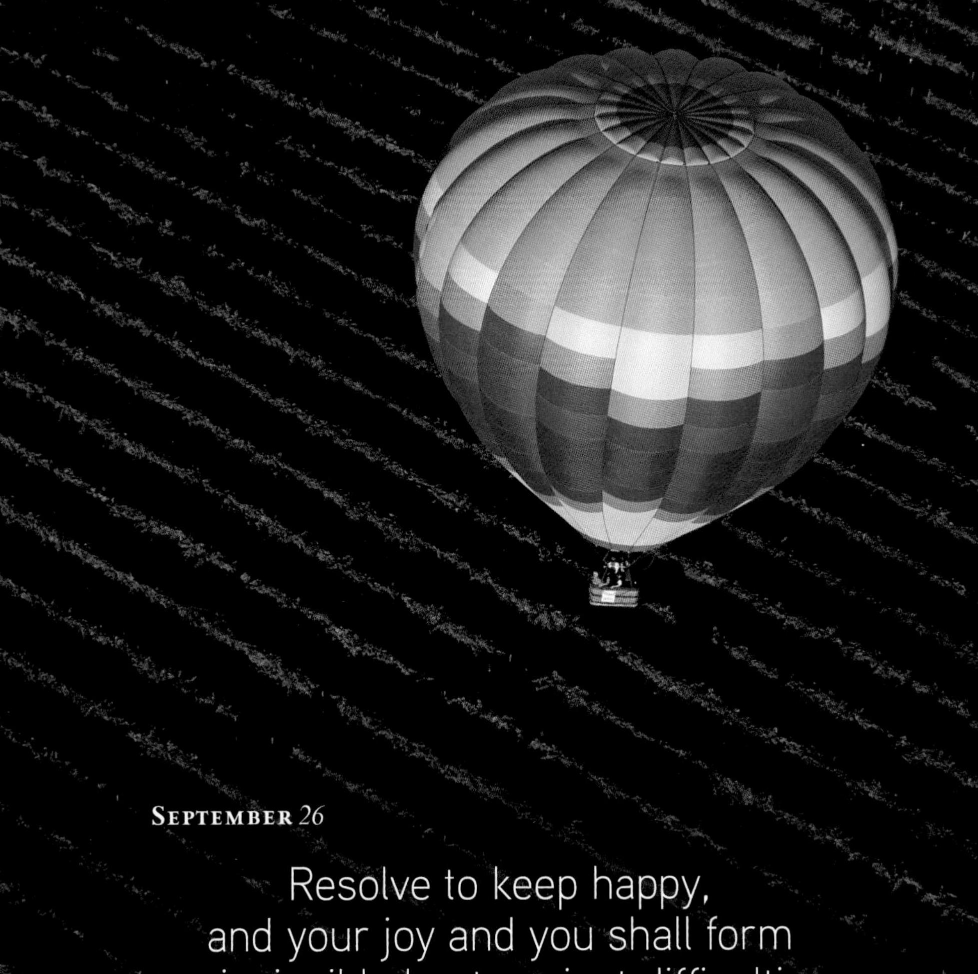

September *26*

Resolve to keep happy,
and your joy and you shall form
an invincible host against difficulties.

~ Helen Keller

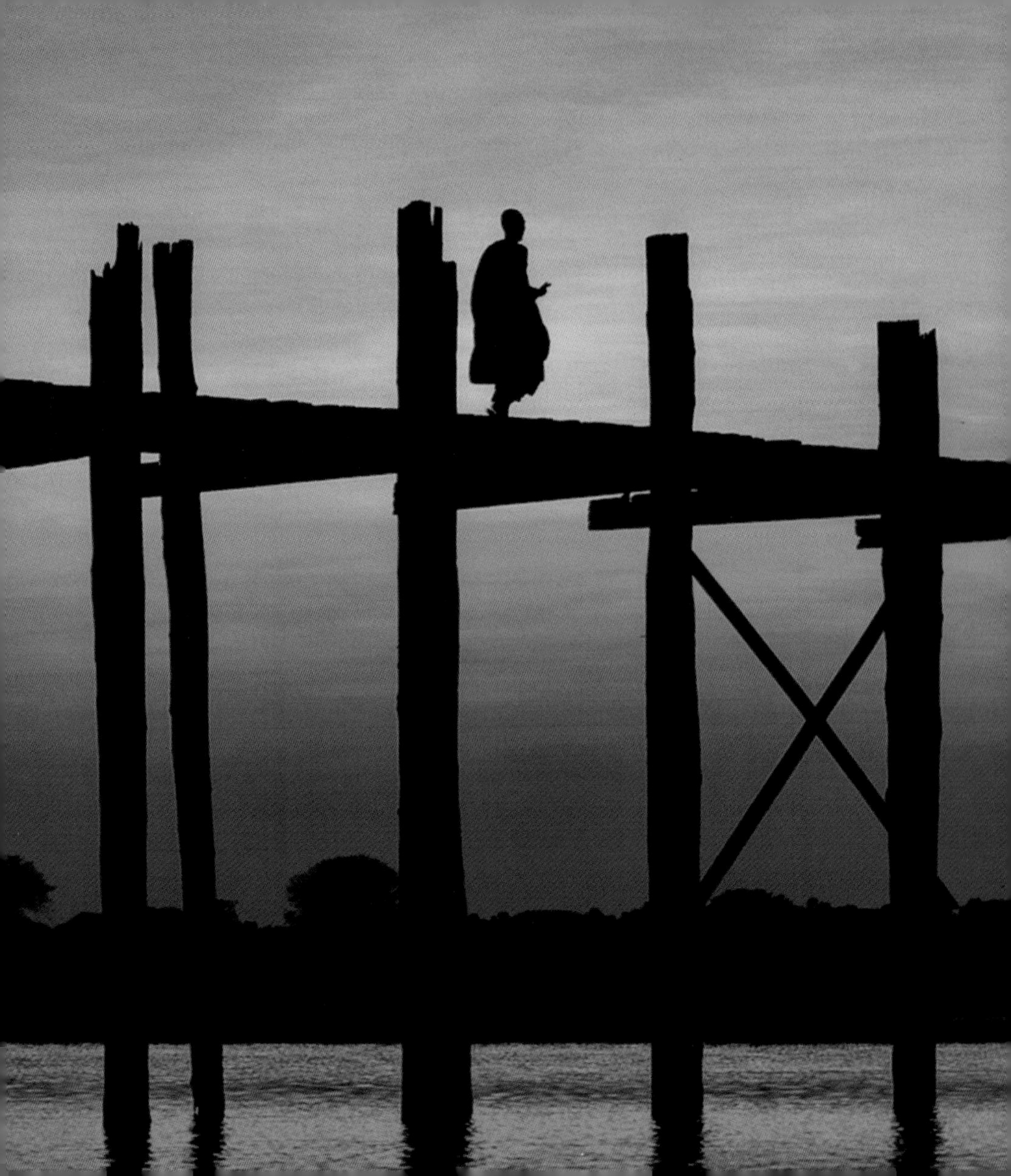

SEPTEMBER 27

With the new day comes new strength and new thoughts.

~ Eleanor Roosevelt

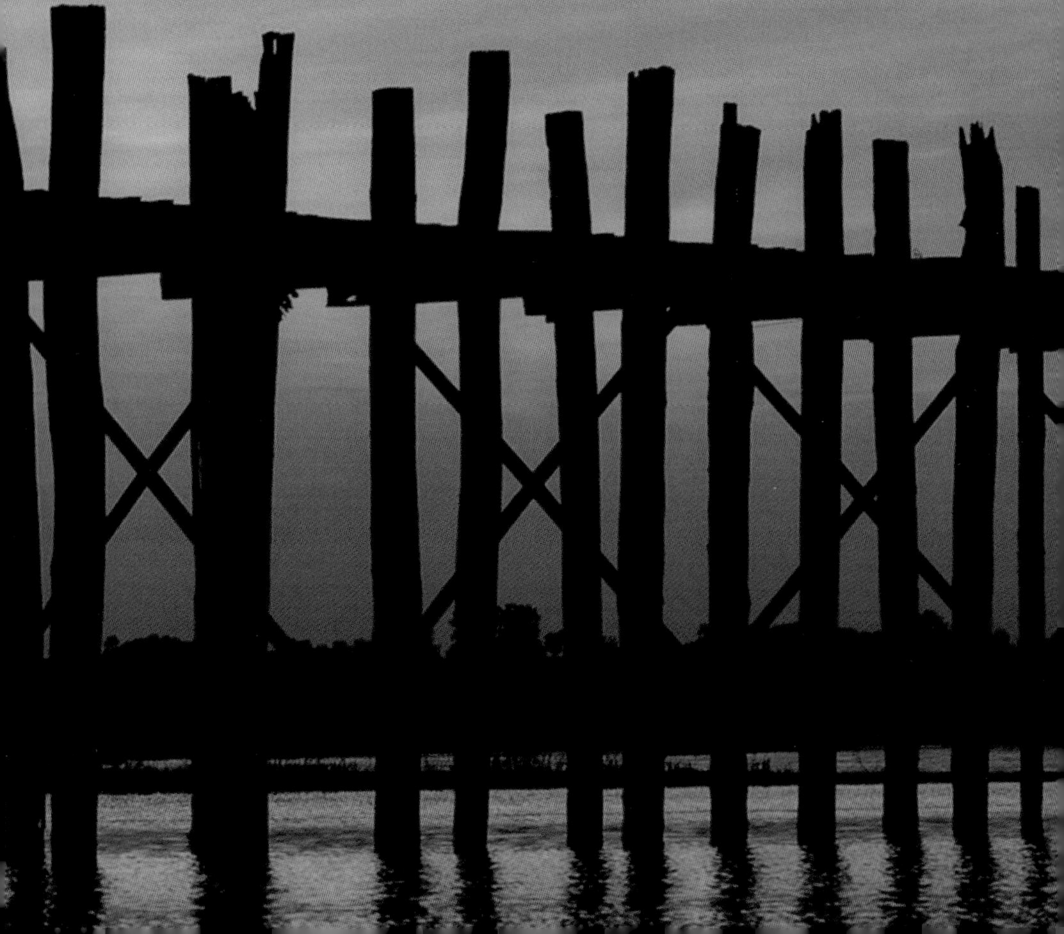

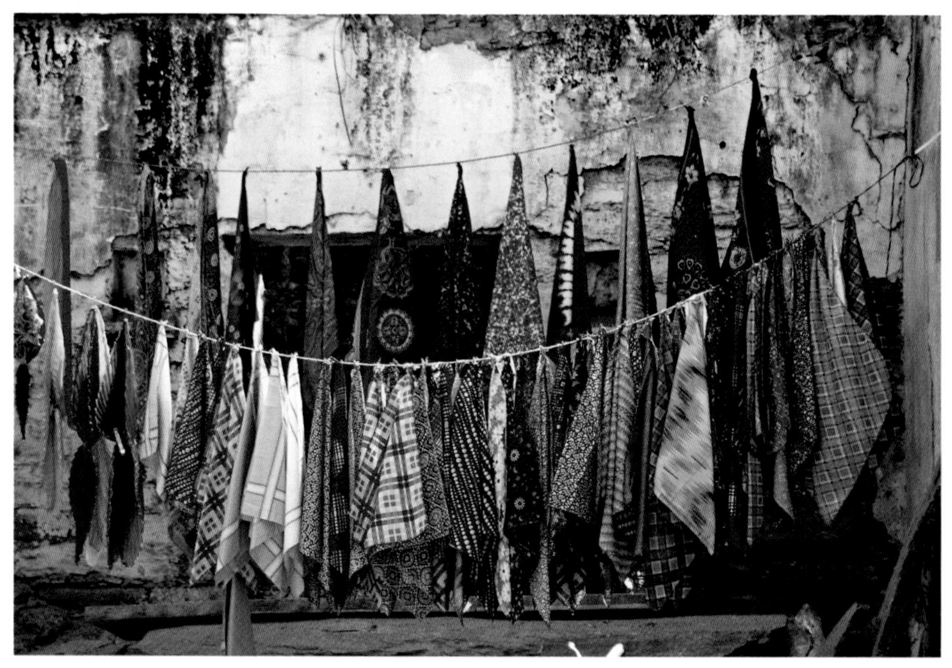

SEPTEMBER 28

Success consists of going
from failure to failure
without loss of enthusiasm.

~ Sir Winston Churchill

September 29

Be regular and orderly
in your life,
so that you may be
violent and original in your work.

~ Gustave Flaubert

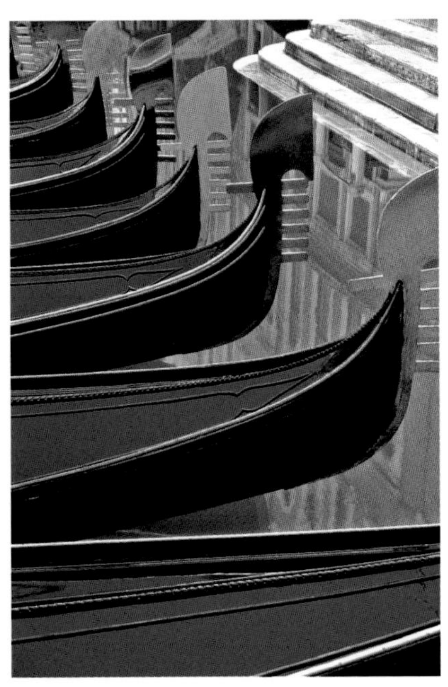

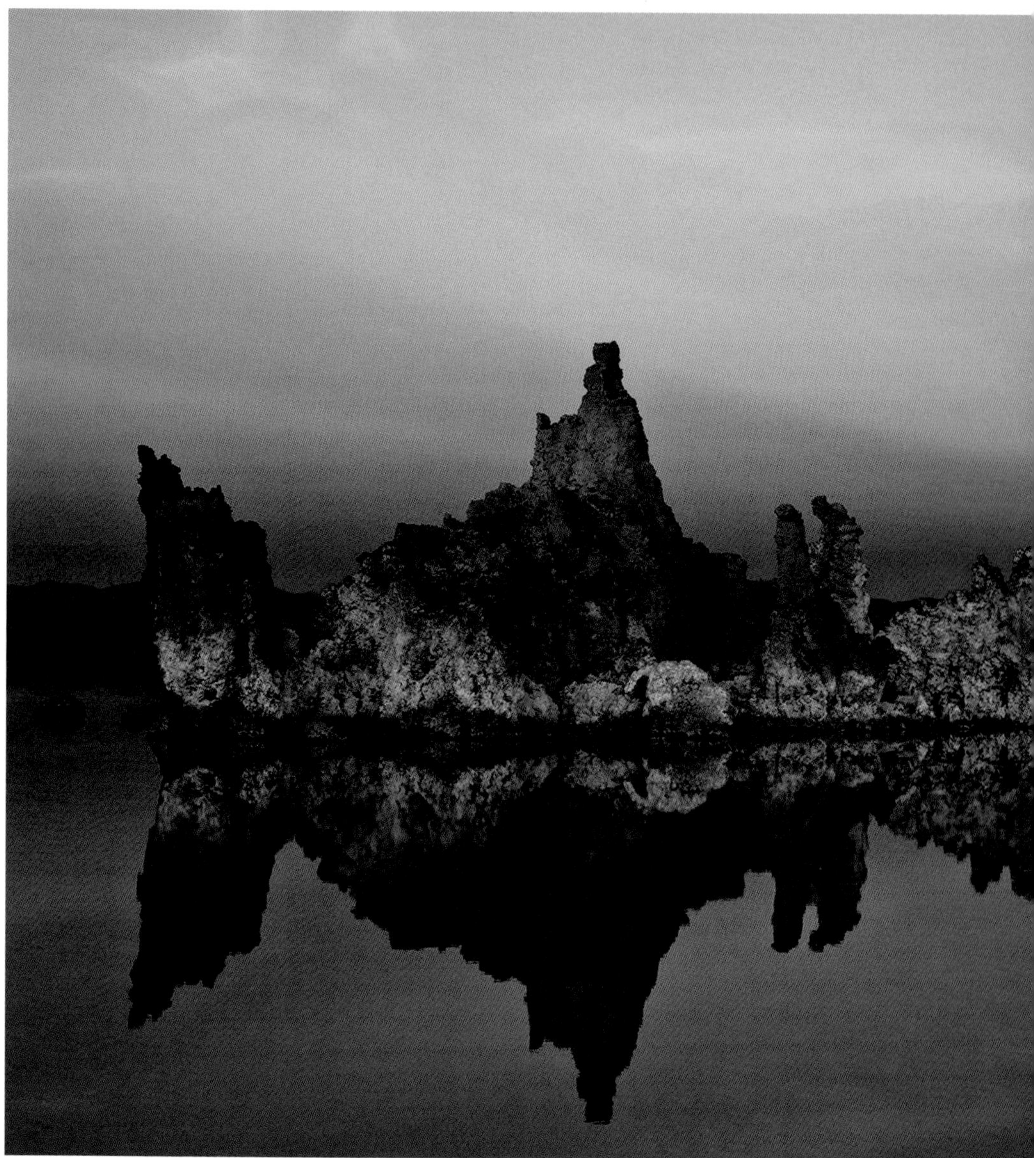

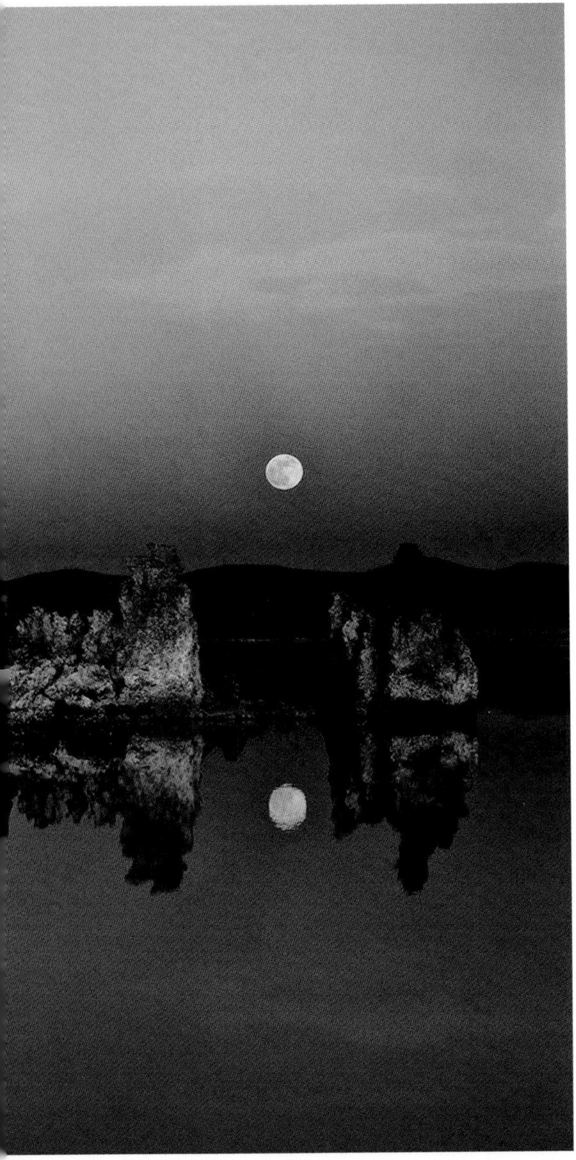

September 30

The purpose of life is a life of purpose.

~ Robert Byrne

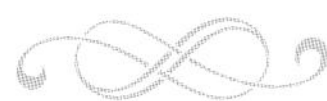

FULFILLMENT

October

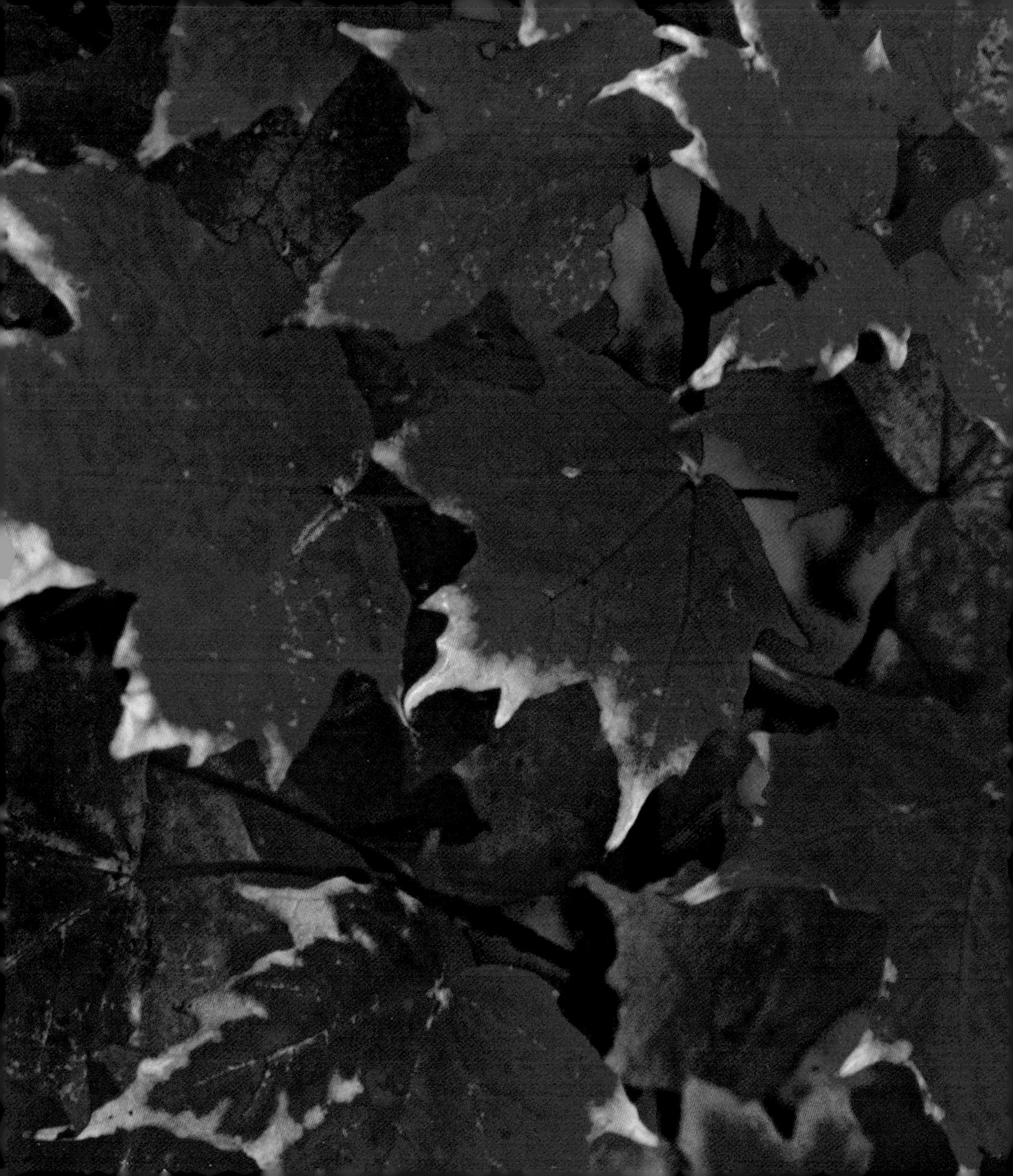

October 1

Let us be grateful to people
who make us happy;
they are the charming gardeners
who make our souls blossom.

~ Marcel Proust

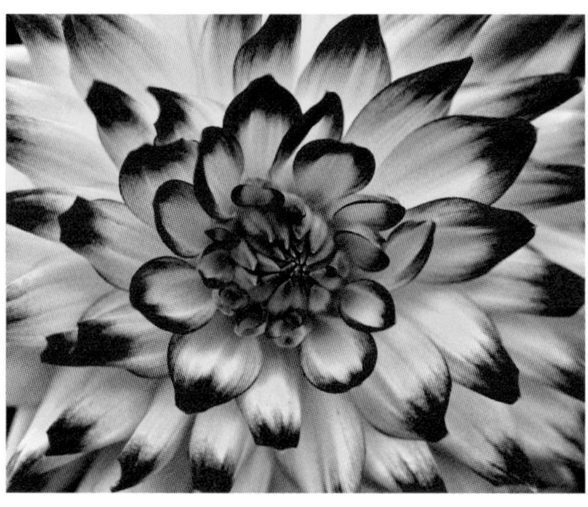

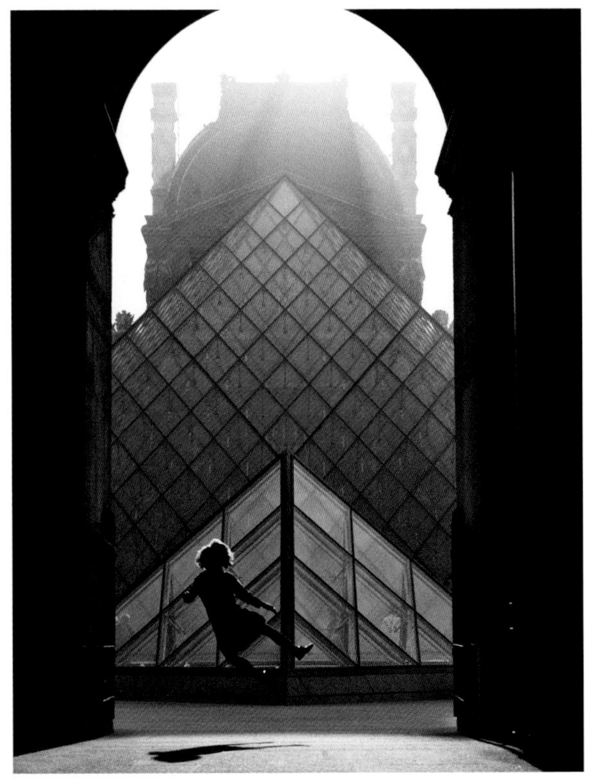

October 2

When we cannot find contentment in ourselves, it is useless to seek it elsewhere.

~ François de la Rochefoucauld

OCTOBER 3

One of the secrets of a happy life is continuous small treats.

~ Iris Murdoch

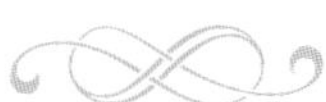

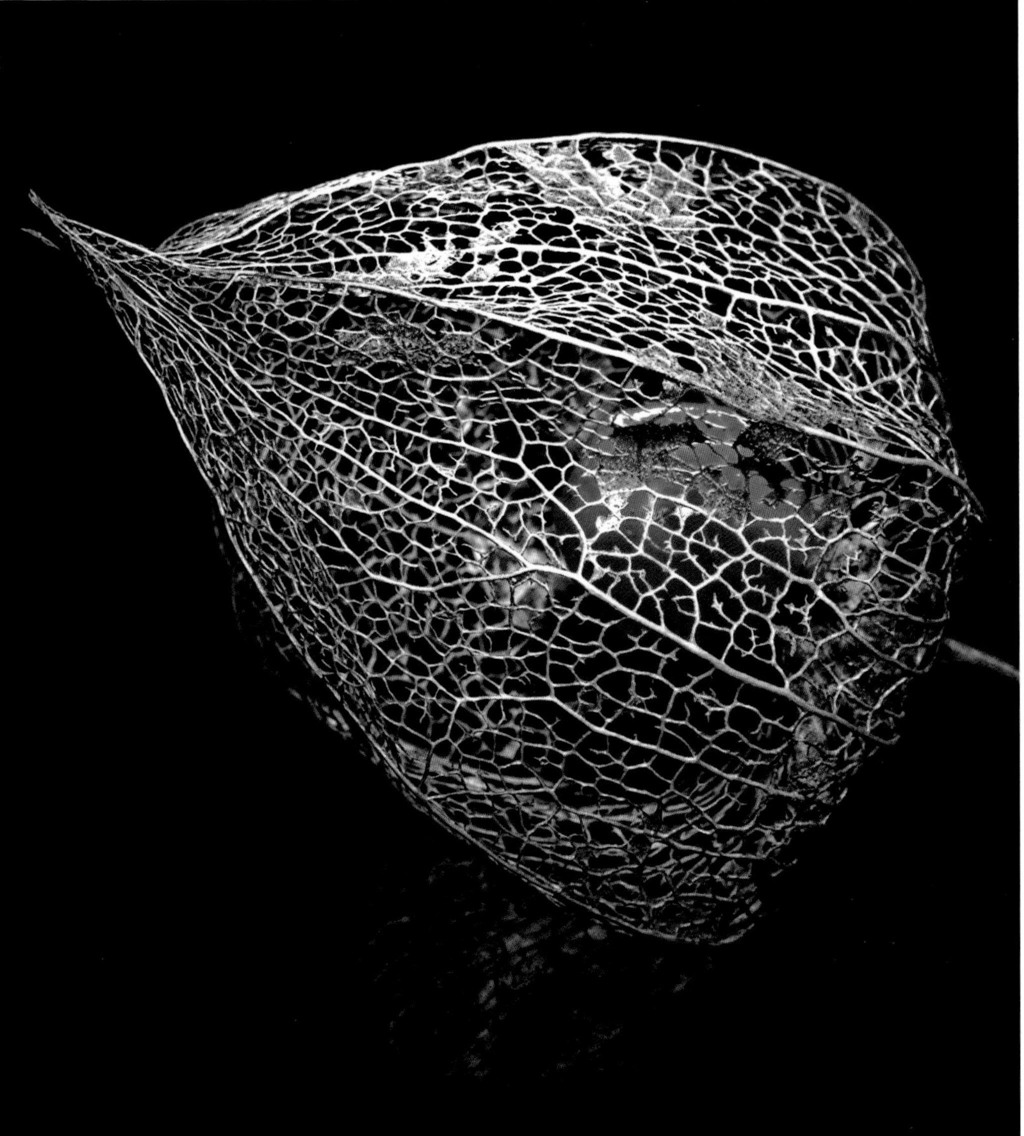

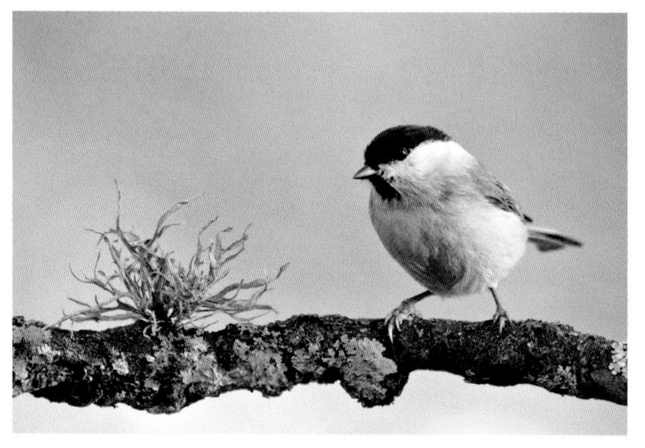

OCTOBER 4

Those who
bring sunshine
to the lives of others
cannot keep it from
themselves.

~ J. M. Barrie

OCTOBER 5

Now and then it's good to pause
in our pursuit of happiness
and just be happy.

~ Guillaume Apollinaire

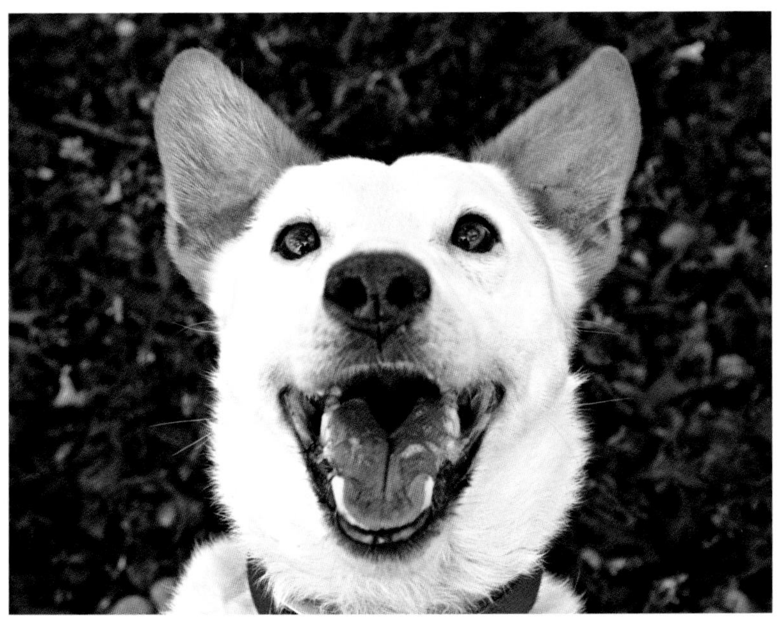

October 6

Your work is going to fill
a large part of your life,
and the only way to be truly satisfied
is to do what you believe is great work.
And the only way to do great work
is to love what you do.
If you haven't found it yet, keep looking.
Don't settle.
As with all matters of the heart,
you'll know when you find it.

~ Steve Jobs

October 7

Anybody who thinks
money will make you happy
hasn't got money.

~ David Geffen

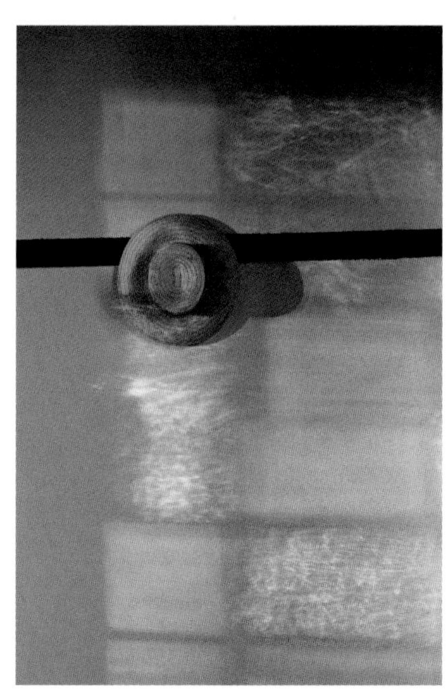

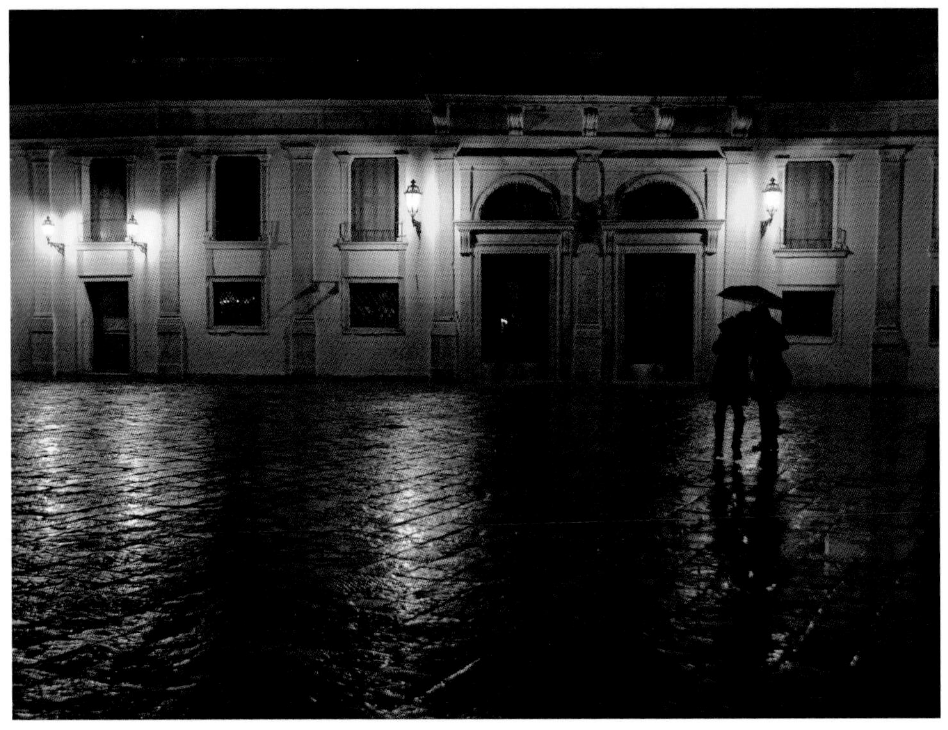

OCTOBER *8*

The grand essentials of happiness are: something to do, something to love, and something to hope for.

~ Alexander Chalmers

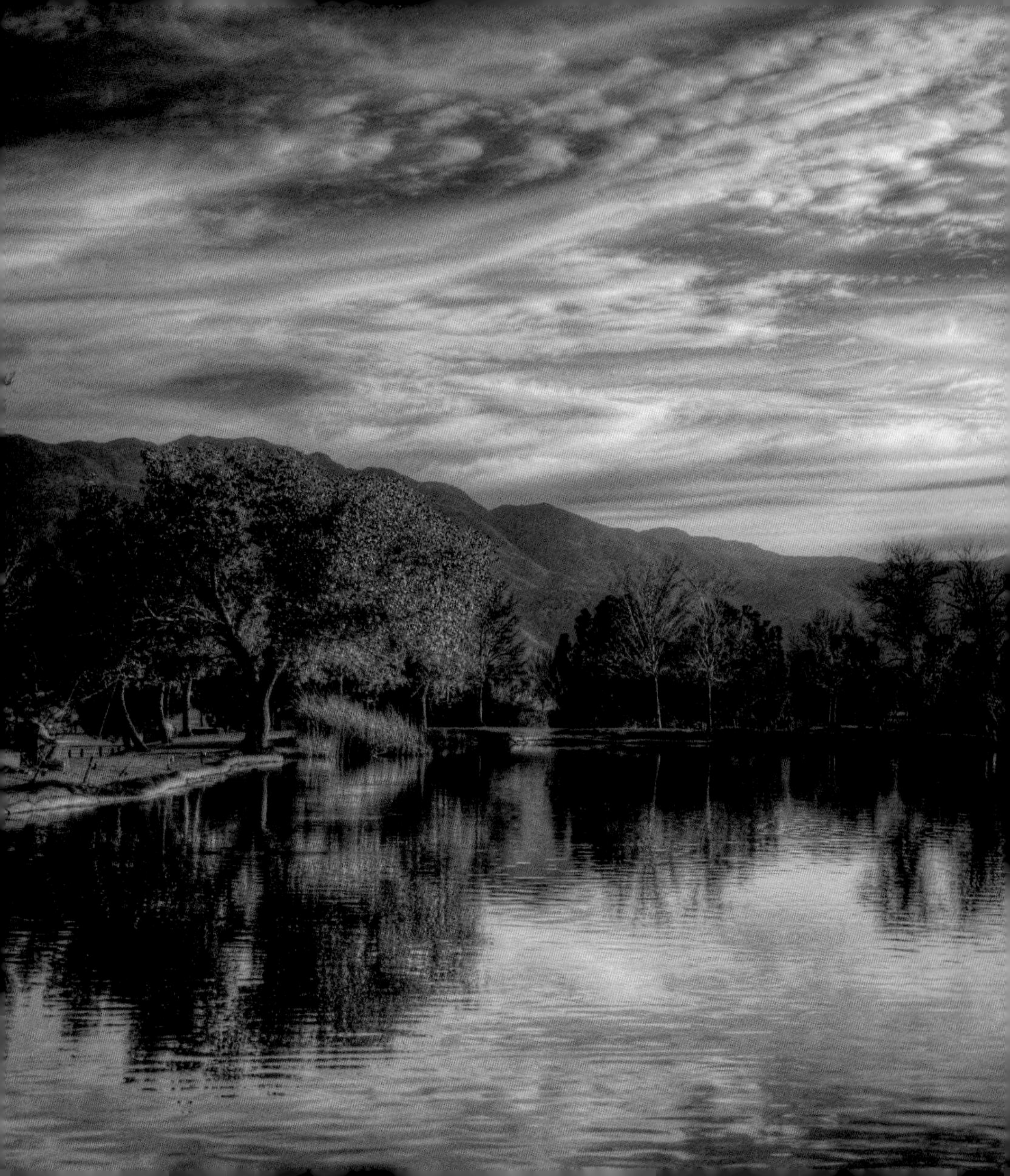

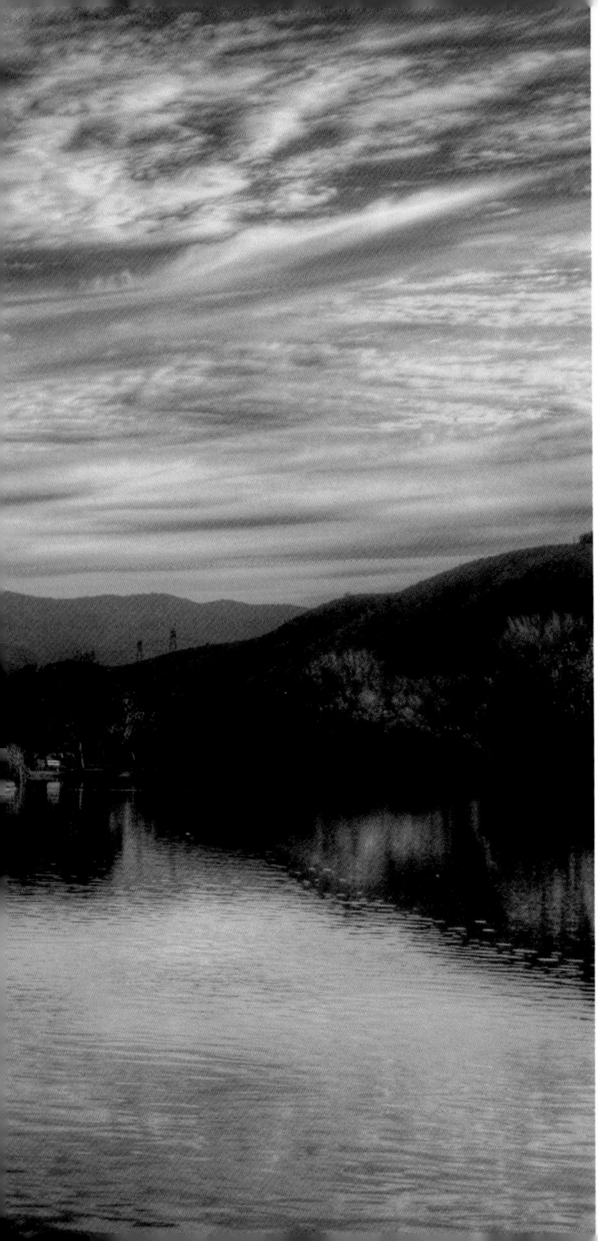

October 9

Ah!
There's nothing
like staying home
for real comfort.

~ Jane Austen

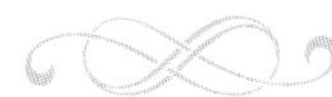

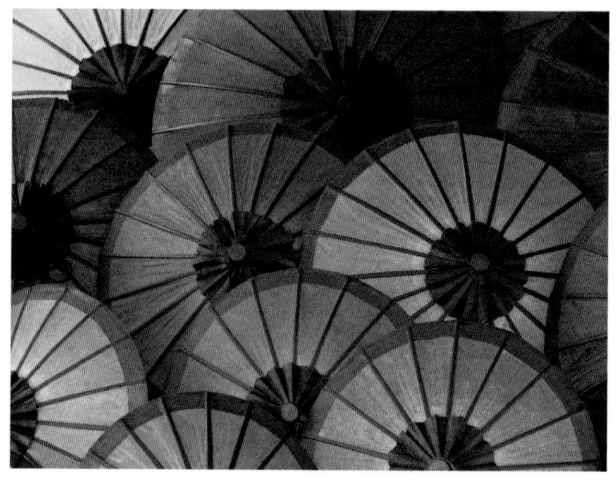

October 10

If only we'd stop trying to be happy we'd have a pretty good time.

~ Edith Wharton

October 11

If you find it in your heart to care for somebody else, you will have succeeded.

~ Maya Angelou

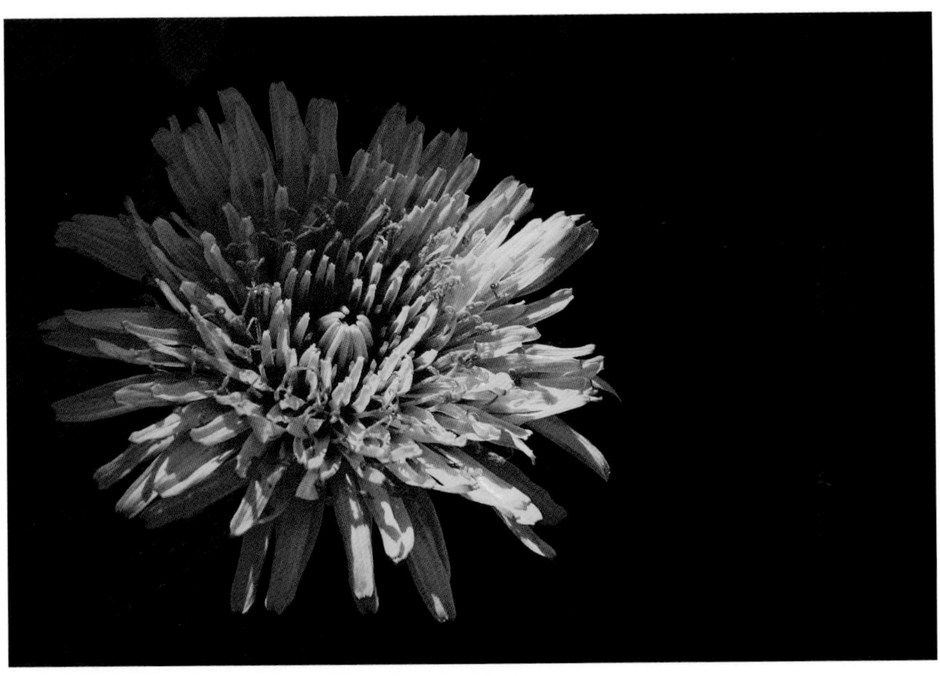

OCTOBER 12

A sure way to
lose happiness,
I found,
is to want it
at the expense
of everything else.

~ Bette Davis

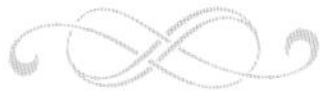

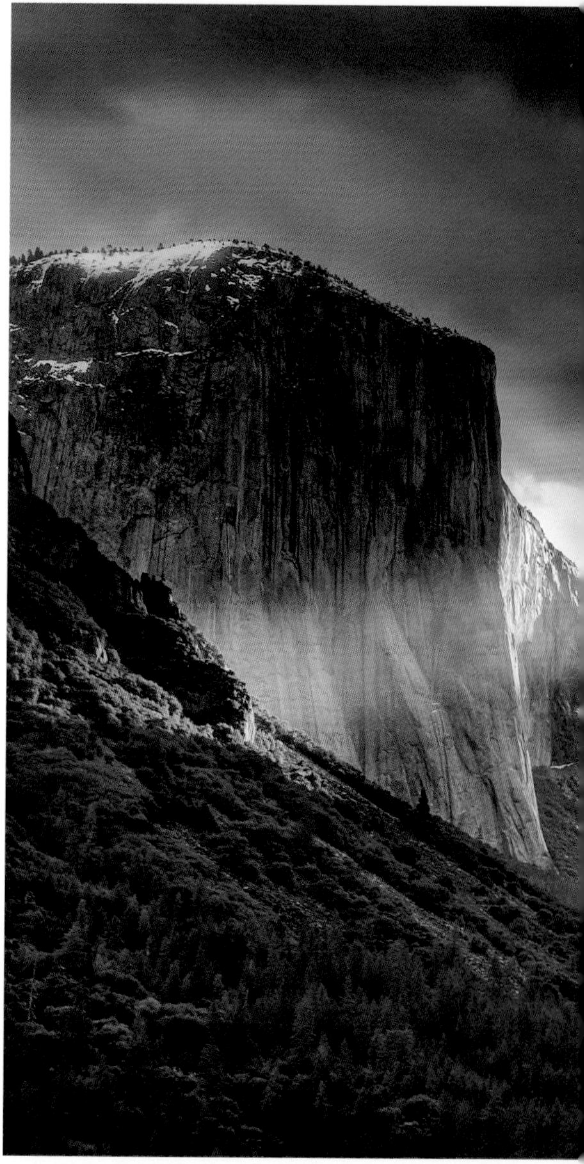

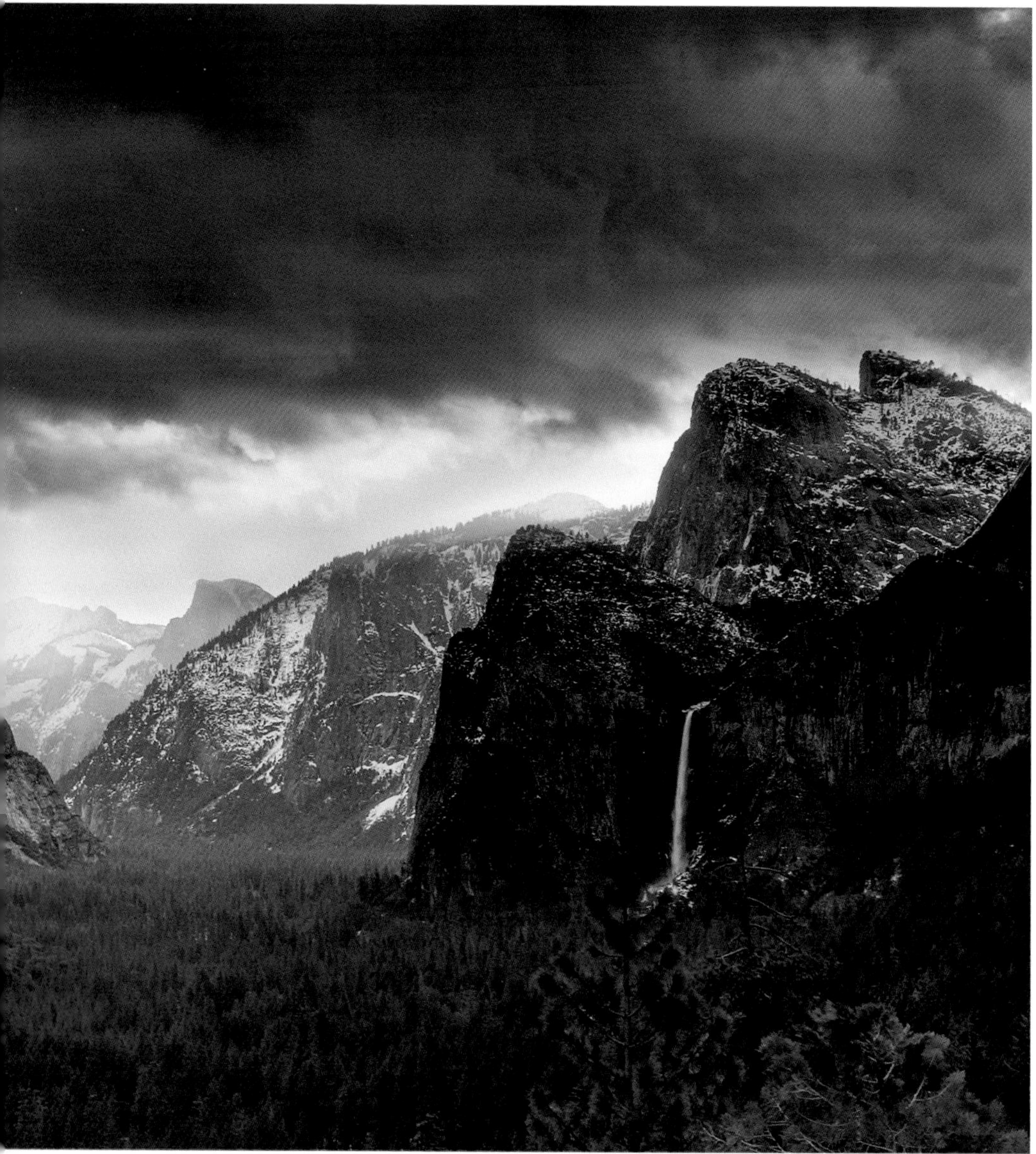

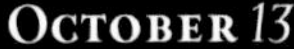

OCTOBER 13

There must be quite a few things a hot bath won't cure, but I don't know many of them.

~ Sylvia Plath

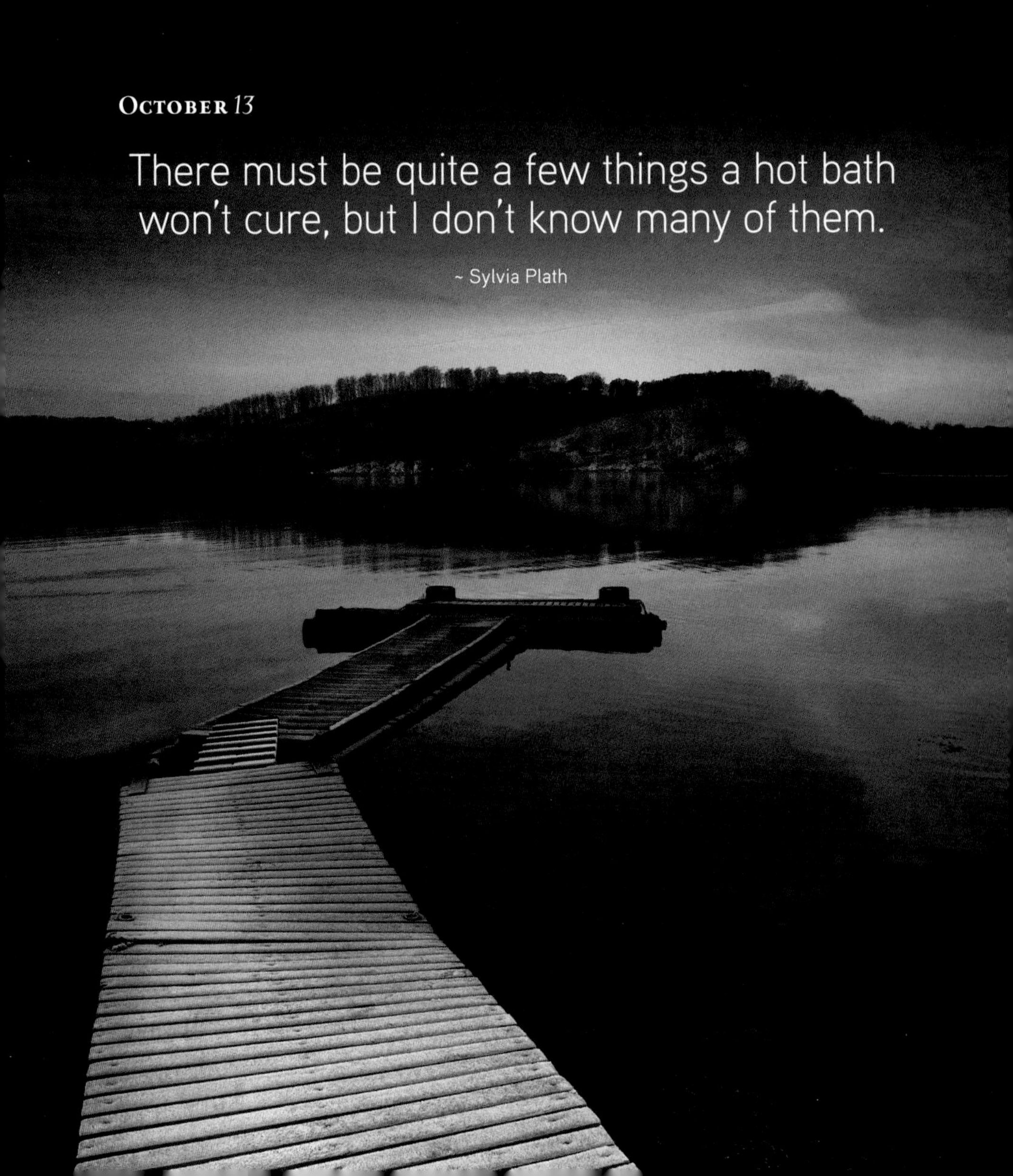

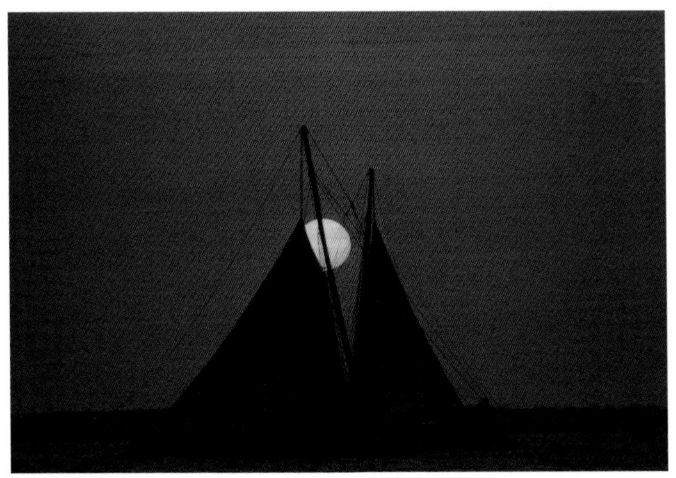

OCTOBER *14*

People tend to think that happiness
is a stroke of luck, something
that will descend like fine weather if
you're fortunate. But happiness is the
result of personal effort.
You fight for it, strive for it, insist upon it,
and sometimes even travel around
the world looking for it.

~ Elizabeth Gilbert

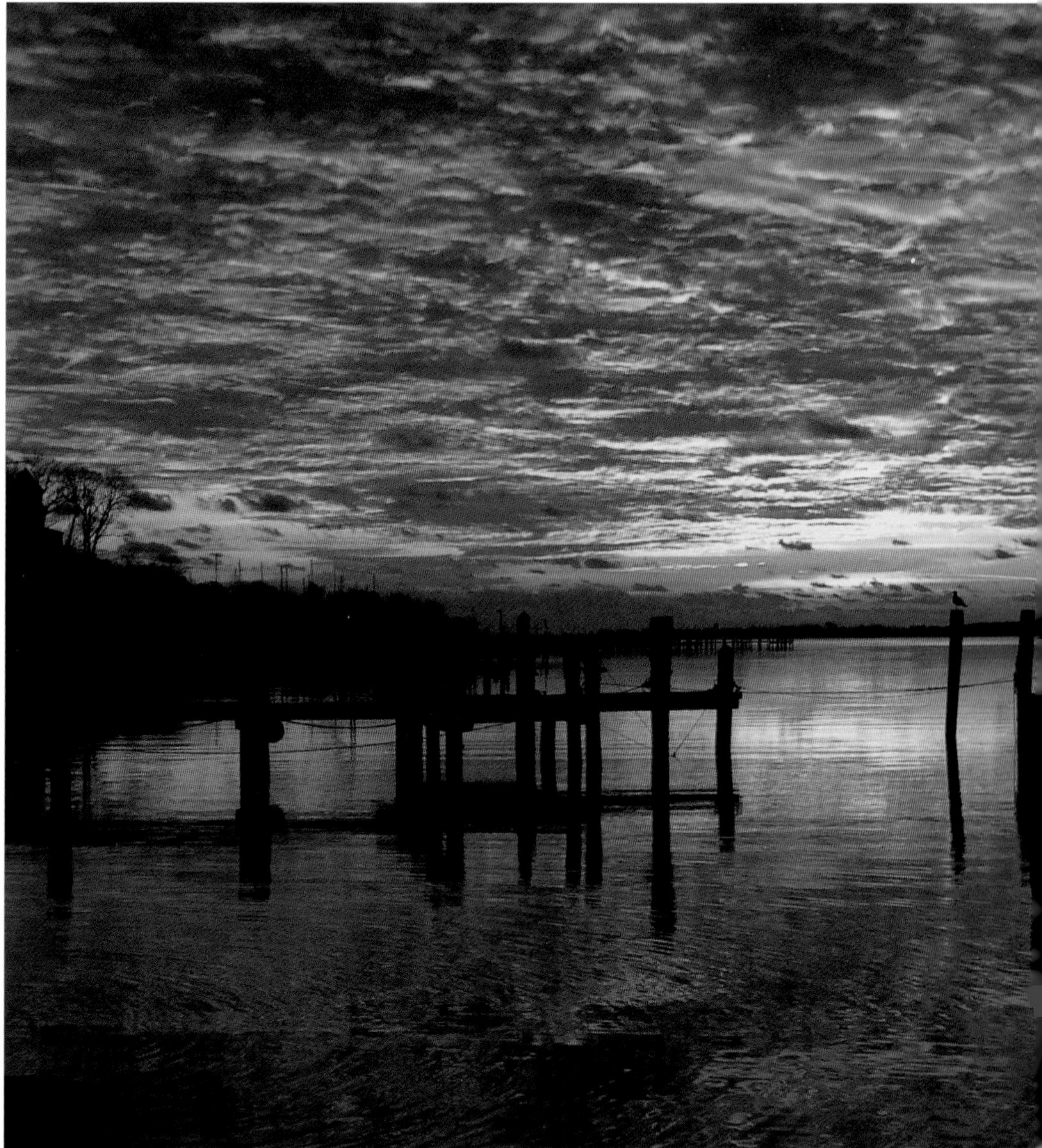

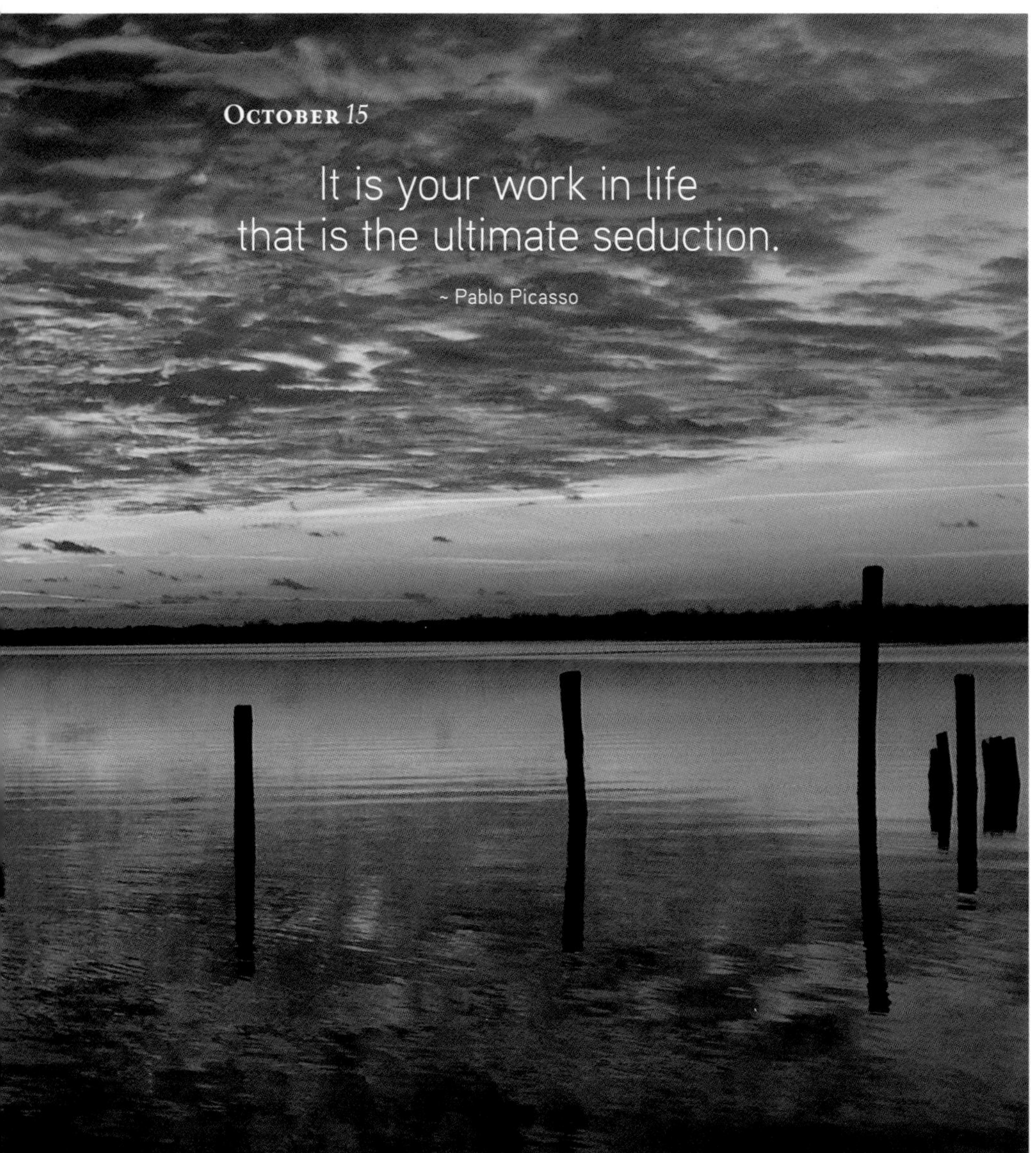

October *15*

It is your work in life
that is the ultimate seduction.

~ Pablo Picasso

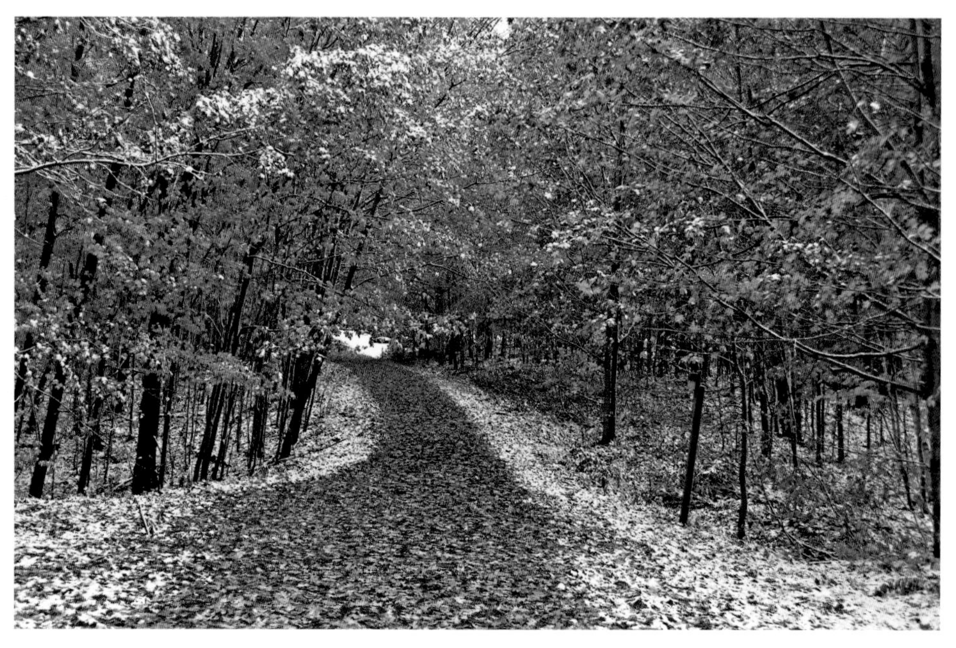

OCTOBER 16

You can never really live anyone else's life,
not even your child's.
The influence you exert
is through your own life,
and what you've become yourself.

~ Eleanor Roosevelt

OCTOBER 17

If you always do what interests you, at least one person is pleased.

~ Katharine Hepburn

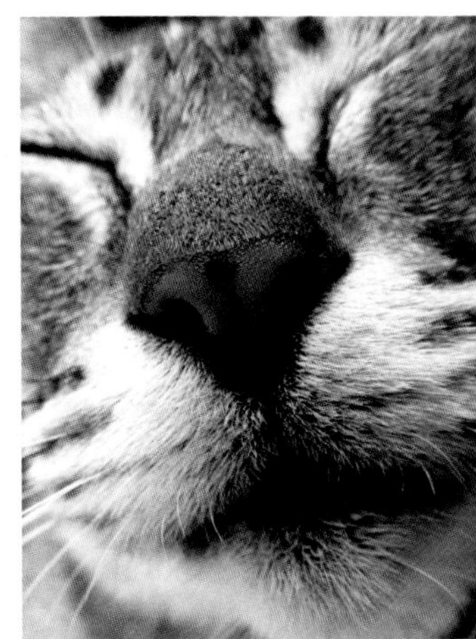

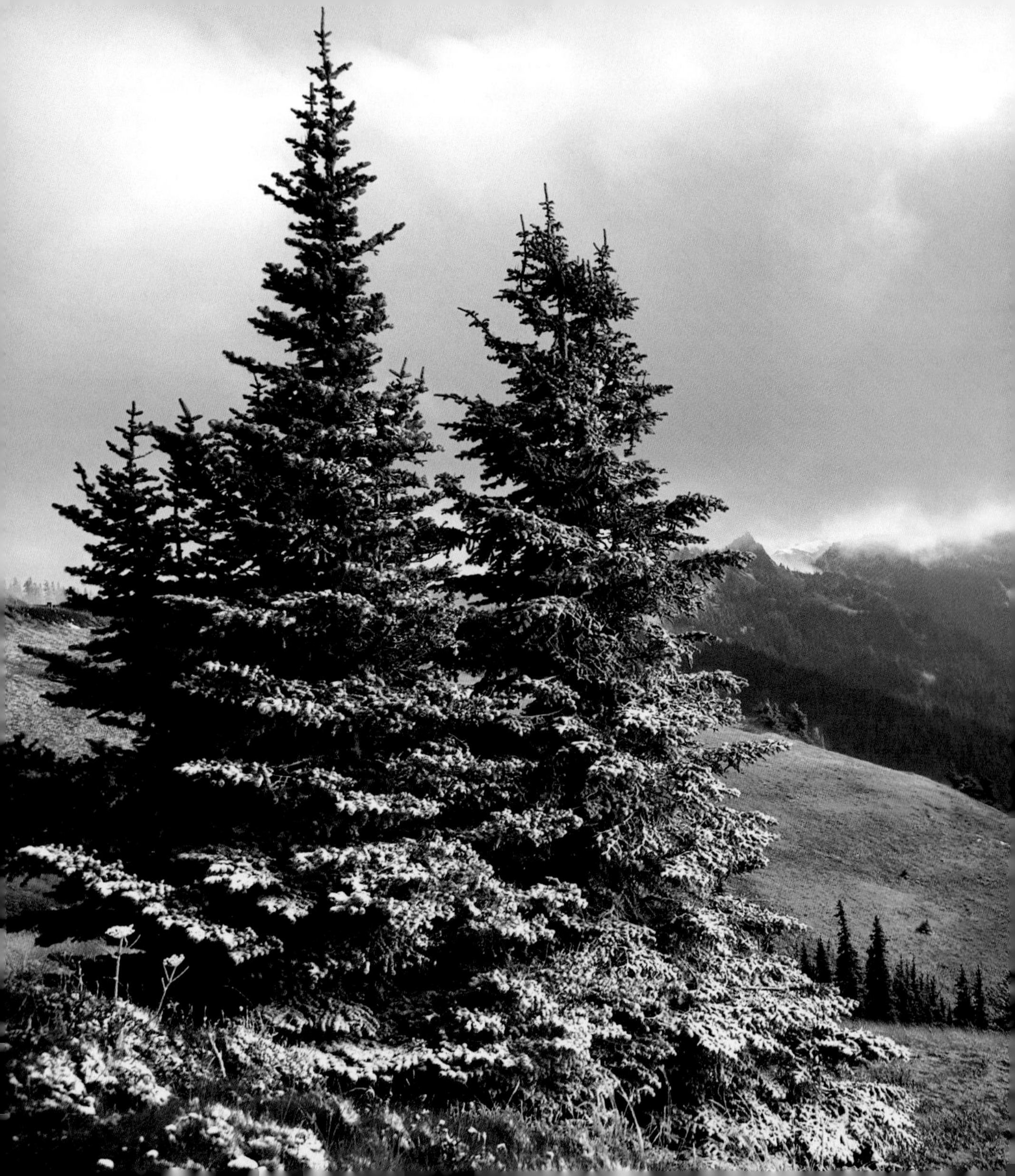

OCTOBER 18

To be without some of the things you want is an indispensable part of happiness.

~ Bertrand Russell

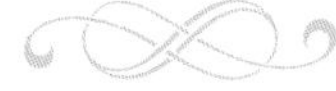

OCTOBER *19*

To find out what one is fitted to do,
and to secure an opportunity to do it,
is the key to happiness.

~ John Dewey

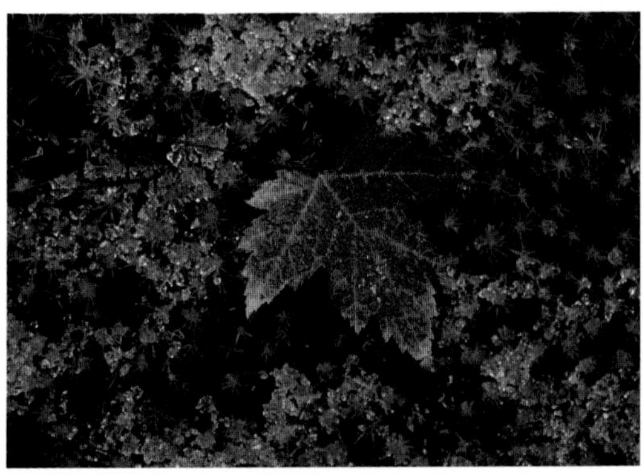

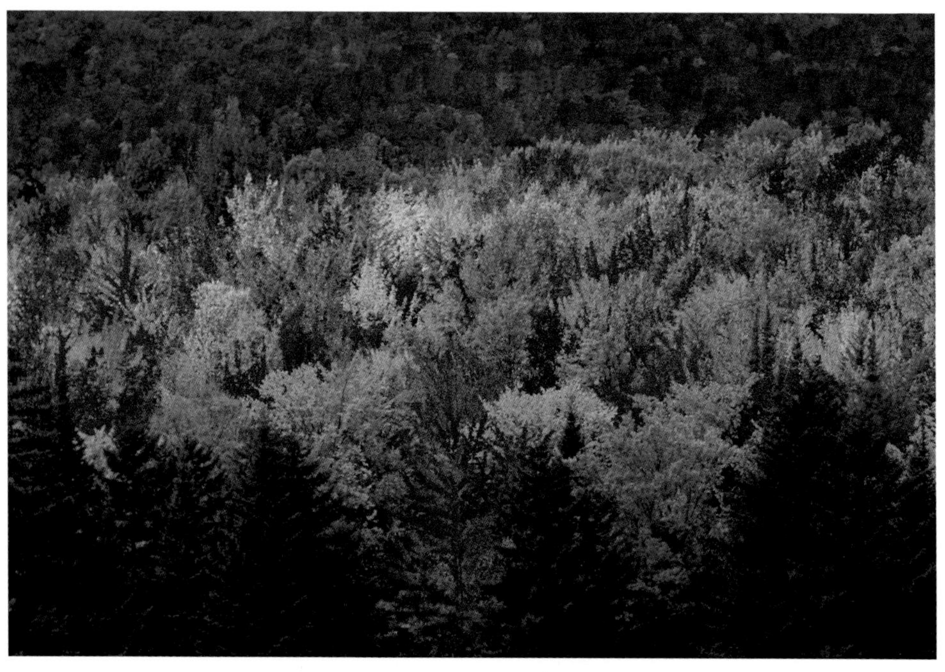

OCTOBER 20

The best way to cheer yourself up is to try to cheer somebody else up.

~ Mark Twain

One is happy as a result of
one's own efforts, once one knows
the necessary ingredients of happiness:
simple tastes, a certain degree of courage,
self denial to a point, love of work—and
above all, a clear conscience.

~ George Sand

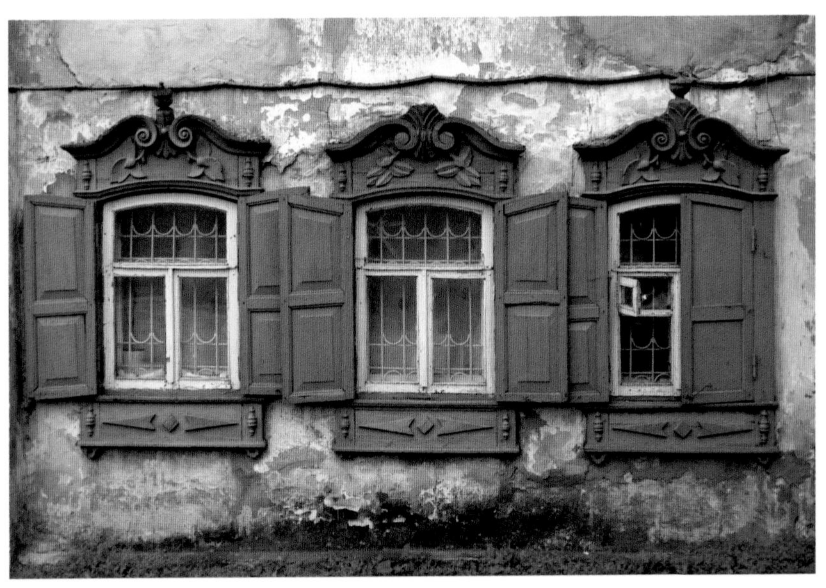

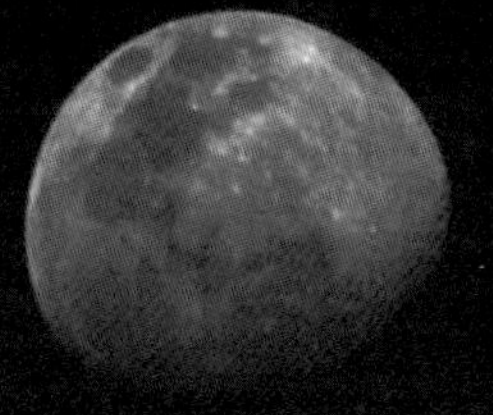

OCTOBER *22*

Far and away the best prize that life has to offer is the chance to work hard at work worth doing.

~ Theodore Roosevelt

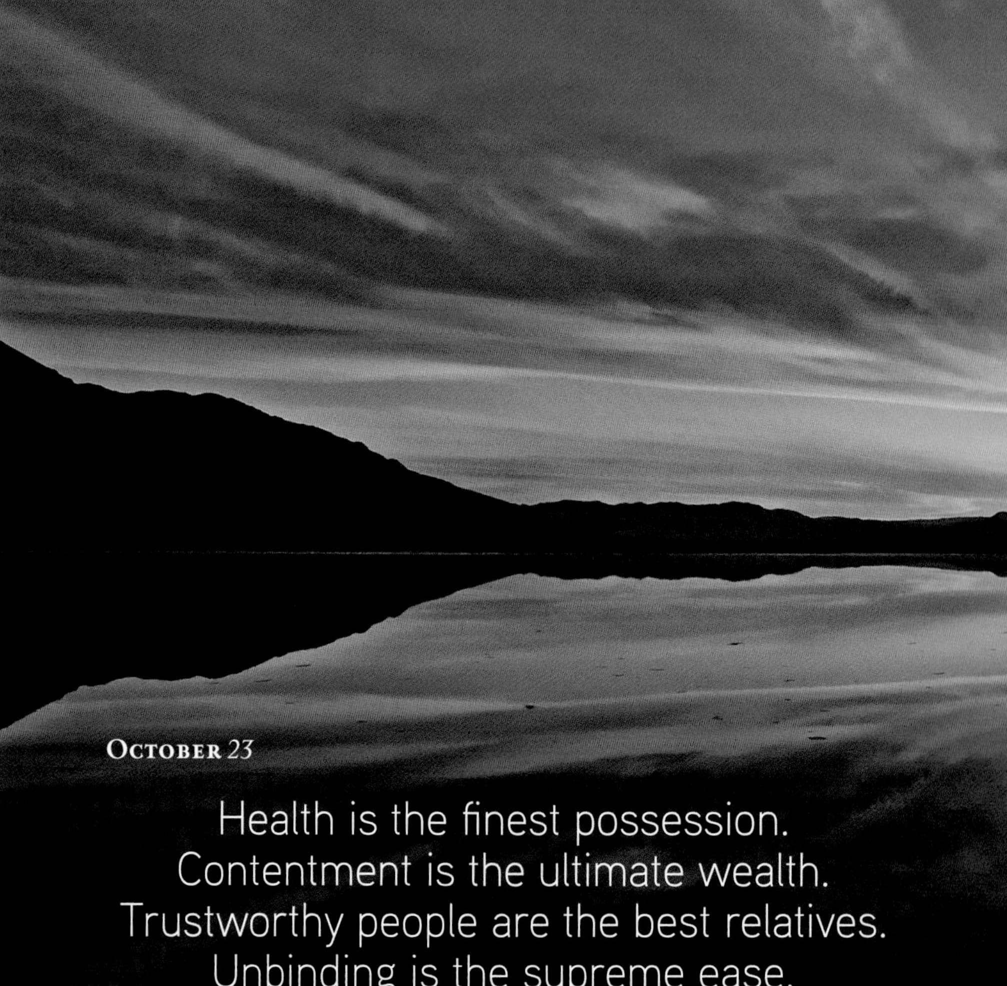

October 23

Health is the finest possession.
Contentment is the ultimate wealth.
Trustworthy people are the best relatives.
Unbinding is the supreme ease.

~ Buddha

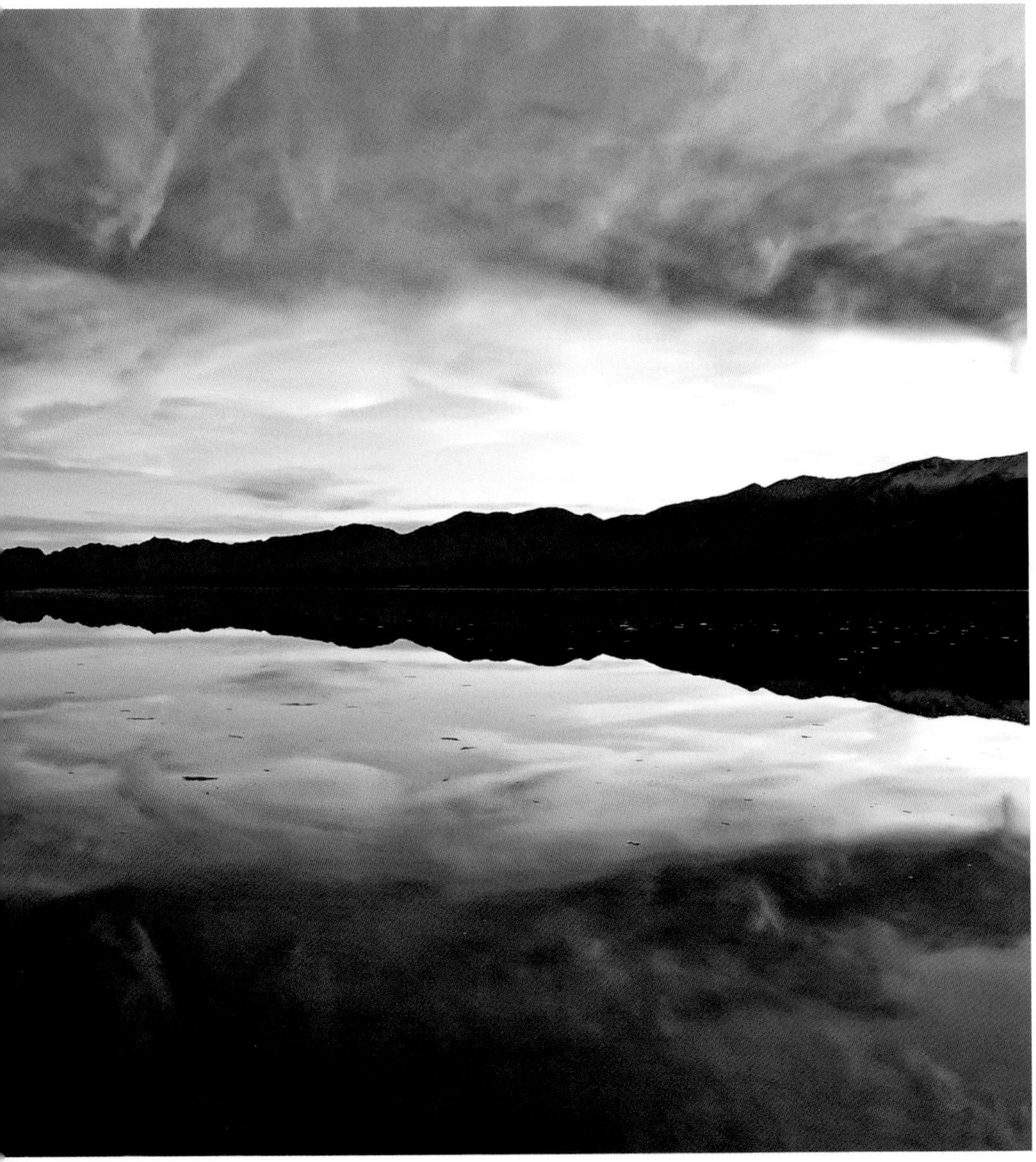

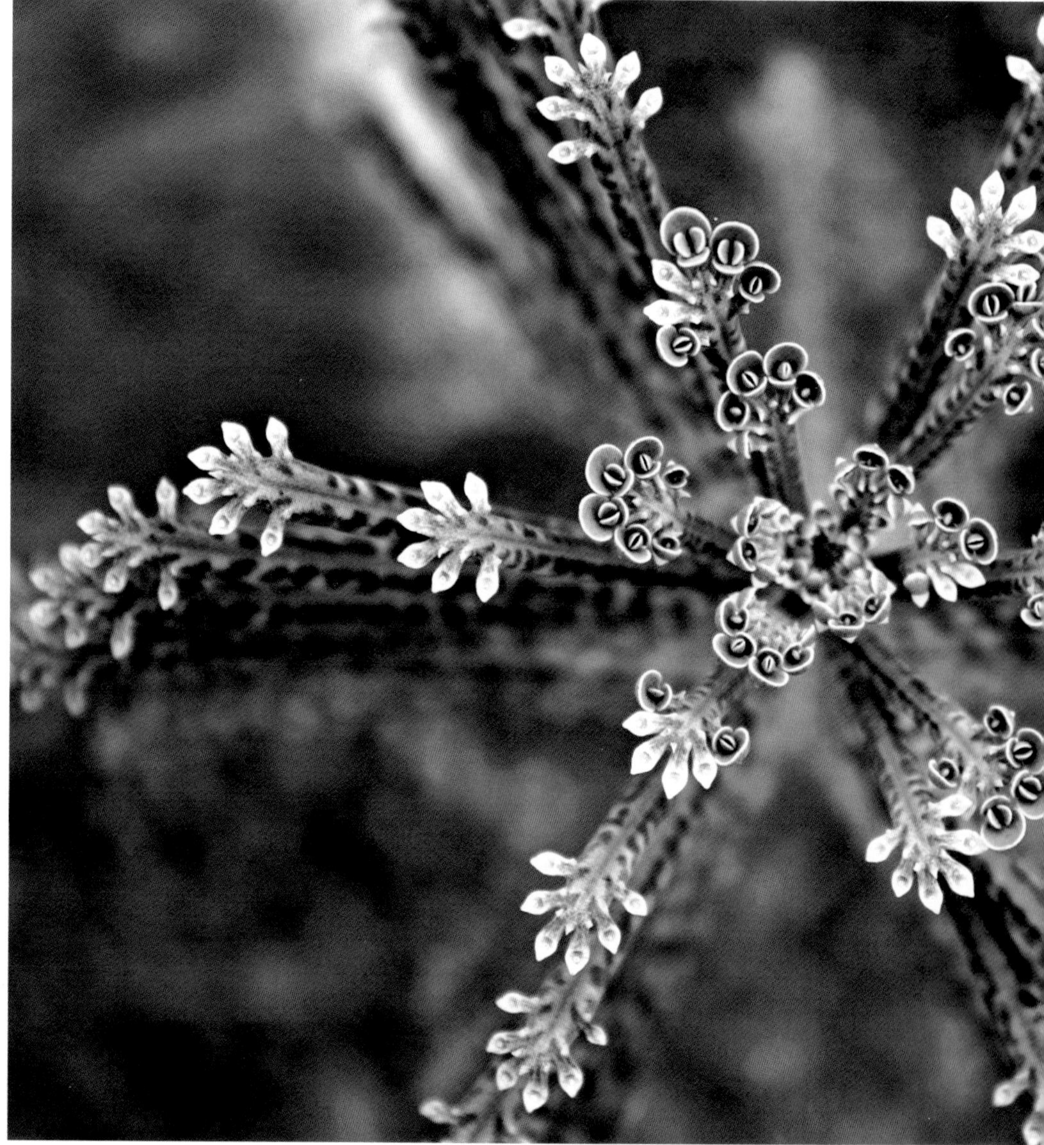

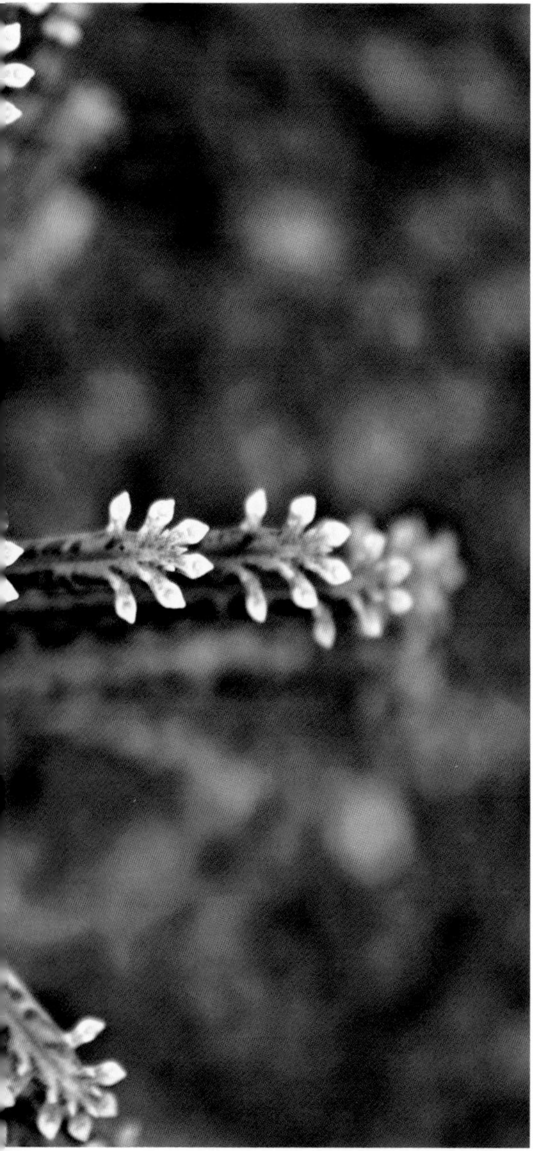

October 24

In order that people
may be happy
in their work,
these three things
are needed:
They must be fit for it.
They must not do too
much of it.
And they must have
a sense of
success in it.

~ John Ruskin

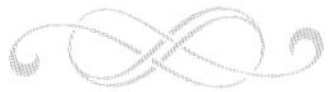

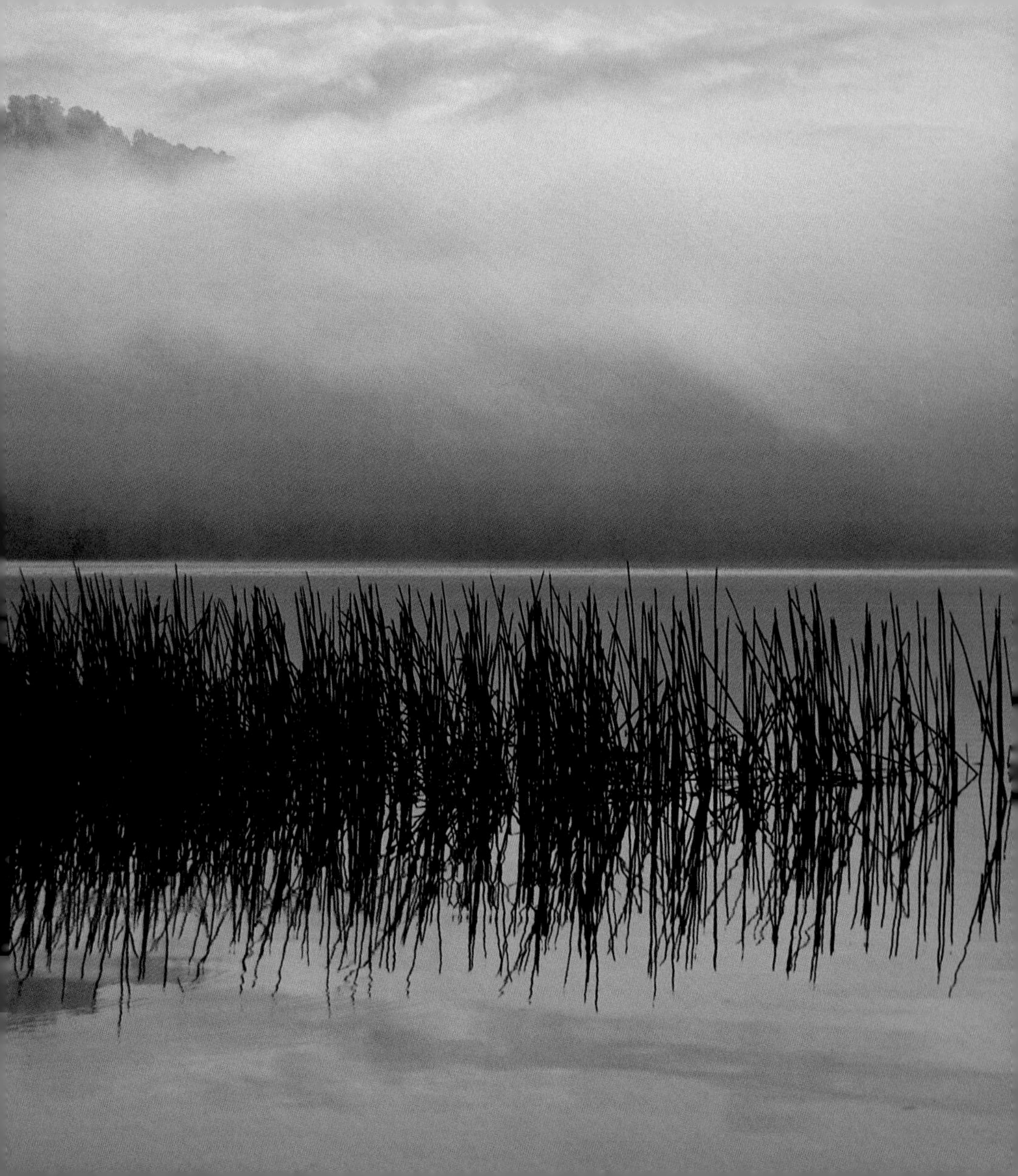

October 25

You will never be happy
if you continue to search for
what happiness consists of.
You will never live if you are looking
for the meaning of life.

~ Albert Camus

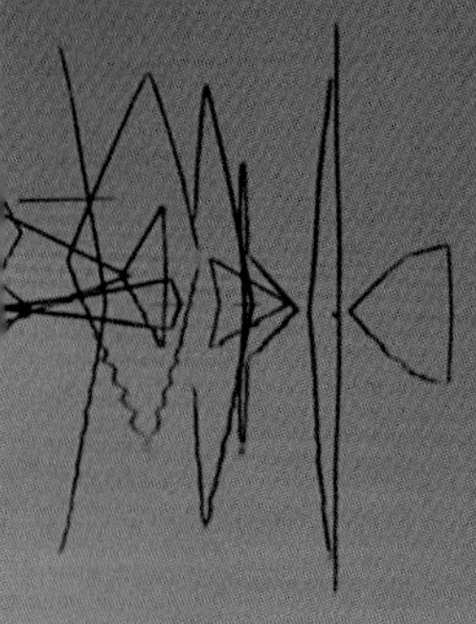

OCTOBER 26

One cannot collect
all the beautiful shells on the beach.
One can collect only a few,
and they are more beautiful
if they are few.

~ Anne Morrow Lindbergh

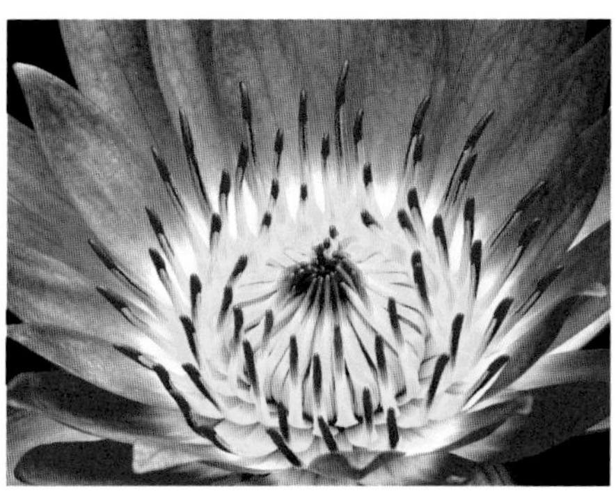

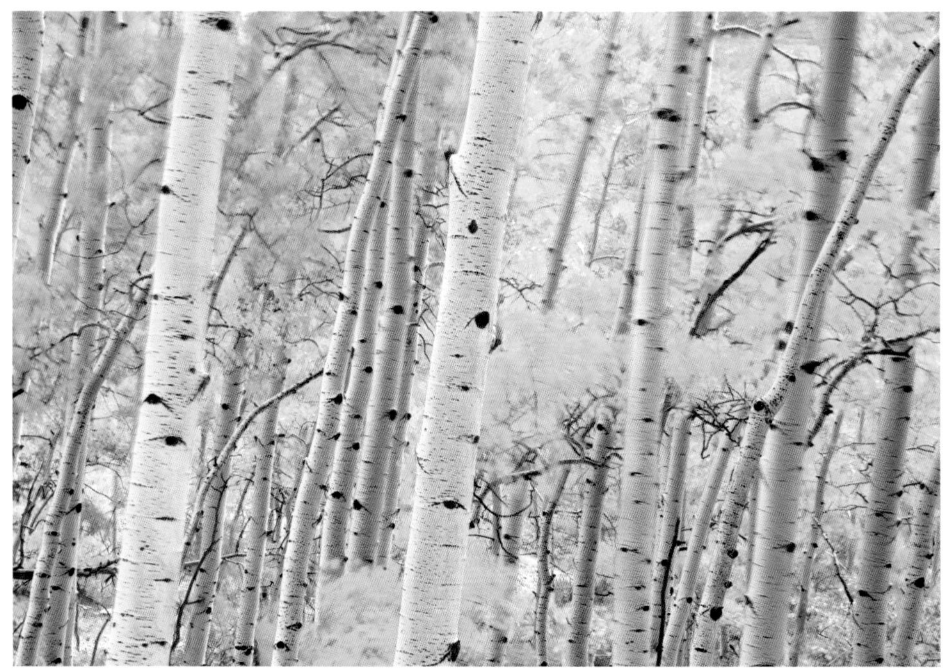

October 27

True happiness consists
not in the multitude of friends,
but in the worth and choice.

~ Ben Jonson

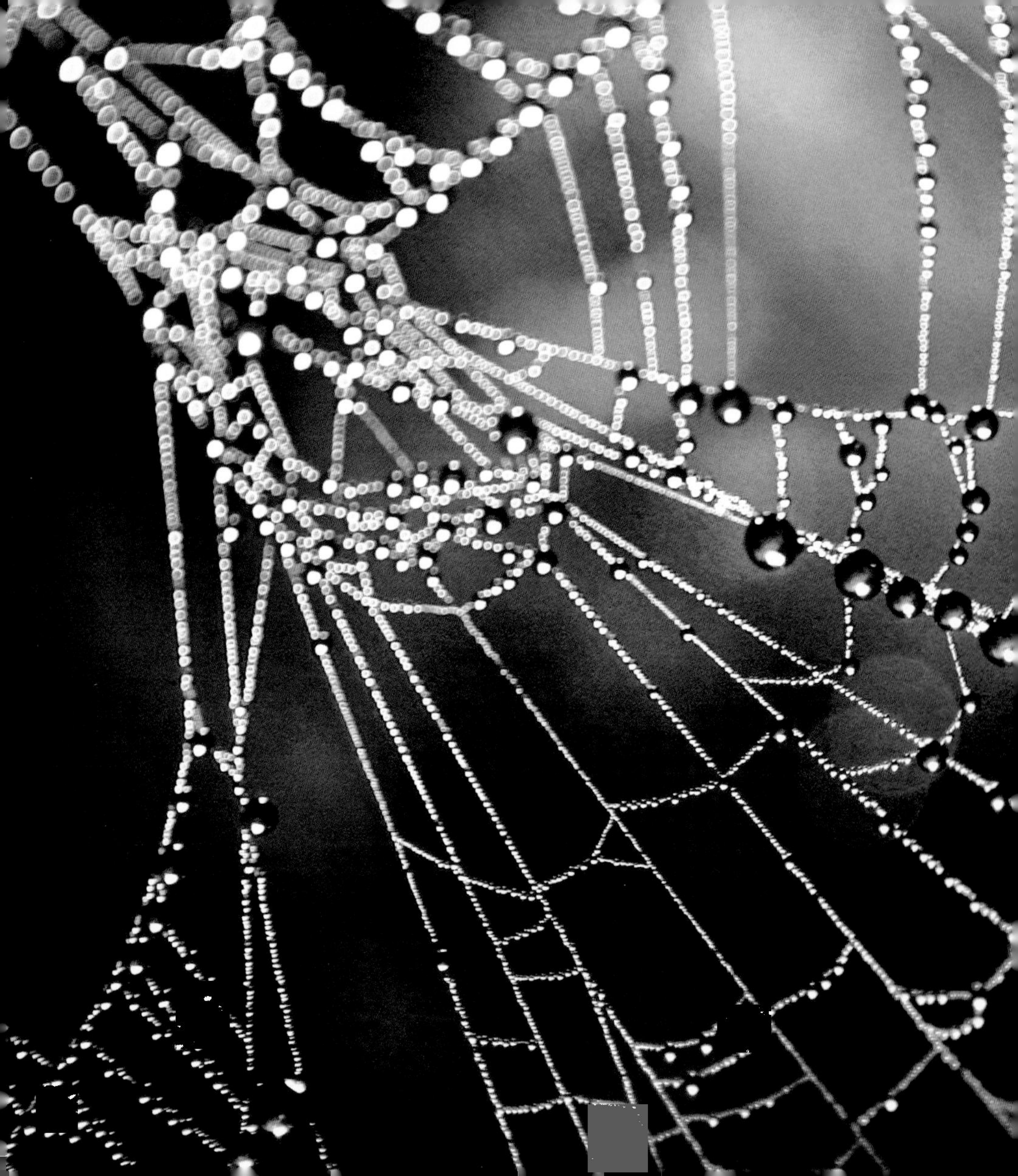

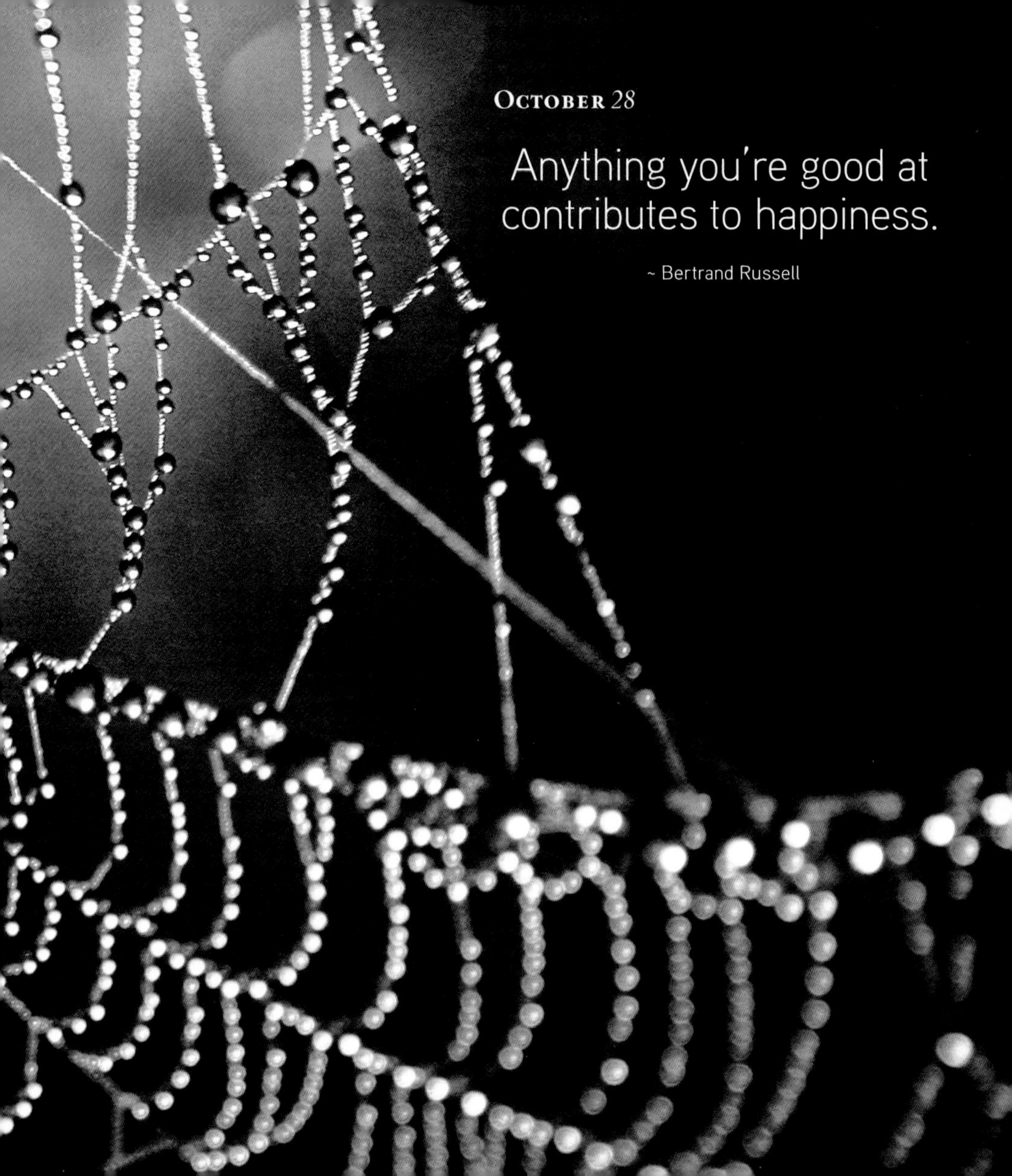

October *28*

Anything you're good at contributes to happiness.

~ Bertrand Russell

October 29

When what we are is what we want to be, that's happiness.

~ Malcolm Forbes

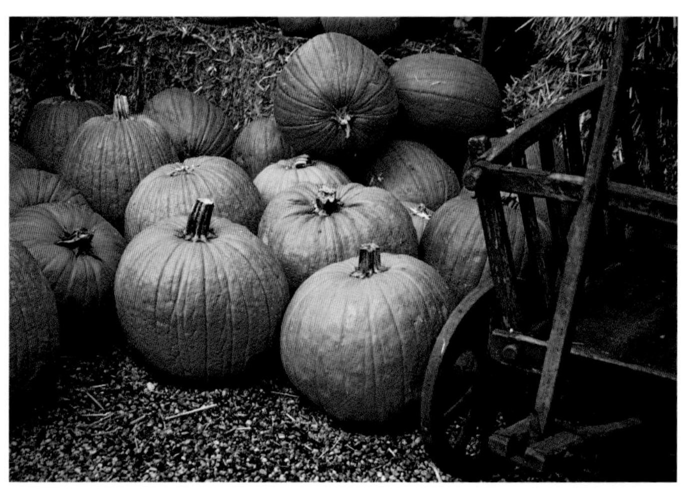

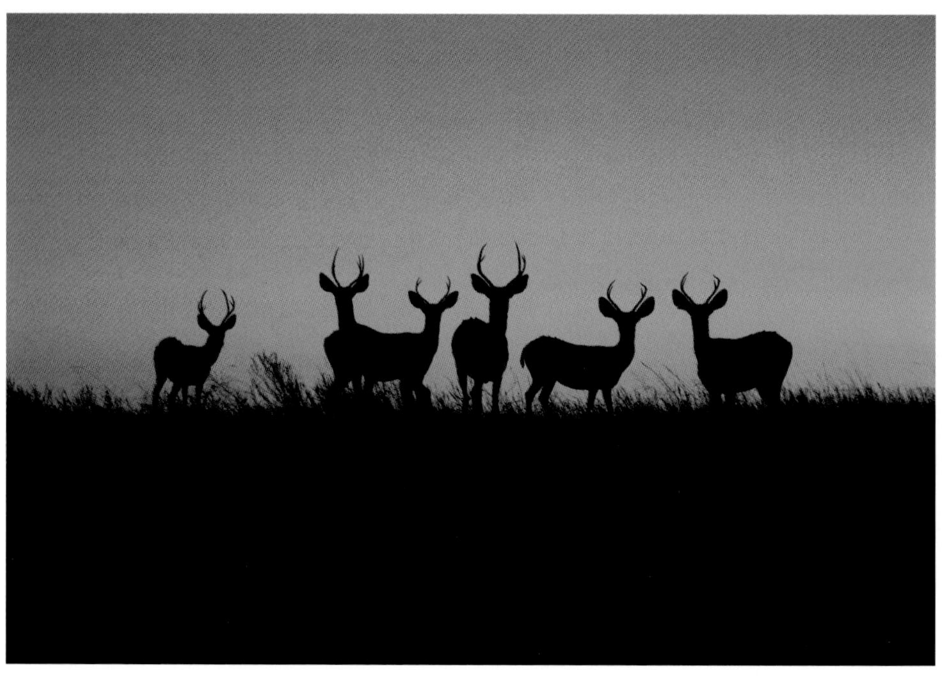

OCTOBER 30

Human happiness and human satisfaction must ultimately come from within oneself.

~ Dalai Lama

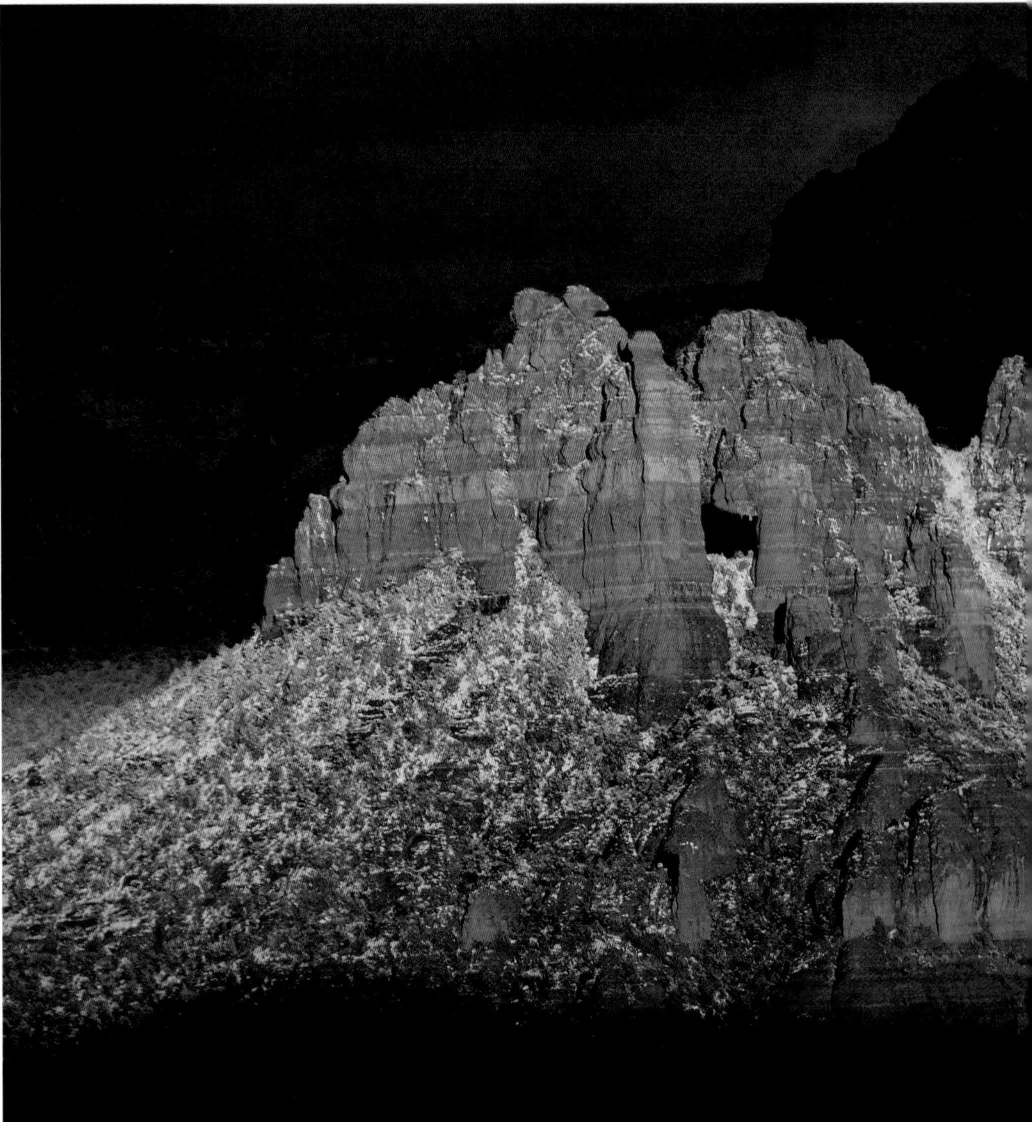

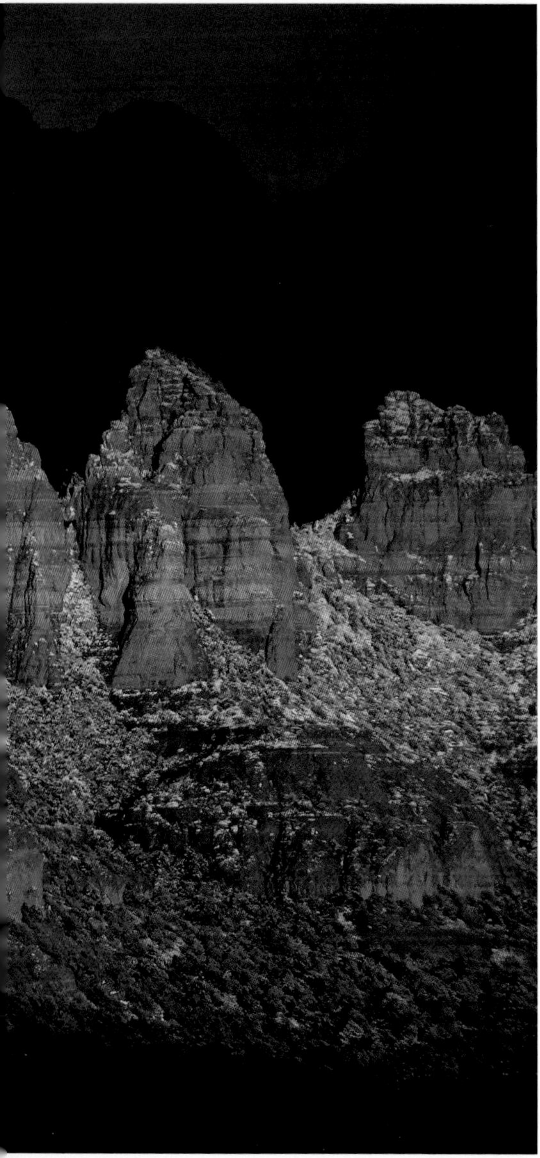

OCTOBER 31

Don't wait around
for other people
to be happy for you.
Any happiness
you get,
you've got to
make yourself.

~ Alice Walker

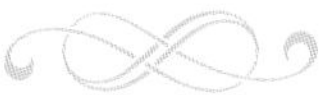

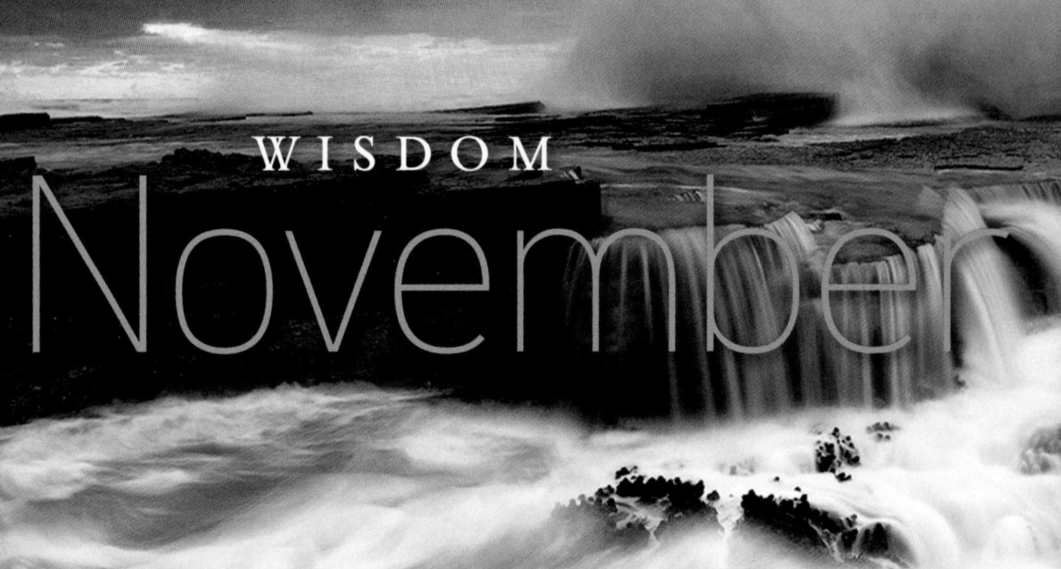

WISDOM

November

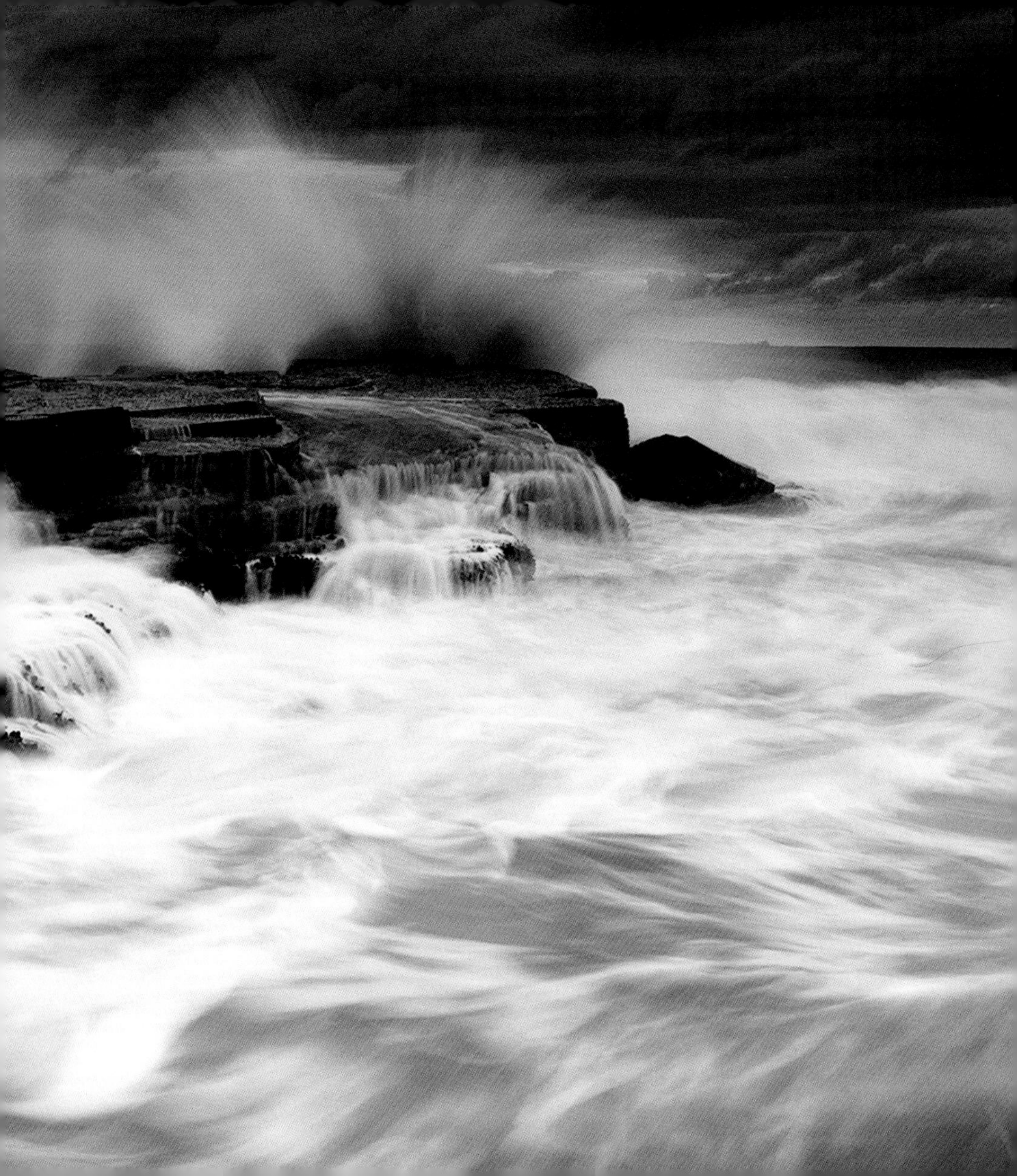

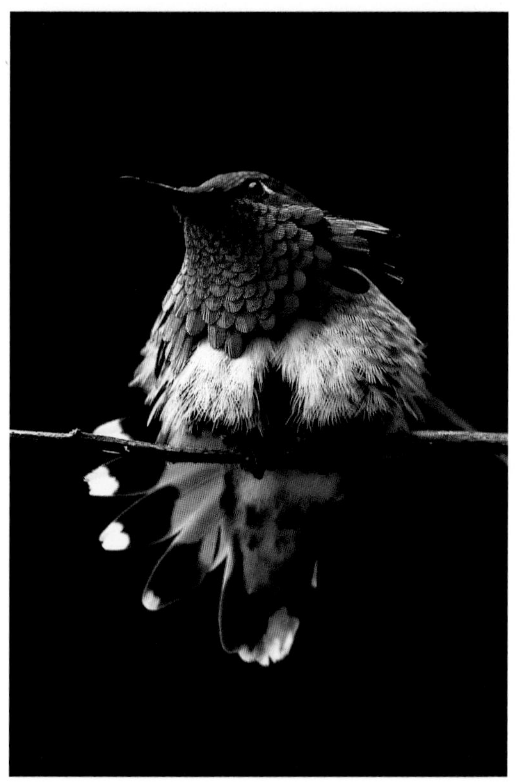

NOVEMBER *1*

The art of being wise
is the art of knowing what to overlook.

~ William James

NOVEMBER 2

Holding on to anger is like
grasping a hot coal
with the intent of throwing it
at someone else;
you are the one who gets burned.

~ Buddha

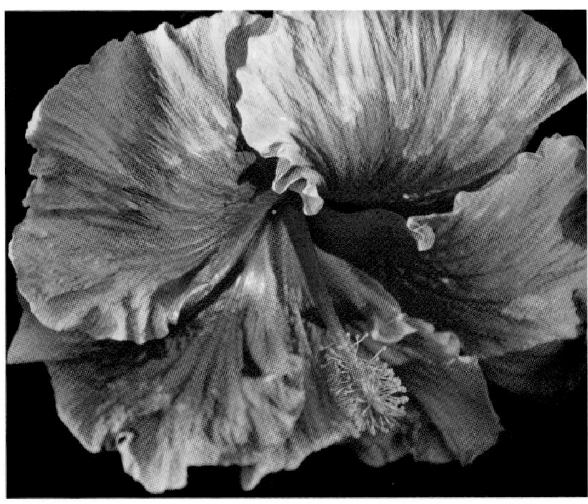

November 3

We choose our joys and sorrows long before we experience them.

~ Kahlil Gibran

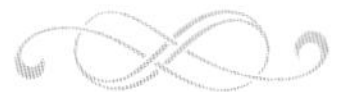

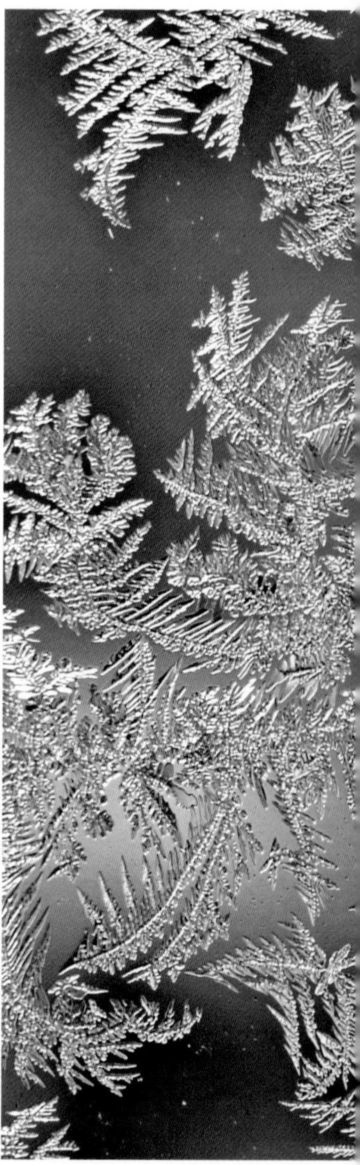

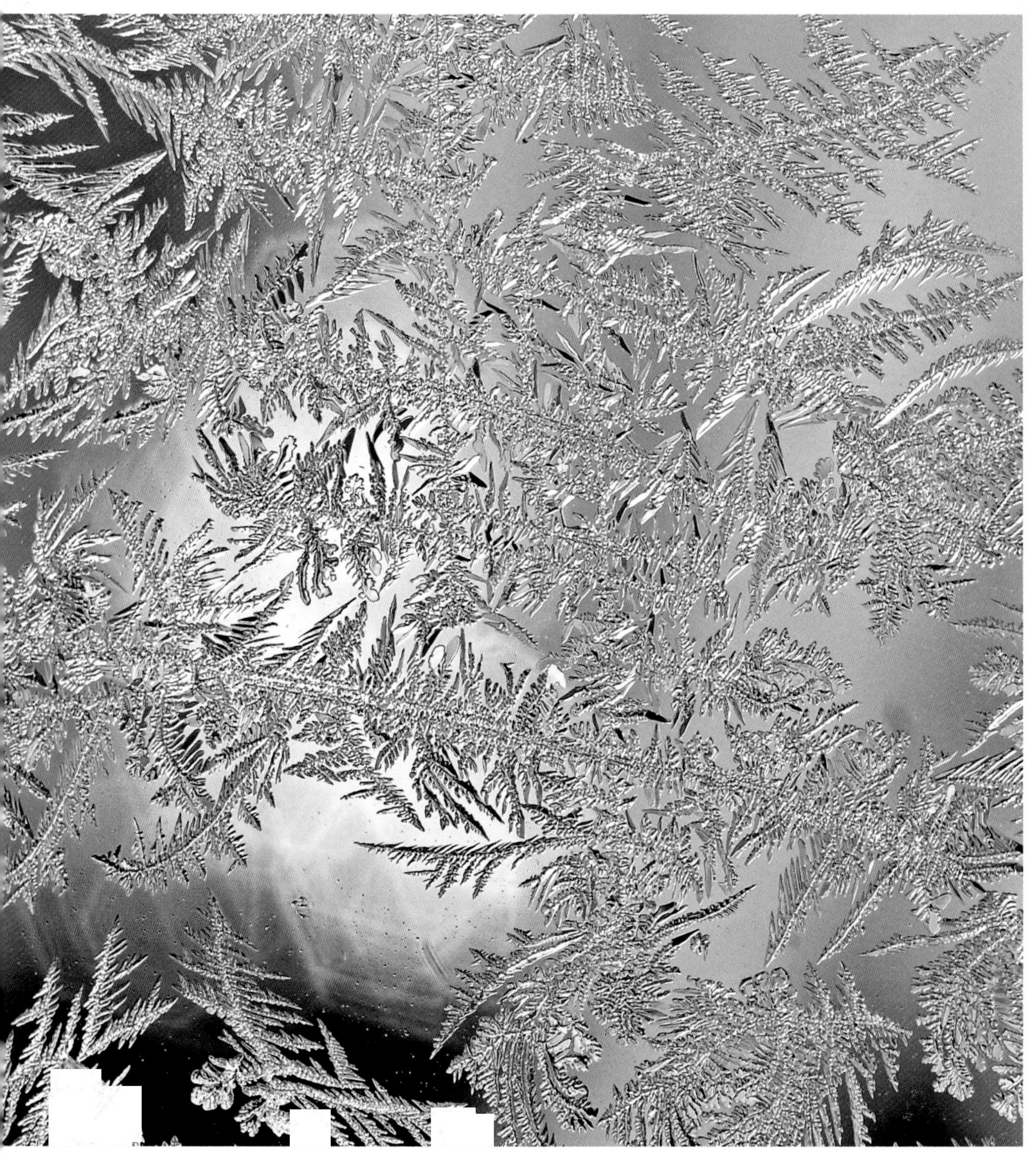

NOVEMBER 4

You can catch health,
happiness, and success
from others
just as easily as
you can catch worries,
bitterness, and failure.

~ Dale Carnegie

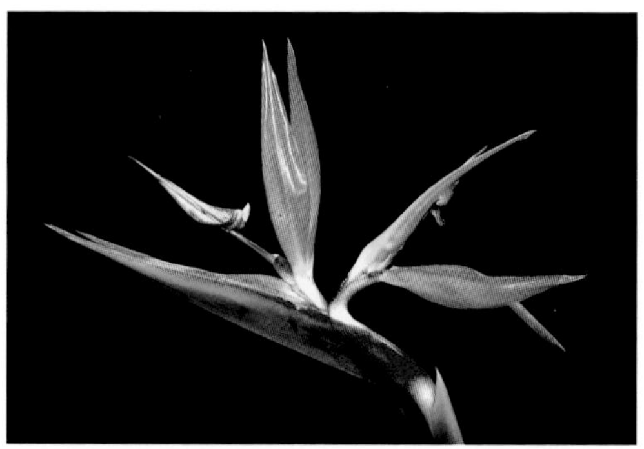

November 5

Not everything that can be counted counts, and not everything that counts can be counted.

- Albert Einstein

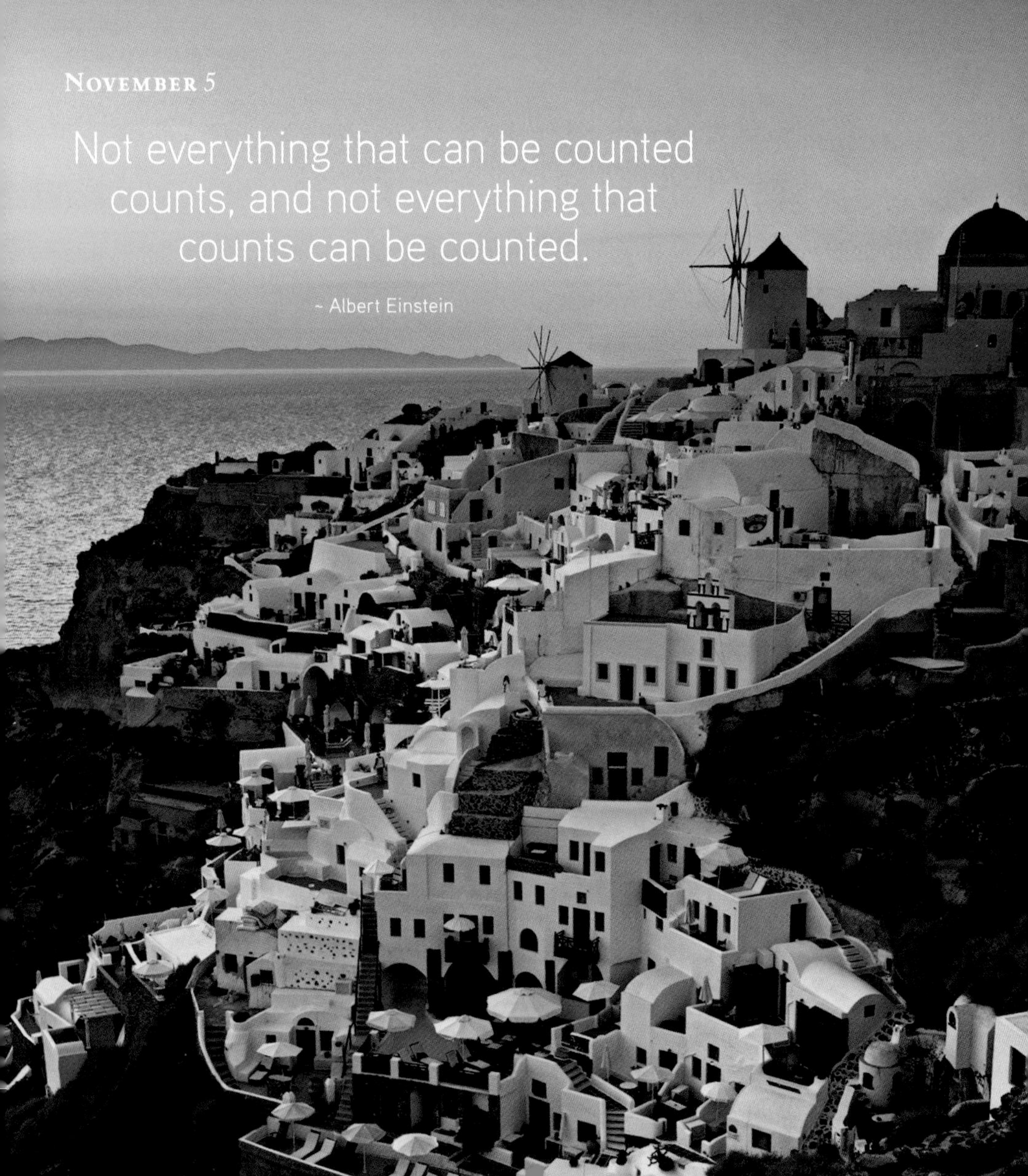

November 6

Sleep is
the best
meditation.

~ Dalai Lama

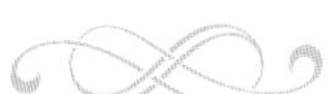

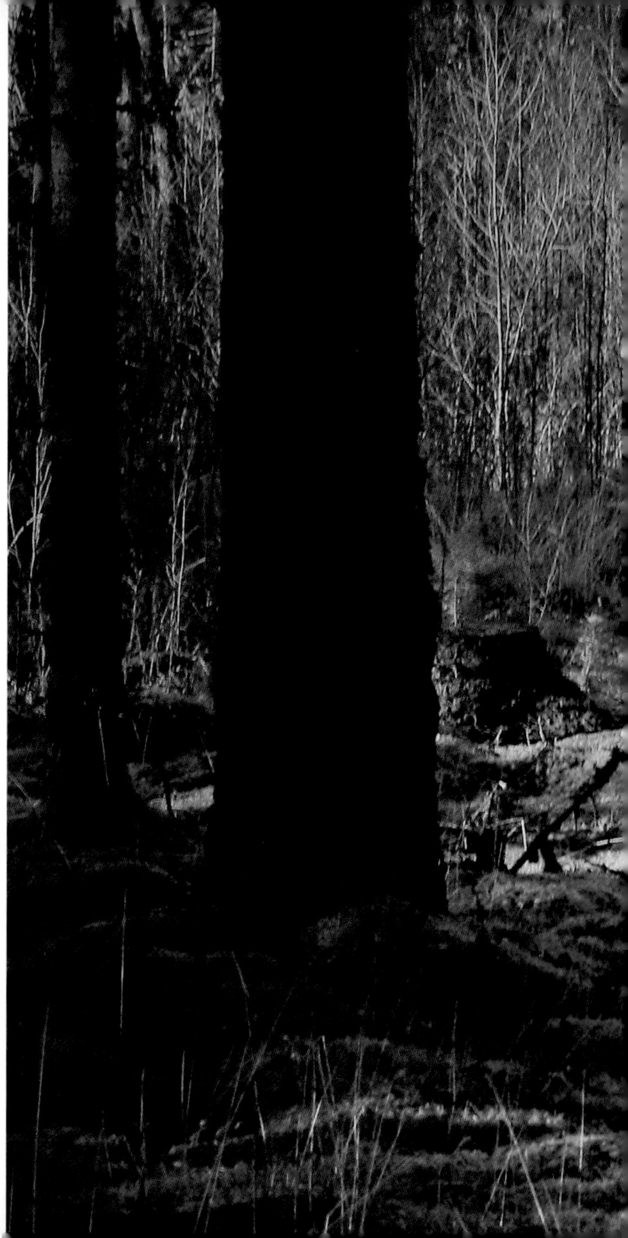

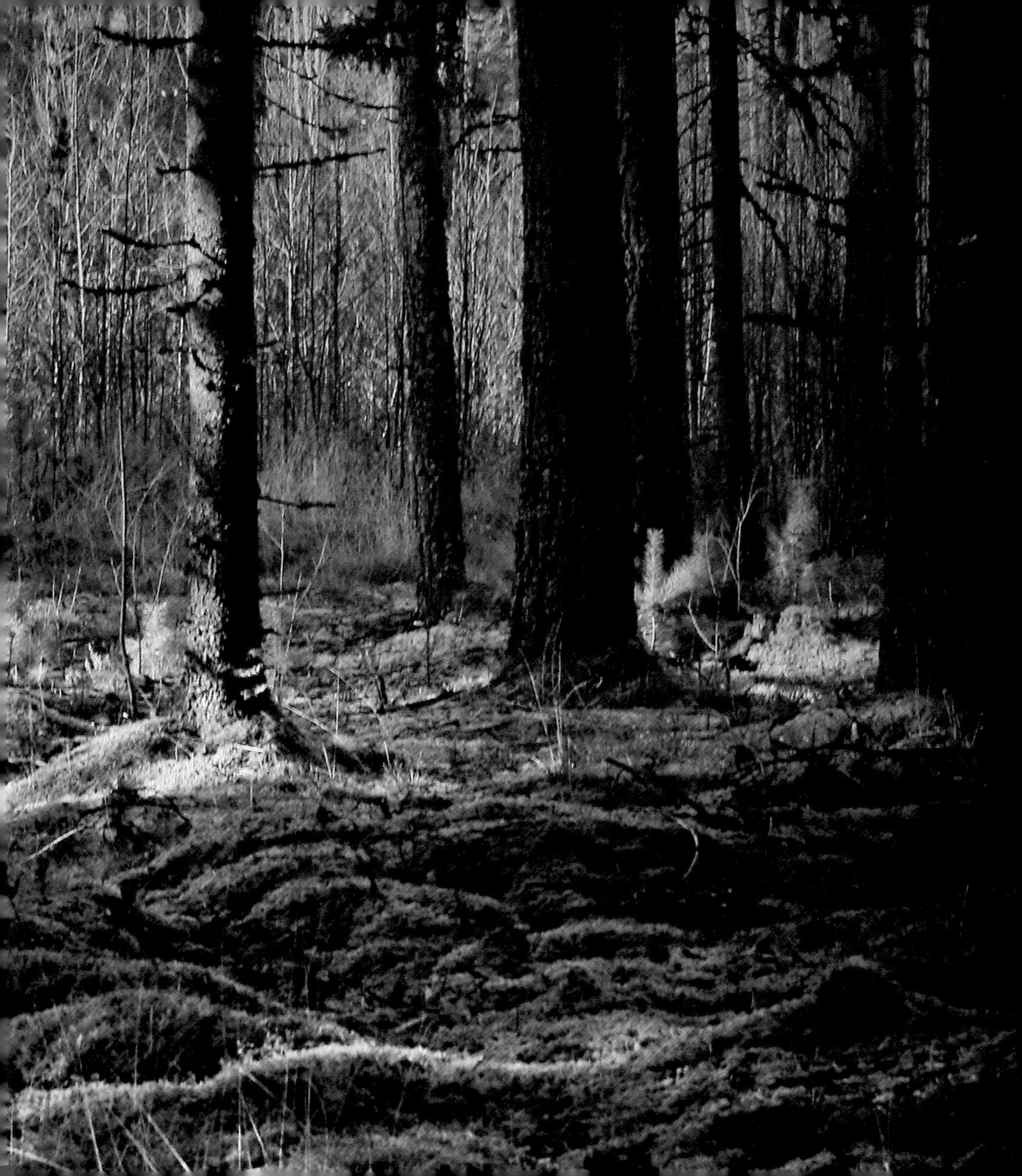

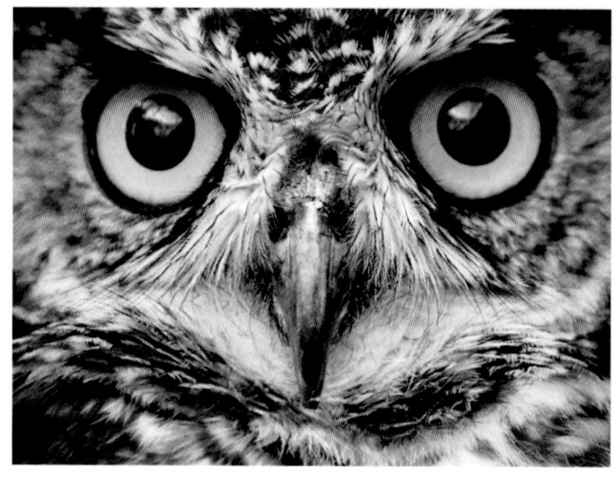

NOVEMBER 7

He that would live in peace and at ease must not speak all he knows or all he sees.

~ Benjamin Franklin

NOVEMBER 8

Perhaps the world's second-worst crime is boredom; the first is being a bore.

~ Cecil Beaton

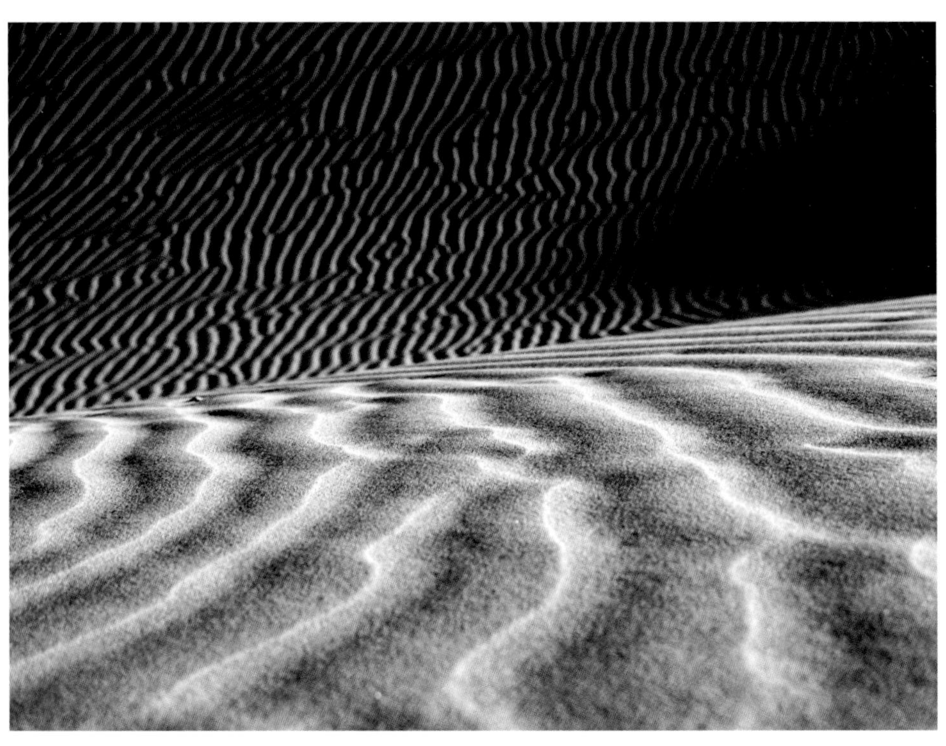

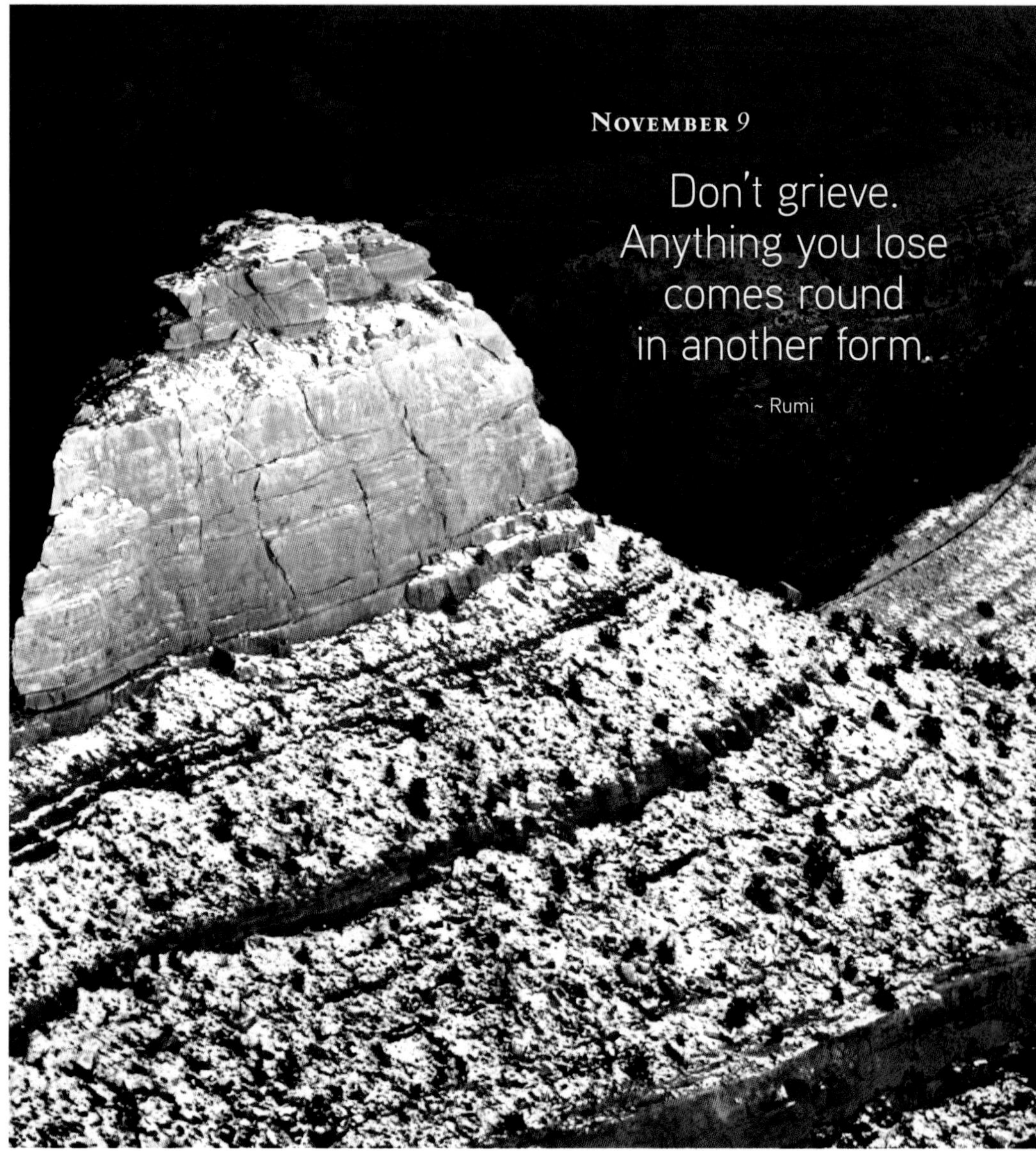
November 9
Don't grieve.
Anything you lose
comes round
in another form.
~ Rumi

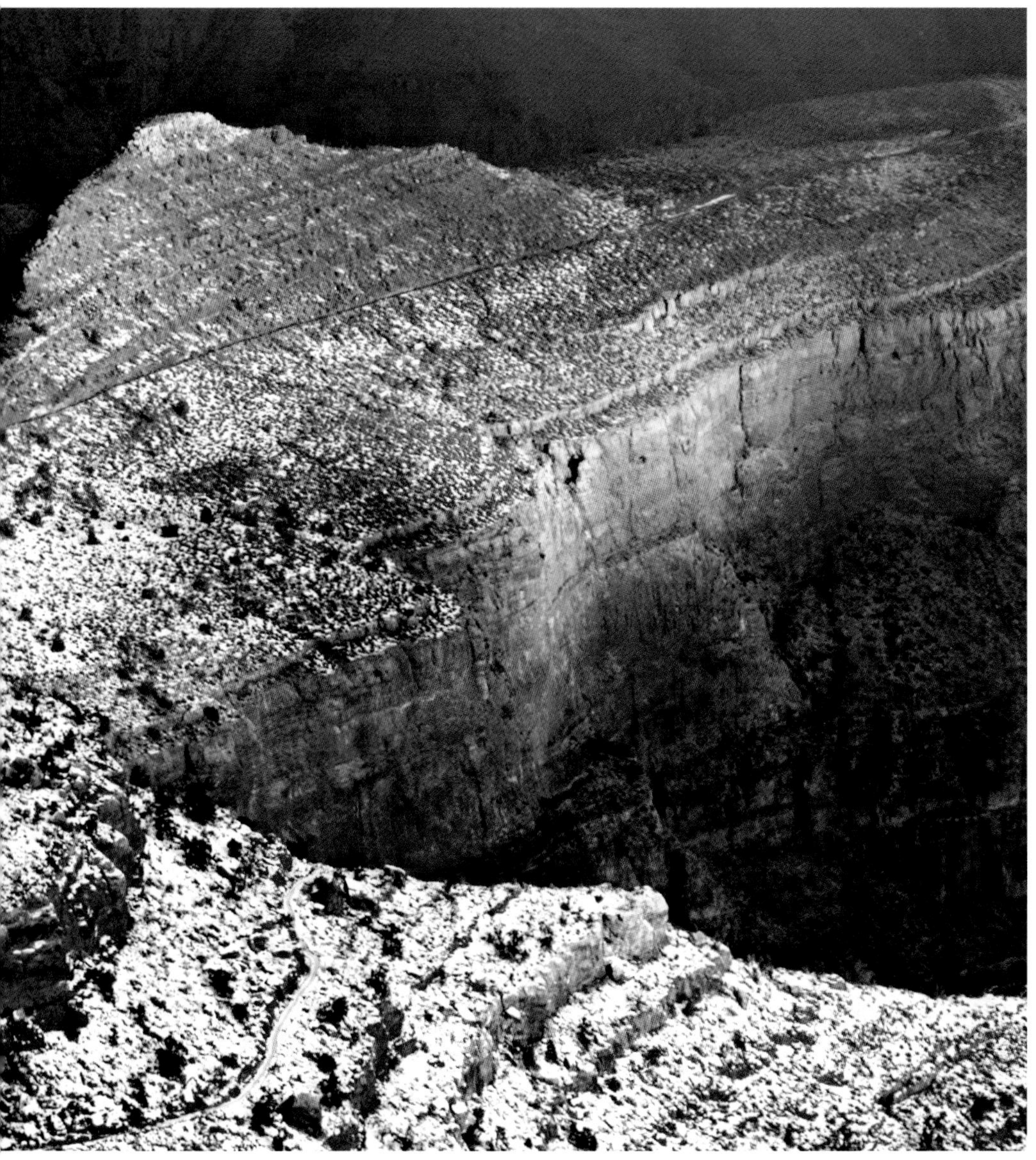

NOVEMBER *10*

Everyone chases after happiness,
not noticing that happiness
is right at their heels.

~Bertolt Brecht

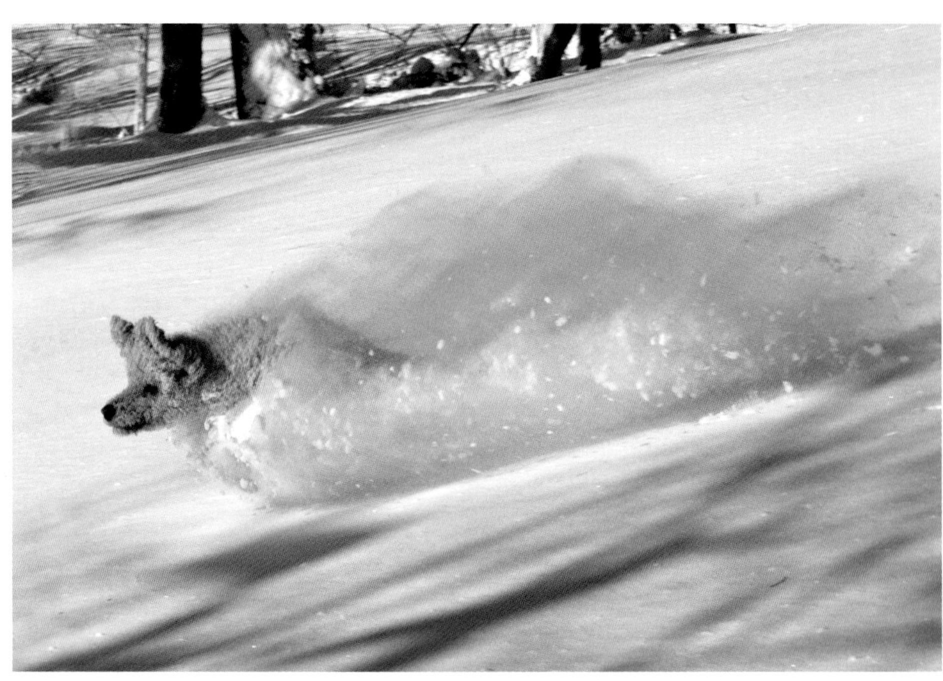

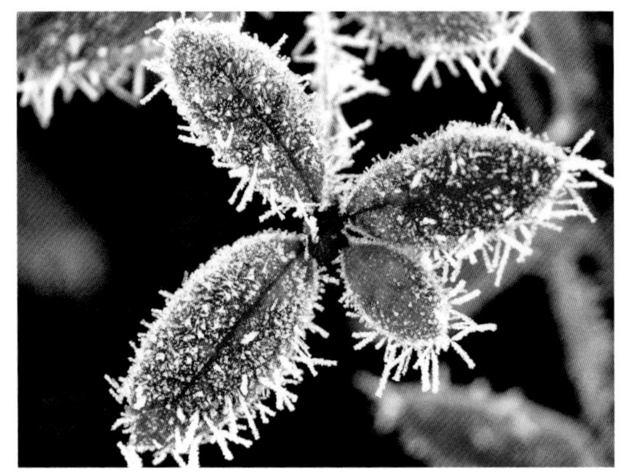

NOVEMBER 11

It is easy to be heavy;
it is hard to be light.

~ G. K. Chesterton

NOVEMBER 12

The most common
way people give up
their power is
by thinking
they don't have any.

~ Alice Walker

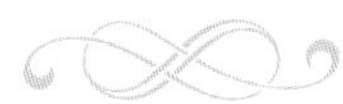

NOVEMBER 13

Crave for a thing, you will get it.
Renounce the craving,
the object will follow you by itself.

~ Swami Sivananda

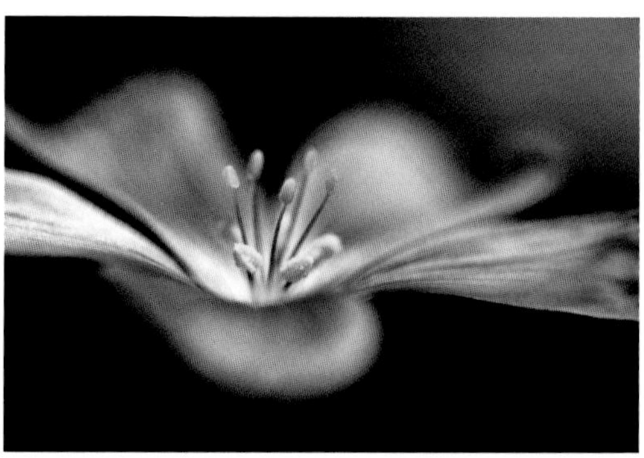

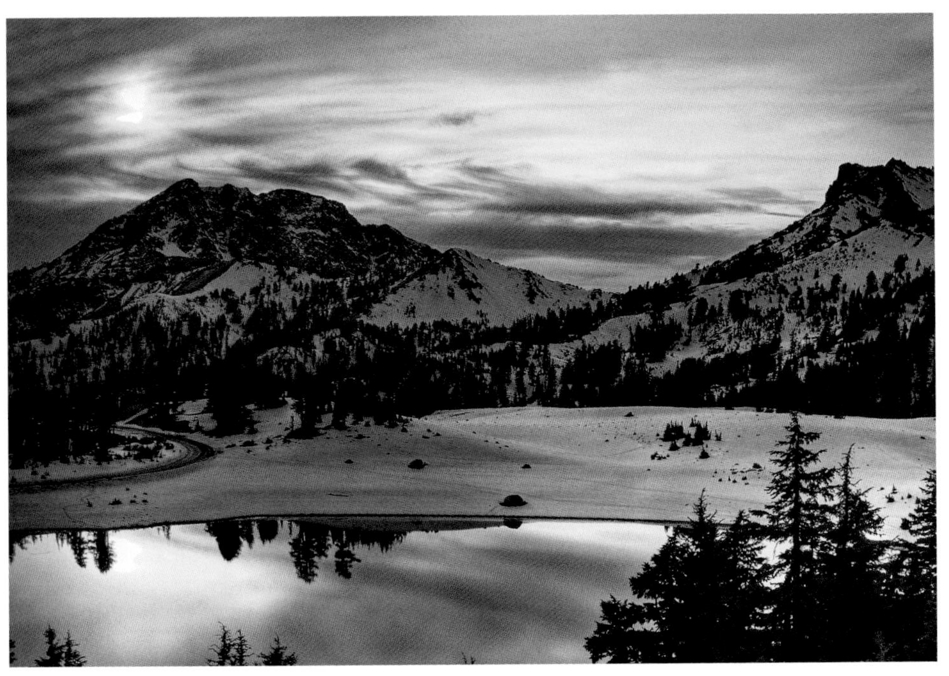

November 14

Whoever is careless with truth
in small matters cannot be trusted
in important affairs.

~ Albert Einstein

November 15

Self-pity
in its early stages
is as snug as
a feather mattress.
Only when it hardens
does it become
uncomfortable.

~ Maya Angelou

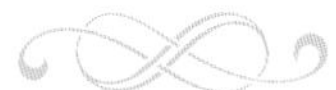

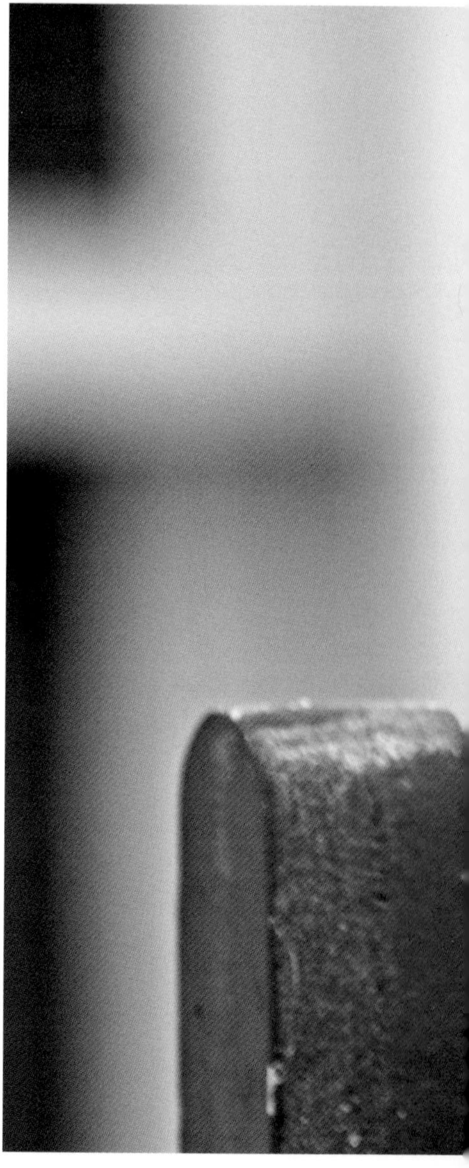

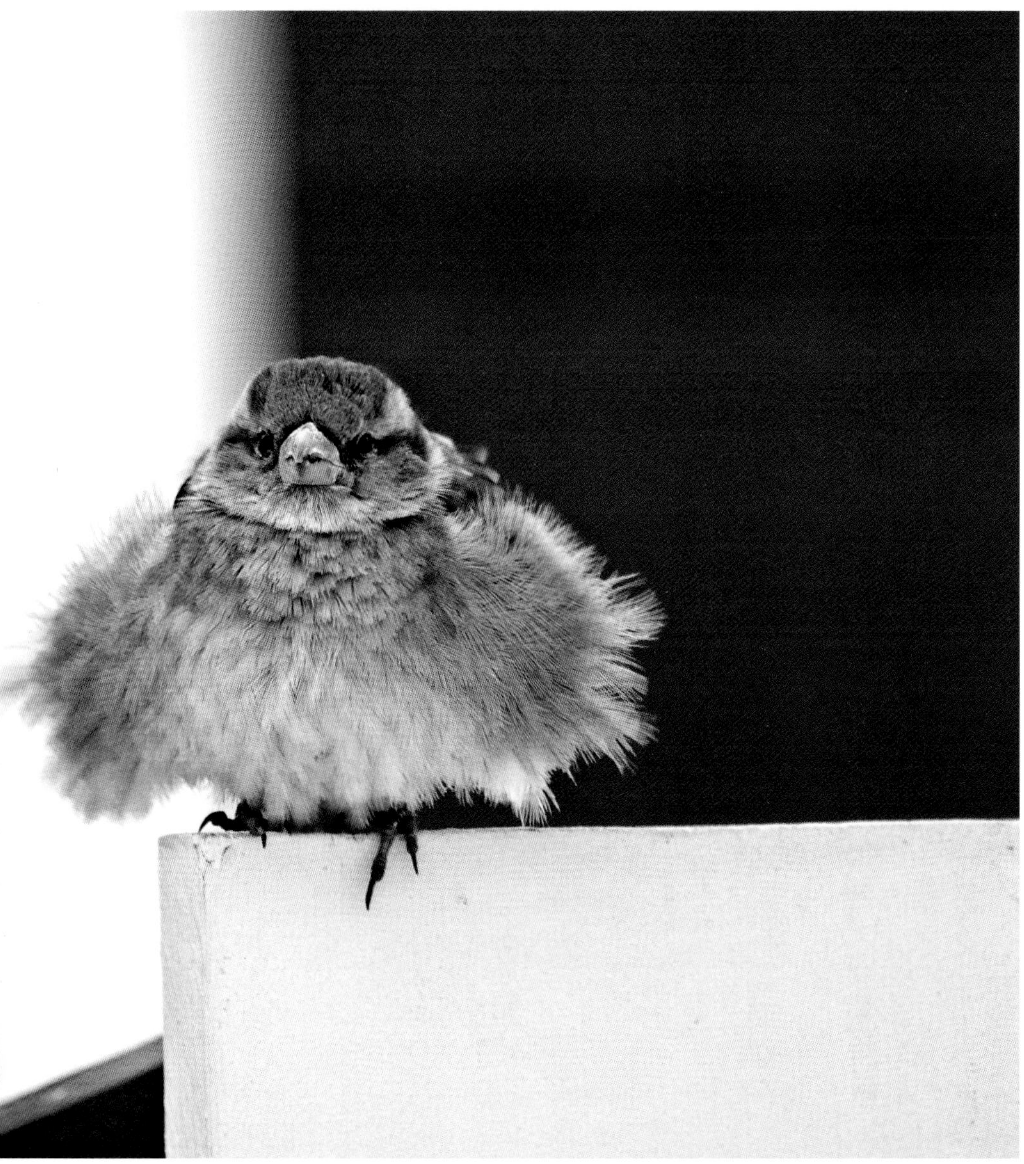

November 16

A girl should be two things:
classy and fabulous.

~ Coco Chanel

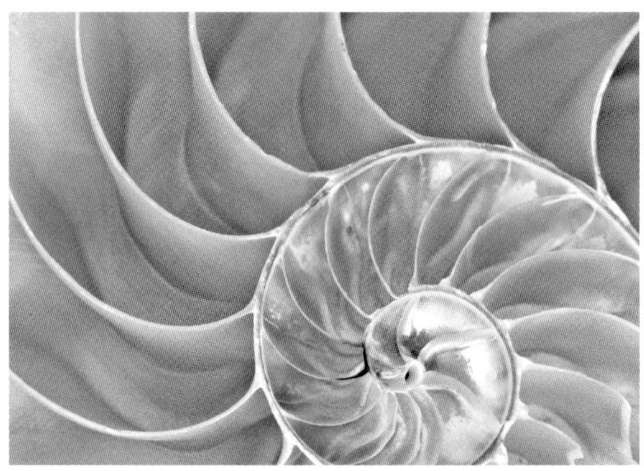

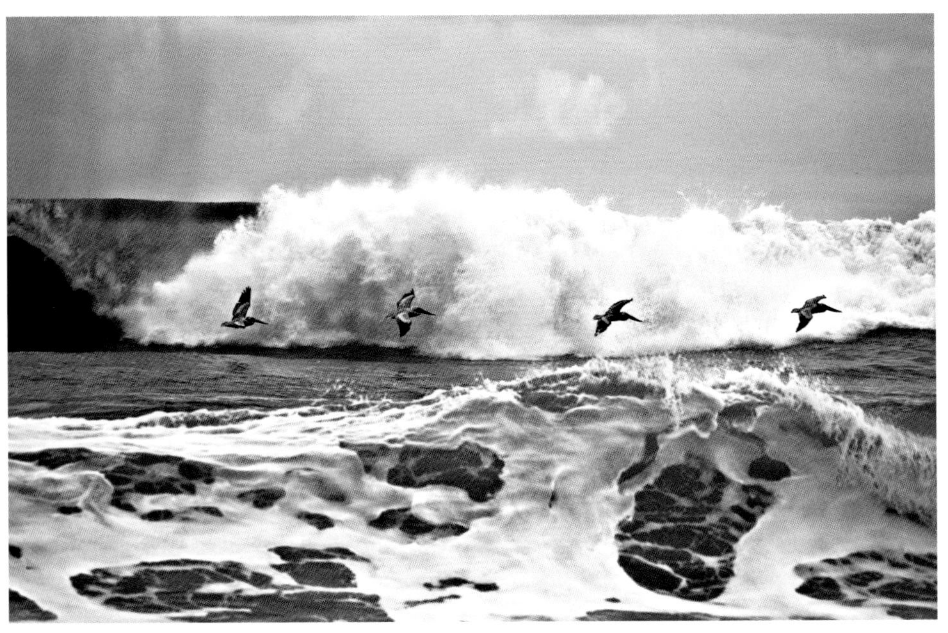

November 17

The person who has lived the most is not the one with the most years but the one with the richest experiences.

~ Jean-Jacques Rosseau

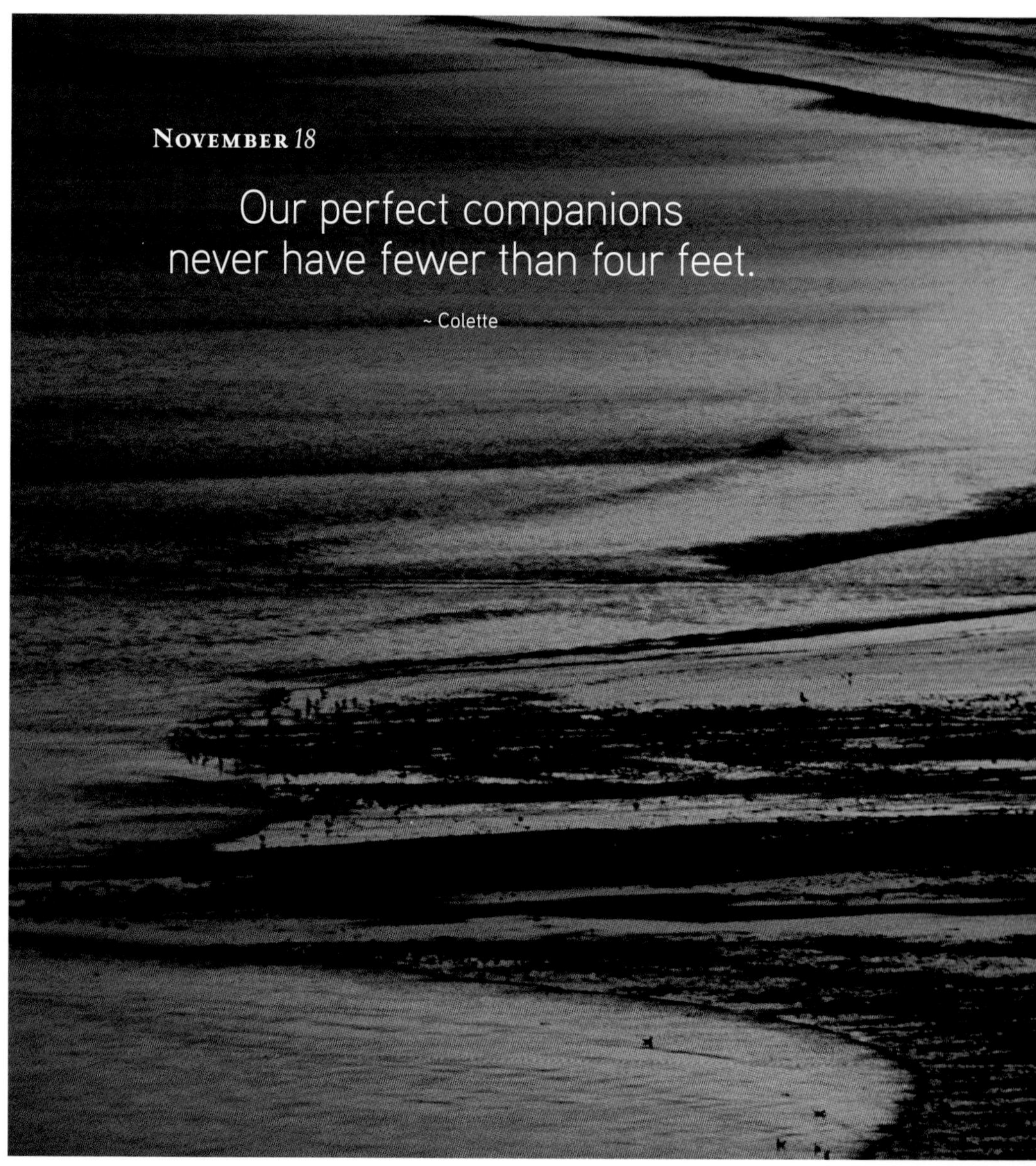

November *18*

Our perfect companions
never have fewer than four feet.

~ Colette

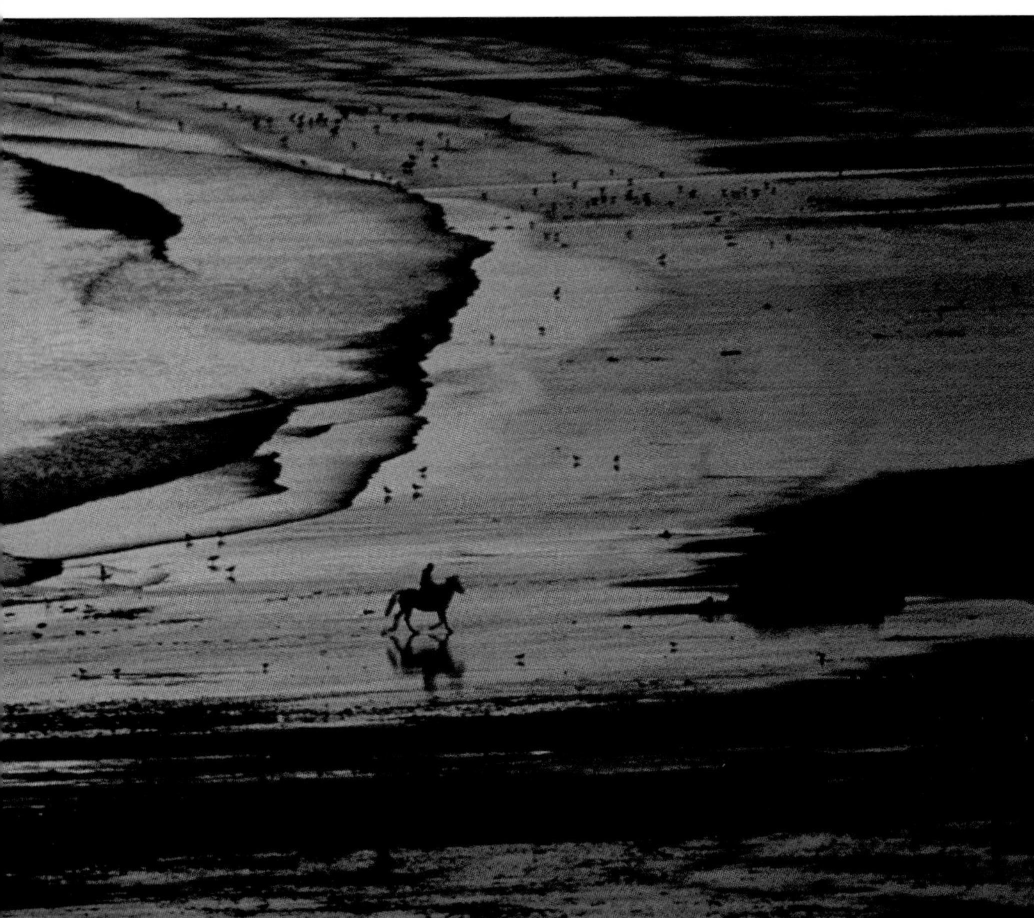

NOVEMBER 19

Things are always in transition.
Nothing ever sums itself up
in the way that we like to
dream about.

~ Pema Chödrön

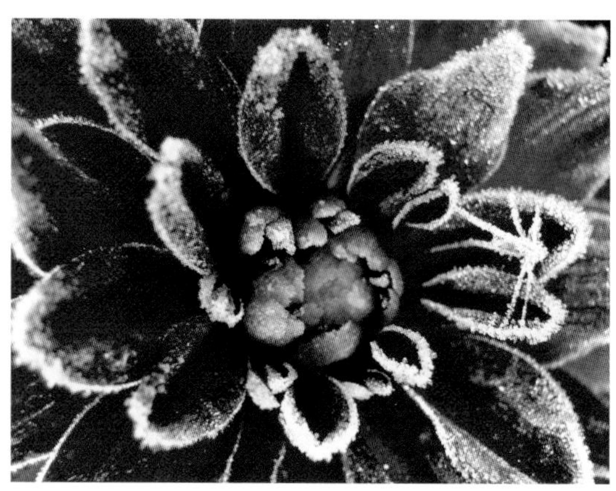

NOVEMBER 20

Happiness often sneaks in through a door you didn't know you left open.

~ John Barrymore

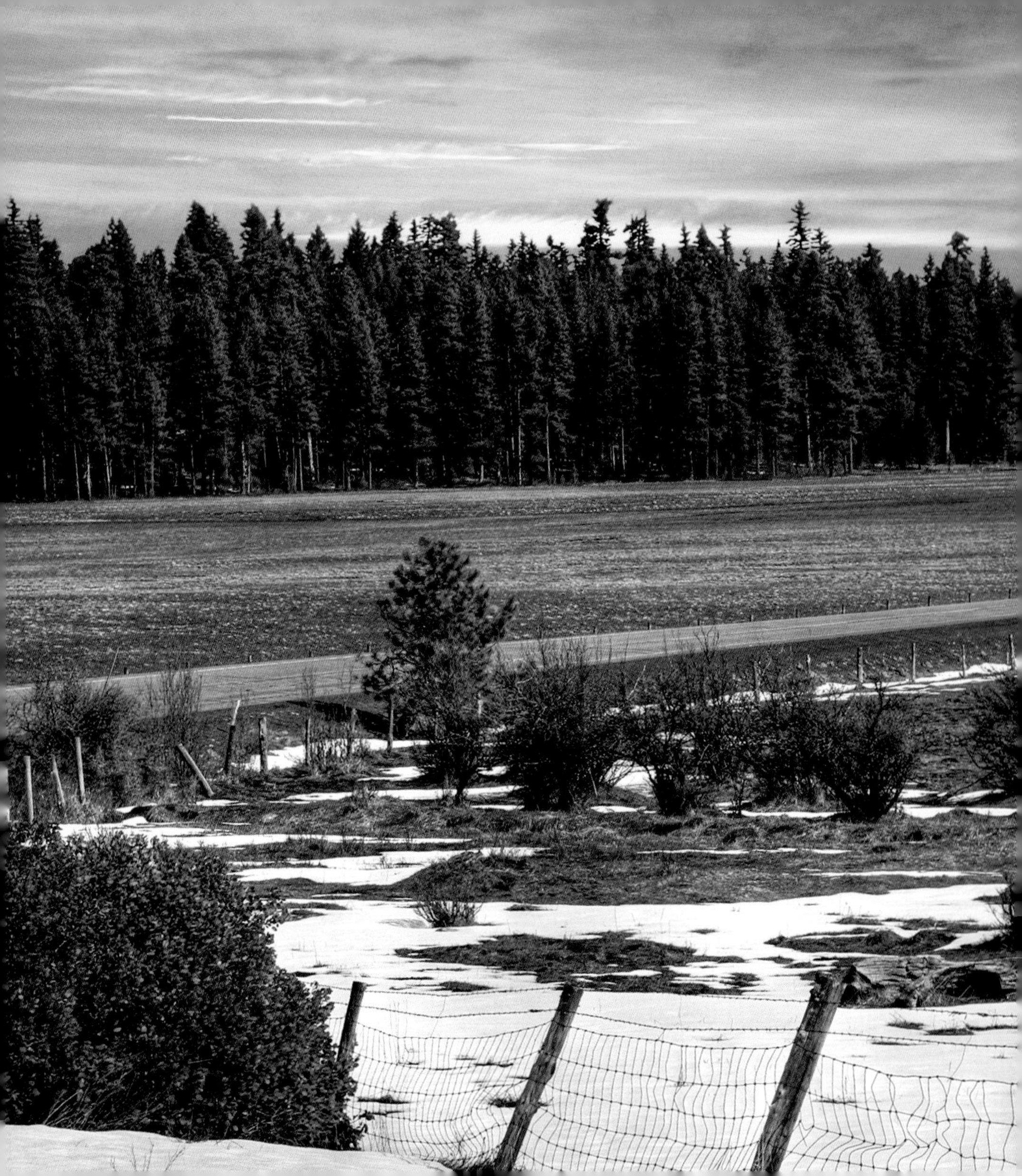

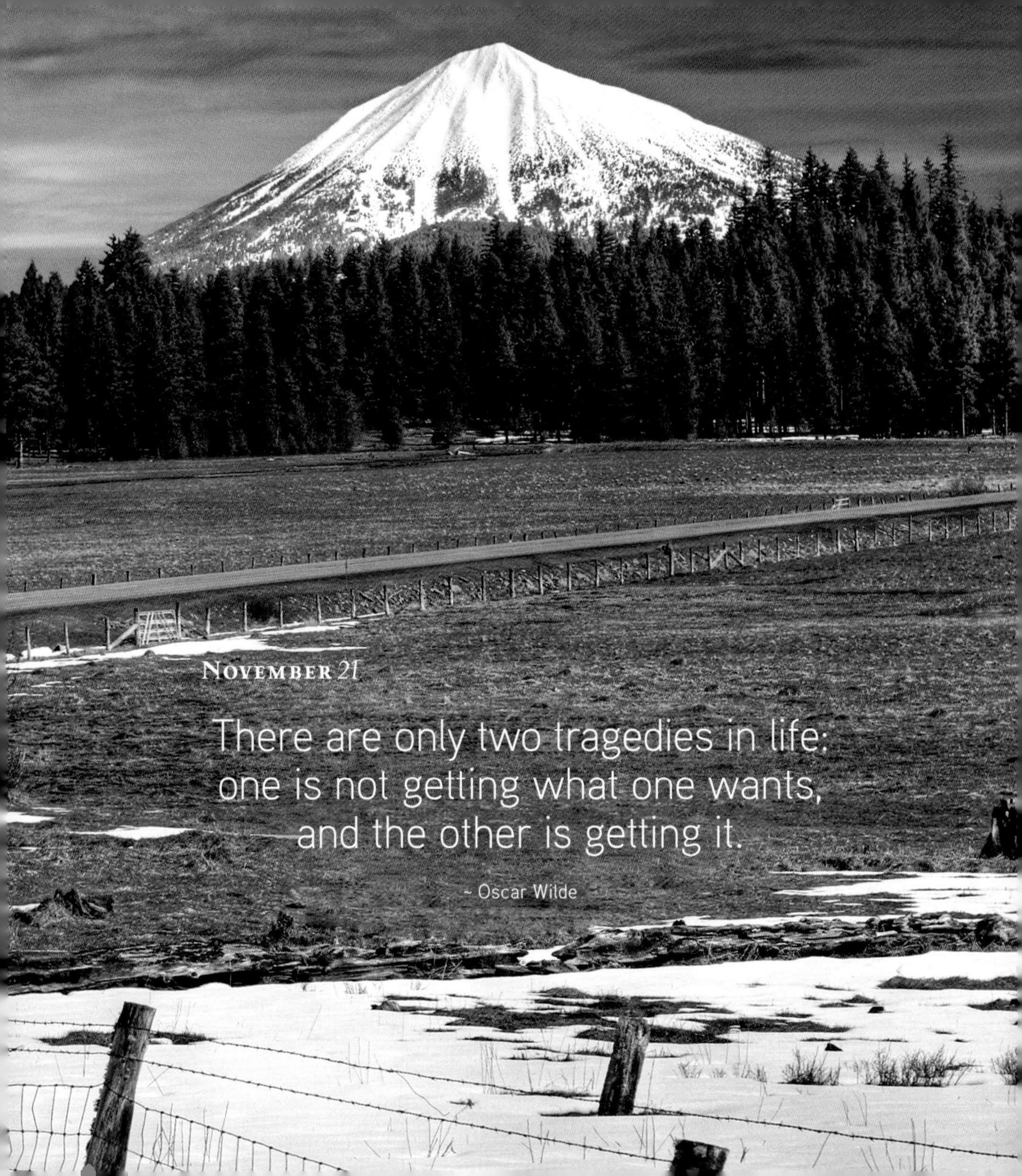

NOVEMBER *21*

There are only two tragedies in life:
one is not getting what one wants,
and the other is getting it.

~ Oscar Wilde

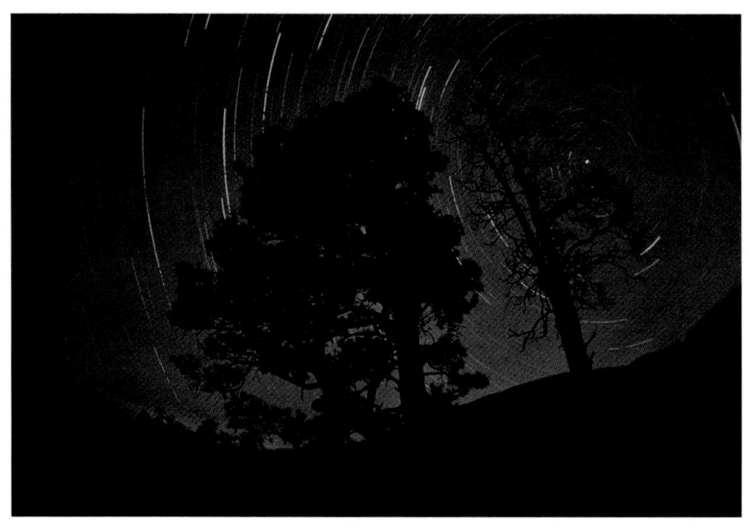

NOVEMBER *22*

The body is a sacred garment.
It's your first and last garment;
it is what you enter life in and
what you depart life with,
and it should be treated
with honor.

~ Martha Graham

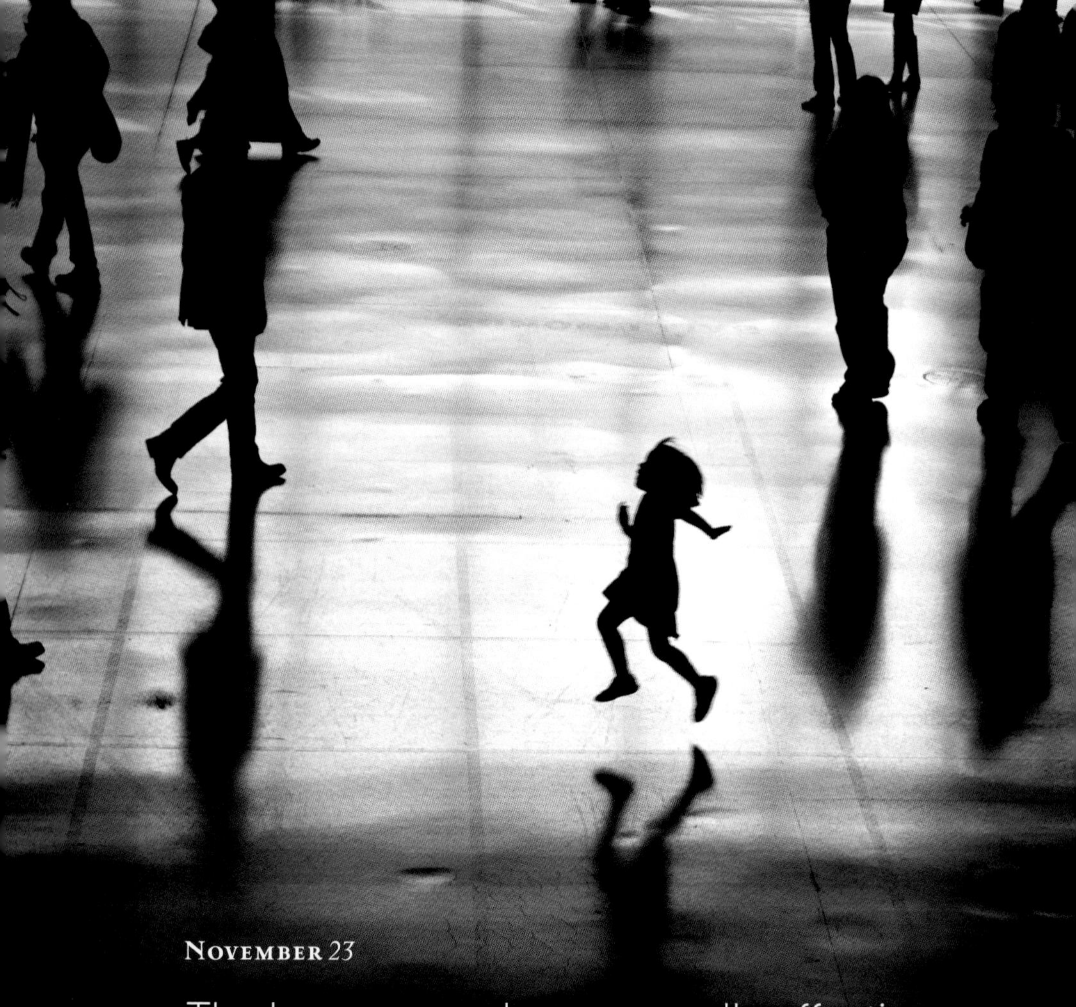

NOVEMBER 23

The human race has one really effective weapon, and that is laughter.

~ Mark Twain

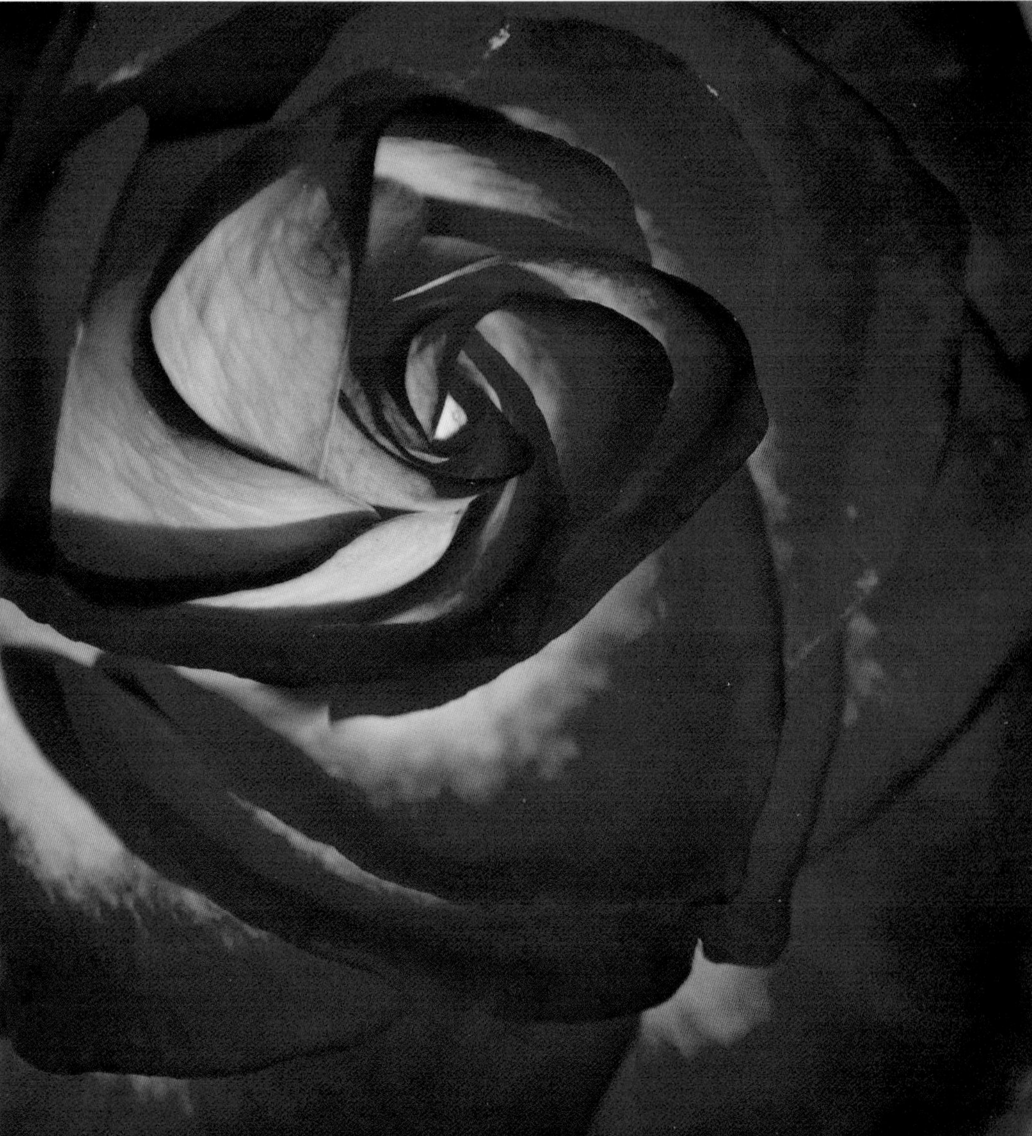

November 24

Instead of comparing our lot with that of those who are more fortunate than we are, we should compare it with the lot of the great majority of our fellow men. It then appears that we are among the privileged.

~ Helen Keller

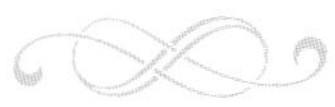

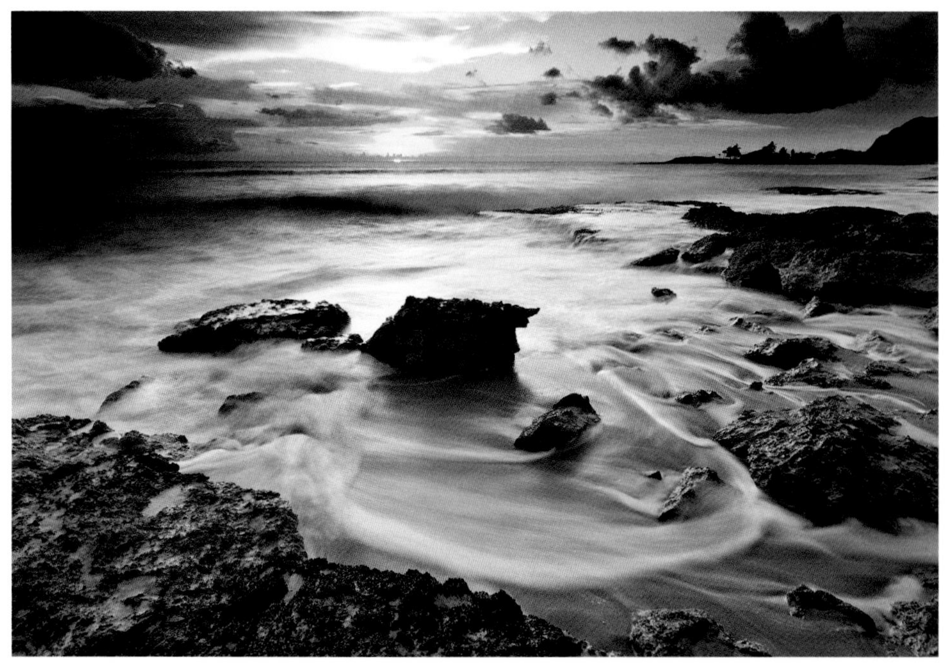

NOVEMBER 25

Forgiveness is a funny thing.
It warms the heart and
cools the sting.

~ William Arthur Ward

NOVEMBER 26

Your successes and happiness
are forgiven you
only if you generously consent
to share them.

~ Albert Camus

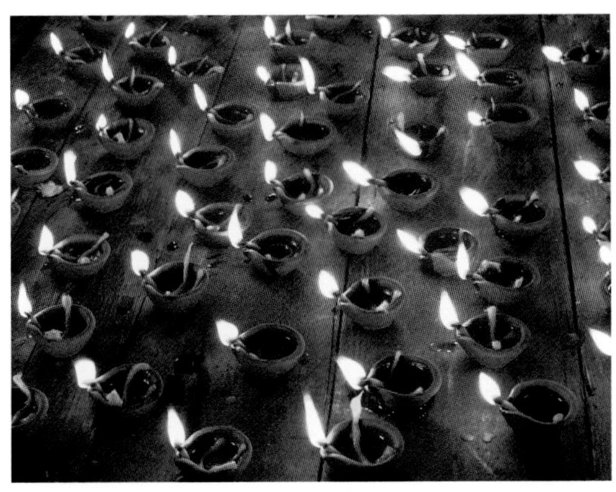

NOVEMBER 27

If you reveal
your secrets
to the wind,
you should not
blame the wind
for revealing them
to the trees.

~ Kahlil Gibran

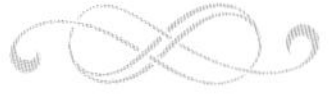

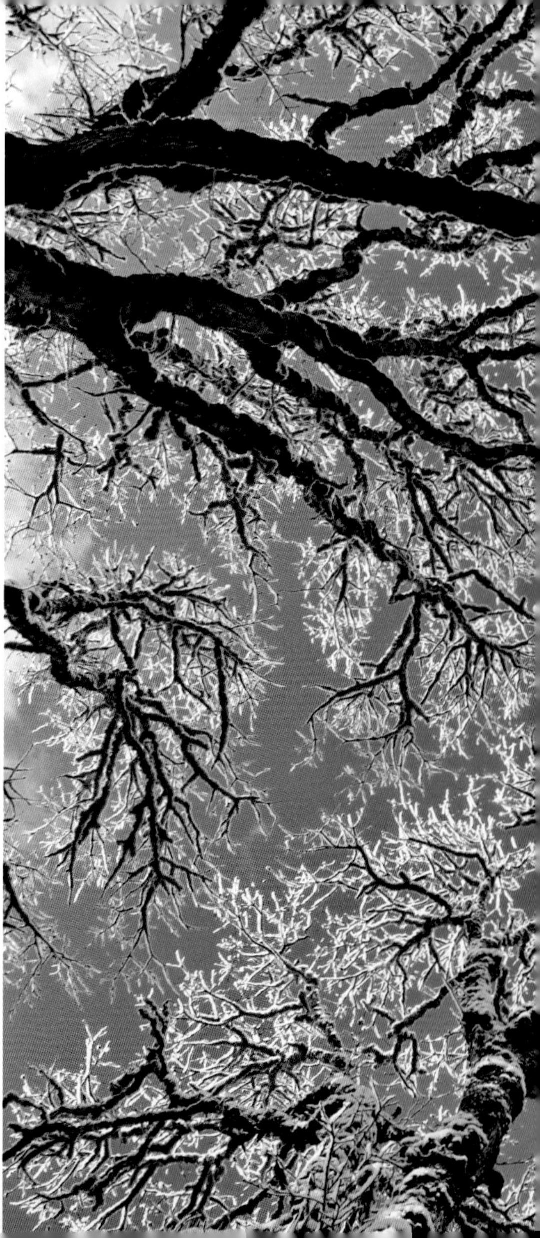

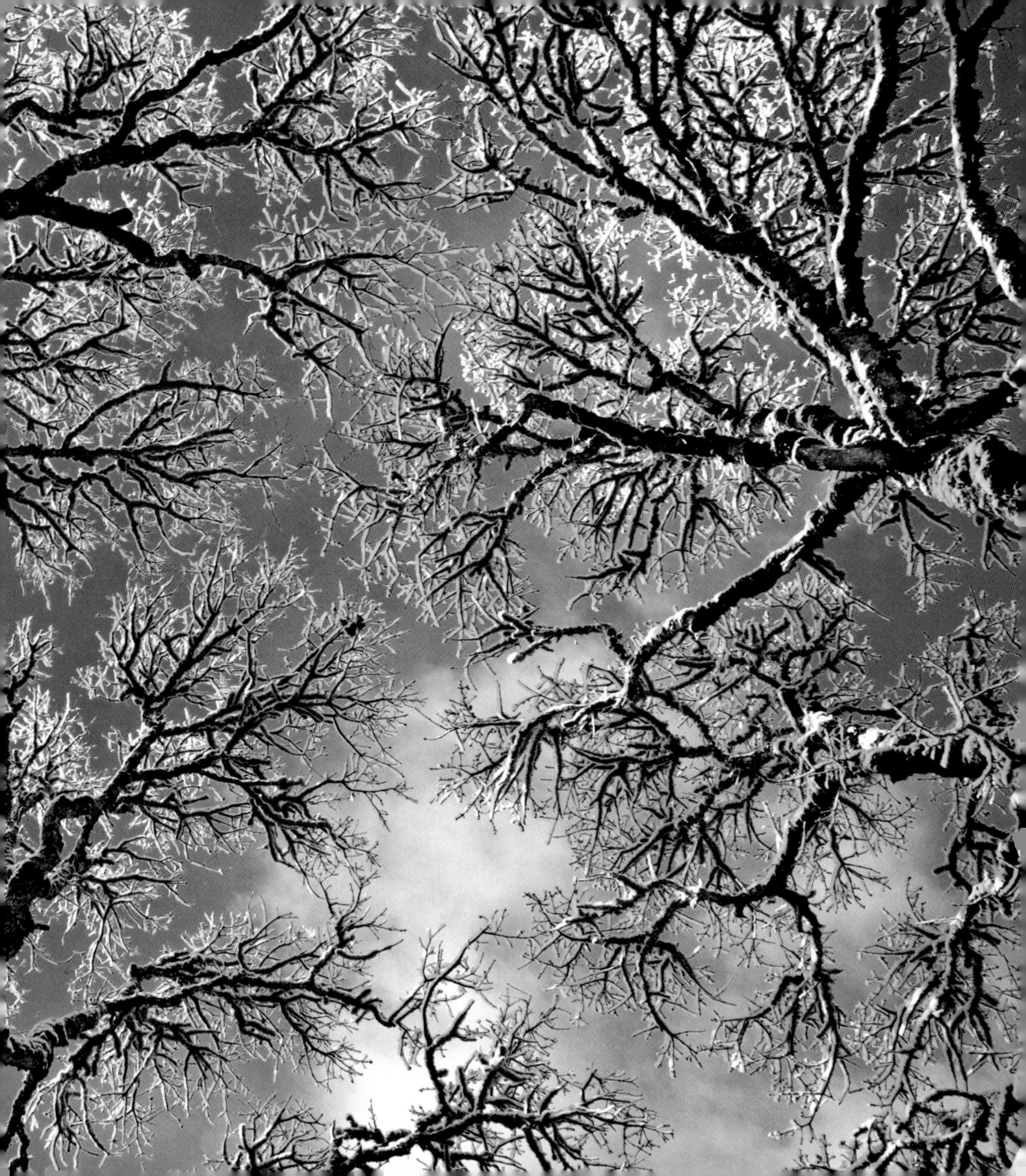

November 28

It is good to have an end to journey toward; but it is the journey that matters, in the end.

~ Ursula K. Le Guin

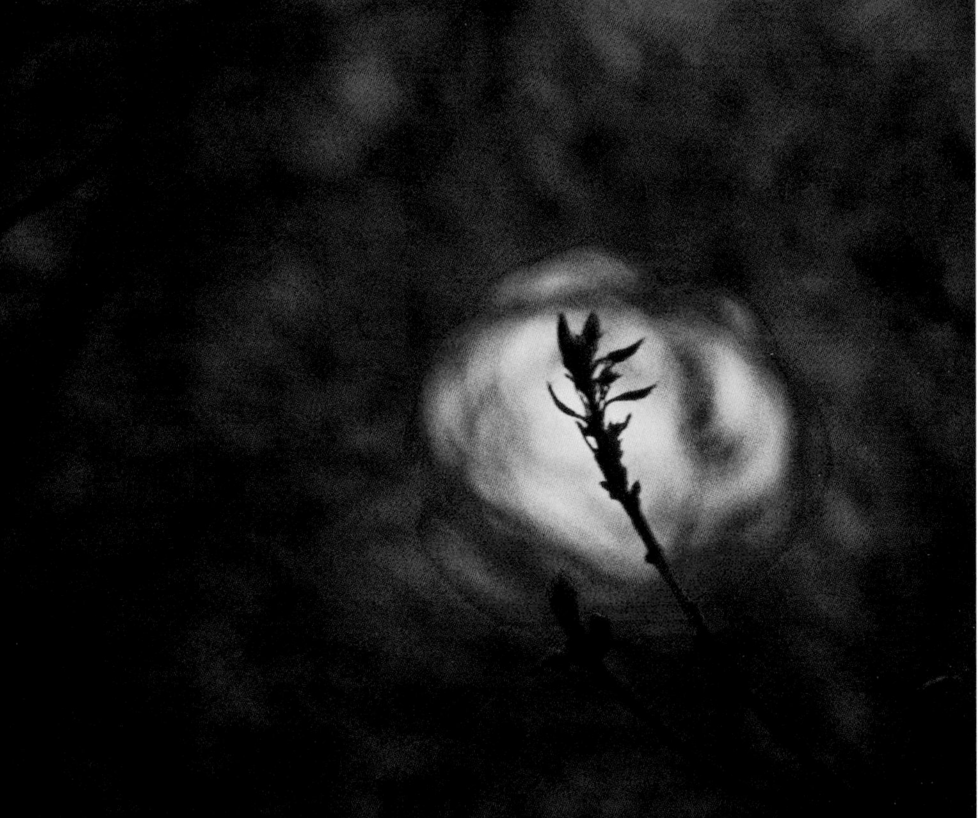

NOVEMBER *29*

Don't worry about losing. If it is right, it happens—the main thing is not to hurry. Nothing good gets away.

~ John Steinbeck

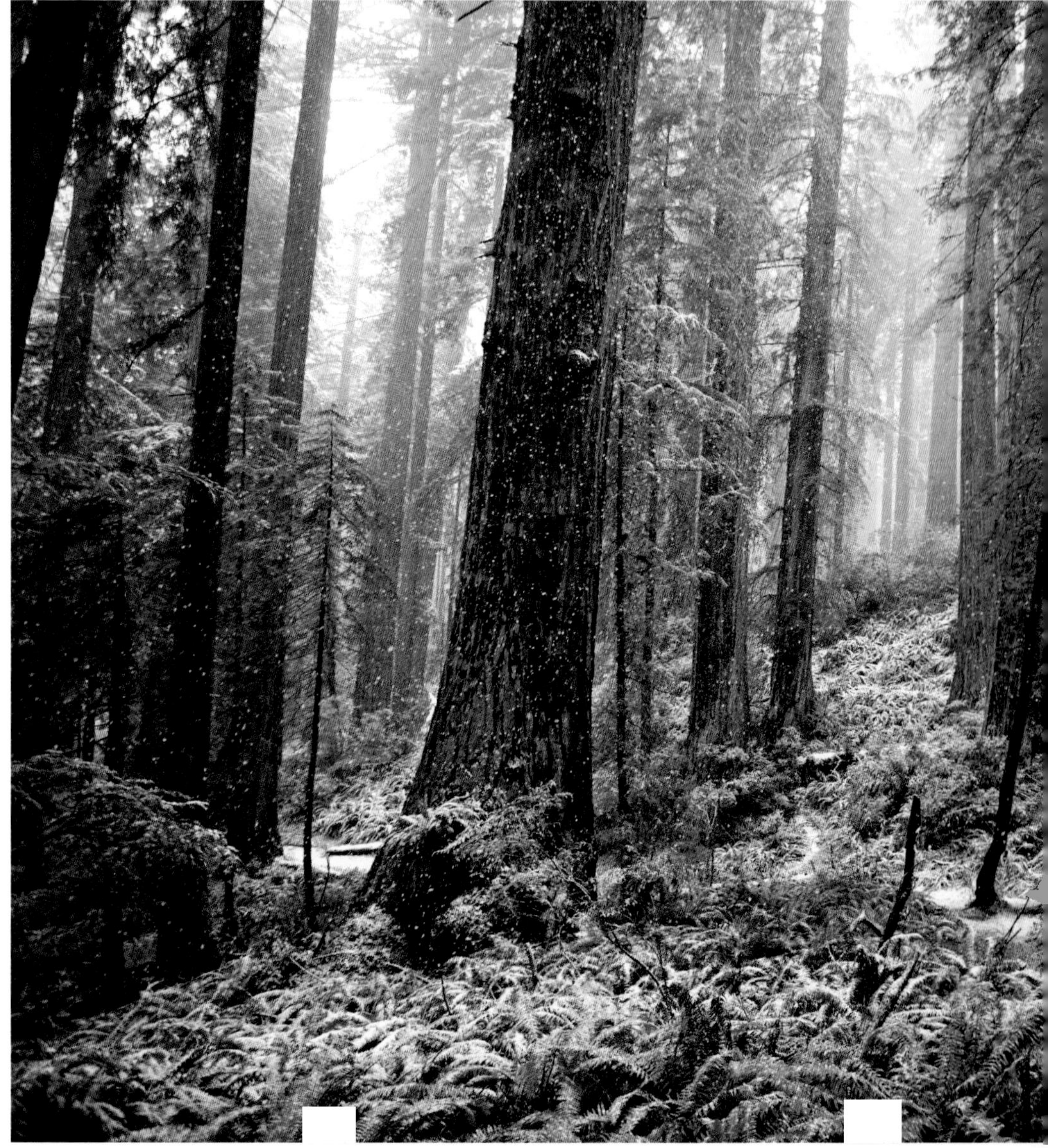

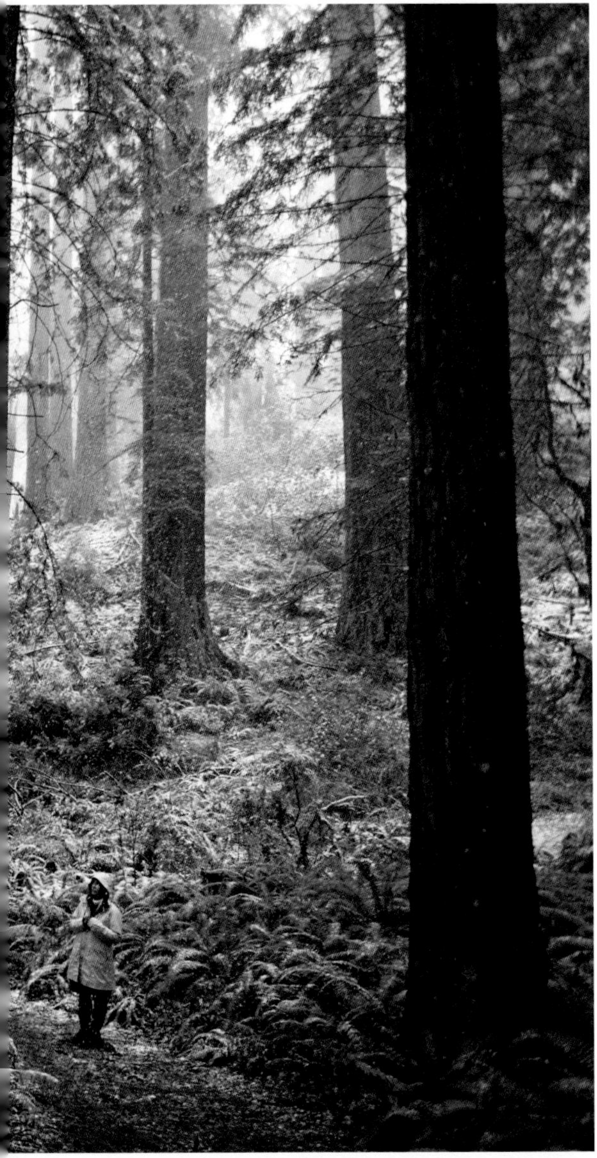

November 30

Look on every exit
as being
an entrance
somewhere else.

~ Tom Stoppard

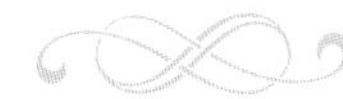

FAITH

December

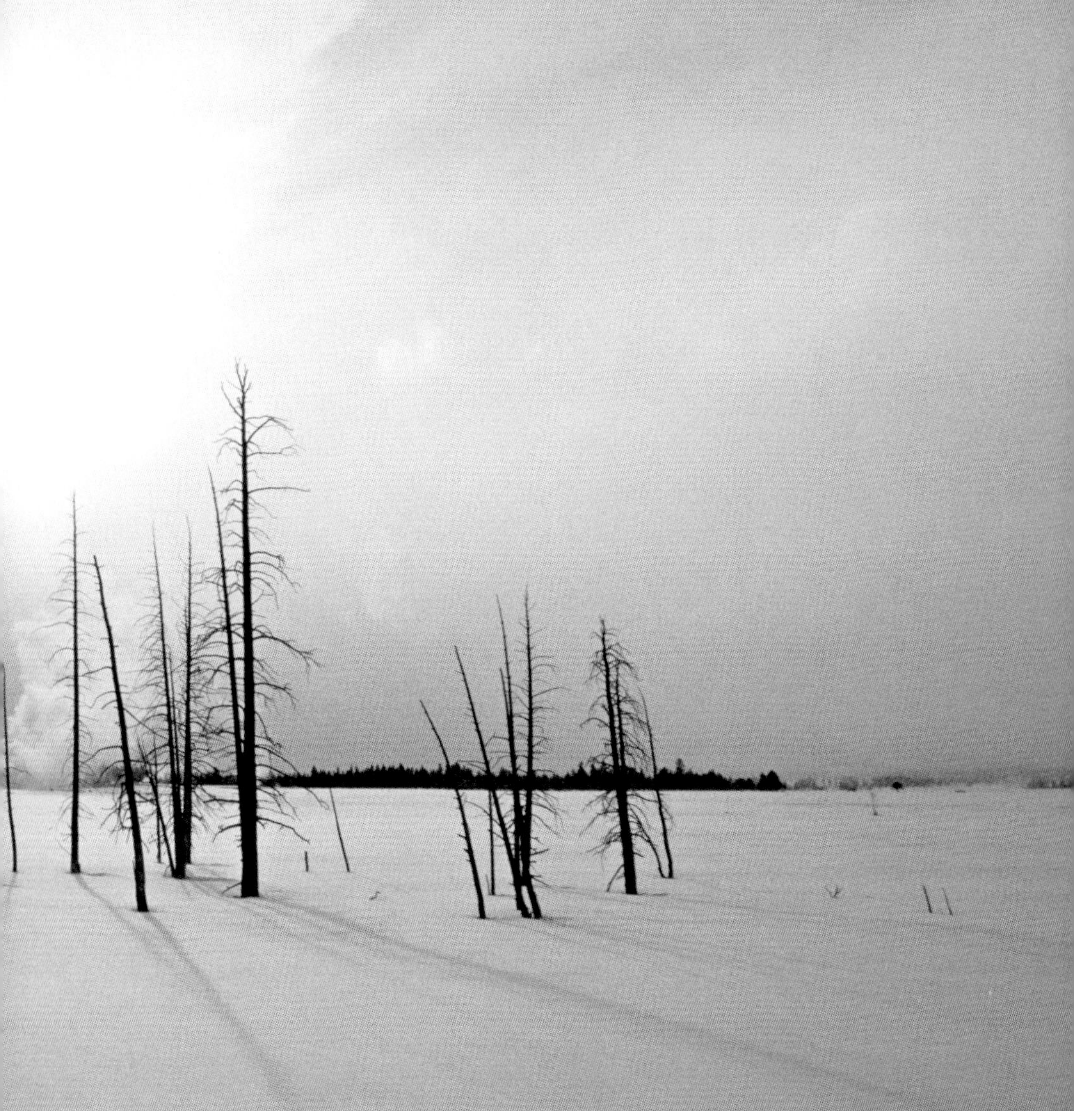

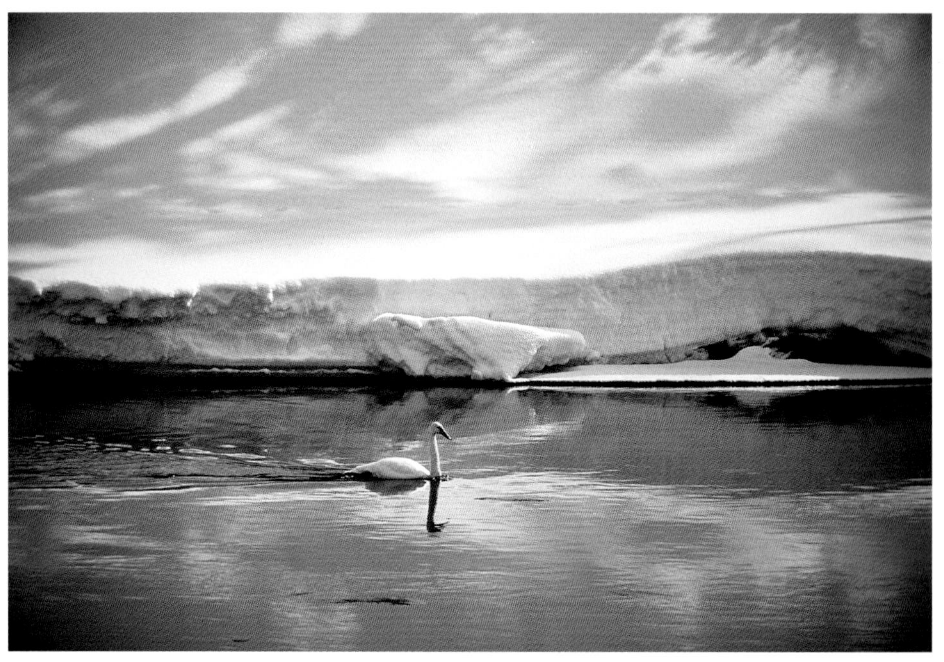

DECEMBER 1

There are two ways of spreading light;
to be the candle
or to be the mirror that reflects it.

~ Edith Wharton

December 2

I don't think of all the misery, but of the beauty that still remains.

~ Anne Frank

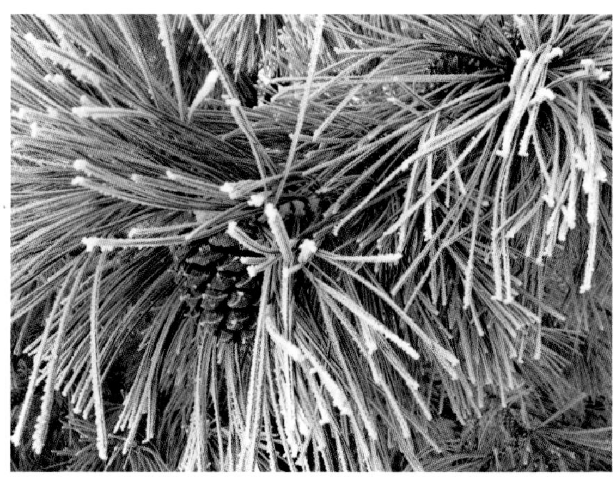

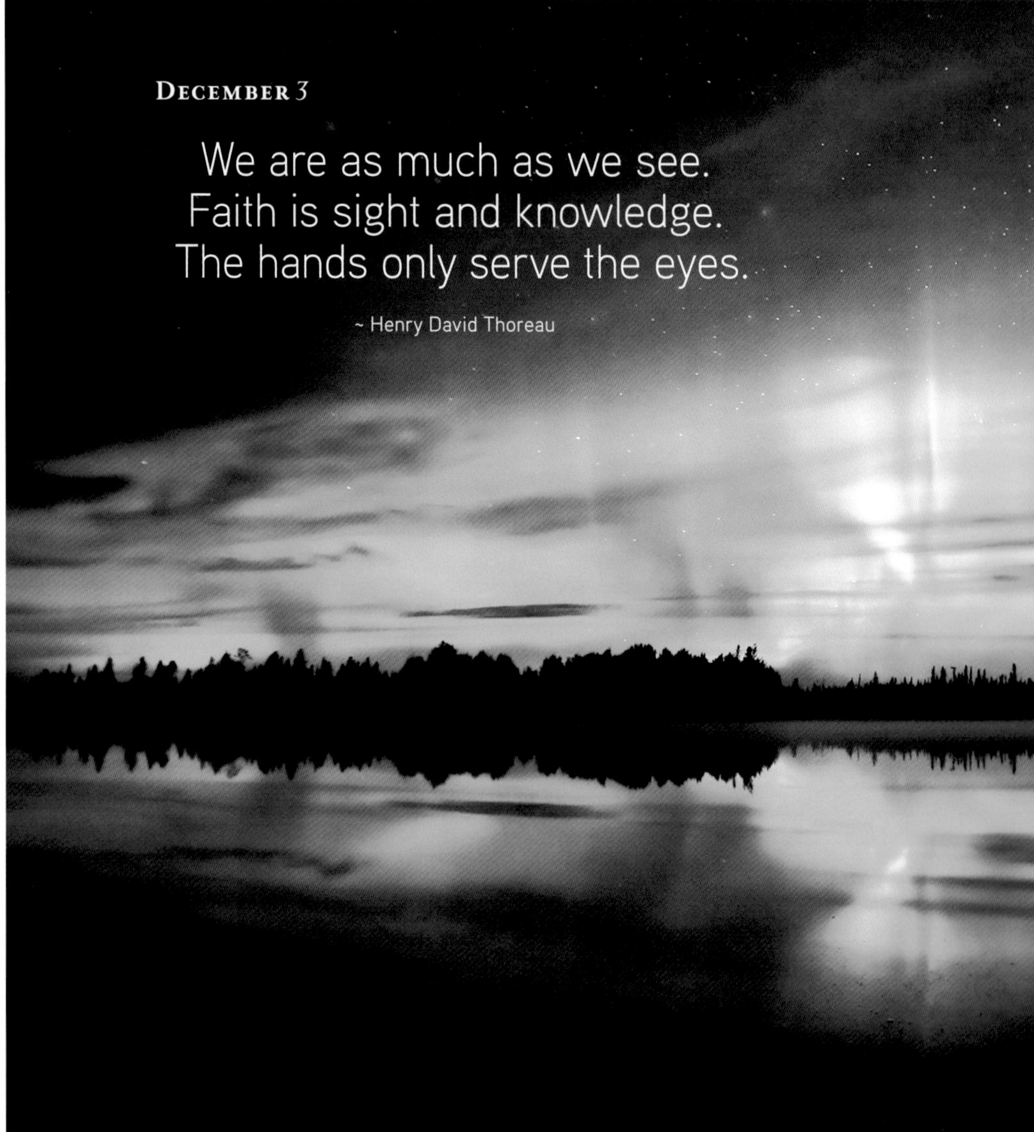

DECEMBER 3

We are as much as we see.
Faith is sight and knowledge.
The hands only serve the eyes.

~ Henry David Thoreau

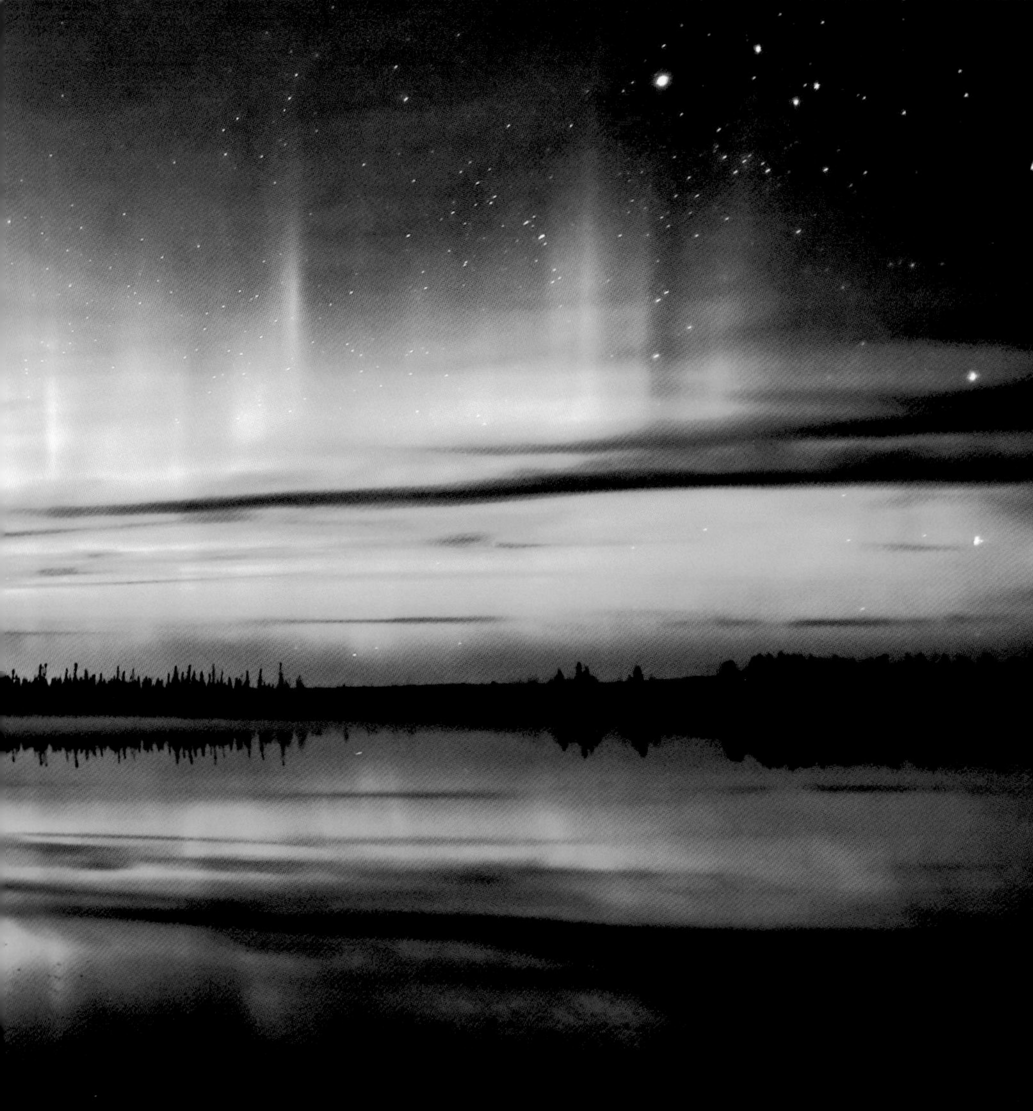

DECEMBER 4

There is not one big cosmic meaning for all.
There is only the meaning we each give to our life.

~ Anaïs Nin

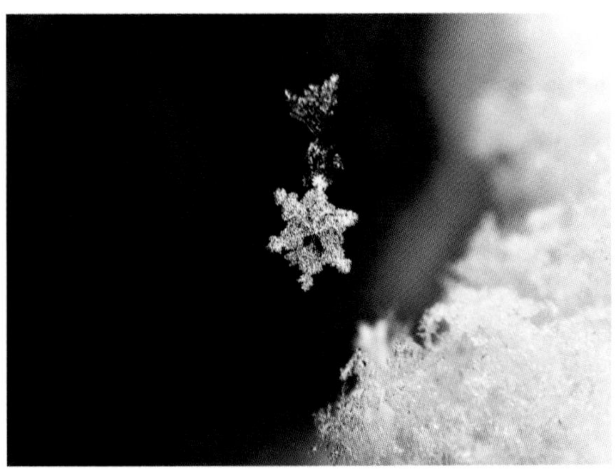

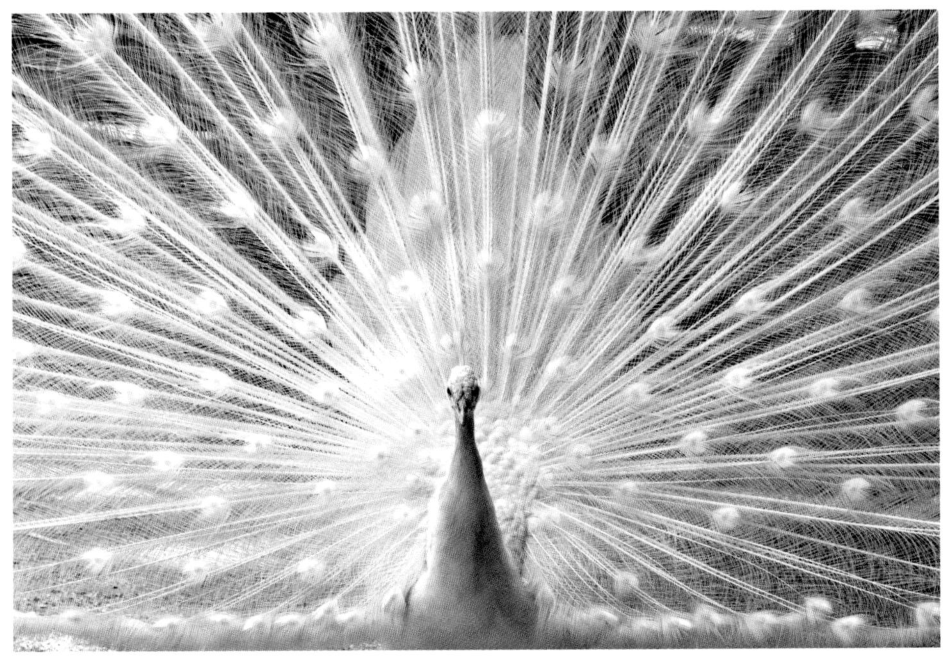

DECEMBER 5

You have been criticizing yourself for years and it hasn't worked. Try approving of yourself and see what happens.

~ Louise L. Hay

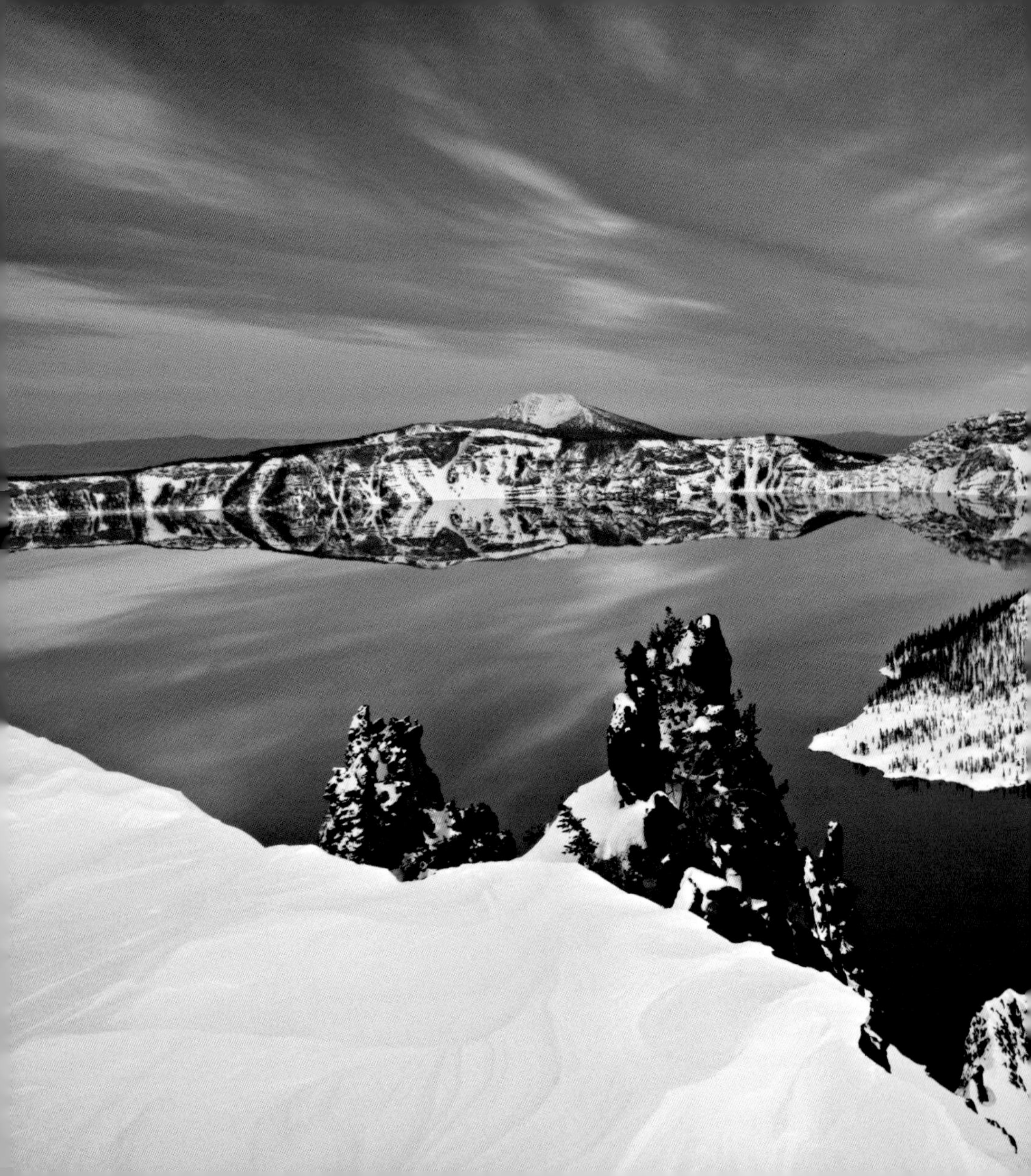

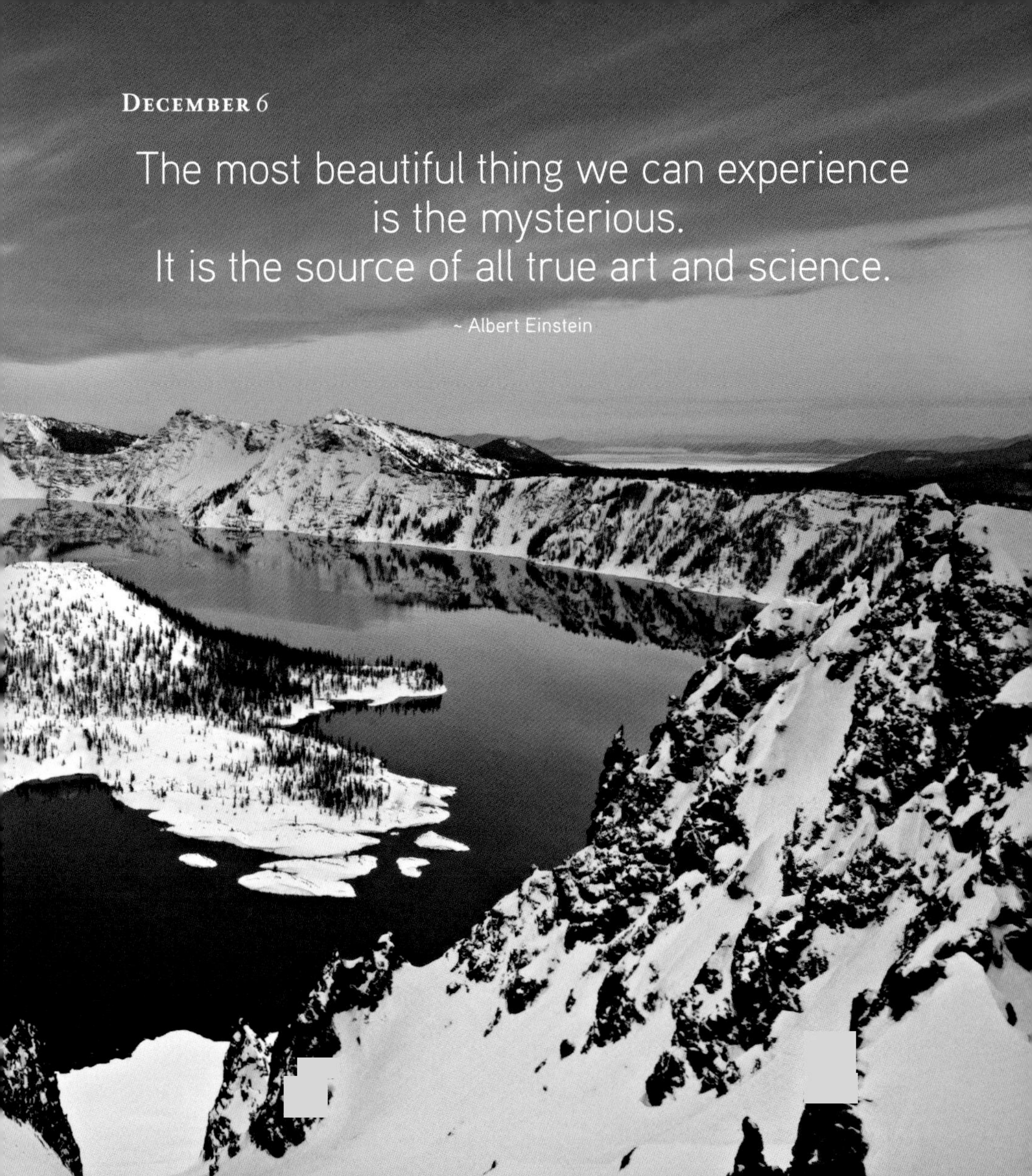
DECEMBER 6
The most beautiful thing we can experience
is the mysterious.
It is the source of all true art and science.
~ Albert Einstein

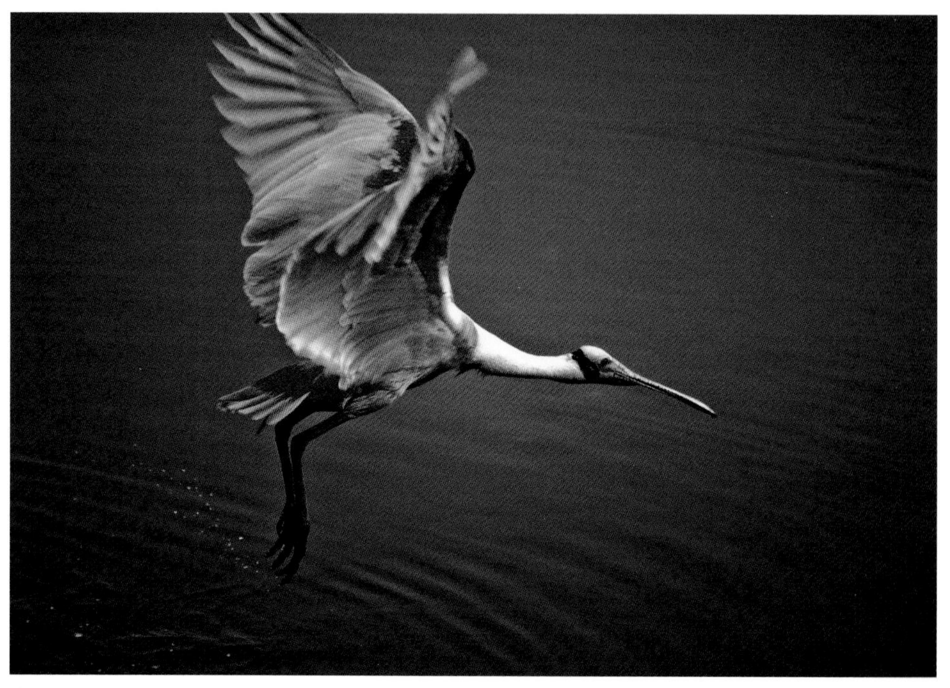

DECEMBER 7

Faith is the bird that feels the light
and sings when the dawn
is still and dark.

~ Rabindranath Tagore

December 8

When you focus on
the goodness in your life,
you create more of it.

~ Oprah Winfrey

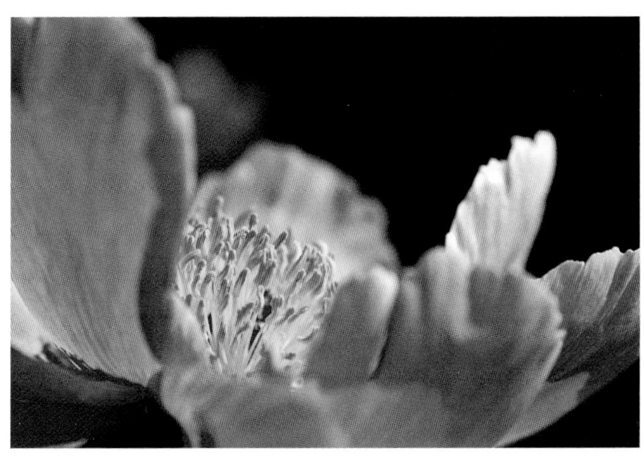

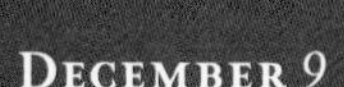

DECEMBER *9*

If you desire faith
then you have faith enough.

~ Robert Browning

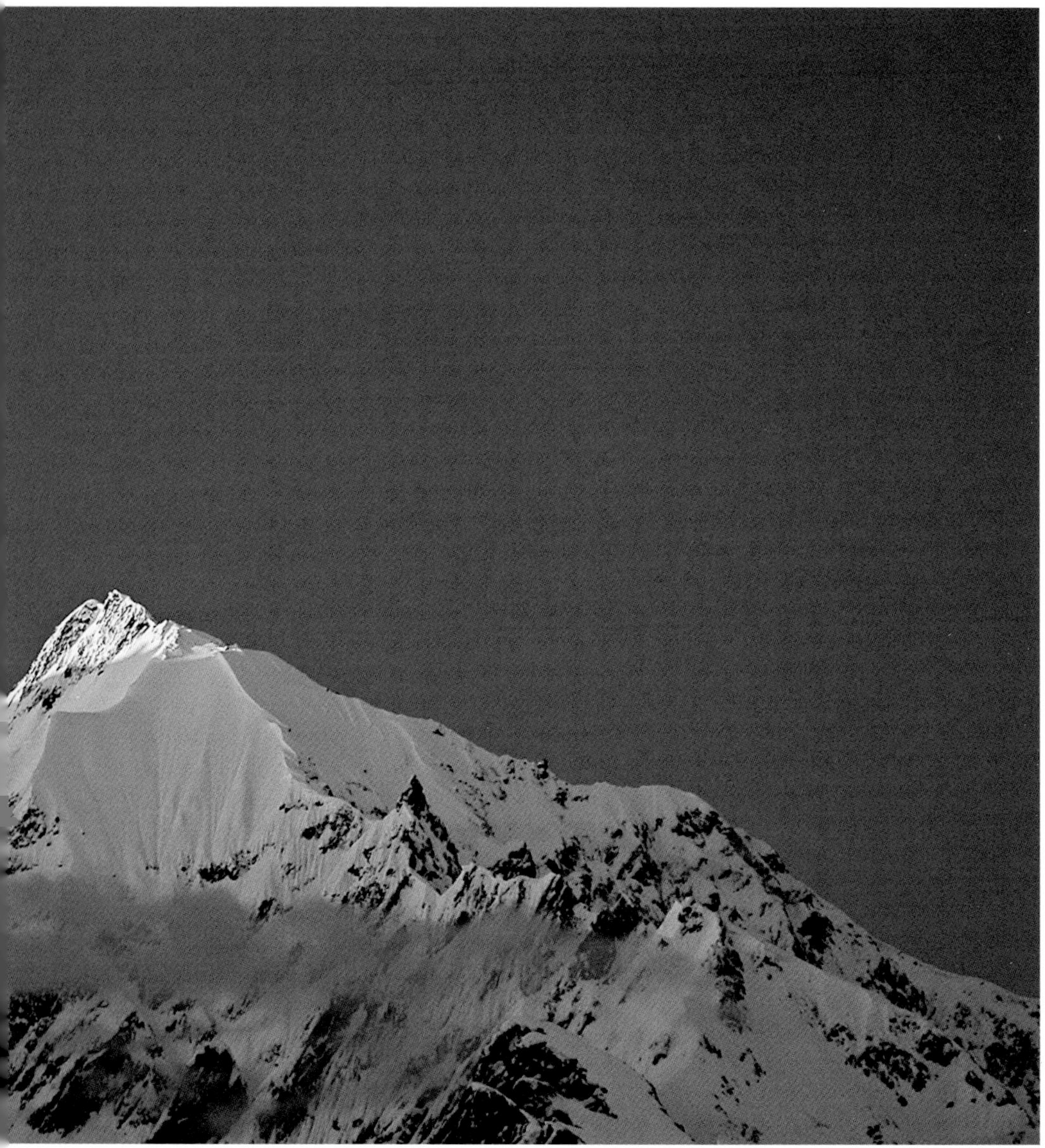

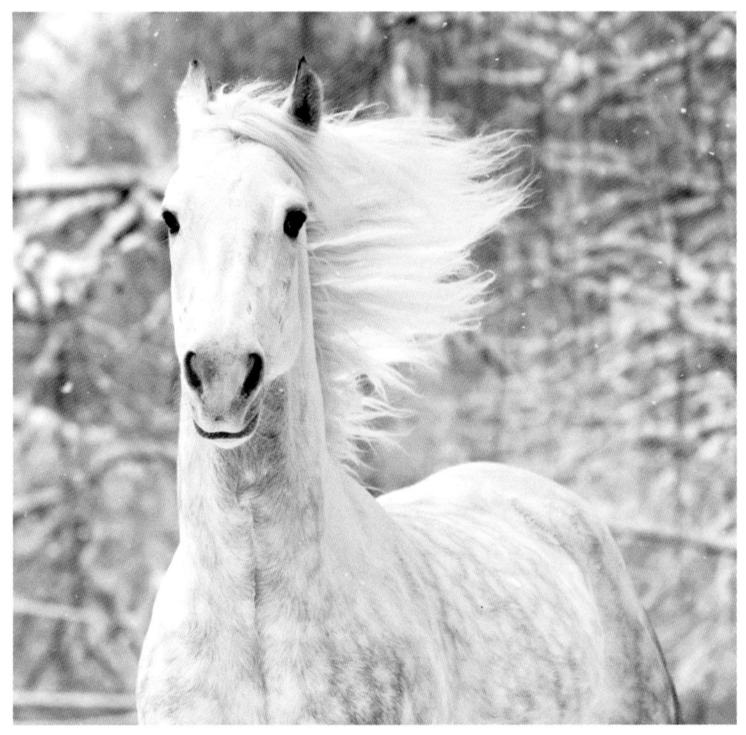

December 10

The best and most beautiful things in the world cannot be seen or even touched—they must be felt with the heart.

~ Helen Keller

December 11

Believe that life is worth living, and your belief will help create the fact.

~ William James

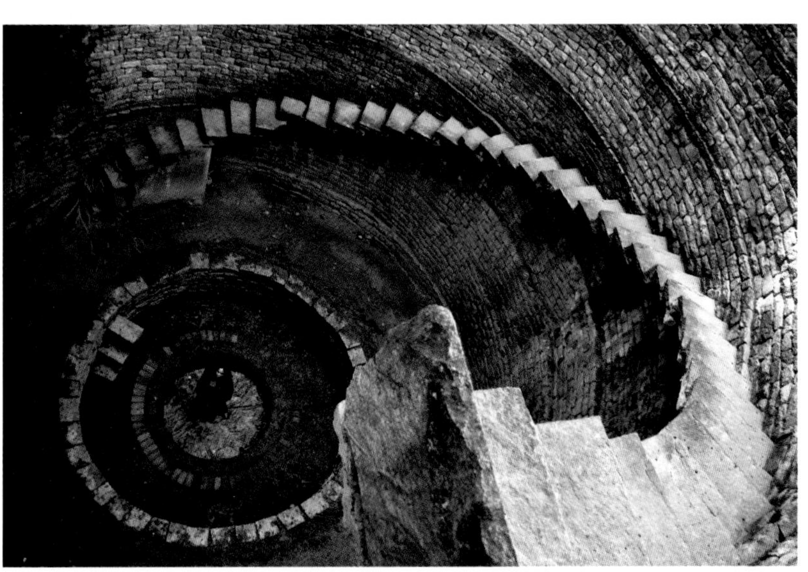

DECEMBER 12

That's the way
things become clear.
All of a sudden.
And then you realize
how obvious
they've been
all along.

~ Madeleine L'Engle

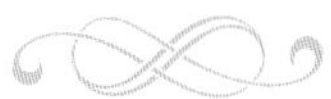

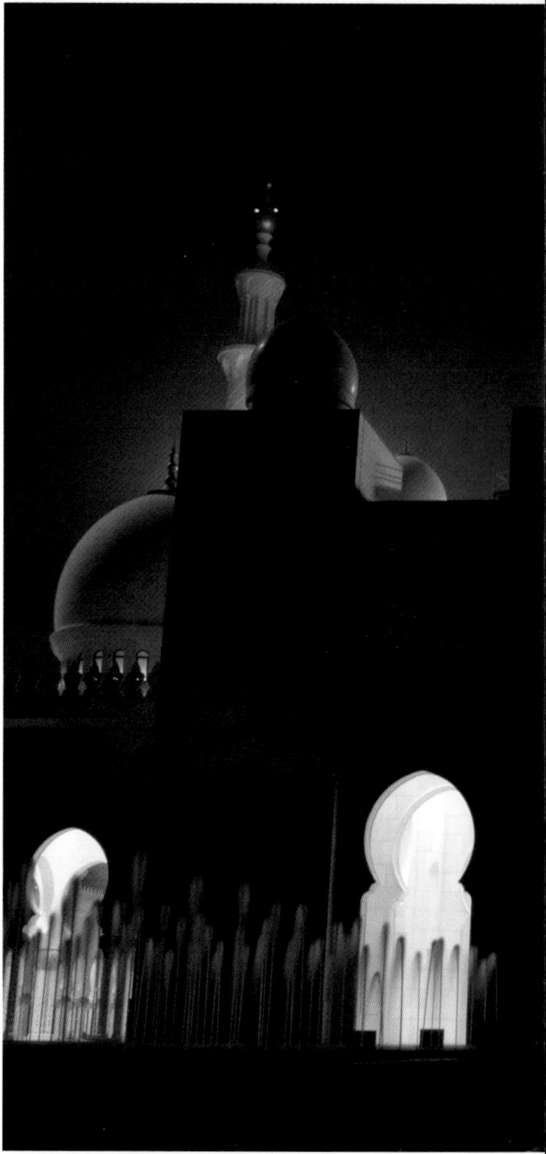

DECEMBER 13

More things are wrought by prayer than this world dreams of.

~ Alfred, Lord Tennyson

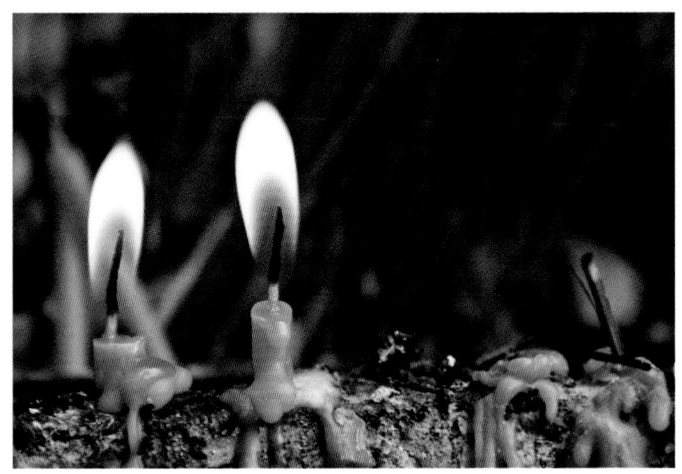

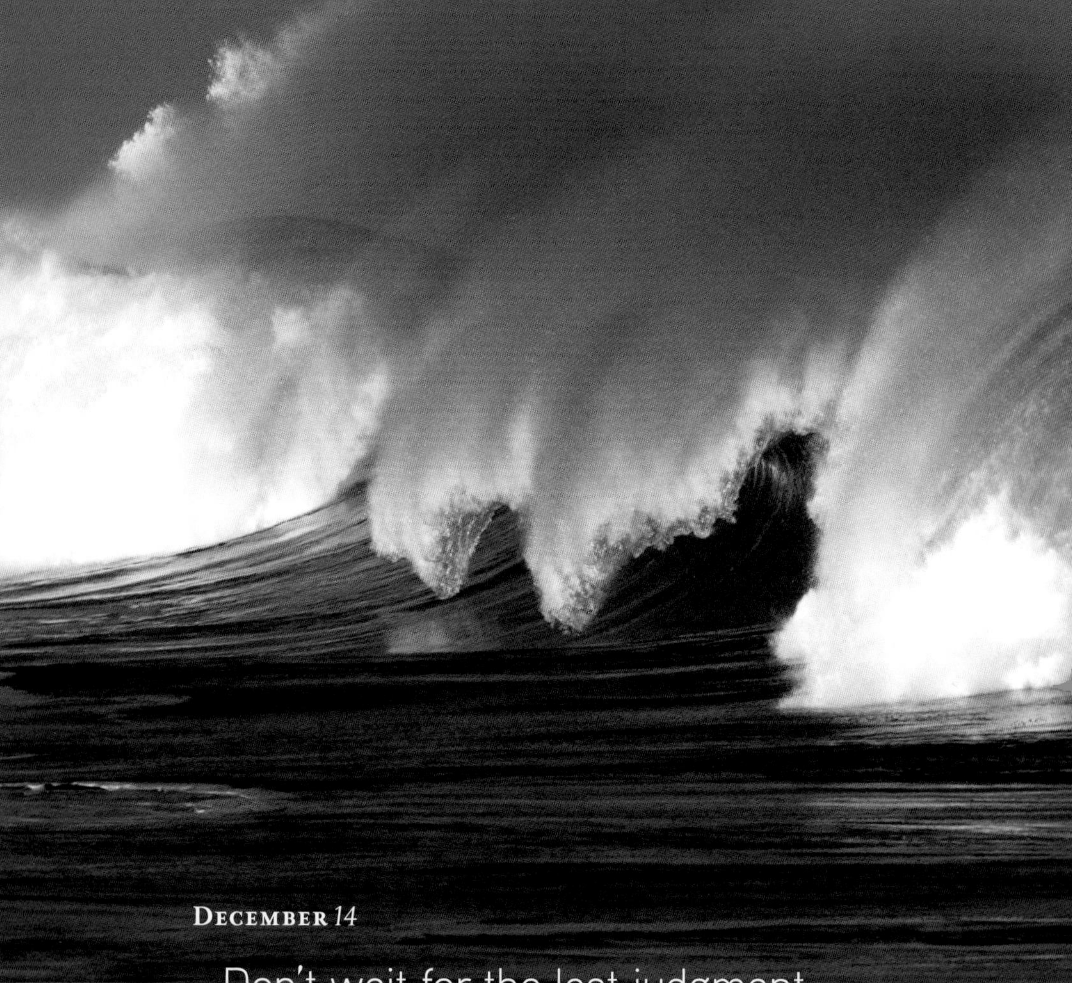

December *14*

Don't wait for the last judgment—
it takes place every day.

~ Albert Camus

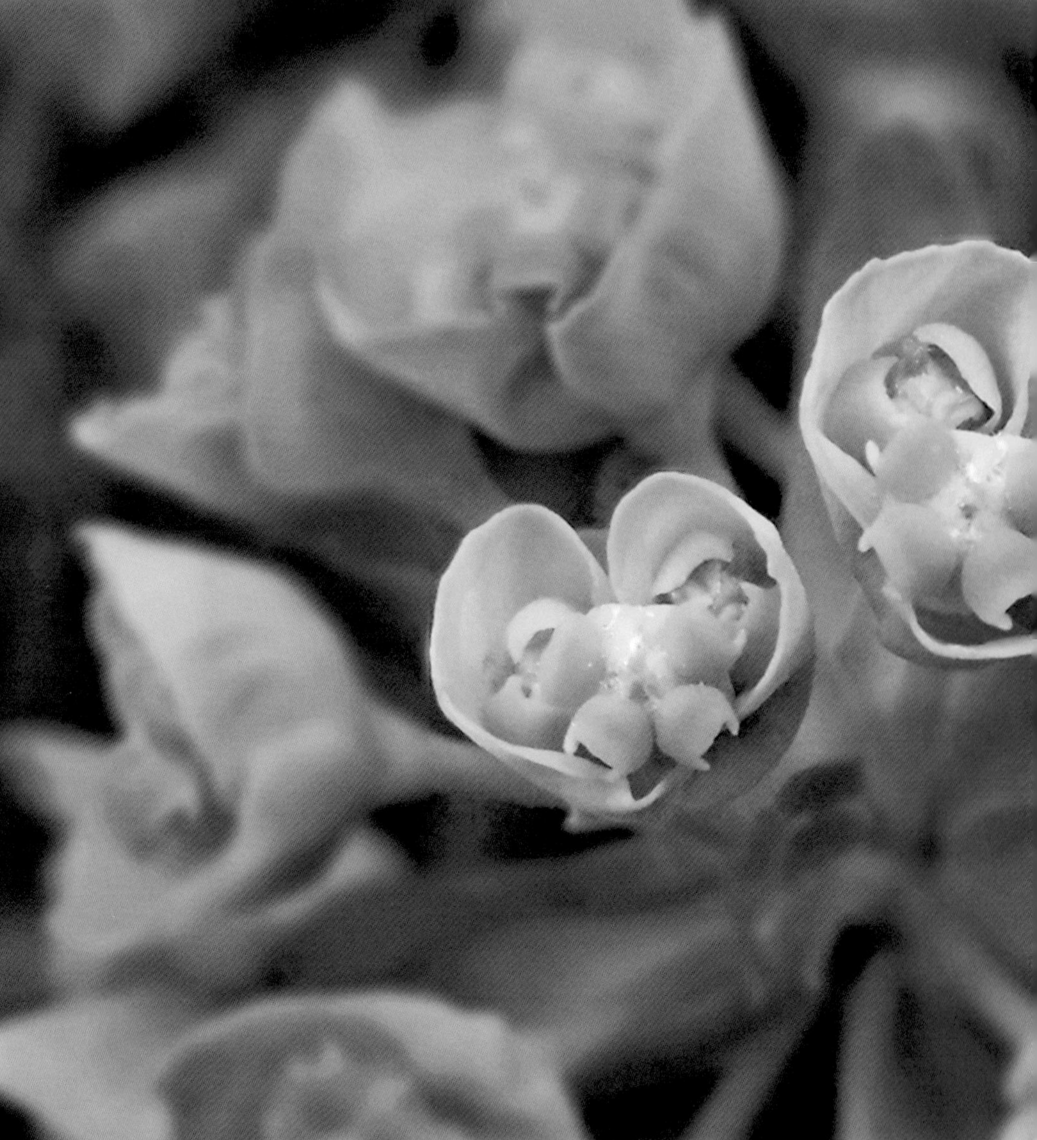

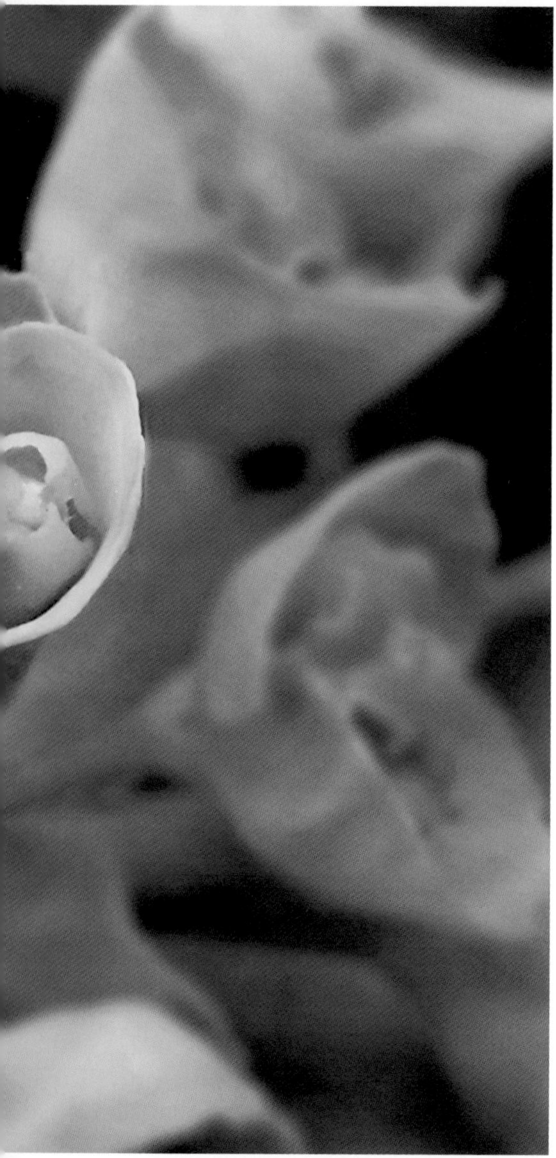

December 15

Love is
an act of faith,
and whoever is
of little faith
is also
of little love.

~ Erich Fromm

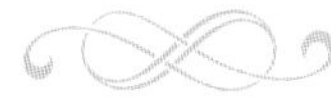

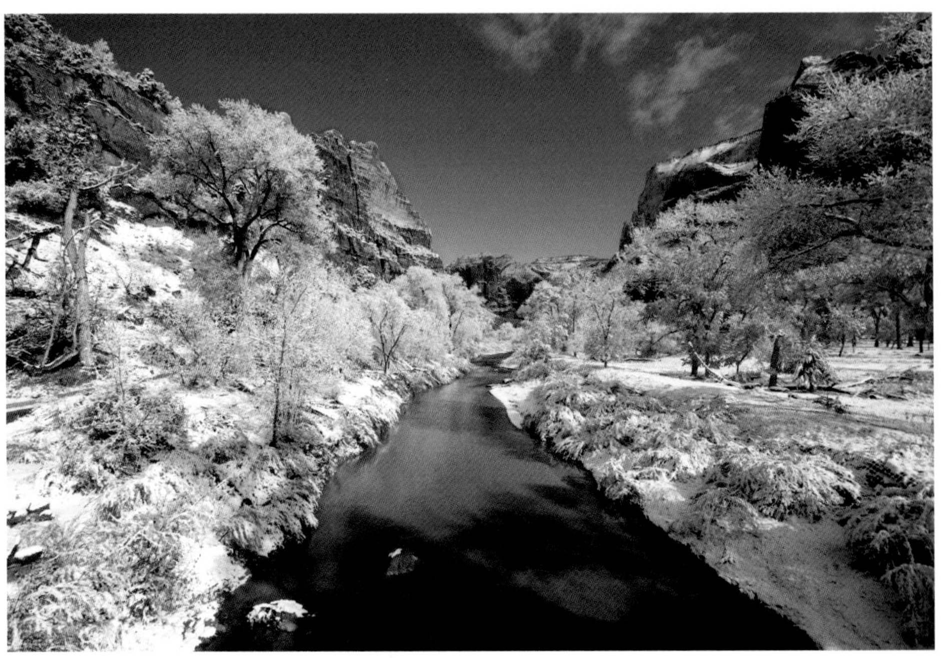

DECEMBER 16

You must learn to be still
in the midst of activity
and to be vibrantly alive in repose.

~ Indira Gandhi

December *17*

You must not abandon the ship in a storm because you cannot control the winds . . . What you cannot turn to good, you must at least make as little bad as you can.

~ Thomas More

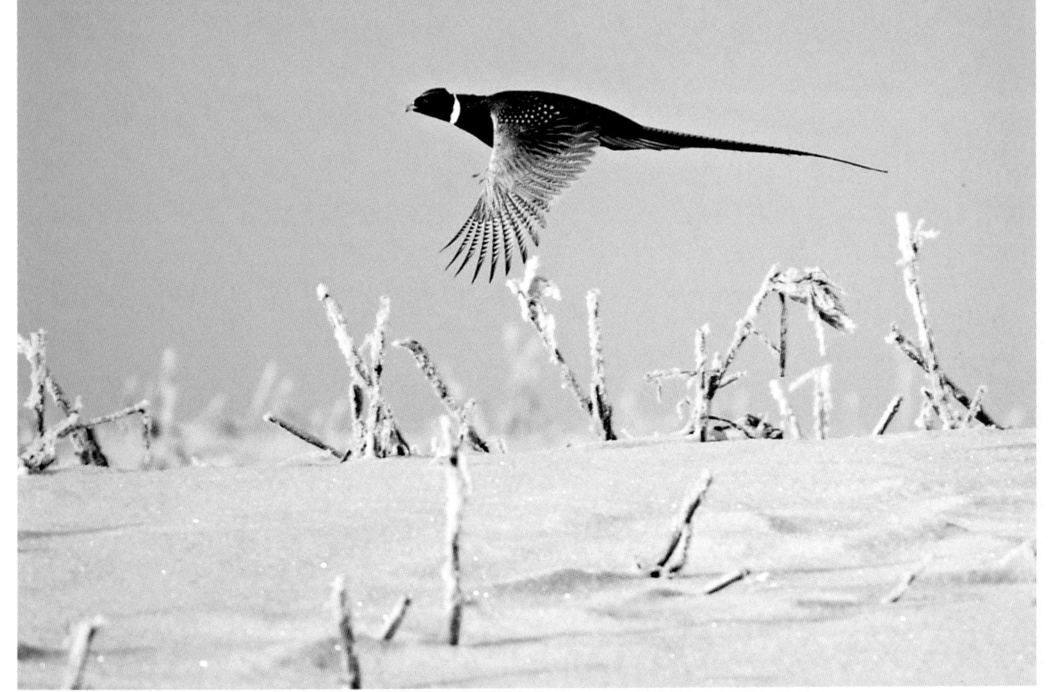

DECEMBER 18

Gratitude
is the fairest
blossom
from which
springs
the soul.

~ Henry Ward Beecher

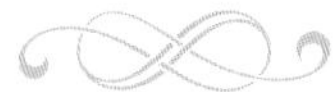

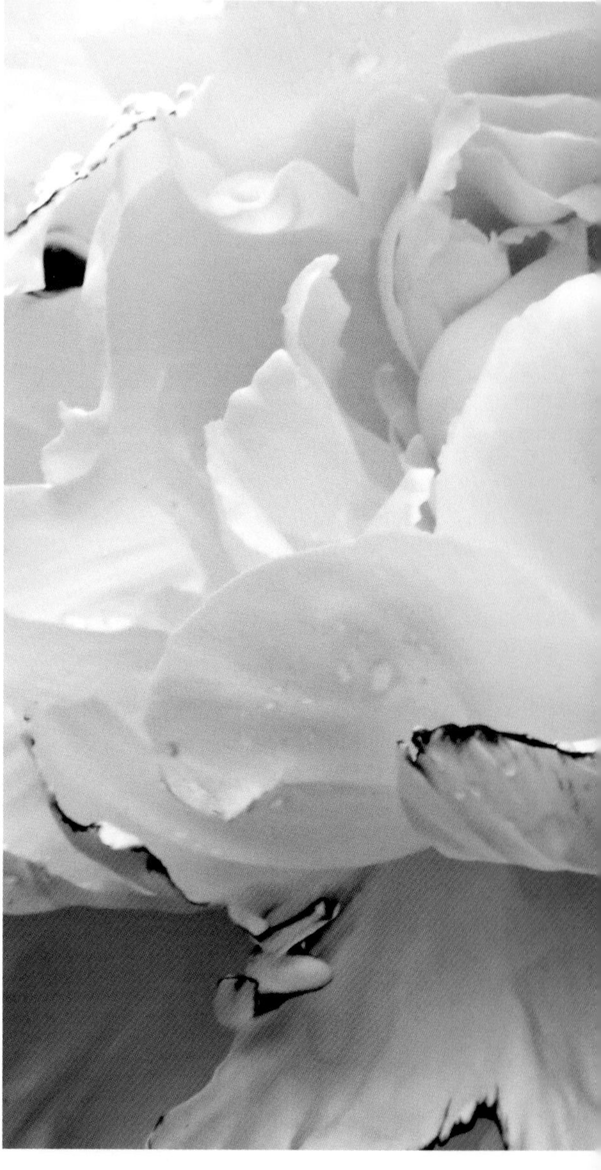

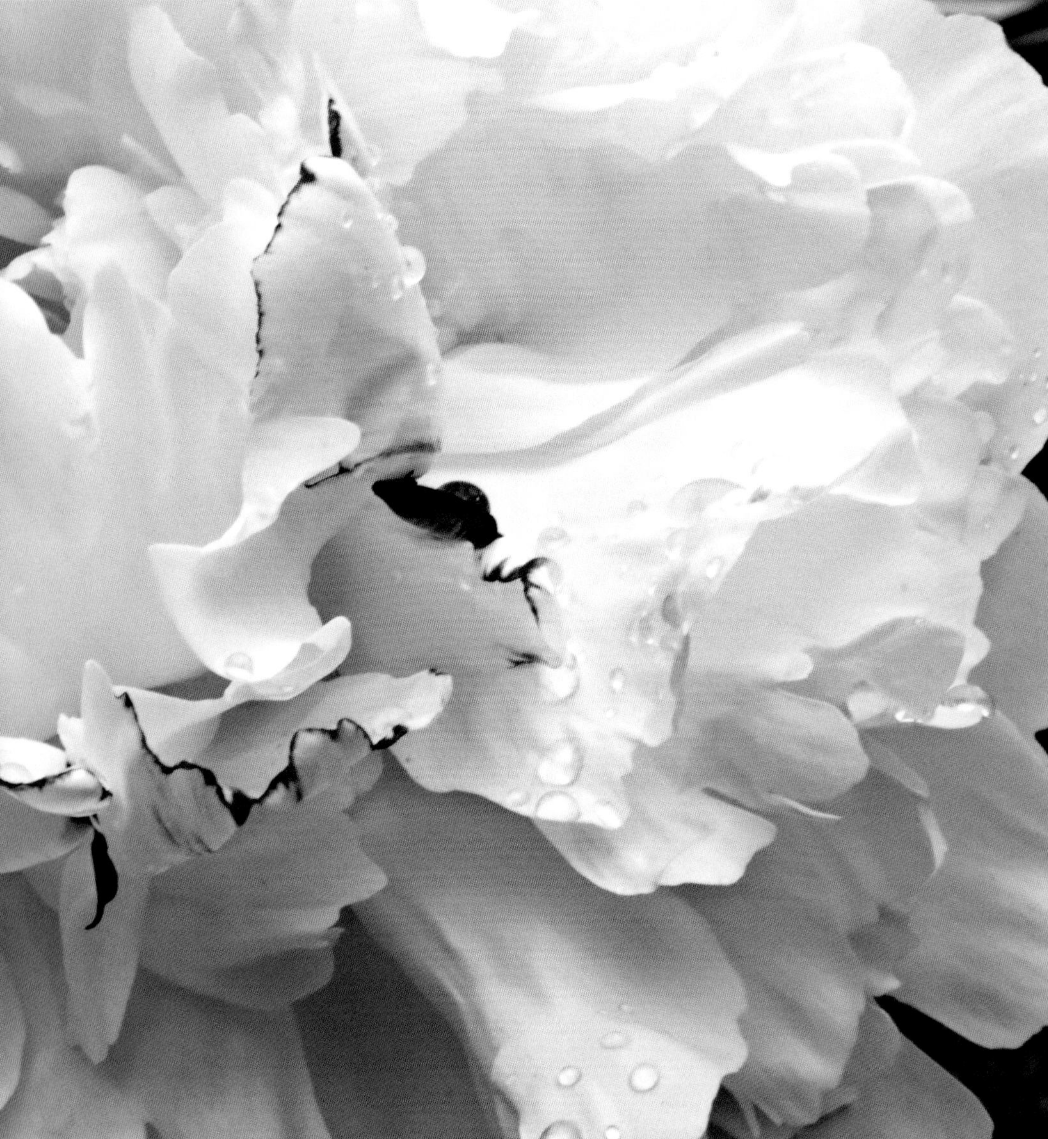

When we do
the best that we can,
we never know what miracle
is wrought in our life,
or in the life of another.

~ Helen Keller

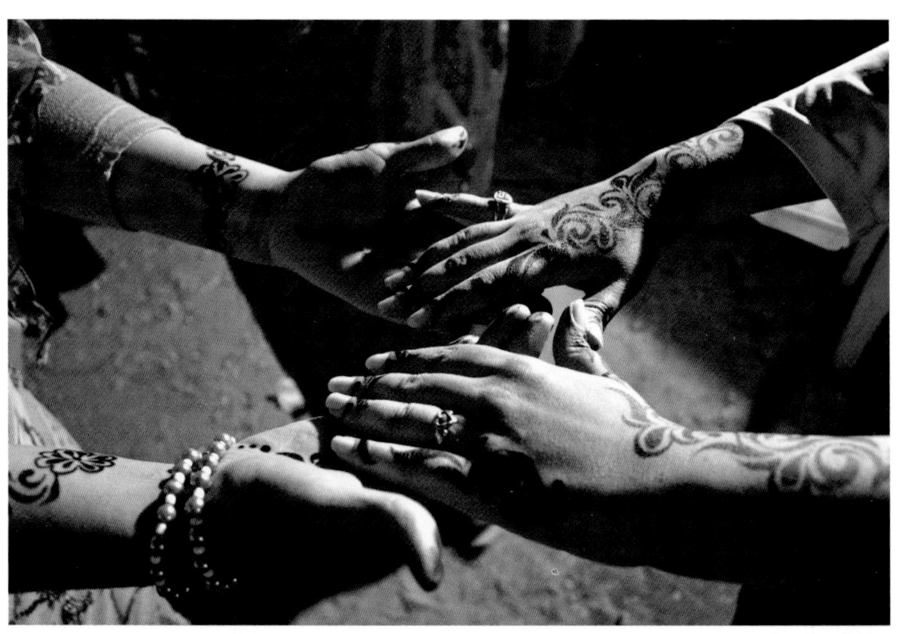

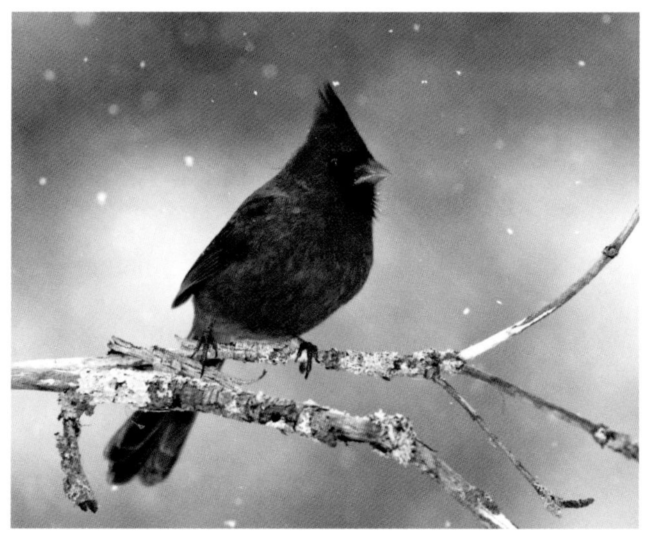

DECEMBER *20*

Be faithful in small things—
because it is in them
that your strength lies.

~ Mother Teresa

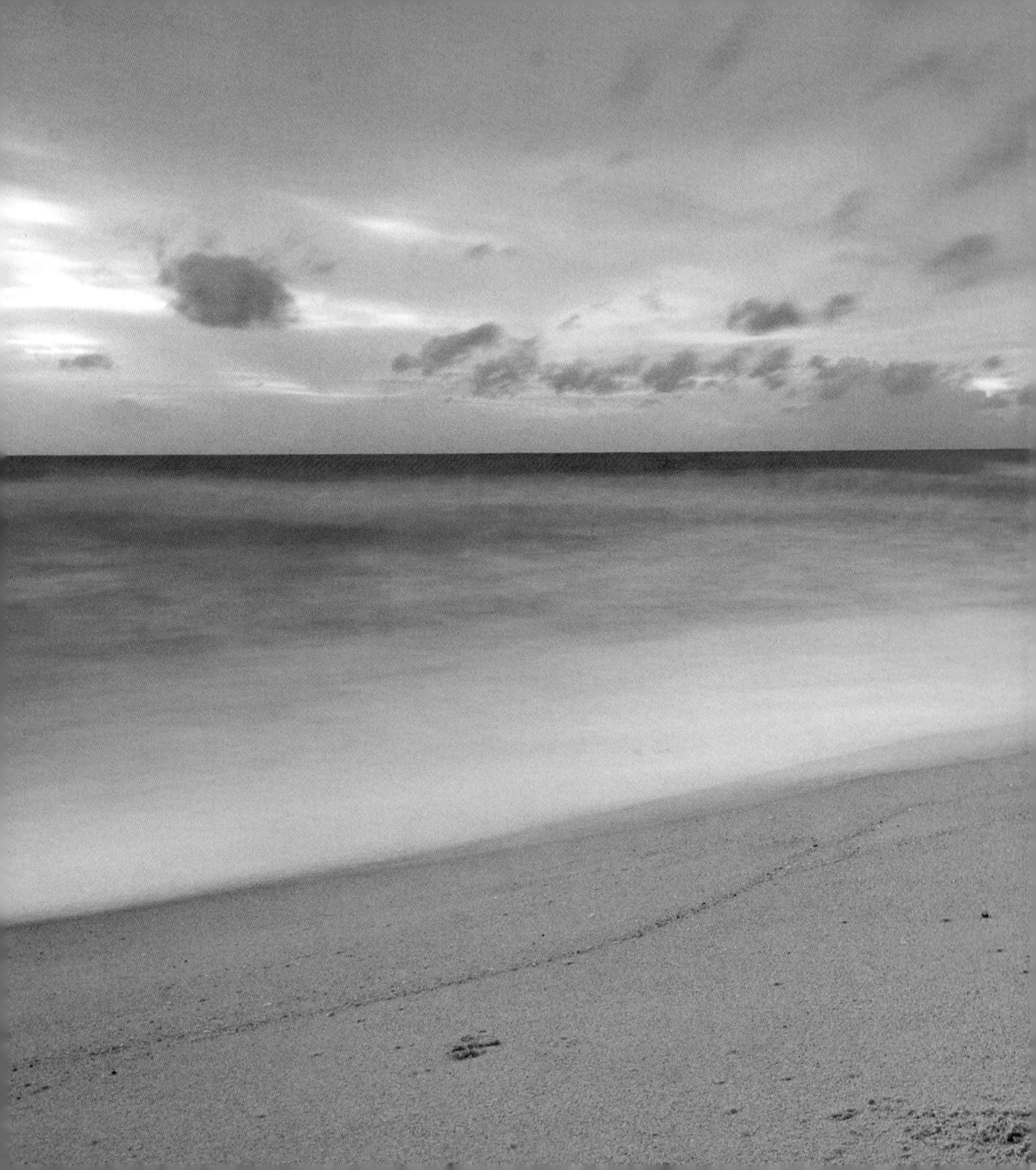

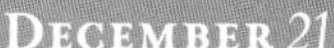

DECEMBER 21

The only faith that wears well and holds its color in all weathers is that which is woven of conviction and set with the sharp mordant of experience.

~ James Russell Lowell

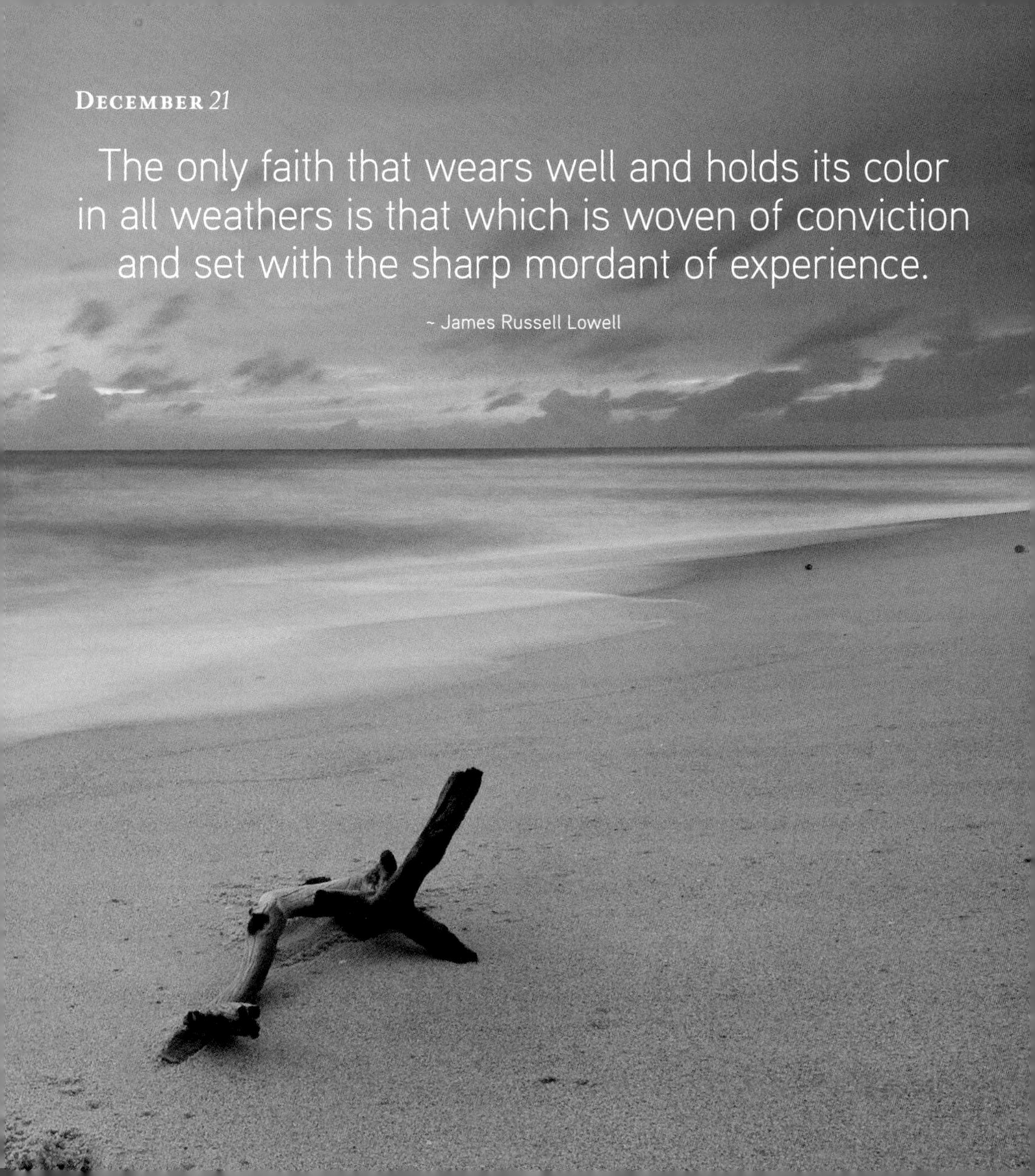

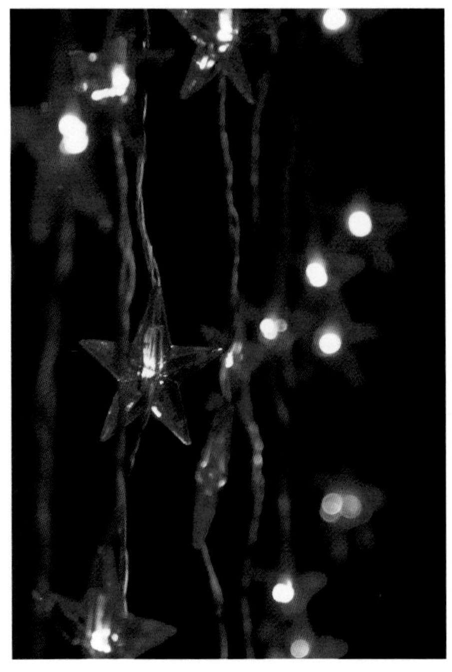

DECEMBER *22*

It is better to light a candle than curse the darkness.

~ Adlai Stevenson

DECEMBER 23

Anything that is of value in life
only multiplies when it is given.

~ Deepak Chopra

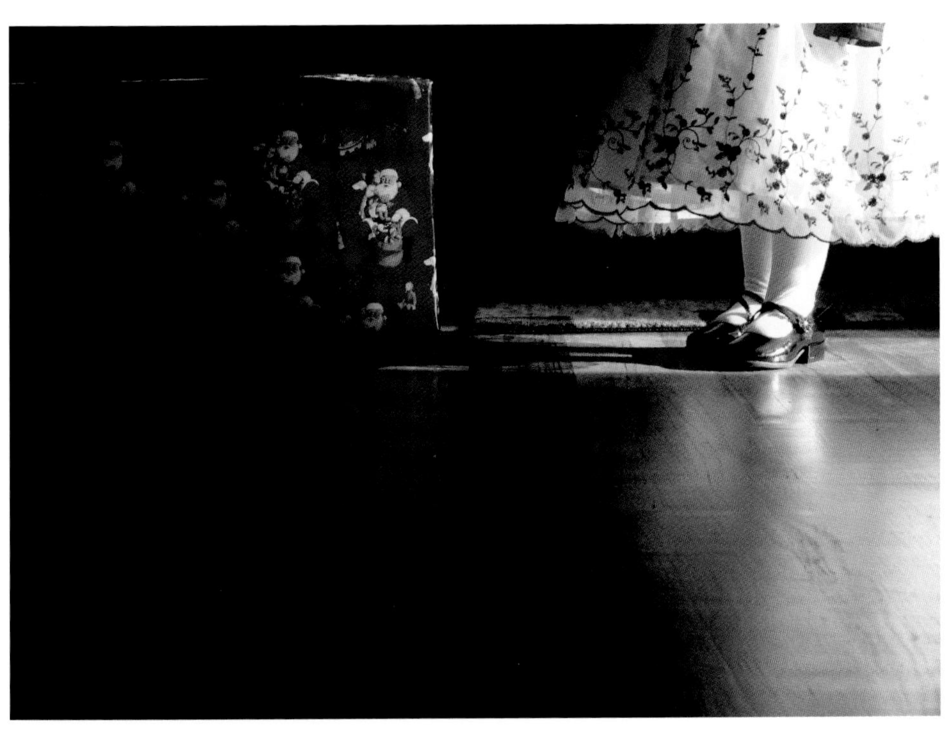

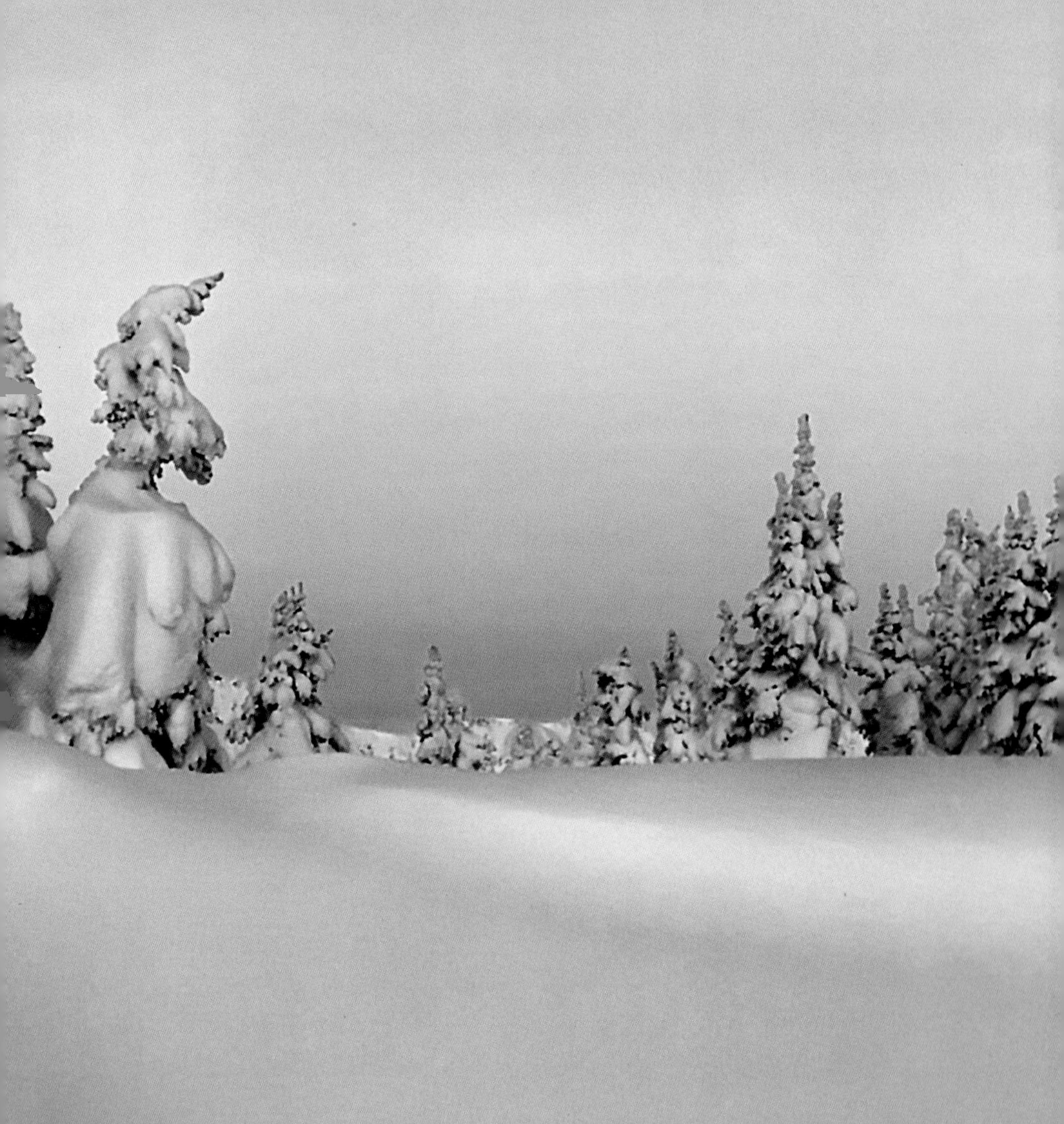

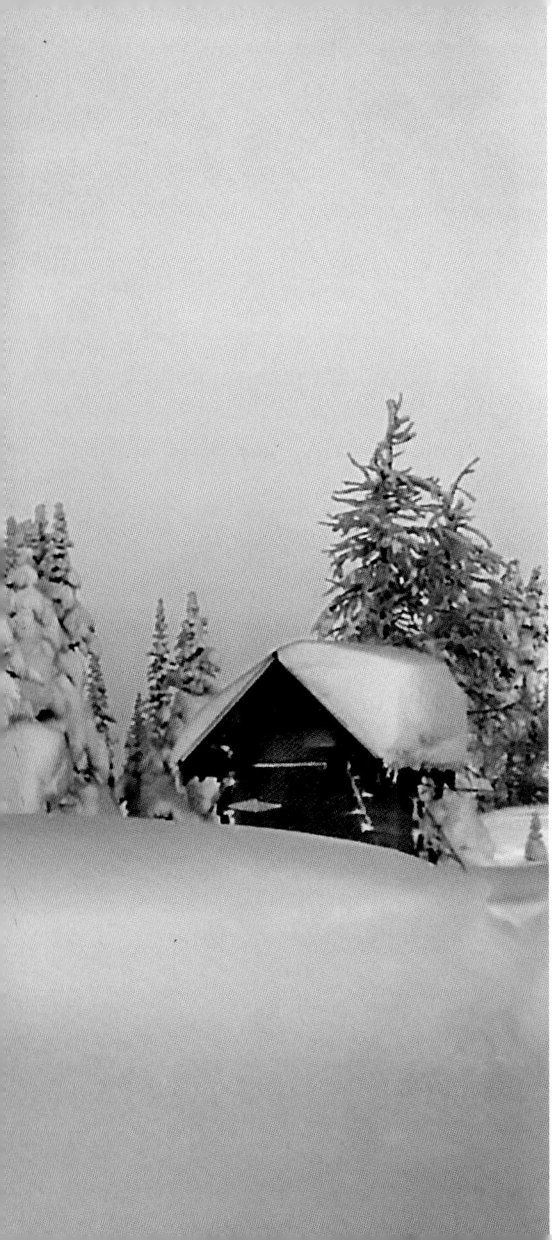

DECEMBER 24

Peace is always beautiful.

~ Walt Whitman

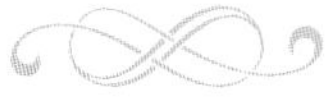

DECEMBER 25

True strength lies
in submission
which permits one
to dedicate his life,
through devotion,
to something
beyond himself.

~ Henry Miller

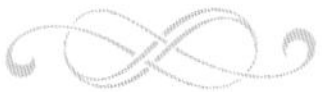

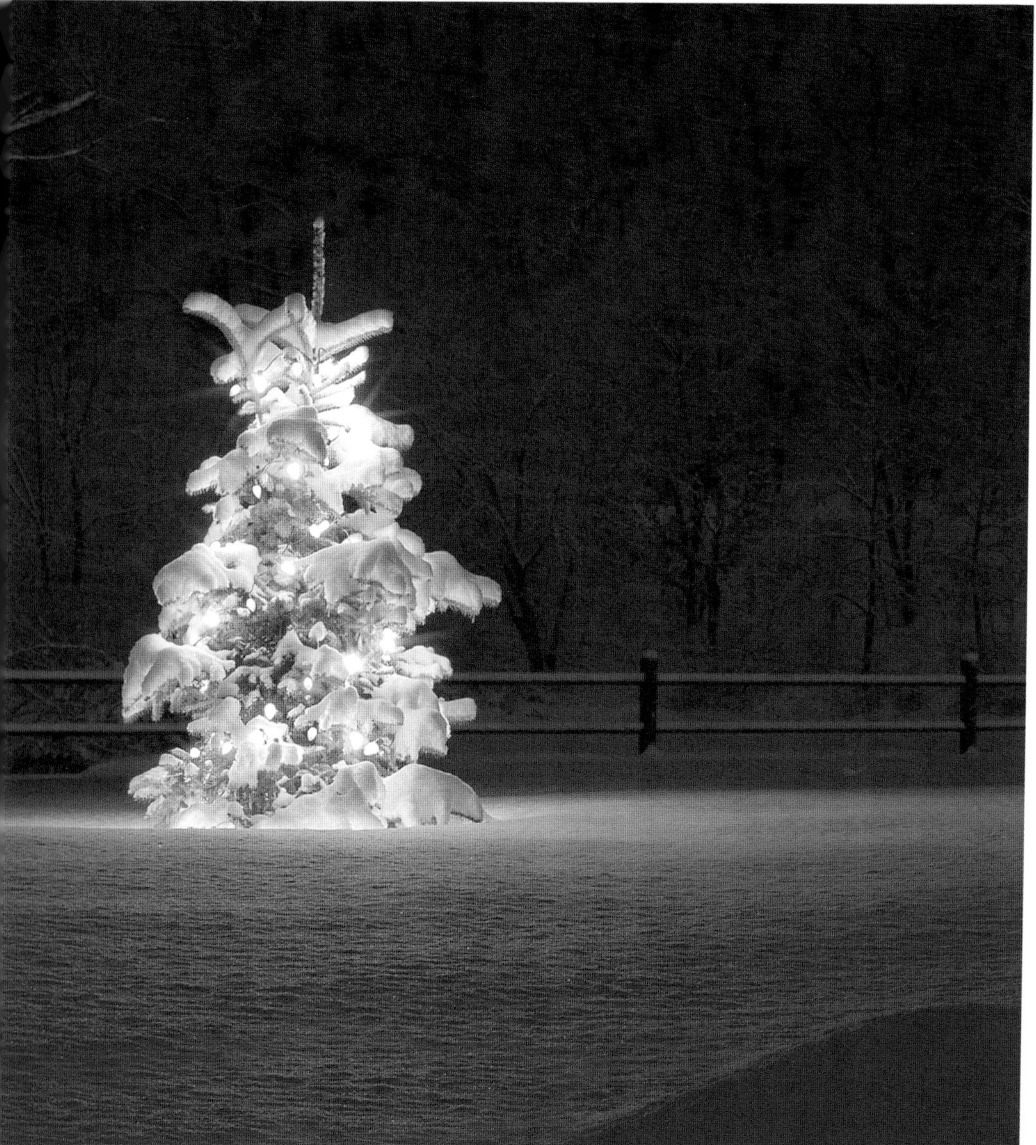

December *26*

Faith is a knowledge within the heart,
beyond the reach of proof.

~ Kahlil Gibran

December 27

Reason is our soul's left hand,
faith her right.
By these we reach divinity.

~ John Donne

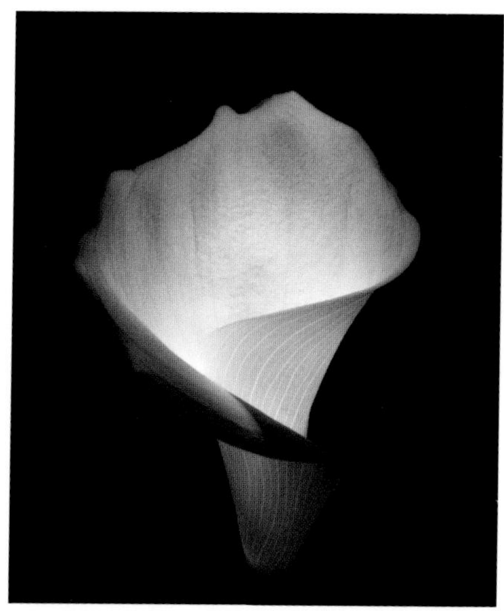

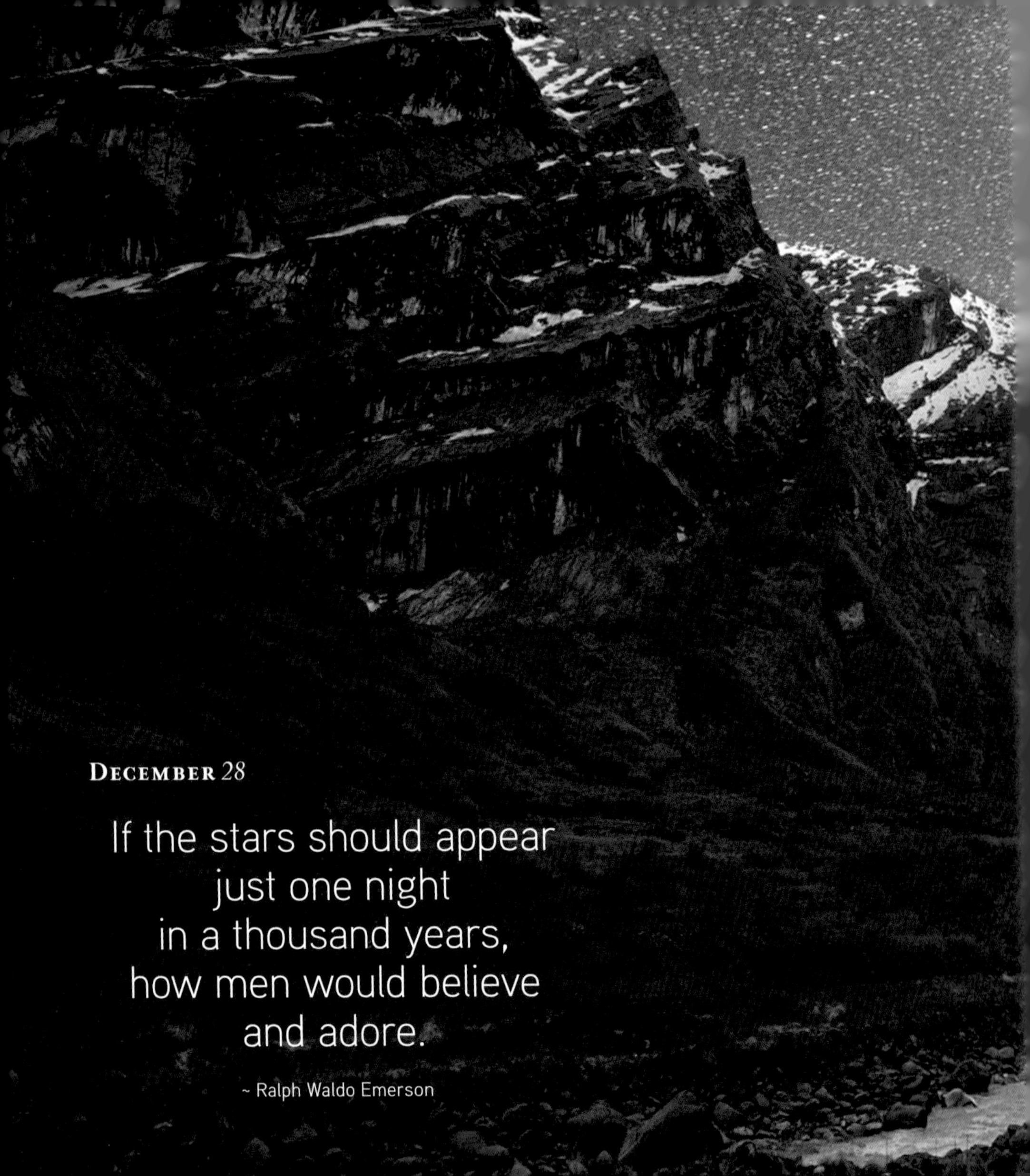

DECEMBER 28
If the stars should appear
just one night
in a thousand years,
how men would believe
and adore.
~ Ralph Waldo Emerson

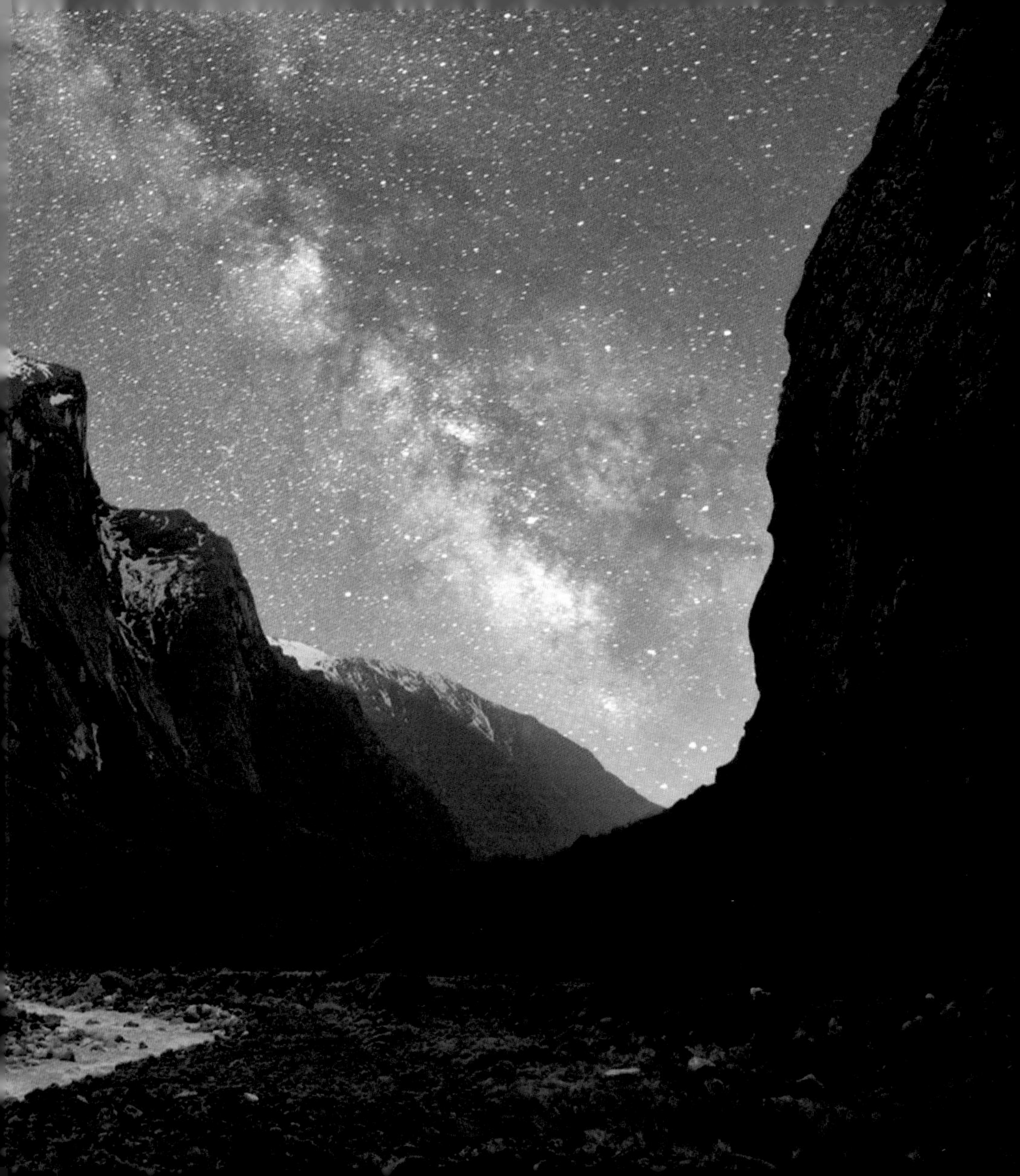

December 29

You can do very little with faith,
but you can do nothing without it.

~ Samuel Butler

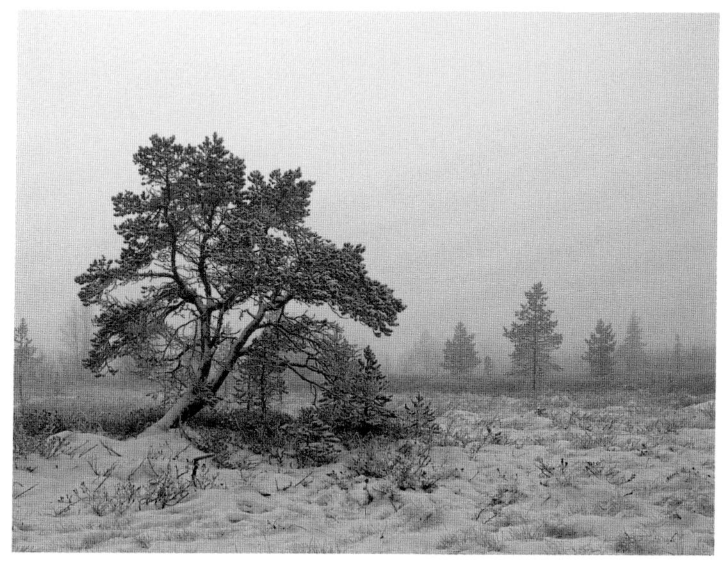

December 30

Faith is not something to grasp;
it is a state to grow into.

~ Mohandas Gandhi

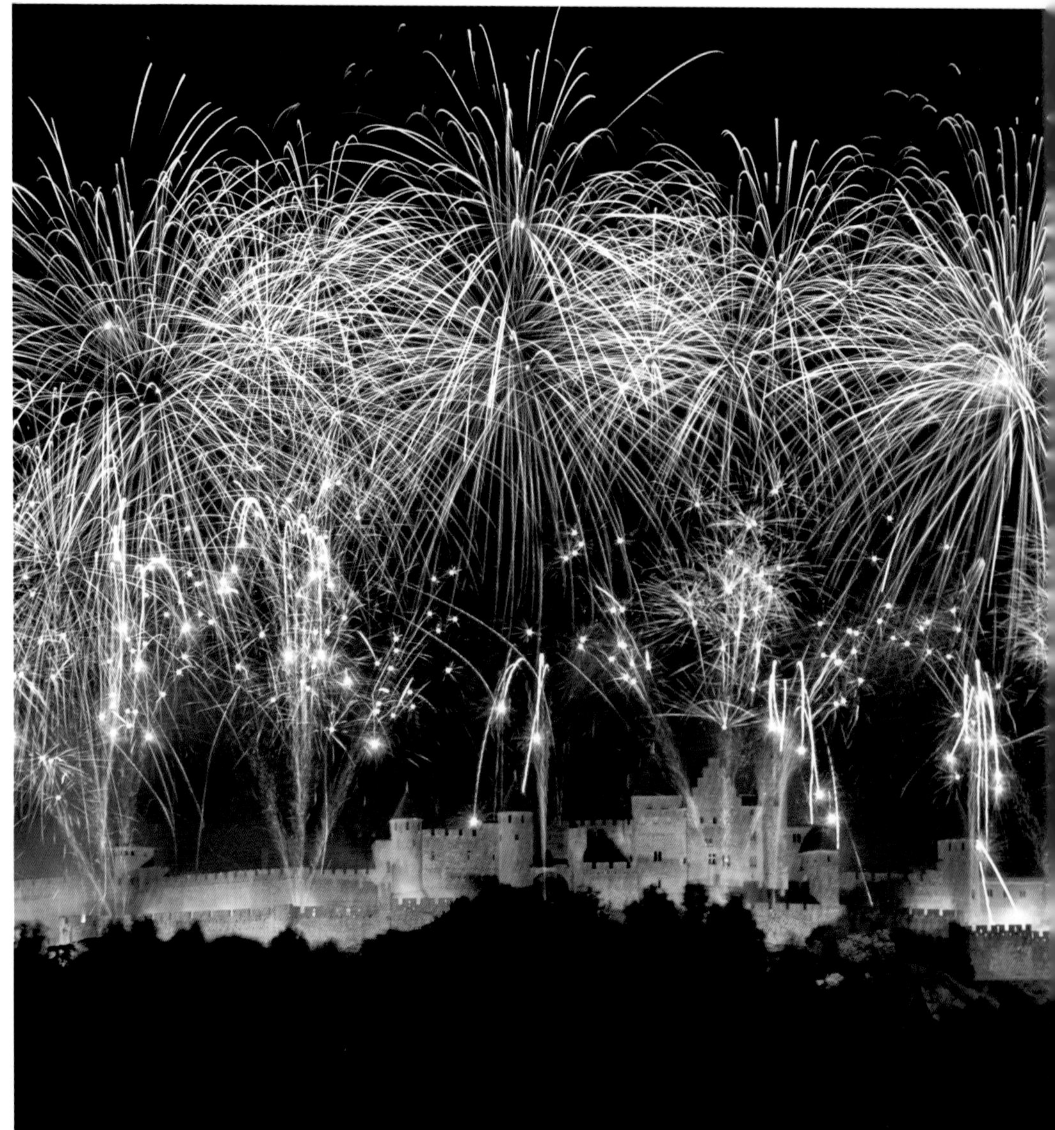

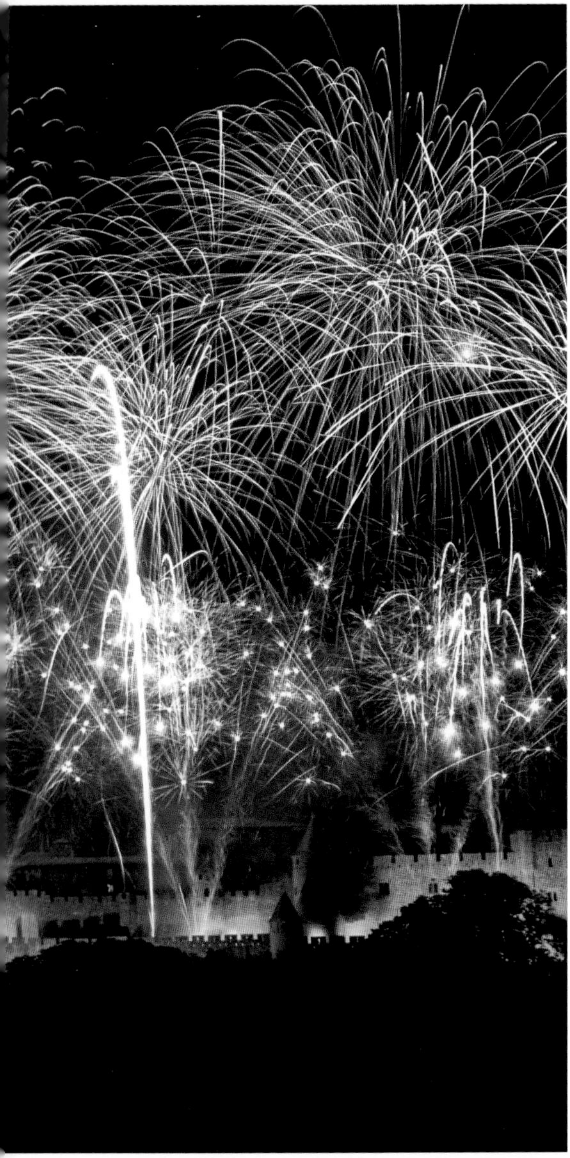

DECEMBER 31

I say,
follow your bliss
and don't be afraid,
and doors
will open
where you
didn't know they
were going to be.

~ Joseph Campbell

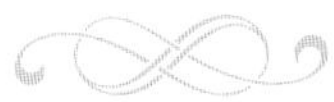

CONTRIBUTOR INDEX

A

Acheson, Dean, *1893–1971.* American statesman and lawyer.

Alcott, Louisa May, *1832–1888.* American novelist.

Alda, Alan, *b. 1936.* American actor.

Andersen, Hans Christian, *1805–1875.* Danish fairy tale author and poet.

Angelou, Maya (Marguerite Johnson), *b. 1928.* American writer and poet.

Apollinaire, Guillaume, *1880–1918.* French poet.

Arbus, Diane, *1923–1971.* American photographer.

Armstrong, Louis, *1901–1971.* American jazz musician.

Augustine, Saint, *354–430.* Algerian theologian and philosopher.

Austen, Jane, *1775–1817.* British novelist.

B

Barrie, J. M. (James Matthew), *1860–1937.* Scottish novelist and playwright.

Barrymore, John, *1882–1942.* American actor.

Barton, Bruce, *1886–1967.* American inspirational author, advertising executive, and politician.

Baruch, Bernard, *1870–1965.* American financier, statesman, and philanthropist.

Baum, L. (Lyman) **Frank,** *1856–1919.* American novelist.

Beaton, Cecil, *1904–1980.* British photographer and costume designer.

Beckett, Samuel, *1906–1989.* Irish novelist, playwright, and poet.

Beecher, Henry Ward, *1813–1887.* American clergyman, social reformer, and abolitionist.

Bonaparte, Napoleon, *1769–1821.* French emperor and military leader.

Boorman, John, *b. 1933.* British filmmaker.

Bradbury, Ray, *b. 1920.* American fantasy, science fiction, and mystery writer.

Brecht, Bertolt, *1898–1956.* German poet and playwright.

Browning, Robert, *1812–1889.* British poet.

Bryan, Arthur, *1923–2011.* British businessman.

Bryan, William Jennings, *1860–1925.* American politician and statesman.

Buck, Pearl Sydenstricker, *1892–1973.* American novelist.

Buddha (Siddhartha Gautama), *563–483 B.C.* Indian spiritual leader and teacher.

Butler, Samuel, *1835–1902.* British novelist and translator.

Byrne, Robert, *b. 1930.* American author.

C

Campbell, Joseph John, *1904–1987.* American mythologist, writer, and lecturer.

Camus, Albert, *1913–1960.* French writer, journalist, and philosopher.

Carlyle, Thomas, *1795–1881.* Scottish satirist, essayist, historian, and teacher.

Carnegie, Dale, *1888–1955.* American inspirational author, lecturer, and teacher.

Chalmers, Alexander, *1759–1834.* Scottish writer, journalist, and publisher.

Chanel, Coco (Gabrielle), *1883–1971.* French fashion designer.

Chesterton, G. K. (Gilbert Keith), *1874–1936.* British journalist, playwright, philosopher, poet, and critic.

Chevalier, Maurice, *1888–1972.* French actor, singer, entertainer, and performer.

Child, Julia, *1912–2004.* American chef and cookbook author.

Chödrön, Pema (Deirdre Blomfield-Brown), *b. 1936.* American teacher, author, and Tibetan Buddhist nun.

Chopra, Deepak, *b. 1946.* Indian medical doctor and spiritual writer.

Church, Francis Pharcellus, *1839–1906.* American journalist and publisher.

Churchill, Winston Spencer, *1874–1965.* British prime minister and statesman.

Colette (Sidonie-Gabrielle), *1873–1954.* French novelist.

Covey, Stephen R., *b. 1932.* American business and inspirational writer.

cummings, e. e. (Edward Estlin), *1894–1962.* American poet, painter, essayist, and playwright.

D

Dahl, Roald, *1916–1990.* British novelist, short story writer, and screenwriter.

Dalai Lama (Tenzin Gyatso), *b. 1935.* Tibetan spiritual and political leader.

Davis, Bette, *1908–1989.* American actress.

de Mille, Agnes, *1905–1993.* American dancer and choreographer.

Dewey, John, *1859–1952.* American philosopher, psychologist, and educational reformer.

Dickinson, Emily, *1830–1886.* American poet.

Diderot, Denis, *1713–1784.* French philosopher and writer.

Dillard, Annie, *b. 1945.* American poet, essayist, and literary critic.

Disraeli, Benjamin, *1804–1881.* British prime minister and statesman.

Donne, John, *1572–1631.* British poet.

Dostoyevsky, Fyodor, 1821–1881. Russian novelist, short story writer, and essayist.

E

Earhart, Amelia, *1897–1937.* American aviator.

Einstein, Albert, *1879–1955.* German-American theoretical physicist.

Eliot, George (Mary Ann Evans), *1819–1880.* British novelist.

Eliot, T. S. (Thomas Stearns), *1888–1965.* British poet and playwright.

Ellis, (Henry) **Havelock,** *1859–1939.* British physician, psychologist, and social reformer.

Emerson, Ralph Waldo, *1803–1882.* American essayist, lecturer, and poet.

Epictetus, *A.D. 55–135.* Greek sage and Stoic philosopher.

Erasmus, Desiderius, *1466–1536.* Dutch humanist, social critic, and theologian.

F

Fitzgerald, Ella, *1917–1996.* American jazz singer.

Fitzgerald, Zelda, *1900–1948.* American novelist.

Flaubert, Gustave, *1821–1880.* French novelist.

Forbes, Malcolm, *1919–1990.* American businessman and publisher.

Ford, Henry, *1863–1947.* American industrialist, inventor, and entrepreneur.

France, Anatole (Jacques-Anatole-François Thibault), 1844–1924. French poet, journalist, and novelist.

Frank, Anne, *1929–1945.* German diarist.

Franklin, Benjamin, *1706–1790.* American inventor, author, politician, diplomat, and scientist.

Fromm, Erich, *1900–1980.* German-American social psychologist and psychoanalyst.

Frost, David, *b. 1939.* British journalist.

Frost, Robert, *1874–1963.* American poet.

G

Galsworthy, John, *1867–1933.* British novelist and playwright.

Gandhi, Indira, *1917–1984.* Indian prime minister and politician.

Gandhi, Mohandas Karamchand (Mahatma), *1869–1948.* Indian civil rights leader.

Garland, Judy (Frances Ethel Gumm), *1922–1969.* American actress.

Geffen, David, *b. 1943.* American record executive, producer, and philanthropist.

Gibran, Kahlil, *1883–1931.* Lebanese-American artist, poet, writer, and philosopher.

Gilbert, Elizabeth, *b. 1969.* American writer.

Giovanni, Nikki, *b. 1943.* American poet.

Goethe, Johann Wolfgang von, *1749–1832.* German novelist, poet, playwright, and philosopher.

Graham, Martha, *1893–1991.* American modern dancer and choreographer.

H

Hale, Edward Everett, *1822–1909.* American writer, historian, and Unitarian clergyman.

Hanh, Thich Nhat, *b. 1926.* Vietnamese Buddhist monk, poet, author, and activist.

Hay, Louise L., *b. 1926.* American motivational writer and publisher.

Hepburn, Audrey, *1929–1993.* British actress and humanitarian.

Hepburn, Katharine, *1907–2003.* American actress.

Hurston, Zora Neale, *1891–1960.* American novelist, essayist, and folklorist.

Huxley, Aldous (Leonard), *1894–1963.* British novelist, playwright, and satirist.

I

Irving, Washington, *1783–1859.* American author, essayist, biographer, and historian.

J

James, William, *1842–1910.* American psychologist and philosopher.

Jobs, Steve, *1955–2011.* American businessman, innovator, and entrepreneur.

Johnson, Samuel, 1709–*1784.* British poet, essayist, literary critic, and lexicographer.

Jong, Erica, *b. 1942.* American novelist.

Jonson, Ben, *1572–1637.* British playwright, poet, and actor.

Jung, Carl (Gustav), *1875–1961.* Swiss psychiatrist and founder of analytical psychology.

K

Kazantzakis, Nikos, *1885–1957.* Greek novelist and philosopher.

Keats, John, *1795–1821.* British poet.

Keller, Helen, *1880–1968.* American writer, lecturer, and activist.

Kennedy, John Fitzgerald, *1917–1963.* American President.

Kierkegaard, Søren, *1813–1855.* Danish philosopher, theologian, and writer.

King, Stephen, *b. 1947.* American novelist.

Koller, Alice, *b. 1925.* American writer and scholar.

Kübler-Ross, Elisabeth, *1926–2004.* Swiss-American psychiatrist and pioneer in near-death studies.

L

Lamb, Charles, *1775–1834.* British essayist and author.

Landers, Ann (Esther Lederer), *1918–2002.* American advice columnist and journalist.

Lao-tzu, *604–531 B.C.* Chinese philosopher.

La Rochefoucauld, François de, *1613–1680.* French memoirist and writer.

Lee, Harper, *b. 1926.* American novelist.

Le Guin, Ursula K., *b. 1929.* American novelist, poet, essayist.

Lenclos, Ninon de (Anne), *1620–1705.* French courtesan and author.

L'Engle, Madeleine, *1918–2007.* American novelist.

Lincoln, Abraham, *1809–1865.* American President.

Lindbergh, Anne Morrow, *1906–2001.* American writer, poet, and aviator.

Longfellow, Henry Wadsworth, *1807–1882.* American poet.

Lowell, James Russell, *1819-1891.* American poet.

Luce, Clare Boothe, *1903–1987.* American playwright, journalist, and editor.

M

Macdonald, George, *1824–1905.* Scottish novelist, poet, and minister.

Marcus Aurelius Antoninus, *A.D. 121–180.* Roman emperor.

McLaughlin, Mignon, 1*913–1983.* American journalist and writer.

Miller, Henry, *1891–1980.* American novelist.

Mitchell, Margaret, *1900–1949.* American novelist.

More, Thomas, *1478–1535.* English philosopher, statesman, and humanist.

Morrison, Toni (Chloe Ardelia Wofford), *b. 1931.* American novelist and poet.

Moreau, Jeanne, *b. 1928.* French actress.

Muir, John, *1838–1914.* Scottish American naturalist, author, and activist.

Murdoch, Iris, *1919–1999.* British novelist and philosopher.

N

Nash, Ogden, *1902–1971.* American poet.

Nevelson, Louise, *1899–1988.* American sculptor.

Niebuhr, Reinhold, *1892–1971.* American theologian, author, and commentator.

Nietzsche, Friedrich, *1844–1900.* German philosopher and poet.

Nin, Anaïs, *1903–1977.* French diarist and novelist.

O

Ortega y Gasset, José, *1883–1955.* Spanish philosopher and essayist.

Orwell, George (Eric Blair), *1903–1950.* British novelist and journalist.

P

Paine, Thomas, *1737–1809.* British pamphleteer, intellectual, and revolutionary.

Parker, Dorothy, *1893–1967.* American satirist, critic, and poet.

Picasso, Pablo, *1881–1973.* Spanish artist.

Plath, Sylvia, *1932–1963.* American poet, novelist, and short story writer.

Plutarch, *A.D. 46–120.* Greek historian.

Proust, Marcel, *1871–1922.* French novelist.

Q

Quindlen, Anna, *b. 1953.* American journalist and novelist.

R

Rilke, Rainer Maria, *1875–1926.* Bohemian-Austrian poet.

Rodin, Auguste, *1840–1917.* French sculptor.

Rooney, Andy, *1919–2011.* American radio and television writer.

Roosevelt, (Anna) **Eleanor,** *1884–1962.* American First Lady, activist, and author.

Roosevelt, Theodore, *1858–1919.* American President.

Rorty, Richard, *1931–2007.* American philosopher.

Rosseau, Jean-Jacques, *1712–1778.* Swiss philosopher and writer.

Rowling, J. K. (Joanne Kathleen), *b. 1965.* British novelist.

Rumi (Jalal ad-Din ar-Rumi), *1207–1273.* Persian poet.

Ruskin, John, *1819–1900.* British art critic and philanthropist.

Russell, Bertrand, *1872–1970.* British philosopher, mathematician, and social critic.

S

Sagan, Carl, *1934–1996.* American astronomer, astrophysicist, and author.

Saint-Exupéry, Antoine de, *1900–1944.* French author, poet, and aviator.

Sand, George (Amandine-Aurore-Lucile Dupin), *1804–1876.* French novelist and memoirist.

Seneca, Lucius Annaeus, *4 B.C.–A.D. 65.* Roman philosopher, statesman, and dramatist.

Sexton, Anne, *1928–1974.* American poet.

Shakespeare, William, *1564–1616.* British playwright and poet.

Shaw, George Bernard, *1856–1950.* Irish playwright.

Sheehy, Gail, *b. 1937.* American journalist and author.

Sivananda, Swami, *1887–1963.* Indian Hindu spiritual teacher.

Smith, Betty, *1904–1972.* American novelist.

Spinoza, Baruch, *1632–1677.* Dutch philosopher.

Spock, Benjamin, *1903–1998.* American pediatrician and author.

Steinbeck, John, *1902–1968.* American novelist.

Steinem, Gloria, *b. 1934.* American feminist, journalist, and activist.

Stendahl (Marie-Henri Beyle), *1783–1842.* French novelist.

Stevenson, Adlai, *1835–1914.* American politician and diplomat.

Stoddard, Alexandra, *b. 1941.* American interior designer and author.

Stoppard, Tom, *b. 1937.* British playwright and screenwriter.

Swaim, Alice Mackenzie, *1912–1996.* Scottish-American poet.

T

Tagore, Rabindranath, *1861–1941.* Bengali poet, novelist, essayist, and composer.

Tennyson, Alfred, Lord, *1809–1892.* British poet.

Teresa, Mother (Agnes Gonxha Bojaxhiu), *1910–1997.* Albanian-Indian nun and religious leader.

Thérèse of Lisieux, Saint, *1873–1897.* French Carmelite nun.

Thoreau, Henry David, *1817–1862.* American author, poet, and philosopher.

Thurber, James, *1894–1961.* American cartoonist and humorist.

Tolle, Eckhart, *b. 1948.* German spiritual teacher and writer.

Tolstoy, Leo, *1828–1910.* Russian novelist and short story writer.

Tubman, Harriet, *1820–1913.* American abolitionist, humanitarian, and suffragist.

Tutu, Desmond, *b. 1931.* South African religious leader and antiapartheid activist.

Twain, Mark (Samuel Langhorne Clemens), *1835–1910.* American novelist and humorist.

U

Updike, John, *1932–2009.* American novelist, poet, and critic.

V

Virgil (Publius Vergilius Maro), *70–19 B.C.* Roman poet.

W

Walker, Alice, *b. 1944.* American novelist, poet, and activist.

Ward, William Arthur, *1921–1994.* American inspirational writer and poet.

Washington, Booker T., *1856–1915.* American educator, activist, author, and political leader.

Wayne, John (Marion Robert Morrison), *1907–1979.* American actor.

Wharton, Edith (Newbold Jones), *1862–1937.* American novelist.

Whitman, Walt, *1819–1892.* American poet, essayist, and journalist.

Wilde, Oscar, *1854–1900.* Irish novelist and dramatist.

Williams, Tennessee (Thomas Lanier), *1911–1983.* American playwright, novelist, and essayist.

Williamson, Marianne, *b. 1952.* American spiritual writer and poet.

Wilson, August, *1945–2005.* American playwright.

Winfrey, Oprah, *b. 1954.* American media personality.

Woolf, Virginia (Adeline), *1882–1941.* British novelist and essayist.

Wright, Frank Lloyd, *1867–1959.* American architect.

Y

Yutang, Lin, *1895–1976.* Chinese novelist, essayist, and translator.

ILLUSTRATIONS CREDITS

Cover and final page, Image Plan/Corbis; title page, JN Nagase/National Geographic My Shot; Table of Contents, Steven Russell Smith Photos/Shutterstock.

January

Opener, Stanislaw Jawor/National Geographic My Shot; 1, Chelsea Marshall/National Geographic My Shot; 2, Doro Schaefer/National Geographic My Shot; 3, Navid Baraty/National Geographic My Shot; 4, Josh Exell/National Geographic My Shot; 5, Antonín Vodák/Shutterstock; 6, Mario Goren/National Geographic My Shot; 7, Andreja Donko/National Geographic My Shot; 8, Buck Lovell/National Geographic My Shot; 9, Robert W. Madden/National Geographic Stock; 10, Cathy Stancil/National Geographic My Shot; 11, Tom Dietrich/National Geographic My Shot; 12, aniad/Shutterstock; 13, Inna Skibinsky/National Geographic My Shot; 14, Patti Waddell/National Geographic My Shot; 15, Robert Turner/National Geographic My Shot; 16, Jim Mandeville/National Geographic My Shot; 17, Cathy Whitehouse/National Geographic My Shot; 18, Morris Altman/National Geographic My Shot; 19, Maciej Gulcz/National Geographic My Shot; 20, Bill Metek/National Geographic My Shot; 21, Jennifer Stockton/National Geographic My Shot; 22, Vphoto/Shutterstock; 23, Rana Dias/National Geographic My Shot; 24, Cui Hong/National Geographic My Shot; 25, Craig Bogden/National Geographic My Shot; 26, Victor Troyanov/National Geographic My Shot; 27, Bang Huei Liou/National Geographic My Shot; 28, Roy Samuelsen/National Geographic My Shot; 29, Cheryl Molennor/National Geographic My Shot; 30, Alex Kosev/Shutterstock; 31, National Geographic Photographer, NGS.

February

Opener, Alejandra Quero/National Geographic My Shot; 1, oliveromg/Shutterstock; 2, Carol Bradfield/National Geographic My Shot; 3, Helen Dittrich/National Geographic My Shot; 4, Laura Goetz/National Geographic My Shot; 5, Suiyang Khoo/National Geographic My Shot; 6, Jamie Urban/National Geographic My Shot; 7, Cynthia Brown Yackenchick/National Geographic My Shot; 8, Robert Welton/National Geographic My Shot; 9, Grant Ordelheide/National Geographic My Shot; 10, Matt Champlin/National Geographic My Shot; 11, Marie Destefanis/National Geographic My Shot; 12, Szilvia Pap/National Geographic My Shot; 13, Alan Poon/National Geographic My Shot; 14, Cameron MacMaster/National Geographic My Shot; 15, Norma Cornes/Shutterstock; 16, Mark Vincent Mueller/National Geographic My Shot; 17, Jodi Cobb/National Geographic Stock; 18, Laura Jean Peterman/National Geographic My Shot; 19, Vitaly Samartsev/National Geographic My Shot; 20, El Choclo/Shutterstock; 21, Roberto Pagani/National Geographic My Shot; 22, Ema Suvajac/National Geographic My Shot; 23, Elaine Malott/National Geographic My Shot; 24, Marco Taddei/National Geographic My Shot; 25, Shyam Prasad/National Geographic My Shot; 26, Gowtham/National Geographic My Shot; 27, thaikrit/Shutterstock; 28/29, Steve Schindler/National Geographic My Shot.

March

Opener, Edward Kennair Jr./National Geographic My Shot; 1, Priit J. Vesilind/National Geographic Stock; 2, Sam Abell/National Geographic Stock; 3, Do Do/National Geographic My Shot; 4, Brett Cohen/National Geographic My Shot; 5, Justyna Korczynska/National Geographic My Shot; 6, Susan Lawton/National Geographic My Shot; 7, Ken Cohen/National Geographic My Shot; 8, Partha Saha, Pratim/National Geographic My Shot; 9, Hema Sukumar/National Geographic My Shot; 10, Chris Dardenne/National Geographic My Shot; 11, Sandor Bernath/National Geographic My Shot; 12, Kavin Ho/National Geographic My Shot; 13, Cheryl Molennor/National Geographic My Shot; 14, Derek Kwan/National Geographic My Shot; 15, Dan Minicucci/National Geographic My Shot; 16, Dale Daniel/National Geographic My Shot; 17, Anton Tsentalovich/National Geographic My Shot; 18, Yohanes B Moa/National Geographic My Shot; 19, Kamala Kannan/National Geographic My Shot; 20, Irawan Subingar/National Geographic My Shot; 21, Francesco Fassi/National Geographic My Shot; 22, Siddhartha Saha/National Geographic My Shot; 23, Timothy Wood/National Geographic My Shot; 24, Heather Boozenny/National Geographic My Shot; 25, Dan Brown/National Geographic My Shot; 26, Deana Steere/National Geographic My Shot; 27, Sandra Zeimyte/National Geographic My Shot; 28, Chuck Bacon Jr./National Geographic My Shot; 29, Martina Kovacova/National Geographic My Shot; 30, Emily Barto/National Geographic My Shot; 31, Steven Stokan/National Geographic My Shot.

April

Opener, Evelyn Tambour/National Geographic My Shot; 1, Thierry Bornier/National Geographic My Shot; 2, Lisa Tremblay/National Geographic My Shot; 3, David Schultz/National Geographic My Shot; 4, April Moore/National Geographic My Shot; 5, Jason Rydquist/National Geographic My Shot; 6, Dave Karnes/National Geographic My Shot; 7, Wei Yun Chang/National Geographic My Shot; 8, Chris May/National Geographic My Shot; 9, Stephanie Seidel/National Geographic My Shot; 10, Sam Abell/National Geographic Stock; 11, Sundar Vembu/National Geographic My Shot; 12, Steve Burling/National Geographic My Shot; 13, Rudy Kellerman/National Geographic My Shot; 14, Charles Powell/National Geographic My Shot; 15, Linda Drake/National Geographic My Shot; 16, Patricia Vazquez/National Geographic My Shot; 17, Raul Vomisescu/National Geographic My Shot; 18, Abhishek Sinha/National Geographic My Shot; 19, Artur Stanisz/National Geographic My Shot; 20, Iouri Dovnarovich/National Geographic My Shot; 21, Sandra van Hoek/National Geographic My Shot; 22, Jeff Dushack/National Geographic My Shot; 23, Weronika Macioszczyk/National Geographic My Shot; 24, Murugesan Anbazhagan/National Geographic My Shot; 25, Veronika Juchnewitsch/National Geographic My Shot; 26, Frank Baker/National Geographic My Shot; 27, Mark Musselman/National Geographic My Shot; 28, Nilesh Bhange/National Geographic My Shot; 29, Maureen Hicks/National Geographic My Shot; 30, Sharon Hitman/Shutterstock.

May

Opener, Lukasz Warzecha/National Geographic My Shot; 1, Donna Castle/National Geographic My Shot; 2, Chris Minihane/National Geographic My Shot; 3, Nitin Prabhudesai/National Geographic My Shot; 4, Tom Dietrich/National Geographic My Shot; 5, John McEvoy/National Geographic My Shot; 6, Gavin Rowlandson/National Geographic My Shot; 7, James P. Blair/National Geographic Stock; 8, Stanislav Shmelev/National Geographic My Shot; 9, Massimo Cavalletti/National Geographic My Shot; 10, Tom Bullock/National Geographic My Shot; 11, Subir Bose/National Geographic My Shot; 12, Paige Boyd/National Geographic My Shot; 13, Michael Neu/National Geographic My Shot; 14, Cheryl Molennor/National Geographic My Shot; 15, Jack.Q/Shutterstock; 16, Jason Wickens/National Geographic My Shot; 17, Mike Hall/National Geographic My Shot; 18, Jennifer Brower/National Geographic My Shot; 19, Jon Wood/National Geographic My Shot; 20, John Seamons/National Geographic My Shot; 21, Barry Hobbs/National Geographic My Shot; 22, Nicholas Crobaugh/National Geographic My Shot; 23, Christian Meyn/National Geographic My Shot; 24, Fabio Sironi/National Geographic My Shot; 25, Troy Lilly/National Geographic My Shot; 26, Peter Racz/National Geographic My Shot; 27, Karl Kryczynski/National Geographic My Shot; 28, Mike Briner/National Geographic My Shot; 29, Sandra Marsh/National Geographic My Shot; 30, Remy Neymarc/National Geographic My Shot; 31, Liliia Rudchenko/Shutterstock.

June

Opener, Joanna Plichcinska/National Geographic My Shot; 1, Peter Pevy/National Geographic My Shot; 2, Alexander Potapov/Shutterstock; 3, Kathleen Walker/National Geographic My Shot; 4, Varsha Chaudhari/National Geographic My Shot; 5, Romain Chassagne/National Geographic My Shot; 6, Xiaomei Sun/National Geographic My Shot; 7, Evelyn Tambour/National Geographic My Shot; 8, Henk Bentlage/National Geographic My Shot; 9, Weldon Schloneger/Shutterstock; 10, Pinto Biswas/National Geographic My Shot; 11, zhuda/Shutterstock; 12, Massimo Cavalletti/National Geographic My Shot; 13, LilKar/Shutterstock; 14, Alexa Hoffman/National Geographic My Shot; 15, Richard Seeley/National Geographic My Shot; 16, Wendy Longo/National Geographic My Shot; 17, Angi Nelson/National Geographic My Shot; 18, He Qustuf/National Geographic My Shot; 19, Narayanan Vijayaraghavan/National Geographic My Shot; 20, Debasish Ghosh/National Geographic My Shot; 21, Juan Manuel Moreno/National Geographic My Shot; 22, asharkyu/Shutterstock; 23, Jason Teale/National Geographic My Shot; 24, Massimo Cavalletti/National Geographic My Shot; 25, Annie Griffiths/National Geographic Stock; 26, Jodi Cobb/National Geographic Stock; 27, Reanna Boudrow/National Geographic My Shot; 28, Jodi Cobb/National Geographic Stock; 29, Jude Walton/National Geographic My Shot; 30, Richard Confucius/National Geographic My Shot.

July

Opener, Sara A. Vera Beltrán/National Geographic My Shot; 1, Andres Bravo Ceron/National Geographic My Shot; 2, Mark Lewer/National Geographic My Shot; 3, Dave Allen Photography/Shutterstock; 4, Jennifer Goulden/National Geographic My Shot; 5, Sandra Pagano/National Geographic My Shot; 6, Mike Gal/National Geographic My Shot; 7, Dale Daniel/National Geographic My Shot; 8, Joshua Howard/National Geographic My Shot; 9, Pam O'Brian/National Geographic My Shot; 10, Stefan Eberhard/National Geographic My Shot; 11, Jeremiah Cunningham/National Geographic My Shot; 12, Ira Runyan/National Geographic My Shot; 13, Betsy Seeton/National Geographic My Shot; 14, Stephen Williams/National Geographic My Shot; 15, April Barci/National Geographic My Shot; 16, Tejas Soni/National Geographic My Shot; 17, Steve van Lingen/National Geographic My Shot; 18, Marie Marthe Gagnon/National Geographic My Shot; 19, Christopher Kiggins/National Geographic My Shot; 20, Sisse Brimberg/National Geographic Stock; 21, Rachel Lee Young/National Geographic My Shot; 22, Nieva Schemm/National Geographic My Shot; 23, Preston Cole/National Geographic My Shot; 24, Giacomo Loffredo/National Geographic My Shot; 25, Mark Roberts/National Geographic My Shot; 26, Dan Price/National Geographic My Shot; 27, Kiersten Miller/National Geographic My Shot; 28, Lindsay Loebig/National Geographic My Shot; 29, Carolyn Pepper/National Geographic My Shot; 30, Sakib Iqbal/National Geographic My Shot; 31, Greg Stafford/National Geographic My Shot.

August

Opener, Abigail Eden Shaffer/National Geographic My Shot; 1, Armen Dolukhanyan/National Geographic My Shot; 2, Bob McCarthy/National Geographic My Shot; 3, Nyain Swe/National Geographic My Shot; 4, Ray Whitt/National Geographic My Shot; 5, Angela Boelman/National Geographic My Shot; 6, Svetlana Eremina/National Geographic My Shot; 7, Subhrojyoti Banerjee/National Geographic My Shot; 8, Sebastian Selzer/National Geographic My Shot; 9, Andrea Guarneri/National Geographic My Shot; 10, Ed Riche/National Geographic My Shot; 11, Bob McCarthy/National Geographic My Shot; 12, Mark Vincent Mueller/National Geographic My Shot; 13, Lorne Rossman/National Geographic My Shot; 14, Thomas Sterr/National Geographic My Shot; 15, Jodi Cobb/National Geographic Stock; 16, Tony Mackrill/National Geographic My Shot; 17, Stephen Cockley/National Geographic My Shot; 18, Mike Criss/National Geographic My Shot; 19, Bill Knudsen/National Geographic My Shot; 20, Marco Taddei/National Geographic My Shot; 21, Elizabeth Ames/National Geographic My Shot; 22, Glennis Siverson/National Geographic My Shot; 23, Allen Aisenstein/National Geographic My Shot; 24, Lawrence Sampson/National Geographic My Shot; 25, Hannah Kost/National Geographic My Shot; 26, Katie McKinney/National Geographic My Shot; 27, Fabrice Milochau/National Geographic My Shot; 28, Lou Hablas/National Geographic My Shot; 29, Thana Thaweeskulchai/National Geographic My Shot; 30, Veronika Kolev/National Geographic My Shot; 31, Rick Campbell/National Geographic My Shot.

September

Opener, Scottyboipdx Weber/National Geographic My Shot; 1, Sylwia Domaradzka/National Geographic My Shot; 2, Renae Tolbert/National Geographic My Shot; 3, Aaron Reed/National Geographic My Shot; 4, Nancy Law/National Geographic My Shot; 5, Toni Jensen/National Geographic My Shot; 6, Bryan Black/National Geographic My Shot; 7, Terrie Scherman/National Geographic My Shot; 8, Neo Wang/National Geographic My Shot; 9, Max Leipold/National Geographic My Shot; 10, D. Ross Fisher/National Geographic My Shot; 11, Daniel Marnell/National Geographic My Shot; 12, Fedor Selivanov/Shutterstock; 13, Chris Dardenne/National Geographic My Shot; 14, Elizabeth McClure/National Geographic My Shot; 15, Mike Briner/National Geographic My Shot; 16, Terry Shoemaker/National Geographic My Shot; 17, Giuliano Mangani/National Geographic My Shot; 18, Mark Duffy/National Geographic My Shot; 19, Jerry Whitten/National Geographic My Shot; 20, Cathy Wyman/National Geographic My Shot; 21, Nicholas McElroy/National Geographic My Shot; 22, Peter Zagar/National Geographic My Shot; 23, Darrell Abolit/National Geographic My Shot; 24, Barb Thornton/National Geographic My Shot; 25, Artur Stanisz/National Geographic My Shot; 26, Sharlyn Nelson/National Geographic My Shot; 27, Jorge de Sousa/National Geographic My Shot; 28, Svetlana Eremina/National Geographic My Shot; 29, Gary Geiger/National Geographic My Shot; 30, Brian Valente/National Geographic My Shot.

October

Opener, Michael Yamashita; 1, Gopal Seshadrinathan/Shutterstock; 2, James L. Stanfield/National Geographic Stock; 3, George Hatzipantelis/National Geographic My Shot; 4, Milda Naujokaitiene/National Geographic My Shot; 5, Jacqueline Abromeit/Shutterstock; 6, Amlan Chatterjee/National Geographic My Shot; 7, Sam Abell/National Geographic Stock; 8, Jodi Cobb/National Geographic Stock; 9, Marvin Walley/National Geographic My Shot; 10, Dimitris Koutroumpas/National Geographic My Shot; 11, Ozan Aktas/National Geographic My Shot; 12, Chikku Baiju/National Geographic My Shot; 13, Scott Murray/National Geographic My Shot; 14, Luis Marden/National Geographic Stock; 15, Edward Brower/National Geographic My Shot; 16, meunierd/Shutterstock; 17, Laurena Francis/National Geographic My Shot; 18, Philip Chen/National Geographic My Shot; 19, Michael Yamashita; 20, Michael Yamashita; 21, Svetlana Eremina/National Geographic My Shot; 22, Tanawat Likitkererat/National Geographic My Shot; 23, Connie Wade/National Geographic My Shot; 24, Elwin Chan/National Geographic My Shot; 25, Daniel Stanek/National Geographic My Shot; 26, Wilma van Hoesel/National Geographic My Shot; 27, Bret Edge/National Geographic My Shot; 28, Kelton Russenberger/National Geographic My Shot; 29, Angela Stanton/National Geographic My Shot; 30, Jeff Stenstrom/National Geographic My Shot; 31, Cherie Tolliver/National Geographic My Shot.

November

Opener, Kieran O'Connor/National Geographic My Shot; 1, Jose Yee/National Geographic My Shot; 2, Erin Carroll/National Geographic My Shot; 3, Heli Heinonen/National Geographic My Shot; 4, John Matzick/National Geographic My Shot; 5, Olegas Kurasovas/National Geographic My Shot; 6, Gunhild Andersen/National Geographic My Shot; 7, Ammit/Shutterstock; 8, Araceli Sanchez/National Geographic My Shot; 9, Angela Carmichael/National Geographic My Shot; 10, Ray Lekich/National Geographic My Shot; 11, Nuvola/Shutterstock; 12, Michael Yamashita; 13, Darrel O'Neill/National Geographic My Shot; 14, Cristina Iacob/National Geographic My Shot; 15, Lillian M. Ford/National Geographic My Shot; 16, HixnHix/Shutterstock; 17, Michael Simpson/National Geographic My Shot; 18, James L. Amos/National Geographic Stock; 19, Deborah Lee/National Geographic My Shot; 20, Bhaskar Mukherjee/National Geographic My Shot; 21, Louis Ruth/National Geographic My Shot; 22, Bruce Dale/National Geographic Stock; 23, Paul Borhaug/National Geographic My Shot; 24, Susan Stanton/National Geographic My Shot; 25, Leon Palmer/National Geographic My Shot; 26, Chhanda Bewtra/National Geographic My Shot; 27, John Hinkle/National Geographic My Shot; 28, William Albert Allard/National Geographic Stock; 29, Dick Durrance II/National Geographic Stock; 30, NG Photographer/National Geographic Stock.

December

Opener, Annie Griffiths/National Geographic Stock; 1, James P. Blair/National Geographic Stock; 2, Sarah Stratton/National Geographic My Shot; 3, Zoltan Kenwell/National Geographic My Shot; 4, Fred Caws/National Geographic My Shot; 5, Phil Pummell/National Geographic My Shot; 6, Tyson Fisher/National Geographic My Shot; 7, David Alan Harvey/National Geographic Stock; 8, Ema Suvajac/National Geographic My Shot; 9, Frank Brace/National Geographic My Shot; 10, Makarova Viktoria (Vikarus)/Shutterstock; 11, Aparna Nori/National Geographic My Shot; 12, Andri Kustiawan/National Geographic My Shot; 13, Tania Lee Crow/National Geographic My Shot; 14, Kuulei Akina/National Geographic My Shot; 15, Chantelle Lamoureux/National Geographic My Shot; 16, John Stone/National Geographic My Shot; 17, Sally Roerick/National Geographic My Shot; 18, Lynn Whitt/Shutterstock; 19, Emily Curtin Phillips/National Geographic My Shot; 20, Steven Smith/National Geographic My Shot; 21, Narong Rattanaya/National Geographic My Shot; 22, CoolR/Shutterstock; 23, Lauren Geary/National Geographic My Shot; 24, Istvan Hernadi/National Geographic My Shot; 25, Kevin Quinn/National Geographic My Shot; 26, Stefan Eberhard/National Geographic My Shot; 27, Jason Groepper/National Geographic My Shot; 28, Anton Jankovoy/National Geographic My Shot; 29, Kevin McElheran/National Geographic My Shot; 30, Scott Wilson/National Geographic My Shot; 31, Martin Castellan/National Geographic My Shot.

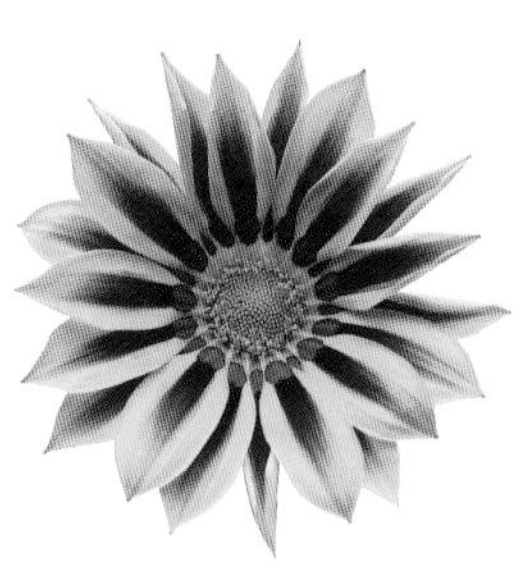